TEXTILES FOR RESIDENTIAL AND COMMERCIAL INTERIORS

TEXTILES FOR RESIDENTIAL AND COMMERCIAL INTERIORS

Jan Yeager
West Virginia University

1817

HARPER & ROW, PUBLISHERS, New York

Cambridge, Philadelphia, San Francisco, Washington,
London, Mexico City, São Paulo, Singapore, Sydney

Sponsoring Editor: Barbara Cinquegrani
Project Coordination, Text and Cover Design, BMR
Text Art: Benjamin Dann
Uncredited Photos: Peter Lessing
Compositor: BMR
Printer and Binder: The Murray Printing Company

Textiles for Residential and Commercial Interiors

Library of Congress Cataloging in Publication Data

Yeager, Jan 1943-
    Textiles for residential and commercial interiors.

    Bibliography: p.
    Includes index.
    1. Textile fabrics in interior decoration.
I. Title.
NK2115.5.F3Y43 1988   747'.5   87-23802
ISBN 0-06-047318-5

87 88 89 90 9 8 7 6 5 4 3 2 1

For Rodger

Contents

Appendixes

List of Tables

Preface

Textiles for Residential and Commercial Interiors is for use by students, educators, extension personnel, practicing interior designers and architects, retailers, and consumers with a professional or personal interest in the selection and serviceability of textile furnishings. The text is designed to expand student knowledge of interior textiles, improve the effectiveness of professionals, and provide answers to consumers' questions.

My intention in writing this work was to overcome the problems facing those who need textile furnishing information. Even when one of myriad sources of information could be located, it generally pertained to a single product and discussed "what," and not "why" or "how." My experiences in teaching an interior textile course confirmed my sense of the need for a comprehensive text. The several excellent introductory textile textbooks available examine textiles with an orientation to apparel; lack of an adequate text dealing with interior textiles has frustrated students and professors alike, and frequently precluded offering a needed course.

I had the following objectives in mind while writing this work:

- To present a consolidated and comprehensive coverage of the textile products available for use in residential and commercial interiors.
- To review consumer product selection criteria influencing the design of interior textile end-products.
- To identify mandatory and voluntary labeling practices used to protect and inform professionals and consumers.

- To review government regulations applying to interior textile product marketing and selection.
- To examine end-use variables that affect product selection.
- To explain product components, manufacturing processes, installation procedures, and maintenance practices affecting textile furnishing serviceability.
- To cover test methods, performance standards, and quality control work used in the industry.
- To review the fire-related behavior of interior textiles and the work already undertaken to widen the margin of safety in the event of fire.
- To increase awareness of product features and installation practices that can help rather than hinder the mobility of those with physical limitations.
- To enhance understanding by including extensive sketches and photographs.

Because readers will have different levels of knowledge about textiles, Unit One focuses on textile fundamentals. Readers having previous formal study of textiles and professionals with knowledge from experience may use this unit for review; others may study the material more thoroughly, to master information built on in later units.

Units Two through Five are divided by end product category. Unit Two discusses upholstered furniture coverings and fillings; Unit Three focuses on window and wall coverings; Unit Four covers soft floor coverings and cushions; Unit Five is devoted to textile accessories and accents. Within each unit, attention is given to the characteristics of the product components and the various operations used in their production. Throughout the work, factors affecting product selection and serviceability are emphasized. The appendixes include a listing of generic class definitions and selected man-made fiber trade names, formulas for metric conversions, a bibliography, and a glossary.

In larger institutions with extensive offerings, *Textiles for Residential and Commercial Interiors* is appropriate for a course to follow completion of introductory textiles and interior design courses. It can be used in either textiles or interior design departments. In smaller institutions where course offerings may be more limited, the text would be useful in an introductory course with an expansive scope, for instance, apparel textiles and interior textiles, or housing and interior textiles. The book's organization permits the selection of units or chapters dealing with topics planned for class discussions.

ACKNOWLEDGEMENTS

When I began this project, there were no works with which I could compare my ideas, style, content, and organization. My work would have reflected a single perspective if it had not been for the help of several reviewers, whom I wish to thank for sharing their time and professional expertise. I am especially indebted to Dr. Carol Avery, Florida State University; Dr. Mary Ann Zenter, Virginia Polytechnic Institute and State University; Dr. Nancy Breen, Syracuse University; and an anonymous reviewer from the University of Illinois for reviewing the entire manuscript. For commenting on selected chapters, I am grateful to Dr. Carol Warfield, Auburn University, and Dr. S. Kay Obendorf, Cornell University. Comments on the proposal were kindly made by some of the above persons, by Dr. Ardis Rewerts of the University of Texas at Austin, and by anonymous reviewers at Iowa State University and the University of Kentucky. I trust the reviewers will appreciate my gratitude when they see their suggestions reflected in the text.

Several persons from the industry provided valuable help, and several firms supplied crucial photographs and illustrations. I am especially grateful to Mr. Richard Ned Hopper of The Carpet and Rug Institute for his thorough reading of Unit Four, Soft Floor Coverings and Cushions. I am also especially appreciative of the help provided by Mr. E. L. Briggs of the Upholstered Furniture Action Council, in his review of Chapter 16, Fire-safety Standards for Upholstered Furniture and Transportation Fabrics.

The reviewers helped me to improve my work and to avoid several glaring omissions; they saved me from more errors than I care to admit. I, alone, however, am responsible for the content.

Completion of this book would not have been possible without the kind and generous help of two friends, Connie Hinzman and Peter Lessing. Connie typed the entire manuscript and many letters. Her accuracy, attention to detail, and willingness to serve beyond the call of duty made my work immeasurably easier. Peter, a geologist by training and a prize-winning photographer by avocation, took scores of photographs of yarns, fabrics, and end-products. Most of the photographs in the book are the result of his expertise and his never-ending patience with my requests for yet more photographs. Every author should be so fortunate.

For his confidence in the merit of the proposed work, I am grateful to Fred Henry, formerly senior editor at Harper & Row. Together with his assistants, Karl Sandin and Diane H. Moran, Fred provided guidance and encouragement during the preparation of the manuscript. I am also appreciative of the help provided by Judith Rothman, editor-in-chief at Harper & Row, and David Crossman and Cathy Cambron, Business Media Resources, for their help in guiding the manuscript through production.

My husband, Rodger, a political scientist, learned more about interior textiles then he had planned. Because of his especially close and long-term association with this work, he has earned the right to be named as co-author. I offer instead my promise immediately to shift my attention to our family life.

one

THE FUNDAMENTALS OF TEXTILES FOR INTERIORS

Unit One focuses on the fundamentals of textiles, with an eye to interiors. Chapter 1 reviews the nature of the industry, including the sequential flow of product manufacturing and distributing. The commercial activities of firms directly involved in the work of the industry are described, as are contributions to the economic health of the industry made by auxiliary enterprises such as trade associations and contract design firms. Chapter 2 identifies criteria influencing interior textile product selection, some of which are mandated by regulatory agencies, and emphasizes that industry members need to work cooperatively to ensure that the products they offer are acceptable to the contemporary consumer.

Following the normal sequence of fabric production, Chapters 3 and 4 focus on textile fibers, Chapter 5 focuses on yarns and yarn substitutes, Chapters 6 and 7 identify methods of fabrication, and Chapter 8 discusses color-related variables and methods of color application. Conversion operations, the final processes in fabric manufacturing, are discussed in Chapter 9.

Chapter 10 covers mandatory, advisory, and voluntary labeling practices relating to textile furnishing products. Their value to informed consumers, designers, and architects in selecting or specifying is noted. The chapter stresses the need for members of the industry to avoid engaging in unfair or deceptive labeling practices, practices that the Federal Trade Commission is empowered to prevent.

Because concern for personal safety and reduced property loss in the event of fire has grown significantly in recent years, the final chapter in the unit examines the involvement of textiles in interior fires. The chapter discusses the responsibilities and powers of the Consumer Product Safety Commission in carrying out the purposes and provisions of the Flammable Fabrics Act, including the establishment of new flammability standards.

chapter *1*

The Interior Textile Industry

- Major Segments of the Industry
- Auxiliary Enterprises
- Factors Affecting the Economic Health of the Industry

The interior textile industry, like the apparel and industrial textile industries, encompasses several segments, each of which is an important link in the chain of production and distribution. Although these segments are composed of many independent firms, there is mutual dependence among firms in different segments: firms in "downstream" segments need suppliers, and firms in "upstream" segments need purchasers. Furniture producers, for example, must have a supply of fillings, linings, and finished fabrics; they must also have interior designers and architects who are willing to recommend their upholstered products to clients and retailers who are willing to offer them to their customers.

Sharing a common goal—operating profitably—all members of the industry work cooperatively to ensure that the end products offered are widely accepted by contemporary consumers. To secure this acceptance and realize their goal, suppliers, producers, and distributors often support and seek assistance from such auxiliary enterprises as trade associations and advertising firms. While such groups are not directly involved in the manufacturing sequence, they can have a major influence on quality, awareness, and selection of the industry's goods.

Although the economic health of the industry and its members is primarily determined by consumer acceptance or rejection of the products available, it is also directly af-

fected by such variables as international trade relations, mortgage interest rates, and energy costs. Industry executives must be aware of and respond to these variables if their firms are to be financially viable.

MAJOR SEGMENTS OF THE INDUSTRY

The major segments of the interior textile industry and their positions in the flow of production and distribution are shown in Figure 1.1. The work of the industry is initiated by natural fiber suppliers and man-made fiber producers; it culminates with the residential and commercial consumer.

Fiber Suppliers and Producers

Natural fiber suppliers recover already-formed or "ready-made" fibers, principally from sheep, silk caterpillars, cotton bolls, and flax plants. The responsibility of the supplier is to assist nature and ensure the production of high yields of quality fibers. To be successful, suppliers must cope with the challenges of today's rising costs of labor, feed, pest-control agents, fertilizers, and transportation. They must also contend with growing competition from foreign suppliers and from man-made fiber producers who are constantly seeking to capture a larger share of the fiber market.

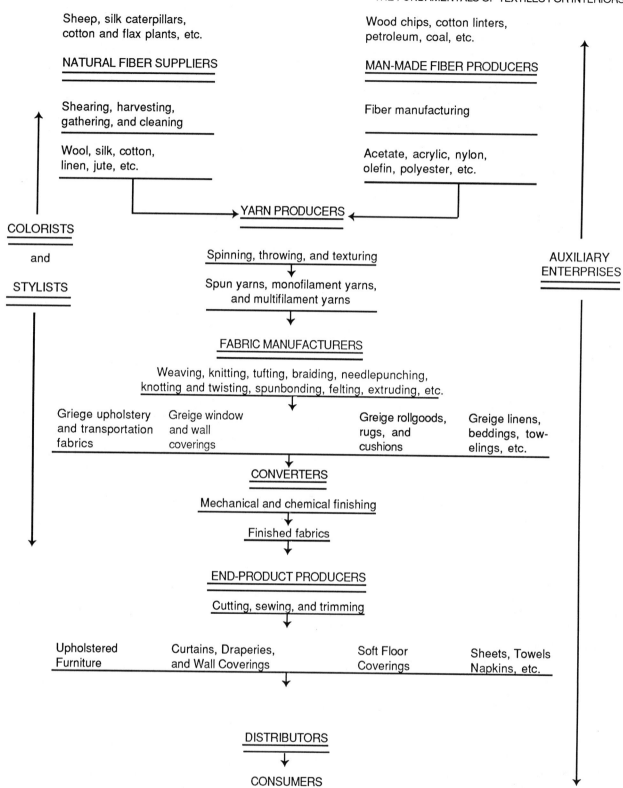

Figure 1.1 The interior textile industry.

Beginning with such natural materials as wood chips, man-made fiber producers manufacture rayon, acetate, and triacetate, and beginning with such natural substances as petroleum and coal, they manufacture acrylic, nylon, polyester, olefin, and several other types of synthesized fibers. Man-made fiber producers are challenged by the rising costs of petroleum and labor, changing trade balances, and persistent competition from natural fiber suppliers.

Fiber suppliers and producers forward staple fibers, filament fibers, and tow to yarn producers. Staple fibers, such as wool, cotton, and linen, are relatively short fibers, measured in inches or centimeters. Filament fibers—silk and man-made fibers—are relatively long fibers, measured in yards or meters. Tow is a bundle of man-made filaments that has been given a two-or three-dimensional crimp or coil but no twist.

Yarn Producers

Yarn producers are responsible for combining fibers into usable yarn structures. Spinsters align, spin, and twist staple-length fibers into spun yarns, and throwsters combine filament-length fibers into untwisted or twisted multifilament yarns. Tow may be directly combined into yarns or it may be reduced to staple-length fibers (Figure 5.3, page 36), which are then spun. Yarn producers frequently employ multiple twisting or plying operations to expand the assortment of yarns available to fabric manufacturers.

Fabric Manufacturers

Fabric manufacturers use a variety of fabrication techniques, including weaving, knitting, knotting and twisting, braiding, and tufting, to combine yarns into fabric structures. They use such techniques as felting, spunbonding, and needlepunching to produce fabrics directly from fibers, bypassing the yarn stage, and they use extruding to produce polymer film sheeting directly from solutions, bypassing both the fiber and yarn stages. With extrusion operations, the man-made fiber/film producer is functioning as the fabric manufacturer.

Fabric producers and textile machinery engineers work cooperatively to develop new equipment and devise more efficient fabrication techniques, continually striving to fulfill two major goals. First, they seek to reduce production time and energy consumption and thus to reduce their manufacturing costs. Second, they work to engineer textile structures that will be accepted by and perform satisfactorily for the ultimate consumer.

After fabrication is completed, the results are still unfinished and often bear little resemblance to fabrics selected by professionals and consumers. These unfinished fabrics, known as greige goods, are forwarded to converters for finishing, or they may first be sent to dyers and printers.

Textile Colorists and Stylists

Textile colorists and fabric stylists may be involved at any stage in the production sequence. Man-made fiber producers may incorporate dye pigments within filaments as they are extruded; dyers may immerse fibers, yarns, or fabrics in a solution of dyestuff. Printers generally apply colorful patterns to greige goods, although they can produce some unique color styles by printing sheets of yarns and tubes of knitted fabric.

Well in advance of production, fabric stylists must identify the aesthetic features preferred by contemporary consumers. They must be alert for slight shifts in the selection of such fashion-related qualities as fabric weight, textural characteristics, and drapability. The must tally the selections of woven-in patterns and printed patterns, noting preferences for simple and elaborate design motifs; for small-scale and large-scale repeats; and for fiber, yarn, and fabric color styling. Stylists must also accurately interpret and forecast trends and anticipate variations, making certain they are suitable for large-scale production operations.

Stylists face another challenge: they must ensure that the fabric's service-related properties meet requirements and expectations. This means that stylists must work closely with converters who can change aesthetic and performance qualities during fabric finishing.

Converters

Converters are fabric finishers; they convert unfinished greige goods into finished fabrics. Using mechanical treatments and chemical agents, they can alter such appearance features as pile yarn orientation and luster and such performance characteristics as water- and soil-repellency, wrinkle recovery, and shape retention. By applying coatings and fabrics to the backs of carpet rollgoods and textile wall coverings, converters can improve the functional characteristics and stability of these structures and facilitate their efficient installation.

End-product Producers

Using fibers, yarns, and finished fabrics, as well as some nonfibrous materials, end-product producers construct items that are ready for immediate use or for installation in an interior setting. Some are specifically produced for use in private interiors—mobile homes, apartments, and other residences. Other products are specifically designed and constructed to withstand the higher levels of use in public or commercial interiors, such as in stores and shopping centers, offices, schools, hospitals, hotels and motels, libraries and public buildings, religious buildings, restaurants and clubs, dormitories, airport terminals, nursing homes, and theaters.

The many interior textile products may be divided into four broad categories, namely upholstered furniture, window and wall coverings, soft floor coverings and cushions, and textile accessories and accents. Among the assortment of products included in each of these categories, there are differences in fiber content, yarn features, fabric structure, color styling, finishes, and product design. In most cases, fabric stylists and end-product designers work cooperatively with producers and marketing specialists to plan the combinations needed to meet a variety of consumer needs and desires.

Domestic producers must compete with one another and with foreign producers; this competition forces them continually to refine their existing products and to develop new and unique items. They must analyze the design, composition, and performance characteristics of their products to confirm that the characteristics offered are those sought by contemporary interior designers, architects, and consumers. At the same time they must contend with the rising costs of materials, labor, and equipment, and seek ways to reduce their consumption, and thus their cost, of energy. Whatever the number and magnitude of the challenges facing them, producers must succeed in meeting them to operate profitably.

It should be noted that some textile firms are organized vertically. These large firms use their own facilities and labor force to complete several sequential production operations. They may, for example, spin yarns, weave fabrics, apply color, convert greige goods, and construct end products. Such corporations normally have the resources needed to support extensive research and development activities and to create and fund effective marketing programs.

Distributors

Several types of retail operations present interior textile products to consumers. Department stores offer home furnishings and household linens, as well as apparel and accessories for all members of the family. Specialty stores offer a limited line of merchandise, such as upholstered furniture or carpet and rugs. Discount stores and factory outlets sell less expensive goods, and mail-order operations offer an ever-expanding assortment of products in a range of prices.

The retailer is sometimes bypassed in the distribution of interior furnishings. An upholstered furniture manufacturer, a wall coverings designer, or a carpet and area rug producer, for example, may elect to maintain a product showroom where merchandise is shown to professional interior designers, architects, and other members of the trade. These professionals select products for their clients that conform with clients' aesthetic preferences, serviceability requirements, and interior furnishings budgets.

Consumers

The consumer is whoever pays for the end product: thus, the consumer may be a person, a group, a corporation, an agency, or an institution. Residential and commercial consumers may prefer to use their own talents and judgments when selecting products, or they may elect to contract for the services of an interior designer or architect. In the latter case, the professionals select, recommend, or specify products, functioning as consultants; their clients, who pay for the merchandise, are consumers.

At this point the work of the industry and the wants and needs of the consumer must coincide. Unless the assortment of products offered by the industry is acceptable to the consumer, the volume of sales will not be high enough for end-product producers to pay their suppliers, cover their operating expenses, and realize an adequate profit. Because a reduction in end-product sales results in a reduction in the amount of fibers, yarns, and finished fabrics needed, it threatens the financial stability of upstream firms as well. Moreover, low profit margins limit the ability of firms to expand. Therefore, all members of the industry strive to ensure that the assortment of products offered conforms with the selection criteria of the contemporary consumer; these criteria are examined in Chapter 2.

AUXILIARY ENTERPRISES

Various enterprises provide valuable assistance to the textile furnishings industry. While their work is primarily intended to generate profit for themselves and for members of the industry, many of their activities are also useful to students, educators, retailers, and consumers. Among the groups serving the industry are trade associations, publishers, advertising firms, and design firms.

Trade Associations

Trade associations are organized to represent, protect, and promote the interests of their members, who provide financial support for the operation and activities of the association. Trade association personnel establish liaisons between their members and various federal and state agencies and legislative bodies. They prepare and distribute educational material and technical literature. They devise marketing programs to increase the recognition and acceptance of their members' products. Some associations also maintain testing laboratories to evaluate and certify the quality of these products.

Some trade associations are composed of firms that compete with one another in the marketplace but also share a common goal. The Man-Made Fiber Producers Association, for example, is supported by several independent firms, each of which is competing for sales orders from downstream firms. At the same time, however, these producers recognize the value of cooperating to provide information about man-made fibers and to extend their use. Other trade associations are made up of firms belonging to different segments of the industry but having a vested interest in the marketing and widespread use of a particular category of products. The Carpet and Rug Institute, for example, works to increase the use of soft floor coverings; Cotton Incorporated works to increase the use of products containing cotton; and The Wool Bureau, Inc. works to increase the use of products containing wool.

Publishers

Writers and publishers provide members of the industry, students, educators, practicing professionals, retailers, and consumers with a wide assortment of articles, books, marketing magazines, technical journals, and trade newspapers focusing on products available for use in interiors. Some of these publications are for the professional preparation of students; some apprise personnel in the industry of new techniques, new products, research findings, marketing plans, and consumer preferences; and some exist to inform the consumer.

Advertising Firms

Industry members use advertising firms and advertisements to introduce and promote new equipment, new components, and new products. Upstream firms direct their advertisements to downstream firms; end-product producers direct their advertisements to members of the trade, to retailers, and to consumers; retailers direct their advertisements to retail consumers. In some cases, the cost of an advertising campaign is shared: for instance, a fiber producer shoulders a portion of the charges assessed for promotions run by an end-product manufacturer.

Design Firms

Interior designers and architects may operate their own firms, be members of partnerships, or be employed by large corporations. In any case, they normally provide services in accordance with the terms of a contractual agreement made with their residential and commercial clients. The frequent use of such a legal document has given rise to the term "contract design" to describe the work of these professionally trained persons.

Contract designers and architects serve as critical links between the industry and the consumer. They have a positive economic effect on the industry when they select new products and when they recommend or specify products that are consistent with their clients' selection criteria. To do their jobs well, they must be familiar with the industry's array of products and be prepared to assess the ability of different products to perform satisfactorily under a particular set of end-use conditions. They must be aware of legal mandates governing the selection and installation of products in a particular facility or in a particular location within a facility. Ultimately, the accuracy with which interior designers and architects recommend or specify products helps determine their professional reputation, and it can have a major influence on the willingness of their clients to be repeat customers of particular interior textile products.

FACTORS AFFECTING THE ECONOMIC HEALTH OF THE INDUSTRY

Several of the factors affecting the work and economic health of the textile industry originate elsewhere in other industries and in government. They nevertheless have a direct impact by favoring or restricting production and expansion in the industry.

Inflation

Inflation (demands exceeds supply and prices rise) makes it necessary for many consumers to alter their spending and savings patterns. Together with high interest rates on personal loans, inflation forces many consumers to postpone purchases of more expensive durable goods, including carpet, upholstered furniture, and automobiles.

Income-related Variables

The demand for textile furnishings is directly affected by the level of income realized by consumers. Their disposable or real income is affected by federal and state income taxes and social security taxes. A reduction in personal income taxes may result in increased savings, reduced interest rates, and an increased demand for durable goods. On the other hand, a reduction in taxes when interest rates are high may result in increased spending for nondurables; consequently, spending for durable goods may continue to be delayed

Fluctuations in the costs of such basic necessities as food, clothing, and shelter, together with the costs of such other things as education and transportation, also influence the demand for interior textile products. These costs alter the discretionary income of consumers, increasing or decreasing the amount of income left to spend on the basis of want rather than need.

Automobile and Gasoline Costs

An increase in the prices of new automobiles or the cost of gasoline encourages many consumers to select smaller passenger cars. A reduction in car size has a negative effect on firms producing automotive carpet, as well as on those firms supplying upholstery, tire cord, and interior roof and trunk linings.

Mortgage Interest Rates and Building Costs

Mortgage interest rates and the costs of building materials directly affect the number and size of new constructions. Of course, high rates and costs have a negative effect, slowing construction and reducing the need for such products as carpet, rugs, upholstered furniture, textile wall coverings, and curtains and draperies. At the same time, the negative impact of such slowdowns may be somewhat tempered by increases in the replacement of these items in existing residential and commercial structures.

Energy Costs and Concerns

Concern for energy conservation and the pressure of rising energy costs encourage many residential and commercial consumers to increase their use of soft floor coverings and textile window coverings as insulation materials. In the industry, such energy-related factors have fostered the develoment of more efficient and economical production techniques and equipment.

Mergers and Acquisitions

Within the industry, mergers and acquisitions can result in companies with greater financial resources, more efficient operations, and a greater number of proficient and skilled personnel. Such large firms are better able to support valuable and necessary research activities, mount effective marketing campaigns, and respond quickly and accurately to changes in consumer needs and wants. They are also more likely to undertake lobbying efforts, the results of which may benefit all members of the industry.

International Trade Relations

An agreement focusing on the international trading of textiles, commonly known as the Multi-Fiber Arrangement (M-F A), began in January 1974, with Western and Far Eastern countries participating. The M-F A encourages participating countries to engage in trade negotiations and to reach bilateral agreements concerning equitable import/export balances. The intention of such agreements is to help firms in each country increase their level of exports without disrupting the domestic markets of firms in the importing country. The agreement gives trading partners legal recourse against a partner who violates an agree-

ment. Prior to mid-1986, the scope of the M-F A included products that were either in chief weight or chief value of cotton, wool, or man-made fibers, or which contained over 17 percent by weight of wool; it did not include those composed primarily of linen, silk, or ramie. However, newly concluded agreements, in effect until mid-1991, have expanded the scope to include selected products made of silk blends (under 70 percent silk by weight), linen, and ramie.

On October 31, 1984, new country-of-origin regulations established by the United States Customs Service, a unit of the Department of Treasury, went into effect. These rules apply to products fully processed in one or more foreign countries and subsequently imported into the United States under the quotas of the M-F A. For quota purposes, the Customs Service designates the country in which there has been a substantial transformation of the product as the country of origin; the product is then counted in that country's import quota. The Customs Service believes these regulations will curb the practice of exporting products to the United States via countries having an unfilled quota or no quota limitation. (These regulations are also used in determining the country of origin of imported goods for the purpose of product labeling. See Chapter 10.)

Other Factors

Other factors influencing the economic stability and expansion of the industry include fluctuations in the cost of raw materials, labor, and equipment. In addition, the cost of compliance with mandatory performance and safety specifications generally necessitates an increase in the price of certain products, which can slow their sales, at least temporarily.

SUMMARY

The primary goal of all firms in the interior textile industry is to operate profitably. All members of the industry recognize that this goal depends on consumer acceptance of the end products offered. They strive to secure the initial and repeated selection of their assorted products. In this effort, they often enlist the support of such auxiliary enterprises as trade associations, advertising and publishing agencies, and contract design firms.

To succeed, a firm must cope with competition from other firms and with various external factors. Among the external factors are mortgage interest rates that may encourage or retard new construction, pressure from foreign producers, and imposed product performance mandates. Whatever challenges are posed by these variables, all industry firms must focus their attention on the wants and needs of contemporary residential and commercial consumers.

chapter 2

Selecting and Evaluating Textiles for Interiors

- Selecting Interior Textile Products
- Evaluating Interior Textiles

Each residential and commercial consumer has a unique set of criteria governing selection of textile end products. Some of these variables relate to appearance and tactile characteristics; some focus on service-related performance; some are concerned with maintenance and installation; and some are necessarily determined by cost factors. Industry firms must be aware of these variables in order to offer products that meet the current selection criteria.

As part of their effort to secure the initial and repeated selection of their products, many firms measure specific properties of the products' components and assess the potential serviceability of the finished items prior to marketing. Initially, this work enables them to make statements about their products' performance on labels and in promotional materials in order to capture the attention of professionals and prospective purchasers. Subsequently, these evaluations help ensure that their goods will continue to exhibit an acceptable level of in-use performance, satisfying consumers and encouraging them to go on selecting the company's products. In many cases, this quality-control work involves the use of standard methods of testing and performance specifications published by scientific and technical associations.

Many producers also evaluate their products in accordance with standards established by various regulatory agencies. Products complying with the design or perfor-

mance specifications set forth in these mandates can be used in interiors that come within the scope of legally binding standards.

SELECTING INTERIOR TEXTILE PRODUCTS

Several characteristics considered in the selection of textile furnishings are listed in Table 2.1. In most cases, the residential or commercial consumer determines the relative importance of these variables, personally deciding whether any compromises can be made. For certain commercial products, however, various regulatory agencies have the authority to require compliance with specific product standards.

Challenges to Members of the Industry

To remain profitable, firms in the industry must constantly monitor consumer selections, noting and quickly responding to changes in consumer preferences. The aesthetic features currently preferred must be mirrored in the products offered; the service-related characteristics expected must be available; any mandated design and performance properties must be exhibited; required maintenance and installation procedures must coincide with those preferred by consumers; and the price of the product, along with any charges for assembly, delivery, and installation, must not exceed the ability or willingness of the consumer to pay.

Table 2.1 CONSUMER PRODUCT SELECTION CRITERIA

	Variable characteristics
Appearance features	color styling: heather, multicolored, solid-colored; scale and detail of motifs, size of pattern repeat color characteristics: hue, value, and intensity level of light reflectance level of light transmittance visual textural features: nonpile, cut pile, uncut pile, smooth surface end product styling: trimmed, plain, traditional, contemporary, life expectancy of fashion elements, coordination with existing interior and current furnishings availability of matching and/or coordinated items
Tactile characteristics	drapability: stiff, fluid hand: smooth, rough, warm, cool, soft, harsh fabric weight
Serviceability expectations	functional properties: insulation, glare reduction, static reduction, fatigue reduction, noise control, mobility improvements, safety enhancement appearance retention: color retention, texture retention, resistance to pilling and snagging, soil hiding, soil repellency durability: abrasion resistance, tear resistance, dimensional stability, repairability
Design and performance mandates	flame resistance structural stability colorfastness wear resistance functional properties: acoustical value, static reduction
Maintenance requirements	cleanability: washable, drycleanable on-site versus off-site cleaning ease of stain removal level of ironing required: none, touch-up, extensive frequency of cleaning
Installation factors	site preparation tools and level of skill needed permanence: movable, removable, permanent
Cost factors	product price accessories prices warranty costs delivery charges installation fees maintenance costs interest charges effect on energy costs professional consultant fees

Challenges to Professionals and Consumers

Whatever textile furnishings are offered in the marketplace, consumers, designers, and architects should be informed when making their selections. They must, for example, consider the factors affecting the apparent color of textiles to ensure that the color characteristics chosen will look the same when seen in the interior setting. They must understand how the components and structural features of a product influence its functional properties and use-life. Consumers and professionals should therefore be aware of inherent and engineered fiber properties, yarn and fabric features, factors affecting color retention, and the effects of finishing treatments and agents. They should be prepared to identify the activities, conditions, and substances to which the item will be subjected in use, and be able to make reliable judgments regarding the ability of the item to perform satisfactorily when exposed to the anticipated stresses and agents. These several product and end-use variables will be discussed in detail throughout this book.

When contract designers and architects are selecting interior textile products for commercial use, they must ascertain which, if any, agency has jurisdiction over the project. They must identify all regulations affecting their selections. They must also confirm that their planned product selections conform with all mandated criteria.

Agencies Regulating Product Selections

Regulatory agencies are outside of the textile industry but have the power to oversee the selection of many of its products. Some of the federal agencies involved in these activities are identified here. The reader must be cautioned that the jurisdiction, responsibilities, and mandates of all regulatory agencies change frequently. Contract designers and architects must contact the various agencies to confirm their current jurisdictions and requirements.

The Federal Housing Administration (FHA). The FHA, a division of the Department of Housing and Urban Development (HUD), has jurisdiction over the materials used in the interiors of such places as elderly and care-type housing, low rent public housing projects, and structures insured by FHA. The minimum standards established for materials used in these facilities are set forth in the Use of Materials Bulletin 44c, which is available from the FHA.

The Social Security Administration (SSA). The SSA, a division of the Department of Health and Human Services (HHS), administers the Medicare and Medicaid programs. In order to participate in these programs, hospitals and extended care facilities must comply with SSA regulations dealing with such things as fire safety and acoustics. Some of these regulations apply to the textile products selected for these facilities.

The General Services Administration (GSA). The GSA oversees the selection of materials for federal facilities. Federal Test Method Standard No. 191A, issued July 20, 1978, describes the general physical, chemical, and biological methods used to test textile fibers, yarn, thread, rope, other cordage, cloth, and fabricated textile products for conformity with mandated and performance specifications. Revised and new test methods are issued as needed.

The Federal Aviation Administration (FAA) and the National Highway Traffic Safety Administration (NHTSA). The FAA and the NHTSA are divisions of the Department of Transportation (DOT). The FAA regulates the selection and installation of textile items in the crew and passenger compartments of airliners, and the NHTSA oversees the selection and installation of textile products in automobiles and certain other vehicles. Flammability standards established by these agencies are discussed in Chapter 16.

There are several other agencies regulating the selection of textile products. Some cities, notably Boston and New York, have stringent flammability mandates, and virtually all states have established criteria related to the flammability of products used in commercial interiors. The reader must again be cautioned that the jurisdiction, responsibilities, and mandates of all regulatory agencies are frequently changed.

The Consumer Product Safety Commission is a federal agency concerned with the flammability of textile products, but the Commission does not set standards pertaining to product selection. Rather, it prohibits the initial introduction of highly flammable products into commerce and thus prevents them from being available for selection. The Commission and its work are discussed in Chapter 11.

EVALUATING INTERIOR TEXTILES

Along with other informed and interested persons, many members of the textile industry participate in the work of several scientific and technical associations. Participants in most of these groups voluntarily share their expertise and opinions to help develop standards pertaining to such things as definitions, recommended practices, methods of testing, classifications, design specifications, or performance specifications. Producers throughout the industry may elect to use these standards when they evaluate their components and end products. Standards related to testing and performance are discussed here.

Methods of Testing

A standard test method prescribes specific procedures to be followed when making a given measurement, for instance, the measurement of yarn distortion after surface friction. A test method details the selection, size, number, and preparation of the test specimens; describes the test apparatus; specifies test conditions; sets forth test procedures; and lists the observations and calculations to be made in analyzing and reporting the test results. Unless specifically stated otherwise, testing is carried out in a controlled atmosphere of 70 ± 2 °F and $65 \pm 2\%$ RH. In order to produce accurate and reproducible results, textile researchers and quality-control personnel must strictly adhere to all details included in a standard test method. Performance comparisons can only be made among specimens tested in a like manner. (While the summaries of test methods provided in later chapters are adequate for discussion, they are not sufficient for carrying out testing. Interested persons can read the full text of standard test methods in such publications as the *AAATC Technical Manual* and the *Annual Book of ASTM Standards.* These publications are listed in the bibliography.) Test methods simulate the conditions to which textile items may be subjected in actual use. Such small-scale laboratory techniques minimize the need for large-scale, long-term, and more expensive evaluation procedures. Standard test methods enable producers efficiently and economically to measure their products' quality and performance.

Many manufacturers use test results as the basis for claims that their products exhibit specific functional and use-life characteristics. They may also analyze test results to determine the advisability of putting their name or other identifying mark on the product label.

Performance Specifications

While analysis of the results of a standard test method may require numerical calculations, it may or may not specify numerical limitations or boundaries pertaining to performance. By contrast, such performance-related requirements are always included in a standard performance specification. These requirements represent the minimum or maximum levels—the limits—of performance that the specimens should exhibit when tested in accordance with the designated method.

Industry members may elect to compare the level of performance recorded for their products with the level recommended in the standard, and, if necessary, to alter the composition or processing of their items accordingly. Compliance with such recommendations ensures that the component or product will exhibit an acceptable level of in-use performance, which in turn will help to secure consumer goodwill and repeat business for the complying company.

Scientific and Technical Associations

Among the many scientific associations involved in establishing standards, five are of particular interest to producers and consumers of textile furnishing. Participants serve voluntarily in four of the five groups.

The American Association of Textile Chemists and Colorists (AATCC). Founded in 1921, AATCC is a technical and scientific society that is internationally recognized for its standard methods of testing dyed and chemically-treated fibers and fabrics to measure and evaluate such performance characteristics as colorfastness to light and washing, shrinkage, water resistance, flammability, and many other conditions to which textiles may be subjected. While it is beyond the scope of AATCC to set standard performance specifications, the test methods help producers and retailers to ensure the marketability and satisfactory performance of textile fabrics.

AATCC maintains a technical center that serves as a test demonstration center. Its laboratory is equipped with all of the testing apparatus used in AATCC test methods; personnel at the center provide technical support to members engaged in the work of the Association. Members receive the Association's monthly journal, *Textile Chemist and Colorist,* which presents information concerning recent developments in dyes, finishes, and equipment used in the wet processing of textiles, and also includes reports of current research activities in the field of textiles.

The American Society for Testing and Materials (ASTM). The term "materials" in this organization's name indicates that materials other than textiles—such as metals, concrete, and acoustical board—also receive attention from the society's members. The Society publishes the *Annual Book of ASTM Standards;* this consists of forty-eight separate books, each focusing on a limited variety of materials, products, or processes. Included in each book are all proposed, tentative, and formally adopted standards, guidelines, and performance specifications developed for use with the specific materials or processes covered.

The work of ASTM is carried out by more than 135 committees. Each major committee is given a letter and number, followed by a general product designation, for instance, D-13 Committee on Textiles. Further numerical designations are used for subcommittees, for example, D-13.21 Subcommittee on Pile Floor Coverings, D-13.56 Subcommittee on Performance Standards for Textile Fabrics. Standards developed by ASTM committees are described as "full-consensus" standards. ASTM members and nonmembers who have an interest in a standard or who would be affected by its application are encouraged to participate in the development of the standard. Each committee and subcommittee has the participation of both producers and users of the products in question, to ensure a balanced representation of all biases and opinions.

The National Fire Protection Association (NFPA). Organized in 1896, the NFPA invites the membership of persons concerned with fire safety. NFPA committees establish standards designed to reduce extent of injury, loss of life, and destruction of property from fire. This work is not limited to the development of test methods and performance specifications for textile products: standards have also been issued for items ranging from household warning equipment to fire fighters' helmets, as well as for the design of egress facilities permitting the prompt escape of occupants from burning buildings or into safe areas within the buildings.

The American National Standards Institute (ANSI). Unlike the other groups discussed here, ANSI is a private corporation, not a voluntary association. ANSI undertakes the development of standards only when so commissioned by an industry group or a government agency. The Institute seeks to reduce the duplication of effort among the many organizations developing voluntary standards and identifies nationally accepted standards. ANSI is the official United States representative to the International Organization for Standardization.

The International Organization for Standardization (ISO). ISO engages in the development of standards to help foster international textile trade. ISO 1139 Designation of Yarns, for example, describes the tex direct yarn numbering system, and is intended to encourage firms throughout the world to identify yarns with their tex number, rather than with their denier or indirect yarn number. (Yarn numbering systems are discussed in Chapter 5.)

Designation and Cross-listing of Standards. Standards developed by the above-mentioned organizations as well as by other associations are issued with fixed designations. For example, ASTM designates standards by the letter assigned to the committee and an identifying number. Immediately following the designation is a number indicating the year of original adoption or of the last revision; a number in parentheses indicates the year of the last reapproval. However it is designated, the latest edition of a standard should always be used in quality-control and research activities.

Standards developed by one scientific association are often shared with and cross-listed by other associations. ASTM E-84 The Standard Method of Test of Surface Burning Characteristics of Building Materials, for example, is also identified as NFPA 255 and as ANSI A2.5. Cross-listing may indicate widespread acceptance of a standard, but it does not change its voluntary status. Standards developed by these scientific and technical associations are recommendations, not mandates. The associations have no power or authority to enforce the use of standard test methods or compliance with standard performance specifications. However, voluntary standards established by these groups are often adopted by local, state, or federal regulatory agencies; the standard then becomes mandatory.

SUMMARY

Residential and commercial consumers consider many variables when they select textile products. The nature and relative importance of these variables is constantly changing. Members of the industry are challenged to identify the current criteria and to offer products that coincide with them.

To ensure that their products will exhibit an acceptable level of in-use performance and satisfy the consumer, most producers of textile components and end-products evaluate their goods prior to shipment. This quality-control work generally involves the use of standard test methods and performance specifications, many of which are developed by members of scientific associations. The use of such standards is voluntary unless they have been adopted by a regulatory agency, in which case products must comply with the criteria set out by the agency before they can be selected for a specific interior.

chapter 3

Textile Fibers

- Fiber Classification and Identification
- Fiber Composition and Structure
- Fiber Production
- Fiber Engineering

Fibers used in contemporary textile furnishings are chemically the same as those used in apparel and industrial textile products. Wool fibers, for example, are used in fine crepe apparel fabrics, durable upholstery coverings, and thick insulation felt for industrial applications; nylon fibers are used in lingerie, carpet, automobile seat belts, and tires; and polyester fibers are used in ready-to-wear apparel, upholstery, drapery, bedding, and tent fabrics. The characteristics that make a given fiber suitable for a particular end-use application are engineered by production and processing techniques.

Whether a fiber is produced by nature or manufactured by man, it is distinguished by its chemical composition and characterized by specific internal and external physical features. Such characteristics are inherent features of natural fibers; they are engineered features of man-made fibers. In either case, these variables make for the appearance, chemical reactions, and performance properties of fibers.

Because their chemical composition distinguishes textile fibers, they are classified and named on the basis of this composition. A review of the nomenclature will serve to introduce the basic vocabulary used to discuss fibers and to label and promote textile products.

FIBER CLASSIFICATION AND IDENTIFICATION

Specific textile fibers are identified by their common or generic name for purposes of discussion or disclosure on a sample or product label. Fibers grouped under the same name are chemically related and tend to exhibit similar properties. Consumers and professionals who are familiar with these names, and with the properties that typically characterize each group, are better equipped to make reliable fiber selections and to identify unnamed fibers.

Classification

A fiber classification system is presented in Table 3.1. Textile fibers are first classified on the basis of how they are produced, whether natural or man-made. Although all man-made fibers are manufactured from natural substances, some of which are inherently fibrous, none can be classified as a natural fiber since the usable fiber form is a product of industrial processing.

Within the two broad fiber groupings, further classification may be made on the basis of general chemical composition, for instance, protein, cellulose, petroleum-based, or mineral. Lastly, fibers are classified by their generic names. For purposes of fiber identification and product labeling, the centuries-old common or family names used for natural fibers are considered their generic names.

Generic names or classes for man-made fibers were established by the Federal Trade Commission in accordance with a congressional directive. Each class is defined in

Table 3.1 **TEXTILE FIBER CLASSIFICATION**

Natural Fibers		
Protein (animals)	**Cellulose (plants)**	**Mineral (rock)**

alpaca (alpaca)
angora (angora
    rabbit)
camel (Bactrian
    camel)
cashmere (Cashmere
    goat)
cattle hair (cattle)
fur fibers (beaver,
    fox, mink,
    sable, etc.)
horse hair (horse)
llama (llama)
mohair (Angora goat)
silk (silkworm)
vicuna (vicuna)
wool (sheep)
	Leaf
	    abaca (Manila fiber)
	    banana
	    pina (pineapple)
	    sisal
	Nut husk
	    coir (coconut)
	Seed
	    cotton
	    kapok
	Stem (bast)
	    hemp
	    jute
	    linen
	    ramie (China grass)
		asbestos

Man-made Fibers		
Cellulose-based	**Protein-based**	**Rubber**
acetate triacetate rayon	azlons[a]	rubber (natural liquid rubber)

Petroleum-based				**Mineral**
acrylic	novoloid[b]	rubber(synthetic)		glass
anidex[a]	nylon	saran	PBI[c]	metallic
aramid[b]	nytril[a]	spandex	sulfar[c]	
lastrile[a]	olefin	vinal[a]		
modacrylic	polyester	vinyon		

[a]These groups are not currently produced in the United States; some may be imported, however.
[b]Name established in 1974.
[c]Name established in 1986.

terms of specific chemical composition. The generic class "acrylic," for example, describes "a manufactured fiber in which the fiber-forming substance is any long chain synthetic polymer composed of at least 85% by weight of acrylonitrile units. . . ." By contrast, the generic class "nylon" specifies "a manufactured fiber in which the fiber-forming substance is a long chain synthetic polyamide in which less than 85% of the amide . . . linkages are attached directly to two aromatic rings." A complete listing of the generic class names and definitions set forth by the Commission, as well as those promulgated by the International Organization for Standardization, is presented in Appendix A.

At this point, it may be useful to highlight the definition of olefin fibers. The name "olefin" is assigned to "a manufactured fiber in which the fiber-forming substance is any long chain synthetic polymer composed of at least 85% by weight of ethylene, propylene, or other olefin units." It should be noted that the frequently used terms "ethylene" and "propylene" identify specific olefin units; they are not generic names. Producers often pair "ethylene" or "propylene" with "olefin," or even incorrectly use the terms alone, to indicate the presence or absence of ethylene units. Ethylene compounds melt at relatively low temperatures, too low to permit their use in virtually any textile furnishings.

The mandatory use of generic names in textile fiber product labeling and promotion is discussed in Chapter 10. Also discussed in that chapter are the powers and responsibilities of the Federal Trade Commission with respect to the commercial activities of the industry.

Identification

Various testing and examination procedures can help expedite the identification of unknown fibers. Among these techniques are solubility and staining tests, measurement of fiber density, microscopic examination, burning tests, and visual examination. Because some of these procedures require special reagents, microscopes, infrared spectrometers, exhaust hoods, and the like, they can only be conducted in an adequately equipped laboratory. On the other hand, the burning test can readily be conducted by designers, architects, retailers, and consumers, all of whom have access to matches.

To conduct a burning test, the following procedure can be used, with caution:

1. Hold several fibers or a yarn from a fabric with metal tweezers over an ashtray to catch ashes and drips.
2. Strike a match away from the body for safety and to avoid inhaling the smoke and fumes.
3. Observe the reaction of the specimen as it approaches the flame, when it is in the flame, and after the ignition source is removed. Note the odor and examine the cooled residue.

Observations from a completed burning test can be compared with the reactions listed in Table 3.2. (Other heat-related fiber properties are identified in Table 4.5 and the pyrolytic characteristics of selected fibers are detailed in Table 11.1.) If a mixture of reactions is noted when a yarn is burned, a blend may be suspected. Visual characteristics may help the observer to separate different fibers in the yarn and repeat the test.

In some cases, the results obtained in a burning test may not permit identification of the generic class of the unknown fiber; the results will, however, always enable the observer to classify the specimen in a meaningful category, such as protein, petroleum-based, or cellulosic. Visual examination may help to support further identification.

FIBER COMPOSITION AND STRUCTURE

All textile fibers, natural and man-made, are relatively fine: that is, they are long and thin and have comparatively high ratios of length to width. This structural feature ensures the flexibility required for manufacturing and end-use serviceability. Differences among textile fibers result not only from their different chemical compositions, but also from variations in the arrangement of their interior units and the nature of their external features.

Molecular Units

With the exception of the inorganic glass and metal fibers, virtually all fibers have carbon (C) and hydrogen (H) atoms. Some fibers, such as cotton, linen, rayon, acetate, and polyester, also have oxygen (O); others, such as wool, silk, acrylic, and nylon, also have nitrogen (N); and wool also has sulfur (S). The various atoms present in each fiber are combined into distinctive molecular fiber-forming units known as monomers (from the Greek *mono,* "one," and *mer,* "part"). Through a process known as polymerization, thousands of monomers are linked by strong chemical bonds into extremely long, chain-like units known as polymers (from the Greek *poly,* "many," and *mer,* "part"). The polymer chains in textile fibers are so long that they are often referred to as "macromolecules" and "linear high polymers."

In the protein fibers, the atoms combine into monomeric units known as alpha amino acids. These monomers can be represented by the generalized formula,

$$HO-\overset{\overset{\displaystyle O}{\|}}{C}-\overset{\overset{\displaystyle H}{|}}{\underset{\underset{\displaystyle R}{|}}{C}}-NH_2$$

By replacing the letter R with specific groupings of atoms, the eighteen or nineteen alpha amino acids found in wood and the eleven or twelve found in silk can be identified. In the natural cellulosic fibers and rayon, the monomeric unit is anhydrous glucose:

Alternate anhydrous glucose units are flipped over in the cellulosic polymer chain. The monomeric units used to form each of the petroleum-based fibers are identified in Appendix A.

Molecular Arrangements

Within textile fibers, the polymer chains assume or are made to assume, different types of arrangements. Four of these arrangements are schematically illustrated in Figure 3.1.

Table 3.2 REACTION OF TEXTILE FIBERS TO HEAT AND FLAME

Fiber	When approaching flame	When in flame	After removal of flame	Residue	Odor
Natural					
Protein					
wool	curls away from flame	burns slowly	self-extinguishing[a]	brittle, small black bead	similar to burning hair or feathers
silk	curls away from flame	burns slowly and sputters	usually self-extinguishing	beadlike, crushable, black	similar to burning hair or feathers
Cellulose					
cotton	does not shrink away, ignites upon contact	burns quickly without melting	continues to burn; afterglow	light, feathery ash, light gray to charcoal in color	similar to burning paper
linen	does not shrink away, ignites upon contact	burns quickly without melting	continues to burn; afterglow	light, feathery ash, light gray to charcoal in color	similar to burning paper
Man-made					
Cellulose-based					
acetate	melts and fuses away from flame	burns quickly with melting	continues to burn rapidly with melting	brittle, irregular-shaped bead, black	acrid (hot vinegar)
rayon	does not shrink away, ignites upon contact	burns quickly without melting	continues to burn; afterglow	light, fluffy ash, small amount	similar to burning paper
Mineral					
glass	shrinks away from flame	melts and glows red to orange	glowing ceases, does not burn	hard bead, white in color	none
metallic pure	may shrink away from flame or have no reaction	glows red	glowing ceases, does not burn, hardens	skeleton outline of fiber	none
coated	fuses and shrinks away from flame	burns according to behavior of coating	reacts according to behavior of coating	hard bead, black in color	characteristic of coating

Table 3.2 (continued)

Fiber	When approaching flame	When in flame	After removal of flame	Residue	Odor
Petroleum-based					
acrylic	fuses and shrinks away from flame	burns with melting	continues to burn with melting	brittle, irregular-shaped bead, black	acrid
modacrylic	fuses away from flame	burns slowly and irregularly with melting	self-extinguishing[a]	hard, irregular-shaped bead, black	acid chemical
nylon	fuses and shrinks away from flame	burns slowly with melting	usually self-extinguishing[a]	hard, tough, round bead, gray in color	celery
olefin	fuses, shrinks, and curls away from flame	burns with melting	continues to burn with melting, black sooty smoke	hard, tough tan bead	chemical or candle wax
polyester	fuses and shrinks away from flame	burns slowly with melting	usually self-extinguishing[a]	hard, tough, round bead, black in color	chemical
saran	fuses and shrinks away from flame	burns very slowly with melting, yellow flame	self-extinguishing[a]	hard, irregular-shaped bead, black	chemical
spandex	fuses but does not shrink away from flame	burns with melting	continues to burn with melting	soft, crushable, fluffy, black ash	chemical
vinyon	fuses and shrinks away from flame	burns slowly with melting	self-extinguishing[a]	hard, irregular-shaped bead, black	acrid

[a]Self-extinguishing fibers stop burning when the source of ignition is removed.

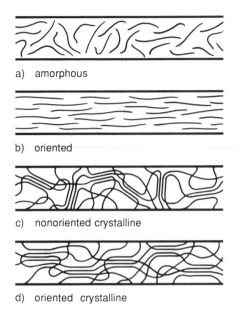

a) amorphous

b) oriented

c) nonoriented crystalline

d) oriented crystalline

Figure 3.1 Molecular arrangements in fibers.

When the polymer chains are not aligned parallel to each other, a disordered, amorphous arrangement exists. When the chains are aligned parallel to the long axis of the fiber, the arrangement is oriented. When the chains are laterally or longitudinally parallel to each other and closely packed, a high number of chemical bonds or attractions, weaker than the main chain bonds, may form between adjacent chains. Such ordered regions are crystalline.

The schematic illustration of an amorphous arrangement shown in Figure 3.1a may remind the reader of cooked spaghetti. This analogy can help us appreciate that fibers, such as wool, that have these highly disordered interiors are characterized by relatively high flexibility and low strength: the stronger chemical bonds linking the monomer units are not aligned lengthwise, the direction of stress in textile fibers. By contrast, fibers with an oriented chain arrangement have their strongest bonds longitudinally aligned, enabling them to bear heavier loads. In any tug-of-war, the winning participants are aligned to offer a collective resistance to the opposing force.

Textile fibers cannot have a totally oriented, crystallized interior arrangement because such fibers would be brittle and inflexible and would snap under stress. Fibers that tend to be highly ordered, such as linen, have relatively low extensibility and flex abrasion resistance. Fabrics composed of such stiff fibers are also less drapable.

External Features

The external features of textile fibers include their cross-sectional shape, their longitudinal configuration, their surface texture, and their length. These features, like molecular composition and arrangement, directly influence the properties of fibers.

Cross-sectional Shape. The cross-sectional shape of a fiber may be basically round, square, flat, or triangular, or it may be multilobal, having from three to five or more lobes with either slightly concave or deeply indented sides. The effects of cross-sectional shape on the look, stiffness, and tactile characteristics of fibers are explained in Chapter 4. The effects of various shapes on the ability of fibers to hide accumulated soil, an important service-related characteristic for fibers used in soft floor coverings, are discussed in Chapter 24.

Surface Texture. The surface of textile fibers may be smooth or wrinkled, somewhat rough, or otherwise irregular. Some typical textures are schematized in Figure 3.2. Together with other external features, texture affects the luster and tactile properties of fabric, aesthetic variables that are relatively important selection criteria for many consumers.

Longitudinal Configuration. Lengthwise, fibers may be fairly straight or twisted, or they may have a two- or three-dimensional crimp or coil. While the form of natural fibers is determined by nature, the form of man-made fibers is often engineered during fiber or yarn processing. The longitudinal configurations of wool, cotton, rayon, and a conventional man-made fiber are illustrated in Figure 3.2.

The longitudinal configuration of fibers affects such aesthetic features as luster and hand. It also affects such performance properties as elasticity, resiliency, and abrasion resistance.

Length. Textile fibers range in length from a fraction of an inch to several miles. Most cotton is 13/16 of an inch in length; most wool fibers are between 1 and 8 inches in length; silk filaments approach 2 miles; and man-made fibers can be manufactured to any continuous length desired.

If other features are equal, longer staples are stronger than shorter staples, and filaments are stronger than staples. In turn, the strength of a fiber helps determine its abrasion resistance.

FIBER PRODUCTION

The production of all fibers, natural and man-made, follows this highly simplified sequence:

atoms → monomers → polymer chains → usable fibers.

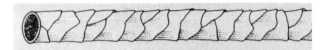

a) overlapping surface scale of wool

b) twisted configuration and wrinkled surface of cotton

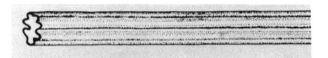

c) straight configuration and irregular surface of viscose rayon

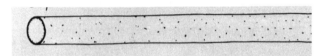

d) straight configuration and smooth surface of conventional man-made fiber

Figure 3.2 Longitudinal forms and surface textures of selected fibers. (Reproduced with adaptations courtesy of Brickel Associates Inc.)

For most natural fibers, this entire sequence is carried out by animals or plants; an exception is asbestos, which is a mineral. For man-made fibers, the chemist becomes responsible for production at the monomer stage, even when nature provides the monomers and polymers.

Natural Fiber Production

The production of natural fibers is accomplished by nature with human assistance but without direct human involvement. Sheep, silk caterpillars, cotton and flax plants, and other organisms synthesize the monomers, form the polymer chains, and produce the usable fibers. The contri-

bution of suppliers is important but limited. They must nurture and protect their animals and plants, keeping their sheep and caterpillars healthy and fed and their cotton and flax plants fertilized, weed-free, and protected from harmful insects. Wool fleeces must be shorn from the sheep, silk filaments must be unwound from the cocoons, linen fibers must be removed from the flax stalks, and cotton fibers must be separated from the seeds in the bolls. Once the fibers are recovered, they must be cleaned, sorted, and graded prior to yarn production.

Man-made Fiber Production

Currently, three major groups of man-made fibers are produced. These include the cellulose-based fibers, the petroleum-based fibers, and the mineral fibers. Virtually all of the fibers included within these groups are manufactured in this sequence:

obtaining fiber-forming substances ➔ forming polymer solutions ➔ incorporating polymer additives ➔ extruding and solidifying filaments ➔ drawing ➔ heat setting.

Obtaining Fiber-forming Substances. Most fiber-forming substances are obtained by one of three techniques: extracting them from fibrous materials, synthesizing them from nonfibrous natural materials, and combining inorganic compounds.

Extracting cellulosic polymers. To produce rayon, acetate, and triacetate fibers, the chemist extracts cellulosic material from such things as wood chips and extremely short cotton fibers known as linters. Although both materials are fibrous, wood fibers lack the flexibility needed for textile processing and end-use applications and linters are too short to spin into quality yarns.

Before acetate and triacetate fibers are produced, acid compounds are used to alter or modify the composition of the extracted anhydrous glucose chains. Because of this change, these fibers are often referred to as modified cellulosic fibers.

Synthesizing monomers. To produce polyester, nylon, acrylic, olefin, and other petroleum-based fibers, the chemist must first synthesize the monomers from such nonfibrous natural materials as oil and coal. Subsequently, the monomers are polymerized in vessels resembling pressure cookers. During this step of the process, the chemist can often control the degree of polymerization, that is, the extent to which the monomers link to form polymer chains. When high strength and abrasion resistance are needed, for example, the chemist will form longer chains.

Because of the initial synthesis of the monomers, the term "synthetic" was formerly applied to these fibers. Negative connotations are sometimes associated with this term, however, and its use has diminished. Today, the term "noncellulosic" is widely used in reference to this group of man-made fibers. Use of this term is limited to the petroleum-based fibers; it does not include such noncellulosic fibers as wool, silk, glass, and metal fibers.

Combining inorganic compounds. Man-made mineral fibers, including glass and metal fibers, are inorganic fibers. Glass fibers are formed by heating silica sand, limestone, and other compounds until they fuse and liquefy; distinctive fiber-forming units are not produced. The resulting solution is normally converted into marbles which can be inspected for clarity.

True metal fibers are made from such substances as gold, silver, copper, and stainless steel. The expense of gold and silver, of course, precludes their widespread use; other structures have been developed to simulate their appearance.

Forming Polymer Solutions. The second step in the production of man-made fibers is the formation of a solution of the fiber-forming substance. In some cases, a solvent is used to dissolve the polymer compound; in other cases, heat is used to melt the substance.

Incorporating Additives. After the polymer solution is formed, the producer may incorporate additives to engineer specific properties. Such additives include dye pigments for superior colorfastness, optical brighteners to improve apparent whiteness and brightness, ultraviolet absorbers to minimize light degradation, flame retardant agents to reduce flammability, delusterants to reduce light reflectance and hide accumulated soil, and antistatic agents to increase electrical conductivity.

Extruding and Solidifying Filaments. Filaments are formed in a mechanical spinning operation. This type of spinning should not be confused with yarn spinning, the combining of staple-length fibers into textile yarn structures.

The spinning operation involves the extrusion of the polymer solution through a device called a spinneret. As schematized in Figure 3.3, a spinneret is similar to a shower head. In the same manner as pressure forces water through a shower head, pressure forces the polymer solution through the minute openings in the spinneret.

The openings in spinnerets are often no more than a few ten-thousandths of an inch in diameter, but their size can be varied to produce finer or coarser filaments. This enables the producer to regulate the flexibility of the filaments, to increase or decrease the area that the filaments will cover, and to control the amount of surface area per

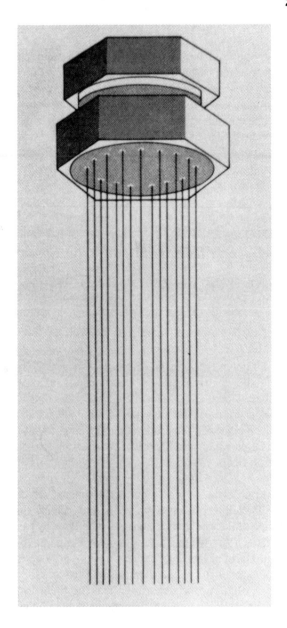

Figure 3.3 Spinneret device for spinning man-made fibers. (Courtesy of Celanese Corporation.)

unit of volume the filaments present for soil adhesion. In some spinning operations, the shape of the apertures is designed to produce filaments with specific cross-sectional shapes.

Three basic spinning techniques are used to extrude and solidify filaments: wet spinning, dry spinning, and melt spinning.

Wet spinning. In wet spinning, a solvent is used to dissolve the polymer. The solution is extruded through the spinneret into a bath where the solvent is extracted and the extruded strands coagulate or harden. Wet spinning is used in the production of rayon and some acrylic and spandex fibers.

The basic wet spinning process has been used continuously since the mid-1920s for the production of conventional viscose rayon fibers. The term viscose comes from the viscous, syrup-like polymer solution formed. In order to compete more effectively in the fiber market, rayon fiber producers have altered the viscose process, including the spinning operation, to produce improved fibers with higher strength and better dimensional stability than the conventional types.

Dry spinning. In dry spinning, a highly volatile solvent is used to dissolve the polymer compound, producing the spinning solution. The solution is extruded through the spinneret into a warm air chamber where the solvent evaporates, solidifying the fine filaments. Dry spinning is used in the production of acetate, triacetate, and some acrylic, modacrylic, spandex, and vinyon fibers.

Melt spinning. In melt spinning, heat is used to melt the polymer, producing the liquid spinning "dope." The liquid is extruded through the spinneret into a cool air chamber where the filaments harden as they cool. Variations in aperture shapes are often used in melt spinning as the filaments retain the shape of the openings. Melt spinning is used for the production of polyester, nylon, olefin, and glass fibers.

Drawing. Because most extruded filaments are disordered, they must be drawn or stretched to increase the orientation of their polymer chains and their degree of interior order. The drawing operation may be carried out by the fiber producer or by the throwster.

Drawing lengthens the filaments and reduces their diameters, aligning the chains and causing them to pack more closely. These changes increase the likelihood that crystalline regions will result from extensive lateral bonding. As the degree of interior order increases, there are parallel increases in strength and stiffness and decreases in extensibility and the rate at which such substances as water, dye, and finishing agents will be absorbed. Producers develop an appropriate balance among these properties by controlling the extent of drawing, always limiting the operation to avoid producing a totally oriented and crystallized arrangement.

Drawing or stretching an extruded filament introduces strain within the fiber, like that created within an elastic band when it is stretched. If an unstabilized drawn filament were exposed to conditions such as water and heat that encourage the release of this imposed strain, the polymer chains would relax, reverting back to the undrawn, amorphous arrangement. This would be accompanied by a shortening of the fiber, a reaction like that of an elastic band returning to its original length after the stretching force re-

leases it. In order to prevent this interior relaxation and loss of length, manufacturers generally stabilize drawn filaments by exposing them to controlled amounts of heat.

Heat Setting. Heat can be used to stabilize or set thermoplastic fibers—fibers that soften and shrink when exposed to a controlled amount of heat, and melt when exposed to an excessive amount of heat. With the exception of rayon and the high-temperature resistant aramid and novoloid fibers, most man-made fibers are thermoplastic.

In the heat setting operation, the fiber is heated to its glass transition temperature. At this temperature, lateral bonds within the fiber are disturbed and the polymer chains can shift their positions. In order to prevent excessive shrinkage, the heated fiber is held under some tension. As the fiber cools, new bonds form to "lock" the polymer chains into their new position, stabilizing the length of the filament.

Heat setting will be postponed until the yarn stage when the filaments are to be given a two- or three-dimensional crimped or curled configuration. It will be postponed until the greige good stage when a three-dimensional, embossed design is planned, or when the converter intends to improve the alignment of the yarns and stabilize the dimensions of the fabric. Whenever heat setting is performed, it must be carried out at approximately 50°F higher than the temperatures that may be encountered later in processing, laundering, or ironing. Exposure to temperatures higher than those used for heat setting will overcome the initial set and stability of the textile item.

FIBER ENGINEERING

Natural fiber suppliers and man-made fiber producers allocate millions of dollars annually toward extensive research and development projects. They support these activities in order to remain competitive and to capture a larger share of the fiber market. The results of this work are fibers with improved appearance and performance characteristics, many of which are specifically engineered for use in interior textile applications.

Natural Fiber Engineering

With natural fibers, appearance and performance engineering must be accomplished by working with already-formed fibers having a given set of inherent properties. Thus, converters, not fiber suppliers, are generally responsible for altering the inherent characteristics of these fibers. While some treatments, such as the application of moth-repellent agents and cross-linking resins, produce chemical changes within the fibers, they are nonetheless introduced during conversion of the greige goods. This work is discussed in Chapter 9.

Man-made Fiber Engineering

For more than a decade, the primary focus of man-made fiber research has been on fiber engineering, not on fiber invention. This work has resulted in the refinement of production procedures and the development or identification of polymer additives that can produce fiber variants. The more recent technological advances, like earlier ones, are often described as belonging to a particular "generation" of man-made fiber development.

Fiber Variants. A fiber variant is chemically related to other fibers in its generic class, but it is distinguished by one or more features. Among several polyester fibers, for example, one variant may have a round cross-sectional shape, a relatively large diameter, and a comparatively high degree of orientation; another may have a pentalobal cross-sectional shape, be inherently flame resistant, and dull; and yet another may be inherently antistatic, have a relatively small diameter, and be bright.

The availability of hundreds of fiber variants enables end-product manufacturers to be highly selective when they choose fibers. In turn, this helps them to offer products that conform closely to the selection criteria of contemporary consumers.

Generations of Man-made Fiber Development. Currently, members of the industry recognize four generations or levels of man-made fiber development. Each new designation has been used to distinguish major scientific breakthroughs from earlier achievements. Such distinctions are used extensively in the promotion of noncellulosic fiber variants, especially those intended for use in soft floor coverings.

First generation. The first level of man-made fiber development is considered to be the level of invention. Following the invention and commercial production of the cellulose based fibers, research chemist Wallace Carothers developed the foundations of high polymer chemistry. His pioneering work led directly to the development of nylon, the first fully synthesized man-made fiber. As knowledge of polymer science grew, fiber chemists manufactured such other fibers as acrylics, modacrylics, olefins, polyesters, spandexes, and vinyons.

Second generation. The second phase of man-made fiber development saw the refinement of the several general groups of fibers. Their aesthetic features were enhanced and their performance properties improved. Some of the technologies used included modification of fiber cross sections for soil hiding, alteration of fiber diameters for controlled stiffness, and inclusion of such polymer additives as delusterants, dye pigments, antistatic agents, and flame retardant compounds. Experimentation and evalua-

tion provided greater understanding of the effects of varied amounts of drawing on fiber performance. Heat setting procedures were perfected and used to improve resiliency and dimensional stability. Texturing methods were developed to introduce multidimensional configurations to smooth, straight filaments, enabling producers to control such things as covering power, resiliency, pill formation, and fiber cohesiveness.

Third generation. The third generation includes such developments as the production of bicomponent fibers, biconstituent fibers, and blended filaments. Bicomponent fibers are made by combining two generically similar compounds into one filament; biconstituent fibers are made by combining two generically dissimilar compounds into one filament; and blended filaments are made by combining two generically dissimilar filaments into a single yarn structure immediately after extrusion. Other developments of this generation include the processing techniques that enable producers to offer man-made fibers having the aesthetic features of natural fibers.

Fourth or advanced generation. The fourth or advanced generation represents the state of the art. With fiber technology becoming increasingly sophisticated, we now see fibers engineered to exhibit specific service-related characteristics, many of which are appropriate for a limited assortment of products. Fiber cross-sectional shapes, for example, have undergone further modification to provide soil shedding as well as better soil hiding and controlled levels of luster in soft floor coverings. Innovative filament compositions and designs have very nearly overcome static problems. Newer polymer additives now provide inherent strain and soil repellency. Fibers having hollow or tubular shapes have been developed to provide higher insulation without added weight. The inventions of the high-temperature and flame-resistant aramid and novoloid fibers are other developments of the advanced generation.

SUMMARY

All textile fibers have a similar physical form; they are relatively long and thin. But there are numerous differences among fibers—their molecular arrangements, cross-sectional shapes, longitudinal configurations, and chemical compositions. Differences in chemical composition serve as the basis for classifying fibers into useful generic groups or classes.

The synthesis and production of all fibers includes the combining of atoms into monomers, the linking of monomers into polymers, and the forming of a fine, usable strand. With natural fibers this sequence is carried out without direct human involvement, but subsequently inherent characteristics may be altered during fabric conversion. With man-made fibers the sequence of synthesis and production is controlled by the fiber chemist and producer, who can introduce specific characteristics during production. Such fiber engineering has become increasingly so-phisticated, enabling the producer to offer fibers that exhibit the aesthetic and performance features preferred or required by residential and commercial consumers.

chapter 4

Fundamental Fiber Properties

- Aesthetic Features
- Physical Properties
- Chemical Properties

Consumers and professionals can obtain greater satisfaction from the textile products they select by first investigating the properties of the component fibers. Such an investigation makes it possible to select the fiber or blend of fibers that offers the best balance of aesthetic and performance features for the anticipated end use conditions.

This chapter covers the aesthetic, physical, and chemical properties of fibers that influence the selection and serviceability of all interior textile products. Fiber properties that chiefly apply only to a limited category of textile furnishings are discussed in later units. It should be noted that all fiber properties may be altered in yarn production, fabric manufacturing, color application, and finishing. Some changes are negative and unavoidable; others are positive and intentional. In any event, the properties exhibited by a fiber in finished fabrics and end products may differ from those that characterize the fiber prior to yarn production.

AESTHETIC FEATURES

The aesthetic features of textile fibers—their appearance and tactile characteristics—are products of their external structural features. Their appearance also depends on the influence of natural colorants and any added colorants and delusterants.

Color

Virtually all natural fibers have some inherent color. Wool fibers are black, gray, tan, yellow, or off-white; silk filaments vary from yellow to off-white; linen fibers range from brown to tan to cream; and cotton fibers are markedly to slightly off-white. When fibers are to be dyed, natural colors are usually removed or neutralized to prevent their interaction with applied colors. However, rich natural colors are often sought after in such items as wall coverings and rugs.

When fiber producers incorporate dye pigments into polymer solutions, the colorants become an integral part of the extruded and solidified filaments. Solution-dyed fibers ordinarily exhibit a relatively high degree of colorfastness.

Luster

The luster of textile fibers depends on the quantity of light waves reflected from their surfaces and the direction in which these waves are traveling. Luster is determined by such features as cross-sectional shape, longitudinal configuration, surface texture, and the presence of delusterants.

Figure 4.1 shows that fiber surfaces reflect some portions of incident light waves, transmit other portions, and absorb still other portions. Fibers with round cross sections and smooth surfaces (Figure 4.1a) typically reflect

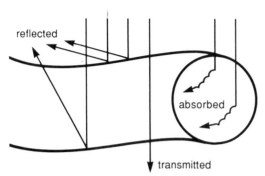

a) man-made fiber having a round shape and smooth surface

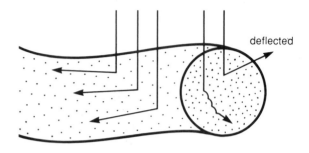

b) man-made fiber having a round shape, a smooth surface, and delusterant particles

c) cotton fiber having a somewhat flat shape and a twisted configuration

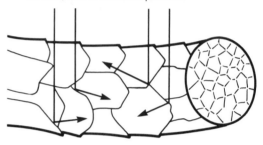

d) wool fiber having overlapping scales and a three dimensional crimp

Figure 4.1 Effects of external features and delusterant particles on fiber luster.

large quantities of rays in one direction, and the surface is therefore bright. Fibers with irregularly-shaped cross sections and rough surfaces typically reflect light rays in several directions: less surface luster appears.

Fibers having crimped or twisted configurations will show reduced levels of reflected light. Although the flat shape of cotton should produce high reflectance, the natural twist interrupts the reflection of rays (Figure 4.1c), giving fabrics composed of cotton low luster. Wool has scales covering the surface of the fiber and a three-dimensional crimp, which scatter incident light rays (Figure 4.1d) to develop a subdued, matte luster. Man-made fiber producers often strive to simulate the luster of wool. In this effort, producers may add titanium dioxide (TiO_2) particles to the polymer solution. As shown in Figure 4.1b, light rays that strike the minute white particles are scattered, resulting in a decreased level of reflectance. Additional techniques used to control the luster of man-made fibers are discussed in Chapters 9 and 24.

Tactile Characteristics

The term "hand" or "handle" refers to the tactile characteristics of a textile structure. These characteristics include such things as the perceived temperature and the level of surface smoothness or roughness.

Whether a fabric has pleasant hand or "feel" is a subjective evaluation that often governs consumer selection.

This important variable is strongly influenced by the external structural features of the constituent fibers. Fibers with irregularly shaped cross sections, textured surfaces, and three-dimensional forms may feel warm and perhaps harsh or rough. By contrast, fibers with round cross sections, smooth surfaces, and straight, nontextured forms may feel cool and slick when touched.

PHYSICAL PROPERTIES

The physical properties of textile fibers are measured in accordance with standard test methods. The test results provide the means for assessing the relative performance of fibers on a number of variables. Several of these performance variables help determine the use life characteristics of end products.

Covering Power

Covering power is the ability of a textile structure to cover or conceal an area without undue weight. The effectiveness with which fibers cover a surface depends on structural features—cross-sectional shape, longitudinal configuration, and specific gravity—and weight.

Fibers having round shapes cover less surface area than do fibers of equal volume with flat configurations. This difference is schematically illustrated in Figure 4.2.

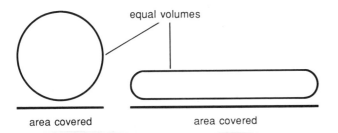

equal volumes

area covered   area covered

Figure 4.2 Effect of cross-sectional shape on covering power.

Fibers with a natural or engineered crimped or coiled configuration cover more surface area than do straight fibers. The effect is more evident when the multidimensional fibers are grouped into yarn structures.

Specific Gravity. In order to obtain maximum cover with minimum weight, a fiber with a low specific gravity should be selected. Specific gravity is the density (mass or amount of matter per unit of volume) of a fiber relative to that of water at 4°C, which is 1. Fibers having specific gravities greater than 1 are heavier than an equal volume of water; those with specific gravities less than 1 are lighter and would float on water. Table 4.1 presents the specific gravities of fibers used extensively in interior textile products.

Table 4.1 SPECIFIC GRAVITIES OF SELECTED TEXTILE FIBERS

Glass	2.50–2.70
Saran	1.68–1.75
Cotton	1.52
Linen	1.52
Rayon	1.50–1.52
Polyester	1.22–1.38
Modacrylic	1.30–1.37
Vinyon	1.37
Wool	1.34
Acetate	1.32
Silk	1.25
Acrylic	1.14–1.19
Nylon	1.14
Olefin	0.91
(polypropylene)	

If the diameters of two fibers are equal, the fiber with the lower specific gravity will cover more area with less weight than will the fiber with the higher specific gravity. Covering power is an especially critical variable when sizable amounts of fiber are used in structures designed to cover large areas, like window, wall, and floor coverings.

Elasticity

Fiber elasticity includes two performance variables, elongation and elastic recovery. Elongation is a fiber's ability to be extended or elongated; elastic recovery is its ability to recover from the extension.

Elongation. Elongation depends on the internal arrangement and external structural features of fibers. Fibers that are highly oriented and crystallized will display minimal elongation, as shown in Figure 4.3a. By contrast, fibers having highly amorphous interiors will tend to exhibit high elongation, with the polymer chains straightening and extending under stress, as shown in Figure 4.3b. This molecular arrangement, and high elongation, are characteristic of wool fibers. The molecular arrangement and thus extensibility of most man-made fibers can be engineered to a great degree by controlling the amount of drawing used in fiber production.

Fibers with a natural or engineered crimp have greater extensibility than do fibers with an essentially straight, nontextured configuration (compare Figures 4.3c and 4.3d). For example, the natural waviness of wool augments the extensibility of the amorphous interior. The elongation of cotton derives largely from the unwinding of the natural twist. Linen not only has high orientation and crystallinity but also lacks a twist, and so exhibits extremely low elongation.

The extensibility of textile fibers is generally measured at the breaking point. In the laboratory, a fiber specimen is held straight, but not stretched, between clamps on a test apparatus. Some equipment used for this work is engineered to exert force and extend the specimen at a constant rate until it ruptures; such machines are known as constant-rate-of-extension (CRE) machines. Other machines apply the load or force at a constant rate; these are called constant-rate-of-load (CRL) machines. Still other machines are designed to move the clamps at a constant rate; these are known as constant-rate-of-traverse (CRT) machines. All these machines may be equipped to record the breaking load or force in grams and the length of the specimen at the point of rupture.

After completion of the test, the elongation of the specimen is calculated and expressed as a percentage of the original relaxed length, using the following formula:

$$\% \text{ Elongation at break} = \frac{\text{length stretched}}{\text{original length}} \times 100.$$

If, for example, a 3-inch length of fiber ruptured when it was 4 inches long, the percent elongation at break is 33.3. (Note that the length stretched is 1 inch, not 4 inches.) Table 4.2 includes elongation measurements for selected textile fibers.

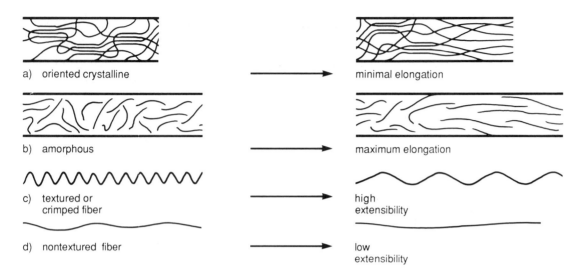

Figure 4.3 Effects of molecular arrangement and longitudinal configuration on elongation.

Elastic Recovery. Elastic recovery measurements indicate how completely a fiber returns to its original length after being strained or elongated. In standard methods of testing, fibers are generally extended 2 percent of their relaxed length, held in the deformed position for 30 seconds, and allowed 1 minute for recovery. In actual use, fibers are normally subjected to greater deformations for longer periods of time.

Fibers having highly disordered interiors typically exhibit an inherent desire to return to their relaxed state. Those having an inherent or heat-stabilized crimp or coil also tend to display better recovery than that shown by noncrimped fibers. Table 4.2 presents the immediate elastic recovery values for several fibers; measurements taken after longer periods would normally show higher recovery.

Resiliency

Resiliency is the ability of a textile structure to recover from deformations other than stretch or elongation. Resilient behavior includes recovery from such deformations as folding, bending, and crumpling, which helps prevent undesirable mussiness and surface wrinkles. Resilient behavior also includes recovery from compression and crushing; a resilient product returns to its original depth after such deformation.

The resiliency of finished fabrics and fillings depends on the behavior of their constituent fibers. If the polymer chains pack closely when the fiber is deformed, new lateral bonds may form and restrict recovery. Such chain packing and bonding is minimized when the polymer chains have large laterally bonded groups, such as those seen in wool. Fibers with relatively strong lateral bonds, such as those present in spandex and wool, and fibers with a natural or heat-set crimp or coil display better recovery. Stiff fibers,

with relatively large diameters and multilobal cross sections, offer greater resistance to deformation and exhibit better recovery than do highly flexible fibers.

The resiliency of textile fibers is generally rated in relative terms: excellent, good, fair, and poor. Table 4.3 lists the relative performance of fibers frequently used in interior textile products.

In order to overcome the inherently poor resiliency of cellulosic fibers, converters employ chemical cross-linking resins. The use of these finishing compounds is reviewed in Chapter 9.

Strength

As explained in Chapter 3, fibers having highly ordered interior arrangements, high degrees of polymerization, and/or longer lengths are generally stronger than shorter fibers with disordered interiors and/or low degrees of polymerization. These variables are givens in natural fibers, but in man-made fibers, these qualities can be engineered during polymerizing, spinning, drawing, and heat setting.

The relative terms "weak" and "strong" are often used to describe the strength of textile fibers. These assessments are based on measurements obtained through laboratory testing. Machines equipped to record the length of test specimens at the break point are also equipped to record the grams of force or load that caused the rupture. This information is used to calculate a specimen's strength or breaking tenacity as the force per unit of linear density required to rupture the fine strand. The value is reported as grams per denier (g.p.d. or g/den) or grams per tex (g.p.t. or g/tex). (Denier and tex indicate weight or mass per unit of length, i.e., linear density. The terms are explained further in Chapter 5.)

Table 4.2 **ELASTIC BEHAVIOR OF SELECTED TEXTILE FIBERS**

Fiber	% elongation at break	% elastic recovery from (X%) strain
Natural		
Protein		
wool	25–35	99–100 (2), 63 (20)
silk	13–31	92 (2), 33 (20)
Cellulose		
cotton	3–7	74 (2), 45 (5)
linen	3	65 (2)
Man-made		
Cellulose-based		
acetate	23–45	48–65 (4)
rayon (conventional)	15–30	82 (2)
rayon (improved)	9–26	95 (2)
Mineral		
glass	3.1–5.3	100 (2)
Petroleum-based		
acrylic	34–50	99 (2)
modacrylic	25–60	100 (1), 55 (10)
nylon	16–65	100 (5), 99–100 (10)
olefin (polypropylene)	14–8	97–100 (2), 95 (10)
polyester	12–67	67–92 (2), 33 (10)
saran	15–25	100 (1), 95 (10)
spandex	500–700	100 (2), 98 (200)
vinyon	18	

The breaking tenacities of several fibers are listed in Table 4.4. Although it is nearly identical to cotton and rayon in chemical composition, linen is stronger than either because of its longer length, higher orientation, and greater crystallinity. The greater tenacity of natural cellulosic fibers when wet is one performance variable supporting their widespread use in toweling.

The noncellulosic fibers exhibit little or no change in tenacity when they are tested wet. This behavior helps make some of these man-made fibers suitable for end products manufactured for outdoor use, such as awnings, lawn furniture, and patio carpet.

Fiber strength is an important variable in textile product performance, but elongation must be considered as well in any judgment of potential serviceability. Elongation is especially crucial to abrasion resistance. A strong fiber with low extensibility may not have good resistance to rubbing, especially when folded or curved. Furthermore, the strength exhibited by a fiber may not be the principal determinant of the strength of the fabric. Weak fibers may be found in strong fabrics, and vice versa.

CHEMICAL PROPERTIES

The chemical properties of textile fibers help determine the end use serviceability of interior textiles. An inherent chemical property may limit the suitability of a fiber for

Table 4.3 **RESILIENCY OF SELECTED TEXTILE FIBERS**

Wool	excellent
Polyester	excellent
Nylon	good
Acrylic	good
Olefin (polypropylene)	good
Acetate	fair
Rayon	poor
Cotton	poor
Linen	poor

Table 4.4 BREAKING TENACITIES OF SELECTED TEXTILE FIBERS

Fiber	grams/denier dry	wet
Natural		
Protein		
wool	1.5	1.0
silk	4.5	3.9
Cellulose		
cotton	4.0	5.0
linen	5.5	6.5
Man-made		
Cellulose-based		
acetate	1.2–1.5	0.8–1.2
rayon (conventional)	0.73–2.6	0.7–1.8
rayon (improved)	2.5–6.0	1.8–4.6
Mineral		
glass	7.0	7.0
Petroleum-based		
acrylic	2.0–3.5	1.8–3.3
modacrylic	2.0–3.5	2.0–3.5
nylon	2.5–9.5	2.0–8.0
olefin (polypropylene)	4.8–7.0	4.8–7.0
polyester	2.5–9.5	2.5–9.4
saran	1.5	1.5
spandex	0.7	
vinyon	0.7–1.0	0.7–1.0

some end use applications, and it may dictate the use of finishing agents. The chemical properties of fibers, like their physical properties, can be measured in the laboratory, following the procedures set forth in standard test methods.

Heat-related Properties

A discussion of the effects of heat on textile fibers can easily become a tangle of confusing terms. This discussion will limit itself to three heat-related properties: thermoplasticity, susceptibility to heat, and heat conductivity. Flammability or combustibility is also a reaction to heat. Because the involvement of textile structures in interior fires has become a significant issue in recent decades, the pyrolytic characteristics of textile fibers are discussed with other fire-related variables in Chapter 11.

Thermoplasticity. Chapter 3 explained that thermoplastic fibers soften when heated to their glass transition temperatures, permitting man-made fiber producers to use heat setting as an engineering tool. In this application, thermoplasticity is a positive fiber characteristic; but thermoplasticity is a negative characteristic when a fiber is heated to its melting point by such items as lit cigarettes, glowing embers, candle flames, and overly hot irons. When such an unfortunate event occurs, the fiber shrinks and melts. Subsequently, the molten polymer cools into an unsightly, hardened mass, producing a permanently damaged area in the fabric that generally must be replaced or repaired by a skilled person.

The softening and melting points of selected thermoplastic fibers are listed in Table 4.5. The table also lists temperatures recommended for ironing fabrics composed of these and other fibers.

The frequent use of "heat sensitivity" as a synonym for thermoplasticity, while not incorrect, often causes confusion. Not all fibers are heat sensitive in this sense of the term; that is, not all fibers soften and melt when heated. However, all fibers are sensitive (or susceptible) to heat—they all decompose, scorch, melt, or otherwise react to elevated temperatures.

Susceptibility to Heat. Although the natural fibers and rayon are not heat sensitive, and thus cannot be permanently set with heat, they are nonetheless susceptible to heat. Exposing natural fibers to elevated temperatures, especially for prolonged periods, may cause degradation and discoloration. For example, excessively high ironing temperatures weaken and scorch cotton and linen.

Heat Conductivity. Heat conductivity and heat transmittance are synonymous terms used to refer to the rate at which a material conducts heat. Most textile fibers have low rates of conduction and contribute to the insulative value of textile structures. While the transfer of heat is influenced by the conductivity rate of the fibers used, it primarily depends on the thickness of the textile structure. This interrelationship is discussed in detail in Chapter 30.

Moisture-related Properties

Two moisture-related properties, absorbency and wickability, affect the serviceability of textile fibers, as well as their suitability for various end use applications. Absorbency also affects the dyeability of fibers.

Absorbency. Comparisons of the abilities of fibers to absorb moisture are based on their moisture regain values, which indicate their abilities to absorb vapor-phase moisture. These values are calculated by the following formula:

$$\% \text{ moisture regain } = \frac{\text{conditioned weight} - \text{dry weight}}{\text{dry weight}} \times 100$$

Dry weight is the weight of the oven-dry specimen.

Conditioned weight is determined after the dry specimen has been kept in an atmosphere of $70 \pm 2°F$ and $65 \pm 2\%$ relative humidity for a period of 24 hours or until the specimen reaches equilibrium.

The increase in conditioned weight over dry weight shows the amount of vapor-phase moisture absorbed by the fiber. The difference is expressed as a percentage of the dry weight. Typical moisture regain values are listed in Table 4.6.

Table 4.5 EFFECTS OF HEAT ON TEXTILE FIBERS

	Softening point °F	°C	Melting point °F	°C	Safe ironing temperature[a] °F	°C
Natural						
Protein						
wool	does not soften		does not melt		300	149
silk	does not soften		does not melt		300	149
Cellulose						
cotton	does not soften		does not melt		425	218
linen	does not soften		does not melt		450	232
Man-made						
Cellulose-based						
acetate	400–445 (sticks 350–375	205–230 177–191)	500	260	350	177
triacetate	482	250	575	302	464	240
rayon	does not soften		does not melt		375	191
Mineral						
glass	1350 +	732 +				
Petroleum-based						
acrylic	450–497	232–258	degrades before true melt		320	160
aramid	does not melt,		carbonizes above 800°F			
modacrylic	300 (shrinks 250	149 121)	degrades before true melt			
novoloid	does not melt,		carbonizes above 5000°F			
nylon	445	229	500	260	350	177
olefin						
polyethylene	230–239 (sticks, shrinks 140–212	110–115 60–100)	260	127	do not iron	
polypropylene	311	155	325–335	163–168	150 (heat cannot be maintained this low on some irons)	66
polyester	460–490	238–254	480–550	249–288	325	163
saran	240–280	116–138	260	127	do not iron	
vinyon	170 (shrinks 150	77 66)	260	127	do not iron	

Sources: Man-Made Fiber Producers Association, *Guide to Man-Made Fibers,; Modern Textile Business,* March 1983.

[a]Reproduced by permission of Burlington Industries, Inc.

Table 4.6 PERCENTAGE MOISTURE RE- GAIN OF SELECTED TEXTILE FIBERS

Wool	16.0
Rayon	13.0
Linen	10.0–12.0
Cotton	8.5
Acetate	6.0
Nylon	4.0–4.5
Acrylic	1.3–2.5
Polyester	0.4–0.8
Vinyon	0.5
Olefin	
(polypropylene)	0.0
Saran	0.0
Glass	0.0

Fibers with high regain values, including wool and the natural and man-made cellulosic fibers, are referred to as hydrophilic ("water-loving") fibers. These fibers are easily colored with aqueous dyestuffs, but they require protective finishes for use in exterior textile products. Fibers with low regain values are called hydrophobic ("water-hating") fibers. These are suitable for use in some outdoor textile applications, but some have virtually no capacity for moisture absorption and are difficult and expensive to dye, limiting their color-styling possibilities.

The moisture absorbency of fibers has a direct effect on their cleanability. Hydrophilic fibers are more easily cleaned as they readily absorb the detergent solution. By contrast, hydrophobic fibers and cellulosic fibers treated with chemical cross-linking resins may require the application of finishing agents or the use of special laundry aids to improve their cleanability.

Wickability. Wickability is the ability of a fiber to transport moisture along its surface by capillary action, as a lamp wick transports flammable fluid upward to the site of the flame. Cotton has inherent wickability, which supports its extensive use in beddings and towelings. Currently, fiber chemists are working to improve the wickability and absorbency of several noncellulosic fibers.

Soil-related Properties

Hydrophilic fibers will have a limited buildup of electrical charges on their surfaces when the level of humidity is relatively high. This lessens their attraction for such airborne soil particles as pet hairs, dust, and lint. On the other hand, these fibers, with the exception of wool, may be more easily stained by water-borne substances, such as the staining agents in grape juice, orange soda, and red wine. In wool, an invisible film, known as the epicuticle, covers the scales and provides temporary protection; staining can be avoided by quickly sponging up spilled fluids.

Some hydrophopic fibers, icluding nylon, polyester, and olefin, are quite resistant to water-borne staining but are subject to oil-borne staining. Converters often apply flourocarbon compounds to greige goods composed of these fibers to minimize this problem.

Recently, fiber chemists and engineers have developed innovative techniques to control the soil-related performance of fibers for use in soft floor coverings. These techniques are discussed and illustrated in Chapter 24.

SUMMARY

The aesthetic, chemical, and physical properties of textile fibers depend greatly on their chemical compositions, the arrangement of their internal units, and the nature of their external features. Residential consumers, contract designers, and architects should consider fiber properties when selecting or specifying interior textile products, to ensure that the constituent fibers exhibit properties suitable for the end use application.

chapter 5

Textile Yarns and Yarn-like Structures

- Yarn Production
- Yarn Classification and Nomenclature
- Designation of Yarn Construction
- Formation of Yarn-like Structures

All textile yarns, like textile fibers, must be relatively long and thin to provide the flexibility required in manufacturing and use. However, yarns can have marked differences in their degrees of twist, textural characteristics, complexity, and relative fineness. The fineness of yarns can be measured and reported in numerical terms. These numbers, along with other notations, are used in designations of yarn construction.

Simple yarns, structures having minimal design value, are typically used in carpet, rugs, towels, sheets, and tabletop accessories. By contrast, decorative complex yarns are often used in textile wall coverings and in upholstery, curtain, and drapery fabrics. Complex yarns have slubs, loops, curls, and other irregular textural effects that add tactile and visual interest. This chapter describes the production and qualities of the widely used simple and complex yarns.

Although most interior textile products are composed entirely of textile yarns or fibers, some are composed in whole or in part of yarn-like structures. Although these components are handled like textile yarns, they are not formed by conventional yarn production processes, and several contain no fibers.

YARN PRODUCTION

One type of yarn, known as a monofilament yarn, is actually manufactured by the fiber producer. In this process, a single filament is treated as a yarn structure. For strength and stability, the filament has a relatively large diameter and is drawn and heat set. Monofilaments yarns are often used in the production of lightweight, transparent window coverings. They are also used as strong sewing thread in the construction of many interior textile products. In this application, the filaments may be clear or smoke-colored so that they will assume the color of the textile structure being sewn and produce an inconspicuous seam.

While man-made fiber producers manufacture monofilament yarns, throwsters produce multifilament yarns and spinsters produce spun yarns. Throwsters may use a texturing process to introduce such characteristics as bulk and cohesiveness to groups of filaments, some of which are then reduced to staple lengths and spun.

Throwing

The great length of silk and man-made filaments allows them to be directly combined or "thrown" together into multifilament yarn structures; no textile yarn spinning process is required. If drawn man-made filaments are supplied, the throwster needs only to gather and twist several of the fine strands. If undrawn filaments are supplied, the throwster must combine drawing and twisting. For a limited number of applications, throwsters will produce untwisted multifilament yarns.

Texturing

Texturing processes introduce multidimensional configurations to otherwise parallel and smooth filaments. Such physical changes may decrease strength, but they can impart elasticity, create a softer, warmer hand, help to simulate a natural appearance, and increase fiber cohesiveness. They also increase the bulk or apparent volume of the grouped filaments to provide greater covering power, as shown in Figure 5.1. In use, fabrics composed of textured yarns have reduced levels of pilling and better dimensional stability and resiliency, and retain their original appearance for a longer period of time than do fabrics made of staple fibers.

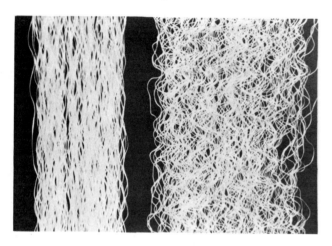

Figure 5.1 Identical skeins of nylon filaments showing increase in apparent bulk or volume produced by texturing. (Courtesy of Fibers Division, Monsanto Chemical Co.)

Among the texturing processes used with interior textile product components are false-twist coiling, stuffer-box crimping, knit-de-knit crinkling, and gear crimping. These processes are schematized in Figure 5.2. Yarns textured by these and other techniques are known as bulked continuous filament (BCF) yarns.

False-twist Coiling. In false-twist coiling, the yarn bundle is twisted, heated, and untwisted in one continuous operation. A heat set coil within each filament results; the yarn itself has no twist (hence the name "false-twist").

Stuffer-box Crimping. This technique is so called because the yarns are rapidly stuffed into a heated, box-like chamber. Because the yarns are withdrawn slowly, they buckle and back up on themselves. The three-dimensional crimp is permanently set by the heat.

Knit-de-knit Crinkling. Knit-de-knit texturing produces a crinkled or wavy configuration. Multifilament yarns are first knitted into a fabric. The fabric is then heat set and subsequently unraveled ("de-knit"). The knitting gauge (the number of loops per inch) determines the size of the yarn waves. This technique is frequently combined with the application of dyestuffs to produce uniquely colored and textured yarns for soft floor coverings (see Figure 28.2, page 303).

Gear Crimping. In this process, intermeshing gears introduce a planar or two-dimensional crimp to filaments. Heat can be used to permanently set the crimped configuration.

When filaments are to be reduced to staple lengths and spun into yarns, they are first grouped into a rope-like bundle known as tow. This untwisted bundle is then textured, generally by gear or stuffer-box crimping, to impart the fiber cohesiveness required for the production of spun yarns. The textured tow is stretched or cut into staple fibers of the desired length, generally from 1 to 6 inches. The staple fibers pictured in Figure 5.3 were cut from gear-crimped tow.

Spinning

Staple-length fibers are converted into usable yarn strands by processing them through various spinning systems, including the cotton, woolen, worsted, and linen systems. Formerly, the system used depended upon the type of fiber being spun; today, as man-made fibers are increasingly used to simulate natural fibers, the choice of spinning systems is largely based on the length of the staples being processed. In any case, the basic procedures used in the several systems are similar, with each successive operation producing a structure that is more yarn-like.

The Cotton System. The following highly simplified summary identifies the basic procedures used in the cotton spinning system and describes the changes produced in each step:

   1. Opening and cleaning: loosening, cleaning, and blending the cotton fibers.
   2. Picking: fluffing the compacted fibers into a loose, disoriented mass.
   3. Carding: initially aligning the fibers in a somewhat parallel fashion and forming a card sliver, a long, loose strand that is approximately 1 inch in diameter.
   4. Combing: further aligning the fibers and separating the shorter staples before forming a comb sliver.
   5. Drawing out: reducing the diameter of the sliver to produce a roving, a long, fine strand that is approximately 1/4 inch in diameter.

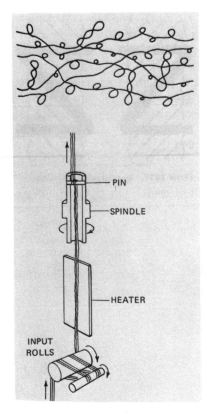

a) false-twist coiling

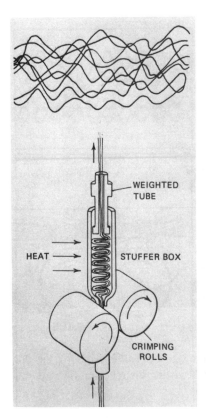

b) stuffer box crimping

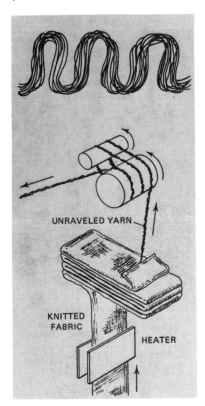

c) knit-de-knit crinkling

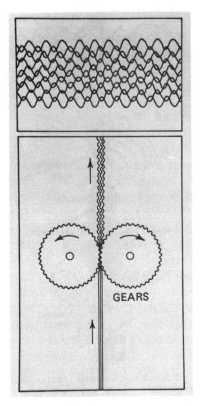

d) gear crimping

Figure 5.2 Yarn texturing processes. (From "Yarns," by Stanley Backer. Copyright © 1972 by Scientific American, Inc. All rights reserved.)

Figure 5.3 Staple-length fibers cut from gear-crimped tow.

6. Spinning and twisting: reducing the diameter of the roving and twisting the resulting fine strand into a usable spun yarn.

The cotton system is used for spinning fibers that are approximately 1/2 inch to 1 1/2 inches in length. Yarns with relatively long and highly aligned fibers are known as combed yarns; those having both long and short staples and relatively little fiber alignment are called carded yarns. Today, polyester and rayon staples, alone or blended with cotton, are frequently spun on the cotton system.

The Woolen and Worsted Systems. The basic equipment in the woolen spinning system is designed to handle fibers from 2 to 3 inches in length; that in the worsted system is designed to handle fibers from 3 to 5 inches in length. Spinsters can adjust the equipment, however, to spin the longer staples frequently used in interior textile yarns. Woolen yarns, like carded yarns, have varied lengths of staples and less fiber alignment; worsted yarns, like combed yarns, contain only long staples that are highly aligned.

Because spun yarns have many fiber ends protruding from their surfaces, their level of light reflectance is less than that of multifilament yarns. Spinsters use this characteristic to advantage when they process staple-length acrylic, nylon, and olefin fibers on the woolen system to produce yarns with a subdued, mellow luster, imitating the much-admired natural luster of wool.

The Linen System. The linen spinning system is designed to align and twist linen tow fibers, which are approximately 12 inches in length, and linen line fibers, which are approximately 24 inches in length. Tow fibers

are spun into relatively heavy yarns for use in such interior textile products as wall coverings, upholstery, and drapery fabrics, while line fibers are spun into fine yarns for use in such items as woven table linens, bed sheets, and lace doilies. Groups of aligned linen fibers, pictured in Figure 5.4, resemble switches of human hair prior to yarn twisting.

Yarn Twisting

Twisting must be used for all spun yarns, and while it is optional for multifilament yarns, it is generally used to stabilize the fine, parallel filaments. Whatever the type of yarn, twist can be specified by its direction and level.

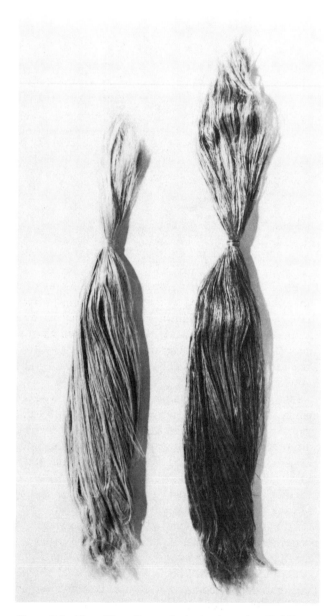

Figure 5.4 Aligned linen fibers prior to drawing out and twisting. (Courtesy of the International Linen Promotion Commission.)

Direction of Twist. The letters S and Z are used to describe the direction of twist in all textile yarns (Figure 5.5). A left-handed or counterclockwise twist is called an S twist; the fibers ascend from right to left and align with the central portion of the letter. A right-handed or clockwise twist is termed a Z twist; the fibers ascend from left to right and again align with the central portion of the letter. Neither direction offers an advantage over the other.

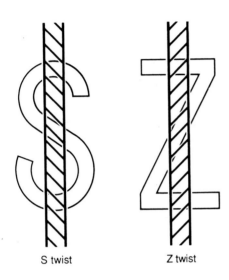

S twist   Z twist

Figure 5.5 Direction of twist in textile yarns.

Level of Twist. The level or amount of twist used in yarn formation is denoted by the number of turns per inch (turns/inch or t.p.i.). Multifilament yarns may have as few or as 2 or 3 t.p.i., while spun yarns often have as many as 30 or 40 t.p.i. Optimum levels have evolved from years of experience and yarn testing by spinsters and throwsters.

Spun yarns with a relatively low level of twist are comparatively soft, large, weak, and dull. Up to a point, increasing the twist will produce a concomitant increase in yarn firmness, fineness, strength, and luster. When more than about 40 t.p.i. are used, kinks and ridges may form, reducing the elasticity and strength of the yarns. Such surface irregularities may deflect incident light waves, dulling the yarns in much the same way as coils dull fibers.

Throwsters and spinsters use a variety of techniques to control the aesthetic features and service-related qualities of yarns and expand the assortment of yarns available to producers and consumers. They may vary the level of twist used, introduce decorative effects, or combine various numbers and types of yarn strands. The resulting yarns are then classified and named on the basis of their structural characteristics.

YARN CLASSIFICATION AND NOMENCLATURE

Yarns produced by throwing or spinning textile fibers are classified and described by the number of their parts and their design features. A brief outline will serve to introduce the classification system used with textile yarns and the extensive number of names used for decorative yarns.

I. Simple Yarns
    A. Single
    B. Ply
    C. Cord
    D. Cable
    E. Rope
    F. Hawser
II. Complex Yarns
    A. Singles
        1. slub
        2. thick-and-thin
        3. speck
    B. Plies and cords
        1. plied slub
        2. flame
        3. flock or flake
        4. spiral
        5. corkscrew
        6. nub
        7. knot
        8. seed
        9. splash
      10. spike or snarl
      11. ratiné
      12. bouclé
      13. loop or curl
      14. gimp

Simple Yarns

Yarns having a smooth appearance and a uniform diameter along their length are classified as simple yarns. Simple yarns may be composed of a single yarn or a number of single yarns twisted or plied together in various ways.

Single, Ply, and Cord Yarns. Simple single yarns are produced in a single spinning or throwing operation, or, in the case of monofilament yarns, in a single extruding operation. Although simple multifilament yarns are composed of multiple filaments, they are classified as single yarns. Simple ply yarns are formed by twisting or plying two or more single yarns together. Simple cord yarns are formed by twisting two or more ply yarns together. These yarns are illustrated in Figure 5.6.

As long as the fineness or size of the components is not reduced, plying increases yarn strength. So that ply and cord yarns will be balanced and smooth, each succes-

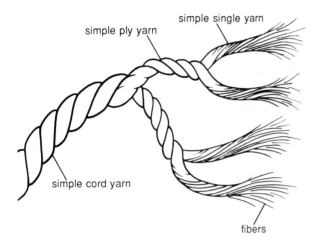

Figure 5.6   Simple single, ply, and cord yarns.

sive twisting or plying procedure uses about half the amount of twist as the previous one and S and Z twists are alternated. The standard practice followed in designating the construction of these yarns is discussed later in this chapter.

Cable, Rope, and Hawser Yarns. When simple cord yarns are plied, the resulting structure is called a cable yarn; when cable yarns are plied, the new structure is called rope; and when rope strands are combined, the structure becomes a hawser, a structure that is strong enough to anchor a ship. Rope structures composed of sisal or hemp fibers frequently appear in hand-woven chair seats. The use of rope and other simple yarns, such as crewel, tapestry, and floss yarns, in interior textile accents is discussed in Chapter 35.

In comparison with complex yarns, simple yarns have minimal design value. Spinsters and throwsters can, however, combine various hues and shades of fibers and yarns to enhance the visual interest of simple yarns. Such distinctive yarn color styles as heather, marled, and ombré, and the methods used to produce them, are described in Chapter 8.

Complex Yarns

Yarns with variations in the level of twist used along their length, three-dimensional decorative features, or components with different fiber contents are called complex yarns. The unique combination of features characterizing each of these decorative yarns determines its yarn name.

Complex Single Yarns. Complex single yarns may be spun or extruded. A slub yarn (Figure 5.7a) is composed of staple-length fibers and has both fine and coarse segments along its length. These differences in diameter are produced by varying the level of twist used in the final spinning operation. Because fewer t.p.i. are used for the coarse areas, they are softer and weaker than the fine areas. As the name suggests, a thick-and-thin yarn also has variations in diameter, but these are less pronounced than those in slub yarns. The slight variations, visible in Figure 5.7b, are produced by varying the extrusion pressure used during the formation of man-made filaments. Duppioni silk filaments have a similar appearance as a result of the irregularities created when two cocoons are spun in contact with one another. A speck yarn (Figure 5.7c) is produced by periodically incorporating small tufts of contrastingly colored fibers during spinning. The colorful tufts interrupt the smoothness of the yarn, creating greater visual interest (see also Figure 23.7, page 250).

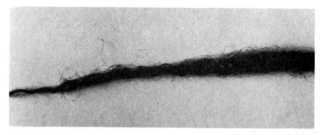

a) slub yarn

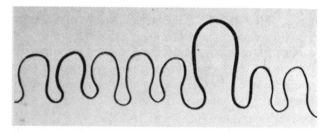

b) thick-and-thin yarn

c) speck yarn

Figure 5.7 Complex single yarns. (Photomicrograph of the thick-and-thin yarn is courtesy of Fibers Division, Monsanto Chemical Co.)

Complex Plies and Cords. Complex plies and cords are formed by twisting together two or more single yarns that may themselves be simple or complex structures. Frequently, distinctive forms of twisting are used to produce complex structures from simple components. Because the basic textural and design features of a complex yarn can be produced by using single or plied components, many textile authorities make no distinction between complex ply yarns and complex cord yarns.

Basic components. As shown in Figure 5.8, complex plies and cords may have three distinct components. The base yarn, which is also known as the core, foundation, or ground yarn, provides stability and determines the yarn length. The effect yarn, which is also known as the fancy yarn, contributes the novelty or decorative appearance. The binder or tie yarn secures the effect yarn to the base yarn. Some complex yarns have only two of these components.

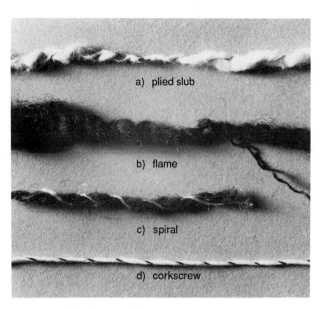

a) plied slub

b) flame

c) spiral

d) corkscrew

Figure 5.9 Complex two-ply yarns.

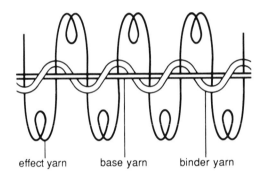

effect yarn   base yarn   binder yarn

Figure 5.8 Basic components of complex ply and cord yarns.

Complex yarn names and descriptions. Complex plies and cords are distinguished by their appearance and structural features. These features determine the name assigned to the yarn.

Plied slub yarns, pictured in Figure 5.9a, are formed by twisting two slub yarns together. As shown in Figure 5.9b, a flame yarn is produced by twisting a simple yarn around a single slub yarn that has large and elongated areas of low twist. Flock or flake yarns have an appearance similar to that of single slub yarns; but in these multicomponent structures, the enlarged segments are created by periodically binding thin bits of roving between plied single yarns. While the removal of fibers from a slub yarn would destroy its stability, removal of the fibers inserted in flock yarns would destroy only their appearance: the plied singles would maintain the stability of the yarns.

The components of spiral and corkscrew yarns differ in their construction, fiber content, level of twist, degree of luster, or size. Together they create a visual spiral. (While plying simple yarns that differ only in color would produce a spiral appearance, such yarns do not come within

the definition of spiral and corkscrew yarns. They would be classified as simple, two-ply yarns.) For greater emphasis on the visual spiral, a spun yarn may be combined with a filament yarn, or a yarn-like metallic strand may be combined with a spun yarn. Although many textile authorities use "spiral" and "corkscrew" as synonyms, a distinction may be made when yarns of different sizes are plied. As shown in Figures 5.9c and 5.9d, "spiral" applies when the heavier yarn twists around the finer yarn, and "corkscrew" when the finer yarn twists around the heavier yarn.

Imaginative forms of plying can produce complex yarns from simple components. Nub yarns, which are also called spot or knap yarns, have tightly compacted projections at irregular intervals along their lengths. These three-dimensional nubs are created by wrapping a simple yarn several times around a base yarn. When bits of tightly compacted and contrastingly colored fibers are incorporated into the nubs, the plied yarn may be called a knot or knop yarn. Seed yarns have tiny nubs and splash yarns have elongated nubs. Examples of yarns with nub effects are shown in Figure 5.10.

Several complex yarns have loop-type textural effects. These include spike, ratiné, bouclé, and loop yarns. Spike or snarl yarns are composed of yarns having different levels of twist. During the plying operation, the more highly twisted yarn is introduced at a faster rate, causing the extra length to form well-defined kinks or loops. Ratiné yarns (Figure 5.11a) have uniformly spaced loops of equal size. In their production, a fuzzy effect yarn is fed faster than the base during the plying sequence, producing small, tightly spaced loops that are almost perpendicular to the

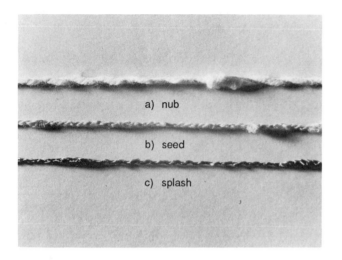

Figure 5.10 Complex yarns with nub effects.

base. Some ratiné yarns are produced with a smooth effect yarn, causing the projections to assume a diamond shape similar to that in rick-rack trim. Bouclé yarns (Figure 5.11b) have pronounced, closed loops that vary in size and spacing. Loop or curl yarns (Figure 5.11c) have open, airy loops. Frequently, the effect yarns are loosely spun of mohair fibers.

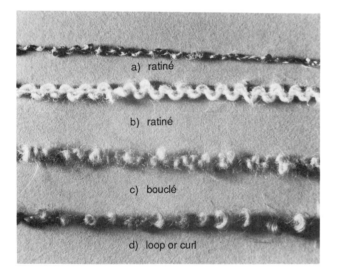

Figure 5.11 Complex yarns with loop effects.

Gimp yarns are formed by spirally wrapping one yarn around another, or by braiding three or more strands around one central yarn; in either case, the core yarn is completely covered. Gimp yarns frequently have yarn-like metallic strands on the exterior; such decorative yarns are occasionally used to embellish towels and such other interior textile items as tablecloths and wall hangings.

Core-spun and covered-core yarns are special types of gimp yarns having a rubber or spandex filament as the core component. When staple-length fibers are spun around the elastomeric filament, the structure is called a core-spun yarn; when filaments are wrapped or braided around the filament, the structure is called a covered-core yarn.

DESIGNATION OF YARN CONSTRUCTION

ASTM D 1244-81 Standard Practice for Designation of Yarn Construction includes recommendations for describing the structural features of simple yarns (the standard does not cover the description of complex yarns). Three basic notations are used to designate the construction: yarn number, direction of twist, and number of components.

Yarn Number

Yarn numbers designate the fineness or size of yarns. They are determined according to various yarn numbering systems, but the number or count of one system can be converted to its equivalent number in other systems.

Indirect Yarn Numbering Systems. In indirect yarn numbering systems, the yarn number or size is based on length per unit of mass (weight), and the yarn diameter decreases as the yarn number increases. These systems are traditionally used for spun yarns.

Cotton count (cc) system. The cc system is used to determine the yarn number of yarns spun on the cotton spinning system. The cc yarn number is equal to the number of 840-yard lengths or hanks of yarn produced from one pound of fiber. For example, a cc of 1 means that one 840-yard hank of yarn was produced from one pound of fiber, while a cc of 50 means that 50 hanks or 42,000 yards of yarn were produced from one pound of fiber.

Linen lea (ll) system. The ll system is used to determine the yarn number of yarns produced on the linen spinning system. In this system, the ll number is equal to the number of 300-yard hanks of yarn produced from one pound of fiber.

Woolen run (wr) system. The wr system is used to determine the yarn number of yarns produced on the woolen spinning system. The wr number is equal to the number of 1,600-yard hanks of yarn produced from one pound of fiber. Some spinsters may choose to use the woolen cut (w/c) system instead of the wr system. In the w/c system, the yarn number is equal to the number of 300-yard hanks of yarn produced from one pound of fiber.

Worsted count (wc) system. The wc system is used to determine the yarn number of yarns on the worsted spinning system. The wc number is equal to the number of 560-yard hanks of yarn produced from one pound of fiber.

Direct Yarn Numbering Systems. In direct yarn numbering systems, the yarn number or size is based on mass (weight) per unit of length, and the yarn diameter increases as the yarn number increases. These systems are generally used with silk and man-made filaments.

Denier (den) system. In this system, the den number is equal to the weight in grams of 9,000 meters of a monofilament or multifilament yarn. A den number of 200, for example, means that 9,000 meters of yarn weighed 200 grams.

Tex system. In this system, the tex number is equal to the weight in grams of 1,000 meters of a monofilament or multifilament yarn. This system is recommended by the International Organization for Standardization. While the system is finding some acceptance for international trade purposes, many experienced technicians are resisting its universal adoption because they are more familiar with the denier and indirect yarn numbering systems.

Because converting yarn numbers or counts determined in one system to equivalent numbers in other systems is laborious and time consuming, selected conversions are presented in Table 5.1. For conversion of yarn counts or numbers not included in the table, readers may consult ASTM D 2260 Standard Tables of Conversion Factors and of Equivalent Yarn Numbers Measured in Various Numbering Systems.

Describing Single Yarns

Information pertaining to the construction of single spun yarns is stated in this order: the yarn number and the numbering system used, the direction of twist, and the amount of twist, e.g., 50cc S 15 t.p.i. For single multifilament yarns, the letter "f" followed by the number of component filaments is inserted after the yarn number, e.g., 10 den f40 S 3 t.p.i. Monofilaments are designated as f/1.

Describing Ply Yarns

Two groups of data are used to describe ply yarns. The first group describes the single yarn components, listing the information as directed in the previous paragraph. The second group describes the ply yarn, stating the number of single yarn components in the plied yarn and the direction and the amount of plying twist. The two groups are separated by a small "x": An example is 50cc S 15 t.p.i. x 2 Z 7 t.p.i.

Describing Cord Yarns

A third group of notations is used to describe cord yarns. This group follows the groups used to describe the single and ply components and states the number of ply yarns and the direction and amount of twist used to form the cord.

Some downstream producers prefer designations of yarn construction to be stated in an order opposite that described, i.e., cord-ply-single or ply-single. Interested readers may refer to ASTM D 1244 for a review of these and other notations.

Table 5.1 YARN NUMBER CONVERSIONS

Cotton count (840 yd per lb)	Linen lea (300 yd per lb)	Woolen run (1,600 yd per lb)	Worsted count (560 yd per lb)	Denier (g per 9,000 m)	Tex (g per 1,000 m)
Coarsest					
0.357	1.000	0.188	0.536	14,890.0	1,654.0
0.667	1.867	0.350	1.000	7,972.0	885.2
1.000	2.800	0.525	1.500	5,315.0	590.5
1.905	5.333	1.000	2.857	2,790.0	310.0
3.333	9.333	1.750	5.000	1,595.0	177.2
3.810	10.67	2.000	5.714	1,395.0	155.0
40.00	112.00	21.00	60.00	132.9	14.80
50.00	140.0	26.25	75.00	106.3	11.80
60.00	168.0	31.50	90.00	88.58	9.84
531.5	1,488.0	279.1	797.3	10.00	1.11
Finest					

Courtesy of Celanese Corporation.

FORMATION OF YARN-LIKE STRUCTURES

Several components incorporated in interior textile products are yarn-like structures. While some of these strands are composed of textile fibers, and are generally referred to as yarns, they are produced with techniques other than throwing and spinning.

Chenille Yarns

Chenille yarns are actually narrow strips cut from a leno-woven fabric. In leno-weave interlacing, illustrated in Figure 6.13 (page 53), pairs of warp (lengthwise) yarns are crossed in a figure-eight fashion around the filling or weft (crosswise) yarns. The warp yarns are simple and highly twisted, and the filling yarns are simple, low-twist strands. After weaving, the fabric is carefully cut lengthwise between the leno-entwined warp yarns, producing fuzzy, caterpillar-like structures (Figure 5.12). Chenille yarns can also be produced by locking precut lengths of fibers between plied base yarns; this avoids the initial weaving operation and cutting procedure.

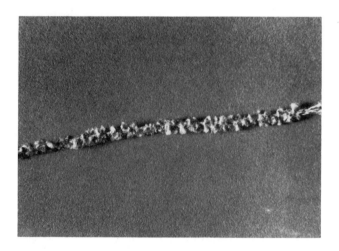

Figure 5.12 Chenille yarn cut from leno-woven fabric.

Felted Wool Yarns

Research projects sponsored by The Wool Bureau, Inc., have led to the development of unique wool yarns for use in soft floor coverings. One technique exposes loosely knitted strands of wool rovings to heat, agitation, and moisture, causing felting shrinkage and converting the strands into yarn-like structures. In this way—by capitalizing on the inherent tendency of wool fibers to shrink and matt together—manufacturers produce wool carpet yarns while avoiding the expense and time involved in conventional spinning, twisting, and plying. This helps to offset the relatively high cost of the fibers in the finished product.

Metallic Yarns

Metallic yarns, in contrast to metal filaments, are formed in various ways. Frequently, silver-colored foil is encased between clear polyester film sheeting. The layered structure is then slit into thin, yarn-like strands. The highly reflective strands may be used alone or in combination with conventional textile yarns.

Polymer Tapes

Polymer ribbons or tapes are produced by extruding a polymer solution as a wide sheet of film, much like sandwich wrap but thicker. The film sheeting is then slit into long strands of the desired width (Figure 5.13). These structures, often referred to as fibrillated ribbons or fibrillated tapes, are usually composed of polypropylene olefin or saran. Fibrillated polypropylene olefin tapes predominate in backing fabrics produced for use with pile floor coverings (see Figure 25.2b, page 270), and they are colored and used extensively as the face yarns in carpet designed to be installed outdoors and in laundry rooms, locker rooms, basements, and barns.

Twisted Paper

Two yarn-like structures are formed by tightly twisting tough sheets of paper. Fiber rush is intended to simulate natural rush, which is described below. Kraftcord is traditionally made of paper produced from cellulose recovered from titiaceous plants, which are related to lime plants. The heavy, cord-like strands are used in the back layers of woven floor coverings (see Unit Four).

Figure 5.13 Fibrillated polymer tapes.

Other Structures

Various natural substances are converted into yarn-like structures and used for such products as hand-woven chair seats and backs. Natural rush strands are produced by twisting two or three flat cattail leaves into a long unit. Sea grass, also known as Chinese grass and Hong Kong grass, is produced by twisting plied strands of grass into a cord; the natural color suggests a resemblance to rope. Cane is retrieved from the rattan, a climbing palm. The outer bark is shaved and cut into various widths, ranging from 1/8 inch or less to 5/16 inch.

SUMMARY

Spinsters use various systems to align and twist staple-length fibers into spun yarns, and throwsters use simple twisting operations to combine filament-length fibers into multifilament yarns. Throwsters may also use a texturing procedure to impose a multidimensional configuration on filaments, increasing their elasticity, cohesiveness, or apparent volume. Spinsters and throwsters can vary the level of twist and employ several plying operations to produce an extensive assortment of yarn styles, many with decorative and distinctive effects.

The construction of simple textile yarns is described in accordance with practices outlined in standards established by such voluntary scientific associations as the American Society for Testing and Materials and the International Organization for Standardization. These designations typically include the yarn number, direction of twist, and number of components. Informed persons can interpret a yarn's designation and learn several important facts about its features without actually examining the yarn itself.

Various yarn-like structures supplement the supply of spun and thrown yarns available to fabric producers. Some of these structures, including felted wool rovings and chenille yarns, are composed of fibers; others are composed of such materials as paper, grass, and film-coated foil.

chapter 6

Fabricating Textiles for Interiors: Weaving

- Biaxial Weaving
- Pile Weaving
- Triaxial Weaving

Fabrications are ways to produce fabrics, and each of the several fabrication techniques used to produce textile fabrics creates a structure with distinctive aesthetic and structural features. Because these features affect the serviceability of the fabric, as well as its installation and maintenance requirements, they influence the suitability of the fabric for various end-use applications. The method of fabrication also has a direct effect on the cost of the end product, an important criterion in the selection of most residential and commercial interior textile products.

With the exception of soft floor coverings, most textile fabrics are produced by interlacing yarns in one of several fabrication operations. Among these operations are biaxial weaving, pile weaving, and triaxial weaving. In biaxial weaving, two or more sets of yarns are interlaced at 90-degree angles to each other, to produce an essentially flat, nonpile fabric. In pile weaving, one or more sets of yarns are interlaced with biaxially woven base yarns to create a pile or depth layer. Three sets of yarns are used in triaxial weaving; the yarns are interlaced at 60-degree angles to produce a nonpile fabric.

BIAXIAL WEAVING

Basic biaxial weaving operations involve the crosswise interlacing of one set of yarns with a second set of yarns that is held parallel and tensioned on a loom. Each successive crosswise yarn is passed over and under selected lengthwise yarns in a predetermined interlacing pattern. To a large extent, the complexity of an interlacing pattern reflects the loom used to produce it. Simple interlacing patterns are executed on simple looms, and complex interlacing patterns are executed on complex looms. In any case, all looms have some common features, and all biaxially woven fabrics have some common components.

Yarn Components and Positions

Most biaxially woven fabrics have one set of lengthwise yarns, known as the warp yarns, and one set of crosswise yarns, known as the filling yarns, the weft yarns, or the woof yarns. (Multiple sets of yarns are used in some decorative biaxial interlacing patterns.) One warp yarn is often referred to as an end, and one filling yarn as a pick. The true bias, which is at a 45-degree angle to the warp and filling yarns, exhibits higher elasticity than other directions in fabric. A quality biaxially woven fabric is grain-straight: all the warp yarns are perpendicular to all the filling yarns (Figure 6.1). Conversion operations used to correct the yarn alignment in off-grain fabrics are discussed in Chapter 9.

Selvages are the narrow (1/4 to 3/4 inch) lengthwise edges of biaxially woven fabric. They are designed to prevent or minimize raveling. Fabrics produced on conventional looms have conventional selvages, whereas those produced on newer types of looms may have tucked-in, compacted, or leno-reinforced selvages (see Figure 6.2).

When composed of thermoplastic fibers, fabrics woven on newer looms often have a fused selvage produced by heat-sealing the edges.

The closeness or compactness of the yarns in biaxially woven fabrics is numerically reported as the thread count. Specifically, thread count is equal to the number of warp and filling yarns in one square inch of greige goods. The number of warp yarns is listed first, e.g., 90 x 84. When one number is given—a frequent practice with bed sheets—a balanced construction, that is, an equal number of warp and filling yarns, can be assumed. (Thread count should not be confused with yarn count.)

The compactness of construction used in weaving helps determine the appearance and serviceability of fabrics, as well as their cost. The compactness of curtain and drapery fabrics, for example, influences their decorative characteristics, their ability to reduce glare, their ability to minimize heat gain and loss, and their cost.

Loom and Weaving Fundamentals

Looms used in biaxial weaving operations vary in width and efficiency, as well as in complexity. Some looms are constructed to weave fabrics in widths of 36, 45, or 60 inches; others to weave narrow trimmings efficiently; still others to weave such wide structures as sheeting, blanketing, and carpet. Today, some looms are capable of weaving multiple widths of fabric simultaneously (see Figure 32.2, page 353).

To execute even a simple interlacing pattern, a loom must have components and control mechanisms to systematically raise and lower specific warp yarns, insert the filling yarns, align each successive filling yarn, and advance the warp yarns and woven fabric as the operation progresses. A complex interlacing pattern requires a loom with additional components and sophisticated control mechanisms.

Parts of a Simple Loom. The component parts of a simple loom are shown in Figure 6.3. Loom beams hold the supply of warp yarns. The warp yarns are threaded through heddles, thin metal strips with eye-like openings.

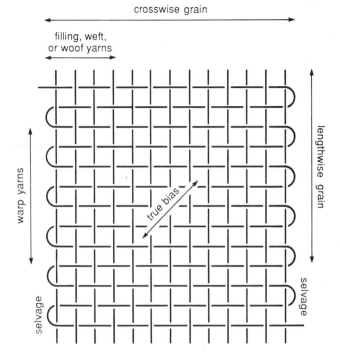

Figure 6.1 Components and features of a grain-straight biaxially woven fabric.

The number of heddles required depends on the complexity of the interlacing pattern, the compactness of construction, and the fabric width. Harnesses hold the heddles and move up and down, shifting the position of selected warp yarns. The reed, a comb-like device with openings called "dents," helps to keep the warp yarns aligned and ensure grain straightness. The number of dents per inch in the reed determines the compactness of the warp yarns. The reed is locked into the beater bar or lay, which moves forward and backward to beat or lay each new pick into position. Cloth beams hold the woven fabric.

On industrial looms, before each warp end is threaded through a heddle, it is threaded through a drop wire, a small, curved metal device. If a strained warp yarn breaks during weaving, its drop wire drops, immediately stopping the operation and preventing an unsightly flaw in the fabric.

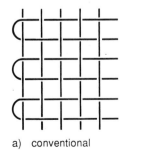

a) conventional

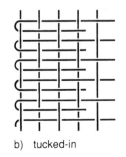

b) tucked-in

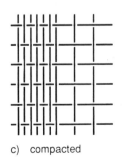

c) compacted

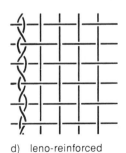

d) leno-reinforced

Figure 6.2 Selvages found on biaxially woven fabrics.

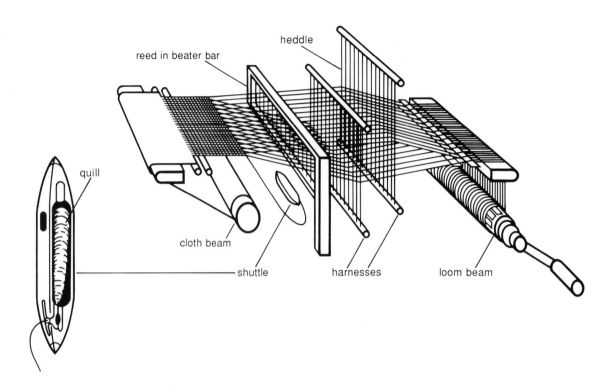

Figure 6.3 Basic parts of a simple loom. (Shuttle is reproduced by permission of Celanese Corporation. Loom is reproduced by permission of Brickel Associates Inc.)

On conventional looms, the filling yarn is wound on a bobbin or quill that is carried by a canoe-shaped shuttle, shown in detail in Figure 6.3. The devices used on newer looms to carry the filling picks are described later in this chapter.

Threading the Loom. In preparation for drawing-in or threading the warp yarns on the loom, large packages of yarn, known as "cheeses," are mounted on a creel frame (Figure 6.4). Hundreds of yarns are taken from the cheeses and wound evenly on a beam. The yarns are then treated with a hot starch or sizing compound in an operation known as "slashing." This treatment makes the yarns smoother and stronger, enabling them better to withstand the weaving stresses. We should note that warp yarns are usually simple yarns. Complex yarns generally lack the strength needed to withstand the weaving tension, and their decorative effects could be abraded by the drop wires, heddles, and reed.

The loom beam full of slashed and dried warp yarns is placed on the loom. Each end is then unwound, threaded through a drop wire, an eye in a heddle, and a dent in the reed, and tied onto the cloth beam. A pattern draft or point design serves as a guide for drawing the warp yarns through the heddles.

Pattern drafts. Pattern drafts or point designs are graphic representations of an interlacing pattern only; they do not indicate yarn size or thread count. Blocked paper is used to record the planned interlacings. Each lengthwise division of the draft paper represents one warp end and each crosswise division represents one filling pick; each block thus represents the perpendicular crossing of the yarns. When an end passes over a pick, the intersection is darkened; when an end passes behind a pick, the intersection is left blank.

The draft of a plain-weave interlacing pattern is shown in Figure 6.5. Because each end passes over and under successive picks in this weave, the draft resembles a checkerboard. It is apparent that more involved interlacing patterns have more elaborate drafts. (See Figures 26.3, page 282, and 31.16, page 340).

Following the draft of the plain weave, for example, the technician would draw-in or thread all even-numbered warp yarns through the heddles on one harness and all odd-numbered warp yarns through the heddles on a second harness. The need for more heddles and harnesses with more complicated interlacing patterns will be understood after the basic weaving operation is reviewed.

Basic Weaving Operation. Whether a simple or a complex interlacing pattern is being woven, the weaving sequence includes four steps: shedding, picking, battening, and taking up and letting off.

Figure 6.4 Warping: winding hundreds of yarns from "cheeses" mounted on a creel frame onto warp beams. (Courtesy of Burlington Industries, Inc.)

Shedding. In shedding, some harnesses are raised, lifting the warp yarns threaded through heddles held by these harnesses, and some harnesses are lowered, lowering the remaining warp yarns. This creates a V-shaped opening called the shed. Mechanized attachments automatically position the harnesses on industrial looms, whereas artisans selectively depress foot-controlled treadles and hand-controlled levers to regulate shedding on hand looms.

Picking. In this step, one or more picks are propelled or carried through the shed. Conventional looms, often called flying shuttle looms, have stick-like attachments that hammer the shuttle and send it "flying" through the shed. Because these looms are comparatively slow and create a great deal of noise, they are being replaced with quieter, more efficient looms.

Newer, so-called shuttleless looms have ingenious devices for inserting the picks. Some use a rapier (from the French for "sword"), a flexible or rigid metal tape, to "thrust" the picks. As shown in Figure 6.6, one rapier carries the pick to the center of the shed. Here, it is grasped by a second rapier and carried through the remaining width of the shed. The rapiers illustrated are flexible, coiling and recoiling during picking.

Other shuttleless looms use a jet of air or a jet of water to "shoot" the picks, and still others use small projectiles to "grip and pull" the picks. As shown in Figure 6.7, a projectile grips a cut end of a pick and is propelled through the shed, pulling the trailing pick into position. When the projectile reaches the far side of the shed, the grip is released, the pick is cut, and the two ends are turned and tucked into the next shed.

Figure 6.5 Draft or point design of plain-weave interlacing.

Battening. In this step, the beater bar or lay moves forward, pushing the inserted pick and aligning it parallel to the other filling yarns. This procedure helps to ensure uniform spacing of the filling yarns and good crosswise grain in the fabric.

Taking up and letting off. The last step in the weaving sequence includes two concurrent procedures. Woven fabric is taken up on the cloth beam, and more warp yarn length is let off from the loom beam.

This four-step sequence is repeated until the supply of warp yarns is exhausted. In each successive shedding operation, however, the positions of the harnesses are changed prior to picking.

Because the number of harnesses limits the complexity of the draft that can be followed in drawing-in the warp yarns, it also limits the variety of sheds that can be formed. More than two harnesses are required for interlacing yarns in patterns other than the plain weave and its variations.

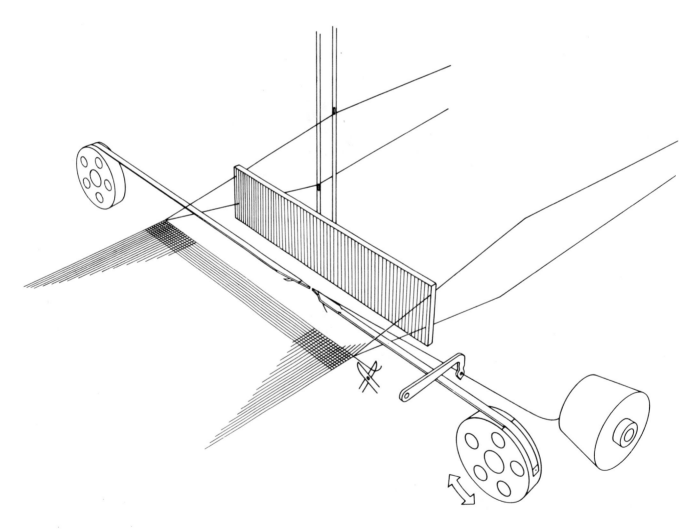

Figure 6.6 Action of flexible metal tapes on a rapier loom. (Courtesy of Sulzer-Ruti, Inc.)

Basic Biaxial Interlacing Patterns

The basic biaxial interlacing patterns include the plain, twill, and satin weaves. Each of these weaves has one or more variations. The variations can be produced by slightly altering the shed patterns used, by varying the number of picks inserted in each shed, and by using warp and filling yarns that have different yarn counts.

The Plain Weave and Its Variations. The plain weave is also known as the tabby or homespun weave. The notation used to describe the interlacing pattern is 1 x 1. This indicates that one warp yarn and one filling yarn alternately pass over one another (see Figure 6.5).

Variations of the basic plain weave include the basket, warp-rib, and filling-rib weaves. The basket variation involves slightly altering the pattern of drawing the warp yarns through the heddles and changing the number of picks inserted in each shed. The rib weaves use an unbalanced thread count or a combination of yarns with different yarn counts.

The basket weave. In the basket weave, two or more warp yarns, side by side, interlace with one or more filling yarns. When two warp yarns altternately pass over and under one filling yarn, the pattern is described as a 2 x 1 basket weave (Figure 6.8a). Interlacing two warp yarns with two filling yarns is a 2 x 2 basket weave (Figure 6.8b). When the loom is threaded for this pattern, the first two warp yarns are drawn through heddles on one harness, the next two warp yarns are drawn through heddles on the second harness, and so on. Each shed has alternating groups of two warp yarns raised and two warp yarns lowered. The 2 x 2 interlacing is then executed by inserting two picks in each shed.

The warp-rib weave. The warp-rib weave creates a rib effect lengthwise in the fabric. The ribs may be produced by combining warp yarns having different counts or

Figure 6.7 Metal projectile used for picking on a shuttleless loom. (Courtesy of Sulzer-Ruti, Inc.)

by using a combination of interlacing patterns. Dimity, a warp-rib woven fabric, is pictured in Figure 6.9, together with a draft of the interlacing pattern. This photograph is a close-up of the dimity shown in Figure 20.6 (page 201).

The filling-rib weave. Filling-rib fabrics generally have a 1 x 1 interlacing, but they are distinguished by crosswise three-dimensional ribs or ridges (see Figure 12.4, page 116). The ribs are produced by cramming (using a higher number of ends than picks per inch) or by incorporating larger yarns in the crosswise direction. These larger yarns may result from extruding filaments or spinning yarns with oversized diameters, plying several single yarns, or grouping several single yarns together without twist.

The Twill and Herringbone Weaves. The interlacing patterns used in twill weaving are more involved

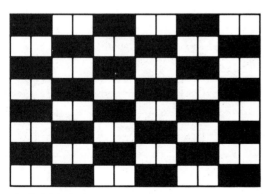

a) 2x1 interlacing

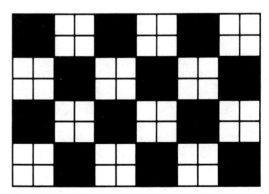

b) 2x2 interlacing

Figure 6.8 Point designs of selected basket-weave interlacings.

than the patterns used in the plain weave and its variations. Looms must have three or more harnesses to execute twill interlacing patterns.

Notations used with twill weaves describe the interlacing pattern of each warp yarn. The 2/1 notation describing Figure 6.10a, for example, indicates that each warp yarn passes or floats over two filling yarns, under one filling yarn, over two filling yarns, and so on. (Students should note the difference between the notation used for the basket and the twill weave, e.g., a 2 x 1 basket and a 2/1 twill.) In a 2/4 interlacing depicted in the draft shown in Figure 6.10b, each warp yarn passes over two filling yarns and under four filling yarns.

Angle and direction of the visual diagonal. To create the visual diagonal characteristic of twill-woven fabrics, each warp yarn must be interlaced one filling yarn above or below the filling yarn interlaced by the adjacent warp yarn. The angle of the visual diagonal depends on the pattern of interlacing and the compactness of construction. Increasing the length of the warp float and increasing the number of warp yarns per inch, for example, increases the angle. The diagonal can be regular (at a 45-degree angle), reclined (at a less than 45-degree angle), or steep (at a greater than 45-degree angle). This diagonal is an appearance feature only; the warp and filling yarns always interlace at a 90-degree angle in biaxial weaving.

As noted in Figures 6.10a and 6.10b, the direction of the visual diagonal is described as either right-hand or left-hand. Left-hand twills have a diagonal pattern that descends from left to right; right-hand twills have a diagonal that descends from right to left.

Even and uneven twill interlacings. In twill interlacings, each warp or filling yarn must float or pass over a minimum of two yarns before interlacing. When the warp yarns float over a greater number of filling yarns than they pass behind, they cover a greater portion of the fabric surface, and the fabric is described as an uneven

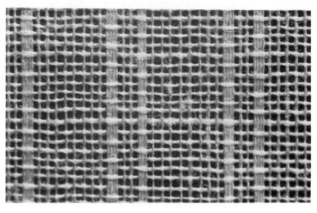

a)   dimity

b)   draft of interlacing pattern

Figure 6.9 Dimity, a warp-rib woven fabric.

warp-faced twill. When the filling yarns float over a greater number of warp yarns than they pass behind, the fabric is described as an uneven filling-faced twill. The difference between a warp-faced twill and a filling-faced twill can be seen by comparing Figures 6.10a and 6.10b. When an interlacing pattern has equal amounts of warp and filling yarns covering the fabric surface, as illustrated in Figure 6.10c, the fabric is described as an even twill.

The herringbone weave. In herringbone interlacings, the direction of the visual diagonal is continually re-

a)   2/1 interlacing
     regular
     right-hand
     warp-faced

b)   2/4 interlacing
     steep
     left-handed
     filling-faced

c)   2/2 interlacing
     regular
     herringbone
     even

Figure 6.10 Drafts and characteristics of selected twill interlacings.

versed across the width of the fabric, as shown by the draft in Figure 6.10c. Lengthwise, successive diagonals repeat in the same direction.

The Satin and Sateen Weaves. Like warp-faced twill fabrics, satin fabrics have floating warp yarns. In satin interlacings, however, a visual diagonal does not appear because adjacent warp yarns do not interlace with adjacent filling yarns.

Satin interlacing patterns require more shed variations than do basic twill patterns. To produce the satin weave depicted in Figure 6.11a, five harnesses would need to be threaded. This pattern is described as five-shaft construction, indicating that each warp yarn is floating over four picks and under the fifth.

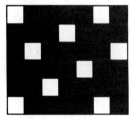 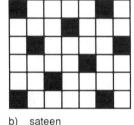

a) 5-shaft satin   b) sateen

Figure 6.11 Drafts of selected satin and sateen interlacings.

Satin-woven fabrics are characterized by high luster and sheen, primarily produced by the reflection of large amounts of light from the smooth, uninterrupted surface areas of the floats, but also frequently augmented by the use of bright fibers. The level of luster will be reduced if abrasion ruptures the floating yarns during use.

The sateen weave. In sateen interlacing, the filling yarns float over the warp yarns. This weave, which is also known as the filling-faced satin weave, is frequently used to produce drapery lining fabrics (see Unit Three).

Decorative Biaxial Interlacing Patterns

The relative simplicity of the basic biaxial weaves and their variations can readily be appreciated when they are compared to the decorative biaxial weaves, in which several simple weaves and multiple sets of yarns are often used. The decorative biaxial weaves include the dobby, the surface-figure, the leno, and the Jacquard weaves. Because decorative appearance features are often important selection criteria, these complex interlacing patterns are used extensively in the production of interior textile fabrics.

The Dobby Weave. Dobby weaving is used to interlace yarns into fabrics having small, geometric motifs. Although the motifs are comparatively simple, dobby looms must have as many as twenty or thirty harnesses to produce the variety of sheds required. The several harnesses are visible in the central portion of the dobby loom pictured in Figure 6.12.

In order to ensure accurate weaving of the motifs, the technician must carefully follow the pattern draft when drawing the warp yarns through the many heddles held by the several harnesses. During weaving, the positions of the harnesses for each shed are mechanically controlled by a unit attached to the side of the loom. This unit has a pattern roll similar to the paper music roll used with player pianos. The holes punched in the pattern roll determine which harnesses will be raised and which harnesses will be lowered, as the holes punched in the music roll determine which keys will be played (Figure 6.12 detail).

The Surface-figure Weaves. Surface-figure weaves are executed on a dobby loom, using extra yarns to produce raised figures while the base fabric is being woven. These interlacing patterns, including dot or spot weaving, swivel weaving, and lappet weaving (Figure 20.11, page 205), are used to produce several curtain fabrics, and the dot or spot technique is used to produce assorted upholstery fabrics (see Figure 12.10, page 119).

The Leno Weave. Looms with special attachments are used for the leno weave, in which paired warp yarns cross as they encircle and secure the filling yarns. As sketched in Figure 6.13, the warp yarns do not twist around one another; one yarn in each pair always passes in front of the second yarn. Although the individual warp yarns are not parallel, the paired groups are, and the structure is essentially biaxial.

The Jacquard Weave. Jacquard-woven fabrics often have extremely complex interlacing patterns combining two or more simple weaves, multiple sets of yarns, and strategically placed colors. Typically, the pattern repeats are large and composed of various motifs, each having finely detailed curved and swirled shapes. It is apparent that the Jacquard loom must have the capacity to form an almost unlimited variety of intricate sheds and to facilitate the selection of specific colors of picks.

As explained earlier, the variety of possible shed patterns can be explained by increasing the number of harnesses. For intricate Jacquard patterns, however, the number of sheds required to complete one repeat may be so large that hundreds of harnesses would be needed. Not only would a loom so equipped be massive in size, but drawing-in the warp yarns would be difficult. To avoid these problems, Jacquard looms have a system of cords and

Figure 6.12 Dobby loom with multiple harnesses for varied shed formation. (Courtesy of Springs Industries, Inc.)

hooks in lieu of harness frames. These cords are visible in the central portion of the loom pictured in Figure 6.14.

Each warp yarn is threaded through a cord heddle that is is linked to a needle by a rod and hook apparatus. In effect, each cord heddle functions as a miniature harness that can be raised and lowered independently of all the other heddles. The position of each cord, and thus of each warp yarn, in a shed is controlled by a programmed card resembling that formerly used with computers or, increasingly, by computer tape. One programmed card is key-punched for each shed in the pattern repeat. Figure 6.14 shows the several cards suspended above the loom.

In the Jacquard weaving operation, a programmed card is brought into position and the needles shift forward. When a needle encounters a hole in the card, the hook is permitted to rise, carrying the warp yarn upward; when a

needle encounters a solid portion of the card, the hook is not permitted to rise and the warp yarn remains down. The picking, battening, and taking up and letting off weaving procedures follow. The second card is then brought into position, and the four-step weaving operation is repeated. This sequence is continued until the pattern repeat is completed. A second repeat is then woven, again using the programmed cards to control the interlacings.

PILE WEAVING

Woven pile fabrics are constructed by interlacing three sets of yarns: one set of warp yarns and one set of filling yarns for the base fabric and one set of warp or filling yarns for the pile layer. In the finished fabrics, the pile

Figure 6.12 Detail of dobby loom control mechanism. (Courtesy of Springs Industries Inc.)

yarns are more or less perpendicular to the base yarns, introducing a dimension of height to otherwise two-dimensional fabrics.

Incorporating Extra Filling Yarns

Filling pile fabrics, including corduroy and velveteen, are produced by incorporating an extra set of filling yarns. Corduroy has length-wise ridges of pile yarns, called wales, whereas velveteen has uniformly spaced pile yarns; the manner of interlacing the pile yarns differs for each fabric.

Producing Corduroy. To produce corduroy, the filling pile yarns are floated over a number of base warp yarns and then interlaced with others. For wider wales, which are often preferred for interior applications, the pile yarns may be floated over five or six base yarns before they are interlaced. Each successive pile yarn must cross over and under the same base warp yarns to ensure that the floats are aligned in lengthwise rows. For high pile den-

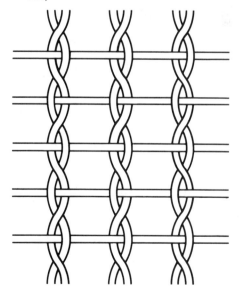

Figure 6.13 Leno-weave interlacing.

Figure 6.14 Jacquard loom. (Courtesy of the American Textile Manufacturers Institute.)

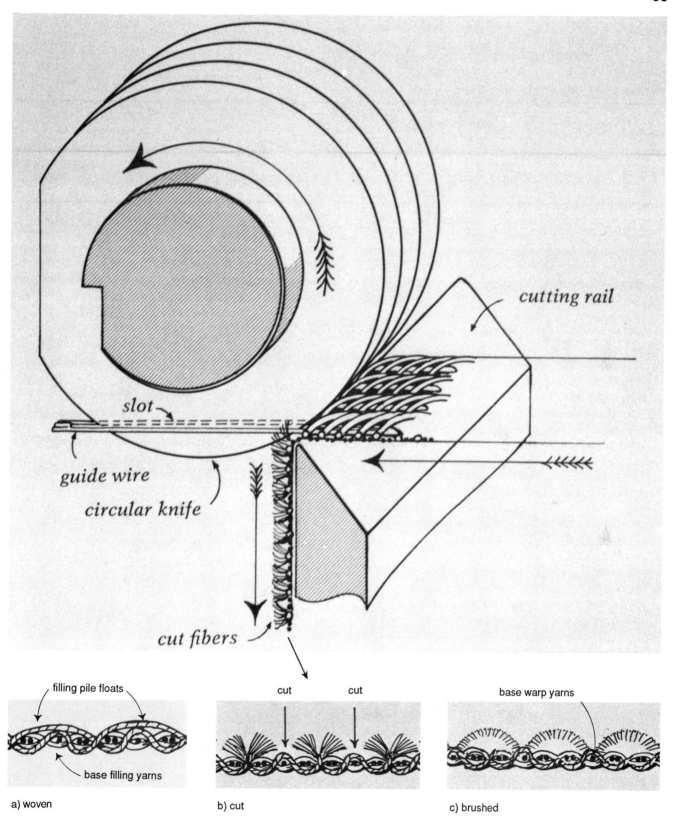

cutting rail

slot

guide wire

circular knife

cut fibers

filling pile floats

base filling yarns

a) woven

cut   cut

b) cut

base warp yarns

c) brushed

Figure 6.15 Production of corduroy, a filling pile fabric. (Courtesy of Crompton & Knowles Corporation.)

sity, two, three, four, or more pile yarns may be interlaced before a base filling is interlaced.

After the weaving operation has been completed, thin metal guides are used to lift the floats as circular knives cut them. When wide and narrow wales are planned, the floats are cut off-center. The surface is then brushed to raise the cut ends, forming the lengthwise wales and exposing the fabric areas that had been covered by the floats. These weaving, cutting, and brushing procedures are illustrated in Figure 6.15.

During fabric conversion, the pile yarns are laid in one direction, introducing a surface feature known as pile lay, pile sweep, or fabric nap. This reorientation of the pile yarns (illustrated in Figure 9.3, page 83) alters the reflective characteristics of the surface, as well as the tactile features. The marked sweep of the pile yarns in the fabric pictured in Figure 6.16 is evident; this novelty corduroy has a patterned pile with some of the floats left uncut for added visual interest.

Figure 6.16 Novelty corduroy having a patterned pile with some filling pile floats left uncut.

Producing Velveteen. Velveteen construction differs from that of corduroy in three major ways. First, the filling pile yarns used are usually much finer than those used in corduroy. Second, each successive pile yarn crosses over and under different base warp yarns to avoid having the floats aligned in lengthwise rows. Third, the pile yarns are floated over no more than two base warp yarns, and more floats are used per inch. Collectively, these construction features produce a short, dense pile layer without wales. As with corduroy, the floats are cut, raised, and laid in one direction after the weaving operation has been completed.

Incorporating Extra Warp Yarns

Warp pile fabrics are made by incorporating an extra set of warp yarns during weaving. Three kinds of weaving operations are used to produce these fabrics.

The Doublecloth Construction Technique. The doublecloth construction technique produces two lengths of velvet in one weaving operation. As shown in Figure 6.17, the pile layers are formed by alternately interlacing the extra set of warp yarns with the base yarns forming the upper fabric and with those forming the lower fabric. The interlacing pattern is controlled to avoid the formation of crosswise wales. As the weaving progresses, the pile yarns joining the two fabrics are cut, and the two fabrics are taken up on separate cloth beams.

The pile yarns may be interlaced in such a manner that the pile tufts have a V-shaped configuration or a W-shaped configuration. In the V pattern (Figure 6.18a), each pile yarn is anchored by one base filling, while in the W pattern (Figure 6.18b), each pile yarn is anchored by three base yarns. The W form is inherently more stable, but the V form can be stabilized by weaving the base compactly and applying an adhesive coating to the fabric back. Using a high pile density with either pattern will improve texture retention and abrasion resistance during the product's use.

The Over-the-wire Construction Technique. The over-the-wire construction technique is used for weaving some pile upholstery fabrics and some carpet. In this procedure, illustrated in Figure 6.19, wires are used to support the pile yarns during weaving. The height of the pile layer can be controlled by the height of the wires used. The wires are withdrawn after several successive rows of pile loops have been woven. If a cut pile surface texture is planned, the wires have a knife blade on one end; the wires have rounded ends if an uncut pile surface is planned.

The Slack Tension Technique. For interior textile applications, only terry toweling is routinely woven by

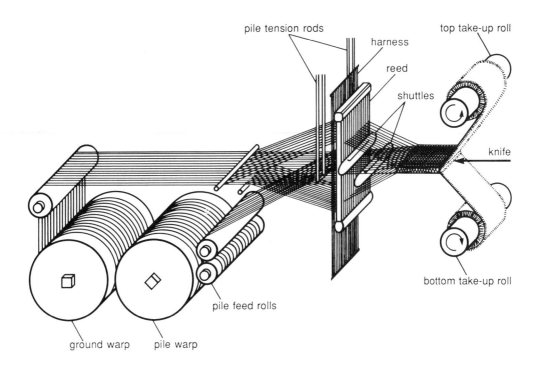

Figure 6.17 The doublecloth construction technique. (Courtesy of Crompton & Knowles Corporation.)

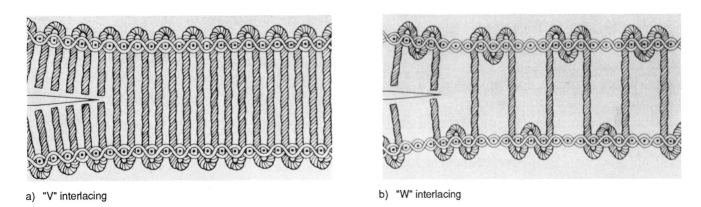

a) "V" interlacing

b) "W" interlacing

Figure 6.18 V and W forms of pile interlacing patterns. (Courtesy of Brickel Associates Inc.)

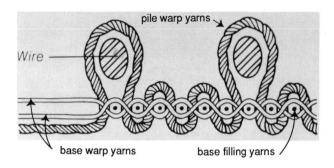

Figure 6.19 The over-the-wire construction technique. (Reproduced with adaptations courtesy of Brickel Associates Inc.).

the slack tension technique. This weaving operation is explained and illustrated in Chapter 32.

TRIAXIAL WEAVING

Triaxial weaving is a relatively new fabrication technique. In this operation, two sets of warp yarns and one set of filling yarns are interlaced at 60-degree angles rather than 90-degree angles. Whereas selected warp yarns are raised and lowered in biaxial shedding operations, in triaxial shedding operations all yarns in each set of warp yarns are alternately raised and lowered. This results in one set of warp yarns always passing over the filling yarns and the other set always passing behind the filling yarns, as illustrated in Figure 6.20.

Triaxially woven fabrics are strong, yet lightweight. This feature, along with stretchability and high resistance to tearing, supports the increased use of these fabrics for upholstered furniture and automobile seat coverings.

SUMMARY

Among the fabrication techniques used to interlace textile yarns or yarn-like structures are biaxial weaving, pile weaving, and triaxial weaving. Relatively simple biaxial

Figure 6.20 Triaxial interlacing pattern.

interlacing patterns, like plain, twill, and satin weaves and their respective variations, can be executed on comparatively simple looms. By contrast, complicated interlacing patterns, like those followed in the dobby, surface-figure, leno, and Jacquard weaves, must be produced on complex looms with sophisticated control mechanisms.

Pile weaving operations use a minimum of three sets of yarns. Two sets are interlaced to form the base fabric, while the third set is simultaneously incorporated to form a pile or depth layer. Such woven pile fabrics as corduroy, velvet, terry, and carpet are used for a wide variety of interior applications.

Three sets of yarns are also used in triaxial weaving operations. In this technique, the yarns are interlaced at 60-degree rather than 90-degree angles. Triaxial weaving is increasingly used by fabric producers to expand the assortment of greige goods available to downstream firms.

chapter *7*

Fabricating Textiles for Interiors: Other Techniques

- Interlooping Yarns
- Inserting Yarns
- Knotting and Twisting Yarns
- Braiding Yarns
- Combining Fibers
- Extruding Polymer Solutions

Besides the techniques used to weave or interlace yarns, several other methods can be used to combine yarns into textile structures suitable for interior applications. Yarns can be interlooped, inserted or embedded, braided, or knotted and twisted. Techniques are also available that use no yarns, enabling producers to combine fibers directly into fabrics, and one technique uses neither yarns nor fibers, allowing producers to convert polymer solutions directly into film fabrics.

In recent years, existing fabrication techniques have been revised and combined, and entirely new processes have been invented, expanding the variety of fabric production methods available to the industry. While the primary goal of this expansion was to control or reduce production time and material costs, textile engineers also sought to enable manufacturers to control the aesthetic, functional, and structural features of their fabrics efficiently. The resulting operations have helped producers respond more quickly and accurately to changing product selection criteria among consumers.

INTERLOOPING YARNS

Three major interior textile fabrications use yarn interlooping operations to produce fabrics: the age-old techniques of knitting and crocheting, and the relatively new technique of chain-stitching.

Knitting

Knitting operations are separated into two major categories, warp knitting and weft or filling knitting, according to the manner in which the yarns are interlooped. Although different stitches are used in these operations, all knitted fabrics have some common features.

Yarn Components and Positions. Rows of yarn loops running lengthwise in a knitted fabric are known as wales, and those running crosswise are known as courses. The wales and course should be at right angles to one another, in much the same way as warp and filling yarns should be perpendicular to one another in biaxially woven fabrics. Unlike woven fabric, in which the true bias offers the greatest elasticity, knitted fabrics are generally most stretchable in the crosswise direction, since the rounded loops expand and contract laterally.

The compactness of construction of knitted fabrics is determined by the gauge used. The gauge is the number of loops per inch or per bar inch (1 1/2 inches) and is controlled by the size of the knitting needles. Along with the size of the yarns used, gauge helps determine the transparency, porosity, and weight of the fabric.

Warp Knitting. Warp knitted fabrics are produced by the simultaneous interlooping of adjacent warp yarns. As shown in Figure 7.1, a portion of each yarn has a diagonal orientation but the wales are essentially parallel. Although courses can be identified, no filling yarns are used.

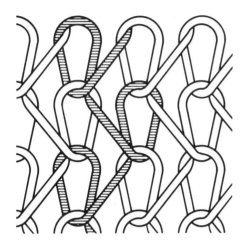

Figure 7.1 Interlooping of adjacent yarns in warp knitting.

Warp knitting is an extremely fast operation, with large machines producing more than four million loops per minute. Warp knitting machines can construct fabrics up to 168 inches in width, but only in flat, rectangular shapes.

Stitches. Two warp knitting stitches, the tricot stitch and the raschel stitch, are commonly used for interior fabrics. The tricot stitch is produced using spring needles, illustrated in Figure 7.2, and one or two guide bars, attachments that guide or shift yarns around the hooked or curved portion of the needles prior to interlooping.

Tricot fabrics are distinguished by the presence of herringbone-like wales on the face of the fabric and by a crosswise rib-like effect on the back of the fabric. Tricot-stitched fabrics have comparatively low stretchability. When these fabrics are made of thermoplastic fibers, heat setting can be used to improve their dimensional stability. Tricot fabrics are used for automobile interiors, upholstered furniture coverings, and wall coverings.

The raschel stitch is executed on a machine that may be equipped with up to thirty guide bars, which select and position the various yarns in preparation for interlooping. Increasing the number of guide bars is equivalent to increasing the number of harnesses on looms; thus, raschel machines are extremely versatile. As shown in Figure 7.3, the needles used have a latch that opens and closes to se-

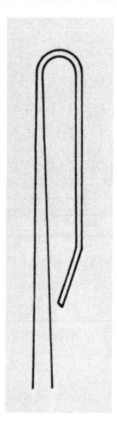

Figure 7.2 Head of spring needle used in tricot stitching. (Courtesy of Celanese Corporation.)

cure the yarn, enabling the manufacturer to use virtually any fiber and any style of yarn.

Raschel-stitched fabrics often have a lace-like appearance and are used as window coverings (see Figure 20.26, page 215). They are also often produced for use as tabletop accessories.

Weft insertion. Warp knitting and weaving are combined in a relatively new fabrication technique known as weft insertion. In this operation, weft or filling yarns are inserted or "woven" through the loops being formed in a tricot-stitching operation. One of the distinct advantages weft-inserted fabrics offer is readily apparent in Figure 7.4. Virtually all of the fabric weight and cover is provided by the weft yarns; thus, the need for the larger and more expensive warp yarns is reduced. Because the transparency and covering power of the fabric can be controlled by the size and character of the weft yarns used, manufacturers are increasingly using weft insertion to produce window coverings (see Figure 20.27, page 215).

Weft or Filling Knitting. In weft or filling knitting (Figure 7.5), fabrics are produced by continuously interlooping one or more yarns from side to side, creating one course after another. No warp yarns are used.

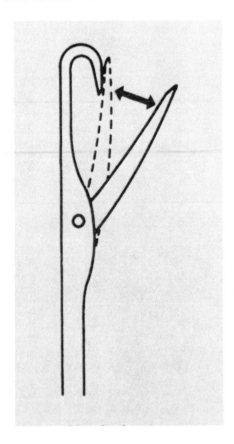

Figure 7.3 Head of latch needle used in raschel stitching. (Courtesy of Celanese Corporation.)

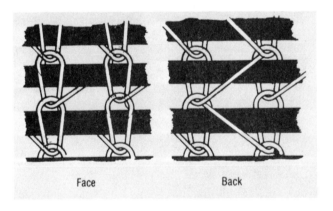

Face   Back

Figure 7.4 Fabric produced by weft insertion. (Courtesy of Celanese Corporation.)

Filling knitting is slower than warp knitting. Approximately three million loops are formed per minute. While warp knitting machines can produce only flat, straight-sided fabrics, filling knitting machines can produce rectangular fabrics, fabrics with a circular or tubular form, and fabrics with a preplanned, angular shape. Knitting flat-to-shape, a procedure used extensively in the production of apparel items, is rarely if ever used in the production of

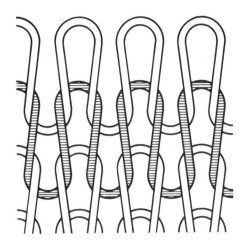

Figure 7.5 Continuous interlooping of one yarn in filling knitting.

interior textile items. Circular knitting, pictured in Figure 7.6, produces the fabric used in the knit-de-knit yarn texturing method explained in Chapter 5.

Stitches. Among the filling knitting stitches used to manufacture interior fabrics are the jersey stitch and the interlock stitch. The jersey stitch, used in some bedsheets, creates herringbone-like wales on the face of the fabric and crescent-shaped loops on the back of the fabric. Knitted pile fabrics, used to make simulated fur bedspreads, are formed by incorporating additional yarns or fibers into a jersey-stitched base fabric.

The interlock stitch is formed by continuously interlooping two yarns. The completed fabric appears to be two interknitted fabrics, as shown schematically in Figure 7.7. Interlock-stitched fabrics are resistant to running and snagging and have high dimensional stability when heat set. These characteristics support the selection of double-knit fabrics—interlock-stitched fabrics with relatively large loops—for use as furniture and wall coverings.

Crocheting

Crocheting can be described as knitting with one needle. The needle is continually manipulated to interloop one yarn into previously formed loops. Artisans use crocheting to make decorative borders for pillowcases and to create such accessories as afghans, doilies, and potholders (see Unit Five).

Chain-stitching

Over the past several years, advances in technology have enabled manufacturers to produce fabrics more rapidly than they could with conventional techniques. In two fast

Figure 7.6 Circular knitting machine. (Courtesy of the American Textiles Manufacturers Institute.)

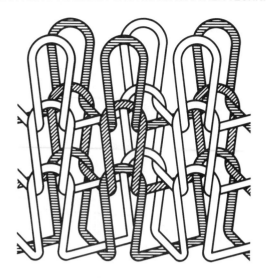

Figure 7.7 An interlock-stitched fabric.

new techniques, stitch-knitting and stitch-bonding, knitting stitches are used as stabilizing chain-stitches.

Stitch-knitting. Stitch-knitting, which is also known as knit-sewing and by the patented name of Malimo, is an innovative fabrication technique. In this operation, webs of yarns are layered and chain-stitched together to produce a usable fabric structure. The chain-stitching is, in effect, "sewing" with knitting stitches, and the rate of fabric production is high. As no abrasive mechanisms (such as drop wires, heddles, or reeds) are used, highly decorative, complex yarns can be incorporated in either fabric direction. This yarn-placement flexibility permits manufacturers to control the level of fabric transparency easily and produce fabrics that vary widely in their visual and textural features. Fabrics produced by this technique are pictured in Figure 20.28 (page 216).

Stitch-bonding. Stitch-bonding operations involve chain-stitching across a fibrous batt, converting the layered webs of fibers into a usable textile structure. A stitch-bonded window covering is pictured in Figure 20.30 (page 218).

INSERTING YARNS

Tufting and fusion bonding operations are used to introduce pile yarns to already-formed fabrics. Both techniques are fast and efficient.

Tufting

In tufting operations, pile yarns are threaded through needles that are mounted across the tufting machine and suspended vertically above the base fabric. As shown in Figure 7.8, the needles punch through the back of the fabric and loopers engage the yarns. As each needle is withdrawn, a pile loop is formed. If a cut-pile texture is desired, the loopers are equipped with oscillating knives.

At this stage, the tufted pile yarns could easily be pulled out as they are only held in the base fabric mechanically. To provide better stability, a thin coating of an adhesive compound is applied to the fabric back.

Tufting has captured a modest portion of the upholstery fabrics market, but it has taken over the soft floor coverings market, accounting for more than 96 percent of all carpet and rugs produced. Readers may refer to Unit Four for an extensive discussion of tufting processes.

Fusion Bonding

In fusion bonding operations, pile yarns are inserted, or, more precisely, embedded, into an adhesive coating that has been applied to a base fabric. This technique, increasingly used in the production of soft floor coverings, is discussed and illustrated in Chapter 26.

KNOTTING AND TWISTING YARNS

Highly decorative lace and macramé fabrics are produced by knotting or twisting intersecting yarns. A major difference between these two kinds of fabric is the size of the yarns used, with macramé items made up of heavier strands.

Lace Making

In the manufacture of lace fabrics, complex machinery is used to twist relatively fine yarns around one another. The yarns in lace fabrics are not parallel and perpendicular; they are instead oriented in various directions. Machine-made lace is used in window coverings, bed coverings, and tabletop accents. Hand-made lace, discussed in Unit Five, is used as trimming for bedding products and is constructed into such items as dresser scarves and doilies.

Producing Macramé

Macramé is usually a relatively heavy fabric constructed by knotting and twisting textile cords. Machine-made macramé is used in vertical blinds (see Unit Three) and hand-made macramé panels are used as decorative hangings.

BRAIDING YARNS

Braiding techniques are similar in some ways to biaxial weaving, triaxial weaving, and twisting operations. As in

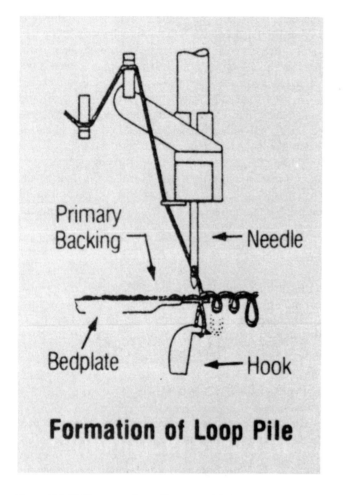

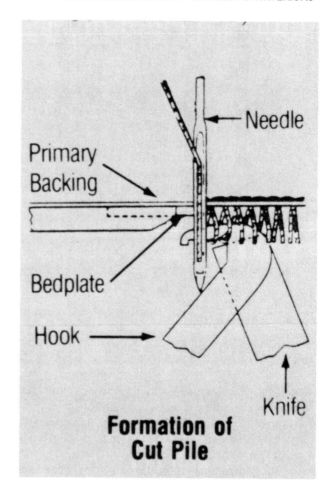

Figure 7.8 Tufting operations. (Courtesy of Celanese Corporation.)

biaxial weaving, the yarn strands are interlaced; as in triaxial weaving, the yarns are interlaced at a less than 90-degree angle; and as in twisting, the direction or orientation of the yarns is continually reversed as production progresses.

To produce flat braids, which are frequently used as trims or converted into rugs, three yarns or yarn-like structures are interlaced (see Figure 26.16, page 292). To produce the circular braids often used as accent tie-backs for draperies, several strands are interlaced around a textile cord or other round structure.

COMBINING FIBERS

Textile machinery engineers and producers have devised new ways to produce fabric structures while bypassing the yarn stage. Techniques such as spunbonding and spunlacing have joined the age-old technique of felting and the ef-

ficient method of needlepunching as ways to combine fibers directly into fabrics.

Bonding Fibrous Batts

In one fabrication, fibrous batts are bonded into essentially flat structures with a paper-like quality. (These structures must not be confused with the three-dimensional fibrous batts produced for use as fillings and paddings. See Unit Two.) Webs of fibers are first layered to form a relatively thin batt. The webs may be layered parallel to each other, as shown in Figure 7.9, at right angles, or randomly. An adhesive must be sprayed over the batt to cause nonthermoplastic fibers to adhere to one another. Heat can be used to soften thermoplastic fibers and cause them to stick together.

Bonded-web fabrics are used as interfacing in upholstery skirts, adding body and weight. They are also used to interface the heading in curtains and draperies, providing

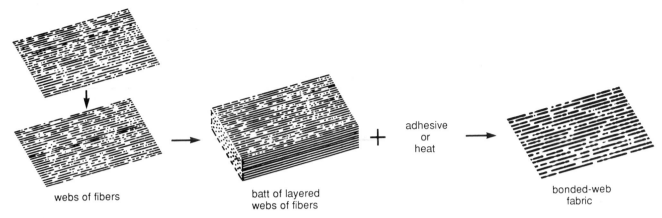

webs of fibers   batt of layered webs of fibers   adhesive or heat   bonded-web fabric

Figure 7.9 Bonding fibrous batts.

support for such treatments as pleats and scallops (see Unit Three).

Felting Fibrous Batts

In the production of felt, wool fibers are cleaned and carded into thin webs, which are then layered at right angles to form a batt. The batt is exposed to controlled heat, agitation, moisture, and pressure. These conditions cause the overlapping scales of the fibers to intermesh and entangle, compacting and shrinking the batt into felt.

Felt is widely used to prevent artifacts from scratching hard-surfaced tabletops. Thick felt is an effective insulation material. To reduce its cost, felt can be produced from a blend of wool and rayon fibers.

Needlepunching Fibrous Batts

The technique of using barbed needles to create a mechanical chain-stitch within a fibrous batt has long been employed in the production of some carpet cushions and saddle blankets. More recently, the method has been refined and used in the production of some carpet, wall coverings, and blankets. For added stability, a loosely woven fabric, called a scrim, or an adhesive may be enclosed within the batt prior to needlepunching. This fabrication technique is pictured in Figure 26.17 (page 293).

Spunbonding Webs of Filaments

Spunbonding converts thermoplastic filaments directly into fabric structures. After the filaments are arranged into a thin web, they are stabilized with heat or chemical binders. For added strength, stability, weight, or reduced transparency, additional compounds can be sprayed over the fine web. Spunbonded fabrics are increasingly used as tablecloths, as coverings for bedding products, and as backings for wall coverings and carpet.

Spunlacing Fibers

Textile fabrics produced by mechanically entangling fibers are referred to as spunlaced fabrics. While an adhesive or other type of binder is generally used with spunbonded and bonded-web fabrics, the fibers in spunlaced fabrics are stabilized solely by fiber-to-fiber friction (Figure 7.10). Today, spunlaced fabrics are used to back textile wall coverings, simulated leather upholstery fabrics, mattress pads, and conforters, and they are also made into pillow coverings.

EXTRUDING POLYMER SOLUTIONS

Polymer solutions can be converted directly into film sheeting fabrics. This is accomplished by extruding the solution through a spinneret that has a narrow slit rather than minute holes. As the polymer ribbon emerges, it is stretched into a thin film or sheet. The thickness of the film can be controlled by varying the extrusion pressure and the amount of stretching. Film sheetings are used for such interior products as simulated leather upholstery coverings, drapery linings, and shower curtains.

SUMMARY

To manufacture the wide variety of interior textile components and fabrics required by end-product producers, a wide range of fabrication techniques is necessarily employed. Several of these techniques enable the fabric producer to interloop, insert, or otherwise combine yarns into greige goods, supplementing the methods used to interlace yarns. Other techniques enable the producer to combine fibers and convert solutions directly into usable structures, avoiding spinning, throwing, and fiber extruding operations. Many of the fabrications reviewed in this chapter are more efficient and less costly than weaving.

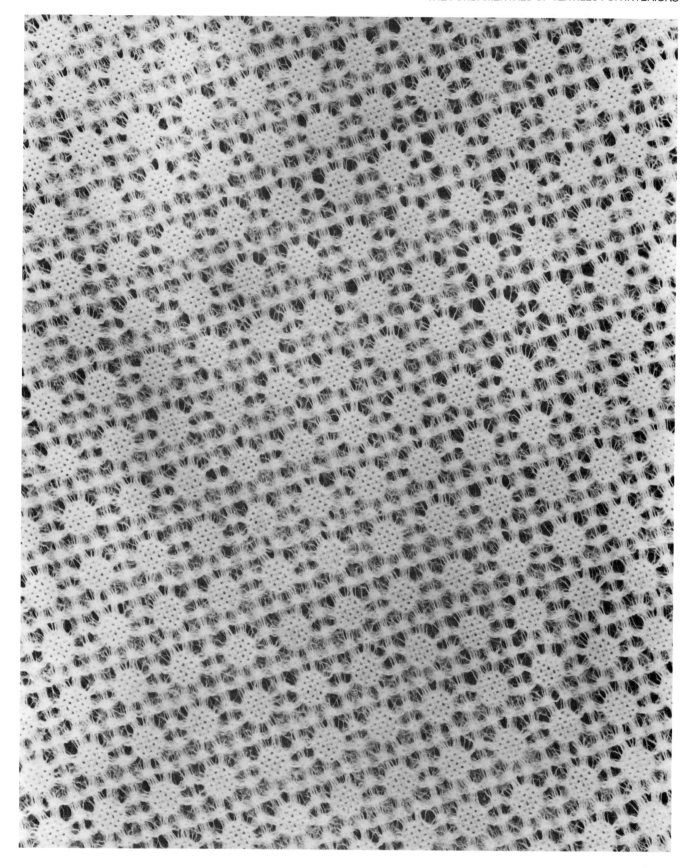

Figure 7.10 Spunlaced fabric. (Courtesy of Burlington Industries, Inc.)

Following the sequence of production outlined in Chapter 1, the greige goods produced by weaving, knitting, tufting, spunbonding, and so on are forwarded to colorists or converters. These members of the industry work to make the goods more attractive and functional, helping to ensure their selection by consumers, contract designers, and architects.

chapter 8

Textile Colorants, Color Perception, and Color Application

- Colorants and Color Perception
- Dyeing Fabrics and Fabric Components
- Printing Greige Goods
- Combining Dyeing and Printing
- Factors Affecting Apparent Color

Interior environments are enhanced when the addition of colored textiles is carefully planned. The planning effort entails an examination of factors that alter the apparent characteristics of the textile colorants. Whatever characteristics are chosen, they will appear different when viewed under different conditions; an obvious example of such a condition is the lighting of a particular environment.

The importance of color-related variables to the selection of interior textile products is reflected in the availability of several methods for applying colorants. These methods may be divided into three major categories: dyeing, printing, and dyeing and printing combinations. Colorists select the method of application that can introduce the color styling features preferred by the contemporary consumer or specified by the contract designer or architect.

Although most natural fibers have some color-producing substances, which may or may not be retained, and most textiles have color-producing substances added, no fibers or other textile structures have intrinsic color. Not until incident light waves are reflected, and interpreted by an observer, will color be perceived.

COLORANTS AND COLOR PERCEPTION

For color to be perceived, incident light waves must first be reflected to the eye. In turn, these rays must stimulate the eye to transmit optical sensations to the brain for interpretation. Only then will the viewer see a particular "color." What the viewer is responding to, in fact, is a concentration of light waves of certain lengths. Because light waves play a critical role in color stimulus and sensation, a brief review of the nature of light will augment our discussion of textile colorants and color perceptions.

The Nature of Light

Light is visible electromagnetic energy, which accounts for a relatively small portion of the electromagnetic spectrum. This spectrum, schematized in Figure 8.1, includes waves of vastly different lengths, but all are very short. At one end are cosmic and gamma rays, which are quite short; at the opposite end are radio and electrical power waves, which are relatively long in comparison with cosmic waves. The actual length of most waves—the distance from the crest of one wave to the crest of the next—is measured and reported in minuscule units called nanometers (nm). One nanometer is equal to one billionth of a meter or to 0.000039 inch.

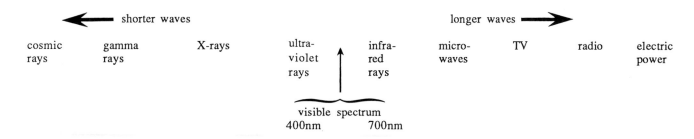

Figure 8.1 The electromagnetic spectrum.

In the central portion of the electromagnetic spectrum is an area known as the visible spectrum. The lengths of waves in this region range from some 400 nm to about 700 nm. When reflected to the eye, these radiations stimulate the eye to send messages to the brain, allowing us to interpret the sensation and see color. While the human eye is not sensitive to wavelengths outside of the visible spectrum, we are aware that some of the so-called invisible rays, for instance, ultraviolet and infrared rays, can have negative effects on colored textiles, altering the reflective characteristics of colorants and degrading the fibers.

Natural and artificial light sources emit all wavelengths within the boundaries of the visible spectrum. They do not, however, have equal mixtures of the various lengths: some have predominantly longer waves, others predominantly shorter waves. Colorants differ in their capacities to reflect the various wavelengths. The length of the waves emitted by the light source together with the length of the waves reflected by the colorant determine the particular color or hue perceived and affect other color characteristics as well.

Color Characteristics

Three color characteristics are determined by the emission, reflection, and interpretation of light waves. These are hue, value, and intensity.

Hue. Depending on the light source, larger quantities of certain wavelengths will be emitted, and, depending on the colorant, larger quantities of certain lengths will be reflected. The length of the waves that predominate in both emission and reflection will determine the particular hue or color perceived. When blue is perceived, for example, the illuminant is emitting a high concentration of waves around 465 nm in length and the colorant is reflecting a high concentration of these waves and absorbing other lengths. When green is perceived, a high concentration of waves around 520 nm is being emitted and reflected; when red is perceived, waves around 650 nm are being emitted and reflected; and so on.

Value. Value and luminosity are synonyms referring to the effect of the quantity of light being reflected from a textile or other surface. Higher levels of incident light and higher levels of reflected light produce lighter hues. Conversely, lower levels of incident and reflected light produce darker hues. When a compound known to reflect all wavelengths, creating white, is used with colorants, a tint is produced and value is increased. When a compound known to absorb all wavelengths, creating black, is used with colorants, a shade is produced and value is decreased.

Intensity. Intensity and chroma are terms used to describe the purity or strength of a color. A blue hue, for example, may appear strong, bright, and clear, or weak, grayed, and dull. Changes in intensity generally produce concomitant changes in value.

The effects of various fiber- and fabric-related variables—such as the presence of delusterants, fiber cross-sectional shapes, and the use of floating yarns—on the luster and brightness of colored textiles were discussed in earlier chapters. The effects of certain finishing agents and processes on color dimensions are described in Chapter 9.

The challenge to the dye chemist is to select a colorant or a mixture of colorants and additives that can create the planned hue, value, and intensity. To accomplish this, the chemist must work cooperatively with fiber, yarn, and fabric producers, as well as with converters.

Colorants

Textile colorants may be dyes or pigments. Dyes or dyestuffs are color-producing compounds that are normally soluble in water. Pigments are also color-producing agents, but they are insoluble in water. The chemical structure of either type of colorant enables it selectively to absorb and reflect certain wavelengths.

Colorants contain groups called auxochromes and groups called chromophores. Auxochromes are responsible for the selective absorption and reflection of light waves: these groups determine the hue. Chromophores control the quantity of waves reflected, influencing the value of the hue. The intensity is controlled by the mixture of colorants and the amount of dyestuff accepted by the fibers.

Some highly amorphous fibers, such as wool, readily accept high amounts of dye; other fibers, especially those with highly crystallized interiors, do not readily accept dyestuffs, and high pressure and temperature or dye-carriers may be required during the dyeing operation. In some cases, the affinity between the fiber and the dyestuff can be improved by the use of special agents known as mordants.

Extensive formal study in the fields of dye chemistry and textile chemistry is necessary for a thorough understanding of colorants and their reaction with or attraction for different fibers. This high level of knowledge is mandatory for the dye chemist, but not for the interior designer, architect, and consumer. Textile chemists and colorists recognize that consumers will prefer fashionable colors to out-of-date ones, and they direct their work accordingly.

Whereas the dye chemist is responsible for the correct match of fiber and colorant, the precise application of the dyestuff or pigment is the responsibility of the dyers and printers. Dyers and printers recognize that adequate penetration of the colorant is needed to produce the planned intensity and to ensure an acceptable level of color retention. They also recognize that accurate placement or registration of all colors will make for better clarity and definition of printed designs.

DYEING FABRICS AND FABRIC COMPONENTS

Dye operations can be carried out at the fiber, yarn, or fabric stage. Most dyeing operations require immersion of the textile into dye liquor, an aqueous solution of dyestuff.

Dyeing in the Fiber Stage

Color-producing agents can be added in the fiber stage by one of two methods, solution dyeing and fiber or stock dyeing. Solution dyeing can be used only with man-made fibers, but fiber dyeing may be used with both natural and man-made fibers.

Solution Dyeing. "Solution dyeing" is synonymous with "dope dyeing." In this operation, dye pigments are added to the polymer solution prior to extrusion. This produces man-made filaments with coloring agents locked inside the fiber. The term "color-sealed" identifies solution-dyed fibers; because the man-made fiber producer adds the color, the term "producer-colored" may also be used.

With the color-producing pigment incorporated as an integral part of the fiber, solution-dyed fibers have comparatively high color retention and stability. The relatively high cost of the pigments, however, precludes the routine use of this technique.

Fiber or Stock Dyeing. Immersing natural or man-made fibers into dye liquor is known as fiber or stock dye-

ing. Because loose masses of the fibers are submerged, the dyestuff can be absorbed more readily and thoroughly than it can when yarns or fabrics are immersed. In yarn structures, fiber packing and twisting may physically restrict the level of dyeing; in fabrics, yarn crossings and structural compactness may present physical barriers. The old phrase "dyed-in-the-wool," meaning "through and through," "deeply ingrained," or "staunchly dedicated," arose from the observation that wool fibers dyed prior to spinning had richer and deeper colors than those produced by dyeing yarns or fabrics.

Fiber dyeing can be used in combination with yarn production to produce yarns having distinctive color styling. When two or more colors of fibers are uniformly distributed throughout a spun yarn, the term "heather" identifies the coloration. A heather appearance can also be produced by throwing different colors of filaments.

The term "marled" identifies the coloration produced by combining two differently colored rovings together in spinning. Although the resulting structure is a single yarn, its visual spiral resembles that produced by plying two differently colored yarns. A marled yarn is pictured in Figure 8.2.

"Ombré," French for "shade," describes color styling in which there is a gradual change in the value of a single hue, for instance, from pink to red to maroon. In yarns, this delicate color style is produced by carefully controlling the introduction of fibers of the appropriate shade or tint during yarn spinning. If the process is well executed, the location of a change is barely perceptible.

Coloring in the Yarn Stage

Adding colorants to yarn structures before fabric formation is known as yarn dyeing. Certain techniques, collectively known as space dyeing, can be used to produce multicolored yarns; these techniques are described later in this chapter. Most yarn-dyeing operations, however, produce single-colored yarns.

Package Dyeing. The equipment used in package dyeing is shown in Figure 8.3. Yarns are first wound on perforated cylinders to form packages of yarn. Several packages are then mounted on posts and lowered into a pressure cooker–like vessel known as a dye beck. Dye liquor is then forcibly circulated throughout each package of yarn. To ensure adequate penetration of the dye, high levels of pressure and temperatures may be used in the operation; this may be necessary when man-made fibers with low moisture regain values, such as polyester, nylon, and acrylic, are being dyed.

Beam Dyeing. Beam dyeing is a second way of dyeing yarns a single color. In preparation for the operation, warp

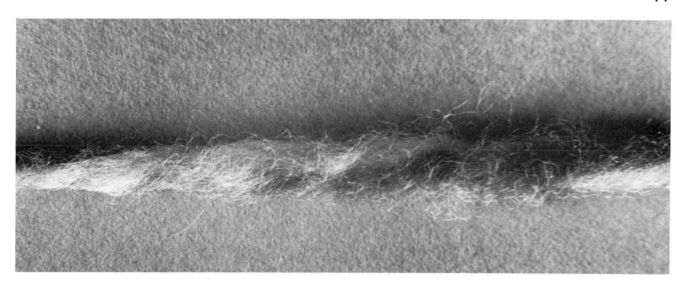

Figure 8.2 A marled yarn.

Figure 8.3 Dyeing packages of yarn in a dye beck. (Courtesy of Fibers Division, Monsanto Chemical Co.)

yarns are wound on a perforated beam barrel. The beam is then loaded into a beam dyeing machine (Figure 8.4), and the dye liquor is circulated through the yarns, from the outside to the inside and from the inside to the outside, via the perforations. The beams of dyed warp yarns, when rinsed and dried, are ready to be placed on a loom, bypassing the unwinding and rewinding operations required after package dyeing.

Skein Dyeing. Immersing long skeins of yarn into troughs filled with dye liquor is known as skein dyeing. This procedure may be employed when the winding and compacting of yarns on cylinders or beam barrels could alter their textural features, or when a relatively small quantity of custom-colored yarn is required. The procedure is rarely used for dyeing large quantities of yarns, however, because it is a relatively slow and therefore costly operation. (Skein dyeing of carpet pile yarns is pictured in Figure 28.1, page 302.)

Single-colored yarns, each dyed a different shade of the same hue or a different hue, are often plied. Such combinations produce a color style described as "moresque."

Space Dyeing. Space-dyeing operations produce multicolored yarns. Unlike heather yarns in which the colors are uniformly distributed throughout the yarns, and unlike ombré yarns in which various values of one color are repeated, space-dyed yarns have differently colored segments along their lengths (see Figure 28.2, page 303). The various hues may be related or contrasting.

Various techniques can produce this color styling. Although some of these techniques are printing rather than dyeing operations, they fall in the category of space dyeing because they create the characteristic coloration. When muted junctures of the selected colors are desired, segments of the yarns will be dipped into or sprayed with dif-

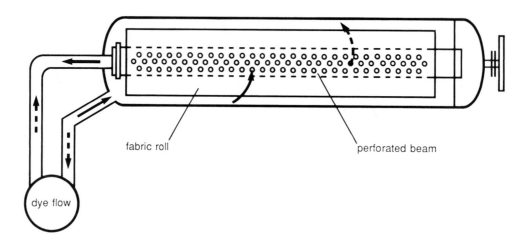

Figure 8.4 Beam dyeing. (Courtesy of Celanese Corporation.)

ferent colors of dye liquor. When well-defined, sharp color junctures are planned, sheets of yarns will be printed. These techniques are explained in detail in Chapter 28.

Although space-dyed yarns, also known as variegated yarns, have long been used in the hand and machine knitting of apparel items, their use in interior textiles, especially in upholstery fabrics and pile carpet, is somewhat recent. (See Units Two and Four.) The styling not only provides visual interest, but the mixture of colors also effectively camouflages the soil that accumulates in use.

Dyeing Greige Goods

Unless colored fibers or yarns were used in fabrication, greige goods bear little resemblance to those offered to residential and commercial consumers. Except for any textural and visual interest contributed by complex yarns or decorative interlacings, such fabrics have virtually no aesthetic appeal. Lacking the critical fashion element of color, such coverings would be summarily rejected by most consumers. For greater consumer appeal, greige goods can be dyed in a conventional piece-dying operation or in a chemically dependent operation known as cross dyeing.

Piece Dyeing. Piece dyeing is carried out after fabrication by immersing the piece goods or greige goods into dye liquor. It produces single-colored fabrics with identical color characteristics on both sides.

Cross Dyeing. Cross dyeing, also called differential dyeing, is a color application process based on chemical variables. The process produces a multicolored fabric from a single immersion in one dyebath formulation. Two or more fibers that are chemically different—classified in different generic groups or variants of the same fiber—are strategically placed in yarns or in greige goods. For a

heather appearance, different fibers are uniformly distributed in the yarns; for plaids or stripes, warp or filling yarns with different fiber contents are used in bands; and for multicolored design motifs, yarns of different fibers are selectively incorporated during fabrication.

A single dyebath is formulated. The dye chemist, often with the aid of a computer, may select specific dyestuffs, each of which will be accepted by one fiber and rejected by all other fibers, or use one dyestuff that will be absorbed in different amounts by related fiber variants. In the former case, each type of fiber or variant has a different hue, and, in the latter case, each variant has a different level of intensity of the same hue. The economic advantage of cross dyeing is readily apparent: "you only dye once."

A second major advantage of cross dyeing is that orders for specific colors can be filled accurately and quickly. Whatever the color mixture ordered, the stored greige goods are ready for immediate dyeing, finishing, and shipping. Without cross-dyeing technology, fibers or yarns would have to be dyed the necessary number of colors in separate dyebaths; then fibers would have to be spun or thrown, and the colored yarns packaged or wound on beams and sent to the mill for preparation of the loom and for winding of the bobbins or cones used for the filling yarns. Shipment would be further delayed by the time required for fabrication and subsequent finishing. Producers who attempt to save time another way—by second guessing the fashion colors of the distant future and coloring fabrics in advance of orders—may find themselves with a sizeable inventory of unpopular colors.

PRINTING GREIGE GOODS

High-speed mechanized operations are generally used to print greige goods when stylists or contract designers specify printed fabrics. Printing requires thicker dyestuffs than those used in dyeing operations. Whereas migration or movement of the dye is required to achieve a uniform level of color in dyed textile structures, such migration in printed goods would result in poor definition of the shapes and details of the motifs. Therefore, the dyestuff used in most printing operations is a dye paste rather than a highly aqueous dye liquor. After application of the dye paste, the textile is exposed to steam, heat, or chemicals to fix the dye in or on the fibers.

Roller Printing

Lighter weight, nonpile fabrics can be printed with engraved metal rollers. The shapes of those portions of the repeat that are to be the same color are etched into the surface of one roller. The number of colors planned thus dictates the number of rollers prepared. As schematized in Figure 8.5, small cylinders revolve through the dye paste and transfer the paste to the engraved rollers. A metal squeegee-like blade, called a doctor blade, then removes the

Although roller printing is an extremely fast operation, its use has diminished because the cost of copper, the metal normally used to cover the rollers, and the cost of the labor needed to prepare the rollers have increased. Growing competition from screen printing has also had an effect.

Screen Printing

Two methods of screen printing, flat-bed screen printing and rotary screen printing, are available for use with textile greige goods. Both methods can deliver large amounts of dyestuff, and both can facilitate the printing of large-scale motifs and pattern repeats. Since most upholstery fabrics are relatively heavy and require large amounts of dye, and since sheetings and curtain and drapery fabrics are often designed with large-scale motifs and pattern repeats, these interior fabrics are very frequently screen printed.

The apparatus and procedures used in flat-bed and rotary screen printing operations differ. Both techniques, however, are based on the principle of a stencil: portions of the printing equipment are blocked to resist the flow of dye.

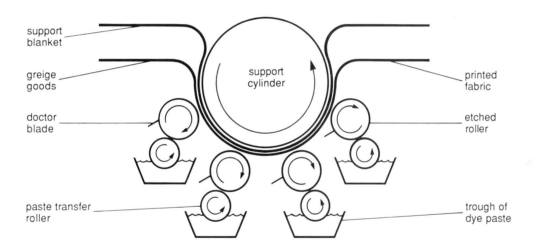

Figure 8.5 Roller printing.

excess dye paste from the smooth, nonengraved surface areas. As the rollers revolve against the fabric surface, the dye paste is transferred and the pattern repeat is completed.

Large areas, whether in the ground or in the design, cannot be roller printed because the revolving motion of the rollers would create waves in the dye, causing poor registration and definition of the design. Coloring large areas of the ground is more readily accomplished by discharge printing, a technique discussed later in this chapter, and coloring large-scale motifs is more effectively accomplished by screen printing. Screen printing must also be used to print pattern repeats whose lengths exceed the circumference of the rollers.

Flat-bed Screen Printing. In preparation for flat-bed screen printing, large rectangular frames are covered with a fine, strong fabric. The compactness of the fabric determines the amount of dye paste allowed to flow through the fabric interstices. Today, nylon and polyester filaments have replaced silk filaments in these fabrics, mostly as a result of the higher cost of the natural fiber. The frames are as wide as the greige goods, generally 45 or 60 inches, and up to 80 inches in length.

Each screen will be used to print one color, so the number of planned colors determines the number of screens that must be prepared. Some areas of each screen are treated with a compound that can prevent or block the

Figure 8.6 Flat-bed screen printing. (Courtesy of Springs Industries, Inc.)

flow of the dye paste; other areas are left untreated to allow the paste to pass through the fabric. The untreated areas on each screen are in the shapes of the designs in the repeat that are to be the same color.

For printing, the screens are aligned and mounted horizontally above the fabric, as shown in Figure 8.6. The dye paste is spread over the screen surface from one side to the other, flowing through the untreated areas and printing the fabric below. The fabric is then advanced and the procedure is repeated. Because each screen adds one color, the fabric must advance under all the screens for the coloration of the repeat to be completed. It is evident that the width of the pattern repeat and the width of the fabric govern the number of repeats that can be printed side by side; the length of the repeat and the height of the screen limit the number of repeats that can be simultaneously printed end to end.

Because large amounts of dyestuff can be passed through the screens, a good level of saturation can be obtained in screen printing heavier flat fabrics and pile structures. When working with pile structures, printers must carefully position the screens to avoid distortion of the pile yarns. (Flat-bed screen printing operations used with pile floor coverings are discussed and illustrated in Chapter 28.)

Rotary Screen Printing. Developed in the early 1960s, rotary screen printing (Figure 8.7) has become the predominant method of printing textile structures. The technique is used to print flat fabrics as well as such three-dimensional structures as velveteen, velvet, and carpet. It is also used to print sheets of warp yarns with motifs and with randomized, space-dyed effects. In addition, it is

Figure 8.7 Rotary screen printing. (Courtesy of Stork Brabant B.V., Boxmeer, Holland.)

frequently used to print the paper used in transfer-printing operations, which are discussed in the following section.

Rotary screen printing is so widely used because several of its features make it economical. It is generally faster and more accurate than other printing techniques, and it produces a more uniform level of coloration when large quantities of goods are being run.

a)   120 holes per inch

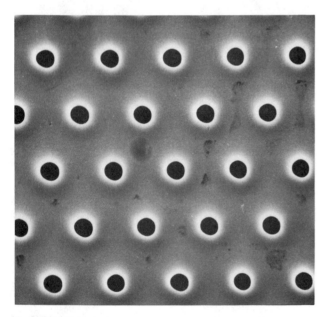

b)   215 holes per inch

Figure 8.8 Photomicrographs of the surface openings in nickel-plated rotary screens. (Courtesy of Stork Screens B.V., Boxmeer, Holland.)

The cylindrical rollers used in rotary screen printing have microscopic openings in their nickel-coated surfaces. While earlier screens had some 120 holes per inch, newer screens have up to 215 holes per inch. As shown in Figure 8.8, the holes in the newer screens are more regular and well defined, and the surface is smoother. These improvements have facilitated more precise control of shaded effects and better definition of design details.

The planned pattern motifs are transferred to the surfaces of the cylinders. The holes in the areas to be printed are left open and those in the adjacent areas are blocked with water-insoluble lacquer. During printing, the dye paste is continually forced from the interior of the cylindrical screen through the minute openings. A diagram of the flow mechanism is given in Figure 8.9.

As shown in Figure 8.10, one color of the repeat is applied by each rotating screen. After the fabric has passed under all screens, all colors and designs will have been added. Some rotary screen printing machines can accept up to twenty screens, so they can print up to twenty colors.

Transfer Printing

Transfer printing, also known as heat transfer printing and sublistatic printing, involves the use of heat to transfer dyestuff from paper to fabric. The technique has long been used to print the outlines of motifs in preparation for hand embroidering, and, more recently, colored motifs have been available as tear-out pages in popular magazines. The technique was adapted for the industrial-scale printing of textile fabric in the early 1970s.

In preparation for this operation, transfer paper is printed by one of three techniques, gravure, flexo, or rotary screen printing (Figure 8.11). "Gravure" identifies roller printing with engraved copper-covered rollers, and "flexo" identifies roller printing with engraved rubber-covered rollers.

For printing, the colored paper is placed face down on the face of the greige goods (Figure 8.12). The dyestuffs used have a higher affinity for the fibers than for the paper; when they are exposed to heat, they sublime, changing from a solid on the paper, to a gas, to a solid on the fabric. The procedure is fast and energy-efficient, and the fabric requires no afterwash because no excess dyestuff remains.

The use of transfer printing as an industrial technique was initially encouraged by widespread consumer acceptance of polyester knits in the 1970s. The inherent elasticity of the fiber and the knitted structure resulted in relatively high relaxation shrinkage following release of the tension used in roller and screen printing operations. The shrinkage caused distortion of the printed patterns. In order to avoid this problem, manufacturers used transfer printing, which requires minimal fabric tensioning.

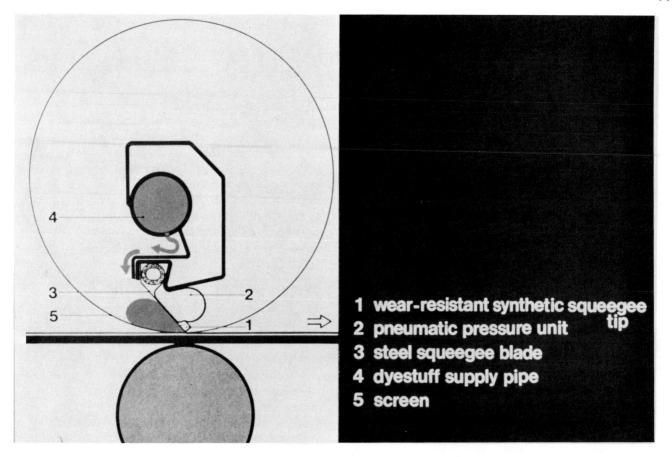

1 wear-resistant synthetic squeegee tip
2 pneumatic pressure unit
3 steel squeegee blade
4 dyestuff supply pipe
5 screen

Figure 8.9 The flow mechanism of a rotary screen. (Courtesy of Stork Brabant B.V., Boxmeer, Holland.)

As long as polyester fiber, especially in knits, continues to increase its share of the window and wall coverings markets and other interior textile markets, the use of transfer printing will no doubt increase as well. However, problems remain: print machinery engineers continue searching for ways to overcome pile distortion, and dye chemists continue working to correct the dyestuff's inadequate penetration of heavier structures.

Pigment Printing

In pigment printing, also known as over printing, water-insoluble pigments are mixed with an adhesive compound or resin binders and applied to textile surfaces. As the pigments are not absorbed by the fibers, the printed designs stand in slight relief. Frequently, white or metallic-colored pigments are printed on a previously dyed surface.

Fusion Printing. Fusion printing is a type of pigment printing used to secure colorants to the surface of fabrics composed of glass fiber. Colored acrylic resins are first printed on the surface of the fabric. Heat is then used to soften the thermoplastic compound and fuse it to the nonabsorbent glass. Like other pigment-printed designs, fusion-printed designs stand in slight relief.

Acid Printing

Acid printing produces a color style known as a burnt-out or etched-out print. In this styling, the motifs and the ground have different levels of transparency. Because this technique is a chemically dependent process and one in which no colorants are added, some textile authorities prefer to classify the procedure as a finishing operation. On the other hand, because the technique produces a patterned effect, other authorities classify the procedure as a printing operation.

Fabrics used in an acid-printing operation must be composed of an acid-resistant fiber and an acid-degradable fiber; a blend of nylon and rayon is typically used. During printing, weak sulfuric acid (H_2SO_4) is printed on selected areas of the fabric, destroying or burning away the acid-degradable rayon. This chemical reaction changes the composition of these areas to 100 percent nylon, creating a

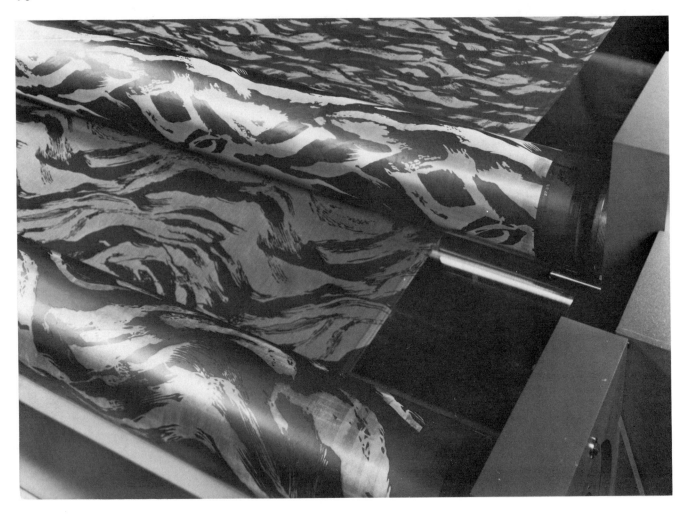

Figure 8.10 Close-up photograph of rotary screen printing. (Courtesy of Stork Brabant B.V., Boxmeer, Holland.)

higher level of transparency than seen in the untreated areas. An etched-out print produced for use as curtain fabric is pictured in Figure 20.25 (page 214).

COMBINING DYEING AND PRINTING

Fabric immersion can be used in combination with a printing procedure to produce interior fabrics having colored backgrounds and noncolored design motifs. Industrial methods involving such combinations include discharge printing and resist printing.

Discharge Printing

Discharge printing is an efficient way to color large areas of the ground and create a pattern. The fabric is first piece dyed, producing the same depth of color on both sides. It is then printed with a reducing agent wherever the design motifs are planned. The agent reduces or discharges

the dyestuff. Recent developments in discharge-printing equipment turn discharging and immediate color printing into one sequential operation. A discharge print is pictured in Figure 20.21 (page 212).

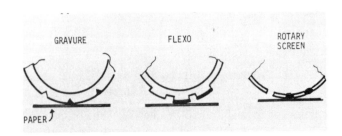

Figure 8.11 Techniques used for printing transfer paper. (Courtesy of Fred Salaff and the American Association of Textile Chemists and Colorists.)

Resist Printing

In industrial resist-printing operations, a water-insoluble compound that will not allow absorption of the dyestuff is first printed on the fabric in the shapes of the planned motifs. When the fabric is subsequently piece dyed, the dye liquor is absorbed only in the areas that are free of the resist compound. Artisans use several hand resist-printing operations to create distinctive interior fabrics. These techniques, including batik, tie-dye, and ikat operations, are discussed and illustrated in Chapter 35.

A colorant may be scientifically selected and precisely applied, but the immediate and long-term appearance of the color may nonetheless be affected by various environmental conditions and end-use activities. Some substances and conditions, such as cleaning agents and atmospheric contaminants, can produce changes in actual color characteristics. These variables, and test methods to measure their effects, are described in later units. The potential effects of various factors on apparent color characteristics are discussed here.

FACTORS AFFECTING APPARENT COLOR

Several factors have no direct effect on colorants but may alter perception of the original color of a product. Some of these factors, including changes in texture and soiling, relate to end-use activities; others, such as the source and quantity of light, are aspects of the interior environment. These variables alter the apparent color characteristics of interior textiles: the actual color characteristics are unchanged.

Light Source

Color may be the most important aesthetic variable in the selection of an interior textile product. Unfortunately, color choices are often made in a setting other than the one in which the product will be used. Inevitably, the lighting in the showroom or retail display area differs from that in the residential or commercial interior. Viewing a colored item in the separate locations, an observer may perceive marked differences in hue and value. If the product is installed in an interior, the harmony and color coordination planned for the space may not be realized.

As mentioned earlier in this chapter, artificial light sources differ from each other and from natural light in the mixture of visible wavelengths they emit. While natural light emits almost equal quantities of all wavelengths, artificial sources emit unequal quantities. Cool fluorescent illuminants, for example, emit large amounts of shorter wavelengths, those resulting in violet, blue, and green hues, and small amounts of red-producing wavelengths.

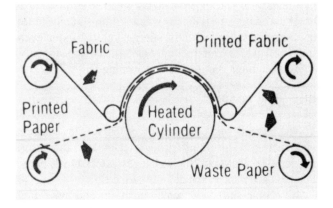

Figure 8.12 Heat transfer printing. (Courtesy of Celanese Corporation.)

By contrast, incandescent illuminants create predominantly longer wavelengths, those producing yellow, orange, and red hues, and they are deficient in blue-producing rays. The source of light thus limits the mixture of wavelengths having the potential to be reflected.

A textile colorant known to reflect a concentration of wavelengths in the red area (around 650 nm) nevertheless appears as a weakened red when viewed under cool fluorescent light and as a strong red when viewed under incandescent light. Similarly, the hue of a colorant known to reflect blue rays is perceived as a strong blue under cool fluorescent light and as a weakened or grayish blue under incandescent sources.

Quantity of Light

The quantity of light incident on a textile directly affects its color characteristics, especially its value or luminosity: increases in the level of light produce apparent increases in the lightness of the surface. The amount of light emitted from artificial illuminants can be controlled by rheostats and the wattages of lamps. The amount of natural light can be regulated by the compactness of the window coverings and the use of exterior awnings. Of course, the size of windows and skylights and their orientation to the seasonal angles of the sun are also very important.

In interior settings, the quantity of light is not limited to that radiating through the windows and emanating from artificial sources. A significant amount can be "reused" or indirect light, that being reflected from light-colored walls, ceilings, doors, and furnishings.

Because natural light and artificial light sources differ in their distribution of wavelengths, it is readily apparent that an increase or decrease in the level of light emitted by any source would affect both the value and intensity of the hue perceived. The apparent changes can be as different as night and day, especially so when strong sunlight in the daytime alternates with dim interior lighting in the evening. Browns, for example, may darken and appear almost black as sunlight diminishes and evening falls.

Changes in Texture

The abrasive and crushing forces that textile structures may encounter during use produce changes in their original textural features. Such changes affect the apparent lightness and darkness of colored surfaces.

As people shift their seated positions and move their arms over upholstery fabrics, they can rupture the yarns and destroy prominent decorative effects. Such physical changes have no effect on the colorants, but the abraded areas appear darker because the pattern of light reflection is altered.

When fibers and yarns used in soft floor coverings are abraded by shoe soles, furniture casters, and the like, their surfaces may be roughened as dirt and sharp-edged grit particles grind severely against the fibers. Deterioration of the smoothness of the fibers and yarns results in deflection of incident light waves and a decrease in apparent value. A decrease in lightness is also apparent when abrasive forces rupture the loops of pile floor coverings and other pile fabrics, because the quantity of light reflected from the fiber ends is less than that reflected from the sides of the yarns in the intact loops.

Textural changes caused by crushing, especially of pile surfaces, may be less readily noticed or less objectionable if the compression is spread uniformly over the surface. But people tend to sit in the central portion of upholstered cushions, to repeatedly lean against the same region of back cushions, and to walk in established traffic patterns. These practices result in localized compression, which may gradually result in a nonuniform pile depth across the textile surface. This creates variations in the apparent value of the surface, with flattened areas appearing lighter and distorted areas appearing darker than undisturbed pile areas. Consumers and professionals can minimize the development of this unsightly effect by selecting pile fabrics made of resilient fibers and having high pile construction densities when a high level of use is expected.

Soil Accumulation

Residential and commercial consumers may be convinced that the original color of their textile product has changed when in fact it is merely masked by soil. As soil accumulates, especially on bright, solid-colored surfaces, the coloration appears duller. As is true for changes in texture, soiling is often localized, with heavier buildup occurring on the arms and seat cushions of furniture and in traffic lanes and entrance areas.

If soil accumulation is expected to be rapid, a multicolored surface that can mask the appearance of soil should be considered. Protective items, such as removable arm covers and walk-off mats, are also available.

Composition and Structural Variables

Different fibers have different color characteristics even when dyed the same color. This difference is the result of the chemical structures of the fibers and dyes used and the affinity the fibers have for the colorants. Increasing or decreasing yarn size causes accompanying changes in the intensity of the chosen hue. Similar effects appear with changes in pile construction density. Contract designers and architects must consider the potential impact on apparent color of specifying composition or construction features that differ from those characterizing the color samples.

Consumers and professionals must be aware that even yarns and fabrics intended to look identical generally have differences in color intensity when dyed or printed in different operations. To avoid this problem, the initial order should include sufficient yardage for the planned project.

SUMMARY

For a particular hue to be perceived, the source of incident light must include a high concentration of wavelengths known to produce the hue, and the colorant used must reflect, not absorb, these waves. Although the dye chemist is responsible for selecting the correct colorant, consumers and professionals are responsible for examining the effects of the lighting conditions on the hue, value, and intensity of the colorant. Whenever possible, a swatch of fabric, a cushion, an arm cover, or a carpet sample should be examined in the end-use setting under a variety of lighting conditions. Consumers and professionals are also responsible for assessing the potential effects that such in-use variables as soil accumulation, abrasion, and crushing may have.

Dyers and printers are responsible for selecting and executing the appropriate method of color application. This method is largely determined by the features that the fabric stylist or contract designer specifies. Fiber dyeing is used when multicolored yarns are needed; yarn dyeing when plaid patterns or other types of woven-in motifs are to be produced; and screen printing when large-scale motifs and pattern repeats are specified. Ultimately, dye chemists, fabric stylists, and textile colorists must be guided by the color and styling preferences of the contemporary consumer.

chapter 9

Converting Interior Textile Greige Goods

- Transforming Surface Appearance
- Improving the Quality and Serviceability of Structural Features
- Engineering Functional Performance

Colored greige goods are more appealing than noncolored goods. However, until the goods are converted into finished fabrics, they may lack the aesthetic characteristics preferred by consumers of interior textile products. The fabrics may also lack structural stability, and they may not exhibit the service-related performance features sought by consumers or mandated by an agency with jurisdiction over their selection and installation.

In many cases, the finishing agents and processes to be used are specified by the fabric stylist, who has monitored consumer preferences for various aesthetic features, functional attributes, and care requirements. Sometimes they are dictated by the contract designer or architect, who may require an interior fabric with a unique appearance characteristic or a specific level of performance in end use. The appropriate selection and proper application of finishes greatly expands the variety of fabrics available to end product producers and consumers.

TRANSFORMING SURFACE APPEARANCE

With appropriate agents and processes, converters can transform the surface appearance of greige goods. When necessary they can remove or neutralize inherent color, and when specified they can control the level of surface luster, alter the fabric form, and embellish the fabric face.

Removing Inherent Color

The inherent colors of natural fibers were discussed in Chapter 4. Unless the stylist specifies their retention, converters remove or neutralize them. When fashion colors are planned, the removal or neutralization precedes the addition of colorants, preventing the subsequent reflection of a mixture of light waves from two sources. When no colorants are to be added, the process precedes other conversion operations to prevent the natural colorants' interfering with the appearance of the finished fabrics.

Bleaching. Bleaching agents remove unwanted color from cellulosic fibers by oxidation. Hydrogen peroxide (H_2O_2) and sodium hypochlorite (NaCLO) are generally used.

Grassing. In grassing, sunlight removes inherent color from linen fibers spread over a grass field. Grassing is slower than other bleaching methods, but is often used to prepare linen fibers for manufacture into fine tabletop products.

Tinting. In contrast to bleaching, which removes color, tinting involves the addition of colorants that neutralize the natural color. Violet tints, for example, may be added to wool to neutralize the yellow hues typically characterizing the fibers. Readers may be familiar with the use of vi-

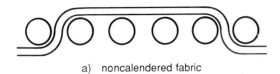

a)   noncalendered fabric

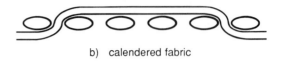

b)   calendered fabric

Figure 9.1 Effect of friction calendering on the cross sections of yarns.

olet or violet-blue tints to neutralize the yellow cast often seen in gray or white hair.

Boiling-off. Silk may be sufficiently whitened by boiling the filaments in a detergent solution. This operation removes sericin, the off-white or yellow gummy compound covering the fine fibers.

Controlling Surface Luster

Whereas man-made fiber producers are responsible for controlling the luster of fabrics composed of their fibers—decreasing it by incorporating delusterant particles in the polymer solution—converters are generally charged with controlling the luster of fabrics composed of natural fibers. The conversion processes involved virtually always increase, rather than decrease, the quantity of light reflected from the fabric surface.

Friction Calendering. With the help of high levels of pressure and heat and a fast rate of revolution, highly polished metal cylinders, known as calendering rollers, can be used to flatten the cross section of the yarns, thus increasing the amount of surface area available to reflect light. This change in the physical configuration of the yarns is illustrated in Figure 9.1. (A similar effect is produced by beetling, a mechanical process explained in Unit Five.)

Glazing. In glazing operations, the surface of greige goods is impregnated with resin, shellac, or wax, and high-speed calendering rollers then buff and polish the surface. Glazing produces a smooth surface texture and a high level of surface luster. Chintz fabrics produced for use as upholstered furniture coverings and curtain fabrics are frequently glazed (see Figure 20.2, page 199).

Schreinering. The schreinering process creates fine hills and valleys on the surface of the fabric. In preparation for this mechanical treatment, calendering rollers are etched with fine, parallel lines that approximate the angle of yarn twist. The number of etched lines may range from 250 to 350 per inch. After schreinering, the modified surface develops a soft luster as light is reflected in different directions from the fine peaks and flattened valleys. The effect is not permanent unless heat or resin treatments are

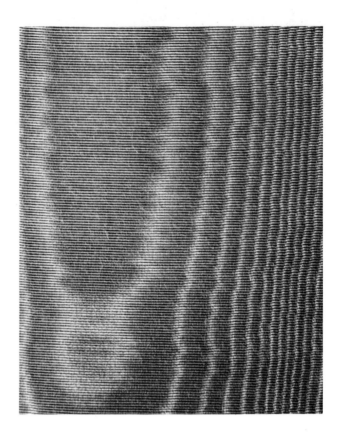

Figure 9.2 Moiré taffeta.

also performed. The use of these treatments is discussed below with embossing operations.

Moiréing. Moiréing is a special type of calendering used on filling-rib woven fabrics. Two fabrics are laid face to face and passed between paired calendering rollers. The pressure causes the mirrored ribs to impact on one another, slightly altering their form and changing the pattern of light reflection. Moiré fabrics are described as having a wood-grain appearance or a water-marked effect (Figure 9.2). Moiré fabrics are also shown in Figures 17.8 (page 180) and 22.7 (page 238).

Introducing Three-dimensional Designs

Embossing, like schreinering and moiréing, involves the use of calendering rollers and alters the form of the

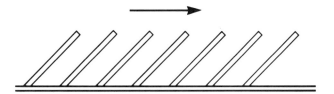 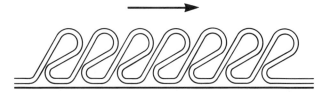

Figure 9.3 Directional pile lay.

greige goods. The changes produced by embossing are, however, greater than those produced by schreinering and moiréing. Embossing creates highly visible three-dimensional surface designs. Whether the changes are slight or marked, their preservation depends on the application of heat or resins.

Embossing. Embossing treatments convert flat, essentially two-dimensional fabrics into three-dimensional structures with convex and concave design forms. The planned designs are first etched into the surface of one calendering roller, which is then paired with a soft-surfaced roller. As the fabric passes between the two intermeshing rollers, it conforms to the etched forms. Greige goods are often embossed for use as decorative curtain fabrics.

Calendering rollers can be heated to emboss, schreiner, or moiré fabrics composed of thermoplastic fibers. In this way, the converter can introduce three-dimensional designs and heat set them in one operation. The heat loosens the strained lateral bonds of the distorted fibers, and the new lateral bonds that form as the fibers cool preserve the imposed configuration.

When fabrics composed of nonthermoplastic fibers, such as cotton and rayon, are processed, chemical crosslinking resins must be applied to preserve the imposed changes. The resins form lateral bonds, linking adjacent polymer chains and stabilizing the distorted configurations of the fibers. This treatment, also used to improve resiliency, is schematized in Figure 9.9 (page 89).

Changing the Orientation of Pile Yarns

Mechanical treatments are used to alter the upright positions of the pile yarns in virtually all pile upholstery fabrics. The realignment affects the reflective characteristics and tactile features of the pile layer.

Brushing, Smoothing, and Shearing. Brushing, smoothing, and shearing operations are used to align, smooth, and level the pile yarns in such fabrics as corduroy, velveteen, and velvet. In brushing, cylinders covered with straight wires revolve against the matted cut-pile surface, raising the pile yarns and aligning them parallel to one another. Brushing is followed by smoothing, laying the pile yarns in one direction. The results of these processes are essentially the same as those produced by combing and brushing hair. Because the angle at which the pile

yarns are oriented to the base fabric is reduced, a surface feature known as pile sweep, directional pile lay, or fabric nap is introduced (Figure 9.3).

After the pile yarns have been brushed and smoothed, they undergo shearing to produce an even pile height. This is accomplished by passing the fabric against a rotating cylinder with a spiral blade. The shearing cylinder is similar to that in rotary lawn mowers.

Obviously, the tactile characteristics of a pile surface will be altered by these operations. The fabric will feel smooth when stroked in the direction of lay and rough when stroked in the opposite direction. And because the quantity of light waves reflected by the sides of the yarns will be significantly greater than that reflected by the cut tips, the level of luster observed will depend on the position of the viewer. The tactile and visual qualities of nap make it imperative that all fabric pieces cut for an item have the same direction of pile lay. Usually pile yarns are oriented downward to help maintain the original appearance.

Crushing. A mechanical finishing operation known as crushing is used on some velvet fabrics. In this operation, the pile yarns in some areas are crushed or flattened, while the pile yarns in the adjacent areas are oriented in various directions. Because each area reflects incident light waves in different quantities and in different directions, the surface has various levels of luster. A crushed velvet upholstery fabric is pictured in Figure 12.24 (page 127).

Embellishing Fabric Surfaces

The appearance of greige goods, especially those to be used as curtain fabrics and tabletop accessories, is often embellished by the addition of fibers or yarns to their surfaces. Yarns are added in an embroidering operation, and fibers are added in a flocking operation

Embroidering. Because hand embroidering, like hand printing, is labor- and time-intensive, machine embroidering is employed to embellish fabric surfaces with motifs resembling those created by artisans. Many machine-embroidered curtain and drapery fabrics are stitched on Schiffli machines. Each of these machines is equipped with more than a thousand needles that operate at right angles to the base fabric. For multicolored motifs, each needle is threaded with a specific color of yarn; control mechanisms similar to those used on the dobby loom are programmed with the planned design shapes and shift the position of the fabric during the embroidering operation. A Schiffli-embroidered curtain fabric is pictured in Figure 20.20b (page 211). Hand embroidering techniques are discussed in Chapter 35.

Flocking. In flocking operations, extremely short fibers, known as flock, are embedded in an adhesive or resin compound. In curtain and drapery fabrics, the flock is generally used to create raised motifs and pattern repeats. In simulated suede upholstery fabrics and some blankets and floor mats, the flock is applied to the entire fabric surface. Both types of flock placement are used in textile wall coverings.

In preparation for flocking, an adhesive or resin is printed on all areas of the greige goods to be flocked. In

tures of greige goods. They can, for example, use a mechanical process to improve the alignment of yarns in biaxially woven fabrics; a heat setting operation to stabilize the shape and form of fabrics composed of thermoplastic fibers; and small flames to minimize the formation of pills on fabrics composed of cellulosic fibers.

Correcting Fabric Grain

When all the warp yarns are not perpendicular to all the filling yarns in a biaxially woven fabric, the fabric is said to be off-grain. Off-grain fabrics have a negative effect on appearance when used in the construction of such end products as upholstered furniture, curtains, draperies, and tabletop accessories. For example, a drapery fabric with a bowed yarn alignment produces treatments that appear to sag, and, as illustrated in Figure 9.5a, an undulating or

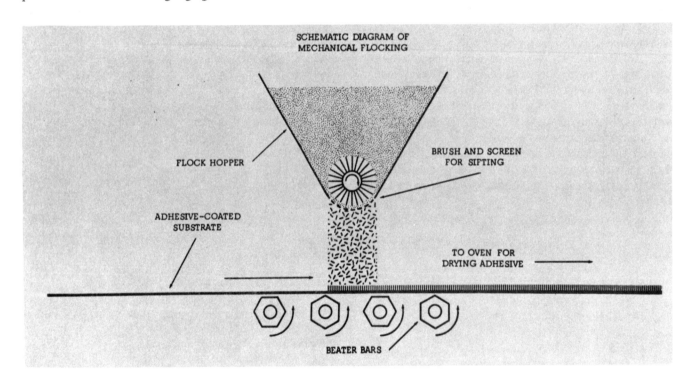

Figure 9.4 Mechanical flocking. (Courtesy of Fibers Division, Monsanto Chemical Co.)

mechanical flocking processes, the flock is then sifted through a screen to the coated surface (Figure 9.4). Beater bars encourage the short fibers to orient themselves perpendicularly to the base fabric. In electrostatic flocking operations, an electrostatic field induces the flock to embed itself into the coating (see Figure 13.3, page 134).

IMPROVING THE QUALITY AND SERVICEABILITY OF STRUCTURAL FEATURES

Converters use finishing procedures to improve the quality and potential serviceability of the structural fea-

waving effect could develop if several widths are used. Fabrics with a skewed yarn alignment produce a lopsided appearance, as shown in Figure 9.5b, and attempts to align crosswise pattern repeats when seaming fabric widths only compound the problem. The negative effects of off-grain upholstery fabrics are illustrated in Figure 14.1 (page 136).

Tentering. To minimize distortions resulting from bow and skew, converters use a mechanical finishing process known as tentering. In this operation, the fabric is mounted full-width on a tenter frame (Figure 9.6). Tension is applied to properly align the warp and filling

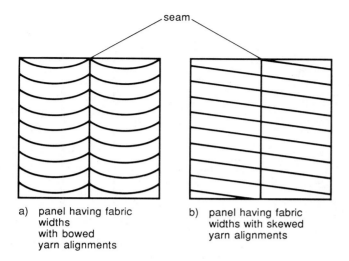

seam

a) panel having fabric
widths
with bowed
yarn alignments

b) panel having fabric
widths with skewed
yarn alignments

Figure 9.5 Effects of bowed and skewed yarn alignments on the appearance of window treatments.

yarns, and the fabric is then steamed and passed through a heated oven and dried. Today, computer-assisted mechanisms often monitor and control the alignment of the yarns during the operation. Small holes are visible in the selvage areas of tentered fabrics, indicating where the fabric was secured by pins or metal clips.

When greige goods are to be printed, tentering should precede the printing operation. Correcting the grain of printed fabrics would distort the shapes of the motifs and the positions of the pattern repeats.

Stabilizing Fabric Shape

A textile structure that maintains its original size and shape after use and care is said to have dimensional stability. Dimensionally stable fabrics do not exhibit "growth"—bagging and sagging from unrecovered stretch—nor do they exhibit shrinkage.

With most interior textile fabrics, there is great concern for the potential problems caused by relaxation shrinkage, and to a lesser extent for those caused by residual shrinkage. Residual shrinkage is shrinkage of the fibers; it generally occurs over time in such frequently laundered items as towels and table linens. Relaxation shrinkage occurs when strained components relax after the stress forces involved in various manufacturing processes are released.

Several processes subject fibers and yarns to stress, deforming and straining them. Extruding and drawing strain the polymer chains in man-made filaments; drawing out and spinning can strain spun yarns; tension exerted on the warp yarns during weaving strains these yarns; bobbin tensioning devices may strain filling yarns; and the pulling and forcing of yarns and fabrics through dyeing or printing and finishing operations can add various amounts of strain.

The behavior of strained fabric components is similar to that of elastic bands that have been stretched, but there is a marked difference between the rates at which the two materials recover from imposed deformations. When the stretching force is released from an elastic band, it will generally exhibit immediate and complete relaxation shrinkage, returning to its original length. By contrast, when manufacturing stress forces are released, textile components relax only gradually and incompletely. Unless the imposed strain has been released or the fabric components have been intentionally stabilized prior to shipment to the end product producer or fabric retailer, full recovery may not occur until sometime during end use, destroying the appearance or fit of the fabric.

Converters encourage relaxation of strained components with heat setting, fulling, and compressive shrinkage operations. The technique used is determined by the fiber composition of the greige goods.

Heat Setting. Fabrics composed of thermoplastic fibers can be stabilized by heat setting. Unless textured yarns have been used, this procedure is normally carried out during tentering of the greige goods to ensure that the strains introduced during fabrication are released.

When heat setting is combined with tentering, converters must correctly align the warp and filling yarns in woven structures. Fabrics that have been heat set off-grain cannot be straightened.

Fulling. Fabrics composed of wool fibers are encouraged to relax by a finishing process known as fulling. The goods are exposed to controlled conditions of moisture, heat, and pressure, which cause the yarns to relax and shrink, resulting in a fuller, more compact fabric. Although this procedure reduces the potential for relaxation shrinkage of the fabrics in end use, it does not reduce the possibility of felting shrinkage. Treatments used to minimize felting shrinkage in bedding products composed of wool fibers are explained in Chapter 33.

Compressive Shrinkage Treatments. The dimensional stability of fabrics composed of cotton can be improved during tentering or with a compressive shrinkage treatment. In compressive shrinkage procedures, the greige goods are laid over a supporting fabric, moistened, and mechanically shifted to encourage relaxation of the yarns. Labeling practices that distinguish fabrics stabilized by such treatments are discussed in Chapter 10.

During tentering, cotton yard goods can be compressed lengthwise by feeding them onto the metal pins at a faster rate than the pins are moving forward. This technique encourages the warp yarns to relax; in some cases, a 10-yard length of fabric can shrink to 8 yards.[1] Crosswise relaxation can be encouraged by reducing the distance between the parallel rows of tenter pins.

Figure 9.6 Tentering frame used to correct fabric grain. (Courtesy of Springs Industries, Inc.)

Heat-setting operations help to minimize bagging and sagging of fabrics composed of thermoplastic fibers; fulling and compressive shrinkage treatments have little or no effect on this performance feature. Wool fibers are highly elastic and fabrics composed of them recover well after being stressed. However, cellulosic fibers, including cotton, linen, and rayon, have comparatively low elasticity and may exhibit excessive growth.

Improving Texture Retention

As explained earlier in this chapter, smoothing and crushing operations are used to alter the positions of pile yarns, producing the depth, directional lay, and reflective features specified by the stylist and preferred by the consumer. The serviceability of pile fabrics depends on the extent to which these features are retained. For long-term retention, the pile yarns must be resilient. In fabrics composed of thermoplastic fibers, heat setting can be used to engineer this performance property. In fabrics composed of cotton, such as corduroy and velveteen, this feature can be improved by using a high pile construction density, a structural characteristic that of course is controlled by the fabric manufacturer, not by the converter. Texture retention can also be improved by blending a resilient fiber such as nylon or polyester with the cellulosic fiber.

Reducing Pilling

Pilling occurs when abrasive forces cause free fibers and fiber ends to roll up into minute balls that are unsightly and a nuisance to remove. While pills composed of some staple-length fibers may be removed by subsequent surface abrasion, those composed of filaments or of strong nylon or polyester staple-length fibers tend to cling tenaciously. In either case, the initial formation of pills can be reduced by singeing the greige goods.

Singeing. Small gas flames are used to burn away loose fibers, bits of lint, and fiber ends from fabrics composed of cotton, linen, and rayon. Fabrics made of thermoplastic fibers cannot be singed with flames because the intense heat would melt the base fabric; instead, hot, smooth metal plates are used, carefully, to soften and shrink the protruding fibers so they can be sheared from the surface. Fabrics composed of wool or silk are not singed because these fibers decompose and form a crusty residue when exposed to flame.

ENGINEERING FUNCTIONAL PERFORMANCE

Converters use numerous finishing agents and treatments to develop specific functional properties—performance features that are not characteristic of the components and cannot be introduced by improving the structural features of the greige goods. These functional properties improve the service-related performance of textile fabrics; they include, for example, retarding the rate and level of soil accumulation, minimizing ironing, and so on. Such properties are primarily service-related, but are frequently important to consumer selection, and may lead to a preference for one firm's product over that of another.

This section discusses functional finishes used with several types of greige goods, some of which may be channeled to upholstered furniture manufacturers, some to bedding product manufacturers, and so on. Functional finishes used with a single type of greige goods, for instance, greige linens or carpet rollgoods, are discussed in later units.

Increasing Apparent Brightness

Optical brighteners are used to overcome the dulling effects produced by the accumulation of soil and soil-detergent mixtures that normally result from improper laundering. Brighteners are fluorescent compounds; whether they are incorporated as an integral part of man-made fibers or adsorbed onto exterior fiber surfaces, they increase reflectance by the same mechanism. Incident ultraviolet rays excite brightener molecules, causing them to reflect more light waves or fluoresce. In effect, brighteners convert invisible wavelengths to visible wavelengths, increasing the apparent, not the actual, whiteness or brightness of fibers and fabrics. The effectiveness of most brighteners depends on the quantity of ultraviolet rays incident on the textile surface.

Increasing Moisture Absorption

To improve the ability of cellulosic fibers, especially cotton, to absorb moisture, converters use a process known as mercerization. This chemical treatment also affects the luster of the fibers and their ability to withstand stress loads and abrasive forces.

Mercerizing. In mercerization, threads, yarns, or fabrics are exposed to sodium hydroxide (NaOH) or liquid ammonia while they are held under tension to prevent excessive shrinkage. This treatment alters various internal and external structural features of the fibers, producing changes in their properties. The degree of orientation is increased, increasing the tenacity of the fibers, and the level of crystallinity is reduced, increasing the moisture absorption. As shown in Figure 9.7, mercerized cotton has a rounded cross-sectional shape and virtually no longitudinal twist. These external features may be compared with the flat shape and highly twisted configuration characterizing unmercerized cotton (see Figure 3.2b, page 20). Although flat cross sections typically reflect higher amounts of incident light than do round cross sections, removal of the twist results in increased luster.

Figure 9.7 Mercerized cotton. (Courtesy of Brickel Associates, Inc.)

Because mercerization improves the absorption, as well as the luster and strength, of cotton, the finish is routinely used on greige towelings and sheetings. Colorants are generally applied after mercerization, using the increased absorbency to develop deep, rich color characteristics.

Repelling Moths

Insects, most notably moth and carpet beetle larvae, thrive on wool fibers after they break the disulfide cross links (—S—S—) contained in the cystine monomer. Moths and beetles prefer to live and breed in dark places, where the larvae will be undisturbed and can sustain themselves on the nutrients obtained from the wool fibers. In unprotected wool carpet the damage is more likely to be seen under rarely moved furniture, and in wool blankets and wool upholstery the attack generally occurs during storage.

Converters render wool fiber durably moth resistant by chemically modifying the disulfide linkage, making the fiber indigestible. Several compounds can be used, including permethrin. Because mothproofing treatments are generally combined with dyeing or finishing operations to control processing costs, the protective agents become integral parts of the fibers. Today, all domestic wool floor coverings are treated to be moth resistant.

Imparting protection from other biological pests, such as bacteria and fungi, may be advisable or mandatory. Compounds used to protect soft floor coverings are discussed in Unit Four, and those used to protect bedding products manufactured for use in hospitals and similar facilities are discussed in Unit Five.

Increasing Water Repellency

Converters can apply silicone compounds to reduce the rate at which textile structures absorb water. Because these compounds offer little or no protection from oily soiling and staining, their use is diminishing in favor of fluorocarbon compounds, which provide both water and soil resistance.

Imparting Soil and Stain Resistance

Many textile authorities differentiate "soil" and "stain" on the basis of how tenaciously the soil or dirt clings to the textile structure. When dirt or other foreign matter is mechanically held and comparatively easy to remove, it is known as soil; when the dirt becomes chemically bonded to the fiber surfaces and is comparatively difficult to remove, it is called a stain. Converters seek to prevent staining by using compounds that enable the fibers to repel or resist soil.

Most finishing agents designed to help textile fibers and fabrics repel or resist soil accumulation are fluorocarbon compounds. These agents make the textile component more oleophobic or oil-hating, as well as more hydrophobic. Rather than spreading over the fabric surface, wetting it and penetrating into the fibers and yarns, spilled water and oily compounds bead up, maintaining their surface tension. As schematized in Figure 9.8a, high surface tension means that the molecules in the foreign matter have a higher affinity for one another than for the fibers. Similar action can be observed when raindrops bead up on a waxed car surface.

Spilled liquids should be absorbed immediately from the surface because the protection is temporary; the rate of absorption is slowed, not halted. As the surface tension gradually lowers, the droplets will spread, as shown in Figure 9.8b, wetting and potentially staining the fabric.

Trade names identifying fluorocarbon finishing compounds include Scotch-gard®, produced by The 3M Company, and Teflon® and ZePel®, produced by du Pont. Fiber.Seal®, owned by Fiber.Seal of New York, Inc., is a stain-resistant polymer resin, the composition of which has not been disclosed.

Improving Smoothness Retention

The extent to which textile fabrics retain their original smoothness in use and after care depends on their ability to recover from the strains and deformations imposed by such stress forces as bending, folding, twisting, and crushing. Fabrics exhibiting a high level of recovery are resilient; in effect, they "remember" their original configuration. Resiliency and "memory" can be engineered by applying heat or by incorporating resins in a durable press finishing operation.

Heat Setting. The application of heat to stabilize the dimensions of fabrics composed of thermoplastic fibers was discussed earlier in this chapter. Heat setting also can be used to help flat fabrics remain smooth and wrinkle-free, minimizing the need for ironing.

Durable Press Finishing. Smooth fabrics composed of cotton, linen, or rayon exhibit extremely poor recovery when crushed, folded, or wrinkled, and remain crumpled and mussed. To compensate for this poor resiliency, converters use durable press finishing treatments with the greige goods.

In these chemical finishing processes, the fabrics are impregnated with a resin or reactant compound, which has generally been a formaldehyde-based substance. Heat is then used to cure the compound, causing it to form strong cross links between the polymer chains within the cellulosic fibers. These bonds, schematized in Figure 9.9, function in the same manner as those found in wool and thermoplastic fibers. They stabilize the positions of the chains and introduce to the fibers the so-called memory for whatever shape and form they were in when heat-cured.

Relatively high amounts of resin must be applied to ensure no-iron performance. While the resin significantly improves the resiliency, it also weakens the fibers, lowering their abrasion resistance and shortening their use-life. The loss in abrasion resistance also can result in a frosted appearance. This unsightly problem occurs when abrasive forces remove some of the resin-weakened cellulosic fibers: as the color carried by the fibers is also removed, the abraded area appears faded and lighter than the adjacent

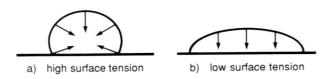

a) high surface tension   b) low surface tension

Figure 9.8 Surface tension and fabric wetting.

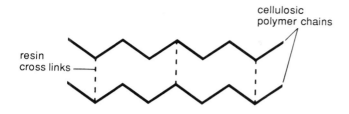

Figure 9.9 Resin cross links introduced into cellulosic fibers to improve their resiliency.

areas. Although frosting is a color-related problem, it is the result of fiber failure, not of colorant failure.

To compensate for the decreased strength and abrasion resistance suffered by the cellulosic fibers, manufacturers often blend them with polyester fiber. The polyester extends the wear-life of the fabric. It does not strengthen the cellulosic components. Together with the potential for loss of the cellulosic fiber, development of a frosted appearance remains a possibility in blends.

Currently, various federal agencies, scientific associations, chemical suppliers, and product manufacturers are investigating the possibility that health hazards may be associated with the use of formaldehyde compounds and their subsequent release from durable press fabrics. Members of the textile industry are now supporting research activities focused on the development and perfection of new durable press finishing agents and procedures.

SUMMARY

Finishing operations are important to the commercial success of all segments of the interior textile industry. They convert greige goods into finished fabrics exhibiting the appearance features, structural qualities, and functional performance properties preferred by contemporary consumers or mandated by regulatory agencies.

The final conversion process is inspection: trained personnel carefully examine the finished fabrics for flaws and defects, rejecting those that contain an unacceptable number of irreparable defects. Together, quality-control tests and visual examinations help to ensure acceptance of the fabrics by end product producers and residential and commercial consumers. These evaluations also help suppliers and producers to determine the advisability of labeling the product with their company name or a name owned by their company. If the qualities of the finished fabrics are unacceptable, their suppliers and producers may be denied the use of voluntary labeling, an effective marketing tool discussed in the following chapter.

NOTE

1. Morris Evans, "Mechanical Finishing," *American Dyestuff Reporter,* Vol. 71, No. 5, May 1982, 36.

chapter 10

Interior Textile Product Labeling

- The Federal Trade Commission
- Mandatory and Advisory Labeling Practices
- Voluntary Labeling Programs

Textile markets are highly competitive: companies must utilize effective marketing techniques to succeed at capturing an adequate share of the consumer market. Several corporations have concentrated their competitive efforts on developing distinctive methods of product labeling. Similar efforts have also been undertaken by trade associations on behalf of their member firms. Often, a name or symbol is added to the label to increase product recognition; sometimes information about such things as quality, reliability, and special performance features is put on the label. The immediate goal of this voluntary, optional labeling is to secure the initial purchase of a firm's products; the long-term goal is to encourage repeated selection of products bearing the firm's label.

Use of voluntary product labeling is optional, but compliance with certain prescribed commercial practices is not. Textile companies must avoid unfair and deceptive marketing practices and activities that would weaken the competitive position of an industry member and restrain trade illegally. To ensure that consumers and members of the industry are protected from abusive practices, the United States Congress and the Federal Trade Commission have established labeling rules and guidelines, as well as antitrust regulations.

THE FEDERAL TRADE COMMISSION

The Federal Trade Commission (FTC) was created by an act of Congress in 1914.* Initially, the Commission was empowered and directed to prevent "unfair methods of competition in commerce." The scope of the Commission's work was expanded by the Wheeler-Lea Act of 1938 also to include "unfair or deceptive acts or practices." An example of such a practice is the failure to disclose that a product or material is not what it appears to be; for instance, disclosure is necessary for a nonleather fabric resembling leather.

Responsibilities and Powers

Improvements in the Commission's operations and revisions of its jurisdiction, responsibilities, and powers have continued over the years. Today, the FTC has the responsibility to investigate commercial trade practices, to encourage voluntary corrective action and compliance, and to commence legal proceedings when necessary. The Commission also has the power to "prescribe interpretative rules and general statements of policy with respect to unfair or deceptive acts or practices in or affecting commerce." This provision has led the FTC to issue various rules and guidelines to be followed in labeling textile products.

*Copies of the Federal Trade Commission Act are available from the FTC, Distribution Branch, Room 270, Washington, D.C. 20580.

The FTC has enforcement and administrative responsibilities for several practices pertaining to the marketing of interior textiles. Within the FTC, the Bureau of Consumer Protection has nine major program divisions that gather and provide information, investigate practices reported to be deceptive, monitor marketplace activities, and enforce federal statutes assigned to them. The Energy and Product Information Division, for example, focuses its work principally on energy policy and conservation, enforcing such rules as the one governing the disclosure of the insulative value (R-value) of home insulation, much of which is glass fiber batting.

Of particular interest to interior textile consumers and producers is the work of the Product Reliability Division. This division is responsible for enforcement of the Magnuson-Moss Warranty Act, which sets forth the procedures to be followed when written warranties are offered. This act and the growing use of warranties for interior textiles are described later in this chapter. Also of critical interest is the work of the Regional Offices Division. The ten offices in this unit are located in major cities nationwide and have exclusive responsibility for enforcing the mandatory fiber product labeling acts passed by Congress, as well as the trade regulation rules prescribed and promulgated by the FTC.

Investigative and Rulemaking Procedures

As noted earlier, the FTC is empowered to investigate marketplace activities and to develop rules affecting the commercial practices of an entire industry. A review of the investigative and rulemaking procedures followed by the Commission will provide greater understanding of the role it assumes in halting unfair and deceptive marketing practices.

The FTC is not authorized to handle individual consumer complaints, but acts when it sees a pattern of marketplace abuse. Complaints from individual consumers may serve to provide the pattern plus the evidence necessary to begin an investigation.

Investigations can begin in many different ways. Complaint letters, scholarly articles on consumer or economic subjects, or congressional requests may trigger an investigation. Investigations are either "public" or "nonpublic." Generally, public announcements will be made of investigations of the practices of an entire industry. An investigation of an individual company will probably be "nonpublic" in order to protect that company's privacy until the agency is ready formally to make an allegation.

After an investigation, the staff may find reason to believe that a business has violated the law. If the case is not settled voluntarily by some official corrective action by the company (a "consent order"), the Commission could issue a "complaint." After that, and if no settlement is reached, a formal hearing is held before an administrative law judge. Members of the public can participate at this point if they have evidence relating to the case. The administrative law judge issues a decision. There may be an appeal to the FTC commissioners. The commissioners' decision may be appealed to the United States Court of Appeals and ultimately to the United States Supreme Court.

After an investigation, the FTC staff may find what it believes to be unfair or deceptive practices in an entire industry. The staff then could make a recommendation to the commissioners to begin rulemaking. If the recommendation is accepted, a presiding officer is appointed, and a notice is published in the *Federal Register,* setting out the proposed rule and what the commissioners believe are the central issues to be discussed. Members of the public can, at this point, comment or testify on the rule or suggest issues to be examined.

The presiding officer conducts public hearings, which include cross-examination on certain issues. After the hearings, the staff prepares a report on the issues. This is followed by the presiding officer's report. Then members of the public have another opportunity to comment on the entire rulemaking record.

The matter then goes before the commissioners who deliberate on the record (which includes the presiding officer's report, the FTC staff report, and the public comments) to decide whether to issue the rule. They can make changes in the provisions of the rule and issue a revised version as they judge appropriate.* This procedure has been followed to establish labeling and marketing rules that apply to various segments of the interior textile industry. Some of these rules are mandatory; others are advisory.

MANDATORY AND ADVISORY LABELING PRACTICES

Labeling rules and guidelines are intended to afford consumers protection, not from any hazardous product, but from such things as misrepresentation of the composition of textile products. There are regulations, such as flammability standards, that focus on safety concerns, but product labeling is not generally required with these mandates. Mandatory labeling rules also serve to protect industry members by specifying acceptable and legal practices for them to follow when engaged in commercial activities.

Fiber Product Labeling Acts

The United States Congress has passed three acts specifically designed to protect consumers and producers from the unrevealed presence of substitutes and mixtures in fi-

---

*"What's Going On at the FTC?" Federal Trade Commission, Washington, D.C., Summer/Fall 1981.

brous products and from misrepresentation and false advertising of the fiber content of textile fiber products. The provisions of these acts are especially important today as fibers can be engineered successfully to simulate the appearance of other fibers: acrylic can resemble wool; rayon can imitate linen; and acetate, nylon, and polyester can look like silk.

Failure to accurately disclose fiber content is an unfair and deceptive act or practice in commerce. Such illegal misbranding can be avoided by strict adherence to the provisions set forth in each act and its accompanying set of rules and regulations. The latter are established and issued by the FTC to help producers, distributors, and consumers interpret the mandates of each act.[*]

The Wool Products Labeling Act of 1939 (WPLA). The WPLA, effective July 15, 1941, focuses on the labeling requirements for products containing any percentage of wool fiber. (The meaning of "wool" in this act is given below.) Interior textile products subject to the provisions of the WPLA include, for example, conventional blankets and underblankets that are composed in whole or in part of wool. Interior textile products that have been specifically exempted include carpets, rugs, mats, and upholsteries.

Products included within the scope of the WPLA must conspicuously display a label or hangtag disclosing the following information:

1. The percentage of all fibers present in amounts of 5 percent or more of the total fiber weight of the product. Those fibers present to the extent of less than 5 percent should be disclosed as "other fiber" or "other fibers." Constituent fibers are identified by the following terms:

"Wool" means the fiber from the fleece of the sheep or lamb or hair of the Angora or Cashmere goat (and may include the so-called specialty fibers from the hair of the camel, alpaca, llama, and vicuna) that has never been reclaimed from any woven or felted wool product. In lieu of the word "wool," the specialty fiber name may be used; "mohair" may be used for naming the fibers from the Angora goat; and "cashmere" may be used for naming the fibers from the Cashmere goat.

"Recycled wool" means the constituent fibers were obtained by reducing (shredding) a previously manufactured product to its original fibrous state and then again subjecting the fibers to the product manufacturing sequence. Legal use of this term was provided by an amendment to the WPLA, effective July 4, 1980. "Recycled wool" replaces the terms "reprocessed wool" and "reused wool." The term "reprocessed wool" was used to identify the resulting fiber when wool had been woven or felted

into a wool product that, without ever having been used in any way by a consumer, subsequently had been returned to a fibrous state. The term "reused wool" was used to identify the resulting fiber when wool or reprocessed wool had been spun, woven, knitted, or felted into a wool product that, after having been used by a consumer, subsequently had been returned to a fibrous state. Labels no longer indicate whether or not remanufactured fibers were previously used by consumers.

"Virgin wool" and "new wool" are synonymous terms. The use of these terms means the constituent fibers have undergone manufacturing only once; they have not been reclaimed from any spun, woven, knitted, felted, braided, bonded, or otherwise manufactured or used product. These terms could not be used, for example, if fibers were recovered from yarns or excess fabric pieces. No quality specifications are included in the definition of these terms.

When natural fibers other than wool or manufactured fibers are contained in wool products, they are identified by their generic names. These names were discussed in Chapter 3.

2. The identifying name or registered number of the manufacturer of the product. Registered numbers are assigned upon application to the FTC, and the assigned number may be used in complying with the provisions of other labeling acts.[**]

3. The country of origin. Country-of-origin regulations have been issued by the FTC and the United States Customs Service. Under the FTC rules, all products entirely manufactured and made of materials manufactured in the United States must bear the label "Made in the U.S.A." For products substantially manufactured in the United States using materials from another country, the label must read "Sewn in the U.S.A. of Imported Components" or words of equivalent meaning. Labels on imported products must include the name of the country where the United States Customs Service determines the product was made. (The country-of-origin regulations established by the Customs Service were discussed in Chapter 1.) These rules apply to products manufactured on or after December 24, 1984. Mail-order catalogs printed after this date also must provide country-of-origin information.

The Fur Products Labeling Act (FPLA). The FPLA, effective August 9, 1952, governs the labeling and advertising of furs and fur products. The term "fur product" means any article of apparel made in whole or in part of fur or used fur. The FPLA's provisions do not apply to products other than apparel products.

The Textile Fiber Products Identification Act (TFPIA). Before World War II, consumers, distributors, and producers had few types of fibers from which to choose in comparison to the number available today. There were the widely used natural fibers, including wool, silk, linen, and cotton, and the less widely used natural fibers, such as jute, hemp, sisal, and camel. Rayon and acetate, initially known as "artificial silk" fibers, were also available. While consumers were familiar with the appearance, general performance properties, and care requirements of most of these fibers, they were not familiar with the characteristics of the several types of synthesized fibers subsequently introduced.

The first fully synthesized man-made fiber, nylon, was unceremoniously adopted for use in toothbrush bristles in 1938, and enthusiastically welcomed in sheer hosiery in 1939. It was available to consumers for only a brief time before World War II required its use to be redirected to the production of war materiel such as parachute fabric and tents. The chemical knowledge gained in the development of nylon, together with advances in production technology, led to the postwar production of an expanding number of man-made fibers.

As each new fiber was developed and manufactured by various companies, each of whom assigned a different name to the fiber, the market became filled with what appeared to be many distinct and unrelated fibers. Consumers, distributors, and producers had no way of knowing the composition of the new fibers, what performance to expect, and what care might be appropriate. Ultimately, growing concern to minimize this confusion, as well as to prevent unfair and deceptive marketing practices (intentional or not), led to the passage of the TFPIA in 1958. The act became effective on March 3, 1960.

Provisions of the TFPIA apply to many textile fiber products, including articles of wearing apparel, beddings, curtains, and casements, draperies, tablecloths, floor coverings, towels, furniture slipcovers, afghans, and throws, and all fibers, yarns, and fabrics. Specifically exempted are such products as upholstery stuffing (unless it was previously used); outer coverings of furniture, mattresses, and boxsprings; and backings of, and paddings or cushions to be used under, floor coverings. Thus, although carpets, rugs, and mats are specifically exempted from the WPLA, the face or pile layers of these floor products are subject to the provisions of the TFPIA. Also, while upholsteries are exempted from the WPLA, they come under the TFPIA when they are marketed in fabric form, that is, when not permanently attached to the furniture frame.

Products included within the scope of the TFPIA must bear a conspicuous label or hangtag displaying the following information:

1. The constituent fiber or combination of fibers in the textile fiber product, designating with equal prominence each natural or manufactured fiber in the textile fiber product by its generic name and percentage in the order of predominance by weight, if the weight of such fiber is 5 percent or more of the total fiber weight of the product. Fibers present to the extent of less than 5 percent of the total fiber weight of the product are designated as "other fiber" or "other fibers," except when a definite functional significance has clearly been established. In the latter case, the percentage by weight, the generic name, and the functional significance of the fiber should be set out, for example, 3 percent spandex for elasticity.

2. The identifying name or registered number of the manufacturer of the product.

3. The country of origin, according to the rules established by the FTC and the United States Customs Service. These regulations were described in the discussion of the WPLA.

Nondeceptive and truthfully descriptive terms are permitted with the generic name, for example, combed cotton, solution-dyed acetate, and antistatic nylon. The information voluntarily provided by this and other forms of permissive labeling is particularly helpful to consumers selecting interior textile products.

If any reference is made in advertising to one fiber used in a blend, then the generic names of all fibers present in amounts greater than 5 percent must be listed. Again, the names must be in descending order according to weight.

When products are labeled in accordance with these acts, consumers are not challenged to recognize fibers by their appearance or to know the performance properties and care requirements of many individual fibers. Instead, they need only become familiar with the features generally characteristic of each generic class of chemically related fibers. We should note that care instructions are not required under the WPLA, the FPLA, or the TFPIA. The disclosure of safe care procedures for finished fabrics and apparel items is governed by a trade regulation rule.

Trade Regulation Rules

Trade regulation rules set out provisions for mandatory and acceptable practices considerd to be in the public interest. Producers following the rules will avoid illegal and unacceptable marketing practices as defined in the FTC Act.

In the marketing of interior textile products, some of the rules apply to a specific market segment. There is, for example, the Trade Regulations Rule Relating to the Deceptive Advertising and Labeling as to Size of Tablecloths and Related Products (see Chapter 34). A second example illustrating specific orientation to one market sector is the Trade Regulation Rule Relating to Failure to Disclose that Skin Irritation May Result from Washing or Handling Glass Fiber Curtains and Draperies and Glass Fiber Curtain and Drapery Fabrics (see Chapter 19).

In April 1974, the FTC gathered comments concerning the advisability of expanding the scope of the Trade Regulation Rule Related to the Care Labeling of Textile Wearing Apparel, which had gone into effect on July 3, 1972. After analyzing the comments, the Commission published, in June 1976, a proposed amended rule recommending the extension of the current rule's coverage to draperies, curtains, slipcovers, linens, piece goods sold for covering furniture or making slipcovers, leather and suede apparel, yarn, carpets and rugs, and upholstered furniture. Oral testimony and written comments were continuously received and analyzed until June 1982; based on these, the Commission did not approve the proposed extensions. The new title of the amended rule, Care Labeling of Textile Wearing Apparel and Certain Piece Goods, reflects this decision. The amended rule became effective on January 2, 1984.*

The role of the FTC should not be construed as strictly adversary in nature. Although it has been assigned exclusive responsibility for enforcing specific congressional acts and for monitoring commerce in general, the Commission also continually strives to inform and educate both the consuming public and industry members concerning fair market practices. Trade practice rules and labeling guides have been helpful to this endeavor.

Trade Practice Rules and Guides

As generally set forth in the introduction of each trade practice rule and guide, the provisions are "interpretive of laws administered by the Commission, and thus are advisory in nature." These rules "are designed to foster and promote the maintenance of fair competitive conditions in the interest of protecting industry, trade, and the public." By complying with the stated provisions, industry members can avoid engaging in unfair and deceptive marketing practices that can lead to litigation.

The major difference between trade practice rules and guides lies in who initiated the proceedings. In the case of trade practice rules, a single industry segment has requested assistance from the FTC in an effort to clarify what trade practices are acceptable. Conferences are then held to provide a forum for all industry members; thereafter, proposed rules are published, responses considered, and final advisory rules published. Guides are the result of proceedings initiated by the Commission, and they supersede several trade practice rules.

Trade practice rules and guides, like trade regulation rules, have a specific and limited scope. There are, for example, guides for the household furniture industry and

guides for the feather and down products industry. These guides are explained in Chapters 13 and 33, respectively.

To ensure that they are using fair and nondeceptive marketing practices, textile firms must label their products in accordance with all applicable acts, rules, and guides. In order to gain a competitive edge in the marketplace, they may also choose to label their products with a distinctive name or logo or to offer a warranty pertaining to in-use performance. The use of such labeling is permissible and strictly voluntary.

VOLUNTARY LABELING PROGRAMS

Voluntary labeling programs are used extensively in the marketing of interior textile products. These programs are primarily intended to increase sales, assisting in the commercial success of all suppliers, producers, and distributors of the labeled product. At the same time, such labeling is helpful to contract designers, architects, and consumers who understand the intention or implication of the various kinds of labeling, such as those relating to nondescriptive fiber names, certification marks, licensing programs, and warranty programs. In virtually all programs, a trademark is a valuable promotional aid.

Use of "TM" and ®

Trademarks are distinctive names, words, phrases, and stylized logos (letters or symbols) that aim at capturing the attention of professionals and consumers. The ownership and use of trademarks is carefully guarded.

Producers and trade associations allocate significant amounts of money, time, and talent to coining names, designing graphic symbols, and writing eye-catching phrases that will be effective trademarks. Once this effort is completed, the chosen name, phrase, or logo appears on product labels and in promotional materials accompanied by the letters "TM." This labeling constitutes basic ownership of the trademark, assuming the person or firm was the first to use the trademark in commerce. Frequently, the user elects to apply for registered ownership of the trademark with the United States Patent and Trademark Office. Following approval of the application, the symbol ® is used in lieu of "TM" to indicate registered ownership.

Trademarks are widely promoted to ensure recognition of the mark by the consumer. At the same time, the use of the mark is carefully controlled. Every effort is taken to protect the reputation of the trademark, as well as to ensure that the legal owner is the only one benefiting from the increased recognition and selection of products labeled with the mark. Unauthorized adoption of a trademark is illegal: in recent years, such piracy has resulted in several multimillion-dollar lawsuits and confiscation of illegally branded goods.

---

*Requests for copies of the rule, and of the Statement of Basis and Purpose, should be sent to Public Reference Branch, Room 130, Federal Trade Commission, 6th and Pennsylvania Avenue, NW, Washington, D.C. 20580.

Fiber Trademarks

Fiber suppliers and producers use trade names and logos to distinguish their products from those of their competitors. Man-made fiber producers use trade names extensively, and apparently their promotional efforts have been successful. Many consumers are more familiar with fiber trade names than with their generic names. A trademarked fiber may be considered unique when in fact several other chemically related fibers produced by other companies are also available. Appendix A lists fiber trade names with their generic classes and the characteristics they designate.

Informed consumers and trained professionals can make valuable use of fiber trade names, especially those that designate a special property. They may, for example, know that solution dyeing has been used when Courtaulds North America labels its rayon fiber with the trade name Coloray®, and they may be reminded that modacrylic fibers are self-extinguishing (i.e., stop burning when the source of ignition is removed) when Monsanto Chemical Company labels a product with the trademark SEF®.

Cotton Incorporated grants permission to qualifying retailers, manufacturers, and mills to use its registered trademark on packaging, hangtags, or in advertisements. The trademark is a stylized design, the Cotton Seal, illustrated in Figure 10.1.

Figure 10.1 The Cotton Seal. (Registered trademark of Cotton Incorporated.)

Some companies license or certify the use of their fiber trade names on end products. Celanese Corporation, for example, permits the use of its trade name Fortrel® with fabrics made of the company's polyester fiber when tested for quality in Celanese laboratories. Another fiber company, Hercules Incorporated, tests the quality and performance of finished carpet containing the company's fiber. If the carpet meets or exceeds standards established by Hercules, the company will certify on the label that the carpet

is made with pile of 100 percent Herculon® olefin fiber. Fiber trademark licensing and certifying should not be confused with other licensing and certification programs applying to textile products.

Certification Marks

Certification marks are coined names and stylized logos that may be used alone or in conjunction with other types of voluntary labeling. They may be used on the labels of end products that conform with fiber content specifications or performance specifications established by the owner of the mark.

Du Pont, a company that produces fibers but not textile end products, has coined several certification marks for use on the labels of yarns, fabrics, apparel, and home textile products composed of the du Pont fibers. "Sayelle," for example, appears on the label of hand knitting yarns meeting fiber content specifications established by du Pont, that is, the yarns are composed of the company's bicomponent Orlon® Type 21 acrylic fiber; "Qiana" is used on fabrics composed of du Pont fiber and conforming with the fiber company's performance specifications; and "Quallofil" is used on the labels of pillows, other sleep products, and apparel items whose fillings are composed of du Pont's Dacron® 113 polyester fiber (see Figure 33.1b, page 359). Another fiber company, BASF Corporation, permits the use of its coined name Zefran® to describe carpet made of the company's fiber whose performance has been quality tested by BASF (see Unit Four).

Some fiber trade associations control or certify the use of their registered trademark logos. The Wool Bureau, Inc., for example, owns and controls the use of the Woolmark and the Woolblend Mark (Figure 10.2). End products carrying these symbols have been quality tested by The Wool Bureau, Inc. for compliance with performance and fiber content specifications.

Licensing Programs

Licensing companies sell the right to use their company-owned processes to producers and converters; they do not process any components or manufacture any end products. Licensing companies do, however, certify the use of their coined names in the labeling and marketing of products. The Sanforized Company, for example, licenses the use of its compressive shrinkage and durable press processes. Producers using these fabric conversion techniques may label and promote their end products with such names as Sanforized®, Sanfor-Knit®, and Sanfor-Set®, tradenames owned by the Sanforized Company.

Consumers, contract designers, and architects must recognize that licensing and certification programs provide assurances, not guarantees. The presence of a licensed or certified name or logo on a label may confirm a specific

PURE WOOL

The sewn-in Woolmark label is your assurance of quality-tested fabrics made of the world's best...Pure Wool.

PURE WOOL PILE

The Woolmark label is your assurance of quality-tested products made of the world's best...Pure Wool Pile.

WOOL BLEND

The sewn-in Woolblend Mark label is your assurance of quality-tested fabrics made predominantly of wool.

Figure 10.2 Registered trademark logos used by The Wool Bureau, Inc. in certification labeling. (Courtesy of The Wool Bureau, Inc.)

fiber content, the use of a particular process, or that the product has met standard performance specifications, but it does not guarantee any features.

Warranty Programs

Today, warranty or guarantee programs are used more frequently in textile marketing than they were in earlier, less economically challenging times. Budgetary pressures have increasingly encouraged designers, architects, and consumers to seek or even demand a legally binding agreement guaranteeing the long-term satisfactory performance of some interior textile products. They are, of course, seeking protection from defective or faulty merchandise and the expense of premature replacement.

In order to meet the demands of professionals and consumers, and thus to remain competitive, several producers of textile components and end products offer written warranties. Fiber companies may, for example, try to enhance their competitive position by voluntarily offering to stand behind products composed of their fiber but manufactured by a downstream firm. This is an especially frequent practice with soft floor coverings.

There are important differences among the various types of warranties. A review of the major types of warranties—spoken, implied, and written—can help to identify and clarify these differences.

Spoken Warranties. Spoken warranties are merely verbal promises, virtually impossible to enforce. Consumers and professionals should have spoken warranties put into writing.

Implied Warranties. Implied warranties are not written; they are rights provided to consumers by state law. These rights include such things as the "warranty of mer-chantability," for instance, that an electric blanket will heat, and the "warranty of fitness for a particular purpose," for instance, that a carpet produced for installation around a swimming pool will not dissolve in water. In states having such laws, implied warranties come automatically with every sale unless the product is sold "as is."

Written Warranties. A written warranty constitutes a legally binding promise that the warrantor is insuring quality and performance and is willing to stand behind the warranted product, assuming it is neither misused nor abused by the warrantee. While written warranties are strictly voluntary, when they are offered they are subject to the provisions of the Magnuson-Moss Warranty Act, passed by the United States Congress in 1975. This act is under the jurisdiction of the FTC.

Like the textile labeling mandates discussed earlier, the Magnuson-Moss Warranty Act serves and protects both producers and consumers. By strictly adhering to the provisions of the act, producers can avoid unfair and deceptive marketing practices. By examining the features included in any warranty offered, and by exercising their rights under the act, consumers can protect themselves from defective products.

The act requires that written warranties offered on consumer products costing more than fifteen dollars must be made available to prospective consumers prior to the sale of the product. The warranty shall "fully and conspicuously disclose in simple and readily understood language the terms and conditions of such warranty." This provision prohibits the use of "legalese" and fine print. Specific information that must be set forth in written warranties includes, but is not limited to, the following items:

1. The clear identification of the names and addresses of the warrantors.

2. The identity of the party or parties to whom the warranty is extended; this is often stated as "original purchasers only."

3. The products or parts covered.

4. What the warrantor will do in the event of a defect, malfunction, or failure to conform with such written warranty, at whose expense, and for what period of time.

5. What the consumer must do and what expenses the consumer must bear.

6. The step-by-step procedure the consumer should take in order to obtain performance of any obligation under the warranty, including the identification of any person or class of persons authorized to perform the obligations set forth in the warranty.

7. The characteristics, properties, or parts of the product that are not covered by the warranty.

Written warranties are required also to carry the designation "full" or "limited." These designations indicate what the warrantor agrees to do for the purchaser, as well as what is expected of the purchaser. An examination of the meanings and implications of these designations will provide greater understanding of warranty labeling.

FULL WARRANTY: The title FULL on a warranty tells you that:

- A defective product will be repaired or replaced for free, including removal and reinstallation when necessary.
- The product will be repaired within a reasonable time period after you have told the company about the problem.
- You will not have to do anything unreasonable to get warranty service (such as return a heavy product to the store).
- The warranty is good for anyone who owns the product during the warranty period.
- If the product has not been repaired after a reasonable number of tries, you can get a replacement or a refund. (This is commonly known as the "lemon" provision.)
- You do not have to return a warranty card for a product with a FULL warranty. But, a company may give a registration card and suggest that it be returned, so long as it is clear that the return of the card is voluntary.
- Implied warranties cannot be disclaimed or denied or limited to any specific length of time.

Warning: The title FULL does NOT mean:

- That the entire product is covered by the warranty.
- That the warranty has to last for one year or any other particular length of time.

- That the company must pay for "consequential or incidential damages" (such as towing, car rental, food spoilage, etc.).
- That the product is warranted in all geographic areas.

LIMITED WARRANTY: The title LIMITED on a warranty tells you that the warranty gives you less than what the FULL warranty gives you. You have to read your warranty to see what protection is missing. For example:

- You may have to pay for labor, reinstallation, or other charges.
- You may be required to bring a heavy product back to the store for service or do something else you may find difficult.
- Your warranty may be good only for the first purchaser (that is, a second owner would not be entitled to any warranty service).
- You may be promised a pro-rata refund or credit which means you will have to pay for the time you owned the product before the defect appeared.
- You may have to return your warranty registration card to get warranty coverage.
- Your implied warranties may expire when your written warranty expires. (For example, a one-year limited warranty can say that the implied warranties only last for one year.)
- The "lemon" provision does not apply to limited warranties, but even under a limited warranty you are entitled to what the warranty promises. If the company cannot do what it has promised to do, the company has to do something else comparable for you.

Warning: The title LIMITED does NOT mean:

- That your product is inferior or will not work as promised.
- That only part of the product is covered. For example, you may have a LIMITED warranty that covers the entire product.
- That the warranty only covers the cost of repair parts. A LIMITED warranty can include labor, too.
- That the warranty will last for any particular length of time.
- That you can only have warranty service done in a few locations.

A product can carry more than one written warranty. For example, an automatic washer can have a FULL warranty on the entire product for one year and a LIMITED four-year warranty on the gear assembly.*

_____

* "Warranties: There Ought To Be A Law," Federal Trade Commission, Washington, D.C., undated.

Sample Labeling

Another form of voluntary labeling used by interior textile product producers that should be highlighted is the use of style, color, and design names on product samples displayed in product showrooms and retail outlets. In most cases, these names are nondescriptive and provide no useful information, but they may have the effect of attracting and holding prospective purchasers' attention. For example, "blue-green" may identify a color accurately, but "sea foam" may sound more enticing; the terms "level, cut-pile" may describe a carpet texture informatively, but "plateau" may seem more interesting; "polka dot" may be readily understandable, but "micro dot" may add contemporary flair; and so on.

It is apparent that the marketing strategy behind this type of sample labeling is the same as that behind the use of a well-known designer's name on product labels. Producers purchase the right to use the name, after confirming that it will be a persuasive and effective marketing aid.

SUMMARY

Members of the interior textile industry must disclose the fiber composition and country of origin of most of their products, using the practices prescribed in the congressional fiber product labeling acts. Members of certain industry segments also must adhere to trade regulation rules, and some are advised also to comply with recommendations set forth in a trade practice rule or in guides. Compliance with these mandates and guidelines helps ensure that producers are not engaged in unfair or deceptive commercial activities related to product disclosures. It also helps ensure that consumers and professionals have useful and accurate information, enabling them to make reliable decisions when they select textile products for interior applications.

To enhance the marketability of their products, many producers use voluntary labeling programs. They may distinguish their products with trade names or certification marks, or they may elect to guarantee their quality or performance. The use of such labeling offers reciprocal advantages for producers and consumers. Producers gain a competitive edge in the marketplace, and consumers are provided more information or protection than is legally required.

chapter 11

Interior Textile Products and Fire

- The Consumer Product Safety Commission
- The Flammable Fabrics Act
- Combustion Processes and By-products
- Fire-related Fiber Properties
- Stages of an Interior Fire
- Flammability Testing

Over the past twenty years, consumers, industry members, and local, state, and federal government personnel have given increased attention to the fire-related behavior of interior textile products. This has resulted in the establishment of flammability mandates applying to interior products intended for use in certain occupancies; such mandates are issued and enforced by various regulatory agencies, several of which were identified in Chapter 1. This attention has also resulted in the establishment of flammability mandates with which specific interior textile products must comply prior to marketing. These mandates were established in accordance with provisions of the Flammable Fabrics Act, a congressional act administered by the Consumer Product Safety Commission.

Residential and commercial consumers should be aware of the role interior textiles play in fires. Understanding fire-related terms and processes and the test methods used in fire-safety work will enable them to widen the margin of personal safety, minimize structural damage, and lessen economic losses in the event of fire. It will also prepare the professional to specify products that conform with mandated selection criteria.

THE CONSUMER PRODUCT SAFETY COMMISSION

The Consumer Product Safety Commission (CPSC) was established as an independent federal agency in late 1972. When the Commission began operation on May 14, 1973, administration and enforcement responsibilities for certain safety-oriented acts, including the Flammable Fabrics Act (FFA), were transferred to it from other federal regulatory agencies. Prior to this transfer, the FFA was administered by the FTC and the United States Department of Commerce.

In carrying out its responsibilities, the CPSC analyzes information and statistics regarding the frequency and severity of injury associated with interior textile and other consumer products. When products are found to pose an unreasonable risk to consumers, the Commission has the power to initiate the necessary proceedings that ultimately may lead to the establishment of a new or revised safety standard. When regulating interior textile products, the CPSC adheres to procedures set forth in the FFA.

THE FLAMMABLE FABRICS ACT

The FFA was passed by the United States Congress in 1953 and became effective on July 1, 1954. This act prohibits the introduction and movement in interstate commerce of articles of wearing apparel and fabrics so highly flammable as to be dangerous when worn by individuals. Congress amended the act in 1967, expanding its scope to include interior furnishings and permitting the establishment of standards for these textile products.

The 1967 Amendment

In addition to expanding the scope of the FFA, the 1967 amendment directed the Secretary of Commerce and the Secretary of Health, Education, and Welfare (now Health and Human Services) to "conduct a continuing study and investigation of the deaths, injuries, and economic losses resulting from accidental burning of products, fabrics, or related materials." Much of the statistical information pertaining to fabric-related burning accidents is provided by the National Electronic Injury Surveillance System (NEISS). The NEISS records personal injury data from more than a hundred hospital rooms throughout the United States and forwards it to the CPSC for analysis.

The 1967 amendment also authorized the Secretary of Commerce to carry out the following activities:

1. Conduct research into the flammability of products, fabrics, and materials.
2. Conduct feasibility studies on reduction of flammability of products, fabrics, and materials.
3. Develop flammability test methods and testing devices.
4. Offer appropriate training on the use of flammability test methods and testing devices.

Much of the investigative work involved is carried out by the federally funded National Bureau of Standards (NBS) in the laboratories of its Center for Fire Research. The NBS does not promulgate standards, but it does provide information to the CPSC and other federal agencies.

When statistical injury data and laboratory test results support the possibility that a new or revised safety standard is needed, it is the CPSC's responsibility to initiate and carry out the following procedures:

1. Publish the notice of a possible need and the proposed standard in the *Federal Register* (prior to April 23, 1976, the notice and proposed standard were published separately).
2. Invite and consider response from affected and interested persons.
3. Publish the final version of the standard in the *Federal Register*.
4. Allow one year for firms affected by the standard to manufacture products meeting specified performance criteria (the CPSC may set an earlier or later effective date if it finds good cause).

5. Prohibit noncomplying products manufactured after the effective date from being introduced into commerce (the CPSC may allow exceptions).

New Standards

Five new standards have been promulgated and others proposed as a result of the provisions of the 1967 amendment. Each new or proposed standard is identified by numbers following the letters "FF" (for flammable fabric) or "PFF" (for proposed flammable fabric). The first number indicates the order in which the standards were proposed; the second number indicates the year in which action was last taken on the standard (note that the second number does not indicate the year in which the standard became effective). Frequently, these designations are used in lieu of the title of the standards. Professionals and consumers should become familiar with the following standards, four of which apply to interior textile products:

FF 1-70   Large Carpets and Rugs
FF 2-70   Small Carpets and Rugs
FF 3-71   Children's Sleepwear, Sizes 0–6X
FF 4-74   Mattresses and Mattress Pads
FF 5-74   Children's Sleepwear, Sizes 7–14
PFF 6-74 Upholstered Furniture
PFF 7-75 Dangerous Categories of Adult Apparel

Standard 1-70 is explained in Unit Four and Standards 2-70 and 4-74 are discussed in Unit Five. The current status of PFF 6-74 is reviewed in Unit Two.

COMBUSTION PROCESSES AND BY-PRODUCTS

Combustion is a chemical process in which oxidation, the combination of oxygen with elements or compounds, produces heat energy. In some combustion reactions, light and such other by-products as molten polymer compounds, smoke, and toxic gases are also produced.

Combustion Processes

Flaming combustion processes are intitiated by pyrolysis, in which heat causes organic compounds to decompose, producing combustible materials. Heat may be supplied by a burning match, a lit cigarette, glowing embers, or an electrical spark. When the kindling or ignition temperature is reached, the combustible materials combine with oxygen, ignite, and produce heat and light in the form of flames. The heat generated by this combustion can promote further decomposition of the textile substance, causing the cyclic process to continue until the structure is consumed.

While a lighted match, which has a temperature of approximately 1,000°F, is a common source of ignition heat for interior textile products, the most common source is a burning cigarette. In recognition of the fire hazard posed by cigarettes, in October 1984 the United States Congress approved funding for a committee to study the feasibility of producing a cigarette that quickly self-extinguishes when no longer being smoked.

Spontaneous combustion occurs when a textile substrate is heated to its kindling temperature without the involvement of a flaming ignition source. Although this is not common with fibers, it is a potential hazard with latex foam compounds, especially when they are being tumbled in a heated dryer. Because cellular latex is a good heat insulator, heat builds up, the relatively low ignition temperature of the material is quickly reached, and it bursts into flame.

In addition to flaming combustion, flameless combustion can also occur. One type of flameless combustion, glowing, is characteristic of cellulosic fibers: after a small area of flame has been extinguished, the fiber continues to be consumed without flames rising. Smoldering is another type of flameless combustion, which may occur with fibrous fillings and battings. This suppressed combustion often produces large volumes of dense smoke filled with deadly toxicants.

By-products of Combustion

Besides the heat energy and light produced during most combustion reactions, burning textiles and other interior materials generate various other products. Among these, toxic gases pose the greatest threat to life.

Molten Polymer Compounds. When thermoplastic fibers are heated to their melting points, the molten polymer compounds produced can play conflicting roles in interior fires. When window and wall coverings contain these fibers, for example, the molten polymer may drip and carry the flames downward. This could be a positive event if the burning fabric self-extinguished and the flaming droplets fell on a noncombustible flooring material. It would be a negative event if the flaming droplets propagated the fire to a flammable floor covering.

Smoke. The amount and density of smoke generated by items undergoing flaming combustion or smoldering can have a major effect on safe exit procedures because smoke reduces visibility and obscures illuminated exit markers. A test method to evaluate smoke density is discussed and illustrated in Chapter 30.

Smoke, not heat or flame, is the primary cause of all fire deaths.[1] Smoke is deadly because of the toxicants it contains.

Toxic Gases. Toxicity studies have shown that varied quantities of six specific gases can be detected after the isolated combustion of commonly used fibers. These gases include carbon monoxide (CO), carbon dioxide (CO_2), hydrogen sulfide (HS), hydrogen cyanide (HCN), nitrogen oxide plus nitrogen dioxide ($NO + NO_2$), and vinyl cyanide (CH_2CHCN).[2] The most toxic of these gases, CO, is present in all fires, whether textiles are involved or not; it causes death by preventing red blood cells from absorbing oxygen.

At the present time, no flammability regulations include specific requirements related to toxic gases, although it may be reasonable to expect such mandates in the future. Currently, some fire-safety researchers are focusing their attentions on the development of a test method to measure the hazards of inhaled toxicants.[*]

FIRE-RELATED FIBER PROPERTIES

As noted earlier, textile fibers must be long and thin for flexibility. This physical form results in high ratios of surface area to volume. Thus, for their volume, all fibers expose a disproportionately large amount of surface area to the atmospheric oxygen needed for combustion reactions. At the same time, their various chemical compositions result in differences in their pyrolytic characteristics and relative flammability.

Pyrolytic Characteristics

As the cyclic combustion process continues, the supply of available oxygen decreases. Without sufficient oxygen in the burning area, and with the source of ignition removed, some fibers self-extinguish. The amount of oxygen required to support the combustion of a fiber is measured and reported as the limiting oxygen index (LOI). Fibers with an LOI above 21 self-extinguish after combustion reduces the level of oxygen below the normal 21 percent concentration and the source of ignition is removed; under the same conditions, fibers having an LOI below 21 continue to burn until they are consumed.

Textile fibers burn at different temperatures and have different heat of combustion values. These values specify the amount of heat energy generated that could cause burn injuries as well as maintain the temperature required for further decompositon and combustion. The heats of combustion, ignition temperatures, and other pyrolytic characteristics of selected fiber groups are listed in Table 11.1.

---

[*] Interested readers may obtain a copy of NBSIR 82-2532, "Further Development of a Test Method for the Assessment of the Acute Inhalation Toxicity of Combustion Products," from the National Technical Information Service, Springfield, VA 22161.

Table 11.1 PYROLYTIC CHARACTERISTICS OF SELECTED TEXTILE FIBERS

| | Temperatures | | | | Heats of combustion (BTUs/lb) | Limiting oxygen index |
| | Decomposition | | Ignition | | | |
	°F	°C	°F	°C		
Fiber						
Natural						
Protein						
wool	446	230	1,094	590	9,450	25.2
			self-extinguishing			
Cellulose						
cotton	581	305	752	400	7,400	17–20
Mineral						
asbestos			fireproof			
Man-made						
Cellulose-based						
acetate	572	300	842	450	7,700	18.4
rayon	350–464	177–240	788	420	7,400	18.6
Mineral						
glass	1,500	815	noncombustible			
Petroleum-based						
acrylic	549	287	986	530	1,300	18.2
aramid	decomposes above 800°F (427°C)					
modacrylic	455	235	will not support combustion; self-extinguishing			
novoloid	decomposes (converts to carbon)		and resists over 5,000°F (2,760°C); does not burn			
nylon	653	345	989	532	12,950	20.1
olefin (propylene)						18.6
polyester	734	390	1,040	560	9,300	20.6
saran	168	76	will not support combustion; self-extinguishing			
vinyon			will not support combustion; self-extinguishing			

Relative Flammability

Relative terms indicate the flammability of textile fibers: fibers are described as flammable, flame resistant, noncombustible, or fireproof. A flammable fiber is relatively easy to ignite and sustains combustion until it is consumed. A flame resistant fiber may have, for example, relatively high decomposition and ignition temperatures, a slow rate of burning, or a high LOI value. Noncombustible fibers do not burn or contribute significant amounts of smoke; they are not fireproof, however, since they can melt and decompose at high temperatures. A fireproof fiber is unaffected by fire. Asbestos is considered fireproof, although it may glow if heated to a sufficiently high temperature. The use of asbestos in consumer products and interior environments is limited, however, because it has been found to be a carcinogen. Table 11.2 includes a listing of the relative flammability of several fibers.

Table 11.2 RELATIVE FLAMMABILITY OF SELECTED TEXTILE FIBERS

Fireproof	Noncombustible	Flame resistant	Flammable
asbestos	glass	aramid	cotton
		novoloid	linen
		wool	rayon
		modacrylic	acetate
		vinyon	triacetate
		saran	acrylic
			nylon
			polyester
			olefin

Reducing Fiber Flammability

Flame resistance is engineered in natural cellulosic fibers by adding flame retardants to the greige goods. These agents are normally based on phosphorous or nitrogen and include various amounts of such compounds as diammonium phosphate $((NH_4)_2HPO_4)$, ammonium sulfate $((NH_4)_2SO_4)$, and boric acid (H_3BO_3). These compounds inhibit or halt the combustion process at some stage in the cycle. Flame resistance is engineered in man-made fibers by incorporating a compound based on chlorine or bromine in the polymer solution prior to extrusion.

STAGES OF AN INTERIOR FIRE

The principal concern of industry personnel, educators, government employees, and others engaged in fire-safety work is not for the damage sustained by textile products or other interior items—burned items can be repaired or replaced—but instead for the reduction of the hazard to life. They strive to minimize the likelihood of initial ignition and, in the event of fire, they seek to make the environment safer by preserving the means for quick and efficient egress from a burning area or structure.

The critical importance of preserving the possibility of safe egress is confirmed when the three distinct stages through which an interior fire progresses are examined. This examination will also confirm the value of early warning systems and automatic sprinkling systems.

Stage 1

A Stage 1 fire is schematized in Figure 11.1. Only the ignited item is burning. The overriding concern is that the fire remain localized. If, for example, a burning cigarette is carelessly dropped onto a carpet or an upholstered chair, the item should be designed to resist ignition or, if ignition occurs, should not propagate or spread the flame throughout the room, making it more challenging to extinguish the fire and more difficult to exit safely.

When a fire is small and isolated, smoke detectors or other alarm systems serve to alert residents. The early warning may enable occupants to contain the fire, preventing its growth to Stage 2.

Stage 2

A fire in Stage 2 is illustrated in Figure 11.2. Here, the fire has spread from the area of origin, igniting other items in its path. As the fire spreads and grows, more heat is generated and the air in the room becomes hotter and hotter. When sufficient heat has built up, all combustible items in the room burst into flames, producing a situation known as flashover.

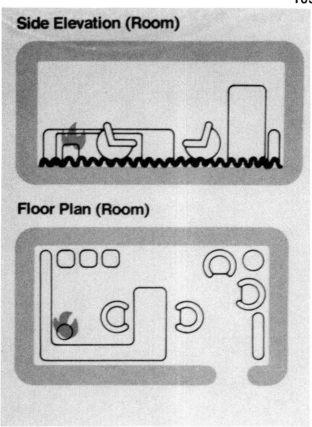

Figure 11.1 Stage 1 of an interior fire. (*Source:* I. A. Benjamin and S. Davis, *Flammability Testing for Carpet,* NBSIR 78-1436, Center for Fire Research, Institute for Applied Technology, National Bureau of Standards, Washington, D.C., April 1978.)

Automatic sprinkling systems, which are usually heat activated, can halt flame propagation, thus minimizing heat buildup and preventing flashover. The Federal Management Agency has found that using smoke detectors and automatic sprinkling systems in all buildings and residences could reduce overall injuries, loss of life, and property damage by at least 50 percent.[3]

Stage 3

In Stage 3 of an interior fire, shown schematically in Figure 11.3, the flames spread beyond the burning room into the corridor or passageway. In addition to the flames, a significant amount of heat may be radiating into the corridor as the fire spills out. If the fire spreads down the corridor, all exits may be blocked.

Fire researchers consider the three stages of fire growth when they design flammability test methods. Members of the Consumer Product Safety Commission and other regulatory agencies consider them when they establish flammability standards for selected interior textile products.

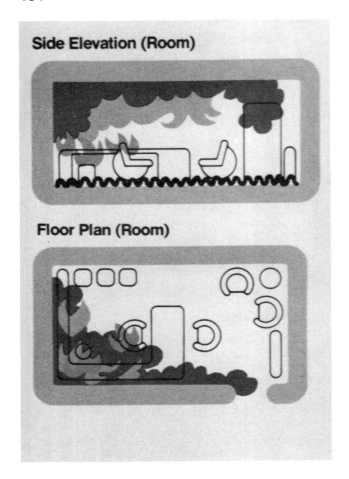

Figure 11.2 Stage 2 of an interior fire. (*Source:* I. A. Benjamin and S. Davis, Flammability Testing for Carpet, NBSIR 78-1436, Center for Fire Research, Institute for Applied Technology, National Bureau of Standards, Washington, D.C., April 1978.)

FLAMMABILITY TESTING

Various types of testing are used to measure the fire-related behavior of interior textile products and components. Currently, small-scale, large-scale, and full-scale procedures are used in this work.

Small-scale Test Methods

Small-scale test methods are used in the laboratory to measure specific flammability characteristics. Like other standard test methods, these are designed to simulate the conditions associated with real-life situations; in some test methods, for example, a lit cigarette is the source of heat for ignition. Small-scale tests enable the producer to make reasonably accurate predictions concerning the behavior of the item being tested in a Stage 1 fire. Several small-scale test methods and their role in performance standards are described in later units.

Large-scale Test Methods

Large-scale test methods are also laboratory procedures, but they use larger test specimens than do small-scale tests. A large-scale test method used on textile window coverings is discussed in Chapter 21, and a large-scale test method used on soft floor coverings is discussed and illustrated in Chapter 30.

Full-scale Testing

Full-scale testing facilities may be constructed to replicate a room or a corridor. Room-size facilities make possible observation of the progressive growth of an interior fire, and they are particularly useful in assessing the involvement of each of several items. Corridor-like facilities can be used to determine the effects various conditions have on a Stage 3 fire; results obtained with them underscore the importance of preserving a safe means of egress.

In the Life Safety Laboratory maintained by Owens-Corning Fiberglas Corporation, a replica of a typical hotel room has been constructed. For the test pictured in Figure 11.4, the room was furnished with conventional, as

Figure 11.3 Stage 3 of an interior fire. (*Source:* I. A. Benjamin and S. Davis, Flammability Testing for Carpet, NBSIR 78-1436, Center for Fire Research, Institute for Applied Technology, National Bureau of Standards, Washington, D.C., April 1978.)

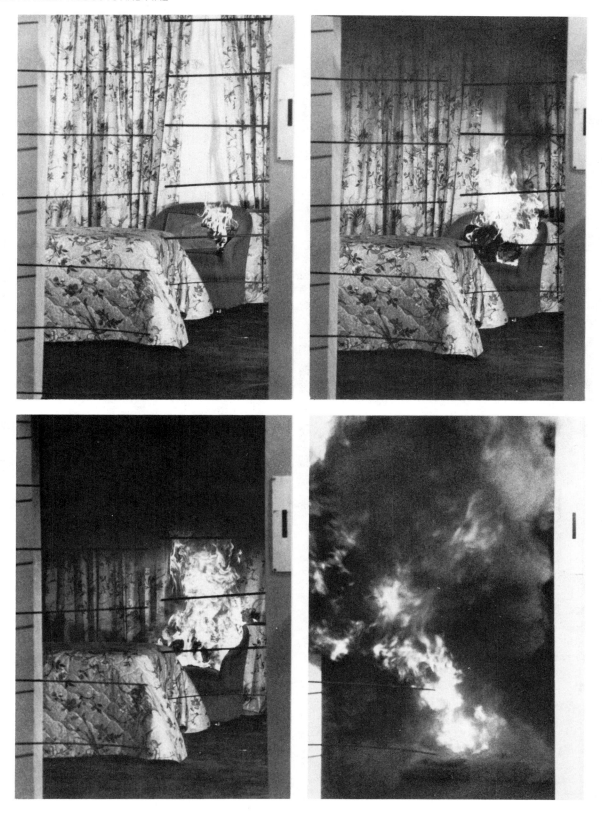

Figure 11.4 Full-scale fire test showing the growth of an interior fire from Stage 1 to Stage 2. The room was furnished with flammable items. (Courtesy of Owens-Corning Fiberglas Corporation.)

Figure 11.5 Full-scale test showing minimal flame propagation in a room furnished with some flame resistant items. (Courtesy of Owens-Corning Fiberglas Corporation.)

opposed to flame resistant, items. Flashover occurred within two and a half minutes after the newspaper-filled brown paper bag on the chair was ignited. For the test pictured in Figure 11.5, beddings composed of specially coated Fiberglas® glass and flame resistant carpet were used. Here, the fire did not spread beyond the immediate ignition site; the growth of the fire from Stage 1 to Stage 2 was prevented.

These investigations show that occupants of a room furnished with some flame resistant items would have more time for safe egress. Both tests make apparent the value of early warning systems and automatic sprinklers.

Additional full-scale room flammability tests are pictured in Figures 16.5 and 16.6 (pages 163 and 164). The former shows a different view of the fire test pictured in Figure 11.4.

Corridor-like testing facilities are maintained by the National Bureau of Standards. Using these facilities, fire researchers have confirmed that the amount of heat radiat-

ing onto a floor covering directly affects the distance flames spread in a Stage 3 fire.[4] Because such spreading may restrict or prevent safe egress, a small-scale test method including radiant heat as a condition is increasingly used to measure the flame spread of floor coverings intended for installation in corridors. The equipment and procedures used in this test are described in Chapter 30.

SUMMARY

In an effort to reduce the threat to life and property posed by flammable fabrics, the United States Congress passed the Flammable Fabrics Act and directed the Consumer Product Safety Commission to monitor the involvement of textile products in burn accidents. As a result, flammability performance standards have been established for carpet, rugs, and mattresses, and a standard has been proposed for upholstered furniture. The test methods adopted in these standards simulate the conditions of real-life situations, so that researchers and producers can make reliable predictions of in-use performance.

Several practices can widen the margin of fire safety beyond that provided by law. Residential and commercial consumers can select noncombustible fibers and fibers with inherent or engineered flame resistance. Smoke detectors can be installed to alert residents before a small fire spreads. When a fire extinguisher is readily available, the fire can then be extinguished, further property damage prevented, and personal injury avoided. Automatic sprinkling systems can be in place to halt the spreading of an uncontained fire, thus lessening the generation of smoke and lethal concentrations of toxic gases and preserving the means of egress to a safe area. Corridors leading to exits must be kept clear and the exits themselves clearly illuminated. Finally, of course, most textiles require an external source of heat for ignition. To reduce the frequency of ignition, consumers must handle the most common source of ignition burning cigarettes, and other smoking materials carefully.

NOTES

1. Federal Emergency Management Agency, "An Ounce of Prevention," U. S. Fire Administration, Washington, D.C., 3.

2. Michael J. Koroshys, "Flammability of Textiles," *American Dyestuff Reporter,* Vol. 58, No. 3, March 24, 1969, 20.

3. Federal Emergency Management Agency, "An Ounce of Prevention," U.S. Fire Administration, Washington, D.C., 4.

4. Francis E. W. Fung, Miles R. Suchmoel, and Philip L. Oglesby, *NBS Corridor Fire Tests: Energy and Radiation Models, NBS TN-794,* National Bureau of Standards, Washington, D.C., October 1973.

two

UPHOLSTERED FURNITURE COVERINGS AND FILLINGS

Unit Two focuses on upholstery coverings and fillings for commercial and residential furniture products. In Chapter 12, statistical profiles detail fiber and yarn usage in upholstery fabrics, including those channeled to transportation applications, and several textile upholstery fabrics are described. The production of nontextile upholstery fabrics, including genuine leather, simulated leather and suede, and vinyl, is reviewed in Chapter 13.

Chapter 14 presents several performance standards developed by members of the upholstered furniture industry. These standards, which are voluntary, recommend test methods and levels of performance and are intended to serve as guidelines for evaluating the end-use serviceability of finished upholstery fabrics. Most of the standards apply to physical attributes, but one is directed to cleanability and can help the consumer detemine what are appropriate cleaning agents. These agents and the proper procedures to follow in maintaining upholstery fabrics also are discussed in this chapter.

Chapter 15 reviews the different materials used to fill furniture, along with their performance characteristics. It also discusses methods of applying outercoverings to furniture framework and their various features.

Because fillings, fabric components, and exterior construction features collectively influence the degree of fire hazard posed by upholstered furniture, the voluntary and mandatory flammability standards currently in effect for these products are discussed in the last chapter in the unit.

chapter *12*

Textile Upholstery Coverings

- Fiber and Yarn Usage
- Nonpile Upholstery Fabrics
- Pile Upholstery Fabrics

Virtually every method of fabrication used to construct apparel fabrics is also used to construct upholstery coverings. Thus, the variety of fabrics available for use on furniture is as extensive as that available for apparel applications. The assortment includes fabrics that are essentially two-dimensional and fabrics that are are markedly three-dimensional. Some fabrics are composed entirely of simple yarns in simple, compact constructions, making for relatively great durability and little aesthetic interest. Others incorporate complex yarns in simple, loose constructions, providing much visual and tactile interest but less durability. Fabric patterns range in complexity, from small, geometric figures to large and elaborately detailed motifs. Pile upholstery fabrics are available in various construction densities and surface textures. Some pile fabrics are woven, some tufted, and some knitted.

Although virtually every natural and man-made fiber is used in textile upholstery fabric, current statistical profiles show that significant portions of the market are held by cotton and the noncellulosic fibers. Disclosure of the fiber composition is particularly appropriate today, as the use of noncellulosic fibers to simulate natural fibers in upholstery applications increases.

FIBER AND YARN USAGE

Currently, man-made fibers appear in most upholstery fabrics, including those produced for use in transportation applications. The dominance of spun yarns in both upholstery and transportation fabrics underscores an apparent preference of consumers and professionals for more decorative coverings.

Fiber Usage in Upholstery Fabrics

Frequently, fabrics manufactured for use as upholstery are also suitable for use as drapery fabric. The techniques used to gather and report statistical data reflect this suitability, since these products are grouped into a single end use category (Table 12.1).

The pattern of fiber usage in upholstery and drapery fabrics is changing. Since 1966, usage has shifted from the natural and man-made cellulosic fibers to the noncellulosic fibers, with usage of noncellulosic fibers increasing from approximately 91 million pounds in 1966 to more than 251 million pounds in 1985 and the market share held by these fibers increasing from 17 to 46 percent. To a large extent, these changes have resulted from the extensive range of features that can be engineered into the noncellulosic fibers, making them more attractive and serviceable.

Over the same twenty-year period, the usage of wool increased from 1.5 to 13.6 million pounds, increasing the

Table 12.1 FIBER USAGE IN UPHOLSTERY AND DRAPERY FABRICS
(million pounds)

| Year | Total fiber | Man-made fibers[a] | | | | | Cotton | Wool | Glass |
| | | Total | Cellulosic | | Noncellulosic | | | | |
			Yarn	Staple	Yarn	Staple			
1966	528.5	332.0	78.7	162.6	79.5	11.2	195.0	1.5	62.7
1984									4.0
1985	542.9	335.1	12.8	70.8	104.6	146.9	194.2	13.6	NA

[a]Man-made fiber end use is divided between cellulosic (rayon plus acetate fibers) and noncellulosic (nylon, polyester, acrylic, olefin, saran, spandex, and textile glass fiber). Yarn includes monofilaments, and olefin "yarn" also includes film fiber and spunbonded polypropylene. Staple includes tow and fiberfill.

Sources: Textile Economics Bureau, Inc., *Textile Organon,* Vol. 43, No. 11, November 1972, 166 and Vol. 57, No. 9, September 1986, 211.

share of the market captured by wool from a mere 0.28 percent to nearly 3 percent. While the natural beauty, resiliency, and inherent flame and stain resistance of wool fibers are valued characteristics, the relatively high cost of the fiber tends to limit its selection. Although the usage of cotton fibers in this period has declined slightly—largely as a result of competition from the noncellulosic fibers—it should be noted that this single natural fiber accounted for nearly 36 percent of the 1985 upholstery and drapery fabrics market.

Fiber Usage in Transportation Fabrics

The end use category of transportation fabrics includes automobile seat upholstery and slipcovers, sidewalls (the vertical portion of car seats), interior roof linings, and sheeting. The cotton poundages include the knit and woven fabric used as the backing for vinyl sheeting. The category also includes convertible automobile tops and re-

placement tops, as well as upholstery used in other modes of transportation, such as airplanes, railroad and subway cars, and buses. It does not include such things as seat padding, window channeling, and carpet and rugs.

The marked shift from cotton to the noncellulosic fibers in transportation fabrics (Table 12.2) can primarily be attributed to the advances made in man-made fiber processing. Such properties as soil repellency, high resiliency, and flame resistance can be directly engineered into man-made fibers, whereas finishing agents and treatments must be used to develop such features with cotton. Again, the relatively high cost of wool precludes its widespread selection, but its inherent flame resistance and resiliency make it an attractive choice when the budget is adequate.

The lack of a more marked increase from 1966 to 1985 in the total number of pounds of fiber used in the transportation market should not be interpreted as indicating a similar lack of growth in yardage production. The effect of fiber density must be considered. Noncellulosic fibers,

Table 12.2 FIBER USAGE IN TRANSPORTATION FABRICS
(million pounds)

| Year | Total fiber | Man-made fibers[a] | | | | | Cotton | Wool |
| | | Total | Cellulosic | | Noncellulosic | | | |
			Yarn	Staple	Yarn	Staple		
1966	83.7	18.7	1.1	7.4	9.4	0.8	65.0	b
1985	85.6	74.3	c	0.8	54.0	19.5	11.3	c

[a]Man-made fiber end use is divided between cellulosic (rayon plus acetate fibers) and noncellulosic (nylon, polyester, acrylic, olefin, saran, spandex, and textile glass fiber). Yarn includes monofilaments, and olefin "yarn" also includes film fiber and spunbonded polypropylene. Staple includes tow and fiberfill.

[b]Nominal amounts used (less than 50,000 pounds).

[c]Little or none of the fiber is used.

Sources: Textile Economics Bureau, Inc., *Textile Organon,* Vol. 43, No. 11, November 1972, 170, and Vol. 57, No. 9, September 1986, 212.

which accounted for some 86 percent of the 1985 market, are not as dense as cotton fibers (see Table 4.1). Thus, a greater amount of yardage can be produced from one pound of noncellulosic fibers than from one pound of cotton. Other factors responsible for this modest growth in fiber usage are the smaller size of many of today's automobiles and the recently depressed state of the domestic automotive industry. As consumers register their preference for more luxurious automotive interiors, however, industry analysts are forecasting an increase in the use of textile fabrics in automobiles, regardless of their size and price.[1] Woven and knitted fabrics are expected to continue replacing vinyl sheeting on seat cushions, seat backs, and door panels, and, with improvements in the lightfastness of automotive fabric dyes, on dashboards as well.

Disclosure of Fiber Composition. Upholstery and transportation fabrics offered to consumers and professionals in piece good form must be labeled in accordance with the provisions of the Textile Fiber Products Labeling Act. As noted in Chapter 10, the Wool Products Labeling Act of 1939 specifically exempts all upholsteries, and the TFPIA specifically exempts permanently incorporated outercovering fabrics.

The scope of the TFPIA also includes slipcovers, antimacassars (fabric covers used to protect upholstery from hair oil), tidies (decorative covers placed on the backs and arms of furniture), swatches, and samples. The required information may be listed on the end of a bolt of yardgoods and on a label or hangtag attached to a slipcover. With swatches less than two square inches in size, the information may appear in accompanying promotional matter. Other swatches and samples may be labeled with the required information or keyed to a catalog, indicating to prospective purchasers where the information can be obtained.

Dominance of Spun Yarns

The dominance of spun yarns in upholstery and transportation fabrics is evident from the data presented in Tables 12.1 and 12.2. Together, natural and man-made staple-length fibers accounted for more than 78 percent of the 1985 upholstery fabric market and for slightly less than 37 percent of the transportation fabric market. More pronounced textural effects and design features, which consumers and designers apparently consider relatively important to selection, can be produced more readily by spinning and plying processes than by throwing operations.

Noncellulosic staple-length fibers are used more extensively than are man-made cellulosic staple-length fibers and wool. To a large extent, this is the result of the increased use of spun yarns of polyester in lieu of spun yarns of rayon and the increasing use of spun yarns of acrylic or polypropylene olefin fibers to replace more expensive woolen yarns.

While the loops, nubs, and other textural features characteristic of complex spun yarns add aesthetic interest to upholstered furniture, prospective purchasers and specifiers should consider the possible effects of end use abrasion on the raised areas. Consumers and interior designers should also evaluate the hand of the fabric to confirm that novelty yarn features are not too harsh or rough for their comfort or that of their clients.

Multifilament Yarn Usage

Multifilament yarns are especially important in the transportation market. Whereas filament fibers accounted for approximately 11 percent of this market in 1966, they captured some 63 percent of the 1985 market. This increase may reflect the expanded use of textile fabrics in commercial transportation vehicles, installations that are subjected to a high level of use. The increase may also reflect the expanding use of textile upholstery in automobile interiors.

Today, filament-length fibers are used in more than a fifth of the upholstery fabrics produced for applications other than transportation vehicles. In order to produce a softer and warmer hand, increase covering power, and minimize the development of unsightly fuzz and pills, throwsters often introduce a three-dimensional form to the filaments by using one of the texturing processes illustrated in Figure 5.2 (page 35). For economy, ease of care, and strength, multifilament yarns composed of nylon are increasingly replacing acetate as a substitute for expensive silk filaments.

When stretch characteristics are needed in a woven upholstery fabric, manufacturers may incorporate a few yarns whose spandex filament cores are covered by fibers identical in color to the other yarns in the fabric. As noted in Table 4.2, spandex fibers have 500 to 700 percent elongation at break and 98 percent recovery after 200 percent strain. The requisite fabric elasticity can often be obtained when the elastomer accounts for as little as 3 percent of the total fabric weight.

NONPILE UPHOLSTERY FABRICS

Greige goods producers, dyers, printers, stylists, and converters work together to manufacture an expansive variety of nonpile and pile structures. Several of these are identified by specific fabric names. Traditionally, fiber composition was an important variable in the descriptions of these fabrics. Today, however, the increased use of the noncellulosic fibers has made fiber content less valuable as a distinguishing characteristic, and more useful descriptions are based on structural and appearance features. This section describes and illustrates nonpile upholstery fabrics.

Biaxially Woven Fabrics

Several relatively simple upholstery fabrics are produced with basic biaxial weaving patterns or a variation of these patterns. Several complex coverings are produced with a decorative dobby, surface-figure, or Jacquard interlacing pattern.

Plain-woven Fabrics. Homespun, tweed, and hopsacking are plain-woven upholstery fabrics. Homespun, pictured in Figure 12.1a, is made of heavy, coarse yarns that resemble hand-spun yarns. The use of complex speck yarns, shown in Figure 5.7c (page 38), adds distinctive color styling to tweed upholstery fabrics. Hopsacking (hopsack), shown in Figure 12.1b, may be made with a plain or a basket weave. This fabric's name is derived from its coarse, irregular yarns, which resemble the rough jute yarns of the gunny sacks use to store hops.

If plain weave and other simple fabrics are produced from smooth, multifilament yarns in loose constructions, converters may apply an adhesive compound, such as polyurethane, polyacrylonitrile, or latex, to the fabric back. The coating helps to prevent yarn slippage and yarn raveling. Yarn slippage is the sliding or "traveling" of warp or filling yarns, shown schematically in Figure 12.2. In patterned coverings, slippage distorts the shapes and details of the design motifs. Yarn slippage may also occur at seam-

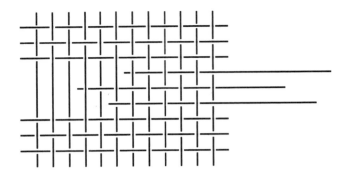

Figure 12.2 Yarn slippage.

lines, with the yarns moving away from the stitching and leaving a gap or opening; a testing procedure for evaluating slippage at seamlines is described in Chapter 14.

Yarn raveling occurs when yarns fall from cut edges of fabrics. This becomes a problem in upholstery when seam allowances have been closely trimmed to reduce bulk and the fabric has been pulled to fit smoothly over the frame and filling. The stress exerted on the seams with use may force the yarns in the narrow seam allowances to slide off the cut edge, weakening the seam and causing the stitching to rupture.

Consumers and interior designers should carefully inspect coated upholstery fabrics to determine whether or not the compound is visible on the face of the fabric. This

a) homespun

b) hopsacking

Figure 12.1 Plain-woven upholstery fabrics.

Figure 12.3 Adhesive backcoating on an upholstery fabric with low thread count.

problem generally occurs only when the coating has been used to compensate for low quality fabric construction. The coating on the fabric pictured in Figure 12.3 is color coordinated with the face yarns to make it as inconspicuous as possible. Because coatings cost less than fibers and yarns, coated fabrics are relatively inexpensive, but may not be durable in use.

Glazed chintz, pictured in Figure 20.2 (page 199), is produced for upholstery applications in somewhat heavier weights than that produced for window treatments. Chintz typically has a floral or geometric pattern printed in bright colors, as well as high surface luster produced by the use of a glazing finishing process. The fabric is often used in removable fitted slipcovers.

Basket-woven fabrics. A 4 x 4 basket pattern is often used to weave rope composed of sisal or other natural materials into chair seats and backs. Basket-woven upholstery fabrics often have warp and filling yarns of different colors. This styling is extensively used with upholstery designed and woven in Scandinavian countries.

Filling-rib woven fabrics. Upholstery fabrics produced with a filling-rib weave, including rep (repp),

faille, bengaline, and ottoman, are pictured in Figure 12.4. The crosswise ribs in these structures are generally covered by fine, crammed warp yarns. Rep has fine ribs, slightly larger than those characterizing taffeta; faille's ribs are slightly larger and flatter still, numbering approximately thirty-six per inch; bengaline has equally sized and spaced ribs, numbering about twenty-four per inch; and ottoman has large ribs that may be equally sized and spaced or varied in size and spacing.

Twill-woven Fabrics. Often different colors or sizes of warp and filling yarns are used to accentuate the visual diagonal of twill-woven upholstery fabrics. This kind of effect is evident in the plaid fabric pictured in Figure 12.5. Some of the blocks have houndstooth checks, jagged or broken check motifs said to resemble the tooth of a hound. Similar fabrics are frequently selected for use on contemporary furniture, especially on items designed for casual residential interiors.

Because the yarn interlacings in twill weaves occur less frequently than they do in plain weaves, higher thread counts can be used to produce strong, compactly constructed twill upholstery fabrics. Such fabrics are serviceable in high-use residential and commercial applications, including transportation installations; various color stylings can add visual interest.

A draft of a twill interlacing pattern used for weaving rope chair seats is shown in Figure 12.6. Although the distance over which the filling yarns float is twice that of the warp yarns, the use of the warp yarns in paired units results in an even twill.

Herringbone-woven fabrics. The reversed diagonals of herringbone twills make for a visual interest that may be enhanced by using different colors or sizes of warp and filling yarns. The effect may be augmented by weaving in narrow bands of warp yarns that are various shades of the same hue in an uneven, warp-faced interlacing pattern, as in the fabric in Figure 12.7. The term "strié" identifies this kind of coloration.

Satin-woven fabrics. Frequently, fine, bright acetate or nylon filaments are thrown into low-twist, multifilament yarns for the production of elegant satin upholstery fabrics. While such fabrics may have silk-like beauty, the low-twist yarns are relatively weak and the floating yarns may be easily snagged. Therefore, the application of these fabrics as furniture coverings should be limited to items that will not be subjected to high levels of use and abrasion. In most cases, upholstery fabric stylists use satin interlacings in combination with other, more durable interlacings, especially in elaborately patterned Jacquard fabrics.

a) rep

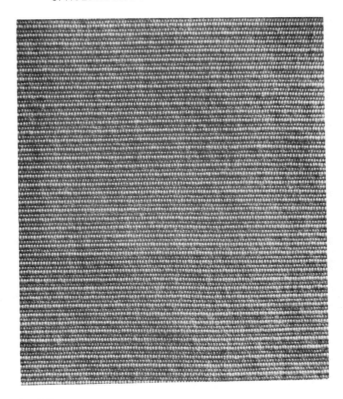

b) faille

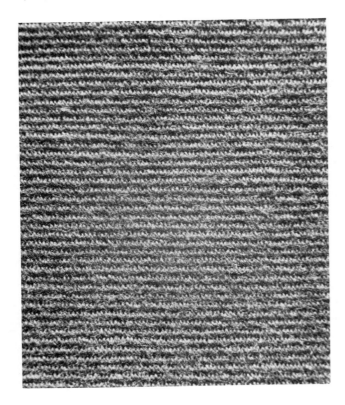

c) bengaline

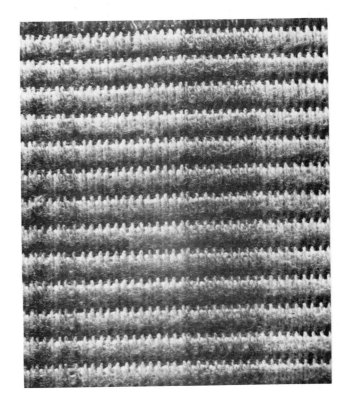

d) ottoman

Figure 12.4 Filling-rib woven upholstery fabrics.

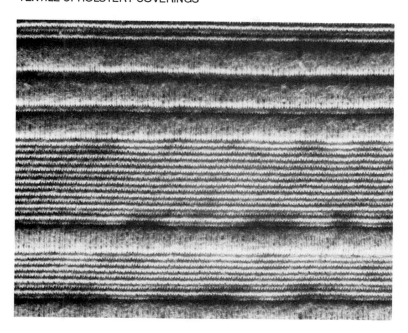

e) ottoman

Figure 12.4 Filling-rib woven upholstery fabrics.

Figure 12.5 Plaid houndstooth upholstery fabric.

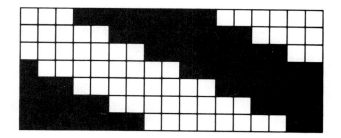

Figure 12.6 Pattern draft for a rope chair seat.

Figure 12.7 Herringbone upholstery fabric with a strié color effect.

Sateen-woven fabrics. A unique upholstery fabric is pictured in Figure 12.8. The interlacing pattern used is sateen, so the warp yarns appear infrequently on the face. The floating filling yarns are chenille and produce a velvet-like appearance and texture.

Dobby-woven fabrics. Some dobby-woven upholstery fabrics use a single color and two distinctly different interlacing patterns, one for the designs and another for the background. The slight difference in height between the designs and the ground highlights the motifs, as does the difference in the quantity of light that the yarns in the two interlacings reflect. Other dobby fabrics have yarns of two colors, one appearing in the background and one appearing in the designs. Some dobby fabrics have several colors for added visual interest.

The goose-eye twill shown in Figure 12.9c illustrates how a basic biaxial weave can be altered to produce a woven-in design. The motifs were formed by selectively reversing the direction of the visual diagonal, creating small diamond shapes said to resemble the eyes of a goose.

Surface-figure Woven Fabrics. One type of surface-figure weave, the dot or spot weave illustrated in Figure 20.11a (page 205), is used to produce decorative upholstery fabrics. In this weave, extra yarns are interlaced to create small, geometric motifs. The visual impact of the motifs is augmented by the use of contrastingly colored base yarns. For stability and weight, the lengths of the extra yarns floating across the back between the motif interlacings are left unclipped, as shown in Figure 12.10.

Jacquard-woven Fabrics. Several distinctive Jacquard-woven fabrics are manufactured for use as furniture

a) face

b) back

Figure 12.8 Chenille "velvet" upholstery fabric.

coverings. They may be produced with two, three, or four sets of yarns, but all have relatively elaborate motifs and multiple interlacing patterns.

Damask is woven from one set of warp yarns and one set of filling yarns. Removal of individual yarns would destroy the details of the motifs, as well as the fabric integrity. Damask fabrics are essentially two-dimensional and generally incorporate one or two colors. When a single

a) dobby bows

c) goose-eye twill

b) dobby squares

Figure 12.9 Dobby-woven upholstery fabrics.

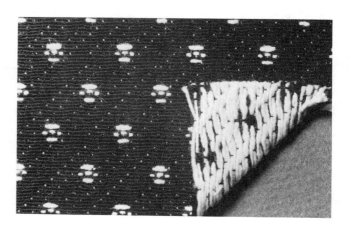

Figure 12.10 Unclipped spot upholstery fabrics.

color is used, the design motifs are highlighted because their interlacing pattern differs from that of the ground. They may be further accentuated by the use of yarns differing in brightness, level of twist, and degree of complexity from the yarns in the ground. The damask fabrics pictured in Figure 12.11 contain both simple and complex yarns.

Frequently, the motifs in damask have a plain, filling-rib, or sateen weave while the ground has a satin, twill, or filling-rib weave. The visual interest of the ground areas in the damask pictured in Figure 12.12 is enhanced by strié color styling.

Armure fabrics are distinguished by small motifs in which the warp yarns float on the face of the fabrics and the filling yarns float on the back, producing a pebbly surface. As in damask, two sets of yarns are used.

Liseré fabrics are woven from two sets of warp yarns and one set of filling yarns. One set of warp yarns is generally identical in color to the filling yarns; together, these form the ground. The second set of warp yarns is composed of a variety of single-colored yarns. In accordance with the planned pattern, different colors of these yarns are wound in bands of various widths on a separate loom beam. During weaving, the Jacquard mechanism raises these yarns and controls their interlacing to produce detailed motifs in lengthwise bands. In many liseré fabrics, the patterned bands are interspersed with satin-woven stripes (Figure 12.13).

Brocade is woven from more than one set of filling or weft yarns; the number of sets is governed by the number of colors that are to appear in the motifs. The extra yarns are generally woven in a filling-faced twill or sateen interlacing pattern, giving the design motifs a slightly raised effect (Figure 12.14). The ground is compactly constructed in a plain, twill, satin, or filling-rib weave.

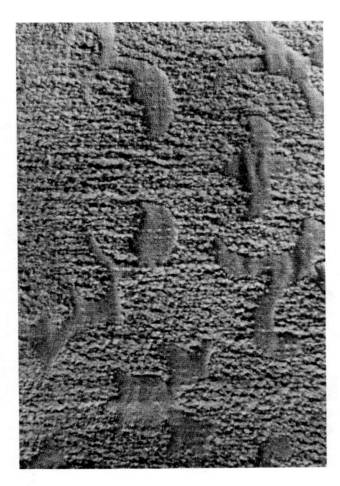

a) chenille damask

b) strié damask

Figure 12.11 Damask upholstery fabrics distinguished by the use of simple and complex yarns.

Figure 12.12 Damask upholstery fabric and close-up of motif.

Figure 12.13 Liseré upholstery fabric.

Figure 12.14 Brocade upholstery fabric.

Brocatelle is often made from one set of fine warp yarns, one set of heavy warp yarns, and two sets of filling yarns. The design motifs are formed by weaving the heavy warp yarns in a satin pattern, producing a more pronounced relief effect than seen in brocade, while the ground is twill (Figure 12.15). The motifs may also be padded by floating extra yarns behind them.

Jacquard-woven tapestry should not be confused with hand-woven tapestry. The two differ not only in their modes of production, but also in the manner in which the filling or weft yarns are handled. In machine-woven tapestry, these yarns are carried from one selvage to the other, interlacing into the face when needed; in hand-woven tapestry, they are interlaced within the perimeter of a design motif and then cut, leaving a short length of yarn handing fringe-like on the back. Machine-woven tapestry may also be made of many sets of yarns.

Like hand-woven tapestries, Jacquard-woven tapestries often have picture-like motifs. Yarns not used in the face of these fabrics are floated across the back, producing a mirror-image pattern of opposite colors (Figure 12.16). The fabric is not reversible, however, because the lengthy floats would be snagged and ruptured in use.

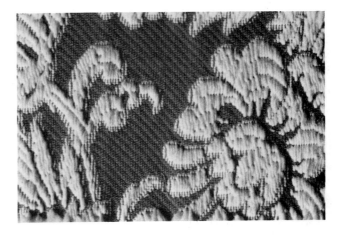

Figure 12.15   Brocatelle upholstery fabric.

Because the motifs and pattern repeats of some machine-woven tapestries resemble those of hand-stitched needlepoint accents (see Figure 35.5, page 384), they are commonly referred to as "needlepoint weave" fabrics. Although the designs of these fabrics are simple and geomet-

a) face

b) back

Figure 12.16   Jacquard-woven tapestry upholstery fabric.

ric, as shown in Figures 12.17 and 12.18a, they cannot be woven on a dobby loom; a Jacquard mechanism is required to control the placement of the various colors and the interlacing of the many sets of yarns.

A distinguishing characteristic of Jacquard-woven tapestries is that the various colors are introduced in crosswise or lengthwise bands. When the colors in a band are not used in the face designs, they are interlaced in the back, creating colored bands or stripes on the back side of the fabric (Figure 12.18b).

Figure 12.17 "Needlepoint weave" tapestry.

Fabrics woven of three or more sets of yarns, including liseré, brocade, brocatelle, and tapestry, may be classified as doublecloth fabrics. Other Jacquard-woven fabrics, including some tapestries, are also doublecloths, but they are further distinguished by the formation of enclosed "pockets," areas where there is no interlacing between two distinct fabric structures that face one another. As shown

schematically in Figure 12.19, the face of the pocket is composed of one set of warp yarns and one set of filling yarns, and the back of a second set of warp yarns and a second set of filling yarns. These pockets may show up in the motifs or in the ground; closure occurs where the positions of the face yarns and the back yarns are shifted at the juncture of the motifs and the ground.

In matelassé, the pockets are formed in the motifs. The mutual interlacing of the multiple sets of yarns is planned to produce the appearance of quilting stitches. When a third set of filling yarns is floated in the pockets, the designs stand out in relief, puffing the fabric and enhancing the quilt-like appearance (Figure 12.20).

Cloque is another doublecloth fabric in which interlacings of the four sets of yarns are planned to simulate the appearance of quilting stitches. As shown in Figure 12.21a, the mutual interlacings, strategically positioned, create a pattern on the solid-colored surface. Unlike matelassé, cloque is an essentially flat fabric, since the pockets are not padded.

Because Jacquard-woven upholstery fabrics have high production and materials costs, they may be comparatively expensive. Nevertheless, their richly patterned surfaces prompt many designers and consumers to give them priority in the furnishings budget.

Triaxially Woven Fabrics

Triaxially woven fabrics (Figure 6.20, page 58) display uniform stretch in all directions and high strength in relation to their weight.[2] Because they easily conform to curves and resist tearing, they are used to cover molded furniture frames and automobile seats.

Knitted Fabrics

Virtually all knitted upholstered furniture coverings are nonpile structures produced by interlooping simple yarns with an interlock stitch (Figure 7.7, page 63). This stitch helps ensure that the fabrics will be serviceable in end use. These fabrics cannot be varied by incorporating complex yarns or by altering structural features, but textile stylists, often with the assistance of a computer, can provide variety by specifying the use of two colors of yarns, Jacquard patterns, printed patterns, heather colorations, or cross-dyed effects.

The elasticity and flexibility of knitted fabrics make them particularly suitable for use as coverings on curved furniture frames. The loops of the fabric open slightly under stress, allowing the fabric to fit smoothly over the filling and frame. Upholstery knits are generally composed of nylon fibers, which can be heat set to impart dimensional stability and resiliency. Moreover, unlike other weft knitting stitches, the interlock stitch is resistant to running and snagging.

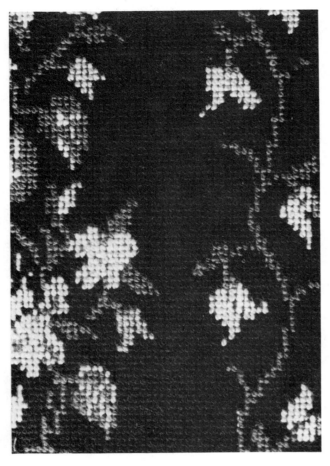

a) face

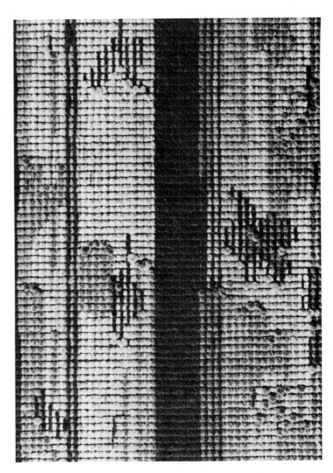

b) back

Figure 12.18 Tapestry showing characteristic color bands on fabric back.

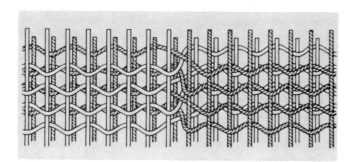

Figure 12.19 Formation of "pockets" in doublecloth Jacquard fabrics. (Courtesy of Brickel Associates Inc.)

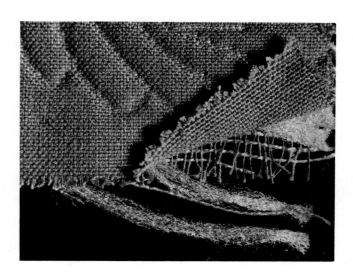

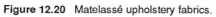

Figure 12.20 Matelassé upholstery fabrics.

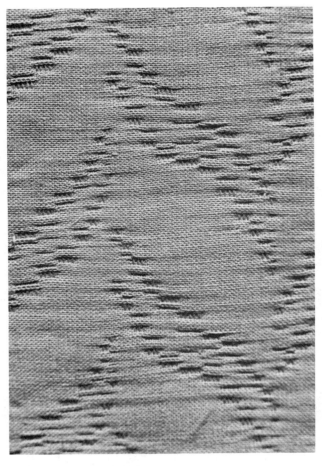

a) face

b) back

Figure 12.21 Cloque upholstery fabric.

PILE UPHOLSTERY FABRICS

The assortment of pile fabrics available for use as upholstered furniture coverings includes several whose pile yarns are uniformly distributed over the fabric surface, as well as several whose pile yarns are strategically placed to create a patterned layer. The techniques used to produce woven pile fabrics were described and illustrated in Chapter 6, and those used to produce knitted pile and tufted fabrics were discussed in Chapter 7.

Woven Pile Fabrics

Two filling pile fabrics, corduroy and velveteen, are used as furniture coverings. Both have a cut-pile surface texture and are normally composed of cotton. The surface of most corduroy upholstery fabric is uniformly covered with relatively wide and densely constructed wales (Figure 12.22).

Figure 12.22 Corduroy upholstery fabric.

Among the upholstery fabrics produced by interlacing extra warp yarns with base yarns are velvet, velour, friezé, and grospoint. With the exception of grospoint and some friezé fabrics, these coverings have cut-pile textures.

Velvet is normally woven to have a uniform pile surface. A variation in velvet upholstery is produced by omitting selected pile yarns and thus exposing some portions of the base fabric. These fabrics, called voided velvets, may have even greater aesthetic interest when a Jacquard mechanism has been employed to control the strategic placement of various colors of pile yarns. In the fabric pictured in Figure 12.23, the voided areas define the shapes of the design motifs forming the pile layer, while Jacquard patterning creates the colored details appearing within each motif. Jacquard patterning may also be used with level-surfaced velvet.

Figure 12.24 Crushed velvet upholstery fabric.

Figure 12.23 Jacquard-patterned voided velvet upholstery fabric.

In most velvet upholstery fabrics, only a slight nap is introduced. In panné velvet, however, a pronounced nap augments the luster contributed by bright fibers, which are often rayon. The effects of pile yarn orientation on surface reflection are readily seen in the crushed velvet pictured in Figure 12.24.

Velour, which is generally produced by the over-the-wire construction technique, has a slightly deeper pile and a more pronounced nap than velvet. Most velour is composed of cotton fibers, which give the fabric a soft, warm hand.

Friezé (frisé) upholstery fabrics normally have a level, uncut-pile surface made of multifilament yarns composed of stiff, strong nylon fibers. For variety, manufacturers may incorporate more than one color of pile yarns, expose areas of the base fabric (Figure 12.25a), or selectively shear some pile loops to vary the level of surface luster (Figure 12.25b).

Grospoint, pictured in Figure 12.26, has a level surface with pronounced loops larger than those characteristic of friezé. Multifilament nylon yarns are often used in the loops to augment their durability. Surface patterns may be introduced by exposing areas of the base fabric and by combining two or more colors of pile yarns. Grospoint fabrics are frequently used for covering office chairs and the bottom and back cushions installed in transportation vehicles.

a) areas of base fabric exposed

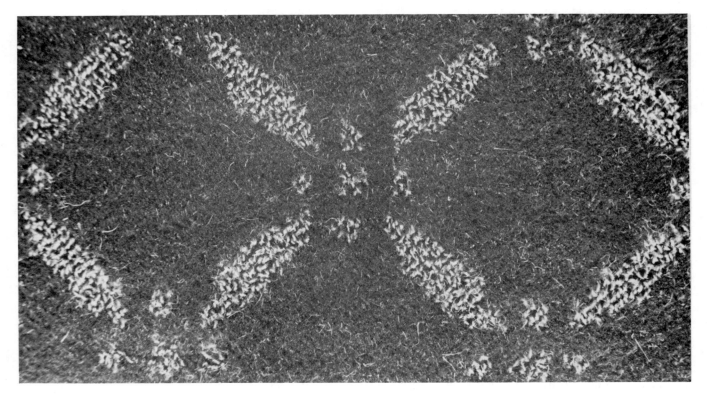

b) cut and uncut surface

Figure 12.25 Friezé upholstery fabrics.

a) uniform surface

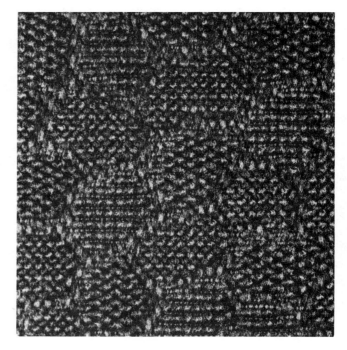

b) areas of base fabric exposed

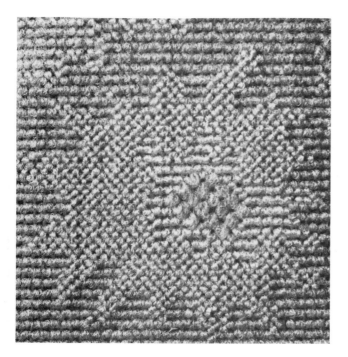

c) patterned surface

Figure 12.26 Grospoint upholstery fabrics.

Knitted Pile Fabrics

A limted number of knitted upholstery fabrics have a pile layer. Generally, these structures are used more frequently as bedcoverings than as furniture coverings (see Chapter 33).

Tufted Fabrics

Over the past twenty years, a number of textile firms have succeeded in engineering tufting machines that can produce the pile construction density required in tufted upholstery fabrics. High density is necessary to prevent exposure of the base fabric, especially on curved areas of furniture. Today, some machines can insert some 400 pile yarns per square inch of base fabric. Together with the high rate of production characteristic of tufting, these developments may result in increased use of the technique for upholstery fabric production.

SUMMARY

Both upholstery and transportation fabrics are predominantly composed of man-made fibers, although a significant amount of upholstery fabric is made of cotton. The widespread use of noncellulosic fibers is largely the result of fiber engineering that enables manufacturers to introduce desirable properties during synthesis and production.

The extensive use of cotton and the growing use of staple-length noncellulosic fibers underscore the importance of complex spun yarns in upholstered furniture coverings. Such yarns contribute decorative interest, but may be ruptured and abraded more readily than simple, smooth yarns.

Many nonpile and pile upholstery fabrics are produced by combining yarns in weaving, knitting, and tufting operations. The balance of the upholstery fabric assortment is produced by converting polymer solutions or raw animal skins into nontextile coverings. These structures are discussed in the following chapter.

NOTES

1. Kenneth Chanko, "Fabric Use in Autos Up, Vinyl Fading," *Daily News Record,* New York, June 14, 1982, 1, 11.

2. Wayne C. Trost, "Triaxial Weaving," *Modern Textiles Magazine,* June 1973, 60.

chapter *13*

Nontextile Furniture Coverings

- Genuine Leather Upholstery
- Vinyl and Simulated Leather and Suede Fabrics

Nontextile furniture coverings are composed of elements other than textile fibers and yarns. Some of these coverings, including simulated leather fabrics, are produced directly from polymer solutions; others, specifically genuine leather fabrics, are converted from the raw skins and hides of animals. It should be noted that leather is composed of a network of tiny fibers, but these fibers are not classified as textile fibers.

Along with the relatively high cost of skins and hides, the lengthy and expensive processing required to convert them into finished coverings puts genuine leather upholstery beyond the financial reach of many residential and commercial consumers. Recognizing this, producers have developed some apparently successful techniques for manufacturing simulated leather coverings. When furniture manufacturers use these coverings, they should follow specific labeling guidelines.

GENUINE LEATHER UPHOLSTERY

The basic structures used in manufacturing genuine leather coverings—raw skins and hides—are "fabricated" by various animals in assorted sizes, shapes, and thicknesses. Skins, retrieved from such small animals as lambs, goats, and calves, are thinner than hides and have an average size that does not normally exceed approximately 9 square feet. Hides, retrieved from such large ani-mals as deer, horses, and cattle, on average reach a maximum size of about 25 square feet. Because heavier and larger pieces of leather are required for upholstery applications, hides are usually selected, and they are processed whole.

Composition and Structure of Raw Hides

The processes used in producing leather upholstery can be better understood if the composition and structural features of raw hide are first examined. As shown schematically in Figure 13.1, raw hide has three distinct sections: the epidermis, the corium, and the flesh layer.

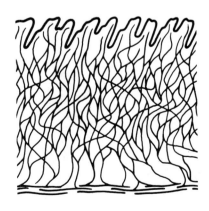

Figure 13.1 Schematic illustration of the cross section of raw hide.

The indentations in the top layer, the epidermis, are the hair follicles or pores. After the hair is removed, the exposed pores are seen as the grain markings, a surface feature found naturally only in coverings produced from the topmost layer of the hide. The central portion of the hide, the corium, is a network of interlaced bundles of tiny fibers composed of a protein called collagen. The fibrous bundles are surrounded by gelatinous matter. The bottommost portion of the hide is flesh tissue.

The processing of raw skins and hides is an involved procedure that may be divided into four major operations: curing and cleaning, tanning, coloring, and finishing. These operations are usually carried out by a single firm in a vertical manufacturing operation.

Curing and Cleaning

Processing begins with curing—salting the raw hides. Curing retards bacterial action, helping prevent putrefaction or decomposition, and it also removes the gelatinous matter from the corium. The hides must be thoroughly cleaned, defleshed, and dehaired before further processing. If the hides are thick enough to be split into multiple layers, the splitting will also be done at this stage, prior to tanning.

Tanning

In earlier times, tanning solutions were often made from tannins extracted from such sources as tree bark. Because these vegetable tanning agents are slow-acting, they are rarely used in commercial tanning operations. Today, tanning solutions are composed of mineral substances, such as chromium-based salts, and oils. The cured and cleaned hides are immersed in the solution, where the tanning agents react with the collagen, rendering the fibers insoluble. The agents and oils fill the spaces that were formerly filled by the gelatinous materials. The hides are now soft, water- and mildew-resistant, and pliable leathers.

Coloring

Coloring may be called for to camouflage an uneven natural color or to introduce currently popular fashion colors. The color may be applied by a piece-dyeing or a surface-dyeing operation.

In piece dyeing, referred to in the leather industry as drum dyeing, the tanned leather is rotated in large vessels filled with dye liquor. Piece-dyed coverings may be described in marketing as having an "aniline finish," a phrase that refers to the use of aniline dyestuffs, not finishing agents. In surface dyeing, pigments are mixed with binding agents and spread or brushed over the surface of the leather; this technique is actually a type of staining and colors the surface portion only.

Finishing

Finishing operations may involve the application of lubricants and softening agents to increase the suppleness of the leather. Imperfect areas of grain may be corrected by gently abrading the surface or by shaving a thin film off the surface. If the natural grain is very imperfect, mechanical embossing operations may be employed to impart attractive markings. Resins, waxes, and lacquer-based compounds may be applied and polished for a glazed finish. The high gloss characteristic of glazed leather is shown in Figure 13.2a. Compounds used in glazing also increase the moisture resistance of the leather.

Finished leather fabrics are labeled with such terms as full-grain leather, top-grain leather, and split leather. Full-grain leather's natural grain markings have not been corrected or altered in any way. Top-grain leather (Figure 13.2b) has undergone minor corrections to its natural grain markings.

Split leather is produced from a central portion of the hide; since the top layer of the hide is not present in split leather coverings, no natural grain markings appear. Split leather may not be as durable as full- and top-grain leathers.

Genuine suede—leather fabric produced with the flesh side of the hide exposed—is not used in upholstery because of its habit of crocking or rubbing off color. Laboratory procedures to evaluate crocking are reviewed in the following chapter.

VINYL AND SIMULATED LEATHER AND SUEDE FABRICS

Vinyl and simulated leather fabrics are produced by extruding or expanding polymer solutions. Simulated suede fabrics are produced with selected finishing operations.

Extruding Film Sheeting

The compounds used most often to create vinyl and simulated leather fabrics include polyvinylchloride and polyurethane. Solutions of these compounds are extruded as film sheeting, using the process described in Chapter 7. To provide the dimensional stability required for upholstery applications, the sheeting is bonded to a supporting fabric, generally a conventional knitted, woven, bonded-web, or spunlaced fabric.

Embossing Grain Markings. The grain markings that distinguish full- and top-grain leathers are introduced to simulated leathers by embossing. This is accomplished

a) glazed leather

b) top-grain leather

Figure 13.2 Genuine leather upholstery.

by pressing a metal-coated die that has been prepared with the desired markings into the surface of the film.

Expanding Polymer Coatings

Polymer solutions may be expanded by incorporating air into the compounds. The effect of this expansion is similar to that produced by whipping cream or egg whites: the apparent, but not the actual, volume is increased. The expanded polymer solution is then applied to a base fabric as a coating. Again, embossing can be used to impart grain markings.

Polymer films and coatings have little or no porosity. Because of this lack of breathability, many people find these fabrics uncomfortable, especially in hot or humid weather.

Simulating Genuine Suede

Upholstery coverings that appear to be genuine suede are actually simulated structures. Two operations, flocking and sueding, are used to produce these fabrics.

Flocking. An electrostatic flocking operation is generally used to produce simulated suede. One of the arrangements illustrated in Figure 13.3 is used. Deposition of the flock is followed by sueding.

Sueding. In sueding operations, sandpaper-covered disks revolve against the flocked surface. Unlike brushing and smoothing finishes, which raise and orient pile yarns in one direction, and unlike napping finishes, which raise fiber ends, sueding roughens the surface, generally orienting the flock in every direction. However, in Ultrasuede®, a simulated suede marketed by the Skinner Division of Springs Industries, Inc., the flock is given a directional lay or nap.

The durability of a flocked and sueded surface is determined by the cohesiveness of the substrate, resin, and flock. The surface must resist abrasive forces and the resin must be stable to cleaning agents.

Simulated leather and suede fabrics are used extensively to cover dining chairs and the seats, backs, and armrests in automobiles. Apart from any damage caused by cutting or puncturing, heavier vinyl and urethane fabrics can withstand the high levels of use in mass transit vehicles.

Labeling Guidelines

As noted in Chapter 10, labeling guides are advisory in nature and are issued to help members of an industry segment avoid unfair and deceptive marketing practices. Included in the FTC Guides for the Household Furniture Industry, which became effective on March 21, 1974, are

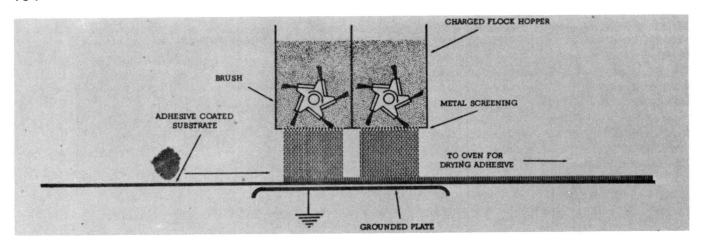

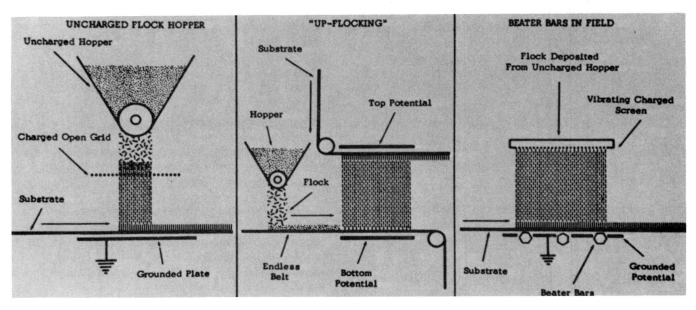

Figure 13.3 Various electrostatic flocking arrangements. (Courtesy of Fibers Division, Monsanto Chemical Co.)

provisions specifically applying to the labeling of non-leather upholstery coverings that resemble genuine leather. They are intended to ensure that the prospective purchaser is not misled by the appearance of the covering.

In marketing, industry members should conspicuously disclose facts concerning the composition of nonleather upholstery coverings. This may be done by disclosing the true composition of the sturcture, for example, vinyl or fabric-backed vinyl, or by stating that the material is not what it appears to be, that is, it is simulated leather, imitation leather, or not leather. Trade names denoting non-leather coverings may not include the words "hide," "skin," or "leather." Homophones of these words, such as "hyde," may be used as long as facts concerning the composition of the fabric are disclosed as described.

SUMMARY

Various techniques are used to convert raw hides and polymer solutions into furniture coverings. Hides undergo lengthy processing, including curing and cleaning, tanning, coloring, and finishing. Polymer solutions may be converted into film sheetings or expanded coatings. To simulate the surface appearance of full- and top-grain leathers, manufacturers emboss films and coatings with grain markings.

Producers have apparently been successful in simulating the appearance of natural leather coverings. The FTC has issued guidelines advising the disclosure of material facts on nonleather structures to ensure that consumers are not misled by the appearance of the simulated fabrics.

chapter *14*

Evaluation and Maintenance of Finished Upholstery Fabric

• Standards for Structural Qualities
• Standards for Physical Performance Properties
• Standards for Color Consistency and Retention
• Maintenance of Outercovering Fabrics

The appearance and serviceability of finished upholstery fabrics are influenced by the characteristics of the components used and the quality of the manufacturing processes employed. Although quality finishing can improve the performance and enhance the visual features of fabrics, it cannot compensate for the use of inferior fibers and yarns, unstable colorants, poor pattern registration, or shoddy fabrication. Similarly, the use of high quality components and fabrication techniques cannot make up for poor fabric conversion. This interdependence encouraged representatives from all segments of the industry to cooperate in establishing sets of standards for finished upholstery fabrics, one for knitted structures and one for woven structures. The latter will be reviewed in this chapter.

The collection of standards established by industry representatives, "Woven Upholstery Fabric Standards," is based on ASTM D 3597-77 Standard Specification for Woven Upholstery Fabrics—Plain, Tufted, or Flocked. This collection includes standards pertaining to various appearance features, such as uniformity of color, shading due to pile distortion, variations in pattern repeats, and colorfastness. Such structural qualities as bow and skew and such performance properties as dimensional stability and cleanability are also covered by standards.

The cleanability standard for upholstery fabric is based on the stability of applied colorants when they are exposed

to water and to solvent according to prescribed testing procedures. Manufacturers may use the results of such tests to help determine what agents should be used in the overall maintenance of a fabric. The need for overall cleaning can be delayed, however, if routine care and immediate stain removal are consistently used to maintain an outercovering.

Use of the industry standards is strictly voluntary; minimum or maximum levels of performance are recommended, not mandated. These standards do, however, identify properties that should be considered when selecting woven upholstery fabrics, and they provide a basis for evaluating quality and predicting end use serviceability.

STANDARDS FOR STRUCTURAL QUALITIES

Industry members came up with two Upholstery Fabric Standards (UFS) concerning the structural qualities of finished upholstery. One pertains to flaws and defects and the other to yarn alignment.

Flaws and Defects

Converters should carefully examine finished upholstery fabrics for the presence of unsightly flaws and defects. According to industry guidelines, flat-woven fabrics, such as lightweight printed cotton fabrics, should have no more than an average of one flaw or defect every 7 linear yards with no more than seven flaws or defects in any 50-yard length. Woven-pile, tufted, and flocked fabrics should have no more than an average of one flaw or defect every 5 linear yards with no more than ten flaws or defects in any 50-yard length.

Yarn Alignment

Problems caused by the use of off-grain upholstery fabrics are illustrated in Figure 14.1. Furniture items appear to be sagging when covered with bowed fabric, and crooked when covered with skewed fabric. These problems are emphasized when colored yarns have been used to create such woven-in linear patterns as stripes and plaids.

Although some properties may be measured by more than one test method, we will discuss here the method that would be recommended in the event of a controversy between a buyer and a seller.

Tear Strength

ASTM D 2262-71 (76) Standard Test Method of Woven Fabrics by The Tongue (Single Rip) Method (Constant-Rate-of-Traverse Tensile Testing Machine) may be used to evaluate the force required to continue or propagate a tear in a fabric under specified conditions. The test

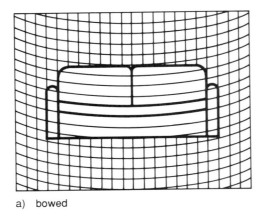

a) bowed

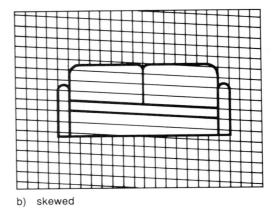

b) skewed

Figure 14.1 Effects of bowed and skewed yarn alignments on the appearance of upholstered furniture items.

Measurements of bow are taken at the maximum point of distortion in three different places along a 3-yard length of fabric, as shown in Figure 14.2 Industry guidelines recommend that the average of these measurements not exceed 0.5 inch.

The measurements of maximum distortion produced by skew are taken parallel to and along a selvage, as shown in Figure 14.3. Three measurements are made in different places along a 3-yard length of fabric; the average of these values should not exceed 1.0 inch.

STANDARDS FOR PHYSICAL PERFORMANCE PROPERTIES

Table 14.1 summarizes the Upholstery Fabric Standards for various physical properties. In most cases, the test methods recommended are those included in ASTM D 3597; they were selected because their results can provide a reasonable basis for predicting end use performance.*

results can predict the likelihood that a small cut or puncture would become a large tear with continued use of the upholstered item.

Test Specimens and Procedures. Test specimens are cut to a size of 3 by 8 inches, with the short dimension corresponding to the direction to be tested. A 3-inch cut is made at the center of and perpendicular to the short side of each specimen, forming two "tongues" or "tails."

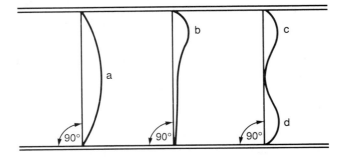

Figure 14.2 Measuring maximum distortion produced by filling bow. (*Source:* Joint Industry Fabric Standards Committee, *Woven Upholstery Fabrics Standards*, 1980, 17.)

* The full text of the test methods may be reviewed in the Annual Book of ASTM Standards, Part 32.

Table 14.1 WOVEN UPHOLSTERY FABRIC STANDARDS FOR PHYSICAL PROPERTIES

UFS number	Property	Test methods	Standard
1979-11	tear strength	ASTM D 2262 ASTM D 1424	category I: 6.0 lbs, min. category II: 4.5 lbs, min. category III: 4.0 lbs, min.
1979-12	elongation (stretch)	UFS 1979-12 (referee method) ASTM D 1682	category I: 2% min. 5% max. category II: 1% min. 5% min. category III: 1% min. 5% max.
1979-13	dimensional stability	ASTM D 3597	warpwise or fillwise 5% shrink, max. 2% gain, max.
1979-14	tensile strength	ASTM D 1682 breaking load- grab method	50 lbs, min.
1979-15	seam breaking strength	ASTM D 3597 (using 7.0 stitches per inch)	warpwise—50 lbs, min. fillwise—50 lbs, min.
1979-16	abrasion	ASTM D 1175 oscillatory cylinder	light duty: 3000 cycles, min. medium-duty: 9,000 cycles, min. heavy duty-15,000 cycles, min.
1979-18	yarn slippage	dynamic seam fatigue method	7,000 cycles, min.

Category I: flat, woven fabrics except lightweight, printed cotton fabrics (less than 8 oz./sq.yd.).
Category II: woven pile fabrics, tufted fabrics, and flocked fabrics.
Category III: lightweight, printed cotton fabrics (less than 8 oz./sq.yd.).
"Light," "medium," and "heavy duty" are explained in Table 14.2.

Source: Joint Industry Fabric Standards Committee, *Woven Upholstery Fabric Standards 1980, 6–7.*

After conditioning the specimens for a minimum of 24 hours in a controlled atmosphere of 70 ± 2°F and 65 ± 2 percent relative humidity, each is successively placed in paired clamps on a constant-rate-of-traverse (CRT) testing machine. One tongue is secured in the jaws of the upper clamp and one tongue is secured in the jaws of the lower clamp; thus, opposite sides of the specimen are exposed to the operator. As the machine operates, the lower clamp moves downward at a constant rate for a distance of 3 inches. The loads required to tear each specimen are automatically recorded.

Analysis of Results. The five peak loads recorded during tearing of a specimen are averaged. The tear strength values for all replicate specimens are then averaged and reported.

Performance Guidelines. The guidelines for tear strength include three levels of performance. The levels are based on differences in the construction and weight of upholstery fabrics. UFS 1979-11 notes that Category III fabrics, lightweight printed cotton structures, are generally rated "delicate"; therefore, these fabrics should not be but-

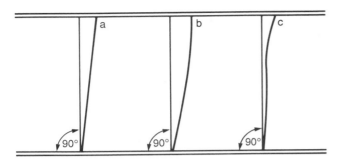

Figure 14.3 Measuring maximum distortion produced by filling skew. (*Source:* Joint Industry Fabric Standards Committee, *Woven Upholstery Fabrics Standards,* 1980, 18.)

toned excessively nor should furniture covered with these fabrics be placed where they will receive heavy use.

Elongation and Tensile Strength

The apparent elongation and tensile strength of upholstery fabrics can be determined in one testing procedure. UFS 1979-12 and 1979-14 specify that ASTM D 1682 Breaking Load-Grab Method be used for these evaluations.

Test Specimens and Procedures. In the breaking load-grab method, only a part of the specimen is gripped in the clamps. Each specimen is 4 inches wide and held in the center by 1-inch wide clamps, as shown in Figure 14.4. To ensure accurate alignment when securing the specimen in the clamps, a line is drawn 1.5 inches from the long edge of the specimen. A constant-rate-of-extension (CRE) or a constant-rate-of-traverse (CRT) testing machine may be used.

Analysis of Results. The breaking load in pounds is recorded for each replicate specimen tested, and the average of these values is calculated and reported. The apparent elongation is expressed as the percentage increase in length based on the distance between the clamps, which is normally 3 inches (% elongation at rupture = [length stretched/original length] x 100).

Performance Guidelines. As detailed in Table 14.1, the UFS guidelines for elongation differ for different categories of fabrics, but a minimum breaking load of 50 pounds is recommended for all fabrics, regardless of construction and weight.

Dimensional Stability

Upholstery fabrics must maintain their original dimensions, within reasonable limitations. With permanently attached, as well as removable, furniture coverings, there should be no prolonged bagging and sagging of the fabric after a person rises from the item; nor should there be excessive growth of the fabric in cleaning. Excessive shrinkage of the fabric in use or cleaning would cause the fabric to become smaller than the filling, distorting the three-dimensional form of the cushions. It would also place stress on the fabric seams and zipper closures, causing them to ripple or split.

Industry representatives recommend that procedures set out in ASTM D 3597 be followed in measuring the dimensional stability of upholstery fabrics. Measurements of the relaxation shrinkage or growth of the specimens are made after exposing them to water; measurements of elastic recovery after extension of the specimens are not made.

Test Specimens and Procedures. In preparation for testing, fabric specimens are cut 12 inches square and marked with sets of three 10-inch gauge distances in both the warp direction and the filling direction, as illustrated in Figure 14.5.

The marked specimens are submerged in distilled water for 10 ± 1 minutes. They are then placed on horizonatal screens and allowed to dry for 24 hours.

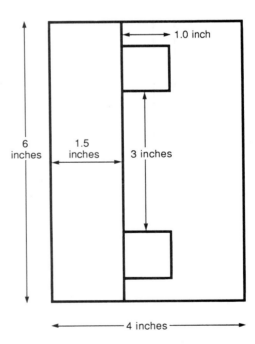

Figure 14.4 Preparation and placement of a specimen for measuring the breaking load and apparent elongation of fabrics by the grab method.

Analysis of Results. The distance between the gauge marks are measured in each direction. Separate averages are then determined for the warp and the filling. The percentage of change is calculated as directed in the following equations:

$$\% \text{ shrinkage} = [\,(A - B)/A\,] \times 100$$
$$\% \text{ gain} = [\,(B - A)/A\,] \times 100$$

where A = distance between gauge marks before wetout, and B = distance between gauge marks after wetout and drying.

Performance Guidelines. According to the UFS guidelines, upholstery fabrics should not exhibit more than 5 percent shrinkage in either fabric direction. The guidelines also suggest a maximum gain of 2 percent in either direction. The reason for this differential is that upholstery fabric is usually under tension; therefore, shrinkage up to 5 percent is generally less objectionable than fabric gain, which produces bagging.

Seam Breaking Strength

ASTM D 3597 specifies the use of ASTM D 434 for the evaluation of seam breaking strength. Although ASTM D 434 includes a statement that the method is not intended for upholstery fabrics, it can be used with modifications. Rather than the specified fourteen stitches per inch, UFS 1979-15 requires seven stitches per inch in the seamline. A CRT or a CRE testing machine may be used, and the force is exerted until the seam breaks or until the fabric yarns break or tear. The UFS guidelines are listed in Table 14.1.

Abrasion

The extensive use of complex yarns and decorative interlacings in upholstery fabric requires that consumers, interior designers, and architects consider the level of abrasion to which the covering will be subjected in end use. This will assist in the selection of a fabric that will be serviceable for a reasonable length of time, minimizing the potential need for premature replacement or recovering of the item.

Depending upon the location and position of the fabric on the furniture item, the covering may be subjected to flat, flex, or edge abrasion. Flat abrasion occurs when the fabric is fairly flat, such as on the seat cushions of automobiles and interior furniture items. Flex abrasion occurs when the fabric is bent or curved and subjected to rubbing action. This is a potential problem with the fabric covering arms and curved portions of seat and back cushions, as well as with that covering prominent welts (see Figure 15.4b, page 154). Edge abrasion may occur where the fab-

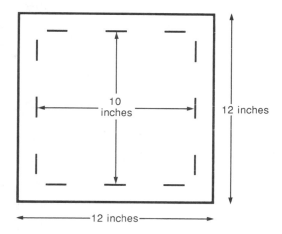

Figure 14.5 Specimen marked for measuring dimensional stability.

ric is folded, as is the case at seamlines, and may be particularly noticeable with plain seams.

Various testing procedures and machines are available to accelerate abrasion for laboratory testing. Some equipment is designed to impart one type of abrasion; others are designed to impart a combination of abrasive actions. Analysis of the effects of the abrasive action may require observation of surface changes, loss in weight, and changes in tensile strength.

Three abrasion testers currently in use are pictured in Figure 14.6 and another, the Taber Abraser, is shown in Figure 30.7 (page 329). The Accelerotor (Figure 14.6a) is the apparatus specified in AATCC 93 Abrasion Resistance of Fabrics: Accelerotor Method. The machine has an impeller and an abrasive liner covering the chamber wall. The fabric specimen is subjected to flexing, rubbing, shock, and compression as it is propelled by the impeller during testing. A fold may be stitched into the specimen to evaluate edge abrasion resistance. The CSI Stoll-Quartermaster Universal Wear Tester (Figure 14.6b) is a multipurpose instrument. It can be used to evaluate resistance to surface abrasion, edge, fold, and projection

a) Accelerotor

Figure 14.6 Testing machines used to evaluate abrasion resistance. (Photograph a is courtesy of the American Association of Textile Chemists and Colorists.)

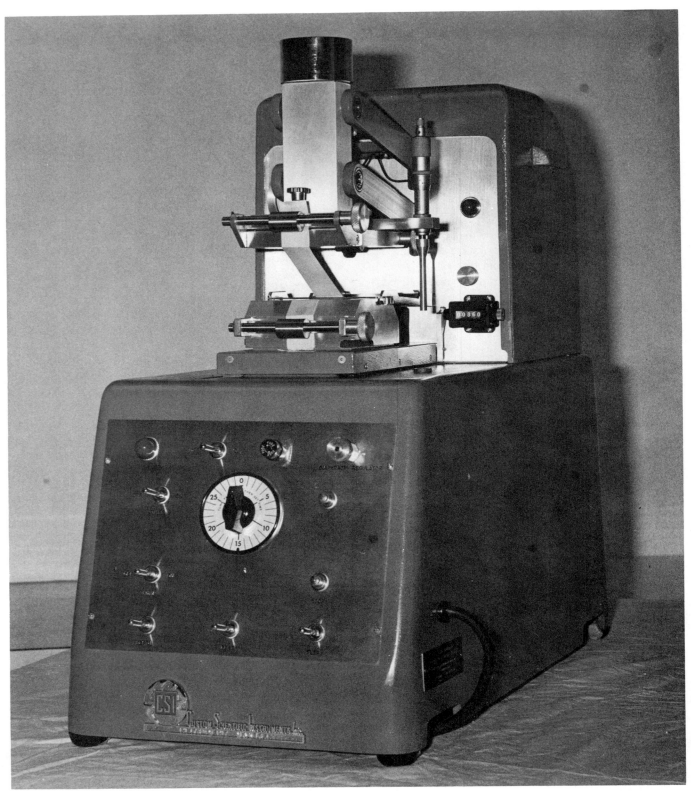

b) CSI Stoll-Quartermaster Universal Wear Tester

Figure 14.6 Testing machines used to evaluate abrasion resistance. (Photograph *b* is courtesy of Custom Scientific Instruments Inc.)

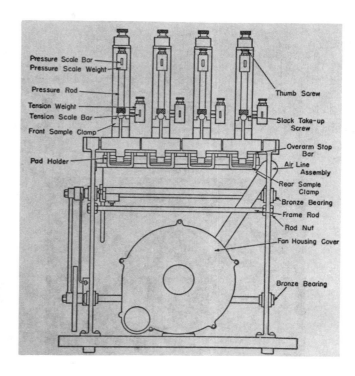

c) Precision Wear Test Meter

Figure 14.6 Testing machines used to evaluate abrasion resistance. (Photograph *c* is copyright ASTM. Reprinted with permission.)

Table 14.2 DESCRIPTIONS OF UFS IN-USE APPLICATION TERMS

Application	Description
"Light," in-use, household applications	Applications where the upholstered furniture is used mainly for decorative rather than functional purposes; for example, several times a month.
"Moderate," in-use, household applications	Applications where the upholstered furniture is used infrequently, such as, for example, once or twice a week in a "formal" living or dining room.
"Medium Duty," in-use, household applications	Applications where the upholstered furniture is used occasionally, every day, for example, for 1 or 2 hours daily.
"Normal," in-use, household applications	Applications where the upholstered furniture is used constantly for several hours or more daily, such as a chair or sofa.

Note: No household furniture fabrics are designed or intended for abusive applications.
Source: Joint Industry Fabric Standards Committee, *Woven Upholstery Fabric Standards, 1980,* 26.

abrasion, and flex abrasion. Attachments can facilitate the evaluation of frosting. Other modifications of the equipment simulate the abrasive wear encountered on welts of upholstered furniture. The Taber Abraser may be selected when specimens are to be subjected to rotary rubbing action.

For the evaluation of the abrasion resistance of upholstery fabrics, UFS 1979-16 specifies the use of ASTM D 1175 Oscillatory Cylinder Method, with modifications set forth in ASTM D 3597. This procedure, frequently referred to as the Wyzenbeek Method, was selected because it has traditionally been employed in the industry. The Precision Wear Test Meter (Figure 14.6c) is used in ASTM D 1175, which is described in the following section.

Test Specimens and Procedures. Test specimens are cut 1.875 by 9 inches. The long dimensions are cut parallel to the warp yarns to test warpwise abrasion resistance and parallel to the filling yarns to test filling-wise abrasion resistance. The specimens are secured in the clamps of the apparatus after conditioning. The specimen supports are then lowered over the curved cylinder, which is covered with stainless steel wire screen abradant. The cylinder oscillates at the rate of 90 cycles (double rubs) per minute, effecting unidirectional rubbing action on the specimens.

Analysis of Results. At the end of 3,000 cycles (double rubs), the specimens are examined for loose threads and wear; slight discoloration from the stainless

steel screen on light colored fabrics is disregarded. If no noticeable change is apparent, the test is continued for another 6,000 cycles and the specimens are again examined. If no noticeable change is apparent, the test is continued for another 6,000 cycles for a total of 15,000 cycles.

Performance Guidelines. As noted in Table 14.1, different levels of abrasion resistance are recommended for light duty, medium duty, and heavy duty applications. As detailed in Table 14.2, these in-use applications are defined in terms of frequency of use.

Yarn Slippage

UFS 1979-18 pertains to yarn slippage at seamlines. While ASTM D 434 may be used for screening purposes, the recommended test method for evaluating yarn slippage is the Dynamic Seam Fatigue Method. In this procedure, the seam is stressed by repeatedly dropping a rubber-faced wheel onto the fabric, parallel to and 1 inch from the seam. As shown in Figure 14.7, the specimen is mounted over a piece of resilient polyurethane foam that forms a simulated seat cushion.

Testing is complete when the specimen has undergone 7,000 cycles (impacts), or when visual evaluation of the seam reveals yarn slippage, yarn breakage, or sewing thread breakage. In the event seam failure occurs before 7,000 cycles have been completed, the industry standard suggests that the seams be reinforced and applications be restricted as set out in Table 14.3. Seams can be reinforced

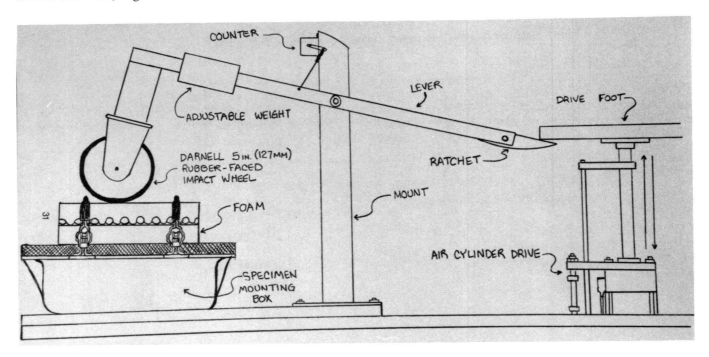

Figure 14.7 The apparatus used in the dynamic seam fatigue test method. (*Source:* Joint Industry Fabric Standards Committee, *Woven Upholstery Fabrics Standards,* 1980, 31.)

Table 14.3 UFS SUGGESTED USES FOR SEAMS EXHIBITING VARIOUS DEGREES OF FAILURE

Degree of failure	Suggested use
1,000 cycles or less	Do not use in upholstered furniture.
1,001–2,000 cycles	Use only with reinforced seams and then only in "light" in-use, household applications (as described in Table 14.2).
2,001–4,000 cycles	Use only with reinforced seams and then only in "moderate" in-use, household applications (as described in Table 14.2).
4,001–6,000 cycles	Use only with reinforced seams and then only in "medium duty" household applications (as described in Table 14.2).
6,001–6,500 cycles	At the 6,000- to 6,500-cycle term, it is advisable to reinforce the structural seams.
Above 6,500 cycles	Seam reinforcement is not needed and the fabric can be used for normal household applications (as described in Table 14.2).

Source: Joint Industry Fabric Standards Committee, *Woven Upholstery Fabric Standards, 1980,* 26.

by inserting an extra layer of fabric in the seamline stitching.

STANDARDS FOR COLOR CONSISTENCY AND RETENTION

Colorfastness refers to the ability of colorants to retain their original properties when they are exposed to various environmental conditions, cleaning agents, and end use activities. Residential consumers and contract designers and architects should be aware of sources of potential harm to colorants and avoid them, if possible. Manufacturers should ascertain the stability of colorants applied to upholstery fabrics and discontinue the use of those failing to exhibit acceptable levels of fastness.

As part of their quality-control work, dyers and printers should examine the uniformity of color characteristics and look for any variability in pattern repeats. Upholstery fabrics exhibiting inconsistent color or pattern placements may be rejected by end-product producers and consumers.

Inconsistencies in Actual and Apparent Color

Sophisticated electronic color meters can be used to detect differences in the color characteristics of fabrics. Standards recommend that the color of a fabric not vary within any single piece or roll, and streaks are unacceptable.

Because changes in the texture of pile fabrics may produce changes in the apparent brightness of the fabric, members of the industry recommend that packaging, storing, and handling of these fabrics be controlled to avoid

distortion of the original pile yarn orientation. Care during processing and shipping can minimize the development of apparent shading problems.

Variations in Pattern Repeats

The variation of pattern repeats should be measured from center point to center point of any contiguous repeats, and a minimum of four measurements should be taken in a continuous length of 50 yards. When pattern repeats are 13 inches or more in length, the variation should not exceed 0.5 inch; when pattern repeats are less than 13 inches in length, the variation should not exceed 0.25 inch.

Fastness Standards

Changes in color characteristics may be described in relative terms—"barely perceptible," "quite noticeable," and so on—but the degree of change can be measured and rated in numerical terms by using standard test methods. Manufacturers of upholstery fabrics may elect to compare the results of such tests with the levels of fastness recommended by representatives of the industry. These standards are listed in Table 14.4.

Colorfastness to Crocking. Rubbing may cause unstable colorants to exhibit a problem known as crocking, the transfer of color from one material to another. The loss or transfer can occur under dry or wet conditions. Crocking may occur in upholstery fabric when, for example, apparel fabric rubs against the colored seat of a chair.

Table 14.4 WOVEN UPHOLSTERY FABRIC STANDARDS FOR COLOR RETENTION

UFS Number	Property	Test methods	Standard
1979-07	Colorfastness to crocking	AATCC 8-1977 ASTM D 3597	dry: class 4, min. wet: class 3, min.
1979-08	Colorfastness to light	AATCC 16-1977 ASTM D 3597	I-VII: class 4, min. (40 hrs.)
1979-09	Colorfastness to burnt gas fumes	AATCC 23-1975 ASTM D 3597	class 4, min. (2 cycles)
1979-10	Cleanability: Colorfastness to water	AATCC 107-1978 ASTM D 3597	class 4, min.: color change
	Colorfastness to solvents	AATCC 107-1978 ASTM D 3597	class 3, min.: staining

Source: Joint Industry Fabric Standards Committee, *Woven Upholstery Fabric Standards, 1980,* 6.

The Crockmeter, pictured in Figure 14.8, is the instrument used in AAATC 8 Colorfastness to Crocking (Rubbing): AATCC Crockmeter Method. During testing, the upholstery fabric is cyclically rubbed by a rod covered with white fabric. Transfer of color from the upholstery surface to the white fabric is evidence of crocking.

The degree of transference is evaluated visually, and a numerical fastness value is determined by comparing the white fabric that covered the rod during testing with pairs of chips on the International Geometric Gray Scale for Evaluating Staining.* As shown in Figure 14.9, there is no difference between the members of the first pair of chips, and the rating is 5; a perceptible difference appears in the second pair, a combination of the white reference chip and a slightly grayed chip, and the rating is 4. The last pair includes a white reference chip and the strongest gray chip: a marked contrast appears, representing a significant level of color transfer.

If no color was transferred from the upholstery fabric surface to the white test fabric, a rating of 5 would be recorded. If transfer occurred, the degree of contrast observed between the unstained and stained areas on the test fabric would be compared with that observed between the paired chips on the scale, and the appropriate number would be assigned. Thus, the higher the reported value, the more stable the colorant and the better the resistance to crocking. The UFS performance guidelines for crocking are listed in Table 14.4.

*The AATCC Chromatic Transference Scale, pictured in Figure 21.6 (page 228), could also be used. The numerical ratings are equivalent to the Gray Scale ratings.

Colorfastness to Light. AATCC 16 Colorfastness to Light sets out several procedures that can be used to evaluate the lightfastness of colored fabrics. There are procedures for accelerated laboratory testing and for extended outdoor exposure testing. Various light sources and testing conditions are specified in each test procedure. Because lightfastness is especially critical for draperies, curtains, and awnings, these test methods are explained in Unit Three.

After completion of the selected lightfastness testing procedure, producers visually evaluate and rate the level of color retention in essentially the same manner as crocking evaluations are made. In this case, however, the International Geometric Gray Scale for Color Change is used. As

Figure 14.8 The Crockmeter testing apparatus. (Courtesy of the American Association of Textile Chemists and Colorists.)

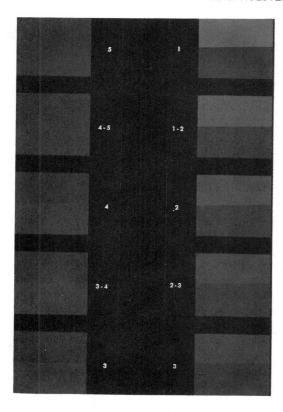

Figure 14.9 International Geometric Gray Scale for Evaluating Staining. (Courtesy of the American Association of Textile Chemists and Colorists.)

Greater numbers of fume fading incidents occur in industrial centers, geographic regions where coal and fuel oil are major heating sources, and densely populated areas where personal automobiles are widely relied on. Automobile exhaust can contain as much as fifty thousand times more nitric oxide than a normal atmosphere. While emission control devices on automobiles and clean air standards are reducing the concentrations of some atmospheric pollutants, the increasing use of fireplaces and wood-burning stoves for home heating is generating greater concentrations of others.

Fume fading is a particular problem in acetate fibers dyed with disperse dyestuffs. After prolonged exposure to oxides of nitrogen or sulfur, certain colors gradually and permanently change hue. Blues turn pink, greens turn brownish yellow, and browns turn red. Solution dyeing is necessary to avoid such changes. The trade name

shown in Figure 14.10, the reference chip is a saturated gray color, and it is successively paired with lighter gray chips.

Numerical ratings are determined by comparing the difference observed between an original and an exposed fabric specimen with that observed between the members of a pair of chips on the scale. Again, the higher the reported value, the more stable the colorant. A rating of 4 or higher after 40 hours of exposure to light is required to meet the standard.

Colorfastness to Burnt Gas Fumes. Atmospheric contaminant fading, ozone or O-fading, fume fading, and gas fading are terms describing the destructive effects of various gases on colored textiles. Gases that commonly cause problems include oxides of sulfur, oxides of nitrogen, and ozone. Exposing colored textiles to various concentrations of these gases may result in weakening or fading of the original color or an actual change in hue. Either type of change in the color characteristics of interior textile products is a two-fold disaster: the harmony among several items in an interior setting is destroyed, and the cost of replacement must be paid.

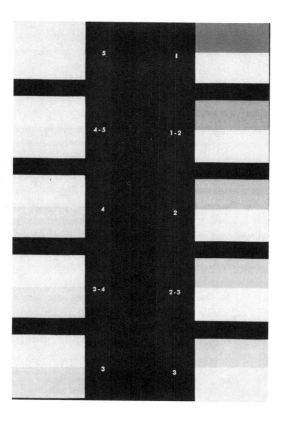

Figure 14.10 International Geometric Gray Scale for Color Change. (Courtesy of the American Association of Textile Chemists and Colorists.)

Figure 14.11 Interior view of a gas exposure cabinet. (Courtesy of Atlas Electric Devices Company.)

Chromspun® is used by Eastman Chemical Products, Inc. to distinguish the solution-dyed acetate fibers the company markets for use in upholstery and drapery fabrics.

AATCC 23 Colorfastness to Burnt Gas Fumes can be used for analyzing the negative effects of various gases, but it is generally used to determine the effects of nitrogen dioxide. The test is conducted in an enclosed chamber, such as the one pictured in Figure 14.11, with controlled concentrations of the gas. After completion of two cycles of testing, the level of color change is determined in the same manner as lightfastness ratings are determined, using the Gray Scale for Color Change.

Cleanability. The standard for the cleanability of upholstery fabric, UFS 1979-10, pertains to the fastness of the colorants when they are exposed to water and to solvents, the agents typically used to clean upholstery. Manufacturers are specifically concerned with the potential for color bleeding and migration (movement of the dyestuff through the fabric components). Bleeding, either to the interior of the covering or onto cleaning cloths, would weaken the surface color. Migration would create various levels of intensity over the surface and could transfer color from one area to another area of a different color.

Colorfastness to water. AATCC 107 Colorfast-
' Water is recommended for evaluating the fastness
d upholstery fabric to water. In preparation for
fabric specimen is backed by a multifiber fab-
 that has narrow bands of six different fi-
fabrics are immersed in distilled water and
sed between glass plates, and heated in
' for 18 hours. After air drying, the
lly evaluated and rated for color
le for Color Change. The mul-
lly evaluated for staining us-

ATCC 107 is also
upholstery fabrics
e paired fabrics
instead of in
d for color

thods
to
nt
-
s

per
ppear-

ance features are retained at an acceptable level for an extended period of time.

MAINTENANCE OF OUTERCOVERING FABRICS

Residential and commercial consumers do not expect an upholstery fabric to retain its new, fresh, clean appearance forever. On the other hand, they do not anticipate that soil accumulation will be so rapid that an unreasonable maintenance program will be required. Consumers also expect that the removal of stains will not be an impossible challenge.

As a preventive maintenance measure, contract designers and other specifiers may request that the surface of upholstery fabrics be laminated with clear or translucent vinyl film sheeting. Although vinylized fabrics can be washed with mild detergent and warm water, they are not waterproof; they are not intended for installation outdoors. Because this treatment produces some variation in color and luster, converters suggest that a treated sample of the fabric be examined by the client before the vinyl application is ordered.

With routine care and immediate stain removal, residential and commercial consumers can assist in the long-term retention of the original appearance of upholstery fabrics. As long as the appearance is satisfactory to the consumer, the need for an overall or restorative cleaning procedure is postponed.

Routine Care

Upholstered furniture products should be frequently and thoroughly vacuumed to remove airborne dust and lint. If possible, loose cushions should be turned and rotated to equalize wear and soiling levels. Protective arm covers and head rests should be cleaned to minimize difference between the appearance of these items and that of other exposed areas.

Simulated leather fabrics with a polyvinylchloride or polyurethane surface may be washed with warm water and a mild soap (not a detergent), and then rinsed with a dampened cloth and dried. As a protective measure, a hard wax can be applied to the surface. However, waxes, oils, and furniture polishes must not be applied to genuine leather coverings as they may damage the finish.

Emergency Action

Prompt action must be taken in the event of spillage or deposition of other foreign matter. Fluids must be immediately absorbed from the surface to confine the area of spillage and to prevent them from penetrating into the fibers and fabric backing. Solid materials, such as candle wax and crayon, should be broken up, scraped, and

Table 14.5 REMOVAL OF SPOTS AND STAINS FROM WOOL UPHOLSTERY

Stain	Detergent or vinegar	Cleaning fluid	Other
Acids			Detergent
Alcoholic beverages	o	o	
Ammonia or alkali	o		
Beer	o		
Bleach	o		
Blood	o		
Butter		o	
Candy	o		Scrape and vacuum
Chewing gum	o	o	
Chocolate	o	o	
Coffee	o		
Cosmetics	o	o	
Crayon	o	o	Scrape and vacuum
Egg	o		
Excrement	o		
Fruit & juices	o		
Furniture polish	o	o	
Glue			Alcohol
Grease		o	Scrape and vacuum
Household cement	o	o	
Ice cream	o	o	
Iodine	o		Alcohol
Lipstick	o	o	
Metal polish	o	o	
Milk	o	o	
Mud	o		
Mustard	o		
Nail polish			Polish remover
Oils		o	
Paint	o	o	
Perfume	o	o	
Salad dressing	o	o	
Sauces	o	o	
Shoe polish	o	o	Scrape and vacuu
Soft drinks	o		
Tar		o	
Tea	o		
Urine	o		
Vomit	o	o	
Washable ink	o		
Wax		o	Scrape an

Courtesy of The Wool Bureau, Inc.

vacuumed to remove as much of the substance as possible before stain removal agents are used.

When stain removal agents are required, they should first be applied as directed to an inconspicuous area of the outercovering. After the agent has been removed and the fabric has dried, the area should be examined for evidence of change in the original color characteristics. If necessary, different agents should be tried until one causing no change in color can be identified.

In order to avoid spreading the stain and overwetting the fabric, stain removal compounds should be applied in small amounts from the outside edges toward the center of the stain. To avoid distortion of the surface texture, the agent should be blotted on, not rubbed into, the foreign matter and fabric. After the stain has been completely removed, the cleaning agent residue must also be removed by rinsing the fabric and blotting it dry.

Water-borne stains can be removed from most textile upholstery fabrics with a mild detergent diluted with warm water, using one teaspoon of detergent per cup of water. Oil-borne stains can be removed with a solvent-type dry cleaning fluid, such as K2r®, produced by Texize.

Table 14.5 lists the stain removal removal agents and procedures recommended for use with wool. Additional stain removal agents and procedures are listed in Tables 31.2, 31.3, and 31.4. Although these are specifically applicable to soft floor coverings, they may also be used with upholstery fabrics. In all cases, however, a pretest should be performed to confirm that the agent will not alter the color of the fabric or the integrity of the fabric structure.

If warm, soapy water does not remove soil from simulated leather coverings, the surface can be cleaned with a cloth dampened with kerosene or naptha. These compounds are flammable and should be used with caution in a well-ventilated area to avoid inhalation of the fumes. Ball-point ink can usually be removed by spraying the stain with hair spray and immediately wiping the surface.

Procedures used to remove stains will also remove accumulated soil. This may result in a localized clean area that can readily be distinguished from adjacent soiled areas. When such differences are apparent, or when large areas are soiled, the entire surface should be cleaned.

Restorative Maintenance

The original appearance of upholstery fabrics can usually be restored by carefully cleaning the fabric surface. Consumers may elect to do the restoration themselves, to send the item to a professional cleaner, or to have a professional cleaner restore the item on-site.

Frequently, upholstery manufacturers voluntarily label their products with a cleaning code. The code to be used is determined by measuring the level of color migration and bleeding caused by water and by solvent, using the standard test methods described earlier in this chapter. UFS 1979-10 includes a specific recommendation that all upholstered furniture should be identified as to its cleanability code, using the letter codes defined as follows:

W—use water base upholstery cleaner only.

S—use solvent base upholstery cleaner only.

WS—can use water base or solvent base cleaners.

X—do not clean with either water base or solvent base cleaners; use vacuuming or light brushing only.

Water-based cleaning agents are commonly labeled upholstery shampoo. These agents are commercially available as foams, concentrated liquids, and dry compounds. Examples of these products include Glamorene®, produced by Glamorene, Inc.; Glory®, produced by Johnson's Wax; Blue Lustre®, produced by Earl Gressmer Company; and Woolite®, produced by Boyle-Midway, Inc.

It should be emphasized that these cleaning codes apply to the outercovering fabric only; it is imperative that overwetting of the fabric be avoided to prevent contact with the filling materials. It must also be noted that zippered covers should not be removed for cleaning or excessive shrinkage may occur and the backing compound may be damaged. Zippers are used to facilitate filling the cushions, not to facilitate cleaning.

Genuine leather coverings may be cleaned with cheesecloth soaked in a solution of warm water and any mild soap. The surface should then be wiped with a slightly damp cloth and dried with a soft cloth.

Salvage Maintenance

In the event that an upholstered furniture covering no longer has an acceptable appearance, even after overall cleaning, consumers may elect to have the item reupholstered. Because such projects involve materials costs, skilled labor charges, and, often, transportation expenses, they may be relatively expensive. For this reason, reupholstering is often restricted to well-constructed items and antique pieces.

SUMMARY

Fiber, yarn, and fabric manufacturers, colorists, converters, and end-product producers have established standards for various physical and color-related properties of finished upholstery fabrics. These standards include suggested methods for testing the fabrics in the laboratory and recommended levels of performance. The test methods were chosen because they provide a reasonable simulation of end use conditions; fabrics meeting the standards based on these methods should therefore display an acceptable level of in-use serviceability.

The original appearance of upholstery coverings can be retained for a longer period of time if vacuuming is routine and removal of stains is prompt. For overall cleaning, informed consumers can interpret the cleaning code frequently, albeit voluntarily, listed on upholstered furniture labels or hangtags. These letter codes are used by manufacturers who accept the Upholstery Fabric Standard for cleanability. Their fabric has been examined for color migration and bleeding after being exposed to water and to solvent.

chapter 15

Construction Features of Upholstered Furniture

- Exterior Construction Features
- Interior Textile Components
- Fillings Used in Upholstered Furniture

Residential and commercial consumers have an almost un-limited variety of upholstered furniture styles from which to choose. All these forms and decorative stylings have some components in common. By definition, an upholstered item has an outercovering that surrounds and con-ceals a filling or stuffing, and such other structural com-ponents as springs, fabric linings, and framework. The various construction techniques for applying outercover-ings expand the range of styling features available to con-sumers.

Filling materials in upholstered furniture serve structur-al as well as functional purposes. Frequently, the in-use behavior of the filling material is more important than that of other components, including the outercovering.

EXTERIOR CONSTRUCTION FEATURES

In addition to the upholstery fabric used to cover the cushions, backs, arms, and sides of furniture items, other fabrics may be used to cover the deck and bottom areas. Bottom fabrics are rarely seen, but deck fabrics may be ex-posed if the furniture has loose pillows. Other construc-tion features, including the styling of the skirt and any surface embellishments, also affect the appearance of an upholstered item.

Deck Fabrics and Bottom Fabrics

The deck of an upholstered item comprises the plat-form, springs, and filling structures that support the seat cushions. To conceal these units and to prevent dust and objects from falling into the deck, a fabric covers the up-permost filling layer. When the fabric is the same as the exposed outercovering, it is referred to as a self-deck treat-ment; it looks like the outercovering in the event cush-ions are separated from the furniture in use. If the outcov-ering is heavy or highly textured, a smoother, lighter weight, less expensive deck fabric may be used; the color of this fabric coordinates with that of the outercovering. When outercoverings have low porosity, as is true for simulated leather fabrics, a porous deck fabric must be used to permit air movement when the seat cushions are compressed.

Bottom fabrics are used underneath the deck to conceal the interior components and give a finished look to the upholstered item if the bottom should come into view. The fabric must be dimensionally stable to prevent sag-ging. Today, spunbonded polypropylene olefin fabrics are frequently used for bottom fabrics. These lightweight fab-rics resist moisture and mildew, do not ravel, and are di-mensionally stable. The spunbonded bottom fabric pic-tured in Figure 15.1 is available in weights ranging from 1.0 to 2.0 ounces per square yard.

Figure 15.1 Accord® spunbonded polypropylene olefin for bottom fabric applications. (Courtesy of Kimberly-Clark Corporation.)

Patterned Fabric Applications

Unless the fabric has an overall design of no particular orientation (as in Figure 15.5), precise fabric cutting and motif positioning are required for upholstery fabrics with woven-in or printed patterns. Attention must first be given to the directional features of the motifs and repeats. These visual characteristics determine whether a fabric should be cut "up-the-bolt" or to "railroad"; the meanings of these terms are schematically illustrated in Figure 15.2 The importance of pattern direction to subsequent placement can be appreciated by examining the floral motifs in the fabric covering the sofa pictured in Figure 15.3. Assuming the linear path of the flowers paralleled the selvages, the flowers would have appeared to grow sideways if the fabric had been cut to railroad.

When a fabric has a main motif, the motif must be centered on the back pillows, as well as on the seat cushions. For maximum aesthetic appeal, distinct patterns can

also be cut and applied in a process known as completion. A completed pattern flows uninterrupted down the back pillows, the seat cushions, the seat boxing, the seat front, and the skirt. With the exception of the skirt, the completion method was used to place the patterned fabric on the sofa pictured in Figure 15.3; the motifs in the fabric were also centered.

Cushion and Pillow Treatments

Three constructions of upholstery cushions and pillows are illustrated in Figure 15.4. The use of a plain seam to join the fabric pieces is called a knife-edge treatment. Inserting a fabric-covered cord into the seam is known as welting. The cords may be covered with the outercovering fabric (see Figures 15.3 and 15.5), or, for greater emphasis, with a contrasting fabric. When welts are planned for items covered with highly textured fabrics, a smooth fabric may be used to cover the cords and increase their abrasion resistance. Wrapping a strip of fabric around the front and sides of cushions is known as boxing. This treatment (shown in Figure 15.3) is generally combined with a zipper closure that enables manufacturers to insert the filling materials easily.

Upholstered cushions and pillows are treated two different ways in the construction of end products. In tight-

a) railroad

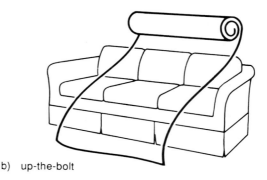

b) up-the-bolt

Figure 15.2 Illustrations of terms describing the directional cutting and placement of patterned upholstery fabric. (Courtesy of Pennsylvania House.)

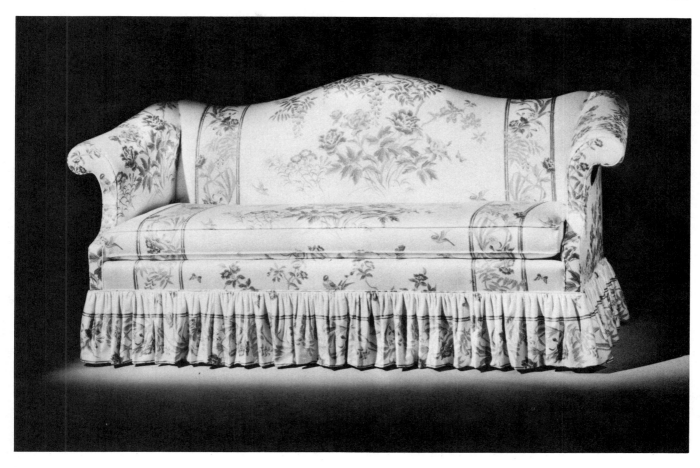

Figure 15.3 Sofa with its main motif centered on back pillow and seat cushion. Except for the skirt treatment, the pattern is completed. (Courtesy of Pennsylvania House.)

pillow construction styles, the pillows are securely attached to the framework and cannot be shifted or removed. In loose-pillow styles (Figures 15.5), the pillows are not secured. Unless a different fabric has been used to cover the backs of the pillows, they can be frequently reversed to equalize wear patterns and soiling levels.

Skirt Options

Several options are available for the treatment of upholstered furniture skirts. Typical construction styles are illustrated in Figure 15.6. The skirt may be flat with single or double kick pleats; it may be shirred (also see Figures 15.3 and 15.5); it may have box pleats; or it may be shirred only at the corners in a princess style. Buttons may be added as decorative accents (see the skirt on the sofa in Figure 15.7).

When a skirt is designed to hang straight and flat, a firm, bonded-web interfacing is generally employed to control the draping quality and to provide support. Skirts may be lined with a spunbonded fabric in order to reduce bulk and weight.

Slipcovers

Many consumers use slipcovers to protect the attached covering from excessive soil accumulation, as well as to change the appearance of the furniture from one season to another. Slipcovers are cut, seamed, and fitted over furniture. Some manufacturers offer upholstered furniture "in-the-muslin": the items are covered in muslin, an undyed, plain-woven fabric composed of carded cotton yarns. Consumers can then order one or more sets of decorative slipcovers.

Arm Covers and Head Rests

Arm covers, also called arm caps and armettes, protect the arms of upholstered furniture from excessive abrasion and soiling. Frequently, these covers are offered optionally. Head rests protect the upholstery fabric from neck and hair oils and hair coloring. They may be cut from the outercoverings, or, as is the case in commercial airliners, buses, and trains, they may be cut from disposable fabric.

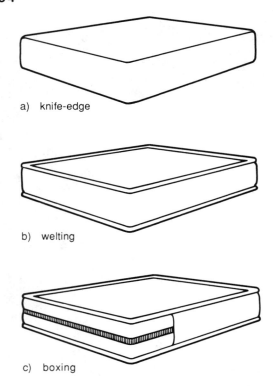

a) knife-edge

b) welting

c) boxing

Figure 15.4 Construction treatments for upholstered furniture cushions and pillows.

Surface Embellishments

The furniture manufacturer can use various treatments to embellish the surface of upholstery fabrics and finished products. These treatments are distinct from others, such as coloring and finishing, which also enrich the surface appearance but are performed on fabric prior to end-product construction.

Quilting is generally offered as an optional fabric treatment. The stitching may be done in parallel rows or on curved and angled lines to create slightly raised design motifs: on pattern fabrics, it may follow the outline of the design motifs (see Figure 33.12, page 372). When the surface is tufted, buttons secure the outercovering and filling tightly in a deeply indented three-dimensional pattern (Figure 15.7). Extensive buttoning should not be used on delicate fabrics with low levels of tear strength. Nailhead trimming may be used to secure heavier coverings, such as genuine leather, to framework. The nails are generally aligned to emphasize the lines of the upholstered item.

To select a product that will retain its original appearance and the stability of its exterior construction features longer, residential and commercial consumers should consider its interior components and construction features. Some of these interior components are often textiles.

INTERIOR TEXTILE COMPONENTS

Within an upholstered furniture item, several textile components, including fabric linings, filling structures, and cords, frequently appear. Textile cords are often used to hand tie or hand knot the several spring units together; the network of cords helps to stabilize the configuration of each spring and to minimize lateral shifting. A fabric lining, such as burlap or spunbonded olefin, is generally laid over the springs to prevent them from penetrating the filling materials. Two layers of filling, one for softness and one for firm support, may be used over the fabric linings. In most cases, the inside vertical walls and the extended portions of the frame will be padded with one or more layers of filling.

The framing material used in upholstered furniture may be hardwood, wood veneer, metal, or molded polymer. Although a discussion of these materials is out of place here, consumers are encouraged to ascertain the soundness and stability of the frame prior to purchase. Special attention should be given to the quality and sturdiness of the framing joints. Consumers should also investigate the composition and structural features of the filling materials used. Often, consumers and interior designers can specify the use of a particular filling material.

FILLINGS USED IN UPHOLSTERED FURNITURE

Three types of filling structures—fibrous battings, foam cushions, and loose particulate materials—are available to stuff or cushion upholstered furniture components and pillows. These structures differ in compressibility, loftiness, resiliency, and flammability. The Federal Trade Commission advises manufacturers to disclose the presence of such filling materials as goose down and feathers and requires disclosure of the presence of previously used filling materials.

Fibrous Battings

Battings are three-dimensional textile structures formed directly from fibers, bypassing the yarn stage. Natural or man-made fibers may be employed.

Cotton Felt. Although batting structures composed of cotton fibers may be referred to as cotton felt, the term is descriptive of the felt-like appearance, not of the processing used. Such structures are produced by layering thin webs of cotton fibers to form a batt of the desired thickness. The natural convolutions of cotton fibers (Figure 3.2b, page 20) help them to entwine and adhere to another, but for added stability the batt may be impregnated with an adhesive or resin.

Figure 15.5 Lounge chair with loose-pillow construction. (Courtesy of Pennsylvania House.)

The use of cotton, as well as kapok and jute, for upholstery fillings has diminished in recent years. These cellulosic fibers have comparatively low resiliency. Supply and delivery problems also hinder the selection of kapok and jute. Moreover, the results of flammability research have encouraged many manufacturers to restrict voluntarily the use of cotton batting that has not been treated to be flame resistant.

Curled Hair Batting. The use of curled horsehair, cattlehair, and hoghair for upholstered furniture filling has been declining. These three-dimensional hair forms can

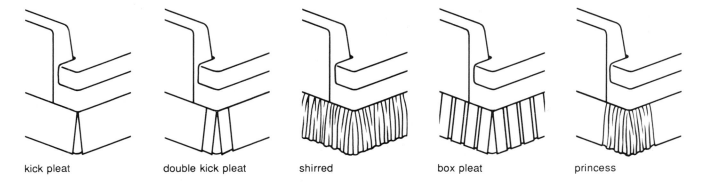

| kick pleat | double kick pleat | shirred | box pleat | princess |

Figure 15.6 Optional skirt treatments. (Courtesy of Pennsylvania House.)

Figure 15.7 Sofa embellished with button tufting. (Courtesy of Pennsylvania House.)

easily be entwined into resilient battings, but they are subject to such moisture- and microbe-related problems as odor and mildew, and, for some people, they can act as allergens. These natural materials, which are by-products of the leather industry, have generally been replaced by man-made fiber structures.

Bonded Polyester Batting. Most man-made fiber batting is composed of staple-length polyester fibers. These fibers are produced by breaking or cutting the crimped filaments in a tow bundle (see Figure 5.3, page 36).

When used in upholstered furniture, batting must not only provide comfort and superior resiliency, but also firm support, a feature not required of fillings for quilts and comforters. To engineer these features, manufacturers frequently combine two distinctly different layers of polyester fibers into one batt. The upper layer contains fine, low denier fibers that are easily flexed and soft, making for comfort; the lower layer contains coarser, stiffer fibers that provide firm support as they resist flexing and compression. For increased stability and greater resiliency, resin is

sprayed throughout the batt, bonding the fibers into position.

Foam Cushions

Three-dimensional foam structures, frequently referred to as slab cushions, often fill upholstered furniture items to preserve their shape and form. Latex and urethane compounds are used to manufacture these cushions.

Latex Foam Structures. Latex foam may be produced from natural rubber or from synthesized rubber compounds. The compound is foamed, creating tiny, air-filled cells, and formed into a slab of the desired thickness. By controlling the quantity and size of the cells, manufacturers can engineer the density of the structure, which in turn determines the degree of firmness or the compression resistance offered by the cushion. Frequently, the latex is vulcanized or heated with sulfur to introduce strong chemical cross links that stabilize the shape and add strength. Latex foam cushions are resilient, but they may exhibit gradual aging and deterioration.

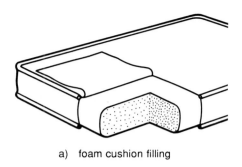

a) foam cushion filling

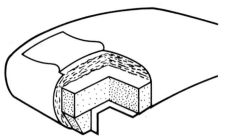

b) foam cushion core surrounded by polyester batting

Figure 15.8 Foam cushion fillings. (Courtesy of Simmons Company.)

Polyurethane Foam Structures. Polyurethane foam is increasingly replacing latex foam in furniture applications. Unlike latex, polyurethane compounds do not exhibit aging, and they are resistant to both microbes and moisture.

During manufacturing, the urethane compound is expanded by heating, increasing the apparent volume and decreasing the density. Structures are produced with lower densities when softness and comfort are the performance features of principal importance, and with higher densities when greater support and resistance to crushing and compression are sought.

As illustrated in Figure 15.8, a latex or polyurethane foam structure may be carefully cut and used alone to fill and impart form to a furniture cushion, or it may form a core unit surrounded by polyester batting. In the latter case, support is provided principally by the foam structure and softness largely by the batting; both components provide resiliency and help the outercovering to maintain its dimensional stability and smoothness.

Loose Particulate Materials

Masses of loose particles are used to fill some upholstered furniture structures. Today, these particles include shredded or flaked latex or urethane foam, feathers, down, and fiberfill. The use of such materials as straw, sawdust, and newspapers has been discontinued because of cleaning and flammability problems. Shredded foam particles are less expensive than slab foam cushions, but they may clump with use. Down, the soft undercoat feathers retrieved from waterfowl, is soft, easily compressed, and lightweight, but the labor costs incurred in retrieving the necessary volume of the tiny feathers make the material

comparatively expensive. Feathers from chickens, turkeys, ducks, and geese are soft and lofty filling materials, but many people are allergic to them. Fiberfill, usually composed of crimped polyester fibers, is lofty and resilient. Polyester offers a cost advantage over down, and unlike down and feathers, man-made fibers are not allergens.

Loose filling materials are frequently enclosed in an inner fabric structure before being inserted into the sewn outercoverings. Today, the inner fabric is often a spunbonded polypropylene olefin fabric.

Service-related Properties

Along with their fire-related behavior, the physical properties exhibited by filling materials greatly influence the serviceability of upholstered furniture items. If, for example, the filling material failed to recover after compression, the cushion would show a deep indentation that would destroy the original design of the item and the smooth appearance of the outercovering.

Compressibility. The ease with which a textile structure can be crushed or reduced in thickness is the measure of its compressibility. All filling structures must be somewhat compressible for comfort. An "overstuffed" chair is specifically designed to be easily compressed under the weight of the seated person; people generally prefer these chairs over straight-backed, noncompressible wooden ones.

The degree of resistance a filling structure offers to being crushed or compressed can be measured in the laboratory. The test apparatus used in this evaluation is pictured in Figure 29.5 (page 305). Structures that require a heavier load, in pounds per square inch, to produce a given deflection or reduction in thickness provide firmer support than those that reach this deflection with a lighter load.

Loftiness. Loftiness is bulk without heaviness. This feature is especially desirable for fillings used in furniture cushions and pillows. If identical cushion or pillow forms are filled, one with down, and one with sawdust, they would have equal thickness and volume. The sawdust-filled pillow, however, would be significantly heavier, thus failing the loftiness test of bulkiness without undue weight. Down and feather filling materials are prized for their inherent loftiness. Even extremely large upholstered cushions filled with these natural materials are light in weight.

To increase the loftiness of fiberfill without increasing the weight, fiber chemists have engineered polyester fibers with hollow interiors (see Figure 33.1, page 359). Hollow fibers are currently used extensively in bedding products, and their use in upholstered furniture items is increasing.

Compressional Resiliency. Compressional resiliency and compressional loft are synonyms that describe the ability of a textile structure to recover from compression deformations. Filling structures must be compressible, but their serviceability depends on their ability to spring back to their original thickness. Without compressional loft or resiliency, fillings would not recover from the force exerted by body weight, and the cushions would develop permanent depressions.

It was noted earlier in this chapter that spraying resin throughout a fibrous batt helps to reduce the compressibility of the structure. This treatment also helps to increase the springiness of a batt, which encourages it to recover after compression.

Flammability. The flammability characteristics of filling materials become very important variables when upholstered furniture catches fire. Because filling materials are always covered by an outercovering, however, their role in upholstery fires must be evaluated in combination with the outercovering and exterior construction features used in a particular item. These fire-related variables are discussed in the following chapter.

Labeling Upholstery Fillings

The Textile Fiber Products Identification Act and two FTC guides have provisions that apply to the labeling of upholstered fillings. Manufacturers should comply with these provisions to avoid engaging in unfair or deceptive commercial practices.

The TFPIA. Although the provisions of the TFPIA do not apply to new upholstery stuffings and fillings, manu-

facturers may voluntarily identify the fiber used by its generic name, and distinguish it with a trade name to make the product more competitive. When the stuffing or filling has been used previously, the product is considered to be misbranded or unfairly and deceptively marketed unless it carries a label or hangtag clearly stating the presence of reused materials. The act does not, however, require the disclosure of the composition of the reused material.

Guides for the Household Furniture Industry. The FTC gives advice in the Guides for the Household Furniture Industry concerning the labeling practices manufacturers should use when they elect to provide information about fillings. To summarize these advisory practices, the information may not be false (e.g., labeling cotton felt as wool felt), nor may it be deceiving (e.g., labeling shredded or flaked latex or urethane foam merely as latex foam or as urethane foam). Furthermore, foam fillings must be specifically identified as latex or urethane foam, not merely as foam.

Interested readers may review the guides for information regarding the labeling of genuine wood, simulated wood, and wood veneer components of upholstered furniture and of such case goods as tables, cabinets, desks, and chests. Students planning careers as professional furniture designers, interior designers, or retailers should become familiar with the guidelines concerning the use of such terms as "Mediterranean," "French Provincial," and "Danish Modern" to describe furniture manufactured in the United States. Consumers and retailers should also understand the recommended use of such descriptive terms as "new," "used," "floor sample," and "discontinued model" in the marketing of upholstered furniture.[*]

Guides for the Feather and Down Products Industry. The Guides for the Feather and Down Products Industry became effective on December 29, 1971. Included in these guides are definitions of the specific terms to be used in labeling feather and down fillings, such as "down," "feathers," "waterfowl feathers," and "nonwaterfowl feathers." Guidelines are also given for the use of such terms as "all down" and "pure down." Other guidelines pertain to the use of damaged and crushed feathers and to the cleanliness of the filling materials.[*] Since feather and down filling materials are used more extensively in bedding products than in upholstered furniture, these guides are reviewed in detail in Chapter 33.

We should note that no labeling provisions have been mandated or recommended for other textile components used in the interior of upholstered furniture. Therefore, the composition of textile cords and fabric linings is rarely, if ever, disclosed.

---

[*]Copies of these guides are available from the Federal Trade Commission, Washington, DC 20580.

SUMMARY

The fabric that covers the exterior of upholstered furniture may be textile or nontextile. Various construction treatments can be used to apply the outercovering, several of which add decorative features to the item. These treatments range from quilting the fabric surface to gathering the skirt to boxing the cushions and pillows.

Upholstered furniture contains various interior components. including springs, framework, fabric linings, and fillings. The fillings may be cotton or bonded polyester batting, latex or urethane foam cushions, or such loose particles as down, feathers, and fiberfill. Manufacturers must disclose the presence of reused filling materials; they should also comply with the labeling practices set forth in guides provided by the Federal Trade Commission.

The end-use serviceability of a piece of upholstered furniture is strongly influenced by the performance characteristics of the filling materials employed. The degree of softness and comfort is primarily determined by the compressibility of the filling; the weight of the cushions is influenced by the loftiness of the filling component; and the long-term retention of the original form and fabric smoothness directly depends on the compressional resiliency of the filling structure.

chapter *16*

Fire-Safety Standards for Upholstered Furniture and Transportation Fabrics

- The UFAC Voluntary Action Program
- Department of Transportation Flammability Mandates

Since the early 1970s, extensive industry research has focused on reducing the hazard posed by upholstered furniture in the event of fire. At first, the work was largely carried out independently by fiber producers, fabric manufacturers, filling materials suppliers, finishing agent suppliers, and end-product producers. The work intensified after the United States Department of Commerce issued a finding of possible need for a mandatory regulation of the cigarette ignition of upholstered furniture. This announcement, made in November 1972, was followed by the drafting of the proposed standard, now designated PFF 6-74. In response, members of the industry formed the Upholstered Furniture Action Council (UFAC) in 1974 to consolidate their research efforts concerning more cigarette-resistant upholstering methods. Through this organization, the industry sought to demonstrate that it could effectively reduce the fire-related hazard of upholstered furniture and that the majority of its member firms would voluntarily participate in a program designed to ensure the production of safer products.

Following a review of the UFAC program, the Consumer Product Safety Commission initially agreed to give the industry one year, beginning December 1, 1979, to intensify the program and demonstrate its effectiveness. After the year was over, the Commission announced its decision to delay further action on a mandatory standard. Therefore, the UFAC program has been continued, and up-

holstered furniture is not currently subject to federal flammability mandates.

In contrast to the voluntary program dealing with upholstered furniture, mandatory flammability regulations apply to transportation fabrics and other textile products used in certain applications, including passenger cars, trucks, buses, and commercial airliners. These regulations are under the jurisdiction of the United States Department of Transportation.

THE UFAC VOLUNTARY ACTION PROGRAM

The UFAC Voluntary Action Program, officially launched in April 1979, is designed to improve the ability of upholstered furniture to resist catching fire from a burning cigarette, the most common source of furniture ignition. The program has four aspects: fabric classification, construction criteria, a labeling plan, and a compliance procedure.

Fabric Classification

Upholstery fabrics are divided into two categories of ignition propensity, based on their ability to resist ignition when exposed to a burning cigarette. The procedures used are outlined in the UFAC Fabric Classification Test Method—1983.

160

Fabric Classification Test Method. In this test method, vertical and horizontal panels are upholstered using the cover fabrics to be tested and 2-inch thick polyurethane foam filling materials. As schematized in Figure 16.1, the panels are placed in the test assembly, and a lighted nonfilter cigarette is placed in the crevice of the assembly and covered with a piece of cotton bedsheeting fabric. The cigarette is allowed to burn its entire length unless an obvious ignition occurs. Three replicate tests are required for each fabric.

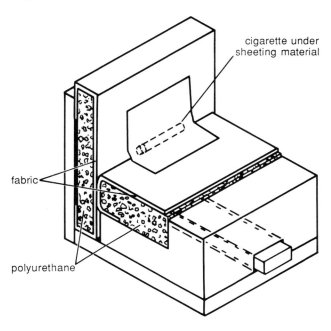

Figure 16.1 The assembly used in the UFAC fabric classification test. (Courtesy of the Upholstered Furniture Action Council.)

If ignition occurs on any one of the three specimens, the fabric is Class II. If no ignition occurs, the vertical char length is measured from the crevice to the highest part of the destroyed or degraded cover fabric. If the char length is less than 1.75 inches, the fabric is Class I; if the char length is equal to or greater than 1.75 inches, the fabric is Class II. This classification determines which construction methods must be employed with the cover fabric to comply with UFAC construction criteria.

Construction Criteria

The UFAC has established five construction criteria to which manufacturers must adhere in order to qualify for participation in the program. Each criterion is paired with a test method to ensure proper compliance. The first four criteria apply to both Class I and Class II fabrics, while the fifth is a further criterion applying to Class II fabrics. The combination of fabric classification with construction method is intended to assure the production of safer uphol-

stered furniture while avoiding the limitation of a large number of upholstery fabrics traditionally available to consumers.

The UFAC construction criteria are as follows:

1. Welt cords must meet the requirements of the UFAC Welt Cord Test Method—1983.

2. Decking substrates must meet the requirements of the UFAC Decking Materials Test Method—1983.

3. Filling material in vertical walls of the seating cavity, as well as in the seat and back cushions, pillows, and bolsters, must meet the requirements of the UFAC Filling/Padding Materials Test Method—1983.

4. Any interior fabric used directly beneath the exposed cover fabric must meet the requirements of the UFAC Interior Fabric Test Method—1983.

5. When Class II fabrics are used with polyurethane foam cushions, a barrier that can pass the UFAC Barrier Test Method—1983 must be used between the cover fabric and the horizontal surfaces of the polyurethane foam cushions.

Manufacturers must confirm that the materials substituted for ignition-prone items meet the UFAC requirements. The materials must be tested in accordance with the appropriate UFAC test method and the test results compared with the acceptance criteria established by the UFAC.

Welt Cord Test Method. In this test, welt cording is placed in the center of a piece of UFAC standard Class II cover fabric that is folded to make an unsewn welt. This cover fabric is a velvet composed of 100 percent cotton; it has no flame retardant finish or backcoating. The welt is placed in the crevice formed by the abutment of the horizontal and vertical panels in the test assembly, which is similar to that shown in Figure 16.1. For this procedure, the panels are covered with UFAC standard Class II fabric, and polyurethane foam is used to fill both the vertical and horizontal panels. As shown in Figure 16.2, a lighted cigarette is placed on the welt and covered with a piece of cotton bedsheeting. Three replicate tests are run. The welt cording is acceptable if no ignition occurs and if the maximum height of the vertical char on any of the vertical panels does not equal or exceed 1.5 inches.

Decking Materials Test Method. In preparation for this test, decking material is cut to size and placed on a plywood assembly base, shown schematically in Figure 16.3. The material may be polyurethane foam, bonded fibrous batting, cotton felt with a flame resistant finish, or some other material produced for use directly beneath the deck fabric. The decking material is covered with UFAC standard Class II fabric and the layered fabrics are held in place by a wooden retainer ring. Three lighted cigarettes

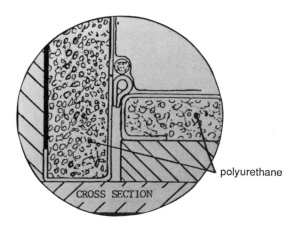

Figure 16.2 Detail of the UFAC welt cord test. (Courtesy of the Upholstered Furniture Action Council.)

are placed on the decking cover fabric and covered with 100 percent cotton sheeting. The cigarettes are allowed to burn their full lengths and the maximum char lengths measured from the cigarettes are recorded. If ignition occurs with one or more cigarettes, or if any char of 1.5 inches or greater occurs, the decking material fails the test.

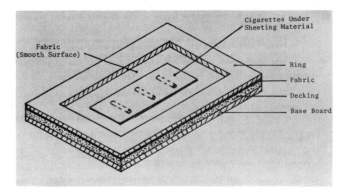

Figure 16.3 The assembly used in the UFAC decking materials test method. (Courtesy of the Upholstered Furniture Action Council.)

Filling/Padding Component Test Method. This test method determines which filling or padding components intended for use in upholstered furniture exhibit sufficient resistance to smoldering cigarette ignition to meet the third UFAC construction criterion. Materials covered by this test method include, but are not limited to, battings of natural and man-made fibers, foamed or cellular fillings or cushioning materials, resilient pads of natural or man-made fibers, and loose filling materials.

The filling material to be tested is used in the vertical and horizontal panels of the test assembly shown in Figure 16.1, in place of the polyurethane. It is covered with UFAC standard mattress ticking, which is composed of 100 percent cotton and has been laundered and tumble-dried once in accordance with prescribed UFAC procedures. One at a time, three ignited cigarettes are placed in the crevice and covered with sheeting fabric. If an obvious ignition occurs on any of the three test specimens or if a vertical char of 1.5 inches or greater is obtained on any of the specimens, the filling material fails the test.

Interior Fabric Test Method. The fourth UFAC construction criterion is intended to confirm that interior fabrics used in intimate contact with outer upholstery fabrics exhibit an acceptable level of performance with respect to cigarette ignition resistance. The assembly used in the required three replicate tests is like that illustrated in Figure 16.1, except that an interior fabric test specimen is placed between the outercovering and the foam filling of the horizontal panels. For this test, the vertical and horizontal panels are covered with UFAC standard mattress ticking. The three lighted cigarettes are again placed one at a time in the crevice and covered. The interior fabric passes the test if no obvious ignition occurs and the vertical char length on any of the three specimens does not exceed 1.5 inches.

Barrier Test Method. The fifth UFAC construction criterion requires that some suitable barrier be placed between Class II fabrics and conventional polyurethane foam in horizontal seating surfaces. This will minimize the likelihood of ignition of the foam in the event a Class II fabric is generating considerable heat as it undergoes decomposition and combustion (see Chapter 11).

Three tests are run using the assembly illustrated in Figure 16.4. The barrier passes the test if no ignition of

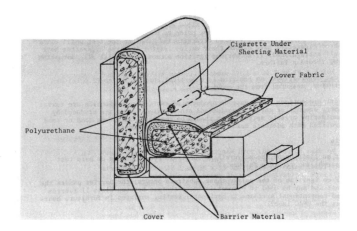

Figure 16.4 The assembly used in the UFAC barrier test. (Courtesy of the Upholstered Furniture Action Council.)

the polyurethane substrate ocurs and if the vertical chars of all barrier specimens are less than 2.0 inches.

The importance of a suitable barrier is underscored by the full-scale fire tests shown in Figures 16.5 and 16.6. The photographs in Figure 16.5 show other views of the fire pictured in Figure 11.4 (page 105). Here, the fire quickly spread, with flashover occurring within two and a half minutes after ignition.

For the test picured in Figure 16.6, the model room was furnished with bedding, window treatments, and wall-coverings of glass fiber fabrics, and the chair had a flame resistant barrier of specially coated glass fiber yarns. In this case, the nylon upholstery burned away, the protective barrier charred but did not burn, and the fire was contained in Stage 1.

A close-up photograph of the chairs used in the above tests is shown in Figure 16.7. It is evident that the presence of the protective barrier in the chair on the right prevented ignition of the foam substrate. The charred area is

substantial, but it should be noted that the ignition source was a paper-filled grocery bag, not an ignited cigarette.

Labeling Plan

The labeling plan devised by the UFAC centers on a hangtag that identifies furniture meeting UFAC criteria. Prospective purchasers are informed that the labeled item has been made in accordance with UFAC methods designed to reduce the likelihood of furniture fire from cigarettes (Figure 16.8).

Compliance Procedure

Participation in the UFAC program is strictly voluntary. The UFAC encourages furniture component suppliers and end-product manufacturers to participate and provides technical assistance to promote compliance. An independent laboratory verifies that materials used in making

Figure 16.5 Full-scale fire test in mock hotel room furnished with conventional items, including a chair having no flame resistant barrier. (Courtesy of Owens-Corning Fiberglas Corporation.)

Figure 16.6 Full-scale fire test in a mock hotel room furnished with flame resistant items, including a chair with a flame resistant barrier between the outercovering and the foam filling. (Courtesy of Owens-Corning Fiberglas Corporation.)

the items carrying the compliance hangtag meet the performance criteria set forth in the program.

Periodically, the results of the verification tests and the level of industry participation are reported to the Consumer Product Safety Commission. By such reporting, the UFAC seeks to demonstrate that members of the industry can and will produce safer upholstered funiture items, eliminating the need for a federal flammability mandate.

DEPARTMENT OF TRANSPORTATION FLAMMABILITY MANDATES

The flammability of upholstery and other textile components used in transportation applications is regulated by two divisions of the Department of Transportation (DOT). The Federal Aviation Administration (FAA) controls the flammability of items used in airplanes, and the National Highway Traffic Safety Administration (NHTSA) oversees the flammability of items used in motor vehicles.

Motor Vehicle Safety Standard No. 302

The Motor Vehicle Safety Standard No. 302 (MVSS 302) became effective on September 1, 1972. This standard is designed to reduce deaths and injuries to motor vehicle occupants caused by vehicle fires, especially those originating in the interior of the vehicle from sources such as matches or cigarettes.*

Scope. The provisions of MVSS 302 apply to seat cushions, seat backs, seat belts, interior roof lining, front and side panels, floor coverings, and other materials used

*The full text of MVSS 302 is available from the National Highway Traffic Safety Administration, 400 Seventh St., SW, Washington, DC 20590.

Figure 16.7 Close-up view of upholstered chairs used in full-scale tests. The chair on the right had a flame resistant fabric of specially coated glass fiber installed as a protective barrier between the outercovering and the foam filling. (Courtesy of Owens-Corning Fiberglas Corporation.)

in occupant compartments of passenger cars, multipurpose passenger vehicles, trucks, and buses.

Test Specimens and Procedures. Whenever possible, each specimen of material to be tested is a rectangle 4 inches wide by 14 inches long. The specimens are conditioned for 24 hours at a temperature of 70°F and a relative humidity of 50 percent and each is then clamped in a U-shaped frame, exposing an area that measures 2 inches wide by 13 inches long. A secured specimen is mounted horizontally in a test apparatus, such as that shown in Figure 16.9. A flame is impinged on the bottom edge of the open end of the specimen for 15 seconds.

Timing of the flame spread is begun when the flame from the burning specimen reaches a point 1.5 inches from the open end of the specimen. The time elapsed for the flame to progress to a point 1.5 inches from the clamped end of the specimen is measured.

Analysis of Results. The burn rate for the specimen is calculated by the following formula:

$$B = 60 \times D/T$$

where B = burning rate inches/minute, D = length the flame travels in inches, and T = time in seconds to travel "D" inches.

Performance Requirements. A material is considered to pass the test and be acceptable for use if the burn rate does not exceed 4 inches per minute. If a material stops burning before it has burned for 60 seconds from the start of timing and has not burned more than 2 inches from the point where timing was started, it also meets the require-

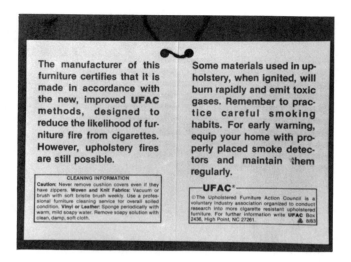

Figure 16.8 UFAC hangtag used on upholstered furniture that complies with UFAC criteria. (Courtesy of the Upholstered Furniture Action Council.)

ments. The NHTSA intends that the rate at which an interior material transmits flame across its surface should not be so rapid as to prevent the driver from stopping the vehicle and all occupants from leaving it before injury occurs as a result of fire.

FAA Paragraph 25.853 (b)

The FAA flammability regulation for textile items used in compartments occupied by the crew or passengers in airplanes is designated as Paragraph 25.853 (b). Other paragraphs in the standard, which was issued on February 15, 1972, concern such items as landing gear systems, escape routes, exit markets, and nontextile interior finishing materials. The general focus of the standard is to improve the crashworthiness and emergency evacuation equipment of airliners.*

Scope. The provisions of Paragraph 25.853 (b) apply to upholstery, draperies, floor coverings, seat cushions, padding, decorative and nondecorative coated fabrics, leather, trays, and galley furnishings. They also apply to such items as acoustical insulation.

Test Specimens and Procedures. The specimens are cut 2.75 by 12.5 inches, with the most critical flammability conditions corresponding to the long dimension. The specimens are conditioned for 24 hours at a temperature of 70°F and a relative humidity of 50 percent; they are then

---

* The full text of FAA Paragraph 25.853 (b) is available from the Federal Aviation Administration, 800 Independence Ave., SW, Washington, DC 20591.

clamped in a U-shaped frame. The secured specimen is vertically suspended in a draft-free test chamber, such as the one shown in Figure 16.10. A flame is impinged on the lower edge of the specimen for 12 seconds and then removed.

Analysis of Results. Three results are determined for each specimen:

1. The after flame time is the time the specimen continues to flame after the burner flame is removed.
2. The afterglow time is the time the specimen continues to glow after it stops flaming.
3. The char length is measured by inserting the correct weight (detemined by the weight of the fabric being tested) on one side of the charred area and gently raising the opposite side of the specimen. The length of the tear is measured and recorded.

Performance Requirements. Materials used in compartment interiors must be self-extinguishing. The average char length may not exceed 8 inches and the average after flame time may not exceed 15 seconds.

SUMMARY

Through the Upholstered Furniture Action Council, members of the upholstered furniture industry devised a program to reduce the cigarette ignition of upholstered furniture. A hangtag identifies items that comply with the

Figure 16.9 Horizontal flammability tester. (Courtesy of United States Testing Co., Inc.)

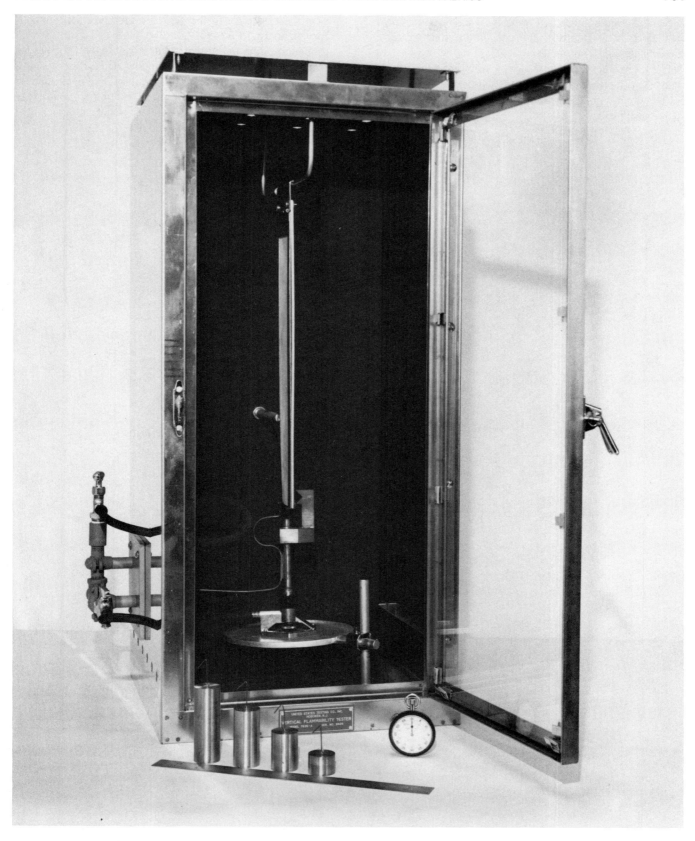

Figure 16.10 Vertical flammability tester. (Courtesy of the United States Testing Co., Inc.)

UFAC program standards. Products so labeled are safer, but they are not fireproof, and consumers must exercise care in using smoking materials.

The Consumer Product Safety Commission is monitoring the effectiveness of the UFAC program and the extent to which supplier and manufacturers are voluntarily participating. The CPSC will use these observations to assess the need for further action on the proposed mandatory standard, PFF 6-74.

Federal flammability mandates are in effect for fabrics used in the interiors of motor vehicles and airliners. These regulations are intended to reduce the immediate threat to occupants by providing more time for egress in the event of fire.

three

WINDOW AND WALL COVERINGS

Unit Three focuses on textiles produced for use in window treatments and as wall coverings. Styles of curtain and drapery treatments, blinds and shades, and shutters and awnings are described and illustrated in Chapter 17. The chapter covers measurements and calculations for determining rod length and placement and the amount of yardage required for constructing lined, two-way draw panels. Chapter 18 discusses the influence of appearance features, functional values, cost variables, and performance mandates on the selection of window treatment styles and coverings. The fibers, yarns, and nontextile elements used in window coverings are identified in Chapter 19. Chapter 20 describes the curtain, drapery, and lining fabrics produced with these components.

Along with the performance guidelines recommended by members of the industry, test methods for measuring various service-related properties of textile window covering fabrics are summarized in Chapter 21. This chapter also reviews procedures for proper maintenance of finished curtain, drapery, and lining fabrics.

Because several fabrics produced for use in window treatments may also be applied to vertical surfaces, the last chapter in this unit, Chapter 22, focuses on textile wall and panel coverings. Attention is given to the selection and installation of these coverings, and to their effectiveness in reducing noise and energy consumption.

chapter 17

Window Treatment Styles

- Curtain and Drapery Treatments
- Blinds and Shades
- Awnings and Shutters

Window treatments include curtains, draperies, blinds, shades, shutters, and awnings, used alone or in combinations. These treatments are decorated with such items as rods, cornices, hold-backs, and valences. The styling features of window treatments impose requirements that consumers and professionals should consider. Some need a highly drapable textile fabric; some require a stiffened fabric; and some, especially those having multiple layers, may demand an unaffordable amount of yardage. Attention should also be given to whether there is a need for hand-drawing, the type and number of rods a particular treatment requires, and the like.

Window treatment styles do not change, but their popularity does. For example, priscilla curtains, illustrated in Figure 17.1e, are always distinguished by ruffles and crisscrossed panels, but at some times they are fashionable and others, not. After any style is chosen, designers and consumers select from a wide variety of components to execute it; thus, identical styles may have dramatically different appearances.

CURTAIN AND DRAPERY TREATMENTS

In general, "curtains" describes relatively sheer, lightweight coverings that are hung without linings, while "draperies" describes heavy, often opaque and highly patterned coverings usually hung with linings. The term "casement" may be assigned to numerous fabrics of medium weight and some degree of transparency. Casement fabrics may be hung as unlined curtains or as lined draperies. Curtains and draperies are normally textile fabrics, but some novel treatments involve such components as strands of glass or wooden beads and polymer film fabrics.

The coverings in some curtain and drapery treatments are hung as stationary, nontraversing panels. Other coverings are hung as traversing panels that can be opened and closed as desired. Additional styling features may be added with the judicious use of decorative headings, trimmings, valences, cornices, and hardware fixtures.

Curtain Treatments

Figure 17.1 shows some typical styles of curtain treatments. Stationary casement panels (Figure 17.1a) are approximately two and a half times wider than the window. The panels are supported by a conventional, nontraversing curtain rod inserted through a casing sewn into the upper edge of the fabric. The casing may be plain or constructed with a heading (Figures 17.3a and 17.3b, respectively). A heading, such as pinched pleats, and a traversing rod convert stationary panels into draw curtains (Figure 17.1b). Panels anchored at their upper and lower edges are known as sash curtains, and are typically used on French doors. As the width of the fabric is increased with respect to the width of the window, the shirred effect becomes more pronounced, reducing inward vision and the degree of light transmission.

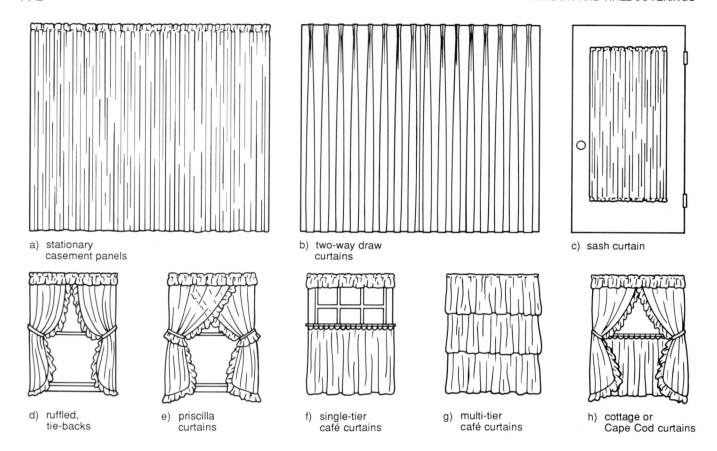

a) stationary
   casement panels

b) two-way draw
   curtains

c) sash curtain

d) ruffled,
   tie-backs

e) priscilla
   curtains

f) single-tier
   café curtains

g) multi-tier
   café curtains

h) cottage or
   Cape Cod curtains

Figure 17.1 Typical curtain styles.

Whereas the panels in ruffled, tie-back curtains (Figure 17.1d) do not cross at their upper edges, the panels in priscilla treatments overlap; priscilla treatments always involve ruffled tie-backs, as well. Ruffled curtain treatments must be carefully chosen to avoid an overdressed appearance. The use of such crisp, transparent fabrics as organdy, voile, and dotted swiss (described in Chapter 20) can help to minimize the visual weight of these treatments, as well as provide the body required for attractive ruffles.

Café curtains may be used alone or in combination with draperies. They are frequently constructed with scalloped headings and hung by rings looped over a rod. Multi-tier café curtains, with each tier normally overlapping the lower tier by about three inches, may be hung by rings or by rods run through fabric casings. When single-tier café curtains are combined with ruffled, tied-back panels, the treatment is labeled a cottage or Cape Cod curtain style (Figure 17.1h).

Drapery Treatments

Typical drapery treatments are illustrated in Figure 17.2. One-way draw draperies are drawn in one direction, stacking on one side of the window; two-way draperies are drawn to stack on both sides.

The panels in tied-back and held-back styles are secured by cords, chains, medallions, and the like, but the panels may be released, if desired. Pouf or bishop's sleeve treatments (Figure 17.2e) have tiers of bouffant or billowed-out areas created by periodically gathering the fabric panels.

When draperies are combined with sheer curtains, they are called "overdraperies," and the curtains are called "sheers" or "glass curtains." The term "glass" here indicates that the curtains hang next to the window glass; it is not describing the use of glass fiber. Combining draperies and curtains increases the cost of a window treatment, but it may also improve interior insulation and acoustics.

Headings

Headings appear at the top of curtain and drapery panels. These treatments finish the upper edge and distribute fullness evenly across the finished width. Figure 17.3 illustrates various styles of headings. Headings may be hand measured and sewn or produced with commercial tape.

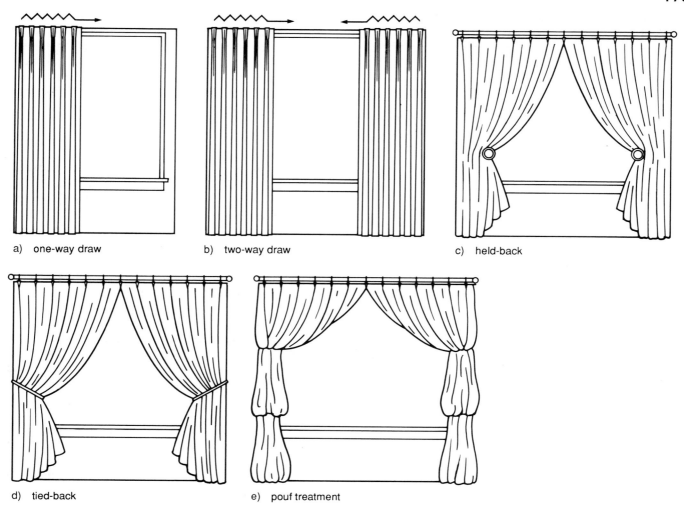

a) one-way draw

b) two-way draw

c) held-back

d) tied-back

e) pouf treatment

Figure 17.2 Typical drapery styles.

Pleats produced with tape are slightly rounded instead of sharply creased, but the hooks can be removed for cleaning.

Sewn headings, in contrast to those formed with tape, should be interfaced with a fabric such as buckram or crinoline. These plain-woven fabrics are stiffened with sizings, starches, or resins and can provide support for the heading treatment. The stability of the stiffening agent to cleaning agents should be ascertained prior to use.

Trimmings

Curtain and drapery treatments may be enriched by the use of ornamental trimmings, such as cords, tasseled or looped fringes, gimps, pipings, rickracks, laces, or galloons (narrow lengths of braid, embroidered fabric, or lace). Some trimmings may be sewn directly to the covering fabric, while others may be used as tie-backs or festoons. A festoon is created by draping an ornamental trim-

ming over a valence rod or other overhead treatment. The use of festoons has diminished in recent years, perhaps because contemporary interiors are often informal.

Overhead Treatments

Overhead treatments cover and conceal panel headings and hardware and enrich window treatments. Valence treatments are executed in fabric; other overhead treatments employ wood or metal.

Simple valences may be pleated, scalloped, or shirred. Since these valences are constructed in the same manner as headings, they are, in effect, short draperies. Very decorative, complex valence treatments may include swags and jabots or cascades (Figure 17.4). A swagged valence is formed by horizontally draping fabric over the drapery heading or a valence rod and securing the fabric at the outer corners; the fabric used should be drapable and fluid. Jabots and cascades are side treatments and one or the other

Table 17.1 ROD LENGTHS NEEDED FOR VARIOUS WIDTHS OF WINDOWS AND STACKBACK SPACES

If the glass is	The stackback* should be	Your rod length and drapery coverage should be (add for overlaps and returns)
38"	26"	64"
44"	28"	72"
50"	30"	80"
56"	32"	88"
62"	34"	96"
68"	36"	104"
75"	37"	112"
81"	39"	120"
87"	41"	128"
94"	42"	136"
100"	44"	144"
106"	46"	152"
112"	48"	160"
119"	49"	168"
125"	51"	176"
131"	53"	184"
137"	55"	192"
144"	56"	200"
150"	58"	208"
156"	60"	216"
162"	62"	224"
169"	63"	232"
175"	65"	240"
181"	67"	248"
187"	69"	256"

Note: Figures are based on average pleating and medium weight fabric. For extra bulky fabrics, add to stackback to compensate for the additional space they require.

*For one-way draws, deduct 7" from stackback.

Courtesy of Kirsch, Division of Cooper Industries, Inc.

is generally used with a swag. Jabots are pleated and the lower edges may be level, or they may be angled as in Figure 17.4. Cascades are gathered and designed to fall in folds of graduated length. In many installations, jabots are hung over the ends of the swag, while cascades are hung behind them. However they are hung, the length of the side treatments should be at least one third that of the window treatment.

Cornices, cantonnières, and lambrequins are rigid overhead treatments constructed of wood or metal. They can be covered with the panel fabric or coordinating fabric, or painted, stained, or left as natural wood. A cornice (Figure 17.5a) is mounted to cover the drapery heading and hardware. Typically, cornices project 4 to 6 inches from the wall and cover one seventh of the treatment length. Adding straight sides and shaped front panels to a cornice board converts it into a lambrequin (Figure 17.5b). A cantonnière fits flush to the wall and has a shaped overhead panel and sides that extend to the floor.

Hardware

The assortment of hardware used with curtains and draperies includes rods, mounting screws and bolts, batons, and fabric weights. Batons are used to manually open and close the panels; fabric weights, placed in the lower hem area, improve the draping quality of the fabric. The assortment also includes such decorative accessories as café rings and clips, chains, and medallions. Medallions are permanently attached to the window frame for use as holdbacks, as shown in Figure 17.2c.

Conventional Rods. A variety of conventional, nondecorative curtain and drapery rods is available today. Conventional rods are comparatively inexpensive, but consumers and contract designers should consider the aesthetic impact of these rods when not covered by the headings. Conventional traversing rods are usually equipped with a system of cords to control opening and closing.

A relatively new style of conventional rods has a height of 2 1/2 inches or 4 1/2 inches. The added depth creates the look of a valence when casings, with or without headings (Figures 17.3a and 17.3b), are shirred over the rod.

Decorative Rods. Decorative curtain and drapery rods are made of wood, metal, or plastic finished to resemble, for example, brass, pewter, gold, or natural wood. Coordinating rings secure the panels. In many cases, matching tie-back chains, hold-back medallions, and various styles of finials (the decorative pieces attached to the ends of rods) are available. Decorative traversing rods may be controlled electrically, by a system of cords, or by batons.

Nontraversing decorative rods are especially useful for supporting macramé and other stationary panels. These panels are hung from wooden or metallic rings looped over the rod. If the panels are to be opened and closed, they should be shifted by a baton and not by pulling on the side hems, which could deform the edge and lead to excessive soiling and wear.

Calculating Yardage Required

The successful execution of a window treatment depends on the accuracy of the measurements taken when determining the amount of fabric required for the project. As is true for any project involving colored textiles, the

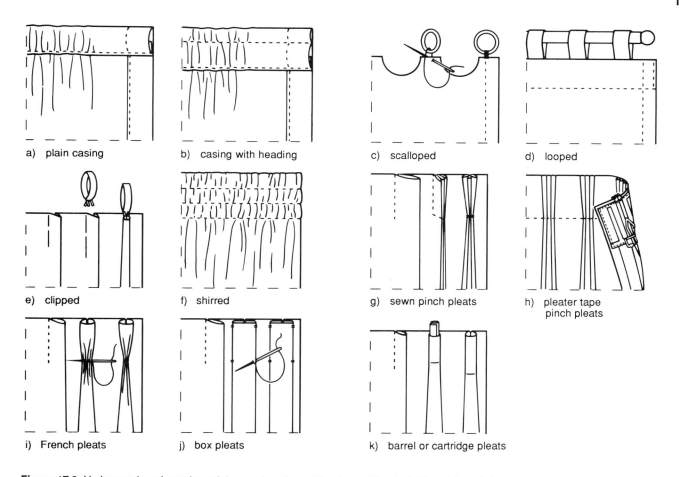

a) plain casing b) casing with heading c) scalloped d) looped

e) clipped f) shirred g) sewn pinch pleats h) pleater tape pinch pleats

i) French pleats j) box pleats k) barrel or cartridge pleats

Figure 17.3 Various styles of curtain and drapery headings. (Courtesy of Reader's Digest Association, Inc.)

amount of fabric initially ordered must be sufficient to complete the treatment. As was noted in Chapter 8, separate orders generally result in the delivery of fabrics with slightly differing color characteristics; even slight differences may prove to be unacceptable.

The following sections summarize the variables that generally should be considered when measuring for curtains and draperies. Other publications, readily available from Cooperative Extension Sevices, product manufacturers, and interior furnishing retailers, may be reviewed for instructions pertinent to specific styles and various overhead treatments. Usually, these materials also include detailed sewing and hanging instructions.

Determining Rod Length and Placement. A yardstick or steel tape should be used for taking all measurements, beginning with those needed to determine the rod length and placement. Before determining the length of the rod, a decision must be made concerning the extent of the outward view desired when the panels are open. For maximum outward vision, it should be possible to stack the panels back beyond the window glass. The values listed in Table 17.1 will help determine the length of the rod needed when full clearance of the glass is preferred. The distances can be adjusted when the panels must camouflage a structural defect and when a portion of the glass is to be used for stackback space.

Rods should be mounted so that the drapery headings will not be visible to the outside. Headings are normally 4 inches in height; thus, the rod should normally be located 4 inches above the top edge of the window glass. Again, if structural defects, such as unequal frame heights, must be camouflaged, the location of the rod can be adjusted. The rod should be installed prior to taking the measurements needed for determining the yardage required.

Determining Panel Length. Lengthwise measurements are taken from the top of conventional rods and from the bottom of the rings on decorative rods. The panels may extend to the window sill, to the apron (the

Figure 17.4 Swagged valence with jabots. (Courtesy of Kirsch, a division of Cooper Industries, Inc.)

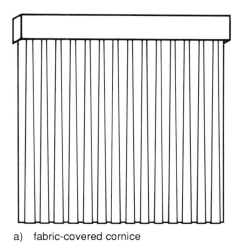

a) fabric-covered cornice

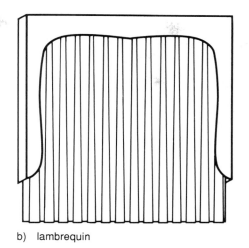

b) lambrequin

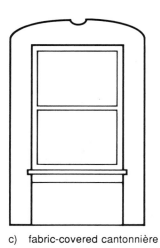

c) fabric-covered cantonnière

Figure 17.5 Rigid overhead and side treatments.

horizontal board below the sill), or to the floor. One inch should be subtracted from the measurement taken to the floor to allow for clearance, especially when soft floor coverings are in place. For distinctive styling and reduced air infiltration, consumers and designers may elect to have the panels stack or mound on the floor, in which case extra yardage must be allowed. For the purpose of this discussion, assume the finished panel will be 85 inches in length.

If patterned fabrics are chosen, extra yardage must be added for matching repeats. The lengthwise measurement must be evenly divisible by the length of the repeat. Thus, assuming the length of the repeat is 18 inches, 5 inches must be added to the measured 85 inches so that it will be divisible by 18. Normally, a full repeat is placed at the lower hem of sill- and apron-length panels, and at the top hem of floor-length panels.

Yardage must now be added for the hem allowances. For unlined panels, a doubled, 4-inch top hem is planned, and for lined panels, 0.5 inch is allowed for top turnover. The lower hem allowance is generally 4 inches, but as a precaution against potential relaxation and residual shrinkage, this figure should be doubled. In the event that in-use shrinkage shortens the panels, the fabric needed for lengthening is readily available. The hem allowance must always be doubled when such fabrics as taffeta, faille, and bengaline are to be used. The numerous fibers in the crosswise ribs of these fabrics, especially if they are cotton or rayon, may swell during cleaning; this increase in the diameter of the ribs would draw up the warp yarns, causing lengthwise shrinkage. Whatever its fiber content, any fabric may exhibit from 1 to 3 percent residual shrinkage, even if it was preshrunk to encourage relaxation shrinkage.

The total cut length of the panel fabric may now be calculated as follows:

finished length of panel	85	inches
+ allowance for pattern matching	5	inches
+ allowance for top hem	0.5	inch
+ allowance for bottom hem	8	inches
= total cut length of panel	93.5	inches

For the lining fabric, no yardage is needed for pattern matching; the bottom hem is generally single and 2 inches deep, and the lower edge is 1 inch above the lower edge of the drapery panel. Again, an allowance may be made for potential in-use shrinkage. The total cut length of the lining fabric may now be calculated as follows:

finished length of panel	85	inches
− lining shorter than panel	1	inch
+ allowance for top hem	0.5	inch
+ allowance for bottom hem	2	inches
= total cut length of lining	86.5	inches

Determining Panel Width. "Fabric panel" is not synonymous with "fabric width." A fabric panel (Figure 17.6a) is formed by seaming a number of fabric widths and, if necessary, a partial width together. "Pleated panel coverage," "pleat coverage," and "coverage" are synonyms that refer to the horizontal distance covered by the pleated area of the panel. Coverage does not include the portion of the panel that covers the overlap at the center, nor the por-

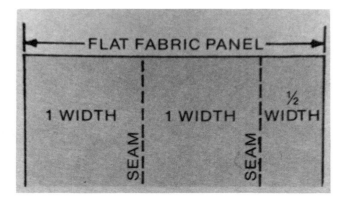

a) fabric panel

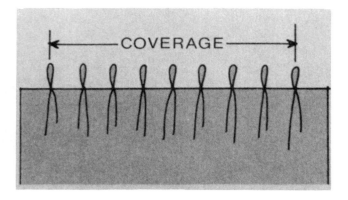

b) coverage

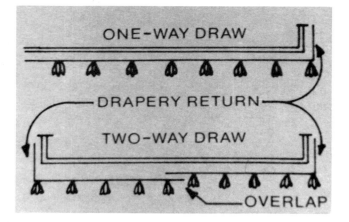

c) overlap and returns

Figure 17.6 Illustrations of terms that describe the measurements taken to determine panel width. (Courtesy of Kirsch, a division of Cooper Industries, Inc.)

tion that covers the return, the bracket extending perpendicularly from the wall at each end of the rod.

For the purposes of discussion, we will assume that the length of the installed rod is 56 inches. For a one-way draw treatment, the panel coverage would be 56 inches, with no allowance required for overlap. For a two-way draw treatment, the coverage for each panel would be 28 inches, and the allowance for overlap is normally 3.5 inches. Yardage must now be added for fullness, a requirement that generally doubles the yardage but may triple it when sheer fabrics are used. The allowance for the return is equal to the bracket projection distance, typically 3.5 inches. Each of the two side hems require an allowance of 2 inches. Of this, 0.5 inch will be used as an allowance when seaming the lining, and 1.5 inches will be turned to show at the side of the lining. The total width of one flat, unhemmed panel for a two-way draw treatment may now be calculated as follows:

coverage	28	inches
+ allowance for fullness	28	inches
+ allowance for overlap	3.5	inches
+ allowance for return	3.5	inches
+ allowance for side hems	4	inches
= total width of one flat panel	67	inches

The values listed in Table 17.2 were calculated in this manner and can be used after coverage is determined. The table also contains guidelines for spacing pleats to control the fullness.

One inch must be allowed for seaming the sides of the lining to the drapery panel. The flat, unhemmed lining is thus cut 3 inches narrower than the flat, unhemmed drapery panel that will be turned 1.5 inches inward on each side.

Determining Yardage Total. If, for example, the width of the covering fabric is 45 inches, one full fabric width and one partial width would be seamed to produce the 67-inch-wide panel. Since a second panel is needed for the two-way draw treatment, we may at first assume four fabric widths are required. In this particular case, half the divided fabric width could be used for each of the two panels and thus, only three fabric widths are required. Such an economical use of fabric is not always possible, especially when allowances must be made for matching crosswise repeats and for seam allowances, but we should be alert to the possibility. For some projects, especially those involving expensive fabric, it may even be desirable to slightly reduce the width of the fabric included in each pleat.

The total amount of fabric to be ordered can be determined by multiplying the total length of the unhemmed

Table 17.2 **FABRIC PANEL WIDTHS AND PLEATING GUIDELINES**

Desired pleated panel coverage	Flat fabric without hens	Hemmed flat fabric	Number of 4" flat spaces between pleats	Number of pleats	Width of fabric in each pleat
16"	43"	39"	4	5	3-1/8"
20"	51"	47"	5	6	3-1/4"
24"	59"	55"	6	7	3-3/8"
28"	67"	63"	7	8	3-1/2"
32"	75"	71"	8	9	3-1/2"
36"	83"	79"	9	10	3-9/16"
40"	91"	87"	10	11	3-5/8"
44"	99"	95"	11	12	3-5/8"
48"	107"	103"	12	13	3-5/8"
52"	115"	111"	13	14	3-5/8"
56"	123"	119"	14	15	3-3/4"
60"	131"	127"	15	16	3-3/4"
64"	139"	135"	16	17	3-3/4"
68"	147"	143"	17	18	3-3/4"
72"	155"	151"	18	19	3-3/4"
76"	163"	159"	19	20	3-3/4"
80"	171"	167"	20	21	3-3/4"
84"	179"	175"	21	22	3-3/4"
88"	187"	183"	22	23	3-3/4"
92"	195"	191"	23	24	3-3/4"
96"	203"	199"	24	25	3-3/4"
100"	211"	207"	25	26	3-3/4"
104"	219"	215"	26	27	3-3/4"
108"	227"	223"	27	28	3-3/4"
112"	235"	231"	28	29	3-3/4"
116"	243"	239"	29	30	3-3/4"
120"	251"	247"	30	31	3-7/8"
124"	259"	254"	31	32	3-7/8"
128"	267"	263"	32	33	3-7/8"

Courtesy of Kirsch, Division of Cooper Industries, Inc.

panel by the number of fabric widths needed. The amount of lining fabric required is calculated in the same manner.

BLINDS AND SHADES

In contrast to curtains and draperies, which are drawn horizontally, almost all blinds and shades are drawn vertically. Some styles of blinds and shades are executed with textile fabric, others with metal or wood, and still others employ textile and nontextile components.

Austrian Shades

Austrian shades (Figure 17.7) are constructed of textile fabric that is vertically shirred to create lengthwise bands of horizontally draping folds. The level of transparency is determined by the compactness of construction of the fabric and the amount of fabric taken up in the gathering.

Balloon Shades

Balloon shades, like Austrian shades, are composed of textile fabric and are vertically drawn. Their name derives from the balloon-like puffs they form when raised. The fullness of the panels may be distributed by shirring the top casing over a rod or by using inverted pleats. In inverted-pleat styling (Figure 17.8), the panels are essentially flat until raised, a feature that makes possible full visual appreciation of the fabric.

Figure 17.7 Austrian shade.

Figure 17.8 Balloon shade with inverted pleats to control panel fullness. (Courtesy of Celanese Corporation.)

Accordion-pleated Shades

Accordion-pleated shades are constructed of woven or knitted fabric that has been stiffened and set in a three-dimensional, folded configuration (Figure 17.9). As the shades are raised and lowered, the folds open and close, the same way the folds in an accordion's bellows open and close when the instrument is played. A 24-inch-long shade takes up only 2-1/4 inches stack-up space when raised, measuring from the top of the headrail to the bottom of the bottom rail; a 96-inch-long shade takes up 3-3/4 inches. The textural characteristics of these shades vary readily with the style of yarn used; their transparency is controlled by the compactness of construction and the selective application of backcoatings. Metallic coatings may be used for insulation, and also for static reduction, which reduces the attraction for dust. These window coverings are frequently used in commercial interiors, generally in combination with drapery panels.

Honeycomb-pleated Shades

A relatively new type of accordion-pleated shade is the honeycomb-pleated shade (Figure 17.10). In these cover-

Figure 17.9 Accordion-pleated shade. (Courtesy of Kirsch, division of Cooper Industries, Inc.)

ings, spunbonded polyester fabrics are permanently pleated and paired to create an insulating layer of air. The outer fabric is always white to provide high heat reflection, and presents a uniform exterior appearance. Because the pleats are smaller than those in conventional accordion-pleated shades, a 24-inch-long honeycomb shade requires only 2 inches of stack-up space; a 96-inch-long shade requires only 3-1/8 inches.

Cascade Loop Shades

A cascade loop shade is shown in Figure 17.11. Horizontal tucks in the fabric panel add visual interest; soft loops, often called architectural folds, form when the shade is raised. Like accordion-pleated shades, cascade loop shades are used extensively in commercial interiors.

Roman Shades

Roman shades hang flat at the window until raised; then, horizontal pleats form. These window coverings may be made exclusively of textile fabric, but frequently they are constructed of woven wood, a combination of wooden slats and textile yarns. The yarns used may vary in color, luster, size, and complexity. To permit the ne-

Figure 17.10 Duette™ honeycomb-pleated shade. (Courtesy of Kirsch, a division of Cooper Industries, Inc. Duette™ is a trademark of Hunter-Douglas.)

Figure 17.11 Cascade loop shade.

cessary folding, the wooden slats always lie across the covering.

Some Roman shades are hand woven, from grasses, cane, or wheat straws crosswise and textile yarns lengthwise. These shades are relatively transparent, but they nonetheless diminish the view into the interior and provide a natural look heightened by the irregularity of the materials and the hand weaving.

A variation of the conventional Roman shade styling is the use of two shades, normally constructed from textile fabric. In these coverings, known as athey shades, one shade is lowered and one shade is raised for full closure.

Roller Shades

A roller shade may be plain or patterned, constructed of a textile fabric or a sheet of polymer film. It may mount at the bottom of the window and unroll upward or mount at the top of the window and unroll downward.

Venetian Blinds

Venetian blinds are made up of horizontal slats or louvers laced together with textile cords. Traditionally, the slats have nearly always been of aluminum coated with cream-colored enamel. Today, wooden louvers, molded polymer slats, and fashion-colored aluminum slats are also available. In recent years, residential and commercial consumers have increasingly shown a preference for relatively narrow slats.

The textile cord system facilitates rotation of the slats to produce the desired level and angle of light and the preferred extent of view inward and outward. The entire covering may also be stacked up at the upper portion of the window.

Vertical Blinds

Vertical blinds, also referred to as vertical venetian blinds, are a relatively new window treatment. In these coverings, the louvers or vanes are suspended vertically from traversing or nontraversing rods. They may be rotated for increased outward vision and inward light transmission. Traversing styles may have a one- or two-way draw.

The louvers or vanes used in vertical blinds may be as narrow as 2 inches or as wide as 6 inches. They may be constructed of metal, wood, woven wood, or macramé. The compactness of construction of woven and knotted structures has a direct effect on the degree of light transmitted when the blinds are closed.

Initially, vertical blinds were almost exclusively used in commercial interior applications. Today, they can also be found in residential interiors, especially in settings having a contemporary design plan.

AWNINGS AND SHUTTERS

Awnings and shutters may be constructed from rigid materials only or from a combination of rigid materials and drapable textile fabrics. These structures can be used as interior and exterior window treatments.

Awnings

Awnings are basically rigid structures that may be composed of metal or molded polymer sheetings or of textile fabric stretched and held over a rigid frame. Awnings are occasionally used for novel interior applications, but primarily as exterior window treatments. Outside windows, they reduce solar heat transmission and provide protection from weather elements.

Textile awning fabric may be used in outdoor applications other than window treatments, for instance, as screens for privacy, windbreaks, and canopies over patios, gazebos, and carports. For all outdoor applications, fabrics must be composed of fibers resistant to sunlight, mildew, insects, water, wind, and atmospheric contaminants. Acrylic, saran, and olefin fibers are often employed, generally solution dyed for superior colorfastness.

Shutters

Decorative, stationary shutters have long framed windows on the exterior of homes and other structures. These panels cannot be unfolded to cover the window glass. Today, folding shutters are increasingly mounted to unfold over the glass, reducing solar heat gain in the summer and interior heat loss in the winter. This current application of shutters is a revival of the practice of using folding shutters on colonial homes for protection from the elements.

Shutters are usually constructed of pine or oak, which is stained or painted the desired color. Stiles are shifted vertically to open and close the crosswise louvers in each rectangular section, and hinges permit the units to be folded and unfolded to control inward and outward vision, the level of light transmission, and heat gain and loss.

Textile fabrics are sometimes used to soften the appearance of wooden shutters. Shirred fabric may be inserted in some sections, or used in lieu of the wooden louvers.

SUMMARY

Window treatment styles range from the relatively simple, with a single component, to the extremely complex, involving multiple layers, an overhead treatment, and decorative accessories. Some treatments are executed with textiles, some with nontextiles, and some with a combination of components.

The style of window treatment and the components to execute it should be decided on only after aesthetic, functional, and cost factors have been considered. When consumers examine these variables before committing themselves—making a purchase or signing a contractual agreement—they will make more informed decisions and be better able to select treatments and components that provide the appearance and functional features they need at a price they can afford.

chapter *18*

Window Treatment Style and Covering Selections

- Appearance Factors
- Functional Values
- Cost Factors
- Performance Mandates

The selection of window treatments and window coverings is influenced by several variables. At the outset, the fenestration—the design, arrangement, and proportioning of the windows and doors in an interior—may limit the range of styles that can be considered. Structural defects needing to be camouflaged impose additional limitations, and so do desires for such functional properties as privacy enhancement and noise or glare reduction. The range of colored covering choices may be narrowed by such conditions as the source and quantity of light and the presence of atmospheric contaminants. Legal mandates may also apply to the covering choices made for certain commercial interiors. In all cases, the selections must be affordable; it must be considered whether multiple fabric components, elaborate hardware fixtures, or extensive trimming will escalate the cost beyond the limit of the furnishings budget. For some treatments, however, future savings in energy could help compensate for the initial cost.

APPEARANCE FACTORS

Window treatment styles and coverings cannot always be selected on the basis of personal preference or professional recommendation alone. The fenestration and any structural defects must be considered first if the setting is to appear attractive. The effects of various factors on color must be examined to assure the realization and retention of the planned appearance.

Aesthetic Preferences

At the outset, consumers' personal preferences limit the range of window treatment styles and coverings they will consider. Some consumers and designers may prefer a treatment that dominates the interior setting; other may prefer a treatment that attracts little attention and can serve as a backdrop for distinctive upholstered items and soft floor coverings. Some prefer an informal treatment, others a formal one. Some may have a taste for a highly decorative fabric in a simple treatment, others for the reverse. As for all product choices, the final selection of window treatment style and materials should also be based on considerations involving more than aesthetics.

Structural Factors

Within an interior space, the fenestration may require that two windows be covered with a single treatment, that treatments on neighboring windows be mounted to equalize differences in height, or that the coverings draw one way or not at all. A small, isolated window may require a large-scale treatment with fabric identical to that used for other windows in the interior to make it appear larger and integrated. Certain types of windows preclude the use of certain treatment styles. Bow windows, for example, cannot be covered with Roman shades or with accordion-pleated shades. Windows that open inward cannot be covered with stationary panels unless the panels and rods are attached to the window sashes.

The large expanses of glass that typify contemporary homes and office buildings may require coverings to control light and heat transmission during the day and to provide privacy and avoid a "black wall" effect at night. Walls in need of repair and windows in need of replacement can be camouflaged by covering them with stationary treatments.

Color-related Variables

Various factors that may affect the apparent color of textile structures were discussed in Chapter 8. These factors, and those affecting actual color, should be considered so that the colors chosen appear the same in the interior and will go on appearing so for a reasonable period of time. Careful consideration will also help assure that the coordination planned between the window treatments and other interior furnishings and wall coverings is realized.

Factors Affecting Apparent Color. It is critically important to confirm the acceptability of any changes in the apparent color of a window covering produced by the lighting conditions in an interior. Professionals and consumers are advised to hang sample lengths of their possible covering choices at their windows, along with any planned shades or linings. If the quantity of incident natural light is judged too high, the consumer may consider adding sheers or exterior awnings.

Because window coverings are normally not subject to the great amounts of abrasion often inflicted on upholstery fabrics and soft floor coverings, changes in texture, and therefore in luster, may be minimal. Because of this, fabrics having prominent relief effects, like those provided by complex yarns, are often appropriate for window treatments. The rate and level of soiling may also be lower with window coverings than with other structures. However, repeatedly opening and closing panels by pulling on their side hems or headings may lead to rapid soil accumulation; and, especially in stationary treatments, airborne dust, smoke, and oily cooking fumes may settle on the fabrics and gradually alter the apparent colors.

Factors Affecting Actual Color. When window covering fabrics are to be installed indoors, concerns arise for lightfastness, gasfastness, and fastness to cleaning agents. When coverings are to be installed outdoors, concern arises as well for the stability of the colorants to weather elements and changing ambient temperature. The accelerated and long-term testing procedures used to ascertain the colorfastness of interior and exterior window coverings exposed to these conditions and substances are discussed in Chapter 21.

Window coverings are continually subjected to solar rays. Sun-related alterations in the structure of dyes produce concomitant changes in the structure of the fibers. To help minimize the degradation of the colorants and the fibers used in decorative panels, the use of permanently attached or separately hung lining materials, and possibly exterior awnings, is advisable.

FUNCTIONAL VALUES

Consumers, contract designers, and architects may elect to restrict their style and covering choices to those that can provide specific functional benefits, such as light control, privacy, insulation, and noise reduction.

Reduction of Glare

The degree of brightness control that window coverings should provide depends on the solar exposure conditions, the type of glass in the window, and the preferences and needs of the people who use the interior space. Windows with a northern exposure are subject to less direct sunlight than those with a southern exposure. Windows with an eastern exposure receive more direct light in the morning, and those with a western exposure more in the afternoon hours. Installing bronze-tinted or reflective-coated vision glass in lieu of clear glass will reduce the level of light transmission, but this reduction may or may not be adequate.

When the degree of transmission fails to coincide with the preferences and needs of the people using the interior, it can be balanced by interior and exterior window treatments. Often, the treatment should be designed to provide varied levels of control throughout the day, ranging from full transmission to total blackout.

The brightness control provided by window treatments is influenced by the color characteristics of the coverings, the number of layers used, the fullness of the panels, the addition of fiber delusterants and fabric coatings, and the fabric openness. Fabric openness is the ratio of the open areas between the yarns to the total area of the fabric. It is apparent from Figure 18.1 that an open fabric would permit more light to pass through than would a semi-open or closed fabric. Openness is not, however, the only variable of fabric composition that affects light transmission. As illustrated in Figure 4.1a (page 26), a portion of the light waves striking a fiber are reflected, another portion absorbed, and the remaining portion transmitted. Light-colored fibers, especially those containing no delusterants, permit more light waves to be transmitted to the interior. Increasing the fullness of the panels reduces this transmission, since more fibers reflect and absorb more waves.

Because the quantity of direct and reflected light varies with the exposure and the hour of the day, consumers may

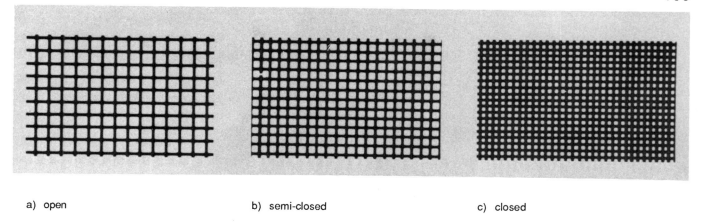

a) open   b) semi-closed   c) closed

Figure 18.1 Levels of fabric openness. (Courtesy of PPG Industries, Inc. 1978.)

elect to use multiple layers of window coverings to widen the range of brightness control options. For maximum flexibility, various combinations of shades, curtains, draperies, and awnings may be used. For total blackout in such interiors as motel rooms, shades or fabrics with opaque coatings may be installed; examples of such fabrics are pictured in Figure 20.32 (page 220).

Controlling the level of brightness may be desirable for aesthetic purposes, but it may be critical to reduce the glare when persons with impaired vision reside or work in the interior. It may also be necessary to reduce the glare for the visual comfort of employees stationed near windows.

Restriction of Inward Vision

Providing privacy has long been a basic function of window coverings. For windows placed so that inward vision must be continually restricted, full, stationary curtains may be selected. Most coverings will reduce the view inward during daylight hours, but a lining or separate curtains may be needed to ensure privacy at night when artificial illuminants brighten the interior. Moreover, when a window faces a private outdoor area, some covering may be considerd to relieve any sense of being open to observation.

Modification of Outward Vision

An exterior view can be modified by a covering with the appropriate degree of openness. As the size of the yarns and the compactness of construction increase, outward vision is decreased. In some settings, complete blockage of an unsightly view may be required; this can be accomplished by combining relatively heavy closed fabrics with opaque linings in stationary mountings.

Reduction of Interior Noise

Three types of sounds may be heard within interiors. Airborne sounds radiate directly into the air from people talking and typing, ringing telephones, video machines, radios, and the like. Surface sounds are produced as people traverse across the floor or push and pull items along it. Impact or structurally borne sounds result from impacts on a structural surface that cause it to vibrate, for instance, walking, jumping, dancing, bouncing balls, knocking on doors, and hammering nails. Of course, several activities, such as walking and vacuuming, create more than one type of sound. Also, most sounds can be transmitted to areas well beyond their origin. From the exterior come sounds from lawn mowers, cars, trucks, buses, airplanes, and the neighbor's dog.

Sounds that we want to hear can be entertaining and enlightening; but if we don't want to hear the sounds, they become noise, which can be annoying and disruptive. Thus, residential and commercial consumers often seek ways to control sounds and prevent them from becoming unwanted noise.

Figure 18.2 illustrates how interior sound can be prolonged and magnified as it is reflected from the floor to the ceiling and from a bare wall to a bare window. Ceiling materials and soft floor coverings will absorb sound that is traveling vertically; window and wall coverings can be installed to absorb sound that is traveling horizontally. (The sound absorption qualities of wall coverings are discussed in Chapter 22.)

The graph in Figure 18.3 shows that the sound absorption quality of drapery fabric decreases as fabric openness increases. The fabrics were tested with 100 percent fullness. The absorption results are reported numerically in terms of noise reduction coefficients (NRC), with higher values indicating greater absorption.

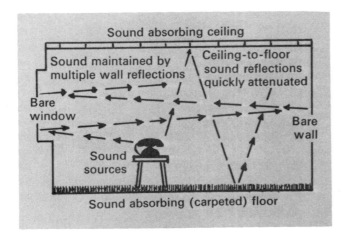

Figure 18.2 Interior sound travel. (Courtesy of PPG Industries, Inc. 1978.)

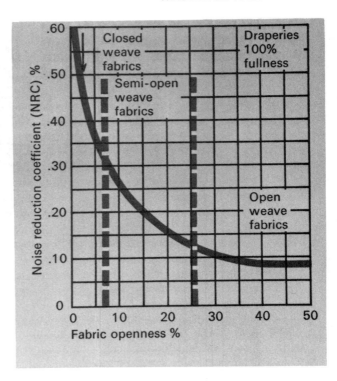

Figure 18.3 Graph of noise reduction coefficient (NRC) versus fabric openness factor. (Courtesy of PPG Industries, Inc. 1978.)

In multibed hospital rooms, fabric partitions are hung primarily to provide privacy; in large, open interiors they are used principally for decoration and to divide space. However, these interior partitions will also lessen horizontally reflected sound if they are constructed of closed, compactly constructed fabrics.

Conservation of Energy

Along with concern for the depletion of energy sources, especially the limited supply of fossil fuels, the pressures of rising heating and cooling costs have impelled consumers and manufacturers to search for ways to reduce energy consumption. Recently, consumer interest and research projects have focused on the role window treatments and other interior textile products can play in this conservation effort. Producers of window coverings and components, research personnel employed by government agencies and universities, and members of trade associations have sought to identify the styles of window treatments and the fabric-related variables that can contribute to the efficient maintenance of interior temperatures.

The thermal performance criteria for window treatments change as the seasons change. In winter, insulation is necessary to reduce heat loss, and in summer rejection of radiant energy is necessary to reduce heat gain. Reviewing the mechanisms by which heat is lost and gained is good preparation for making the appropriate selections of window treatments and components.

Air movement, including wind and forced circulation, causes heat transfer by convection. As wind circulates against exterior surfaces, it will convect heat away; the loss will be more pronounced with higher air speeds and greater differences between inside and outside temperatures. (Convection is the mechanism that causes a bridge surface

to freeze before the rest of the road's surface does.) In an interior, warm air may be drawn between the window coverings and the window glass, where it is cooled, becomes heavier, and flows under the lower edges of free-hanging coverings and back into the room. Air movement is also responsible for drafts, the infiltrations of cold air through structural openings such as cracks between window and wall frames and wall joints.

Conduction is the movement of thermal energy through solids, liquids, and gases. Insulation resists thermal transfer and stems conduction. In residential and commercial structures, heat energy will be conducted through the walls, doors, floors, and roof areas as well as the windows. However, from 25 to 50 percent of the heat generated in residences may be lost through the windows alone.[1]

The extent to which windows and window treatments retard heat loss in the winter, and heat gain in the summer, can be be measured and the results reported numerically in terms of U-values. U-values indicate how much heat actually does pass outward in winter and inward in summer. To become familiar with U-values, we can examine the values for various types of windows; these values are approximate and vary with construction, thickness of the glass, and the presence of tints or coatings. Single-pane window glass has a U-value of 1.13, double panes with 3/16 inch of insulating air space between them have a U-value of 0.41, and triple panes with a total of 5/8 inch insulating air space have a U-value of 0.35. A U-value of

1.13 BTU/ft²-hr-°F means that 1.13 British thermal units of heat pass through each square foot of window configuration every hour for each Farenheit degree of difference between inside and outside temperatures.

Because air is a poor heat conductor and a good heat insulator, window coverings should be installed to provide a tight enclosure that will entrap dead air between the fabric and the glass, similar to the enclosure between the panes in double- and triple-pane windows. The dead air will retard conduction, and the sealed covering also helps to prevent warm air from being drawn against the window. The installation of a free-hanging, traversing drapery treatment has been found to be minimally effective; it only reduced the winter U-value of a single-pane window from 1.13 to 1.06.[2] By contrast, the use of a tight-fitting closed drapery may reduce the value to 0.88.[3] Similarly, the use of a tight-fitting lining, sealed around the perimeter of the window, has been found to be more effective than a free-hanging lining. Furthermore, the thermal performance of drapery fabrics with different degrees of openness was found to be essentially equal when combined with the same sealed lining.[4]

Multilayered roller shades, many of which are not unlike the familiar mattress pad, can be used for their insulative value, especially in passive solar homes. Dead air is trapped between the layers; again, thermal efficiency improves when the edges of the shade are sealed to restrict air flow.[5]

With Roman shades constructed of woven wood, an increase in the quantity of complex yarns was found to increase the insulative quality.[6] Conventional venetian blinds and vertical blinds, especially those made of metal, are comparatively ineffective in reducing winter heat loss, because of the small gaps remaining between the closed louvers and the high conductivity of the metal components. On the other hand, their louvers can easily be angled to let in sunlight and increase heat gain during daylight hours in winter.

Interior shutters without louvers can contribute significantly to energy conservation, provided they fit tightly and are used consistently. Similarly, covering a window with an insulating panel of such material as expanded polystyrene, expanded polyurethane, cork, or plywood will effectively reduce winter heat loss. A 1-inch-thick panel of expanded polyurethane over a single pane of glass was found to produce a U-value of 0.14.[7]

To minimize air infiltration, weatherstripping and caulking compounds should be used to seal any cracks around structural joints. For added protection, consumers and designers may use drapery panels of extra length and width. In these treatments, the draperies extend over the wall joints on each side of the windows, and the panels stack on the floor, acting as infiltration barriers.

Radiation is the transfer of heat in the form of waves or rays. Waves radiating against the exterior surfaces of win-

dows include those emanating directly from the sun, as well as those reflected from the sky and such other surfaces as the facades of neighboring buildings, paved parking areas, streets, and sidewalks. As schematized in Figure 18.4, some of the incident waves are rejected, some absorbed, and some transmitted. Of the rays transmitted through the outdoor glass, various portions will be rejected, absorbed, and transmitted by the indoor glass. Finally, various portions of the rays transmitted through the indoor glass will be rejected, absorbed, and transmitted by the draperies.

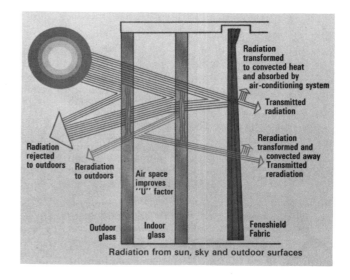

Figure 18.4 Typical heat rejection pattern. (Courtesy of PPG Industries, Inc. 1978.)

Clearly, window treatments that can be opened and closed provide the flexibility needed to control seasonal solar heat gain. On sunny winter days, the coverings can be opened to increase the level of heat transmission; on sunny summer days, they can be closed to increase the level of heat rejection. Solar heat gain in the summer, of course, warms the interior and increases the air conditioning load.

The effectiveness of windows and window coverings in reducing the level of radiant energy transmitted into the interior can be measured and the results reported numerically in terms of the shading coefficient (S/C). To calculate the S/C, the total amount of heat transmitted by a window and covering combination is divided by the total amount of heat transmitted by a single pane of clear 1/8-inch-thick glass. S/C values indicate how well a window and covering reduce heat gain, with lower values indicating more effective control; the actual amount of heat gain is reported in terms of the U-value.

A single pane of clear 1/4-inch-thick glass has a S/C of 0.93; adding a tint reduces the value to 0.67, and using double panes and a reflective finish further lowers the value, to 0.30 (Table 18.1). While drapery treatments produce insignificant reductions in the S/C value of insulated reflective glass, they produce significant decreases in the values of clear and tinted vision glass. The most significant reductions in these cases are produced by closed, light-colored draperies.

Conventional venetian blinds and vertical blinds are relatively ineffective in retarding winter heat loss, but they are quite effective in reducing summer heat gain. When combined with a single pane of clear glass, light-colored venetian blinds reduce the S/C to 0.55 and white vertical blinds reduce the value to 0.29.[8] Various types and colors of roller shades are also highly effective in reducing heat gain. As shown in Table 18.2, a white opaque shade reflects up to 80 percent of the incident solar energy. In contrast, a dark opaque shade absorbs some 88 percent of the energy. In turn, this absorbed heat will be transferred into the room, a negative effect in the summer but a positive effect in the winter.

Exterior shutters and awnings can be highly effective in reducing solar heat gain. Light colors should be used for both types of coverings for high reflection and low absorption of radiant energy. Heat absorbed by these coverings can be transferred through the windows to the interior: for maximum effectiveness, awnings must be correctly angled over the windows to reflect all direct rays.

Protection of Other Interior Furnishings

The radiant energy of the sun not only warms and brightens interior space; it also weakens textile fibers and, as discussed earlier in this chapter, changes their apparent and actual color characteristics. To protect other textile and nontextile furnishings, window coverings can be drawn to minimize light transmission. This will, of course, subject the window coverings themselves to higher levels of radiant energy. The replacement cost of the window treatments, however, is normally less than that of other furnishings, and relatively inexpensive curtains and linings can be used to protect more expensive overdraperies.

COST FACTORS

Various cost-related factors must be considered prior to final selection of window treatments. Together with the initial costs of the materials, labor, and accessories required, residential and commercial consumers should consider financial variables related to replacement and maintenance.

Initial Costs

The initial cost of a window treatment is not limited to the cost of the outercovering; it also includes the cost of

Table 18.1 SHADING COEFFICIENTS FOR GLASS WITH DRAPERIES

Type of glass (shading coefficient glass only)	I_D	I_M	I_L	II_D	II_M	II_L	III_D	III_M	III_L
1/4" clear (0.93)	0.72	0.68	0.65	0.68	0.61	0.56	0.64	0.54	0.46
1/4" tinted (0.67)	0.53	0.50	0.49	0.51	0.47	0.44	0.48	0.44	0.39
Insulating glass (0.54) 1/4" clear + 1/4" tinted	0.43	0.42	0.41	0.42	0.39	0.36	0.40	0.35	0.33
Insulating glass, reflective coated (0.30)	0.28	0.27	0.27	0.27	0.26	0.26	0.27	0.26	0.25

Classification of Fabrics: I—open weave; II—semi-open weave; III—closed weave; D—dark color; M—medium color; and L—light color.
Courtesy of PPG Industries, Inc., 1978.

Table 18.2 PERCENTAGE LIGHT TRANSMISSION, REFLECTION, AND ABSORPTION BY VARIOUS ROLLER SHADES

Shade characteristics	Light transmitted	Light reflected	Light absorbed
light color, translucent	25	60	15
white opaque	0	80	20
dark opaque	0	12	88

Source: S. Robert Hastings and Richard W. Crenshaw, "Window Design Strategies to Conserve Energy," *National Bureau of Standards Building Science Series 104,* U.S. Department of Commerce, June 1977, 403.

any linings, curtains, shades, and shutters to be used. The choice of a relatively narrow fabric with a comparatively high price per yard, elaborate styling, and fuller panels will escalate the materials cost. The cost is higher still when solution-dyed fibers and such treatments as flame resistant finishes and reflective coatings are specified. Custom projects involve separate charges for consultations with the designer and for measuring, cutting, sewing, trimming, and installing. Whether consumers choose ready-made coverings, elect to have a custom-designed treatment, or plan to construct the treatment themselves, added costs include those for the rods and any tie-backs, hold-backs, or overhead treatments.

Residential and commercial consumers should ascertain whether their new treatment qualifies for energy tax credit. This credit is offered by Congress as an incentive to consumers to reduce their energy consumption voluntarily by selecting materials known to be effective insulators. They may also balance the initial cost of the treatment against any energy savings that will be realized during the use-life of the treatment. Regardless of potential savings, however, the total cost and terms of payment—whether due in full on delivery or made in installments with interest charges—must coincide with the ability of the purchaser to pay. Financial institutions may permit the cost of some window treatment projects to be included in long-term mortgage obligations.

Replacement Costs

When selecting window treatment styles and coverings, consumers should consider the initial cost in relationship to the expected use-life. The use-life of textile coverings is affected by fiber and fabric variables, styling features, exposure conditions, and care; the average use-life generally ranges from three to five years. Because linings can extend the service-life of drapery fabrics for a year or more, consumers may determine that linings are especially cost-effective. Solution dyeing, although a comparatively expensive color application technique, should be used whenever coverings composed of acetate are installed in areas

having high concentrations of atmospheric pollutants. This will avoid the expense and disruption associated with the premature replacement of a covering that has changed hue.

Unless new hardware is required, replacement costs are normally limited to the cost of the new materials and the labor costs incurred for construction and installation. In some cases, charges may also be assessed for removing the existing treatments.

Maintenance Costs

Several variables related to fabric composition, such as the type of fiber used, the dimensional stability of the fabric, the use of durable press resins, the stability of the colorants, and the structural characteristics of the coverings, are the main determinants of what cleaning method should be used to maintain a window treatment. By considering these variables, consumers can determine whether laundering or dry cleaning is required; if the more expensive dry cleaning is called for, consumers may elect to reconsider their covering options.

Elaborate styling and multiple components, such as shades, curtains, draperies, and swags, will increase maintenance cost, since charges are incurred for the commercial laundering or dry cleaning of each covering and component. Wide, long panels are also more expensive to clean than are narrow, short panels. Separate charges may be assessed for removing and transporting the coverings to the cleaning plant, for ironing and reforming the folds, and for returning and rehanging the treatment. Of course, the anticipated frequency of cleaning—determined to a large extent by the appearance required by the owner—must be considered when estimating long-term maintenance costs.

PERFORMANCE MANDATES

Interior designers, architects, and specifiers must ascertain whether an authority with jurisdiction over materials used in a particular facility has established any mandates governing the performance characteristics of window coverings installed there. Today, various city, state, and federal agencies have established flame resistant requirements for the coverings to be installed in several types of commercial interiors. In many cases, the coverings must be tested in accordance with the procedures outlined in NFPA 701 and comply with the flame resistance requirements listed in the standard. The test methods and performance criteria in NFPA 701 are explained in Chapter 21.

Draperies installed in commercial airliners must comply with FAA Paragraph 25.853 (b). The scope, test specimens and procedures, and performance requirements of this mandate were explained in Chapter 16. Currently, no federal flammability mandates exist for textile and nontextile window coverings intended for installation in residential interiors.

SUMMARY

To ensure reliable judgments and sound decisions in selecting window treatment styles and coverings, residential and commercial consumers should consider several factors, some of which may limit their choices. They should examine the fenestration of the interior to determine which styles can be considered and which would be unworkable. They should consider the immediate and long-term effects of various color-related variables to verify that the planned appearance will be realized and retained. They should determine the need for such functional qualities as glare reduction, energy conservation, privacy enhancement, and view modification. They should also investigate the properties of the fibers and yarns used, the characteristics of the fabric structure, and the effects of the various finishing agents and processes employed. Then they should limit their choices to styles and coverings that are capable of providing the necessary or desirable characteristics.

Professionals must ascertain whether the coverings they select for a commercial interior have to comply with any performance mandates. All consumers must have sufficient funds to cover the cost of the project; for some projects, the initial cost may be partially offset by energy tax credits and energy savings.

NOTES

1. G. Cukierski and Dr. D. R. Buchanan, "Effectiveness of Conventional, Modified, and New Interior Window Treatments in Reducing Heat Transfer Losses," *Proceedings of the Fourth National Passive Solar Conference,* American Section of the International Solar Energy Society, University of Delaware, Newark, Del., 402–406.

2. Rollin C. Dix and Lawan Zalman, "Window Shades and Energy Conservation," Mechanics, Mechanical and Aerospace Engineering Department, Illinois Institute of Technology, Chicago, Illinois, December 1974, 13; quoted in S. R. Hastings and R. W. Crenshaw, "Window Design Strategies to Conserve Energy, " *NBS Building Science Series 104,* Washington, D.C., June 1977, 5–7.

3. ASHRAE, *ASHRAE Handbook of Fundamentals,* American Society of Heating, Refrigeration, and Air Conditioning Engineers, New York, 1974, 395.

4. Cukierski, *op. cit.,* 404.

5. *Ibid.*

6. *Ibid.,* 403.

7. ASHRAE, *op cit.,* 361.

8. *Ibid.,* 402.

chapter *19*

Window Covering Components and Properties

- Textile Fibers Used in Curtains and Draperies
- Yarns Used in Window Covering Structures
- Nontextile Materials Used in Window Coverings

With the increased use of such nontextile materials as wood, and with the expanded color styling of metal components, the variety of window covering structures offered to today's residential and commercial consumers has been greatly expanded. The major portion of the assortment, however, continues to be composed of textile fibers and yarns. Noncellulosic fibers are used more frequently than other fibers, but a significant quantity of cotton fiber and modest amounts of rayon and acetate are also used. Both spun and filament yarns are available, ranging from fine, simple, single structures to coarse, complex, multi-unit structures.

Certain fiber properties and certain yarn features have a great impact on the appearance and serviceability of window treatments. Professionals and consumers should consider these characteristics, as well as those of nontextile materials, when they are specifying or selecting window coverings.

TEXTILE FIBERS USED IN CURTAINS AND DRAPERIES

Although their importance varies greatly, virtually all of the major groups of fibers are used in textile window coverings. Fortunately, legal mandates require that information pertaining to fiber composition be available to prospective purchasers. These disclosures enable informed

consumers and professionals to assess the properties of the fiber or fibers and select the fiber or blend that offers the best balance of features for their interior or exterior window treatment.

Statistical Profile of Fiber Usage

As noted in Chapter 12, the fact that several fabrics are used for upholstery and drapery applications leads statisticians to gather and report fiber usage in these products together. The date presented in Table 12.1 reveal the growing use of the noncellulosic fibers, as well as the extensive use of cotton fiber, in these interior fabrics. The cotton poundage listed in the table also includes the cotton fiber used in the production of drapery linings.

The growing dominance of the noncellulosic fibers in the drapery and upholstery markets is mirrored in the curtain fabric market. The usage of noncellulosic fibers in curtains rose from 11.2 million pounds in 1966 to 75.6 million pounds in 1985, more than a 575 percent increase (Table 19.1). Whereas cotton and the man-made cellulosic fibers held over 75 percent of the 1966 market, they held only 25 percent of the 1985 market. Technological advances in fiber engineering and yarn processing and the increased use of polyester fibers to compensate for the poor resiliency of cellulosic fibers are largely responsible for the continued growth in usage of synthesized fibers.

Although the quantity of wool used in curtain and drapery fabrics is not sufficient to warrant listing in statistical reports, its use should be noted. Currently, a limited number of casement fabrics composed of wool are designed and

Table 19.1 FIBER USAGE IN CURTAINS
(million pounds)

| | | Man-made Fibers [a] | | | | | | | |
| | Total | | Cellulosic | | Noncellulosic | | | |
Year	Fiber	Total	Yarn	Staple	Yarn	Staple	Cotton	Wool
1966	45.7	21.0	6.7	3.1	11.2	[b]	24.7	[c]
1985	100.6	87.8	2.0	10.2	31.5	44.1	12.8	[c]

Glass:

Year	Total
1966	1.8
1984	0.0
1985	0.0

[a]Man-made fiber end use is divided between cellulosic (rayon plus acetate fibers) and noncellulosic (nylon, polyester, acrylic, olefin, saran, spandex, and textile glass fiber). Yarn includes monofilaments, and olefin "yarn" also includes film fiber and spunbonded polypropylene. Staple includes tow and fiberfill.

[b]The noncellulosic staple data are tabulated in the noncellulosic yarn column.

[c]Little or none of the fiber is used.

Sources: Textile Economics Bureau, Inc., *Textile Organon,* Vol. 43, No. 11, November 1972, 166, and Vol. 57, No. 9, September 1986, 211.

produced for commercial applications, principally in order to capitalize on the inherent flame resistance of the fiber.

The quantity of glass fiber used in curtains and draperies has steadily declined, falling from more than 64 million pounds in 1966 to only 4 million pounds in 1984. None was used in curtains in 1985, and the quantity used in draperies in 1985 is not available (see Tables 12.1 and 19.1). Although glass fiber is noncombustible, it may cause skin irritation. It also has extremely low flex abrasion resistance and relatively high density.

Fiber Properties Affecting Serviceability

Fiber properties that have a critical influence on the selection and serviceability of textile window coverings include density, elastic modulus, stiffness, sunlight resistance, and chemical resistance. Of course, inherent fiber properties can be effectively altered by the use of polymer additives and finishing agents and treatments.

Density. As has already been noted, glass fiber has a relatively high density. The specific gravity of glass, 2.50, is higher than that of all other fibers commonly used for interior applications (see Table 4.1). Thus, window coverings of glass would weigh more than identical fabrics composed of other fibers. For this reason, glass fiber generally has been used in open casements (see Figure 19.4).

Elastic Modulus. The initial resistance to deformation stress exhibited by a fiber is known as its elastic modulus.

A fiber may have high initial resistance and then yield readily as the stress load increases. Such a response is typical of spandex fibers and partly accounts for their success in foundation garments and swimwear. Spandex's superior elastic modulus provides the necessary holding power, but the fiber can be extended five to seven times its relaxed length by higher stress loads before rupturing.

Unlike spandex fibers, conventional rayon fibers have a low elastic modulus, especially when they are wet or when the level of humidity is relatively high. Under these conditions, the fibers may readily yield to the stress of their own weight and that of the absorbed moisture and lengthen. This lack of fiber stability would cause the panels in curtains and draperies to sag; when the humidity decreases, the fibers and the fabric would shorten again. This phenomenon, variously termed "the elevator effect," "the yo-yo effect," and "hiking," may be quite pronounced with loosely constructed fabrics.

Rayon fiber producers have engineered high wet modulus (HWM) fibers that resist deformation under humid conditions. Fabrics composed of these fibers will not exhibit the elevator effect, and can be laundered as well. An example of a HWM rayon fiber is Avril®, produced by Avtex Fibers, Inc.

Stiffness. The degree of stiffness or flexibility exhibited by fibers directly affects fabric draping quality, which is especially important in curtains and draperies. Consumers and designers generally handle and shake sample fabrics and ready-made panels and make subjective evaluations about their drapability or fluidity. Pleats and folds in panels composed of stiff fibers like linen and higher denier glass may not hang freely and evenly, causing the panels to have bows or bulges.

Fiber stiffness also affects the flex abrasion resistance of curtain and drapery fabrics. This is an important property for fabrics that will rub against furniture, walls, window frames, or companion panels as they are repeatedly opened and closed. Because fibers displaying low flexibility and elasticity may split and break when subjected to such stress, it may be advisable to use them in stationary panels or in infrequently opened casements.

Earlier, the high stiffness and low flex abrasion resistance of conventional, high denier glass fibers resulted in a problem known as fibrillation, the breaking off of minute slivers of glass from the filaments when they were handled or laundered in an automatic washer. The minute particles were similar to the "angel hair" used in holiday decorations, and caused skin irritation. To minimize the problem, extremely low denier glass fibers are now being manufactured.

Sunlight Resistance. Because fabrics and other textile components used in interior and exterior window treat-

ments are exposed to the sun's rays for prolonged periods of time, the sunlight resistance of the fibers used is a crucial service-related property. Consumers and professionals may be more familiar with the negative effects of sunlight on the color component of textile products than with the concurrent loss in fiber tenacity. All fibers are weakened or tendered by sunlight, but some are degraded more rapidly. Over time, the radiant energy of natural light alters the interior structure of fibers, breaking their chemical bonds and reducing the length of their polymer chains. The damage caused to fibers is somewhat analogous to that caused by sunburning the skin, and in both cases prolonged exposure increases the extent of the damage.

The rate and extent of fiber damage by sunlight is influenced by several factors, including fiber composition, length of exposure, intensity of the light, atmospheric conditions, the presence of colorants, and the use of polymer solution additives. Delusterants can act as catalysts and speed fiber deterioration; ultraviolet absorbers, on the other hand, can effectively protect the fiber from harmful rays. Usually colorants accelerate the rate of fiber degradation by light while at the same time their own structure and characteristics are negatively affected by the radiant en-

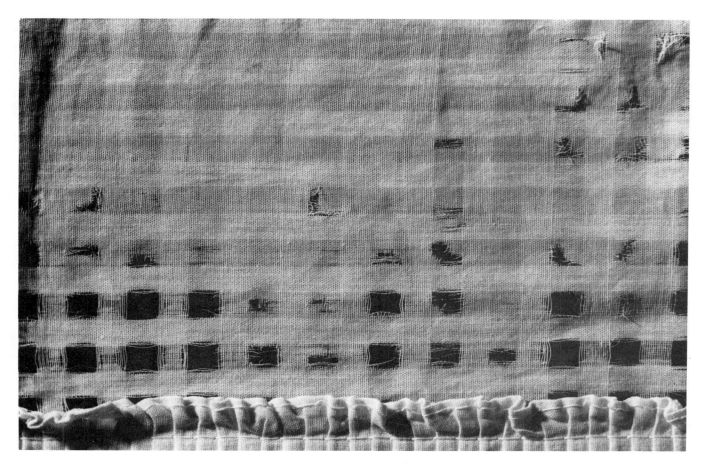

Figure 19.1 Accelerated fiber degradation by textile colorants. The degradation is greatest in the gingham checks, which are made up of both colored warp yarns and colored filling yarns.

Table 19.2   SUNLIGHT RESISTANCE OF SE-LECTED TEXTILE FIBERS

glass	Excellent
acrylic	
modacrylic	
polyester	
linen	
cotton	
rayon	to
triacetate	
acetate	
olefin	
nylon	
wool	
silk	Poor

Source: Norma Hollen, Jane Saddler, and Anna L. Langford, *Textiles,* 5th ed., New York: Macmillan, 1979.

ergy. This is vividly shown in Figure 19.1, where fabric damage is greatest in the checks having colored warp yarns and colored filling yarns.

Table 19.2 compares the sunlight resistance of selected textile fibers. An "excellent" rating indicates slower, and a "poor" rating more rapid, deterioration. Glass fiber is rated as having excellent resistance; it has nevertheless been found to lose approximately 50 percent of its wet tenacity after three years of exposure to natural light.[1]

The loss in tenacity suffered by fibers exposed to light may not become evident until the fabric is cleaned. Consumers may wish to hold the owner of the cleaning establishment responsible for what actually is the result of already-weakened fibers rupturing under cleaning procedures. For this reason, cleaners may ask customers to sign a statement releasing the firm from responsibility in the event the fabric deteriorates.

Chemical Resistance. Various pollutant gases can destroy colorants (see Chapter 14) and, after combining with moisture, they also can destroy textile fibers. When vapor-phase moisture within fibers, yarns, or folds in panels reacts with such gases as sulfur oxide and nitrogen oxide, weak sulfuric acid (H_2SO_4) and weak nitric acid (HNO_3) will be formed. Indoors, droplets of these compounds may be described as "interior acid rain." Gradually, the acids attack the chemical bonds within the fibers, interrupting the polymer chains and weakening the fibers. The effects of this degradation may not become evident until laundering or dry cleaning, and they may be more pronounced with cellulosic fibers.

Fiber Labeling Mandates

Currently, two labeling mandates include provisions that apply to textile fibers used in window covering fabrics. One mandate pertains to fiber composition; the other concerns the potential skin irritation that may result from glass fiber fibrillations.

Disclosure of Fiber Composition. The provisions of the Textile Fiber Products Identification Act apply to all curtain, casement, and drapery fabrics and the products made from them. All curtains, casements, and draperies, or any portions of these items that would otherwise be subject to the act, made principally of slats, rods, or strips composed of wood, metal, plastic, or leather, are excluded. Thus, the fiber composition of certain textile components, such as the yarns used in woven wood shades, is not required to be disclosed.

Cautionary Labeling with Glass Fiber Products. Recognizing the problem of fibrillation with higher denier glass fibers, the FTC issued a trade regulation rule that requires the use of special labeling with glass fiber window coverings. The provisions of the rule, which became effective on January 2, 1968, apply to glass fiber curtains, draperies, and fabrics. These products must carry a tag or label cautioning purchasers that skin irritation may result: (1) to the exposed skin of persons handling such glass fiber products; and (2) from body contact with clothing or other articles, such as bed sheets, which have been washed (a) with such glass fiber products, or (b) in a container previously used for washing such glass fiber products unless the glass particles have been removed from such container by cleaning.

YARNS USED IN WINDOW COVERING STRUCTURES

The yarns used in curtains, draperies, and other window coverings are as varied as those used in upholstery fabric. Spun yarns dominate the market, but a number of filament structures are used in curtain fabrics. Yarn choices depend on several appearance and service-related variables.

Dominance of Spun Yarns

The data listed in Table 19.1 reveal that about 67 percent of the fibers used in curtain fabrics have been spun into yarns. (Relatively few of the staple-length fibers included in the data are used directly in the production of stitch-bonded and spunlaced curtain fabrics; see Chapter 20.) As noted in Chapter 12, spun yarns show an even greater dominance in the drapery and upholstery fabrics market, with a 78 percent share of the total. Filaments are

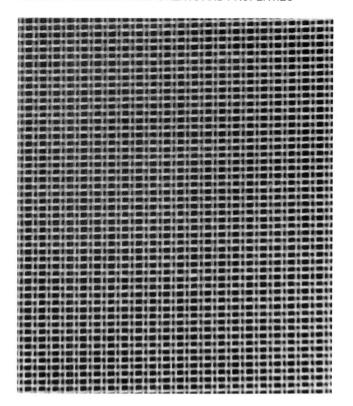

Figure 19.2 Ninon curtain fabric produced with fine, simple multifilament yarns.

used most often in curtain fabrics as a result of the demand for sheer, yet strong and stable, panels.

Variables Influencing Yarn Selection

Fabric stylists specify yarns for curtains, draperies, and other window coverings after considering the appearance and functional characteristics preferred or required by contemporary consumers. They also take into account the qualities the structures should exhibit when used in various treatments.

Planned Visual and Textural Features. For coverings planned to have minimal textural interest, manufacturers use simple yarns in the fabrication operation. Fine monofilament or multifilament yarns are used, for example, to produce the smooth surfaces characterizing ninon, a plain-woven fabric pictured in Figure 19.2, and marquisette, a leno-woven fabric pictured in Figure 20.14 (page 206). Simple yarns are also generally used when printing or decorative interlacings are planned.

Complex yarns are frequently employed to add visual and textural interest to curtain and drapery fabrics. Seed yarns, for example, appear in the novelty marquisette curtain fabric pictured in Figure 19.3a, and bouclé yarns in the drapery fabric pictured in Figure 19.3b.

Relatively coarse and irregular yarns can be made to simulate the appearance of hand-spun yarns. This is typically seen in such curtain and drapery fabrics as osnaburg and monk's cloth (Figures 20.4 and 20.5, pages 200 and 201).

Woven wood coverings may be constructed with simple ply or cord yarns contrasting with or matching the color of the wooden slats. They may also be constructed with a variety of highly decorative, complex yarns that are variously colored to coordinate with other interior furnishings. In these coverings, the yarns are often incorporated in lengthwise bands to create stripes that augment the visual and textural interest of the shade.

Planned Functional Attributes. As was explained in Chapter 18, the openness of a window covering fabric has a major influence on the functional performance of the treatment. Openness controls the efficiency of fabric in reducing interior noise, in restricting the view inward and modifying the view outward, and in controlling the amount of light and radiant energy transmitted to the interior. Manufacturers often consult with contract designers and architects to identify the functional properties needed or desired by their clients and then determine the appropriate degree of openness for a particular fabric.

In all textile coverings except those composed of glass fiber, the requisite openness can readily be produced by balancing the size of the yarns and the compactness of construction used. Because glass fiber has a high specific gravity, increasing the size of the yarns or the compactness of construction would result in a comparatively large increase in fabric weight; increasing the diameter of the yarns would also increase the likelihood of fibrillation. To avoid these problems, manufacturers of glass fiber window coverings often use loop or curl yarns (Figure 5.11d, page 40) to engineer the desired degree of fabric openness. The airy projections of these complex yarns effectively cover the surface area and increase the opacity (Figure 19.4).

Intended Use of the Covering. All window coverings intended to be used as free-hanging panels must be drapable, but those fabrics intended for such valence treatments as swags, jabots, and cascades must be exceptionally so. The importance of this drapability in these applications is readily apparent in the treatment in Figure 17.4 (page 176). Fabric manufacturers generally use fine, low-twist, multifilament yarns in a satin weave to produce good drapability.

Fabrics produced for curtains, especially ruffled curtains, often are made from fine, high-twist yarns that introduce a crisp hand and provide the body needed to support the folds of the ruffles and the tie-back panels. Fine, soft yarns are selected for fabrics intended to be used in such window treatments as sash curtains and Austrian

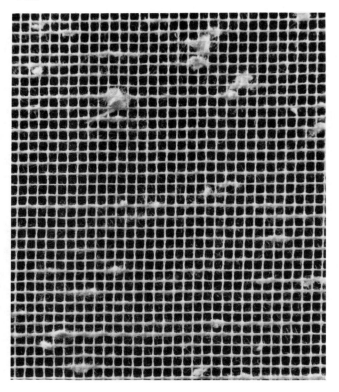

a) marquisette having seed yarns

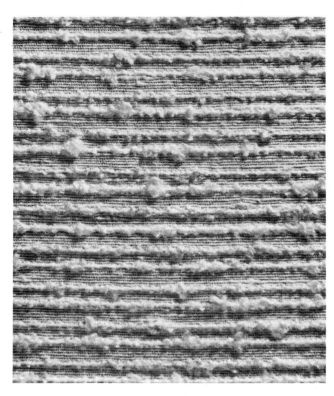

b) drapery fabric having bouclé yarns

Figure 19.3 Complex yarns add visual and textural interest to curtain and drapery fabrics.

shades; these yarns produce soft, rounded folds that enhance the shirred effect while preserving the preferred level of transparency. Fabrics intended for awnings or other exterior treatments are often composed of relatively large, high-twist yarns strong enough to resist rupturing when the fabric is stretched over the framework and when it is repeatedly stressed by wind gusts.

NONTEXTILE MATERIALS USED IN WINDOW COVERINGS

The assortment of nontextile window coverings in earlier years was basically limited to structures composed of wood or metal. More recently, the assortment has been expanded to include structures composed of molded polymer compounds and natural grasses.

Metals and Polymer Materials

Formerly, only cream-colored, enamel-coated aluminum slats were used for venetian blinds. The aluminum slats now come in a wide variety of fashion colors, which makes these blinds more appealing to designers and consumers. A contemporary flair has also been introduced to some of these blinds by constructing them of slats composed of molded polymer compounds.

Metal, glass, and plastic beads are occasionally strung into chains and hung vertically as stationary, panel-like treatments. Metals, generally aluminum, are also frequently used for exterior shutters, awnings, and canopies.

Polymer compounds, such as polyvinylchloride, are extruded as film sheeting for use in manufacturing conventional roller shades. Frequently, printed film sheeting is used for matching shades and wall covering.

Woods

The slats of roman shades, venetian and vertical blinds, and shutters are frequently made of pine, but more expensive structures may be constructed of oak. The wood is first kiln dried to minimize the potential for cracking and splitting; it is then sanded and stained, or painted a fashion color.

Grasses

Although grasses are not used extensively in window coverings, they are hand woven into Roman shades. The variations in thickness and surface texture that grasses exhibit make for a contemporary covering with a natural look.

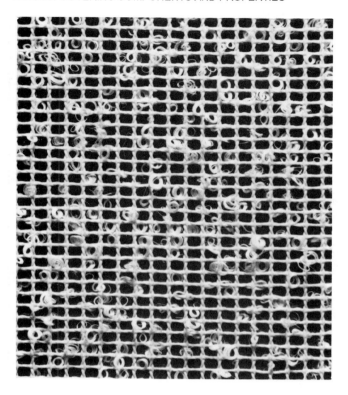

Figure 19.4 Loop yarns reduce openness but add little weight to leno-woven casement composed of glass fiber.

SUMMARY

Although noncellulosic staple-length fibers dominate the textile window coverings market, a significant quantity of cotton fiber is also used. The fiber composition of curtains, draperies, and fabrics must be disclosed. This disclosure enables informed consumers and professionals to consider fiber properties in relationship to the planned end-use.

The yarns used in window covering structures are chosen for their visual and textural features and the necessary or desirable functional properties they exhibit. Also important is whether the covering is intended for an interior or exterior treatment. Besides textile yarns, such nontextile materials as wood, natural grasses, and plastic expand the assortment of window coverings available to today's residential and commercial consumer.

NOTE

1. Esther M. Cormany, "Service Qualities of Sheer Curtain Fabrics," *Journal of Home Economics*, Vol. 51, No. 10, December 1959, 873.

chapter *20*

Window Covering Fabrics and Lining Materials

- Woven Curtain and Drapery Fabrics
- Knitted Window Covering Fabrics
- Knotted and Twisted Window Coverings
- Coverings Formed from Fibrous Webs
- Drapery Lining Materials

Several techniques used to fabricate upholstery coverings are also used to fabricate textile window coverings. Because window coverings are normally subjected to less abrasion than upholstery coverings, however, additional techniques are available for fabricating a greater variety of window coverings. Some of these methods enable manufacturers to incorporate decorative surface features more economically; others facilitate the production of fabrics with maximum openness as well as high dimensional stability; and still others expedite production and thus reduce the product's cost.

Working together, fabric manufacturers and converters produce drapery fabrics with permanently attached linings. They also produce a vast amount of textile fabric for use in separately hung lining panels. Both types of material help to protect the decorative drapery panels from sunlight and degradation; some materials also help to reduce noise, heat transfer, and light transmission.

WOVEN CURTAIN AND DRAPERY FABRICS

The aesthetic features of some textile window covering fabrics take precedence over their functional attributes; the converse is also sometimes true. In the production of most fabrics, however, manufacturers seek to strike a balance between appearance and function while also producing a stable structure. A wide variety of interlacing patterns is necessarily used in the production of curtain and drapery fabrics. Various surface embellishment techniques further expand the assortment.

Fabrics with Simple Biaxial Interlacings

The basic biaxial interlacing patterns and their variations were explained in Chapter 6. This section describes and illustrates the several curtain and drapery fabrics constructed using these weaves. These fabrics are defined by such characteristics as yarn structure, interlacing pattern, color styling, finish, and hand. Shifts in fiber usage have diminished the value of fiber composition as a distinguishing characteristic for curtain and drapery fabrics, as is also true for upholstery fabrics.

Plain-woven Fabrics. The plain weave is used to produce several curtain and drapery fabrics that have distinct differences in their appearance features, tactile characteristics, and performance attributes. These variations derive from yarns that differ in size, design features, level of twist, or color styling, from different thread counts, and from coloring methods and finishing procedures.

When it is composed of fine, combed cotton yarns, batiste has a soft hand, is translucent, and is normally solid colored. Resins and preshrinking treatments may be employed to introduce resiliency and dimensional stability to fabrics made of these natural fibers. Batiste that is woven of yarns composed of polyester has a crisp hand, is transparent, and is often white in color. Heat setting may be used to impart dimensional stability and resiliency to these fabrics. Batiste fabrics are effectively used in all styles of curtain treatments (Figure 17.1, page 172) and in Austrian shades (Figure 17.7, page 179). Polyester batiste is increasingly replacing cotton batiste in the production of tambour-embroidered curtain panels, pictured in Figure 20.19.

Calico, formerly made exclusively from cotton fiber, is now generally composed of cotton and polyester for improved resiliency and dimensional stability. The fabric has a balanced thread count (approximately 78 x 78) and small, colorful, printed design motifs on a solid-colored ground (Figure 20.1). Calico is particularly appropriate for multi-tier café curtains, because the short panels require short pattern repeats and the extensive gathering would camouflage large design motifs.

Chintz (Figure 20.2) is glazed to add body and high surface luster. Most chintz fabrics have colorful, printed designs, but some are solid colored. The fabric, which has relatively low drapability, is frequently used in single- and multi-tier café curtains.

Figure 20.2 Chintz fabric with a glazed surface.

Cretonne, a drapery fabric infrequently used in recent years, is produced from coarse yarns. It is characterized by large, printed motifs, relatively high stiffness, and a dull surface.

Gauze or theatrical gauze has a slightly higher thread count than cheesecloth; stiffening agents are used to impart body. Originally produced for use in stage settings, the transparent fabric may be dyed and used for stationary or traversing curtain panels in residential and commercial interiors.

Ninon (Figure 19.2, page 195) is used for sheer draw or stationary curtains, generally in combination with over-draperies. Close examination of the fabric shows that every third warp yarn has been omitted to increase the transparency of the fabric. Ninon's interlacing pattern is 1 x 1, not 2 x 1, which the paired spacing of the warp yarns may first suggest (Figure 20.3).

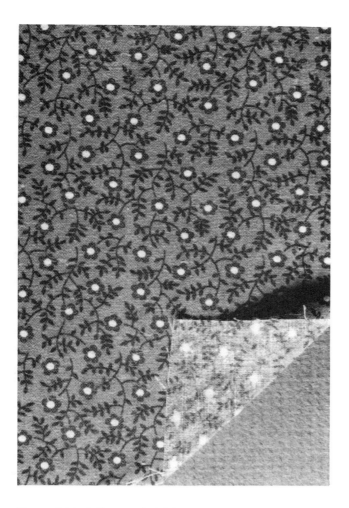

Figure 20.1 Calico curtain fabric.

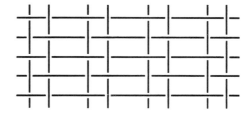

Figure 20.3 Yarn spacing in ninon curtain fabric.

Organdy, produced when an all-cotton fabric is exposed to a weak solution of sulfuric acid, is characterized by transparency and a parchment-like hand. In order to partially offset the weakening effect of the acid, the fabric is first mercerized to increase the strength of the fibers. Organdy is now also made of monofilament nylon, which requires no acid treatment. The sheer cotton or nylon fabrics are effective in most styles of curtain treatments.

Osnaburg is composed of coarse, carded cotton yarns. These are bleached only a little, if at all, to preserve the natural off-white color of the yarns, which are interspersed with bits of dark-colored fibers. Osnaburg was originally produced for use as grain and cement sack fabric; its unrefined look is apparent in Figure 20.4.

Voile is a transparent fabric woven of highly twisted yarns composed of cotton or a blend of cotton and polyester fibers. The fabric has a crisp hand and is generally white in ruffled curtains and printed in other styles. Voile may be flocked with small dots that convert the fabric into dotted swiss (Figure 20.18).

Basket-woven fabrics. Two basket-woven fabrics, namely monk's cloth and duck, are commonly used for window treatments. Monk's cloth (Figure 20.5) is usually produced in a 4 x 4 interlacing pattern, but a 2 x 2 pattern may be used. The yarns are spun to simulate those found in the fabric traditionally used for monk's robes. For use in window coverings, the fabric is generally bleached and occasionally dyed to create a refined, contemporary appearance.

Duck, also known as canvas, may be constructed in a 2 x 1 basket interlacing or in a plain weave. The fabric is often made from strong, two-ply yarns for use in exterior awning treatments. To make duck and other textile awning fabrics waterproof, converters coat them with vinyl solutions, rubber-based materials, or other synthesized compounds. These agents fill the yarn and fabric interstices, making the structures nonporous.

Filling-rib woven fabrics. Taffeta, faille, and bengaline are produced for use in window treatments. Faille and bengaline (described and pictured in Chapter 12) have slightly larger ribs than those in taffeta. Taffeta's smooth yarns are usually composed of bright acetate fibers; often a wood-grain or water-marked surface design is introduced by moiréing. A moiré taffeta fabric is used for

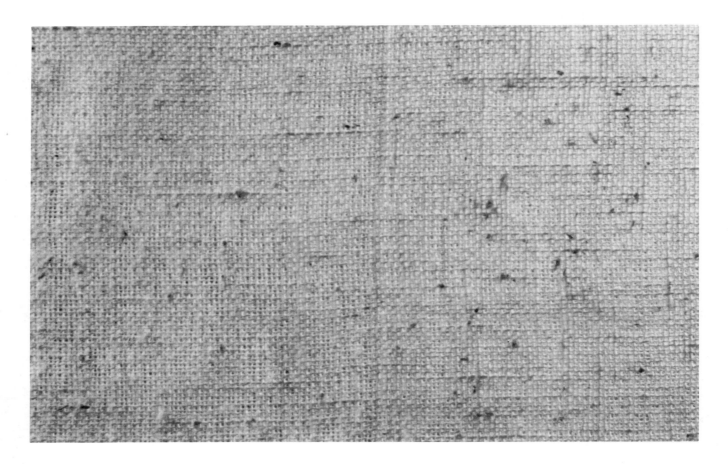

Figure 20.4 Osnaburg window covering fabric.

Other curtain fabrics, such as pique and Bedford cord, also have lengthwise ribs, but their interlacing patterns are too complicated to be executed on a two-harness loom. To make these fabrics, a dobby loom with multiple harnesses for increased shedding variations is a necessity.

Twill-woven Fabrics. Twill interlacing patterns are rarely used alone in the construction of curtain and drapery fabrics. Instead, they are generally combined with other interlacing patterns in decorative weaving procedures, including dobby and Jacquard operations.

Satin- and Sateen-woven Fabrics. Multifilament yarns composed of bright acetate fibers are often woven in a satin interlacing to produce highly drapable, lustrous drapery fabrics. Such fabrics are especially suitable for swagged valences, jabots, and cascades (see Figure 17.4, page 176).

Antique satin (Figure 20.8) has simple warp yarns and complex single slub filling yarns. The slub yarns float over the face of the fabric in a sateen interlacing. When high luster is desired, the fabric is composed of bright acetate, and, for low luster, cotton is used. Antique satin enjoys great popularity among contemporary designers and consumers.

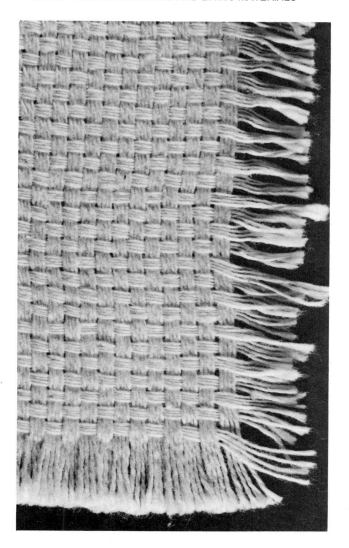

Figure 20.5 Monk's cloth, a basket weave window covering fabric.

the balloon shade pictured in Figure 17.8 (page 180) and as the wall covering pictured in Figure 22.7 (page 238).

Warp-rib woven fabrics. In dimity, a sheer fabric used for curtains, a lengthwise rib effect may be produced by periodically placing one large warp among fine yarns, or, as shown in Figures 6.9 (page 50) and 20.6, by periodically placing a group of warp yarns among fine yarns. Fine, combed cotton yarns produce a smooth surface; they are generally mercerized to increase luster and fiber strength. The degree of fabric openness is similar to that of organdy and voile. The dimity pictured in Figure 20.6 exhibits marked filling skew.

The roller shade fabric pictured in Figure 20.7 has a lengthwise rib effect produced by combining fine and coarse yarns. Called ribcord, the fabric may be coated on the back with a vinyl compound to increase its opacity.

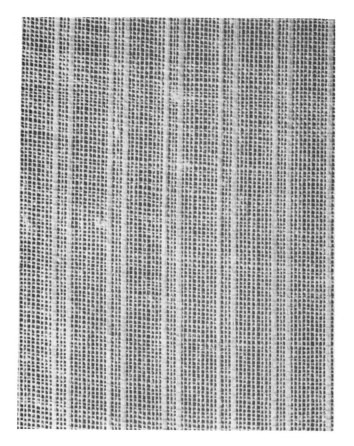

Figure 20.6 Dimity, a warp-rib weave fabric.

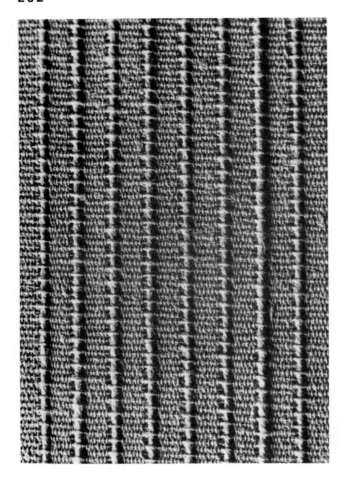

Figure 20.7 Ribcord, a warp-rib weave fabric used in roller shades.

Simple biaxial interlacing patterns are also used in the production of woven wood and woven grass window coverings. These structures simply employ wood slats or grass strands, rather than textile yarns, as their crosswise elements.

Fabrics with Decorative Interlacing

Several decorative interlacing patterns, including the dobby, dot or spot, and Jacquard weaves, produce fabrics suitable for use in window treatments as well as in upholstery applications. Additional complex interlacing patterns, including the leno, swivel, and lappet weaves, are used in curtain and drapery fabrics; the relatively low abrasion resistance or low covering power characterizing these weaves precludes their use in upholstery coverings.

Dobby-woven Fabrics. The multiple harnesses and control mechanisms on a dobby loom facilitate the production of novelty curtain fabrics with geometric features woven into the base fabric. Fine lengthwise ribs are found

in plain or pinwale piqué; larger ribs are found in Bedford cord; small, diamond-shaped designs are characteristic of birdseye piqué; and the grid of a waffle iron is replicated in waffle piqué. Examples of the pique fabrics are pictured in Figure 20.9.

As shown in the cross-sectional sketch of pinwale piqué presented in Figure 20.10, extra warp yarns, called stuffer yarns, can be used to support the tunnel-like ribs or wales. Stuffer warp yarns may also appear in Bedford cord, and stuffer filling yarns in birdseye piqué.

The low drapability of these fabrics makes them more suitable for tailored curtain panels than for ruffled and shirred styles. Scalloped headings are especially effective with these fabrics.

Surface-figure Woven Fabrics. Special attachments can be added to dobby looms to facilitate surface-figure weaving. As schematized in Figure 20.11, surface-figure woven fabrics have raised figures or motifs produced by incorporating extra yarns in various ways.

Dot- or spot-woven fabrics. In dot or spot weaving, extra yarns are periodically interlaced with the base yarns to create a small dot or figured spot. Between the decorative figures or dots, the extra yarns are floated on the back of the fabric. When the floating yarns are left in place, the fabric is known as an unclipped dot or spot fabric; when the floating yarns are cut away, the fabric is known as a clipped dot or spot fabric. When the base fabric is sheer, the floats should be clipped to avoid linear shadows, especially when the fabric is intended for use as a window covering. Either side of a clipped dot or spot fabric can be used as the face side (Figure 20.12). The floating yarns should be left unclipped in opaque fabrics to minimize the possibility that the dots or spots will be removed by in-use abrasion and cleaning.

Swivel-woven fabrics. In swivel weaving, extra yarns periodically swivel around or encircle the base yarns to create small, secure dots. Some imported dotted swiss is produced with this interlacing technique, but the relatively slow rate of production precludes its widespread use.

Lappet-woven fabrics. In lappet weaving, hundreds of needles are used to interlace extra warp yarns. The needles are shifted laterally to create a zigzag surface pattern that resembles hand embroidery (Figure 20.13). Lappet fabrics, like swivel fabrics, are woven at comparatively slow rates.

Leno-woven Fabrics. Because the crossed warp yarns effectively lock the filling yarns into position and minimize yarn slippage, the leno weave is particularly useful for interlacing fine, smooth yarns into stable window

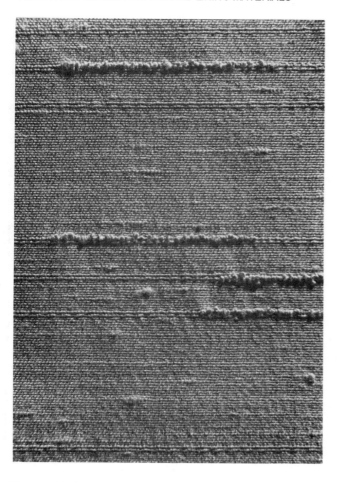 

Figure 20.8 Antique satin drapery fabrics.

a) plain or pinwale piqué

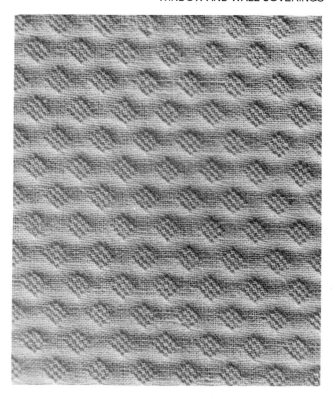

b) birdseye piqué

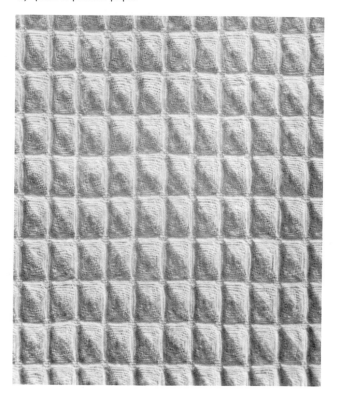

c) waffle piqué

Figure 20.9 Dobby-woven curtain fabrics.

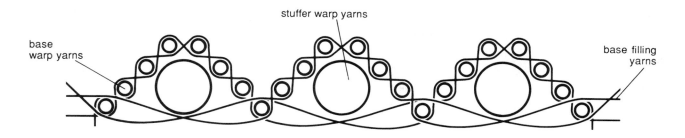

Figure 20.10 Cross-sectional view of pinwale piqué with stuffer warp yarns.

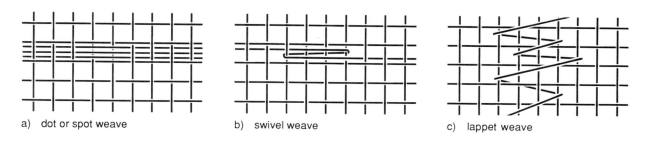

a) dot or spot weave   b) swivel weave   c) lappet weave

Figure 20.11 Surface-figure weaves.

Figure 20.12 Clipped dot curtain fabric.

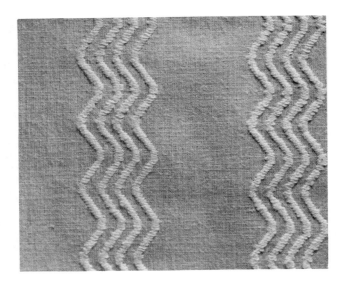

Figure 20.13 Lappet-woven curtain fabrics.

covering fabrics. Marquisette (Figure 20.14) is a transparent leno-woven fabric composed of fine monofilament yarns; the lightweight fabric is used extensively in stationary or traversing curtain panels. Mosquito netting is also transparent and compactly constructed; it is used as a curtain-like bed canopy in tropical climates, forming a barrier against mosquitos.

The stability and novel appearance of leno interlacing enables manufacturers to produce a wide variety of highly decorative, leno-woven fabrics. The visual interest of the casement pictured in Figure 20.15 is enhanced by the use of slub yarns.

Jacquard-woven Fabrics. Such Jacquard-woven fabrics as damask, brocade, and tapestry (Figures 12.12, 12.14, and 12.16, pages 121–122) are produced for use in drapery treatments as well as in upholstery. The damask drapery fabric pictured in Figure 20.16 has linear motifs that are complimented by the strié color styling of the ground.

Another distinctive Jacquard-woven drapery and upholstery fabric is called lampas. The fabric is characterized by elaborate woven-in designs typical of the seventeenth and eighteenth centuries. The detailed motifs are created by combining satin and sateen interlacings (Figure 20.17). In many lampases, two sets of identically colored warp yarns are combined with one or more sets of variously colored filling yarns.

Fabrics with Pile Interlacings

Such pile-woven fabrics as corduroy, velveteen, and velvet, which were described in Chapter 12, may be used for interior window treatments. Corduroy works well in single-tier café curtains and casual draperies, and velveteen

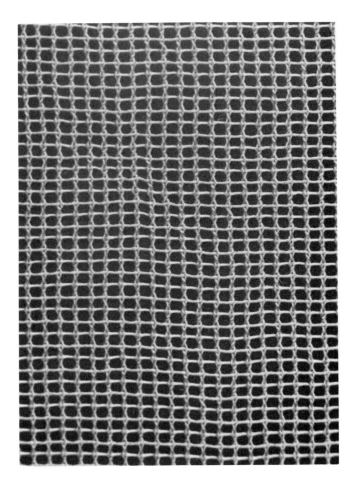

Figure 20.14 Marquisette, a leno-weave curtain fabric.

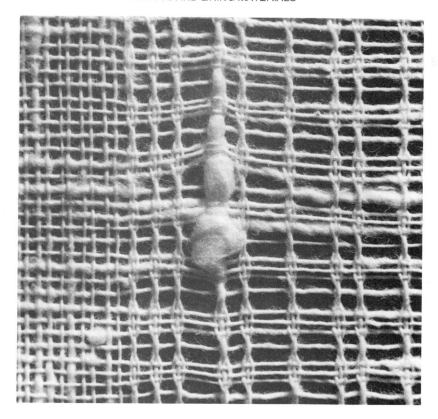

Figure 20.15 Leno-woven casement fabric.

Figure 20.16 Strié damask drapery fabric.

Figure 20.17 "Venice Art" lampas, multicolor motifs on lacquer red ground. Made in Italy of 81 percent rayon, 15 percent silk, and 4 percent nylon. (Courtesy of Scalamandré.)

Figure 20.17 Detail

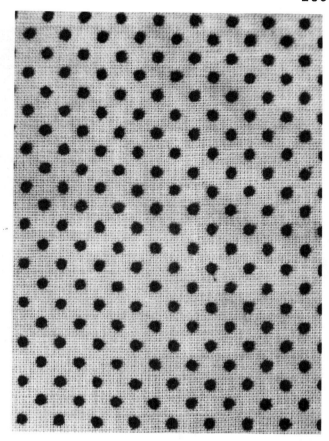

Figure 20.18 Flocked dotted swiss curtain fabric.

and velvet are effective in formal drapery treatments. When considering these fabrics for use in any style of treatment, designers and consumers should make a subjective evaluation of their "visual weight," assessing whether or not the three-dimensional texture will be appropriate or too imposing. They should also determine whether extra strong rods and additional brackets will be required to support the panels constructed from these comparatively heavy fabrics.

Fabrics with Surface Embellishments

Converters can embellish the surfaces of already-woven fabrics to produce distinctive coverings for curtain treatments. They may use a flocking or an embroidering operation.

Flocked Fabrics. Flocked dotted swiss fabric (Figure 20.18) is less expensive than that produced by spot or swivel weaving. Frequently, the base fabric is voile.

Embroidered Fabrics. Tambour-embroidered curtain fabric is distinguished by chain-stitched, lace-like designs.

The stitching (shown in detail in Figure 20.29) resembles that created by artisans. Frequently, mirror-image panels with finished edges (Figure 20.19) are produced from such fabrics as batiste and organdy.

Eyelet curtain fabric is produced with an embroidery machine used to stitch around holes created in the greige goods (Figure 20.20a). These holes used to be produced by destroying cotton fibers with sulfuric acid; today, knives are used. The eyelet pictured in Figure 20.20b has a scalloped edge, a decorative feature often selected for single-tier café curtain treatments.

Fabrics Distinguished by Color Styling

Many textile window covering fabrics are distinguished by the decorative features of their yarns or the structural features introduced during fabrication; others are distinguished by their color styling. Among the latter group of fabrics are blotch prints, warp prints, toile de Jouy prints, pigment prints, and burnt-out prints.

Roller printing has traditionally been employed to create a color style known as a blotch print. The ground of

Figure 20.19 Tambour-embroidered curtain panels. (Courtesy of Henry Cassen.)

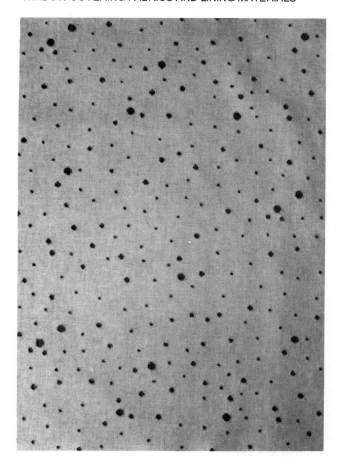

a) prior to embroidering

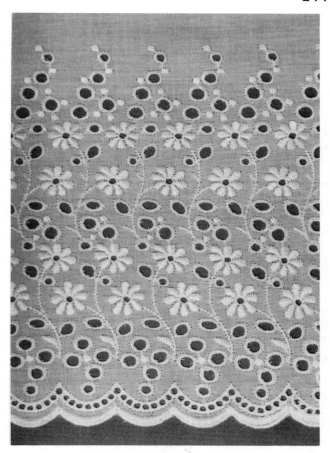

b) after embroidering

Figure 20.20 Eyelet curtain fabrics, before and after embroidering.

the fabric is printed, leaving undyed, white design motifs. In contrast to discharge prints, blotch prints do not exhibit the same level of color intensity on both sides of the fabric; this difference is evident in Figure 20.21.

Figure 20.21 Blotch and discharge prints.

A warp print color style is produced by first screen printing a web of warp yarns; the colors are applied in precise, well-defined motifs and pattern repeats. The subsequent interlacing of the printed warp yarns with neutral-colored filling yarns will develop a striated appearance (Figure 20.22) similar to that seen in ikat prints (see Figure 35.17, page 393).

Toile de Jouy prints have monochromatic color styling. The motifs have a picture-like quality (Figure 20.23). Thick, white pigment mixtures are used to produce pigment print curtain fabrics (Figure 20.24). These opaque compounds add visual interest and reduce fabric openness. Opaque pigments were also used to print the fabric pictured in Figure 20.27.

Etched-out or burnt-out prints are distinguished by different levels of transparency in the same fabric. After acid has been used to burn away the rayon fibers, only nylon

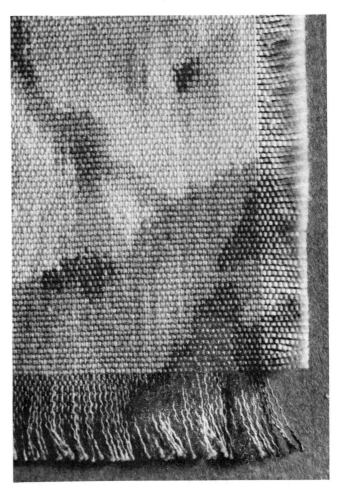

Figure 20.22 Warp print drapery fabric.

remains in the highly transparent areas of the burnt-out print curtain fabric pictured in Figure 20.25.

KNITTED WINDOW COVERING FABRICS

Knitting is a relatively fast and economical method of combining yarns into fabric structures that is increasingly employed in the fabrication of window coverings. Specific levels of fabric openness can be produced by balancing the gauge and type of yarns used. High dimensional stability, non-run performance, and design flexibility are provided by raschel stitching; many curtain and casement fabrics are produced with this interlooping technique. Two variations of conventional knitting procedures, weft insertion and stitch-knitting, are also used.

Raschel-stitched Fabrics

The multiple guide bars and latch needles (Figure 7.3, page 61) on the raschel machine facilitate the production

Figure 20.23 Toile de Jouy prints with monochromatic color styling and picture-like motifs.

Figure 20.24   Pigment print ninon curtain fabric.

Figure 20.25   Burnt-out print curtain fabric.

of a variety of window covering fabrics, ranging from delicate, lacy curtain structures to heavy, elaborate interlooped casements. A raschel-stitched fabric is pictured in Figure 20.26.

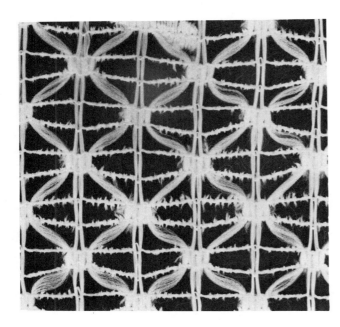

Figure 20.26 Raschel-stitched casement fabric.

Fabrics Produced by Weft Insertion

Because the transparency and covering power of a fabric can effectively be controlled by the size and character of its weft or filling yarns, manufacturers are increasingly using weft insertion to produce window coverings. In the casement fabric pictured in Figure 20.27, the manufacturer has inserted various lengths of weft yarns to develop an integral pattern with different levels of fabric openness. Opaque pigments are frequently printed on the surface of such fabrics to reduce their transparency and enhance visual interest.

Stitch-knitted Casements

Chapter 7 explained the use of knitting stitches to anchor webs of yarns in stitch-knitting operations. Examples of casement fabrics produced this way are shown in Figure 20.28.

Because the stability and integrity of stitch-knitted fabrics can be lost when loops of the chain-stitching are ruptured, they should not be selected for panels that will be subject to abrasion. Panels of these fabrics must not be opened and closed by hand, and they must be cleaned with care.

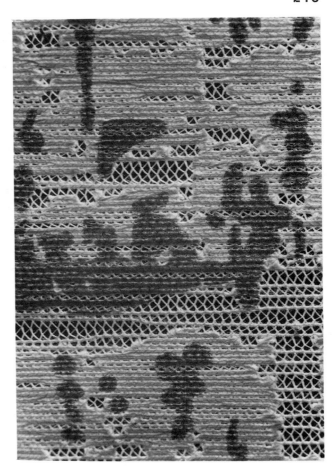

Figure 20.27 Casement fabric produced by weft insertion.

KNOTTED AND TWISTED WINDOW COVERINGS

Lace, net, and macramé window coverings are fabricated with knotting and twisting operations. Designers and consumers desiring an airy, delicate, and highly ornamental lace fabric for a window treatment must be aware that the panels are likely to sag. Their stability can be improved when the fabric is made from thermoplastic fibers and properly heat set.

Appliqués may increase the visual interest of net curtain fabrics. The fabric pictured in Figure 20.29 has had its surface interest further augmented by the Tambour embroidering that secures the appliqué.

The use of macramé structures as window coverings is limited because of their weight, stiffness, and bulkiness. Wide macramé panels may be hung flat as stationary, decorative treatments. Narrow macramé strips may be used as the louvers or vanes in vertical blinds.

Figure 20.28 Stitch-knitted casement fabrics.

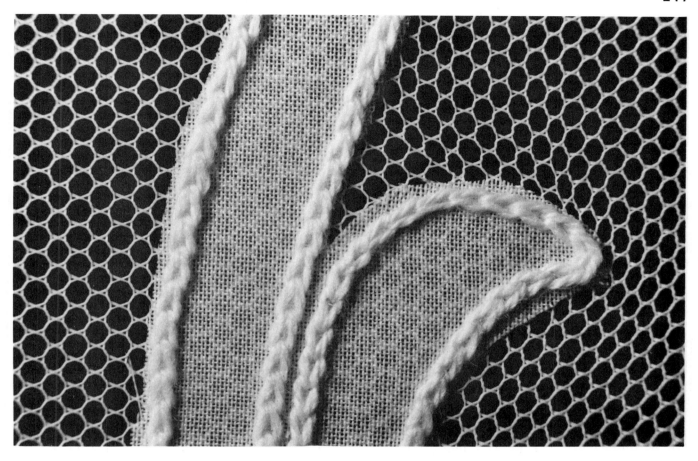

Figure 20.29 Tambour-embroidered appliqué on bobbinet curtain fabric. (Courtesy of Henry Cassen.)

COVERINGS FORMED FROM FIBROUS WEBS

The stitch-bonding and spunlacing techniques explained in Chapter 7 enable manufacturers to produce window coverings directly from fibers. Because these techniques bypass spinning operations, such coverings may be less expensive than those fabricated from yarns.

A stitch-bonded window covering fabric is pictured in Figure 20.30. The surface of this fabric has been printed; for this reason, it may require close examination to confirm that it is not a conventional textile structure.

Figure 20.30 Stitch-bonded window covering.

Manufacturers can produce spunlaced curtain fabrics with open, airy constructions by manipulating the positions of the fibers. Such fabrics may be treated as disposable, especially in care-type facilities where maintenance expenses are higher then replacement costs.

DRAPERY LINING MATERIALS

Two types of lining materials, coatings and film sheetings, may be permanently attached to the back of drapery fabric. These multicomponent fabrics, known as self-lined drapery fabrics, often display specific functional attributes. Other types of linings, virtually all of which are textile fabrics, are hung separately, behind the drapery panels.

Permanently Attached Lining Materials

Converters frequently apply foamed acrylic compounds to the back of drapery fabrics to increase their insulative value (Figure 20.31). The air-filled cells of these coatings retard heat loss by convection as the compound restricts the flow of air through the yarn and fabric interstices. The insulative value of window treatments using these fabrics largely depends, however, on how tightly the panels are mounted (see Chapter 18). Acrylic polymers, which have high resistance to sunlight, provide the added benefit of slowing the rate at which the sun's radiant energy degrades the fibers and colorants in treated fabric.

The amount of light transmitted through a window covering fabric is inversely related to its opacity or level of openness: increasing the opacity of the structure decreases the level of light transmission. In certain interiors, such as hospitals and similar facilities, coverings may need to be highly opaque to block most of the incident rays and provide partial blackout. In other interiors, such as rooms used for viewing films, the coverings must be fully closed or fully opaque, blocking all incident rays and providing total blackout.

Converters can increase the opacity of greige drapery fabrics with coatings and film sheetings. For total blackout, a vinyl coating may be spread over the surface (Figure 20.32a) or vinyl film sheeting may be bonded to a base fabric (Figure 20.32b). The vinyl component is frequently fashionably colored for greater aesthetic appeal. In many motel and hotel rooms, especially those operated by national chains, these multicomponent structures are the only window covering, functioning as both covering and lining.

Separately Hung Lining Fabrics

Linings designed to be installed as separately hung panels are generally textile fabrics. Virtually all of these fabrics have a plain- or sateen-interlacing pattern, but a variety of surface appearance features and service-related properties are introduced by the use of finishing agents and processes.

Plain-woven Lining Fabrics. A great deal of lining fabric is produced from simple, single yarns of cotton combined in a plain- weave interlacing pattern. The greige goods are then finished in various operations, the first of which is bleaching. Silicone compounds may be applied for water-repellent performance. The silicone slows the rate of moisture absorption, minimizing the wetting of the fabric from moisture condensed on panes and frames

Figure 20.31 Drapery fabric having an aerocellular acrylic backcoating for increased acoustical and insulative values.

a) vinyl coating laminated to base fabric

b) vinyl film sheeting bonded to base fabric

Figure 20.32 Opaque window coverings providing total blackout.

and from rain that blows in when windows are inadvertently left open. It may also help to minimize the staining and streaking that can occur when moisture combines with smoke and oily cooking residues that have settled on the fabric; more effective protection against soiling and staining can be provided, however, by fluorocarbon compounds. Compressive shrinkage treatments may be employed to encourage relaxation shrinkage; chemical cross-linking resins may be used to improve appearance retention. Greige lining fabrics finished with some or all of these conversion processes are often marketed with a registered trade name: an example is Roc-lon®, owned by the Roc-lon Corporation, Inc.

Challis (challie) is a soft, drapable lining fabric produced from spun yarns of rayon or acetate fibers. During conversion, chemical cross-linking resins may be applied for improved resiliency, and fluorocarbon compounds may be added for water and soil repellency. Frequently, the man-made cellulosic fibers are engineered to be flame resistant; acetate is often engineered to be sunlight resistant, as well.

Sateen-woven Lining Fabrics. Much of the fabric in separately hung drapery lining panels has been produced with the sateen weave. These sateen linings are composed of fine, combed cotton yarns, bleached to whiteness or piece dyed. The soft luster produced by the floating yarns may be augmented by friction calendering or schreinering (see Chapter 9). At first glance, schreinered sateen lining may appear to have a fine twill interlacing: the "hills" suggest a visual diagonal. Close inspection, however, confirms the presence of floating filling yarns and proves the apparent diagonals to be three-dimensional protrusions of the fabric.

The luster that the floating filling yarns contribute to sateen will last until the yarns are ruptured. The reflective characteristics introduced by calendering and schreinering operations, however, will eventually be altered by cleaning processes.

Metallic-coated Lining Fabrics. One side of plain- or sateen-woven lining fabrics may be sprayed with a mixture of metallic or metallic-colored particles and resin binders. The silver-colored particles that coat the lining in Figure 20.33 not only increase opacity for a dimout (partial blackout) effect, they also increase the level of solar heat rejection. These reflective coverings may be particularly beneficial in large windows with southern exposures.

SUMMARY

Primarily because window coverings do not have to withstand the same high level of abrasion as upholstered

Figure 20.33 Metallic-coated, reflective textile lining fabric.

furniture coverings, window covering fabrics are manufactured using a more extensive variety of fabrication techniques. Some fabrics, especially those produced in stitch-knitting, stitch-bonding, weft insertion, and spunlacing operations, are relatively inexpensive, and their transparency and covering power is readily controlled.

Other curtain and drapery fabrics, including those produced by knotting, twisting, and surface-figure weaving, display distinctive design features. Still other fabrics, such as those made in leno-weaving and raschel-stitching operations, exhibit a high degree of openness and dimensional stability and virtually no yarn slippage.

Drapery lining materials, whether permanently attached or separately hung, present a uniform appearance to outside viewers and reduce the negative effects of radiant energy on the fibers and colorants used in the decorative panels. They can also provide such functional benefits as insulation, noise reduction, and greater control of light transmission.

chapter 21

Evaluation and Maintenance of Finished Window Covering Fabrics

- Standards for Physical Performance Properties
- Evaluations of Colorfastness
- Evaluations of Flame Resistance and Smoke Generation
- Maintenance of Window Covering Structures

Laboratory tests conducted on greige goods help to evaluate the potential quality of textile curtain, drapery, and lining fabrics. Reliable assessments of actual quality, however, must be based on tests conducted on the finished fabrics themselves. Results of these tests reflect the effects of the agents and processes used to transform the greige goods' surface appearance, improve performance, and minimize care requirements. Even though producers can make textile window coverings easier to care for, it is up to residential and commercial consumers to use a three-part maintenance program that will prolong fabrics' use-life.

Manufacturers and converters evaluating the flame resistance of finished window covering fabrics often employ test methods developed by members of the National Fire Protection Association. When evaluating other performance characteristics, they often use the test methods and performance guidelines recommended by representatives of all segments of the window covering industry, as covered in ASTM D 3691 Standard Performance Specifications for Woven, Lace, and Knit Household Curtain and Drapery Fabrics.*

*The full text of ASTM D 3691 may be reviewed in the *Annual Book of ASTM Standards,* Part 32.

STANDARDS FOR PHYSICAL PERFORMANCE PROPERTIES

Because the satisfactory end use performance of textile window covering fabrics depends on their physical performance, members of the industry set out performance guidelines for such characteristics as dimensional stability, distortion of yarn, and fabric strength in their recommended standard. Guidelines also concern the level of appearance retention that durable press curtain and drapery fabrics should exhibit.

Dimensional Stability

Sagging and shrinking must be minimized in textile window covering fabrics to preserve the appearance and the usefulness of the treatments they compose. In swagged valences and such treatment styles as priscilla curtains and Austrian shades, sagging would destroy the balance of the laterally draping folds. In straight, free-hanging panels, sagging could cause the lower part of the fabric to stack on the floor. Sagging is more likely to occur in fabrics composed of conventional rayon (see Chapter 19), and in fabrics of loose construction, especially when low-twist, spun yarns are involved or the yarns are variously angled, as in lace fabrics.

Shrinkage of the overdraperies in treatments having multiple layers could expose the lower edge of the curtains to the interior, and shrinkage of the lining panels could expose a portion of the overdraperies to the exterior. If the panels shrank, fabric transparency would be reduced and the tight closure that maintains an insulating layer of dead air between the covering and the glass might be destroyed.

Converters can use compressive shrinkage processes and heat-setting operations to stabilize curtain and drapery greige goods. Laboratory tests evaluate the effectiveness of these treatments. Specimens of the stabilized fabric are prepared as illustrated in Figure 14.5 (Page 139), except they are larger and the inner markings are 18 inches apart. The specimens are laundered in accordance with AATCC 135 Dimensional Changes in Automatic Home Laundering of Durable Press Woven or Knit Fabric, or they are dry-cleaned in accordance with ASTM D 2724 Testing Bonded and Laminated Apparel Fabrics. The performance guideline in ASTM D 3691 states that the fabrics should not change more than 3 percent in their lengthwise and crosswise dimensions after being laundered five times or dry-cleaned three times.

Distortion of Yarn

Evaluating the propensity of yarns to shift or distort in such open curtain fabrics as voile, ninon, and marquisette is important. This characteristic should also be examined in satin-woven fabrics with smooth yarns. The shifting or slipping of one set of yarns over the other produces areas having different levels of transparency (Figure 12.2, page 114); in patterned coverings, a stain-like appearance may develop. ASTM D 1336 Test for Distortion of Yarn in Woven Fabrics measures the extent to which this unsightly characteristic occurs in woven curtain and drapery fabrics.

Test Specimens and Procedures. As directed in ASTM D 1336, five specimens are cut slightly larger than 4 inches by 8 inches, with their longer dimension parallel to the set of yarns having the greater resistance to shifting. The operator determines this direction by exerting a shearing motion on the fabric with the thumb and forefinger. After conditioning, a specimen is clamped into a rectangular carriage frame and placed between two frictional drums on the testing device (Figure 21.1). The weight of the upper drum is adjusted to provide a total force of 1 pound when sheer curtain fabrics are being tested, and a total force of 2 pounds when conventional weight woven fabrics are being tested. The carriage is then shifted so that the drums produce a shearing action on the specimen.

Analysis of Results. After the specimen has been removed from the carriage and allowed to relax for 15 minutes, the widest opening of each shift mark, or distorted yarn group, is measured as shown in Figures 21.2a and 21.2b. Nonmeasurable openings, illustrated in Figures 21.2c and 21.2d, are described and reported. The average of the five measurements is calculated and reported.

Performance Guidelines. According to the performance specifications included in ASTM D 3691, sheer and conventional weight woven window coverings should exhibit a maximum distortion of 0.1 inch.

Fabric Strength

Performance guidelines for three types of fabric strength measurements are included in ASTM D 3691. Breaking strength and tear strength measurements are made with woven curtain and drapery fabrics; bursting strength measurements are made with knitted and knotted and twisted fabrics.

Breaking Strength. The breaking strength (load) of woven curtain and drapery fabrics may be evaluated in accordance with the procedures outlined in the grab method of ASTM D 1682 Tests for Breaking Load and Elongation of Textile Fabrics. (This test method was described in

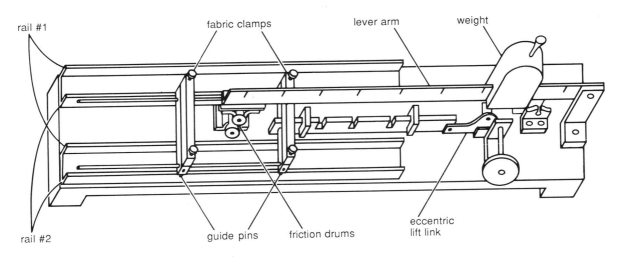

Figure 21.1 Fabric shift tester. (Reprinted, with permission, copyright American Society for Testing and Materials.)

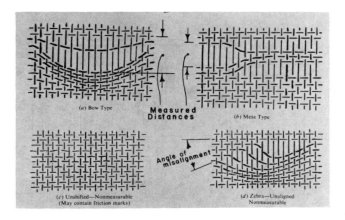

Figure 21.2 Measurable and nonmeasurable shift openings. (Reprinted, with permission, copyright American Society for Testing and Materials.)

Chapter 14.) Sheer fabrics, such as batiste, dimity, ninon, and voile, should withstand a minimum load of 15 pounds before rupturing, and conventional weight woven coverings should withstand a minimum load of 20 pounds.

Tear Strength. The tear strength of woven curtain and drapery fabrics may be evaluated as directed in ASTM D 2262 Test for Testing Strength of Woven Fabrics by the Tongue (Single Rip) Method (Constant-Rate-of-Traverse Tensile Testing machine). This procedure measures the force required to continue a tear in the specimens. (See Chapter 14.) Sheer curtain fabrics should require a force of at least 1 pound to propagate the tear, and conventional weight woven fabrics should require at least 1.5 pounds.

Bursting Strength. Bursting strength measurements are made only on fabrics having nonaligned yarns; in this case, they are made on knit and lace curtain and drapery fabrics. ASTM D 231 Testing and Tolerances for Knit Goods is the specified test method.

In this test, a conditioned specimen is secured under an O-shaped plate. A force is exerted against the specimen by a polished, hard steel ball. The test is completed when the ball bursts through the specimen. The maximum force required to burst each specimen is recorded. The average of all replicate tests is then calculated and reported. Knit and lace curtain and drapery fabrics should resist a minimum force of 20 pounds per square inch.

Durability of Backcoatings

A performance requirement for backcoatings used on drapery fabrics is included in ASTM D 3691. The coating

should exhibit no evidence of cracking or peeling when the fabric is subjected to prescribed laundering and dry-cleaning tests.

Appearance Retention

Textile window coverings are repeatedly folded and bent as panels are opened and closed. They also are folded, bent, twisted, and crushed during cleaning. To help curtain and drapery fabrics composed of cotton, linen, or rayon to recover from such treatment, converters apply durable press or chemical cross-linking resins. As long as treated fabrics retain their smooth appearance in use and care, ironing can be avoided.

Members of the industry have established recommended levels of performance for fabrics with a durable press finish. After specimens of the fabric have been laundered five times as directed in Test IIB of AATCC 127, their appearance is compared with that of three-dimensional plastic replicas (Figure 21.3). Smoothness progressively increases from the first to the fifth replica; each specimen is assigned the number of the replica it most closely resembles. Knit, lace, and conventional weight woven curtain and drapery fabrics should have an average minimum rating of 3.5, and woven sheer fabrics should have an average minimum rating of 3.0.

EVALUATIONS OF COLORFASTNESS

Manufacturers and textile colorists use various testing procedures to ensure that colored interior and exterior window covering fabrics exhibit acceptable levels of fastness when exposed to potentially destructive conditions and substances. The test methods in ASTM D 3691 are used on textile coverings intended for use in residential interiors. The fastness guidelines set forth in the performance standard apply to residential fabrics, but contract designers, architects, and other specifiers may refer to the recommended performance values when making decisions about fastness requirements in their commercial projects. Test methods other than those in ASTM D 3691 may be employed on textile fabrics for outdoor applications. Colorists should always discontinue the use of fugitive colorants, those found to exhibit an unacceptable level of fastness.

Colorfastness to Light

Although the radiant energy of all spectral rays—visible and invisible—can have a negative effect on textile colorants, ultraviolet waves have been shown to be particularly destructive. Because natural light has a higher quantity of these short waves than do artificial illuminants, concern for color retention is generally focused on the stability of textile colorants to sunlight. Such stability is

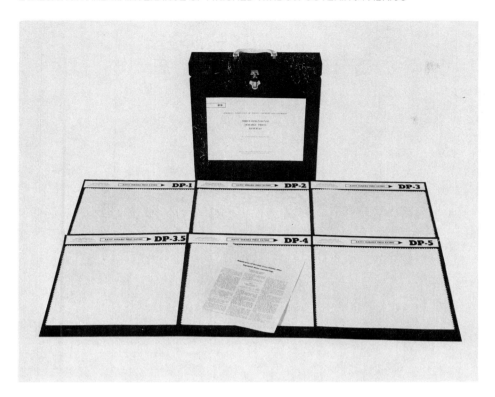

Figure 21.3 Three-dimensional plastic fabric replicas used to evaluate the appearance retention of durable press fabrics. (Courtesy of the American Association of Textile Chemists and Colorists.)

critical in colorants used in curtains and draperies, and in all textiles installed outdoors, in passive solar residences, and in commercial buildings with large expanses of glass. It is especially important in colorants for textile products installed in a southern exposure.

When solar rays strike a colored textile surface, the heat energy excites the dye molecules and gradually changes their chemical structure. Continued alteration of the molecular structure reduces the ability of the dyestuff to produce its original color characteristics. The textile develops a faded appearance: strong, bright, and pure hues become weak, dull, and grayed.

Several test methods have been developed for evaluating the effects of radiant energy, alone or in combination with moisture and heat, on the colorants used in textile products. Some methods are accelerated laboratory procedures; others are long-term outdoor tests.

Lightfastness of Interior Fabrics. Accelerated testing for lightfastness can be performed with the Fade-Ometer® (Figure 21.4), using one of two different lamps. A glass-enclosed carbon-arc lamp produces light energy throughout the visible spectrum, and is the light source specified in AATCC 16A Colorfastness to Light: Carbon-Arc Continuous Light. Because this lamp is somewhat deficient in ultraviolet rays below 350 nm, its use is diminishing, and it is not recommended for use in evaluating

textiles to be installed outdoors. A xenon-arc lamp more closely simulates natural light and gives a more accurate evaluation when correlating to end use performance. This lamp is specified in AATCC 16E Colorfastness to Light: Water-cooled Xenon-Arc Lamp, Continuous Light, the method increasingly used for determining the lightfastness of window coverings intended for interior installation.

For testing with either light source, fabric specimens are mounted in holders, which are suspended in the apparatus and rotated for several hours. The number of hours of exposure (calculated as the standard fading hours, SFH, or standard fading units, SFU or FU) recommended for window coverings is 60.

After completion of an accelerated test, the color retention of the specimens is visually evaluated and numerically rated. The number is determined by comparing the difference observed between an original and exposed specimen with that observed between a pair of standard gray chips on the Gray Scale for Color Change, pictured in Figure 14.10 (page 145). A minimum lightfastness rating of Class 4 is recommended for dyed and printed curtain and drapery fabrics produced for installation in residential interiors.

Lightfastness of Exterior Fabrics. A Weather-Ometer®, manufactured by Atlas Electric Devices Company, is used for the accelerated laboratory testing of

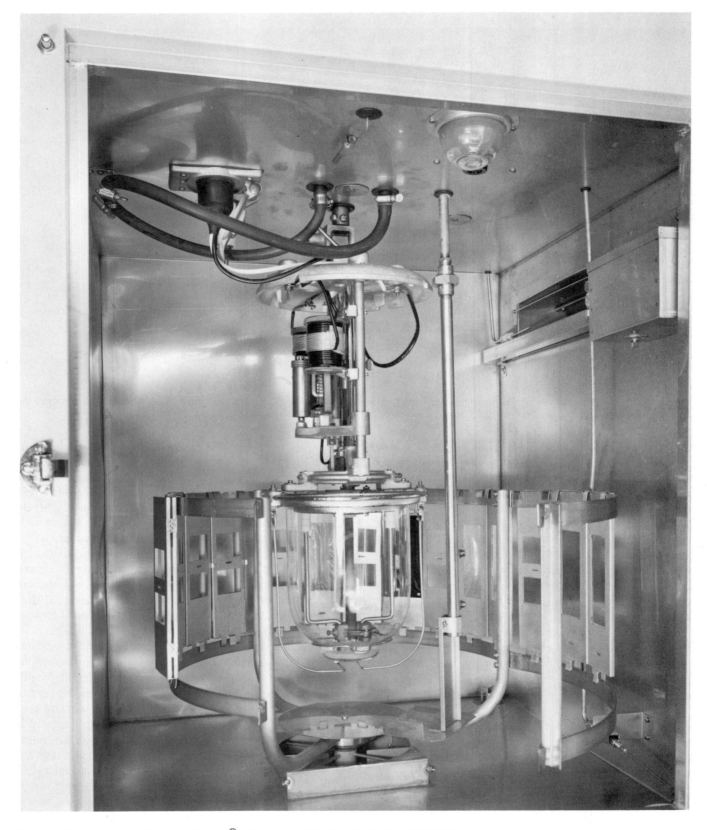

Figure 21.4 Interior view of the Fade-Ometer®. (Courtesy of Atlas Electric Devices Company.)

textile fabrics to be installed outdoors. This unit effectively simulates the natural outdoor environment, since it facilitates temperature and humidity changes.

For extended outdoor testing, specimens may be fully exposed, or they may be mounted behind glass (Figure 21.5). Depending on the conditions anticipated in the end use setting, the fabrics may be exposed continuously for 24 hours a day, placed in an enclosed cabinet to permit testing at elevated temperatures, or tested near the ocean for an analysis of the effects of salt atmosphere on the colorants.

The level of color retention exhibited by exterior fabrics tested in the laboratory or outdoors may be rated on the basis of the Gray Scale for Color Change. Because the exposure conditions may have degraded the fibers as well as the colorants, measurements are also often made to determine changes in such properties as strength and dimensional stability.

Colorfastness to Atmospheric Gases

The fastness of colored window coverings to controlled concentrations of gases, such as nitrogen dioxide (NO_2) and sulfur dioxide (SO_2), can be evaluated by following the procedures in AATCC 123 Colorfastness to Burnt Fumes. This test method was described in Chapter 14; the apparatus used to expose the specimens is pictured in Figure 14.11 (page 146). Curtain and drapery specimens are exposed and evaluated before and after one laundering or dry-cleaning. The Gray Scale for Color Change is used to evaluate the amount of fading or color change, and a minimum Class 4 rating is recommended for acceptable performance.

The negative effects of ozone (O_3), a strong oxidizing agent, on colored window fabrics can be assessed through the procedures outlined in AATCC 129 Colorfastness to Ozone in the Atmosphere under High Humidities. After one cycle of exposure, the specimens should have a minimum Class 4 rating when compared to the paired chips on the Gray Scale for Color Change. [*]

---

[*]The reliability of AATCC 129 as a test for predicting in-service fading due to ozone was investigated and confirmed in a three-year study. See Melvin R. Nipe, "Atmospheric Contaminant Fading," *Textile Chemist and Colorist,* Vol. 13, No. 6, June 1981, 18–28.

Figure 21.5 Outdoor testing facility used to evaluate the effects of natural light on textile colorants. (Courtesy of South Florida Test Service, Inc., a subsidiary of Atlas Electric Devices Company.)

Colorfastness to Crocking

Although crocking—the transfer of color from one material to another—is a more serious problem in upholstery fabrics, certain situations may lead to crocking problems in colored curtain and drapery fabrics. Color transfer may occur when the fabrics rub together or are handled during shipping, sewing, hanging, opening, and closing.

The colorfastness of solid colors to dry and wet crocking is evaluated by the AATCC 8 Colorfastness to Crocking (Rubbing): AATCC Crockmeter Method. This method was described in Chapter 14; the apparatus used to rub the specimens is pictured in Figure 14.8 (page 144). For printed fabrics, the procedures in AATCC 116 Colorfastness to Crocking (Rubbing): Rotary Vertical Crockmeter Method should be followed.

After the test is completed, the AATCC Chromatic Transference Scale (Figure 21.6) is used to evaluate the amount of color transferred. This scale is a card with six colors, neutral gray, red, yellow, green, blue, and purple, mounted in each of four horizontal rows. In each of six vertical rows, the chroma or intensity of each hue is varied, beginning with an extremely light tint and ending

with a moderately deep shade. The vertically aligned chips are separated by holes in the card.

For evaluation, the stained fabric is placed behind the card and visually examined through the holes. The observer shifts the card until the chroma or intensity of the stain is judged to be similar to that of a color chip, and the number of the row in which this chip is located is assigned to the fabric. Dry tests should yield a minimum rating of 4, wet tests a minimum rating of 3.

Colorfastness to Laundering and Dry Cleaning

When dyed and printed curtain and drapery fabrics are laundered or dry cleaned, the colorants should not exhibit unacceptable levels of fading, bleeding, or migration. A faded appearance may result when the colorants are oxidized by bleaching agents or when the dyestuff bleeds from the fabric. Excessive bleeding of the dyestuff into the cleaning solution may stain (in effect, dye) other articles in the load. A stained appearance may also result when the dyestuff migrates or moves through the fabric. Product manufacturers and textile colorists use laboratory test methods to evaluate the potential for excessive fading and

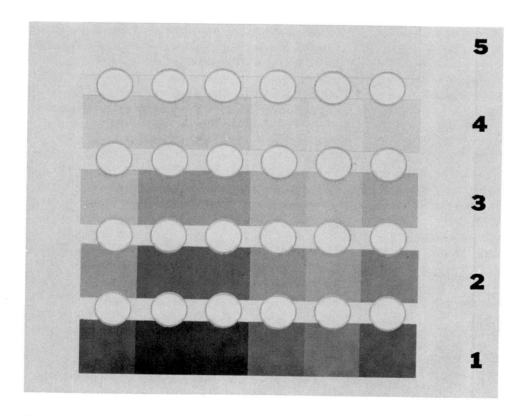

Figure 21.6 AAATC Chromatic Transference Scale. (Courtesy of the American Association of Textile Chemists and Colorists.)

staining and to determine what type of cleaning agents should be used.

Accelerated testing for colorfastness to laundry and dry-cleaning agents can be conducted with a Launder-Ometer® (Figure 21.7). This apparatus contains stainless steel jars to hold the specimens and the specified cleaning solution. During testing, the jars are rotated to simulate agitation. Washfastness evaluations are made following the procedures described in Test IIA of AATCC 61 Colorfastness to Washing, Domestic, and Laundering, Commercial: Accelerated. In this testing, multifiber test fabric is paired with some specimens to facilitate evaluation of staining. The effect of repeated dry cleanings is assessed by following the testing procedures outlined in AATCC 132 Colorfastness to Dry Cleaning.

After completion of either testing procedure, the fabrics are evaluated for color change using the Gray Scale for Color Change; a rating of 4 is recommended for acceptable performance in end use. The multifiber test fabrics are evaluated for staining using the Gray Scale for Staining, which is pictured in Figure 14.9 (page 145). A minimum rating of 3 is recommended.

EVALUATIONS OF FLAME RESISTANCE AND SMOKE GENERATION

Industry representatives did not include flammability guidelines in ASTM D 3691, and the Consumer Product Safety Commission has not established a flammability standard with which curtains and draperies must comply prior to their introduction into commerce. However, various regulatory agencies have set forth mandatory flammability standards for window coverings selected for use in

Figure 21.7 Interior view of the Launder-Ometer®. (Courtesy of Atlas Electric Devices Company.)

certain commercial interiors. In many cases, these mandates are based on recommendations included in the NPFA 101® Life Safety Code®.*

NFPA 701

NFPA 701-1977 Standard Methods of Fire Tests for Flame Resistant Textiles and Films may be used to evaluate the effectiveness of polymer additives and finishing compounds in reducing the flammability of textile window coverings. Two test methods, both of which may be used to measure the ignition propensity of fabrics to be installed indoors or outdoors, are set out.

Scope. NFPA 701 is intended for use with textiles and films treated with flame retardant agents or composed of flame resistant man-made fibers. Fabrics expected to retain their flame resistant qualities through dry cleaning, laundering, weathering, or other exposures to water are subjected to accelerated exposure procedures prior to testing. Treated awning fabrics, for example, would be exposed to simulated weathering conditions and then tested.

Small-scale Test Method. The small-scale test method can be used to evaluate the flame resistance of fabrics that do not exhibit excessive shrinkage or melting when exposed to a flame.

Test specimens and procedures. Ten specimens of the covering are cut 2.75 inches by 10 inches. Five have their long dimension in the direction of the filling and five in the direction of the warp. The specimens are

*Life Safety Code® and 101® are Registered Trademarks of the National Fire Protection Association, Inc., Quincy, Mass.

then conditioned in an oven at a temperature of 140 to 145°F for 1 to 1-1/2 hours, or, if they would melt or distort in the oven, they are conditioned at 60 to 80°F and 25 to 50 percent relative humidity for a minimum of 24 hours. Each specimen is then placed in an open-ended specimen holder and suspended in a vertical flammability tester, similar to the apparatus pictured in Figure 16.10 (page 167). The flame from a burner is then applied to the lower edge for 12 seconds.

Flame resistance requirements. In order for the covering material to pass the small-scale test, the specimens must meet the following requirements:

1. No specimen shall continue flaming for more than two seconds after the test flame is removed from contact with the specimen.
2. The vertical spread of flame and afterglow (smoldering combustion) on the material, as indicated by the length of char or the measurement from the bottom of the sample above which all material is sound and in original condition, shall not exceed the values listed in Table 21.1.
3. At no time during or after the application of the test flame shall portions or residues of textiles or films that break or drip from any test specimen continue to flame after they reach the floor of the tester.**

Large-scale Test Method. The large-scale test may be selected for use with covering materials that show ex-

** Reprinted with permission of NFPA 701-1977, Standard Methods of Fire Tests for Flame Resistant Textiles and Films, Copyright©1977, National Fire Protection Association, Quincy, MA 02269. This reprinted material is not the complete and official position of the NFPA on the referenced subject, which is represented only by the standard in its entirety.

Table 21.1 PERMISSIBLE LENGTH OF CHAR OR DESTROYED MATERIAL—NFPA 701 SMALL-SCALE TEST

Weight of treated fabric being tested (ounces per square yard)	Maximum average length of char or destroyed material for ten specimens (inches)	Maximum length of char or destroyed material for any specimen (inches)
over 10	3-1/2	4-1/2
over 6 and not exceeding 10	4-1/2	5-1/2
not exceeding 6	5-1/2	6-1/2

Reprinted with permission of NFPA 701-1977, Standard Methods of Fire Tests for Flame Resistant Textiles and Films, Copyright © 1977 National Fire Protection Association, Quincy, MA 02269. This reprinted material is not the complete and official position of the NFPA on the referenced subject, which is represented only by the standard in its entirety.

cessive melting or shrinkage when tested by the small-scale test. This method is also useful for evaluating the fire behavior of coverings hung in folds, as is typical in window treatments.

Test specimens and procedures. Specimens of the covering material may be tested in single, flat sheets or they may be hung with folds. For flat testing, ten specimens, 5 inches by 7 feet, are cut. For testing with folds, four lengths of the covering, each cut 25 inches by 7 feet, are folded longitudinally to form four folds, each approximately 5 inches wide. In either case, half the specimens have their long dimension in the direction of the warp and half have their long dimension in the direction of the filling. The specimens are conditioned as described for the small-scale test.

The specimens, flat or folded, are suspended in the tester, which is a sheet-iron stack 12 inches square and 7 feet high. The lower edge of the specimen is 4 inches above the burner tip and an 11-inch flame is held under the specimen for two minutes.

Flame resistance requirements. In order for the covering material to pass the large-scale test, the specimens must meet the following requirements:

1. No specimen shall continue flaming for more than two seconds after the test flame is removed from contact with the specimen.
2. The vertical spread of burning on the material in single sheets shall not exceed 10 inches above the tip of the test flame. This vertical spread shall be measured as the distance from the tip of the test flame to a horizontal line above which all material is sound and in original condition, except for possible smoke deposits.
3. The vertical spread of burning on the folded specimens shall not exceed 35 inches above the tip of the test flame, but the afterglow may spread in the folds.
4. At no time during or after the application of the test flame shall portions or residues of textiles or films that break or drip from any test specimen continue to flame after they reach the floor of the tester.*

In the event of fire, fabrics meeting the flame resistance requirements included in the small- or large-scale test methods would not be likely to propagate the flames to the floor, wall, and ceiling. This reduces the threat of a Stage 1 fire growing into a Stage 2 fire.

* Reprinted with permission of NFPA 701-1977, Standard Methods of Fire Tests for Flame Resistant Textiles and Films, Copyright ©1977, National Fire Protection Association, Quincy, MA 02269. This reprinted material is not the complete and official position of the NFPA on the referenced subject, which is represented only by the standard in its entirety.

NFPA 258

NFPA Research Test Method 258-1982 Smoke Generation of Solid Materials may be used to assess the rate of smoke production and the time at which specific smoke levels are reached under the test conditions applied. Because smoke generation criteria are included more often in flammability standards for soft floor coverings than for curtains and draperies, this test is described in Unit Four.

MAINTENANCE OF WINDOW COVERING STRUCTURES

By planning and following an appropriate maintenance program that includes preventive, routine, and restorative practices, residential and commercial consumers can effectively prolong the use-life of window treatments, especially those containing textile components. Manufacturers are not required to provide care instructions, but several voluntarily include them on their product labels. Such instructions are often based on the results of the colorfastness to laundering and dry-cleaning tests described earlier in this chapter.

Preventive Maintenance Measures

Preventive maintenance techniques not only preserve the original appearance of window coverings, but may also reduce the weakening suffered by the fibers. Care should be taken to avoid allowing rainwater to blow in on linings and other fabric layers and to prevent panels from hanging in contact with framework on which water condenses. Water, including vapor-phase moisture, may combine with soil present on the fibers and cause staining of the fabric. Water may also combine with pollutants and oily cooking fumes to form weak acids that attack and weaken the fibers (see Chapter 19). When gases and cooking fumes are present, especially in high concentrations, the coverings should be frequently cleaned to prevent accumulation of these acids.

An effort should be made to keep the level of relative humidity around coverings composed of conventional rayon fibers as constant as possible. This will avoid or minimize the development of the elevator effect, the sagging and shrinking problem described in Chapter 19.

Neither textile nor nontextile panels should be allowed to flap in the wind. This could result in tearing and abrading of textile fabrics, splitting and cracking of wood components, and bending of aluminum louvers.

Routine Care Practices

Textile fabric panels, especially those that are stationary or laterally draped, should be vacuumed or tumbled in an automatic dryer, using low heat or none at all, to remove airborne soil. This is especially important for coverings composed of hydrophobic fibers, whose tendency to build up electrical charges increases the fibers' attraction for airborne soil. The louvers and vanes in blinds and shutters and the surfaces of roller shades should be routinely vacuumed to remove accumulated dust.

Restorative Maintenance Procedures

Curtains and draperies are not included in the scope of the FTC trade regulation rule related to care labeling, but many producers elect to provide a cleaning code. Usually, the cleaning code letters for upholstery fabrics are used for curtains and draperies as well. These letters and their meanings were described in Chapter 14.

Unless specifically stated on the label or in literature accompanying glass fiber curtains, draperies, and fabrics, those products must not be dry-cleaned or laundered in an automatic washer because the agitation promotes fibrillation. Because soil is held only on fiber surfaces and in yarn and fabric interstices, it may be removed by immersing the coverings in a bathtub or in a commercial cleaning tank filled with a detergent solution. After rinsing, the nearly dry panels should be rehung to dry.

Fabrics with a durable press finish may be laundered in an automatic washer. Strong oxidizing bleaches, such as chlorine compounds, should not be used. In high concentrations, these agents may be retained by the fibers, turning the fabric yellow and further weakening the cellulosic components. The laundered panels should be tumbled with low heat in an automatic dryer until dry, followed by a cool-down cycle and prompt removal.

Excessively high heat should not be used on any fiber. Recommended ironing temperatures are listed in Table 4.5. Unfortunately, consumers often find that iron dials are divided by fiber type or by finish, not by specific temperatures. Moreover, the same setting on different irons may produce quite different temperatures. Consumers and professional cleaners should be alert for signs of fiber and fabric damage. For fabrics composed of thermoplastic fibers, the slightest amount of fabric shrinkage and the slightest resistance of the soleplate to gliding are indications that the ironing temperature is too high.

Commercial and residential consumers may consider having their textile window coverings cleaned by a professional cleaner. This is advisable when long, heavy panels with multiple folds require large cleaning tanks and special pressing equipment. Frequently, laundry and dry-cleaning firms offer removal and rehanging as optional services. Consumers can determine for themselves whether the value of these services overrides the burden of the additional charges.

SUMMARY

As part of their quality-control work, producers and converters may subject curtain and drapery fabrics to prescribed laboratory test methods, measuring such properties as bursting strength, flame resistance, and appearance retention. The results of these tests can be compared with the performance guidelines established by members of the industry or the performance mandates of a regulatory agency. Different standards of performance have been set for fabrics with different construction features. If necessary, manufacturers may alter their choice of components or construction methods to improve the quality of their products.

Textile colorists may elect to evaluate the fastness of colorants used in interior and exterior window covering fabrics, following the procedures outlined in an accelerated or a long-term test method. Tests expose the colored fabrics to such conditions and substances as artificial light, natural light, atmospheric contaminants, and cleaning agents. The use of dyes and pigments that exhibit unacceptable levels of color retention in appropriate tests should be discontinued.

The original appearance and condition of curtain and drapery fabrics and other window covering structures can be well maintained by following a planned program. The program should include preventive measures, routine practices, and the use of appropriate procedures when restorative cleaning is needed. Frequently, producers voluntarily provide care instructions with textile window coverings.

chapter 22

Textile Coverings for Walls and Panels

- Components and Constructions
- Selection and Serviceability
- Installation Techniques

In large, open interiors, textile fabrics often cover panels or partitions positioned to define work areas. In other interiors, textile structures cover all or part of the surfaces of permanent walls. In both applications, the coverings provide visual and tactile interest and some measure of noise reduction. In certain cases, wall coverings are installed also to increase insulation.

A variety of textile structures is produced exclusively for use on vertical surfaces. Many fabrics produced for use as window and upholstered furniture coverings, and several pile structures produced for use as soft floor coverings, can also be used as wall and panel coverings. Frequently, contract designers and consumers elect to use the same fabric to cover the walls, windows, and upholstered furniture in an interior.

COMPONENTS AND CONSTRUCTIONS

Because textile wall coverings are primarily expected to provide visual and tactile interest, and are subjected to few stresses in use, distinctive components and construction techniques are appropriate for them. Virtually all fabrics chosen for wall and panel coverings, however, carry some backing applied to impart dimensional stability and facilitate installation.

Fibers and Yarns

Natural fibers, including wool, silk, linen, jute, and cotton, are extensively and effectively used in wall and panel fabrics. Often, the inherent color variations of these fibers help stylists to design yarns and coverings with a warm and rich appearance. Stylists also capitalize on the natural surface irregularities of these fibers to produce distinctive textural characteristics. Such color and textural variations appear in the linen blend covering in Figure 22.1.

The high stiffness and low elasticity of linen limit its use in certain textile furnishings, but these properties contribute high dimensional stability to wall coverings, helping to minimize their sagging. When flame resistance is mandated or desired, designers and architects can specify the application of flame retardant compounds to fabrics composed of linen, cotton, or rayon, or they may elect to use wool or glass fibers.

To reduce the cost of coverings composed of some natural fibers, producers frequently blend them with viscose rayon. Although viscose rayon has poor dimensional stability, the use of a backing or coating can overcome the problem, and some coverings are composed entirely of this relatively inexpensive cellulose-based fiber.

Of the noncellulosic fibers, polypropylene olefin fibers have an extremely low specific gravity. They may be used to produce lightweight coverings resembling those composed of wool (Figure 22.4).

Figure 22.1 Laminated wall covering enriched by the natural color and texture of linen fibers. (Courtesy Sommer® Coverings, division of Allibert, Inc.)

Simple and complex yarns are used alone or in combination. The decorative effects of complex yarns are often emphasized by placing the yarns individually in a parallel arrangement on a backing fabric. This technique highlights the varied features of the yarns (see the coverings in Figure 22.2).

Eye-catching reflections appear in wall coverings when they incorporate bright man-made fibers, silk, metal filaments, and metallic yarns. In some coverings, spiral yarns containing metallic strands are plied with simple yarns strategically positioned to create reflective highlights as viewers pass the wall.

Construction Techniques

Because wall and panel coverings are not subjected to significant levels of abrasion or repeated flexing, the assortment of coverings offered to contemporary consumers includes a number of distinctively constructed fabrics as well as fabrics produced by conventional weaving and knitting procedures.

Weaving. Flat-woven wall covering fabrics range from those produced with a simple biaxial interlacing pattern to those produced with a decorative dobby or Jacquard weave. The visual and tactile interest of these fabrics is often enhanced with flocking or embroidering. Woven pile fabrics,

Figure 22.2 The use of variously colored complex yarns in single layers increases the visual and textural interest of these wall coverings. (Courtesy Sommer® Coverings, division of Allibert, Inc.)

such as corduroy and velvet, and woven or tufted carpet are also available.

Frequently, fabric stylists design woven coverings with relatively little compactness of construction, so that the backing are visible. Figure 22.3 shows a jute covering in which the backing's trellis print can be viewed through the face fabric, and the surface's visual interest is augmented.

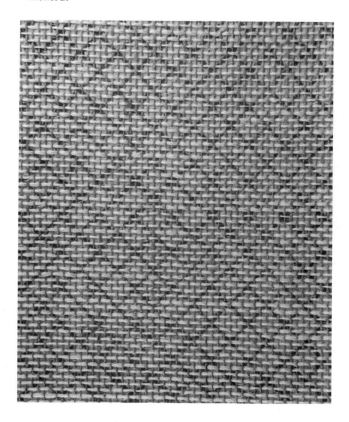

Figure 22.3 Open woven jute covering permits view of the printed pattern on the backing. (Courtesy Sommer ®Coverings, division of Allibert, Inc.)

Knitting. For high dimensional stability, most knitted wall coverings are produced with a tricot or interlock stitch. Such fabrics readily conform to curved surfaces.

Needlepunching. Webs of fibers may be layered into a batt and stabilized by needlepunching (Figure 26.17, page 293). For increased visual and textural interest, the level surface may be punched or embossed to create a three-dimensional, patterned configuration (Figure 22.4). This alteration in fabric form may produce an appearance resembling that of more expensive woven pile fabrics. Such structural changes may also improve the acoustical value of the coverings, making them especially suitable for covering panels in open office interiors. Measurement of the acoustical benefits of wall and panel coverings is discussed later in this chapter.

Laminating. Frequently, a single web or layer of textile yarns is laminated or glued directly to a paper base. In such structures, the parallel yarns may be closely or widely spaced, and the yarns may be fine or coarse, as in the laminated coverings in Figures 22.1 and 22.2.

Backings and Finishes

Various backings and finishing agents are used with textile wall and panel fabrics. Some of these serve both functional and aesthetic purposes.

Sueding. Genuine suede could be used to cover walls and panels, but such applications would be expensive. Manufacturers do, however, offer simulated suede coverings (Figure 22.5). Not only is the materials cost of the simulated suede lower, but so is the potential for crocking when people inadvertently rub against the surfaces.

Backings. Acrylic foam, vinyl spray, paper, gypsum, or a spunlaced or spunbonded fabric must be applied to the back of most textile fabric coverings to prevent the application adhesive from striking through and producing a stained appearance. Spunbonded backings, normally composed of polypropylene olefin fibers, are designed to be strippable, a feature attractive to residents anticipating a move.

Gypsum, a high density, uncrystallized plaster, may be used to coat the back of open-weave burlap wall covering. When applied, the compound is soft, permitting the coverings to be rolled for shipment. After contact with the special adhesive that secures the fabric to the wall, the coating crystallizes and sets into a hard backing. The compound, available in numerous colors, fills fabric interstices and hides any surface defects.

Functional Finishes. For increased safety in the event of fire, textile wall and panel coverings may be treated with a flame retardant compound. To reduce the rate of soil accumulation and to protect the coverings from unsightly staining, fluorocarbon compounds may be applied. For maximum protection against soil accumulation, fingerprints, atmospheric contaminants, and general abuse, and to make the surface washable, textile wall coverings may be laminated with a clear or transluscent vinyl film. This treatment, also used on upholstery fabric, was described in Chapter 14.

SELECTION AND SERVICEABILITY

Textile wall coverings often serve primarily aesthetic or primarily functional purposes in an interior, but both purposes may be furthered if attention is given to certain selection and serviceability factors. In certain interiors, at-

Figure 22.4 Needlepunched wall covering with a three-dimensional, pile-like surface.

tention to the fire performance of the covering is mandated.

Interior Enrichment

The coverings pictured in this chapter show how much textile structures for installation on vertical surfaces can differ in color styling, textural features, tactile characteristics, construction, and weight. This wide assortment permits consumers and designers to select a covering that provides the ambiance and decorative impact they seek.

Because dyestuffs applied to different types of substrates inevitably show differences in color characteristics, a precise color match between fabric and paper is normally impossible to obtain. Consumers and designers can avoid a mismatch by having their upholstery or window fabric backed for application as a wall covering, rather than installing coordinated wallpaper.

Functional Values

Textile wall coverings may be selected to fulfill specific functional needs. They may, for example, provide some measure of acoustical control or of insulation.

Noise Reduction. Bare walls can reflect sound waves and prolong duration of noise (Figure 18.2, page 186). Textile-covered interior panels or partitions placed throughout open areas interrupt the horizontal travel of sound waves; some of the sound generated within each enclosure can be contained this way. Textile coverings on permanent walls help reduce the amount of waves reflected back into the interior, as well as the amount transferred through the walls to adjoining rooms.

The acoustical benefits of textile structures used on vertical surfaces should be analyzed with testing equipment that can simulate the construction characteristics of the wall or partition and the technique for installing the covering. In one series of tests sponsored by The Carpet and Rug Institute, for example, various carpet specimens were mounted on standard wall constructions. One mounting system (Figure 22.6) places the face of the carpet approximately 2 inches from the structural wall, and accommodates approximately 1.75 inches of filler. The effectiveness of the coverings in reducing noise is numerically reported in terms of a noise reduction coefficient (NRC); higher values indicate greater sound absorption.

When a loop pile carpet with a pile weight of 23 ounces per square yard and no backcoating was tested in this mounting, a NRC of 0.90 was recorded; when a cut-

Figure 22.5 Simulated suede wall covering. (Courtesy Sommer® Coverings, division of Allibert, Inc.)

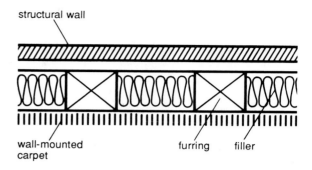

Figure 22.6 A wall sound absorption test. (Courtesy of The Carpet and Rug Institute.)

pile carpet having a pile weight of 44 ounces per square yard and having a backcoating was tested, a NRC of 0.70 was recorded. These results show that the structural features of textile coverings directly influence their acoustical properties. Thus, residential and commercial consumers should request actual test results from product manufacturers when selecting wall and panel coverings primarily for noise control.

Energy Conservation. Increasingly, residential and commercial consumers control heat transfer and reduce air infiltration by installing textile structures as interior wall finishes. As is true for acoustical evaluations, assessments of the insulative value of textile coverings must be conducted using a mounting that simulates the construction features of the structural walls and the techniques used to install the covering.

One technique that increases the insulative value of textile wall covering installations is the application of a padding behind the fabric. The cost of the materials and labor incurred in installing these "upholstered walls" may be balanced against potential savings in energy charges.

Interior designers, architects, and specifiers must consult with representatives of the agency that has jurisdiction over a facility to ascertain whether the materials se-

lected for the interior must meet noise or insulation criteria. They must also determine whether the materials are covered by flammability mandates.

Flammability Requirements

City, state, and federal agencies require that materials used inside certain occupancies conform to the requirements of the NFPA 101®Life Safety Code®. As detailed in Table 30.6 (page 324), material installed as an interior finish (in contrast to an interior floor finish) on building surfaces must exhibit a Class A, B, or C rating, depending upon the type of occupancy and area of installation. The ratings are determined by testing the coverings in accordance with the procedures outlined in ASTM E-84, which is equivalent to NFPA 255. This test method is described and illustrated in Chapter 30.

INSTALLATION TECHNIQUES

Textile coverings are generally installed over structural wall surfaces with one of four techniques: shirring, stapling, using an adhesive, or using premounted supports.

Shirring

Shirring is a simple and inexpensive technique for covering walls with nonbacked textile fabrics. After yardage has been allowed for fullness and pattern matching, if necessary, the fabric widths are seamed and the top and bottom edges are finished with a casing. The casing may be plain or constructed with a heading (Figure 17.3, page 175). Conventional curtain rods are then inserted through the casings and positioned on the walls to support the shirred fabric.

Stapling

When the wall surface is smooth, the edges of textile fabric coverings may be stapled directly to the structural material. Seaming can be avoided by covering the joins with decorative tape or braid or with rigid molding (Figure 22.7). When the wall is rough and damaged, lath strips must first be nailed to the top, bottom, and sides of the wall and next to the framework of the doors and windows. After the fabric is stapled to the laths, decorative tape or braid may be glued over the edges to conceal the staples. Because the lath strips support the fabric a small distance from the wall surface, surface irregularities are concealed.

Figure 22.7 Joins of moiré wall covering concealed by rigid molding. (Courtesy of Celanese Corporation.)

Using an Adhesive

Textile structures having a paper or foam backing may be handled in essentially the same manner as wallpaper is handled in the hanging procedure. With paper-backed textile structures, the adhesive is generally applied to the paper; with foam-backed structures, the adhesive is generally applied to the wall.

Using Premounted Supports

As the use of textile structures on walls has increased, specialized mechanisms have been developed to add tension and support to the coverings. In one such system, the fabric is held in wall-mounted channels by locking clips. Another features loop and hook fasteners. The covering is backed with a soft fabric with tiny loops over its surface; the mounting strips have tiny hooks on their surfaces. Contact between the loops and hooks secures the fabric to the wall, and the raw edges are tucked into channels in the strips. Sewn seams are avoided by tucking the fabric edges into parallel panels built into double strips.

SUMMARY

Webs of textile yarns and textile fabrics may be used as interior wall finishes for decorative purposes, noise reduction, and energy conservation. Professionals must confirm the acoustical and insulation values of the textiles prior to installation. Some coverings are composed of natural fibers with their inherent color characteristics; some are composed of man-made fibers; and some contain metal filaments and metallic yarns Most textile coverings for use on walls and panels are woven, knitted, needlepunched, or laminated. Paper or foam backings are applied to prevent strike-through of an application adhesive.

Some wall covering installations, such as shirring and stapling, may be successfully executed by a nonprofessional. Other installations, however, should generally be left to an experienced, skilled person.

four

SOFT FLOOR COVERINGS AND CUSHIONS

Unit Four focuses on soft floor coverings and cushions. Chapter 23 offers a review of several variables affecting the selection of carpet, rugs, and cushions for residential and commercial interiors. In Chapter 24, statistical profiles detail fiber usage in today's soft floor coverings, and several fiber and yarn properties influencing floor performance are discussed. Chapter 25 explains tufting, the dominant carpet construction technique. Other machine techniques are examined in Chapter 26, and hand techniques are reviewed in Chapter 27.

Chapter 28 illustrates and explains methods used to apply color to carpet and rug fibers, yarns, and greige goods. The composition, construction, and performance properties of carpet and rug cushions are considered in Chapter 29. Chapter 30 summarizes procedures to measure functional characteristics and performance properties of carpet and carpet and cushion assemblies; it also identifies items included in carpet specification lists. Finally, the installation and maintenance of soft floor coverings is reviewed in Chapter 31.

chapter 23

Selection Criteria for Soft Floor Coverings

- Appearance Features
- Serviceability Expectations
- Design and Performance Mandates
- Cost Factors

Several of the selection criteria listed in Table 2.1 apply to the selection of soft floor coverings. The nature and importance of these qualities are determined by personal preference, professional recommendation, and anticipated in-use conditions and activities. In some cases, certain design and performance characteristics are prescribed by regulatory agencies.

Soft floor coverings cannot be selected on the basis of appearance features alone. The near environment should be attractive, but it must be safe and functional. Because the functional and safety characteristics of floor coverings are influenced by the features of the combined carpet and cushion assembly, attention must be given to the structure and properties of both layers. Special attention should be given to the selection and installation of floor covering assemblies in locations frequented by people with physical or visual limitations. Interior floor finishes should not be hazardous barriers; they should help, not hinder, mobility.

As is true for any other consumer purchase, the total cost of a planned floor covering project must be affordable. The initial materials costs, the installation charges, and the long-term maintenance expenses must all be considered. In many cases, use-cost analyses, which reflect these financial variables, may show carpet and cushion assemblies to be more economical than other flooring materials.

APPEARANCE FEATURES

Residential and commercial consumers have widely varying and constantly changing tastes in the size, shape, color, and texture of soft floor coverings. The visual impact and tactile interest of these features are primary concerns, but consideration must also be given to variables such as end-use lighting and yarn size if the planned appearance is to be realized, and to soiling if the appearance is to be retained. Anticipated traffic levels and safety concerns may preclude the choice of certain appearance features.

Sizes and Shapes

Some soft floor covering products, including rollgoods and modules, are designed to cover all of the floor space within an interior. Other products are designed to define a limited area, such as an entrance foyer or the space under a furniture grouping. The particular style chosen determines the method of installation. Generally speaking, a securely fastened or anchored floor covering is referred to as carpet, and a loosely laid structure is called a rug. The term broadloom is frequently used to identify rollgoods that are more than 54 inches wide. The term does not describe the method of construction, and it carries no implication about quality.

Wall-to-wall Carpet. Wall-to-wall carpet covers the entire floor space, baseboard to baseboard (Figure 23.1). As is true for other consumer purchases, certain compromises are inevitable when one style of floor covering is selected over another.

A wall-to-wall installation has some negative features:

- The initial cost is higher as more square yardage is required.
- Costs are incurred for installation.
- It must be cleaned in place.
- Repair of large damaged areas is difficult.
- It cannot be shifted to equalize traffic patterns and soiling.
- Extra yardage may be required for matching patterns.
- It is difficult to remove for relocation.

On the other hand, a wall-to-wall installation has these positive features:

- It is securely anchored to prevent shifting.
- There are no loose edges to cause tripping.
- There is no "curb" effect for wheelchairs if low level pile is used.

- Potential for energy conservation is maximized.
- The room may appear larger.
- It can camouflage worn or uneven floors.
- No special preparation of the floor is usually required.
- It may improve the resale value of a building.

Some manufacturers offer broadloom rollgoods with rug-like designs strategically placed. Such goods provide the appearance of a loose-laid rug, but can be securely attached to the floor, an advantage in high traffic areas in commercial interiors.

Carpet Modules. Carpet modules are relatively new forms of soft floor coverings. Their use is increasing, especially in commercial installations. Carpet modules are also known as squares or tiles, and are generally 18 inches square. Some are designed to be glued directly to the floor with a permanent or a releasable adhesive; others are manufactured to be extra heavy and stiff so that when they are free-laid, gravity holds them in place. When correctly in-

Figure 23.1 Wall-to-wall installation of rollgoods. (Courtesy of The Wool Bureau, Inc.)

stalled, the surface has many of the same features as wall-to-wall carpet since the squares are laid across the entire floor space. The installation pictured in Figure 23.2 illustrates the design flexibility offered by carpet modules.

Carpet modules have some limiting characteristics:

- Initial materials costs are high.
- Edge curl can occur with low quality tiles.
- Butted joints can separate with improper installation.

They also offer some distinct advantages, especially when releasable or no adhesive is used:

- Loss of materials during installation is minimal.
- They are easily rotated to equalize traffic and soiling patterns if releasable or no adhesive is used.
- They may be replaced if damaged.
- They may be lifted for access to underfloor service trenches.

Room-size Rugs. Room-size rugs are intended to be loose-laid, coming within 12 inches of each wall. Room-fit rugs are designed or cut to come to or within one or two inches of the walls. Either of these rugs can be cut to follow the contours of a room, with their raw edges finished by serging (machine overcasting), fringing, binding with twill-woven tape, or with a seam-sealing cement. Because these floor coverings can easily be rolled up for moving, they are especially attractive to people who rent and to those who anticipate frequent relocation.

Room-size rugs are often available in such standard sizes as 9 feet by 12 feet and 12 feet by 15 feet. Rugs have some negative features:

- They may have to be cut to fit an unconventional perimeter.
- Cut edges require finishing.
- Unsecured edges may cause tripping.
- A "curb" effect may be presented to wheelchair drivers.

They also have some positive features:

- They are available in standard room sizes.
- No installation is required if standard size fits room contour.
- They are easily moved to a new location.
- They are highly decorative.

Runners. A runner is a long, narrow form of a room-fit rug installed in hallways and on stairs. Runners are normally 27 inches wide, cut to any length, and serged or fringed on the cut ends. On stairs, runners can be held in place with brass rods securely anchored at the back of the treads (Figure 31.6, page 335).

A special form of runner is the walk-off mat used in entrance areas subjected to high traffic levels. These mats are intended to capture tracked-in dirt and grit, protecting the carpet from abrasion and apparent changes in color caused by such materials. For safety, walk-off mats should be heavy and stiff enough to prevent edge curl, which could cause tripping.

Area Rugs. The rising popularity of area rugs can partly be explained by the extensive range of sizes and shapes available on today's market. Whatever the spatial need, an area rug can be chosen to fill it. These floor coverings are available in such sizes as 27 inches by 54 inches, 4 feet by 6 feet, and 6 feet by 9 feet. There are square, round, oval, rectangular, octagonal, and free-form shapes; the rug may or may not have fringe. Coupled with the wide variety of constructions, fiber contents, textures, and colorations, these features can make for much design appeal. Some consumers and designers lay area rugs directly on smooth floors, especially on fine hardwood; others lay them over wall-to-wall carpet to define a furniture grouping or accentuate a living area; and still others hang them as decorative wall accents.

The selection of an area rug involves considering their drawbacks:

- They are hazardous to persons having limited vision or mobility.
- They may shift or slide on smooth floors.
- They tend to "walk" off thick cushions and move on carpet.

However, area rugs are attractive:

- They come in an extensive variety of sizes, shapes, designs, and textures.
- No installation is required.
- They are easily moved.

Scatter Rugs. Scatter rugs are small rugs, often 2 feet by 3 feet or smaller. They are used in the home where traffic and soiling are concentrated, such as inside the entrance area and in front of sinks. Novelty scatter rugs serve as decorative accents and are available in imaginative shapes ranging from a dog's paw print to an orange slice. These floor coverings are also relatively inexpensive. However, they are easily tripped over and they slide on smooth surfaces. Their use should be limited, especially when persons with visual or physical limitations use an interior.

Surface Texture

Besides their length and width, most textile floor coverings have a noticeable third dimension, that of depth,

Figure 23.2 Carpet module installation. (Courtesy of Milliken and Company.)

produced by a pile or wear layer. Variations in the visual and tactile characteristics of pile layers depend on differences in pile sweep, pile height, pile thickness, pile construction density, and yarn twist, as well as whether the pile tufts have been cut or not.

Pile Sweep. Pile sweep is schematicized in Figure 9.3 (page 83). The greater the slant of the pile yarns, the more prominent the nap or lay of the pile layer. This feature determines the quantity of light a floor covering reflects, which increases as the angle decreases. Therefore, when pile floor coverings are installed, care must be taken that the nap goes in the same direction (see Chapter 31).

Pile Height. Height is the length of the pile tufts above the backing; the length of that part of the pile yarn incorporated in the backing is excluded. Pile height is normally reported in decimal form, and is routinely supplied to contract designers, architects, and others specifying floor covering variables. Pile heights typically range from 0.187 to 1.250 inches.

Pile Thickness. Pile thickness is the average thickness of the pile material above the backing. Because thickness measurements are made on finished floor coverings, they reflect any pile sweep introduced during conversion operations.

Pile Construction Density. Pile construction density is determined by the closeness of the pile tufts in the wear layer. A dense construction has closely spaced tufts; a sparse construction has widely spaced tufts (Figure 23.3). Density has a major influence on the surface appearance, texture retention, and wear-life of pile structures.

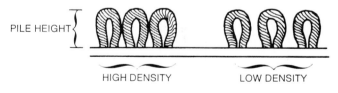

a) uncut tufts

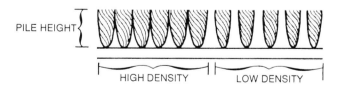

b) cut tufts

Figure 23.3 High and low pile construction densities. (Courtesy of Allied Fibers.)

Consumers and professionals can make an eyeball evaluation of construction density by flexing a carpet or rug and judging how much backing is exposed, that is, how much the structure "grins" (Figure 23.4); lower densities produce broader smiles. Pile construction density and potential exposure of the backing are especially critical factors to examine when selecting carpet for installation on stairs.

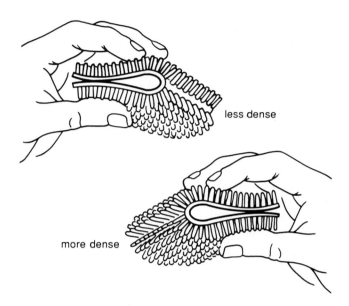

less dense

more dense

Figure 23.4 "Eyeball" evaluation of pile construction density.

Cut and Uncut Pile. The yarn loops in some soft floor coverings are cut, producing independent tufts. In other coverings, the loops are left uncut (see Figure 23.3).

Yarn Twist. The level of twist used in pile yarns has a major influence on the appearance of soft floor coverings. Higher levels create well-defined yarn ends, and lower levels create flared tips (Figure 23.5). Differences in twist level are largely responsible for the appearance differences observed among one level cut pile surface textures (Figures 23.6a through 23.6f).

NEAT TIPS

FLARED TIPS

TIGHT TWIST   LOOSE TWIST

Figure 23.5 Effect of twist level on the appearance of pile yarns. (Courtesy of Allied Fibers.)

A brief outline will help sort out the wide variety of textures available in pile floor coverings today. Differences among these surfaces are a result of variations in the textural characteristics described above.

    I. One Level Cut Pile Styles
        A. Velour
        B. Plush
        C. Saxony
        D. Friezé
        E. Shag
        F. Splush
        G. Tip shear
    II. One Level Loop Pile Styles
    III. Multilevel Loop Pile Styles
    IV. Multilevel Cut and Loop Pile Styles
        A. Sculptured
        B. High-low
        C. Random Shear

One Level Cut Pile Styles. Several cut pile styles have a uniform level across their surfaces. These styles differ among themselves in pile height, pile density, and yarn construction, however.

Velour surfaces are fine, short, dense constructions that are relatively new textures for soft floor coverings (Figure 23.6a). Their production has been made possible by the development of machinery and fabrication processes that can yield high pile construction densities, for example, fusion bonding. High density allows pile height to be decreased without diminishing the important variable of pile yarn weight (see Chapter 25). Velour surfaces normally have a pile height of 0.25 inch.

The pile yarns in plush, also called velvet and velvet plush, surfaces (Figure 23.6b) range in height from 0.625 to 0.750 inch. The pile yarns have relatively low levels of twist: the cut yarn ends blend together for a luxurious, velvet-like look and feel. In use, these textures exhibit shading effects when the orientation of the pile yarns is physically changed. When occasional foot traffic or vacuum cleaning alters the direction of the pile yarns, the effect is normally temporary; the yarns gradually recover their original positions. In areas where directional traffic patterns cross or where pivoting action is common, the pile layer will be repeatedly crushed in opposing directions, and the effect may be permanent. In such areas, a darker area may appear as an irregularly shaped circle, somewhat like a large stain: the pile yarns are oriented in

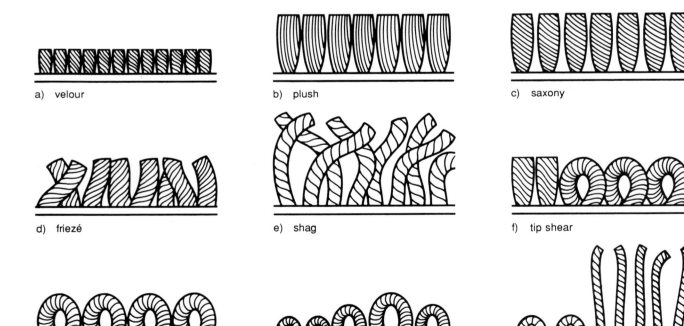

a) velour   b) plush   c) saxony

d) friezé   e) shag   f) tip shear

g) one level, loop   h) multilevel, loop   i) multilevel,
                                               cut and loop

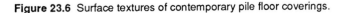

Figure 23.6 Surface textures of contemporary pile floor coverings.

one direction inside and outside of the circle, and in the reverse direction along the outline. This appearance problem is variously described as pile reversal, watermarking, shading, and pooling.

Saxony textures (Figure 23.6c) have approximately the same pile height and density as that seen in plush. However, saxony yarns have a higher twist level that is heat-stabilized to reduce the amount of flaring at the tips of the cut yarns. Rather than blending together in a continuous surface, each yarn end is well defined, and the set twist minimizes splaying and improves thickness retention. Apparently, the improved yarn stability and resilience exhibited by saxony textures have increased their popularity. These surfaces now account for approximately 60 percent of the residential market.[1]

Friezé textures, also known as twist textures, are constructed of yarns having maximum twist for high stability and wear-life. Each yarn is clearly visible, since the high twist defines each yarn and encourages it to seek its own direction of orientation in the lower density pile (Figure 23.6d).

The height of pile yarns in shag surfaces (Figure 23.6e) goes up to approximately 1.250 inches. The pile density is lower than that in plush and saxony textures; the longer pile yarns are responsible for covering the backing.

Splush textures have a pile height and a pile construction density between those typically used for plush and shag surfaces. The production of splush has diminished in recent years, largely as a result of an increased preference for saxony textures.

Tip shear surfaces are produced by selectively shearing the oppermost portion of some yarn loops (Figure 23.6f). Subtle differences in luster appear because more light is reflected from the smooth loops than from the sheared fibers. Frequently, low pile, densely constructed floor coverings are sheared to camouflage future soil accumulation.

One Level Loop Pile Styles. In the past, carpet with a short, level loop pile (Figure 23.6g) was normally seen only in such commercial settings as restaurants, airport terminals, and hospitals. Many professionals and consumers thought this surface had an "institutional" appearance. Today, improved color styling and yarn texturing have helped to make the uniform surface more appealing (see Figure 24.9, page 266), and residential use of this durable, wear-resistant surface has increased.

Multilevel Loop Pile Styles. Multilevel loop pile styles show noticeable differences in the height of their pile yarns (Figure 23.6h). The variations may be random or planned to create a pattern. These surfaces are quite durable if density is reasonably high.

Multilevel, Cut and Loop Pile Styles. Various surface constructions are produced by combining cut loops, uncut loops, and multiple pile heights (Figure 23.6i). These include sculptured, high-low, and random shear textures.

Sculptured surfaces have a definite three-dimensional appearance. In most cases, the higher loops are all cut and the lower loops all uncut for an embossed effect. Normally, the cut pile areas are dominant, and the visual impact is strong and formal. The exquisite texture of some custom floor coverings is produced by hand sculpturing dense, cut pile surfaces.

High-low is the name given to some multilevel cut and loop styles with an informal appearance. Sometimes, the higher tufts have the appearance of shag textures.

Random shear textures differ from tip shear textures because they contain multiple levels of pile yarns instead of a single level. They differ from sculptured surfaces in that the uppermost portions of some of the higher yarn tufts are sheared, not all of them as in sculptured coverings.

Surface Coloration

Soft floor coverings may or may not dominate the aesthetics of an interior. A carpet or rug may have a subdued, solid-colored surface and serve as a backdrop for other, more distinctive furnishings; or it may have detailed designs or bold graphic colorations whose strong visual impact attracts attention. Residential consumers are generally free to choose color stylings that please them; contract designers and architects may be limited by the preferences of their clients, but they are able to use their professional training to recommend colorations. Whoever chooses the color styling, the possible effects of end-use conditions and activities on the color must be anticipated.

Color Styling. The color styling of soft floor coverings ranges from solid-colored surfaces in dark, deep hues to finely detailed designs in light, intense hues. Preferences for various color characteristics and styles in carpet and rugs fluctuate in the same cycles that hold for other fashion merchandise, such as apparel and cars. Avocado green surfaces, for example, were treasured in the 1950s; today, they enjoy about the same favor as doubleknit leisure suits.

Solid-colored surfaces can be produced in any combination of color characteristics preferred by the professional or consumer. Distinctive multicolored stylings are produced with heather, Berber, space-dyed, and moresque yarns. Authentic Berber yarns, a type of speck yarn hand spun by peoples of northern Africa, contain the deep black, rich brown, and grays of the wool retrieved from the sheep. Simulated Berber yarns (Figure 23.7) are produced by blending dyed, staple-length acrylic fibers.

A carpet of space-dyed pile yarns is shown in Figure 23.8; another is pictured in Figure 28.2b (page 303). The varied coloration adds visual interest; its potential

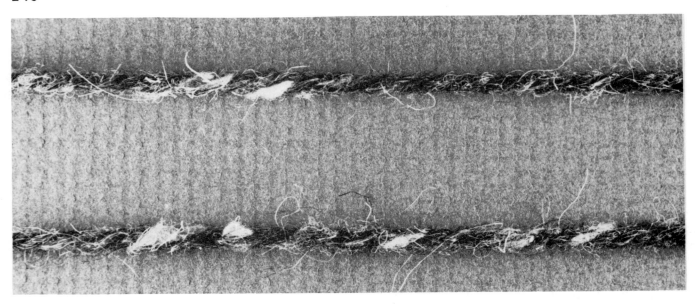

Figure 23.7 Simulated Berber yarn composed of staple-length, fiber-dyed acrylic fibers.

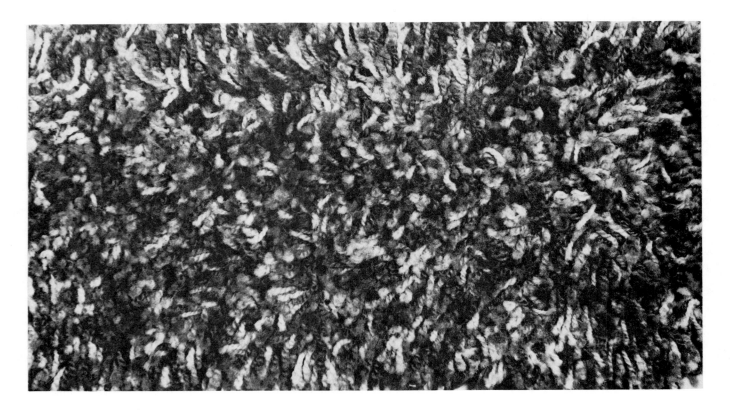

Figure 23.8 Shag carpet with space-dyed color styling.

effectiveness for masking the appearance of soil and stains is apparent. Other multicolored effects can be produced with operations such as TAK and gum printing, described in Chapter 28.

Patterned floor coverings may have designs created with colored fibers and yarns during construction or printed on the greige rollgoods. The almost infinite variety of patterns and colors available in stock lines can be expanded by custom design and color work. Some commercial carpet producers, in fact, maintain an inventory of floor coverings in a range of neutral colors, so that contract designers and architects can order the addition of distinctive motifs in specific colors.

Factors Affecting Apparent Color. The various conditions and activities that may affect the surface color should affect the choice of a soft floor covering. (Factors affecting apparent color were discussed in Chapter 8; those affecting actual color are identified in Chapter 30.) Special attention should be given to the potential effects of soiling on the apparent surface color. For locations where the covering will undergo much spillage and tracked-in dirt, a darker, multicolored surface may be called for, to mask the appearance of soil. In some locations, it may even be advisable to coordinate the carpet color with the color of the soil in the area.

When heavy traffic is anticipated, consumers and professionals should select floor coverings whose components and construction features will encourage thickness retention and provide abrasion resistance. This can help to minimize the development of a patchy surface luster in use.

SERVICEABILITY EXPECTATIONS

Service-related considerations influence the selection of soft floor coverings. Some of these concern the functional benefits carpet and rugs can contribute, and others, their use-life characteristics.

Functional Properties

Many residential and commercial consumers seek to camouflage structural defects, reduce noise, or conserve energy with soft floor coverings. They may also be looking for improved safety and mobility for people with visual or physical limitations.

Camouflage Worn and Uneven Floors. Increases in building material costs and mortgage interest rates have encouraged many people to renovate and refurbish older structures. Such structures may be sound but have worn or uneven floors. Installing a carpet and cushion assembly

can help to fill uneven spaces and hide damaged floor areas. This property of soft floor coverings is both functional and aesthetic.

Add Comfort and Reduce Fatigue. The comfort provided by soft floor coverings may also be deemed an aesthetic and functional quality. The tactile pleasure of stepping onto a deep pile, cushioned surface is clear in contrast to the lack of give characteristic of such smooth, hard, nonresilient surfaces as slate and quarry tiles.

The compressibility of textile floor coverings enables them to absorb and cushion the impact forces of walking. For people who spend the major portion of the working day on their feet—homemakers, nurses, production managers and technicians, waiters and waitresses, bank tellers, and sales personnel—the cushioning effect of carpet can be critically important. It may lessen orthopedic problems, reduce fatigue, and increase productivity.

Increase Safety. The compressibility of soft floor coverings contributes comfort; it also is responsible for increasing the margin of safety. When falls are cushioned, the severity of injury can be reduced. This criterion is especially important to the selection of carpet and rugs for use in interiors where older persons work or reside.

Textile floor coverings may reduce the frequency of falling. They provide a slip-resistant surface for better footing, and they do not have the "slippery when wet" problem characteristic of some hard, polished floorings.

Improve Interiors for People with Handicaps. Textile floor coverings can be useful for people with mobility and sight impairments while enriching the interior space with their warmth and beauty of color and texture. Careful attention must be given to their selection and installation, however, to ensure that they do not become barriers. The Veterans' Administration has made recommendations for the design of residences for use by veterans with physical handicaps: "Low pile, high density carpet may be installed in any appropriate location. In addition to its aesthetic qualities, carpet greatly reduces sound transmission and serves to cushion accidental falls." [2]

Soft floor coverings can provide a slip-resistant surface for persons using canes and crutches. Slip resistance is especially critical for swing-through movement, when body weight is transferred to the crutches. All carpet and rug edges must be securely attached to the floor to prevent tripping and to minimize the movement of the carpet surface under force.

Wheelchair users need soft floor coverings with a low pile so that no curb effect is created. Pile should be dense and minimally compressible, allowing for easy movement of the chair over the surface. Shaggy, loose constructions tend to entrap the wheels and restrict forward movement.

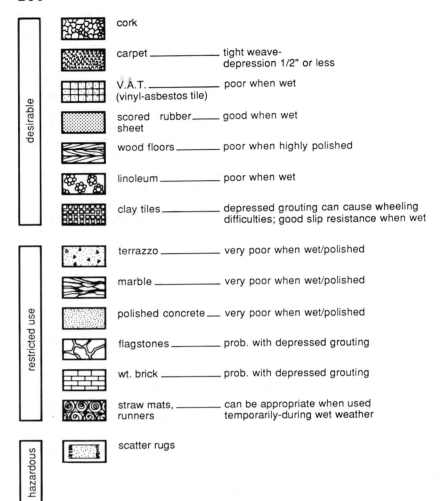

desirable

cork

carpet ——————— tight weave-
depression 1/2" or less

V.A.T. ——————— poor when wet
(vinyl-asbestos tile)

scored rubber——— good when wet
sheet

wood floors ———— poor when highly polished

linoleum ——————— poor when wet

clay tiles ———— depressed grouting can cause wheeling
difficulties; good slip resistance when wet

restricted use

terrazzo ———————— very poor when wet/polished

marble ——————— very poor when wet/polished

polished concrete —— very poor when wet/polished

flagstones ———— prob. with depressed grouting

wt. brick ————— prob. with depressed grouting

straw mats, ———— can be appropriate when used
runners   temporarily-during wet weather

hazardous

scatter rugs

Figure 23.9 Paving suggestions for interior floor space to be accessible to persons of limited mobility. (*Source: Design Criteria: New Public Building Accessibility, PBS (PCD): DG5,* General Services Administration, Washington, D.C., December 1977, 103.)

Cushions may be separate and thin, permanently attached to the carpet back, or not used. Shearing, the movement of the carpet and cushion in opposite directions, can occur when the chair is driven over the surface. Shearing can be avoided, and warping or rippling can be minimized, by gluing the carpet directly to the floor.

Figure 23.9 compares several interior floor coverings' usefulness to people of limited vision or mobility. Depressed grouting in some coverings can hinder mobility. Surfaces that become slippery when wet should only be used selectively.

For people who are blind or have limited sight, certain carpet and rug features can provide cues for increased orientation and mobility. Orientation skills and cues help persons with diminished sight to identify their location within an environment; mobility skills and cues enable them to travel through the space. Total or partial loss of vision does not result in a more acute sense of smell or touch, or more sensitive hearing; but persons with impaired vision become more aware of their other senses and more perceptive with them. Patterns of variance in the texture underfoot may aid in orientation, helping the person to feel where he or she is within the interior. The surfaces must have marked textural differences if they are to be detected; an example would be carpet alternated with a smooth flooring such as tile or linoleum. Different surfaces can also provide auditory cues. The edges of carpet and rugs can serve as a "shoreline," guiding a cane traveler.[3]

Carpet and rug surfaces lack any capacity for the glare and bright reflections characteristic of highly polished smooth surfaces, which are troublesome to persons with a visual limitation. For accent and demarcation, such as at the nosing of stairs, red-yellow, as opposed to blue-green, colors are more effective.[4] Some persons with limited vision may see differences in value or intensity better than they see differences in hue.[5]

Before modifying any environment for use by people of limited sight or mobility, their advice and counsel should be sought. Help can also be obtained from professional organizations, several of which are listed in Appendix C.

Reduce Noise. Noise abatement is often one of the more important functions of floor coverings and cushions. Along with the tests used to measure the acoustical values of carpet, alone and in combination with cushions, various factors influencing this property are identified in Chapter 30.

Conserve Energy. Extensive research has shown that certain structural features of carpet and cushions increase thermal resistance. Research has also shown that certain appearance features can increase light reflectance, decreasing the quantity of light needed from artificial illuminants. These features are discussed in Chapter 30.

Use-life Characteristics

When selecting one of today's textile floor coverings, consumers and professionals should focus their attention on the variables that govern appearance or newness retention, retention of the original color and texture. Fortunately, minimal attention can be given to questions of wear caused by abrasion: the loss of significant amounts of fiber as a result of abrasive wear has largely been overcome by the use of nylon and improved processing.

If rapid changes in appearance are to be avoided or minimized, the fiber properties, yarn characteristics, and construction features of soft floor coverings must be chosen in light of anticipated end-use conditions. Traffic conditions, for example, vary for different interior locations. High levels of traffic are normally expected in such areas as corridors and lobbies, and low levels in such spaces as executive offices and rooms within apartments (Table 23.1).

In most cases, a soft covering intended for use in areas of little traffic would not be serviceable where traffic is heavy. Early replacement, accompanied by annoying dislocation, interruption of normal activities, and a second outlay of money and time, would be necessary. Conversely, selecting a carpet engineered for use in a commercial corridor for installation in a residential interior may entail a higher initial investment than necessary. It may also require postponement of the inevitable redecorating desired when tastes and styling preferences change. Quality control and performance evaluations, a routine part of the production efforts of industry firms, provide assistance in making suitability decisions. Testing enables producers to label their products with specific performance data and recommendations pertaining to installations, for instance, whether the products are suitable for low traffic, residential interiors or for high traffic, commercial interiors (see Chapter 30).

Multicolored surfaces may camouflage accumulated soil. But if large amounts of soil are anticipated, consideration should also be given to the selection of fibers engineered to hide, repel, or shed soil and finishes designed to repel soil and minimize staining. These finishes and engineered fiber qualities are discussed with other service-related variables in later chapters in this unit.

DESIGN AND PERFORMANCE MANDATES

Various local, state, and federal regulatory agencies have established mandates pertaining to the design and performance of textile floor coverings selected for use in certain commercial interiors (see Chapter 2). Mandates pertain to such structural characteristics as pile height and pile construction density and such functional properties as noise reduction, as well as to flammability.

Table 23.1 TRAFFIC RATINGS FOR SELECTED INTERIOR SPACES
L-M denotes light-medium traffic; H denotes heavy traffic.

Area (by major category)	Traffic rating	Area (by major category)	Traffic rating
Educational		**Commercial**	
Schools and colleges		Banks	
administration	L-M	executive	L-M
classroom	H	lobby	H
dormitory	H	teller windows	H
corridor	H*	corridors	H*
cafeteria	H	Retail establishments	
libraries	L-M	aisle	H*
Museums and art galleries		check-out	H
display room	H	sales counter	H
executive	L-M	smaller boutiques, etc.	H
lobby	H	window & display area	L-M
		Office buildings	
		executive	L-M
Medical		clerical	H
Health care		corridor	H*
executive	L-M	cafeteria	H
patients room	H	Supermarkets	H
lounge	H	Food services	H
nurses station	H		
corridor	H*	**Recreational**	
lobby	H	Recreational areas	
		clubhouse	H
Multi-residential		locker room	H
Apartments, hotels and motels		swimming pool	H
lobby/public areas	H*	recreational vehicles	H
corridors	H	boats	H
rooms	L-M	Theaters and Stadiums (indoors)	H
Religious		Convention Centers	
Churches/temples		auditorium	H
worship	L-M	corridor	H*
meeting room	H	lobby	H
lobby	H		

*If objects are to be rolled over an area of carpet, the carpet should be of maximum density to provide minimum resistance to rollers. For safety, select only level loop or low, level dense cut pile. (Courtesy of Fibers Division, Monsanto Chemical Co.)

Specific regulations must be followed when selecting and installing carpet and rugs in interiors mandated by congressional action to be accessible and usable by persons with handicaps. The Architectural Barriers Act of 1968 requires certain federally owned, leased, or funded buildings and facilities to be accessible to people of limited mobility. Coming under the scope of the act are such structures as United States post offices, federally assisted housing units, several military facilities, and federal government buildings. Enforcement of the standards set forth in the act is under the jurisdiction of the Architectural and Transportation Barriers Compliance Board (ATBCB). This board was created under section 502 of the Rehabilitation Act of 1973; subsequent amendments expanded its work to include responsibility for establishing minimum guidelines and requirements for accessible designs. The Department of Defense, the Department of Housing and Urban Development, the United States Postal Service, and the General Services Administration must establish guidelines consistent with those prescribed by the ATBCB.

A revised edition of the ATBCB Minimum Guidelines for Accessible Design, which became effective on September 3, 1982, includes specific provisions governing the selection and installation of carpet and carpet tiles. Several of these provisions are based on the specifications developed by the American National Standards Institute. Among other things, ATBCB requires that carpet tile used on an accessible ground or floor surface have a maximum combined thickness of pile, cushion, and backing height of 0.5 inch. If carpet is used, then it should also meet this requirement, but in no case shall the pile height exceed 0.5 inch.* (Recall that pile sweep can reduce the thickness of a pile layer without affecting pile height.)

COST FACTORS

Three basic elements of cost must be considered when selecting and specifying soft floor covering assemblies: the initial purchase price, installation charges, and maintenance expenses. For the purpose of comparing various types of carpet, cushions, and hard-surfaced floorings, the total use-cost or life-cycle cost of each should be amortized according to its life expectancy. In this way, the important impact of maintenance expenses and the length of the product's use-life are taken into account.

Initial Purchase Price

The purchase price of carpet and cushion materials is normally given in dollars per square yard. Residential and commercial consumers must confirm whether the quoted price is for the carpet only, the cushion only, or for the assembly. Of course, the dollar figure must be multiplied by the number of square yards required, including any extra amount that may be needed for matching pattern repeats and for fitting and trimming (see Chapter 31).

Installation Charges

A number of cost variables are involved in installation. The cost of site preparation should be detailed: there may be per square yard charges assessed for removing the existing floor covering, for filling cracks and smoothing rough areas, and for reducing the amount of moisture and alkaline concentration, if necessary. Charges for installing the new carpet may be separate from those for installing the new cushion.

Maintenance Expenses

The cost of maintaining a flooring material at an attractive level of appearance is a critical factor in commercial installations. The major cleaning expense is generally the cost of labor; thus, the more time required for maintaining a flooring material, the greater will be maintenance costs. Other maintenance expenses include the purchase and repair of equipment and the continual replacement costs of expendable cleaning supplies.

The results of an investigative project sponsored by The Carpet and Rug Institute showed that the annual amortized cost (initial cost per square foot of the material divided by years of life expectancy) of purchasing and installing reinforced vinyl tile is significantly less than that of carpet, sheet vinyl, and terrazzo. When maintenance expenses were considered, however, the annual amortized life cycle or use-cost of carpet was significantly less than that of other flooring materials.*

Life-cycle Costing

Several producers of commercial carpet have established life-cycle costing programs. A life-cycle cost analysis compiles materials, installation, and maintenance costs. Such figures are prepared for each flooring material being considered by the designer or architect, and then form the basis for making use-cost comparisons.

Lending institutions may permit the cost of the soft floor covering assembly in certain new constructions to become part of the mortgage obligation. In such cases, the tax savings on the portion of interest attributable to the carpet and cushion may be considered in the life-cycle analysis. Depreciation and capital investment credits may be additional factors to analyze in the costing of a project.

---

*The full text of the ATBCB Minimum Guidelines for Accessible Design may be reviewed in the Federal Register, Vol. 47, Wednesday, August 4, 1982, 33873–33875.

* A description of this investigative project is available from The Carpet and Rug Institute.

Similar tax-related assessments can be made when replacement installations involve interest charges.

SUMMARY

Several variables affect the selection of soft floor coverings. Decisions must be made about appearance features such as size, shape, surface coloration, and surface texture. Consideration must be given to various factors influencing apparent color of the surface. Prospective purchasers may seek floor covering assemblies providing such functional benefits as noise control, insulation, and usefulness to persons with limited mobility or impaired sight. Professionals must confirm that their selections conform with any applicable design and performance mandates. Ultimately, residential and commercial consumers must be sure that initial costs and long-term maintenance expenses do not outstrip their budgets.

Today, the satisfactory in-use performance of textile floor coverings depends on the level of appearance or newness retention exhibited by the surface; wear or abrasion resistance has been successfully engineered by fiber and floor coverings producers. Consumers and professionals should therefore investigate composition and construction qualities that will maintain an acceptable appearance and texture, and they should select those best suited to end-use conditions.

NOTES

1. Alan W. Morse, quoted in "Complex Colorations Expand Carpet Design Potential," *Modern Textile Business,* April 1983, 10.

2. Department of Veterans' Benefits, Veterans' Administration, *Handbook for Design: Specially Adapted Housing, VA Pamphlet 26-13,* Washington, D.C., April 1978, 28.

3. John Templer, and Craig Zimring, "Accessibility for Persons with Visual Impairments," Access Information Bulletin, National Center for a Barrier Free Environment, Washington, D.C., 1981.

4. Ibid.

5. John Duncan, et al., compilers, "Environmental Modifications for the Visually Impaired: A Handbook," *Journal of Visual Impairment and Blindness,* Vol. 71, No. 10, December 1977, 442–455 (reprint).

chapter *24*

Fibers and Yarns Used in Textile Floor Coverings

- Fibers Used in Carpet and Rugs
- Fiber Properties Affecting Floor Performance
- Yarn Features Affecting Serviceability

The performance of a textile floor covering will not be totally determined by a single feature, but certain performance properties are strongly influenced by one component. A fiber characteristic or a yarn feature has the primary influence on some service-related properties. The level of static voltage generated by carpet and rugs, for example, is largely determined by the inherent or engineered electrical properties of the fibers used. The development of fuzz on the surface of pile floor coverings depends on the ability of the yarns to maintain their original level of twist. This chapter discusses these and other fiber and yarn properties with a strong effect on floor covering serviceability.

Current statistical profiles show that noncellulosic fibers have captured the major portion of the soft floor coverings market. The growing consumption of these fibers began in the early 1950s when producers began shifting from weaving with wool to tufting with nylon. The more economical production operation and the less expensive fiber made textile floor coverings more affordable, enabling increased numbers of homeowners, builders, and commercial firms to choose them in lieu of linoleum, tile, and oak flooring. The growing market encouraged fiber and yarn producers to engineer fibers and yarns specifically for use in carpet and rugs.

FIBERS USED IN CARPET AND RUGS

Carpet and rug producers used nearly 2.6 billion pounds of textile fibers in 1985.[1] Of this large amount of fiber, approximately 83 percent was incorporated into face or pile yarns, and the balance was used in the backings. The fiber composition of face yarns and backing structures is markedly different.

Fiber Usage in Face Yarns

The relative importance of cotton, wool, and man-made fibers in face yarns is shown in Table 24.1. The changing patterns of fiber consumption in recent years are apparent from these data.

The rate of growth exhibited by the noncellulosic fibers has been phenomenal. In 1966, noncellulosic fibers controlled roughly 65 percent of the domestic carpet and rug face yarn market, leaving approximately 16 percent to the man-made cellulosic fibers, 15 percent to wool, and 4 percent to cotton. Today, noncellulosic fibers account for 99 percent of the market; wool, cotton, and rayon share the remaining 1 percent.

Disappearance of Wool. Long considered to be the finest and most luxurious of the face fibers, wool dominated the floor coverings market for centuries. Recently, however, the consumption of wool has so steadily declined that it has all but disappeared from the domestic market. In 1960, 210 million pounds of carpet wool were

Table 24.1 FIBER USAGE IN FACE YARNS
(million pounds)

Year	Total fiber	Man-made fibers[a]						Cotton	Wool
		Total	Cellulosic		Noncellulosic				
			Yarn	Staple	Yarn	Staple			
1966	766.9	622.0	1.5	118.5	211.3	290.7	28.9	116.0
1970	1,122.1	1,026.0	0.5	76.7	355.5	593.3	16.0	80.1
1985	2,149.5	2,125.9	b	1.3	1,057.5	1,067.1	11.7	11.9

[a] Man-made end use is divided between cellulosic (rayon plus acetate fibers) and noncellulosic (nylon, polyester, acrylic, olefin, saran, spandex, and textile glass fiber). Yarn includes monofilaments, and olefin "yarn" also includes film fiber and spunbonded polypropylene. Staple includes tow and fiberfill.

[b] Little or none of this fiber is used.

Sources: Textile Economics Bureau, Inc., *Textile Organon,* Vol. 43, No. 11, November 1972, 166, and Vol. 57, No. 9, September 1986, 211.

consumed in the United States.[2] Twenty-four years later, as shown in Table 24.2, only 50.7 million pounds were consumed, of which 81 percent was in imported wool floor coverings. This decline has been accompanied by an increase in the price of foreign carpet wool: all wool fiber used in carpet and rugs is imported because domestic wool is too fine for these products.

The decrease in the use of wool has not come about because of any serious deficiencies in the properties or processing of the fiber. The initial challenge was on the basis of cost; the continuing challenge is from the lower cost and improving quality of man-made fibers. If cost is no consideration, many people believe that the beauty, inherent soil and flame resistance, and excellent resiliency of wool support its choice.

Dominance of Nylon. Nylon dominates the assortment of fibers used in face yarns. Together, nylon filament and staple fibers captured nearly 74 percent of the 1985 market.[3]

Fiber Usage in Backing Structures

Most of the fiber produced for carpet and rug backing structures is directed to fabrics for backing tufted goods. A smaller amount of fiber is used for the yarns in the backing layers of other constructions.

In 1985, nearly 426 million pounds of man-made fibers and 6.5 million pounds of cotton were used in backing structures. Polypropylene olefin was dominant, but minor amounts of nylon and polyester were also used.[4] Some

Table 24.2 SUPPLY AND DEMAND OF WOOL IN CARPET AND
RUGS IN THE U.S.
(million pounds, scoured basis)

	Carpet wool consumption	Imports of carpets	Exports of carpets	Total	% imports of total
1971	77.7	9.2	1.2	85.7	10.5
1972	79.2	12.3	1.1	90.4	13.5
1973	43.1	13.6	1.9	54.8	25.0
1974	19.4	12.5	2.5	29.4	42.5
1975	16.6	11.4	1.9	26.1	43.5
1976	15.5	14.1	2.3	27.3	51.5
1977	12.8	14.8	2.0	25.6	58.0
1978	13.2	13.9	0.7	26.4	52.5
1979	10.9	13.9	0.3	24.5	56.5
1980	10.4	16.9	0.3	27.0	62.5
1981	10.7	18.1	0.2	29.0	62.5
1982	10.3	20.7	0.2	30.8	67.0
1983	10.7	28.5	0.1	39.1	73.0
1984	9.9	40.9	0.1	50.7	81.0

Source: Textile Economics Bureau, Inc., *Textile Organon,* Vol. 56, No. 12, December 1985, 255.

cotton yarn appears in the back of woven constructions and in fabrics used to back small, tufted rugs and mats, but none is used for tufted rollgoods. Other backing materials include foam rubber, kraftcord, vinyl, latex, and jute. Because jute is imported and susceptible to problems with moisture, domestic producers have largely replaced it with olefin.

Disclosure of Fiber Composition

The fiber composition of the pile layer of soft floor covering must be disclosed in accordance with the provisions of the Textile Fiber Products Identification Act. Backing fibers and yarns are exempt.

FIBER PROPERTIES AFFECTING FLOOR PERFORMANCE

The selection of carpet and rug fibers should be based on an evaluation of both engineered and inherent properties. Virtually every inherent property can be engineered or altered for improved performance. Unless a particular feature is mandated, residential and commercial consumers may weigh appearance and performance benefits against any added cost.

Abrasion Resistance

Abrasion of a soft floor covering can come from the movement of shoe soles, pets, furniture, and equipment across the structure. Abrasion may not only cause changes in the apparent luster of the surface; it can also diminish the wear-life.

Abrasive rubbing, especially when coupled with accumulated grit, can cause carpet and rug fibers to rupture, as though they had been sawn by a serrated knife blade. As split fibers are gradually removed, worn and tattered areas develop and expose the backing. This unsightly problem is more likely to develop first in areas where rubbing actions are concentrated, such as on the nosing of stairs and at pivotal points in traffic paths.

The ability of a fiber to resist abrasion depends largely on its toughness, which is determined by the strength and elongation of the fiber. To a large extent, producers can engineer the necessary toughness by controlling the drawing and heat setting operations used with thermoplastic fibers. Because nylon has excellent abrasion resistance, several manufacturers using the fiber are able to offer long-term warranties against significant fiber loss and wear.

Absorbency

Several carpet fibers, including acrylic, polyester, and polypropylene olefin, have comparatively low moisture regain values (see Table 4.6). If other characteristics are appropriate, these fibers may be used in carpet to be installed outdoors. Drawing and heat setting are used to increase the crystallinity and reduce the absorbency of nylon, making the fiber suitable for use in such products as synthetic turf for sports stadiums. Fibers with comparatively high regain values, such as wool, may have reduced static problems when the level of relative humidity is high, but they absorb more moisture and require longer drying times when exposed to wet cleaning agents.

Fibers used in the backing layers of structures to be installed below-grade (below ground level) should have low absorbency to resist microbe damage and odor. Olefin fibers' lack of absorbency supports their selection for such installations; the moisture-induced degradation exhibited by jute makes it inappropriate for such a use.

Microbe Resistance

Protecting soft floor coverings from the deterioration, discoloration, and odor development caused by microorganisms is an area of on-going research in the floor coverings industry. For floor coverings installed in damp areas, the growth of odor-causing mildew and bacteria should be inhibited; for carpet and rugs exposed to pets, the retention of odors in the structure should be prevented. Carpet installed in hospitals, nursing homes, and similar facilities should be resistant to a variety of bacteria and fungi, so that the structures will remain odor-free and will not harbor microbes that could spread disease and slow patient recovery.

Biological resistance has been engineered into nylon carpet fibers by incorporating antimicrobial agents into the polymer solution or by adding them early in the production sequence. Examples of trade names indicating that microbe resistance has been introduced include Microfresh®, owned by du Pont; HaloFresh®, owned by Allied Fibers; Zeftron® 500 ™ ZX, owned by BASF Corporation; BioFresh®, owned by Burlington Industries, Inc.; and Slygard™, owned by Dow Corning.

Moth Resistance

Unless wool carpet and rug fibers are treated to be moth resistant, they may be attacked by moth larvae and carpet beetles (see Chapter 9). All domestic wool floor coverings are treated to repel these insects, but residential and commercial consumers must examine the labels of imported products to confirm the use of such treatments.

Optical Properties

Carpet fiber producers recognize that consumers generally prefer brightness over dullness, and sheen over shine. To engineer the preferred optical properties, producers developed various cross-sectional shapes and controlled the amount of delusterant added to the polymer solution.

Because fibers with round cross sections and smooth surfaces typically reflect light waves in one direction (Figure 24.1a), they produce shiny brightness like that produced by glass tree ornaments. To reduce the shine while preserving luster and brightness, fiber engineers created concave shapes, some with marked indentations (Figure 24.1b) and some with slight ones (Figure 24.1c). Light waves striking the indented surfaces are scattered or reflected in several directions, producing sheen, not shine. Deep indentations and prominent lobes create the same unidirectional reflection that characterizes smooth, round shapes.

Various amounts of a delusterant, such as titanium dioxide (TiO$_2$), can be added to reduce the luster of man-made fibers. Light waves striking the minute, white particles are deflected, dulling the fiber (see Figure 24.2b). Incorporating too much delusterant, however, results in a muddy or chalky luster.

Some producers have combined a slightly concave, trilobal cross section with a small quantity of delusterant to simulate the natural luster of wool. A photomicrograph of such a fiber is shown in Figure 24.6a.

Soil-related Properties

Residential and commercial consumers are extremely critical of textile floor coverings that rapidly accumulate high levels of soil. To overcome such problems and satisfy consumers, fiber chemists and engineers have manipulated fiber cross-sectional shapes and experimented with different polymer additives. Their efforts have been directed to the development of three properties: soil hiding, soil shedding, and soil repellency.

Soil Hiding. Soil hiding is the ability of a fiber or coloration to hide or camouflage dirt. The carpet will look cleaner than it is, in contrast to soil magnification in which fibers magnify accumulated soil and the surface looks dirtier than it is. The peculiar problem of soil magnification occurs when soil particles reflect incident waves through round, nondelustered fibers (Figure 24.2a). Industry researchers first sought to overcome this problem by adding delusterant compounds. As the amount of delusterant was increased, the soil-hiding power also increased, but an undesirable muddiness would at some point become apparent in the luster. Researchers then created various non-round cross-sectional shapes that produce an acceptable level of soil hiding as well as the preferred luster and sheen.

Light waves are diffused from a multilobal design (see Figures 24.1b and 24.1c). Although deeply indented or "leggy" shapes effectively hide soil, their highly concave sides provide crevices or spaces where dirt particles can become entrapped, making their removal more difficult. The modified trilobal design illustrated in Figure 24.1c avoids this problem.

An innovative approach to soil hiding is the introduction of microscopic voids, also referred to as conduits or tunnels, lengthwise within fibers. The interior voids deflect incident waves, obscuring the appearance of soil. Du

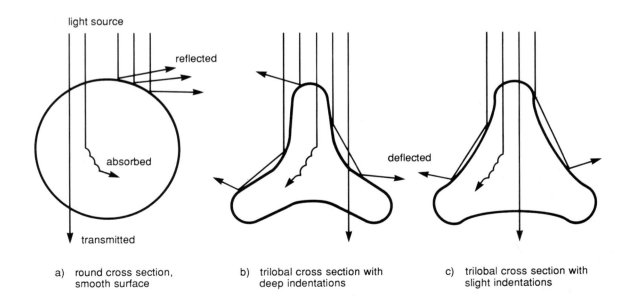

a) round cross section,   b) trilobal cross section with   c) trilobal cross section with
    smooth surface   deep indentations   slight indentations

Figure 24.1 The effects of cross-sectional shapes on optical properties.

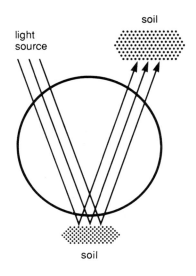

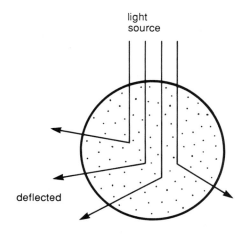

a)   soil magnification by transparent, round cross section

b)   soil hiding by delusterant particles

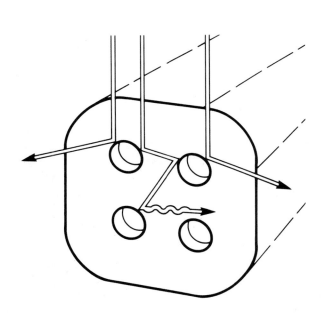

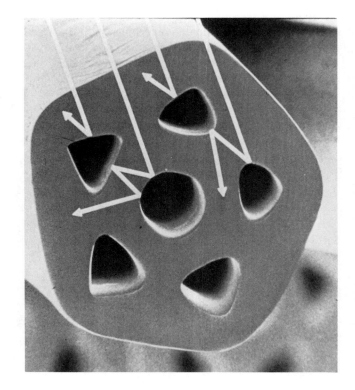

c)   soil hiding by voids and a rounded-square cross section

d)   soil hiding by voids and a pentalobal cross section

Figure 24.2 The effects of cross-sectional shape on soil magnification and soil hiding. (Illustration *c* is courtesy of E.I. du Pont de Nemours & Co., Inc. The photomicrograph in *d* is courtesy of BASF Corporation Fibers Division.)

Pont produces carpet nylon with the rounded-square shape illustrated in Figure 24.2c, and distinguishes it with the trademark Antron® XL. BASF Corporation produces carpet nylon with the pentalobal shape and microscopic voids shown in Figure 24.2d, and distinguishes it with the trademark Zeftron® ATX.

Soil Shedding. Continuing the research towards achieving control of soiling problems, Monsanto Chemical Company has developed a soil-shedding fiber distinguished by the trade name Untron® Z. The trilobal fiber has a micro-rough surface that reduces soil adhesion; the producer has stated that the micro-ridges effectively "tee up" soil for easy shedding or removal. Soil's behavior on this fiber is roughly similar to that of a decal that fails to adhere to a rough surface.

Soil Repellency. Recently, carpet fibers have been engineered for built-in soil repellency, the ability to reduce initial attraction for soil and to retard the rate of soil accumulation. This is accomplished by chemically modifying the fiber. Generally, a fluorocarbon compound is incorporated in the polymer solution. Because this compound lowers the critical surface energy of fibers, dirt, dust, and grime do not readily adhere to their surfaces, and spilled liquids bead up rather than pass into the fibers. Examples of soil-repellent carpet fibers include Anso® IV nylon pro-

duced by Allied Fibers, Trevira® Pentron™ polyester produced by Hoechst Fibers Industries, and Zeftron®500™ ZX nylon produced by BASF Corporation.

Soil repellency can also be introduced by coating the surfaces of the fibers with fluorocarbon compounds. The agents may be applied to the filaments at the point of extrusion or sprayed over the fibers during conversion of the greige goods. In the latter case, converters must see that placement of the compound is not limited to the upper portion of the pile yarns. Examples of trade names indicating the application of soil-repellent compounds include Milliguard® Carpet Protector, owned by Milliken and Company, R9000 Soil Shield®, owned by Armstrong World Industries, and Scotchgard® and 3M Brand Carpet Protector, supplied by The 3M Company.

In contrast to this chemical approach, a physical approach for reducing the quantity of soil accumulated involves the extrusion of fibers with an extra large denier per filament (dpf). The larger diameter covers more carpet surface area so fewer of the filaments are required for carpet production. Such carpet structures reportedly have "25 to 30 percent less surface area per square yard for soil to adhere to."[5] Whereas conventional carpet nylon often has a dpf of 15, Ultron® 3D, produced by Monsanto Chemical Company, has a dpf of 20; Anso® IV HP nylon, produced by Allied Fibers, has a dpf of 36; and Antron® XL, produced by du Pont, has a dpf up to 34. Figure 24.3 com-

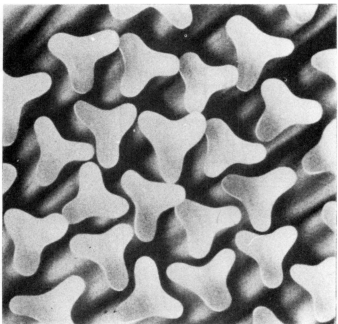

Figure 24.3 Comparison of the size of Antron ® XL nylon, pictured on the left, with that of conventional carpet nylon. (Courtesy of E.I. du Pont de Nemours & Co., Inc.)

pares the size of Antron® XL nylon with that of conventional carpet nylon.

Static Propensity

The electrical properties and absorbency of fibers, rather than the way they are incorporated into a covering, determine the level of static generated by a soft floor covering. For this reason, the principal approach to static control is through fiber engineering. Conductive elements sometimes play a part in backings and backcoatings as well. The mechanism of static development should be reviewed for a good understanding of the techniques devised to control static.

Static Development and Voltage Levels. Static development is initiated by the frictional heat energy created by the rubbing of shoe soles on carpet and rug fibers. The heat energy causes negatively charged electrons to transfer from the fiber surfaces to the body, where they accumulate. When the person touches a good electrical conductor, such as a metal doorknob, the accumulated electrons rapidly flow from the body to the conductor. It is the sudden discharge of this high energy potential that results in an electrical shock.

The buildup of electrical energy on the body can be plotted graphically as shown in Figure 24.4. As a person walks, increments of electrical charge build up, reaching equilibrium or the steady state after a period of 10 to 20 seconds, or after twenty to thirty steps. Fortunately, the voltage level does not keep increasing over time: some electrons are released into the surrounding air and some are transferred back into the carpet. If the person stops walking, the charge rapidly dissipates.

The level of voltage on the body when contact is made with a conductor determines the severity of the shock. Almost no one is sensitive to the discharge of 2,500 or fewer static volts. When the charge level is between 2,500 and 3,500 static volts, almost everyone will feel a shock, and the lower end of this range is known as the threshold

of human sensitivity. As the charge level increases above 3,500 static volts, people are likely to experience an increasingly severe shock.

Fiber Properties Affecting Voltage Buildup. Fibers are not inherently static or antistatic. Static is generated only when the separation of dissimilar materials, here shoes and fibers, results in the transfer of electrons. Certain fiber properties do, however, influence the availability of electrons and the ease with which they are removed.

Electrical properties. Electrical conductivity and resistivity are terms of opposite meaning that describe the relative ease with which a fiber conducts or resists the flow of electrons. The continual movement and rapid dissipation of electrons over large areas are critical influences on static development. All fibers allow for some degree of flow and some degree of resistance. Specific resistivity values can be used to rank textile fibers; however, these numerical values range widely, and because conductivity and resistivity are relative, the use of such terms as good and poor is more meaningful.

Fibers that keep electrons flowing, minimizing their accumulation, are classified as conductors, in contrast to insulators. Olefins, acrylics, and modacrylics are conductors. Metal fibers are especially good conductors. Fibers that offer higher resistance to the flow of electrons are insulators. These fibers, which include nylon, wool, and polyester, allow "pools" of electrons to form on their surfaces, readily available for transfer.

Fibers have other electrical properties that help to determine their static propensity. They vary in their tendencies to develop their own electrical charges. The triboelectric series for fibers presented in Table 24.3 helps make this clear. "Tribo" is Greek for "rubbing"; the series shows the relative ease with which fibers allow electrons to be rubbed from their surface atoms, leaving a positive balance. Fibers listed at the positive end of the series release electrons relatively easily, that is, release occurs with low

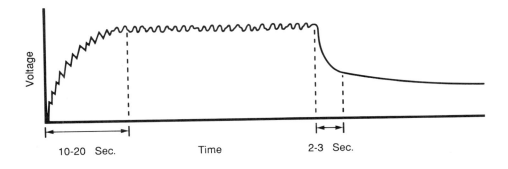

Figure 24.4 Static voltage buildup versus time. (Courtesy of Fibers Division, Monsanto Chemical Co.)

levels of frictional heat energy. The reverse is true of fibers listed at the negative end of the series.

Table 24.3 TRIBOELECTRIC SERIES FOR SELECTED TEXTILE FIBERS

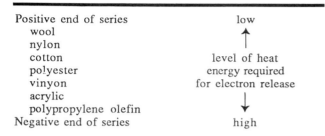

Sources: Adapted from D. J. Montgomery, *Solid State Physics*, 1959, 9, 139, quoted in W. R. Harper, *Contact and Frictional Electrification*, Oxford University Press, 1967, 352. Position of vinyon provided by Avtex Fibers.

The amount of heat energy available to cause electron release is determined in great part by the manner of walking. Slow, light-footed walking generates less heat energy than a rapid, heavy gait. Great amounts of heat energy and high levels of electron release accompany scuffing and shuffling since these movements involve vigorous rubbing of the fiber surfaces.

Like fibers, shoe sole materials vary in the ease with which they release electrons. When a fiber and sole material are paired, the potential for electron transfer is greater the more widely separated the materials are on the triboelectric scale. Neolite, for example, is fairly close to polyester and olefin on the scale. When neolite soles are paired with these fibers, neither fiber nor sole releases electrons readily, and voltage buildup is minimal. Pairing neolite soles with wool or nylon, however, would result in high electron transfer. Of course, if everyone everywhere wore the proper sole materials for the carpet fibers present, the need for static control measures might be overcome—an interesting concept, but an unreasonable expectation.

Absorbency. Fibers displaying high moisture regain values will show fewer static problems when the level of humidity is relatively high. Moisture encourages the flow of electrons and limits their pooling on fiber surfaces. It must not be assumed, however, that fibers having little or no capacity to absorb water vapor will automatically have the most marked static problem when relative humidity is low. Olefins, for example, have a moisture regain value of 0.0 percent, but they require higher levels of heat energy for electron release than many fibers do and they are conductors, not insulators.

Controlling levels of relative humidity is a year-round, routine practice in such interiors as computer rooms and medical facilities. This control helps ensure that sensitive equipment does not malfunction as a result of extra electrical signals picked up from the floor covering. The ability to increase relative humidity is particularly helpful in the winter months, when interiors may have levels as low as 5 to 10 percent. Some consumers find, however, that higher humidity levels result in condensation forming on windows, and some would rather not pay for a humidity-producing unit or its energy consumption.

To summarize, the following sequence leads to static shock:

Pooling of electrons on fiber surfaces → release and transfer of electrons to the body → accumulation of more than 2,500 static volts of energy on the body → sudden discharge of the built-up energy from the body to a conductor → shock.

It is apparent from this sequence that static problems could be lessened at the outset if the pooling of electrons were minimized. As well as by regulating the relative humidity, static control in textile floor coverings is accomplished, in fact, by incorporating conductive elements, several of which are conductive fibers, to minimize pooling.

Fibers Used to Control Static Generation. Electrical conductivity can be increased by periodically incorporating fine metal filaments in floor coverings. It may also be increased by periodically incorporating a textile fiber engineered for improved conductivity. The aim is to prevent the level of voltage buildup from exceeding the threshold of human sensitivity.

Fibers with additives. One of the first techniques devised to improve fiber conductivity was to add a compound, such as polyethylene glycol, to the polymer solution prior to extrusion. Such additives can contribute soil-hiding as well as static reduction properties.

Coated filaments. By enclosing a nylon filament in a sheath of a conductive material, such as silver, and plying these coated filaments with other fibers, some companies have developed an effective way to prevent electron pooling. X-Static®, marketed by Sauquoit Industries, Inc., is produced in this manner.

A similar technique is used to make Zefstat® products, produced by BASF Corporation. In these structures, however, the positions of the components are reversed. The conductive material, aluminum, forms the core and a colored polymer compound is used as the coating.

A third variation, no longer much used, involved coating a nylon filament with carbon black paste, a highly conductive compound. The use of this technique has diminished because heavy traffic gradually removed the antistatic coating. The coating was also visible in lighter-colored pile layers.

Metal fibers. Metal fibers placed at regular intervals in textile floor coverings effectively drain away electrons. These extremely fine fibers, in staple or filament form, can be added by themselves, spun with staple carpet fibers, or thrown with multifilament yarns. The fibers' fineness ensures their flexibility. Examples of fine stainless steel fibers are Brunsmet®, produced by Brunswick Corporation, and Bekinox®, produced by the Bekaert Steelwire Corporation. When spun yarns of Bekinox® are plied with wool, nylon, or polyester yarns, the blended yarns are distinguished by the name Bekitex.®

Conductive filaments. Some fiber producers have capitalized on the conductivity of carbon black by incorporating the compound into nonuniform filament structures. These filaments are categorized as biconstituent or conjugate fibers, fibers composed of dissimilar compounds.

Du Pont has developed a conductive filament whose core of carbon black is surrounded by a round sheath of nylon. This fiber is combined with several soil-hiding nylon fibers (Figure 24.5).

Monsanto Chemical Company has engineered a conductive fiber that incorporates carbon black as a "lightning rod" down the side. This conjugate fiber is 5 percent carbon black and 95 percent nylon. The round cross-section fiber is plied with soil-hiding trilobal Ultron® nylon to form the yarn bundle used in carpet production. Photomicrographs of this fiber are shown in Figure 24.6.

Specific Gravity

The weight and cost of textile floor coverings relates to the fibers' specific gravity. An analogy can demonstrate how this is so. Drinking straws represent olefin fibers, wooden chopsticks represent nylon fibers, and glass stirring rods represent polyester fibers; these items, with their obvious differences in density, were chosen to reflect the specific gravities of the fibers (see Table 4.1). If equal weights of the three are given, as Figure 24.7 shows, the lowest amount of cover will be provided by the polyester "rods" and the highest amount by the olefin "straws." To develop coverage equal to olefin's, more or larger nylon and still more or larger polyester fibers would have to be used. Needless to say, the weight of the floor covering would increase in either case, as probably would also its cost; the actual cost difference would depend on the differ-

ence in the costs of the fibers at the time of production. As fiber engineers improve the absorption and dyeability and reduce the heat sensitivity of olefin fibers, their use in interior floor coverings will no doubt increase.

The relationship between fiber density and denier is partly responsible for the success of nylon over polyester in the face yarn market. Figure 24.8 shows a nylon fiber and a polyester fiber of equal deniers. Manufacturers could produce more carpet—cover more surface area with fewer filaments and less weight—with nylon than with polyester. Increasing the diameter of the polyester to equal that of the nylon would also increase the polyester's weight and cost. Because stiffness increases and resiliency improves as diameters grow larger, it follows that a polyester carpet must be heavier and thus more costly than a nylon carpet to provide the necessary texture retention. One industry representative has reported that "polyester carpet cannot be made in low weights and must be used at 36 to 40 ounces per square yard in order to give good floor performance. Thus it can never compete with nylon in the low end market of 12 to 20 ounces per square yard range."[6]

YARN FEATURES AFFECTING SERVICEABILITY

The appearance and floor performance of carpet and rugs relates to several yarn features, including some structural characteristics and the stability of the yarn twist. Often, spinsters and throwsters can produce the desired appearance and expected service-related properties by manipulating these features.

Structural Characteristics

Virtually all carpet and rug yarns are constructed as simple, relatively heavy structures. Spun yarns are dominant, but a sizeable amount of bulked continuous filament (BCF) yarns is also used.

Design Features. Complex yarns, except for speck yarns, are not used in floor coverings because loops, curls, and other irregular textural effect would readily be abraded and snagged. Decorative appeal, however, can be introduced by other variables, including color styling, pile height, and yarn twist.

Form. From the data listed in Table 24.1, it can be estimated that spun yarns account for approximately 51 percent of the face yarn market. For good floor performance two- or three-ply spun yarns are produced from staple fibers 4, 6, or 8 inches long. Longer lengths help to reduce the number of protruding fiber ends and to increase yarn strength, and thus to minimize the problems of shedding, fuzzing, and pilling induced by abrasion during use.

Figure 24.5 Antron® III filament with a conductive carbon black core combined with soil-hiding filaments. (Courtesy of E.I. Du Pont de Nemours & Co., Inc.)

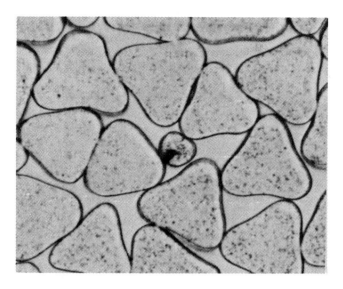

a) cross-sectional view

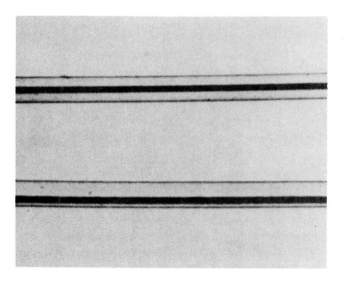

b) longitudinal view

Figure 24.6 Photomicrographs of conductive fiber used with Ultron® nylon. (Courtesy of Fibers Division, Monsanto Chemical Co.)

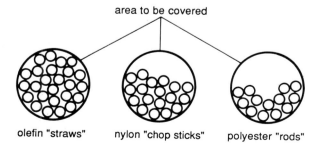

Figure 24.7 Schematic representation of the effect of specific gravity on covering power.

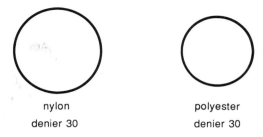

Figure 24.8 Effect of fiber density on denier and fiber diameter.

Most multifilament carpet yarns are textured, using the false-twist coiling or knit-de-knit crinkling techniques. Recently, there has been some shifting from spun to BCF yarns.[7] Because most of the filament ends are buried in the yarn bundle, BCF yarns, like longer staple spun yarns, exhibit less pill formation. In combination with heather color styling, BCF yarns often have a wool-like appearance (Figure 24.9).

Size and Weight. The average denier of filament carpet yarns composed of nylon, the dominant carpet fiber, has been decreasing over the past several years, as shown in Table 24.4. The reduction in diameter has largely resulted from changes in fashion styling preferences—most notably a shift toward the finer velour surface texture—but rising raw material costs have had a major impact as well.

Although the average denier of filament nylon yarns has been decreasing, some carpet yarns and some carpet fibers are being manufactured with extra high denier counts. These extra large yarns, which have denier counts as high as 7,000, are used in floor coverings intended for installation in commercial interiors that undergo heavy traffic.

Pile Yarn Integrity

Pile yarn integrity refers to the ability of the face yarns to maintain their stability and resist the effects of abrasion. Loop pile yarns should not rupture, and cut pile yarns should not splay or untwist. Such abrasion-induced changes would be accompanied by changes in the apparent luster wrongly suggestive of colorant failure. Concomitant changes would be observed in the original textural characteristics: for example, fuzziness would replace smoothness.

When cut pile yarns fail to maintain their original level of twist, they are said to splay, flare, or "blossom," as

Figure 24.9 Level loop carpet of Marquesa® Lana polypropylene olefin BCF yarn having a wool-like appearance. (Courtesy of Amoco Fabrics and Fibers Company.)

Table 24.4 DOMESTIC SHIPMENTS OF NYLON CARPET FILAMENT YARNS BY DENIER
(million pounds)

	1979	1980	1981	1982	1983	1984	1985
1,199 and finer			138.4	138.0	212.1	275.3	294.7
1,200–1,499	479.2	460.6	331.7	300.9	385.4	354.5	356.4
1,800 (1,500–1,900)	131.2	149.4	88.9	65.3	83.9	85.5	89.9
2,600 (1,901–2,700)	100.7	84.8	55.5	40.0	44.4	43.2	58.3
2,701 and coarser	21.4	19.7	19.1	15.3	8.8	11.7	16.1
Total domestic shipments	732.5	714.5	633.6	559.5	734.6	770.2	815.4
average denier	1,506	1,503	1,448	1,423	1,398	1,396	1,412

Source: Textile Economics Bureau, Inc., *Textile Organon,* Vol. 57, No. 3, March 1986, 56.

Figure 24.10 Yarn splaying.

shown in Figure 24.10. Because incident light waves are reflected from the small tips of the multiple, disoriented fibers, areas of splayed yarns appear duller than surrounding areas. Surface luster will also vary when fibers that are part of loop pile yarns are snagged and ruptured.

Pile yarn integrity can be improved with the use of abrasion-resistant fibers, BCF yarns, and more highly twisted and heat stabilized yarns. Higher pile construction densities also exert a positive influence on the integrity of the yarns in a covering over time.

SUMMARY

Fiber producers, yarn spinsters and throwsters, and converters are capable of engineering specific features into carpet fibers and yarns. Wool fibers, for example, can be chemically modified to resist moth attack. Man-made fibers can be drawn and heat set to increase their strength and abrasion resistance. Noncellulosic fibers can be extruded with cross-sectional shapes that hide and shed soil, and with larger diameters that reduce soil adhesion and improve texture retention. Carpet and rug fibers can also be engineered to resist microbes and reduce static voltage buildup. Yarns can be textured, to reduce pilling, and heat set, to minimize splaying and increase appearance retention.

The choice of inherent and engineered fiber and yarn properties should be made in anticipation of traffic conditions and in the light of budgetary limits. It should also entail consideration of construction variables that affect floor performance; these variables are discussed in the following chapter.

NOTES

1. Textile Economics Bureau, Inc., *Textile Organon,* Vol. 57, No. 9, September 1986, 211.

2. ———, Vol. 43, No. 12, December 1972, 188.

3. ———, Vol. 57, No. 3, March 1986, 62, 63.

4. ———, Vol. 57, No. 9, September 1985, 216.

5. Robert M. Axtell, quoted in "Industry Looks to Summer Markets with Optimistic Air," *Modern Textile Magazine,* Vol. LXIII, No. 5, May 1981, 22.

6. Robert G. Turner, "The Dynamic Carpet Industry," *Textile Chemist and Colorist,* Vol. 13, No. 3, March 1981, 16.

7. *Textile Organon,* Vol. 56, No. 2, February 1985, 23.

chapter 25

Construction of Floor Coverings: Tufting

- Basic Components of Tufted Floor Coverings
- Tufting Operations
- Structural Qualities of Tufted Constructions

Body construction techniques employed with textile floor coverings may be divided into two broad categories: those that create pile structures and those that create nonpile structures. Nonpile structures are produced by such methods as braiding, weaving, and needlepunching. Weaving produces pile structures, as well. Other pile structures are produced by such methods as tufting, knitting, and fusion bonding. For pile structures, surface textures or constructions do not go hand in hand with body constructions; identical textures can be produced by any of several techniques.

The division of body construction techniques on the basis of usage and economic importance is useful and meaningful. This separates tufting, which accounts for more than 96 percent of the approximately one billion square yards of floor coverings produced annually, from other industrial techniques and from hand operations.[1] The dominance of tufted floor coverings is largely the result of the economic advantages offered by high-speed, wide-width tufting machines, and by the use of nylon instead of nonresilient cotton and expensive wool fibers. It has also resulted from improvements made in the quality of tufted carpet that have enabled designers and architects increasingly to specify tufted floor coverings for commercial interiors, including areas of heavy traffic.

Because tufted floor coverings are used so extensively, residential consumers and professionals should understand their structural qualities. This will prepare them to make informed decisions and reliable judgments concerning the suitability of tufted structures for various installations. Contract designers, architects, and other specifiers will also thus be prepared to interpret structural data supplied by producers.

BASIC COMPONENTS OF TUFTED FLOOR COVERINGS

Whether a carpet or rug is machine tufted or hand tufted, the principal components are the same. Tufted constructions include pile or face yarns, a primary backing, a layer of adhesive, and a secondary backing (Figure 25.1).

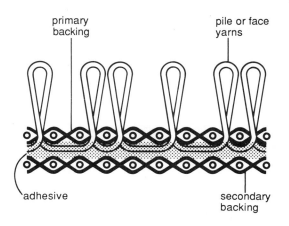

Figure 25.1 Components in tufted constructions.

269

a) plain woven jute

b) plain woven olefin

c) spunbonded olefin

Figure 25.2 Typical primary backing fabrics.

Pile or Face Yarns

The composition and structural characteristics of face yarns used in pile floor coverings were discussed in Chapter 24. Spun yarns and nylon fibers dominate.

Primary Backing Fabric

Typical primary backing fabrics are pictured in Figure 25.2. Although jute formerly dominated the market, it has largely been replaced by olefin. Woven jute fabrics are dimensionally stable unless they are overwetted during cleaning or flooding. Because they retain moisture and may rot and mildew, they should not be used with floor coverings installed below-grade where ground moisture can move through the floor to the carpet back. Because jute is imported from tropical areas, supply and delivery problems have often plagued producers using jute.

Plain-woven fabrics of yarn-like tapes or ribbons of olefin (Figure 25.2b) have high stability unless heated above 338°F. These fabrics are impervious to moisture; they resist mildew and the development of odors. To minimize raveling, a thin butyl coating is frequently applied to bond the warp and filling yarns. Some examples of these backings include Baxon®, produced by Exxon Chemical Company, and PolyBac®, produced by the Patchogue Plymouth Division of Amoco Fabrics and Fibers Company.

When low pile construction densities are planned, producers can use a plain-woven olefin backing with a "nylon cap," produced by needlepunching a thin nylon batt into the backing (Figure 25.3). Because nylon fibers accept dye more readily than olefin fibers, the needlepunched fibers can be colored to coordinate with the face yarns. In the event the backing is exposed in use, any difference in color between the face fibers and the backing is masked. Fuzzback®, produced by Exxon Chemical Company, and

Figure 25.3 Plain-woven olefin backing with a needlepunched "nylon cap" to minimize color differences between pile yarns and backing.

Figure 25.4 ActionBac®, a leno-woven olefin secondary backing, with spun filling yarns for improved adhesion. (Courtesy of Amoco Fabrics and Fibers Company.)

PolyBac® FLW, produced by Amoco Fabrics and Fibers Company, are examples of this style of primary backing.

Spunbonded olefin fabric (Figure 25.2c) exhibits no fraying or raveling and is not susceptible to problems from moisture. During tufting, the filaments are pushed aside; thus, the needle is only minimally deflected, which helps ensure uniform pile height and tuft placement. Some examples of these backings include Loktuft®, produced by Hercules, Inc., and Typar®, produced by du Pont.

Secondary Backing Fabrics

Secondary backing fabrics, also referred to as scrims, must adhere well and provide high dimensionsl stability. Fabrics composed of jute are naturally rough and adhere well; spunbonded fabrics are smooth and have poor adhesion.

A leno-woven fabric composed of olefin fibers is specifically manufactured for use as a secondary backing. The leno interlacing minimizes edge raveling, and the spun filling yarns provide the necessary roughness for adhesion of the fabric. ActionBac®, produced by Amoco Fabrics and Fibers Company, is an example of this construction (Figure 25.4).

Some manufacturers use a glass fiber scrim to reinforce a vinyl secondary backing. This combination has high dimensional stability and virtually no moisture-related problems. An example of this backing is Milliback®, produced by Milliken and Company.

Permanently attached foam rubber cushions may be used as secondary backings, eliminating the need for a separate cushion. Secondary backings may or may not be used with commercially produced, hand-tufted carpet and rugs.

Adhesives

The most frequently used adhesive is synthetic latex; approximately 12 ounces per square yard are applied to most tufted floor coverings.[2] Some carpet producers are replacing latex adhesives with molten thermoplastic compounds, such as Unibond®, used by Lees Commercial Carpet.

To control electrical charge buildup, tufted carpet producers may incorporate a conductive compound into the adhesive used to secure the secondary backing, or they may sandwich an antistatic coating between the primary backing and the adhesive. Gafstat®, owned by the Gaf Corporation, is an example of a trade name identifying employment of the latter technique. Some carpet producers combine a conductive compound in the adhesive or backing fabric with an antistatic component in the pile layer. Dataguard® is the trade name used by Lees Carpets to identify their commercial carpet protected in this manner.

Tufted carpet producers may also incorporate a flame retardant compound into the adhesive. To be effective, the coating must penetrate the primary backing.

TUFTING OPERATIONS

Unlike most weaving operations, tufting is a relatively simple and uncomplicated process. Pile yarns are inserted into an already-formed primary backing fabric, and surface textures and construction densities can easily be varied.

Forming the Pile Layer

Pile yarns are supplied from cones mounted on a creel frame erected in back of the tufting machine. So that they will not tangle, the yarns are fed through thin plastic tubes, visible in the upper portion of the photograph in Figure 25.5, to tension control devices and the tufting needles. The tension controls determine the quantity of yarn supplied to the needles, helping ensure the production of the planned pile height.

Many needles are aligned crosswise on the machine. The number of needles required depends on the width and the planned crosswise density or gauge. Gauge is the fractional distance between adjacent needles; it can be converted to a needle count, which is the number of needles per crosswise inch on the machine. A gauge of 1/8 inch is equivalent to a needle count of eight; a gauge of 1/10 inch is equivalent to a needle count of ten. To prepare a tufting machine to produce carpet 12 feet wide, with a gauge of 1/10 inch, 1,440 needles must be aligned and threaded with pile yarns (12 feet x 12 inches = 144 inches; 144 inches x 10 needles = 1,440 needles).

Figure 25.5 Commercial tufting machine. (Courtesy of The Hoover Company.)

The sequence used to form loop pile floor coverings is schematized in Figure 7.8a (page 64). Threaded with pile yarns, the needles descend through the back of the primary fabric. Working in a timed relationship with the descending needles, loop pile hooks rock forward, catching and holding the yarn loops while the needles ascend. The pile layer is then formed on the face of the primary fabric. One crosswise row of tufts is produced in each tufting cycle.

When a pile surface is planned, a knife blade is attached to the pile hook, which cuts the loops, forming one U-shaped tuft from each loop (Figure 7.8b, page 64). For either loop or cut pile coverings, the descend and ascend tufting cycle is followed by the advancement of the primary backing a predetermined distance and the repetition of the cycle.

The number of tufts or stitches per inch determines the distance the primary backing is advanced after each tufting cycle, and thus governs the lengthwise density. Typically, the number of stitches per inch ranges from four to eleven. If, for example, a stitch of eight is selected, the crosswise bank of needles would punch into the fabric eight times in each lengthwise inch, and there would be 1/8 inch between each crosswise row of tufts.

Modern tufting machines are capable of completing more than 500 tufting cycles per minute. Depending upon width, density, and surface texture, this capability can translate into the production of more than 1,000 square yards of cut pile carpet in 8 hours, and about twice that amount of loop pile carpet.[3]

In comparison to machine tufting, hand tufting is an extremely slow and expensive process. It is only used for custom orders requiring a relatively small amount of yardage. Hand tufting is done with a hand-held, electrically powered tufting gun (Figure 25.6).

Creating Multilevel Surface Textures

Various attachments are available for tufting multilevel surfaces in random and patterned shapes. Differences in pile height are achieved by controlling the quantity of yarn supplied to the needles prior to their descent. The needles and loop hooks continue to operate in the conventional manner.

Roll-type Attachments. Roll-type attachments control the speed at which yarns flow over rollers as they are fed to sections of needles, by various mechanisms, ranging from clutches and gears to light-sensitive devices. When the speed of the rolls is held constant, the amount of yarn feeding to the needles is constant, and a level surface will be produced. When the speed is slowed, the amount of yarn feeding to the needles is reduced; then, as the hooks hold the loops while the needles ascend, the "missing" quantity of yarn is robbed mechanically by tension from the previously formed loops. Thus, the just

Figure 25.6 Custom tufting with a hand-held, single needle gun. (Courtesy of Cabin Craft Products.)

completed loops have greater pile height than the previously formed loops. This pattern of supplying insufficient yarn and robbing the pile loops is continued until the planned low pile area is completed.

Scroll-type Attachments. In scroll-type pattern attachments, photoelectric cells control the amount of yarn fed to each needle. As shown in Figure 25.7, the planned high and low pattern shapes are painted on the surface of a translucent drum; the painted opaque areas define the high pile areas and the unpainted translucent areas define the low pile areas. The position of the drum on the tufting machine can be observed in Figure 25.5.

During the tufting sequence the center of the drum is lighted; as it rotates, light is transmitted only through the transluscent areas. The transmitted light activates a photoelectric cell that slows the yarn-feed roll speed. This in turn reduces the yarn supply and a shorter pile height is formed.

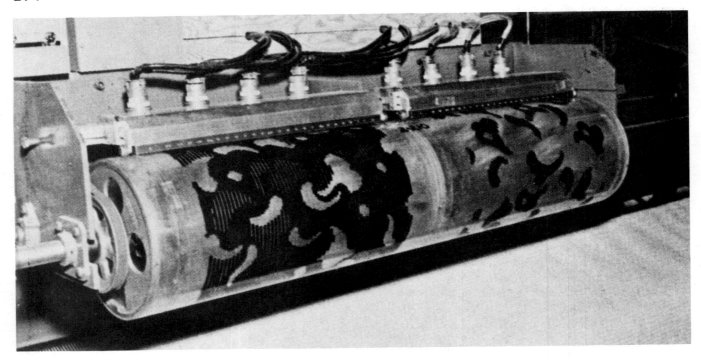

Figure 25.7 Pattern drum attachment used for multilevel, patterned tufted carpet. (Courtesy of The Hoover Company.)

Slat-type Attachments. Two forms of slat-type pattern attachments have been developed for use in tufting operations. In one system, pile yarns are fed to the needles over a rotating bank of metal slats with a pattern of notched areas cut into the outer edge of each slat; one slat is required for each crosswise row of tufts. When a pile yarn encounters a notched area, it is subjected to less tension and will form higher loops. When the pile yarn encounters an uncut area, its flow is restricted, and it will form a shorter loop.

In another slat-type system, two sets of notched slats rotate and intermesh. As the yarns flow between the intermeshing slats, they conform to the depth of the notches. In this case, deeper notches cause less deflection in the path of the yarn, so less yarn is reeled off from the cones on the creel, resulting in lower loops. Unnotched slats deflect the yarn to a greater extent, reeling off more yarn and developing higher loops.

In recent years, the use of roll- and slat-type pattern attachments has diminished with consumer preference for multilevel surface textures. The use of these attachments has also diminished as manufacturers have adopted newer equipment, such as video machines, that can more efficiently control pile height variations.

When tufting of the pile yarns is completed, several operations are required to convert the greige carpet into finished carpet. Among these, tip shearing, random shearing, and hand carving create even more variety in surface texture.

Applying an Adhesive and Scrim

Unless the tufted pile yarns are permanently anchored in the primary backing, they could easily be pulled out when snagged. In cut pile styles, this would show up as an empty space the size of the space once occupied by the removed tufts. In loop pile styles, pulling the continuous length of yarn would expose a lengthwise line of backing void of tufts, as illustrated in Figure 25.8.

In preparation for application of the adhesive, the back of the primary fabric is beaten to drive the pile yarn segments tightly against the fabric base. The coating is then applied uniformly across the back, securely binding the yarns into their positions. The secondary backing is then rolled onto the adhesive coating.

Most tufted broadloom carpet is manufactured in 12-foot widths. The yardage may be in rollgood form or cut into small rugs and mats. The products are converted and then subjected to quality testing.

STRUCTURAL QUALITIES OF TUFTED CONSTRUCTIONS

As part of their quality-control programs, tufted carpet producers evaluate such structural features as the strength

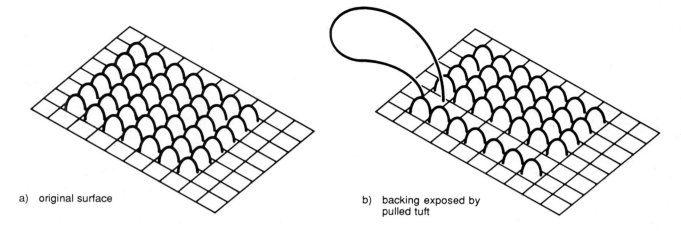

a) original surface

b) backing exposed by
    pulled tuft

Figure 25.8 Potential problem with poorly anchored pile yarns.

of the bond between the primary and secondary backings and the pile construction density. Several also measure various weight-related characteristics, for use in selection guidelines that coordinate minimum weight values with anticipated traffic levels.

Bundle Penetration

Visual examination enables carpet producers to estimate how thoroughly the adhesive penetrates the pile yarn bundle. A high degree of bundle penetration helps to prevent individual staple or filament fibers from being pulled out of the yarns and rubbed into fuzz and pills on the carpet surface.

Delamination Strength

Another crucial function of the adhesive coating is to develop a strong bond with the secondary backing. Good adhesion is especially important to prevent delamination or separation of the backings when they are subjected to heavy stress forces. The movement of heavy equipment or the flow of much traffic across a carpet surface can have a "snowplow" effect, crushing and pushing the structure, which in turn can cause shearing, the movement of the primary and secondary backings in opposite directions. Unless the bond between the two fabrics is strong, shearing can cause delamination. Delamination could result in bubbling, rippling, and straining at the seams.

The strength of the bond between the backings may be measured in accordance with the procedures outlined in ASTM D 3936 Standard Test Method for Delamination Strength of Secondary Backing of Pile Floor Coverings. As shown in Figure 25.9, stress is exerted on the specimen clamped in the jaws of the test apparatus. The force

required to separate the components is measured for each of three specimens; the average is then reported in pounds per inch of specimen width. Values frequently range from 2.5 to 8.33 pounds per inch.

Tuft Bind

Tuft bind testing may be carried out in accordance with the procedures outlined in ASTM D 1335 Standard Test Method for Tuft Bind of Pile Floor Coverings. The force required to pull one loop pile tuft from a floor covering is measured by first anchoring the structure in clamps, as shown in Figure 25.10. A hook is inserted into the test loop, and the loops on either side of the test loop are cut. Force is then exerted by raising the hook. Three replicate tests are run, and the average force required to remove the tufts is reported in pounds-force. Values typically range from 4.5 to 20 pounds. This procedure can also be used on cut pile structures: a tweezer-like device is clamped onto one side or leg of a cut loop.

Tufts Per Square Inch

Although the "eyeball" method illustrated in Figure 23.4 (page 245) can roughly evaluate pile construction density, a more reliable technique is to determine the actual number of tufts per square inch. Producers measure and report the necessary lengthwise and crosswise values separately on data and specification sheets.

Gauge, needle count, and number of tufts or stitches per inch were explained earlier in this chapter. Typical gauge and needle count conversions are listed in Table 26.1 (page 287). The number of tufts per square inch may be calculated by multiplying the needle count by the number of stitches per inch. If other construction features are

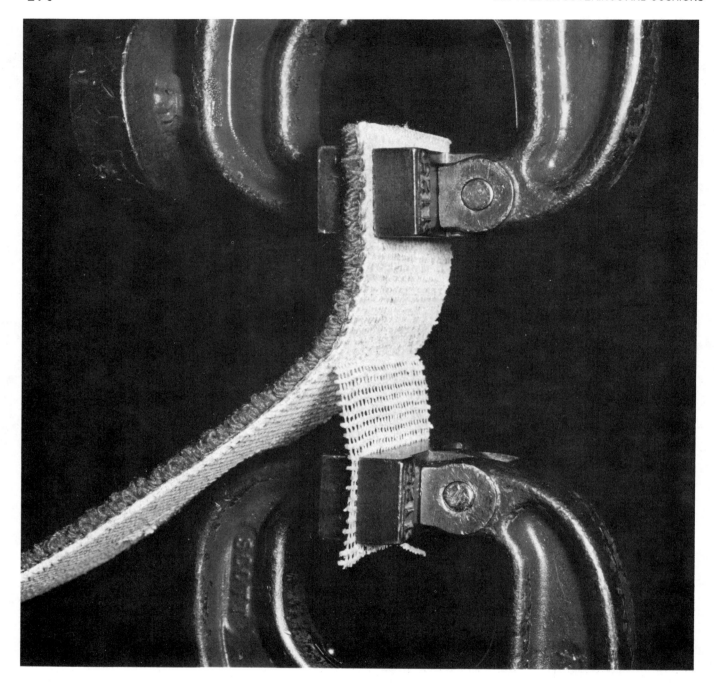

Figure 25.9 Measuring secondary back adhesion strength. (Courtesy of BASF Corporation Fibers Division.)

equal, carpet and rugs with higher construction density values should exhibit better durability and texture retention.

The important influence of construction density on thickness retention can be appreciated by reviewing a simple principle of physics. When a stress load is distributed over a large, rather than a small, number of supports, the force or load each must bear is minimized. The same idea is behind the "magic" we see when a performer lies on a bed of nails without injury to the skin: each one of many nails supports an extremely small portion of the body weight, so the skin is not punctured. To pursue the analogy, each tuft in a pile floor covering may be considered equivalent to one nail; as the number of tufts is increased,

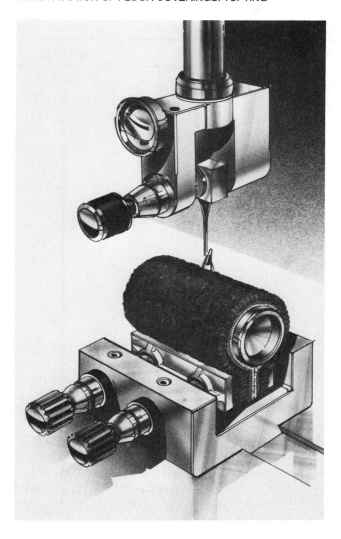

Figure 25.10 Measuring tuft bind strength. (Courtesy of Lees Commercial Carpet Company.)

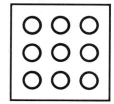 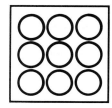

Figure 25.11 Equal pile construction densities having different sizes of yarns.

the load each must support is reduced. Denser construction also helps to reduce yarn flexing within the pile because adjacent tufts support one another.

Pile construction density values are important, but they should not be used alone to predict thickness retention. For example, each square in Figure 25.11 has the same number of pile tufts, but the size and thus the weight of the yarns in each is significantly different. Evidently, accurate predictions of serviceability must also include weight factors.

Weight-related Factors

In general, as the weight of a textile floor covering increases, so do its quality, its potential texture retention, and its wear-life. For this reason, producers of tufted carpet and other soft floor coverings generally report various weight-related measurements. These include pile yarn weight, effective face weight, total weight, density factor, weight density, and HUD/FHA density. The challenge to students and practicing professionals is to understand the differences among these measurements. Professionals must also be aware that minimum weight values are often part of design standards established for certain commercial interiors.

Pile Yarn Weight. Pile yarn weight is the weight of the yarns used in the wear layer and those portions of the pile yarn that extend into the backing layer. Pile yarn weight values are expressed in ounces per square yard or in grams per square meter.

Several construction variables are reflected in pile weight values, including fiber density, yarn weight, pile height, and pile construction density. Pile yarn weight values are among the better references for judging the potential serviceability of similarly constructed floor coverings. To compare floor coverings of different constructions, however, consideration should be given to the proportional distribution of the pile yarns between the wear layer and the backing layer.

Effective Face Yarn Weight. The effective face yarn weight is a way to express the weight of the pile yarns in the wear layer, excluding those in the backing. Because fusion bonded structures (discussed in Chapter 26) contain a relatively small amount of their pile yarns in the backing layer, producers of these carpets often report the effective face yarn weight.

Total Weight. The total weight of a floor covering includes the weight of the pile yarns as well as the weight of the backing yarns, backing fabrics, and backcoatings. Table 25.1 illustrates how weight measurements and other construction variables should be coordinated with traffic conditions for good performance. (Traffic classifications for various areas within several commercial interiors are listed in Table 23.1.) Since the weight values listed are minimums, increasing them should provide increased floor

Table 25.1 RECOMMENDED CONSTRUCTION STANDARDS FOR CARPETS OF HERCULON® OLEFIN

	Light traffic	Medium traffic	Heavy traffic
Gauge (pitch)	1/8 (216)	1/8, 1/10 (216, 270)	1/8, 1/10, 5/64 (216, 270, 346)
Rows or stitches	7	8	8 or above
Pile height	1/4 in. or below	1/4 in. or below	1/4 in. to 3/8 in.
Pile yarn weight	16.0 oz./ sq. yd. min.	18.0 oz./ sq. yd. min.	28.0 oz./ sq. yd. min.
Total weight	55 oz./ sq. yd. min.	57 oz./ sq. yd. min.	65 oz./ sq. yd. min.

Courtesy of Hercules Incorporated.

performance; but such increases should always be balanced against concomitant increases in cost.

Density Factor. The density factor or density index is a calculation that reflects both pile construction density and yarn size (denier). The following formula is used to calculate this factor:

Density factor = yarn size x needle count x stitches per inch

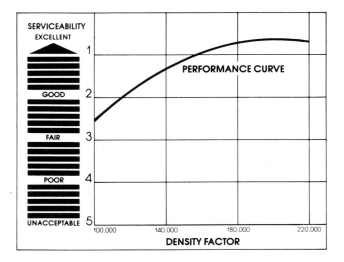

Figure 25.12 Relationship of density factor to floor performance. (Courtesy of Allied Fibers.)

Increasing the density factor will increase floor performance, up to a point: the relationship is shown in Figure 25.12.

The usefulness of pile yarn weight, effective face yarn weight, and total weight measurements is limited in that they do not reflect the true pile density (mass or amount of matter per unit of volume). Consider, for example, two carpets that have the same pile yarn and identical pile construction densities, but different pile heights. The carpet with the higher pile would weigh more, but would have lower true density. On the other hand, if two carpets only differed in their yarn size, the carpet containing the heavier yarns would not only weigh more but would also have a higher true density. The density factor also does not reflect true density because it does not consider pile height. It is apparent that structures with equal construction densities and yarn sizes, but different pile heights, will have identical density factors; but increasing the pile height will in fact reduce the true density. Therefore, measurements that reflect the true density are often reported.

Average Density and Weight Density. Average density and weight density measurements take pile height (finished thickness) into consideration and thus can indicate the true density of floor covering structures. Minimum density values may be recommended or required in some settings. Required minimum values are set out, for example, in the HUD/FHA Use of Materials Bulletin 44c (see Chapter 2). Commercial specifiers must select a floor covering that has been certified to meet or exceed the minimum requirements in effect at the time of the project work. Certification must be carried out by an independent laboratory administrator approved by HUD/FHA. The bulletin offers these formulas for calculating average density and weight density:

(D) = average density = $\dfrac{36\,(W)}{(t)}$, where

(W) = average pile weight in ounces per square yard, and

(t) = average pile thickness in inches.

(WD) = weight density = $W\,(D)$

Weight-related features not only affect texture retention, but also such functional values as noise control and insulation. Test methods for evaluating these and other service-related properties are discussed in Chapter 30.

SUMMARY

Constructing pile floor coverings through tufting operations is relatively fast and economical. The economic advantages of machine tufting, of course, may be overridden by the selection of more expensive fibers, yarns, and finishes and by the use of higher pile construction densities. Costs can also escalate when production runs are small and specialized, as is generally the case with custom work made to order. The costs will also be higher for small, unique orders that must be hand tufted, a comparatively slow, labor-intensive process.

In their quality-control programs, tufting firms generally measure and evaluate such structural qualities as the strength of the bond between the primary and secondary backing fabrics, the pile construction density, and the weight and density of the pile layer. Tufting firms use the results of these evaluations to help secure the widespread selection of their floor coverings.

NOTES

1. G. Robert Turner, "The Dynamic Carpet Industry: Today and Tomorrow," *Textile Chemist and Colorist*, Vol. 13, No. 3, March 1981, 15, 16.

2. Cecil Davis, "Fine Gauge Tufting," *Modern Textile*, June 1973, 60.

3. The Singer Company, Cobble Division, *Handbook of General Information on Yardage Tufting Machines and Their Use*, Tenn., n.d., 6.

chapter 26

Construction of Floor Coverings: Other Machine Techniques

- Weaving Pile Floor Coverings
- Fusion Bonding Operations
- Other Machine Operations

Commercial weaving of textile floor coverings began in the United States in the late 1700s. The principal product was a nonpile, yarn-dyed, reversible structure called Ingrain. Gradually, this rug began to replace the braided and hand-woven rugs made in the home. Pile carpet was imported until the mid-1800s, when the power loom was adapted for the domestic production of a patterned, loop pile carpet known as Brussels. Over the years, other techniques and looms augmented the production capabilities of domestic manufacturers. In addition to Ingrain and Brussels carpet, cut pile constructions, such as Wilton, Axminster, velvet, and chenille, also became available. Together, woven floor coverings dominated markets until the mid-1950s, when large-scale tufting operations were widely adopted.

In addition to tufting and weaving operations, other machine techniques, including fusion bonding, flocking, and needlepunching, are used to produce contemporary carpet and rugs. Although machine techniques other than tufting produce only a relatively small portion of today's residential and commercial floor coverings, even small percentages translate into millions of square yards.

WEAVING PILE FLOOR COVERINGS

Several methods of weaving are employed in the manufacture of pile floor coverings. Among these, major differences exist in the structure and operation of the looms, the nature of the surface patterns formed, and the degree of interlacing complexity involved. Some yarn components are, however, common to all forms of woven pile structures.

Basic Components

Most woven pile floor coverings contain chain warp yarns, stuffer yarns, filling shots, and pile yarns. These yarns are illustrated schematically in Figure 26.1.

Filling shots or weft shots are crosswise yarns used to anchor the pile warp yarns. The shots are generally of polypropylene olefin, jute, or cotton, and the pile yarns may be spun or multifilament yarns of any fiber. For added

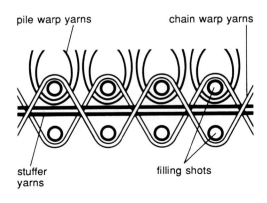

Figure 26.1 Basic components of woven pile carpet and rugs.

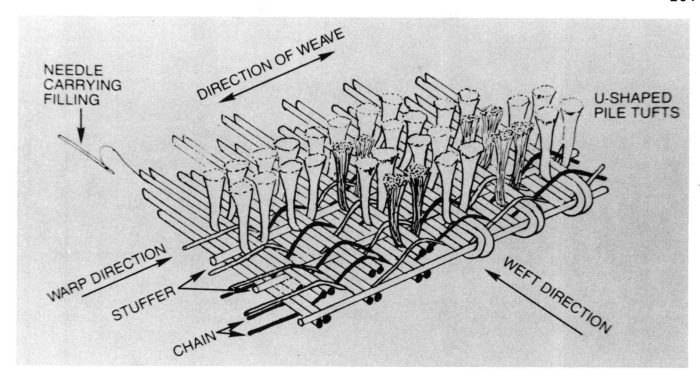

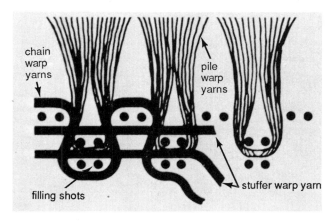

Figure 26.2 Cross-sectional sketches of Axminster carpet with paired filling shots. (Courtesy of Mohawk Carpet.)

body and weight, extra warp yarns, called stuffers, are inserted in a plane in the back layer. Stuffers are normally kraftcord or stiff jute yarns. Chain warp yarns pass over and under the shots, securing all components of the structure tightly together. The zigzag configuration of these yarns in most woven floor coverings makes them easy to recognize. Today, chains are generally composed of polyester, not cotton.

Unlike tufting, in which the pile layer is added to an already-formed base fabric, weaving operations form the pile and backing layers simultaneously. Some methods, such as velvet weaving, are relatively simple procedures that have only limited design capabilities; others, including

Axminster and Wilton, are quite complicated and virtually unlimited in the range of designs they can produce. Weaving operations are comparatively slow and labor-intensive, however, so they are used less frequently than tufting by domestic producers.

Axminster Weaving

Two schematic illustrations of Axminster carpet are shown in Figure 26.2. A distinctive feature is the use of paired filling shots, with either two pairs used per tuft row, as shown in the upper sketch, or three pairs per tuft row, as shown in the lower sketch. This makes the crosswise direction of the carpet somewhat rigid and inflexible, a distinguishing characteristic of Axminster floor coverings.

Preparation for Axminster weaving is lengthy and involved; the more intricate and complex the design and pattern repeat to be woven, the more complicated preparation becomes. First, a colored print design displaying the full length and width of one pattern repeat is prepared. A portion of the design prepared for weaving an intricate Oriental pattern is shown in Figure 26.3. Each small block represents one pile tuft. Clearly, the colored tufts must be woven precisely in their planned positions, or the motifs will be irregular and flawed.

When the design is ready, skilled technicians assemble cones of yarns colored according to its specifications.

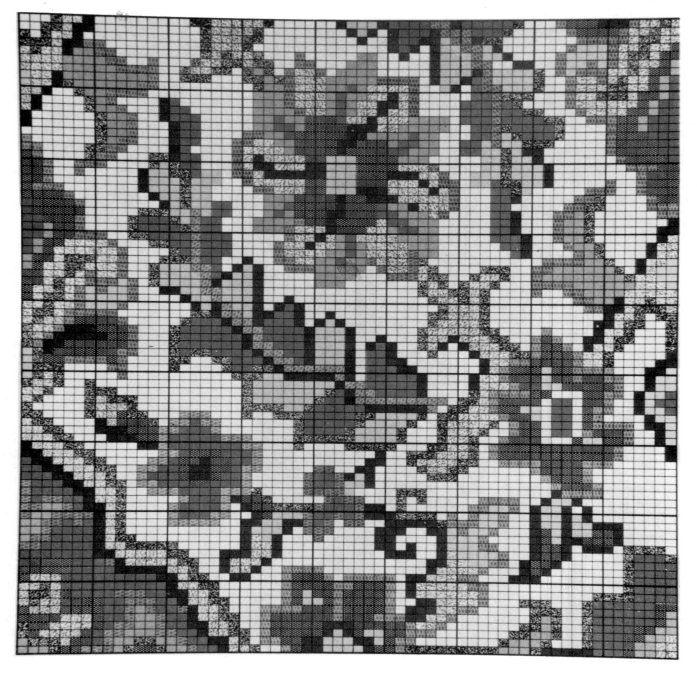

LATTICE ORIENTAL, pattern #10   18" wide repeat   set match

POSITION 1   POSITION 2   POSITION 3   POSITION 4   POSITION 5   POSITION 6   POSITION 7   POSITION 8   POSITION 9

Figure 26.3 Point design for a portion of an Axminster pattern repeat. (Courtesy of Mohawk Carpet.)

They then wind the various colors of yarns onto 3-foot-long spools, following the sequence printed on one crosswise row of the point design. For a repeat 18 inches in width, the sequence would be used twice on each spool. Spools are linked end to end to form a bracket. If the carpet is to be woven 12 feet wide, four spools are used, and the sequence would be repeated eight times across the bracket.

The number of yarns wound on each spool is determined by the pitch. Pitch is the number of pile units (loops or cut, U-shaped tufts) per 27 inches of width; it commonly ranges from 162 to 216. The pitch method of reporting crosswise density in woven carpet has persisted from earlier times when looms were narrower: carpet was woven in 27-inch widths and seamed as often as necessary. If a carpet is to be 12 feet wide and have a pitch of 189, a total of 1,008 tufts will form each crosswise row. This is calculated as follows: 12 feet x 12 inches = 144 inches; 144 inches divided by 27 inches = 5.33, that is, there are five and a third of the 27-inch segments in the carpet width; and 5 1/3 x 189 tufts = 1,008 total tufts. Each bracket thus carries 1,008 yarns, and each 3-foot-long spool carries one third of the total, or 336 yarns.

After the first bracket is completed, spools are wound with yarns according to the sequence shown in the second row of squares on the draft paper. The process continues until one bracket has been prepared for each crosswise row in the pattern repeat. The number of brackets required is governed by the length of the repeat and the planned lengthwise density.

The number of rows per inch—the number of crosswise rows of tufts per lengthwise inch—in an Axminster carpet is commonly within the range of seven to ten. If, for example, a count of eight rows per inch is selected, eight brackets would be prepared for weaving 1 lengthwise inch of carpet. A repeat 25 inches long would then require 200 brackets.

In preparation for weaving, the multiple brackets are positioned in proper order on the loom (the brackets are in the central portion of the photographs in Figure 26.4b). Yarn from the first bracket is rolled off, lowered into position, and the stuffers, chain warp yarns, and pairs of weft shots are integrated with the pile yarns, locking them into the structure. The amount of yarn reeled off is determined by the planned pile height. The pile yarn is cut, the bracket is moved away, and the second bracket is lowered. A complete cycle of all the brackets would produce the length of one repeat; a second cycle would produce another length, and so on.

Wilton Weaving

Formerly, loop pile carpet woven on a Jacquard loom was called Brussels, and cut pile carpet was called Wilton.

Today, all pile floor covering woven on a Jacquard loom is called Wilton.

The number of colors of pile yarns used in the pattern is used to describe the carpet; for instance, a three-frame Wilton has three colors, a six-frame Wilton has six colors, and so on. When the variously colored yarns are not required to form part of the surface design, they are carried in a plane in the backing layer (Figure 26.5). The presence of such "dead and buried" yarns distinguishes Wilton constructions. Although the hidden lengths contribute weight, cushioning, and resiliency, they also add to the materials cost.

An enlarged section of a point design for a three-frame Wilton carpet is shown in Figure 26.6. The shed for weaving the first crosswise row would be formed by raising a red, a blue, and a green yarn. A blue and a green yarn would be lowered below the red yarn; a green yarn and a red yarn would be lowered below the blue yarn; and a red and a blue yarn would be lowered below the green yarn. The shed for weaving the second crosswise row would be formed by raising a blue, a green, and a red yarn. A red and a green yarn would be lowered behind the blue yarn, and so on. One cone of yarn must be supplied for each color appearing in each lengthwise row of pile tufts. Weaving the three rows of carpet represented in the draft would require nine cones of yarn, one of each color for each row.

The total number of cones of yarn required for Wilton weaving is determined by the carpet width, the pitch, and the number of colors planned. If, for example, a three-frame Wilton is to be woven 12 feet wide with a pitch of 189, a total of 3,024 cones would be required, assuming

a)

Figure 26.4 Weaving action on an Axminster loom. (Courtesy of Mohawk Carpet.)

b)

c)

Figure 26.4 Weaving action on an Axminster loom. (Courtesy of Mohawk Carpet.)

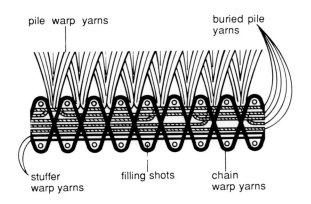

Figure 26.5 labels: pile warp yarns, buried pile yarns, stuffer warp yarns, filling shots, chain warp yarns

Figure 26.5 Cross-sectional sketch of a Wilton carpet. (Courtesy of Mohawk Carpet.)

green	red	blue
blue	green	red
red	blue	green

Figure 26.6 Enlarged portion of a point design for a Wilton carpet.

each color is used in each lengthwise row. Since there are 1,008 pile units in each crosswise row, the total is calculated by multiplying 1,008 by 3, which equals 3,024.

To reduce yarn costs, a system of "planting" colored pile yarns may be employed: an added color of yarn is periodically substituted ("planted") for one of the basic pile colors. Planting can cause a three-frame Wilton carpet to appear to be a four-frame structure; an investigation of the backing, however, would uncover only two buried pile yarns behind each tuft.

Jacquard carpet weaving is similar to other Jacquard weaving operations (see Chapter 6 and Figure 6.14, page 54). In carpet weaving, however, the Jacquard attachment controls the pile yarns, not the base yarns; additional harnesses are used to control the chain warp yarns; and additional loom beams are used to hold the chain and stuffer

yarns. As shown schematically in Figure 26.7, wires are inserted into the shed formed by the pile yarns, and weft shots are inserted into the separate shed formed by the chain warp yarns. The reed moves forward, pushing the wire and shot against the already-woven carpet. The heddle-like cords holding the raised pile yarns then descend, lowering the pile yarn over the wires. A weft shot is carried across the carpet, above the pile yarns and below the chain warp yarns. Then, a new pile yarn shed is formed, the harnesses reverse their positions, and the sequence is repeated.

The pile loops are formed over wires whose height determines the pile height. If a cut pile is planned, the wires are equipped with knives on one end; as the wires are withdrawn, they cut the loops. If a looped pile texture is planned, the wires will have rounded ends.

Since one wire is used for each crosswise row of pile tufts, the lengthwise density of Wilton carpet is reported as the number of wires per inch. Typically, this number is

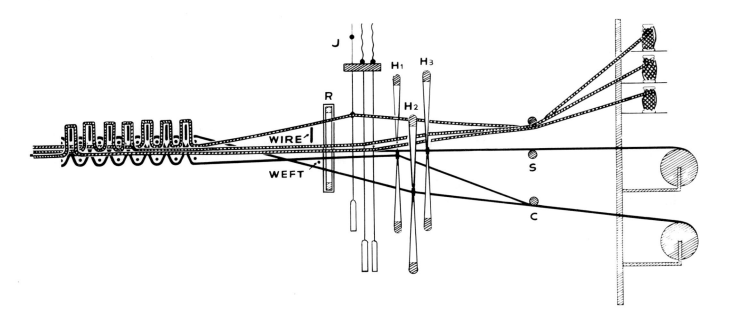

Figure 26.7 Diagram of Jacquard carpet weaving. (Courtesy of The Hoover Company.)

within the range of seven to ten. The crosswise density commonly ranges from a pitch of 189 to 252, but it may be as high as 270 or 346.

Velvet Carpet Weaving

Velvet weaving is an over-the-wire construction technique (Figure 6.19, page 58) used to produce velvet carpet. This use of "velvet" must not be confused with its use to name a surface texture nor with its use as a name for an upholstery fabric.

Velvet weaving is one of the least complicated methods of producing pile carpet. As in Wilton construction, the wire height determines the pile height. Again, the wires may or may not have knives on their ends (use of the term tapestry to distinguish loop pile velvet carpet has been discontinued). Unlike Wilton weaving, however, no Jacquard attachment is used, so intricate details and elaborate patterns are not possible. Appearance variations may be created by combining cut and loop textures, by incorporating different colors of pile yarns in bands of various widths, or by employing pile yarns with distinctive color styling.

The cross sections in Figure 26.8 show two structural forms of velvet carpet. In Figure 26.8a, the pile yarns are anchored by the upper filling shots only. In Figure 26.8b, they are held by both the upper and lower filling shots: the carpet constructed this way would be described as a "woven-through-the-back" velvet. If other construction variables are the same, a woven-through-the-back velvet is more serviceable because the pile tufts are more securely bound and the total weight is greater. The carpet back in either type of velvet weave may be coated with latex or a thermoplastic compound for greater stability.

The pitch of velvet carpet ranges from 165 to 270. The number of wires per inch ranges from a low of seven to a high of ten.

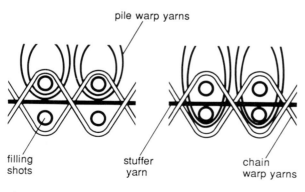

Figure 26.8 Cross-sectional sketches of velvet carpets.

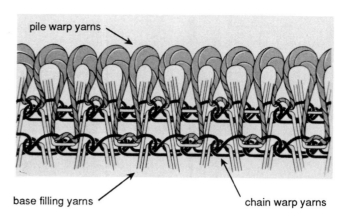

Figure 26.9 A woven interlock carpet. (Courtesy of Mohawk Carpet.)

Woven Interlock Carpet

The woven interlocking process is similar to other carpet weaving operations in that the pile and backing layers are formed simultaneously. It is distinctive in that the chain warp yarns in interlock carpet are interlooped, not interlaced, around the base filling yarns (Figure 26.9). Moreover, whereas conventional warp knitting operations use only warp yarns, woven interlocking combines base warp and base filling yarns. Because of these features, carpet manufactured by this technique is increasingly known as "woven interlock" carpet, rather than as knitted carpet.

Woven interlocking is faster than weaving but slower than tufting. When interlocking and tufting were both being increasingly adopted for carpet production in the early 1950s, more manufacturers devoted attention to the faster, simpler technique of tufting, a tendency still prevalent today.

Loomed Carpet

Loomed carpet is a relatively simple structure. It is produced with the over-the-wire construction technique, using wires of 0.15 inch in height. Because loomed carpet has no chain warp yarns and no stuffer yarns, it is more similar to grospoint upholstery fabric than to other woven floor coverings. The construction density is high, but most of the weight and resiliency come from the sponge rubber cushioning material attached to the back. The use of this kind of carpet has diminished in favor of more attractive and serviceable floor coverings produced by newer techniques.

Chenille Carpet Production

Two completely separate weaving operations are required to manufacture chenille carpet. The producer must first manufacture chenille "yarns," using the leno-weaving

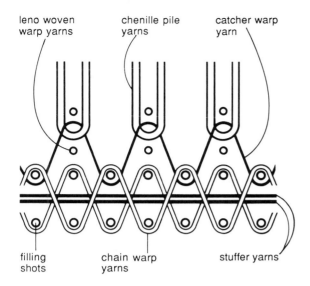

leno woven warp yarns

chenille pile yarns

catcher warp yarn

filling shots

chain warp yarns

stuffer yarns

Figure 26.10 A chenille carpet.

and fabric-cutting processes described in Chapter 5. The chenille strips are folded for use as pile yarns; the leno-entwined warp yarns form a base and the extended filling yarns form a V shape.

Figure 26.10 details the structural components of a chenille carpet. In addition to the stuffer, chain warp, and filling shots normally found in woven pile carpet, chenille carpet also has catcher or binder warp yarns to secure the chenille pile yarns to the base components.

Chenille carpet is comparatively expensive: the production sequence is involved and time-consuming, and an additional yarn component is required. Because of its cost, this construction technique is rarely used today, and not at all by domestic producers.

Pile Construction Density

The number of tufts per square inch in woven floor coverings can easily be calculated by dividing the pitch value by 27. The resulting figure, the number of pile units per crosswise inch, is equivalent to the needle count with tufted constructions. Conversions of several com-

monly used pitch and needle counts are listed in Table 26.1.

After pitch has been converted, the resulting value is multiplied by the number of rows or wires per inch. Direct comparisons can then be made with tufted constructions.

FUSION BONDING OPERATIONS

A significant portion of the recent research efforts of some commercial carpet producers has been channeled to the improvement of fusion bonding operations. Some operations are used for the production of rollgoods, which will be installed wall-to-wall; others are used for the production of carpet, which will subsequently be die-cut into modules.

Basic Components

Fusion bonded structures have a minimum of three components: pile yarns, adhesive, and a primary backing (Figure 26.11). The adhesive, which is generally a vinyl compound such as polyvinylchloride (PVC), is placed on the face of the backing, which may be woven jute or a

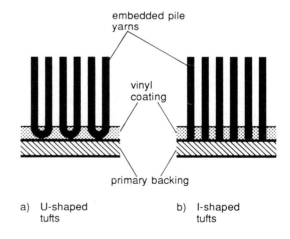

embedded pile yarns

vinyl coating

primary backing

a) U-shaped tufts

b) I-shaped tufts

Figure 26.11 Fusion bonded floor coverings.

Table 26.1 Pitch and Needle Count Conversions

pitch	108	143.9	172.8	180	189	216	243	252	256	270	346
needles	4	5.3	6.4	6.6	7	8	9	9.3	9.5	10	12.8
gauge	1/4	3/16	5/32		9/64	1/8	1/9			1/10	5/64

Note: Unless gauge conversions are whole number fractions, they are omitted.
Courtesy of Fibers Division, Monsanto Chemical Co.

nonwoven glass fiber fabric. The pile yarns are embedded or implanted into the vinyl; they are not woven or tufted through the primary backing.

Fusion bonded carpet has approximately 5 to 8 percent of the total pile yarn weight embedded in the adhesive; tufted structures may have 15 to 30 percent of the pile yarn weight enclosed in the primary backing; and woven constructions may have 20 to 50 percent of the total pile yarn weight interlaced in the backing layers. Thus, fusion bonded carpet and modules can have more of the yarn available to the wearing face. Together with denser gauge fusing capabilities, this feature helps producers to engineer fusion bonded floor coverings, even those having fine velour textures, to withstand the high levels of traffic encountered in commercial installations. The processing is slower than tufting, however, and the vinyl compound is more expensive than tufting substrates.

Multifold Implantation

Fusion bonded floor coverings having U-shaped tufts (Figure 26.11a) are produced in a vertical or a horizontal operation. Because the pile yarns are continually folded as they are fed into the vinyl, these processes are known as "multifold implantation" operations.

Vertical Fusion Bonding. In vertical fusion bonding operations (Figure 26.12) two separate primary backing fabrics are coated with vinyl as they enter the bonding apparatus. They are then brought to a parallel, vertical position, approximately 0.50 inch apart. Yarn creels mounted above the unit supply pile yarns, which are folded and fed between the coated fabrics, becoming embedded in the coatings. As the structure continues downward, it passes through a chamber that is heated by infrared lamps to cure and set the vinyl. Below this chamber, a reciprocating knife blade slices through the folded yarn, producing two identical lengths of cut pile carpet. In order to produce a uniform pile height and sharp definition of surface patterns, the carpet is sheared prior to final inspection.

Horizontal Fusion Bonding. Horizontal fusion bonding is a two stage operation, as shown in Figure 26.13. In stage 1, folded pile yarn is embedded into PVC that is flowing onto the back of a glass fiber mesh fabric. After heat-curing, the carpet is ready for the second stage: in this, the tops of the pile loops of the carpet are embedded into PVC on a second primary backing. Heat is again used to cure and set the vinyl and a knife blade slices through the pile, producing identical lengths of level cut pile carpet.

For added weight and stability, woven secondary backings are generally added to fusion bonded rollgoods intended for wall-to-wall applications, whether produced vertically or horizontally. Heavy gauge vinyl and glass fiber

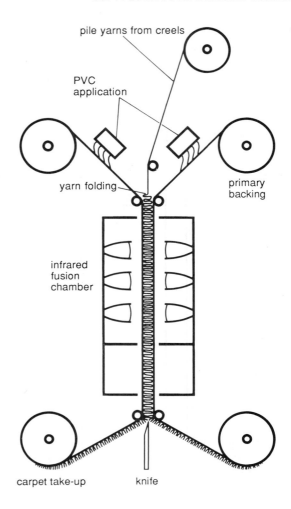

Figure 26.12 A vertical multifold implantation fusion bonding process.

scrims are often used with goods to be cut into modules (see Figure 31.5, page 335).

Single End Implantation

Fusion bonded floor coverings whose cut pile yarns are embedded in vinyl at one end are said to have I-shaped tufts (Figure 26.11b). They are manufactured in a single end implantation process (Figure 26.14). In the first stage of this operation, precisely cut lengths of pile yarn are embedded into the vinyl compound. Here the compound is applied to the face of the glass fiber fabric, rather than to the back. The tips of the heat-cured carpet are then embedded into PVC that coats a second fabric. As in other fusion bonding operations, a knife cuts through the pile and identical lengths of cut pile carpet are rolled on cylinders.

A special use of fusion bonding is the production of entrance mats made of coir fibers. Figure 26.15 provides a close-up view of the implantation of the ends of the fibers in PVC. The superior stiffness of these fibers helps them

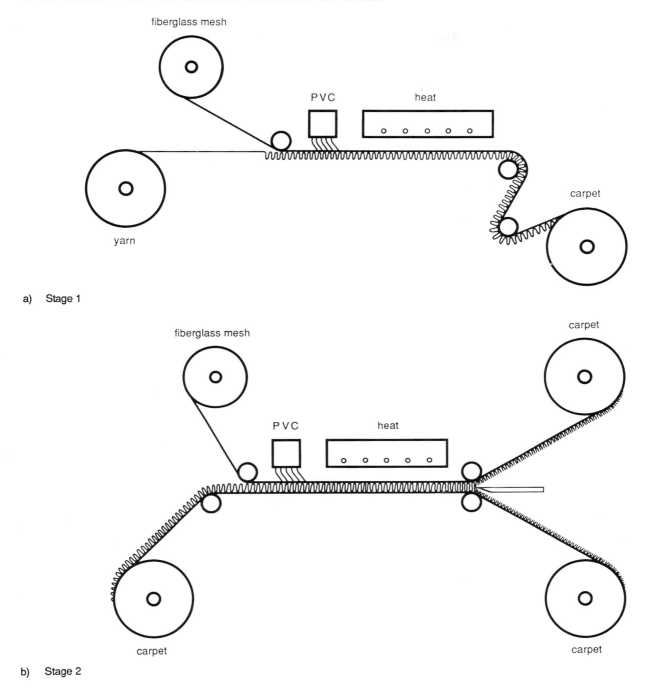

a) Stage 1

b) Stage 2

Figure 26.13 A horizontal multifold implantation fusion bonding process. (Courtesy of Interface Flooring Systems, Inc.)

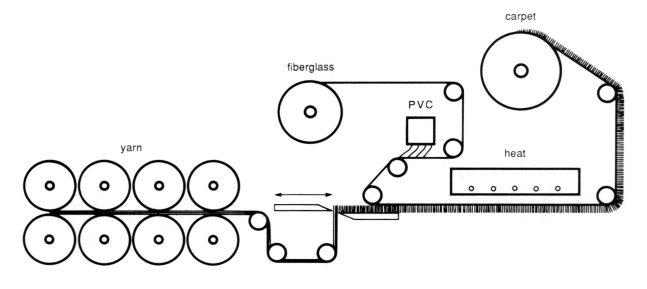

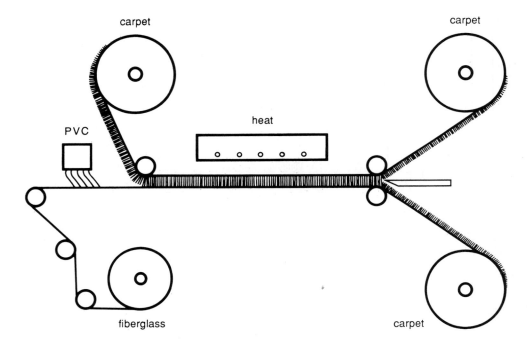

Figure 26.14 A horizontal single end implantation fusion bonding process. (Courtesy of Interface Flooring Systems, Inc.)

Figure 26.15 Close-up view of coir fibers implanted into a liquid plastisol (PVC) layer and then heat fused to form an entrance mat material. (Courtesy of USCOA International Corporation.)

function like hundreds of miniature brushes, efficiently cleaning shoe soles and protecting the interior carpet from excessive amounts of tracked-in dirt. Coir mats generally range in total thickness from 0.68 to 1.2 inches. Some producers offer coir rollgoods and carpet modules, as well as mats.

OTHER MACHINE OPERATIONS

Machine operations other than tufting and fusion bonding are also used to produce soft floor coverings. These include braiding, flocking, and needlepunching.

Braiding

Braided rugs are constructed of braided components; the rugs themselves are not braided. The braids in the rug in Figure 26.16a were formed by interlacing three groups of plied simple yarns; the braids in the rug in Figure 26.16b were formed by interlacing three chenille yarns. In both rugs, core yarns composed of waste fibers were incorporated for weight, body, and cushioning. It is also possi-

ble to enclose yarn-like strands of sponge rubber for these purposes.

Braided strands are assembled side by side in a round or oval shape; machine zigzag stitching links adjacent braids. In a few rugs, flat braids are handled as conventional yarns and interlaced in a plain-weave pattern.

Flocking

Fibers with relatively high denier counts, ranging from 30 to 60, are used for flocked floor coverings. The fibers must be straight and nontextured so that they may be embedded in the adhesive coating in very large quantities. In preparation for the flocking operation, the fibers are cut into uniform lengths, ranging from 0.08 to 0.25 inch, and placed in a charged hopper. As shown in Figure 13.3 (page 134), the flock is drawn into the adhesive coating on a substrate as it passes over a grounded plate. Often, the substrate is heavy-gauge vinyl sheeting.

Because electrostatic flocking draws the fibers vertically into the adhesive, the quantity of fibers per square inch can be greater than that in mechanical flocking. This high density provides better abrasion resistance and durability, per-

a) braids of simple plied yarns

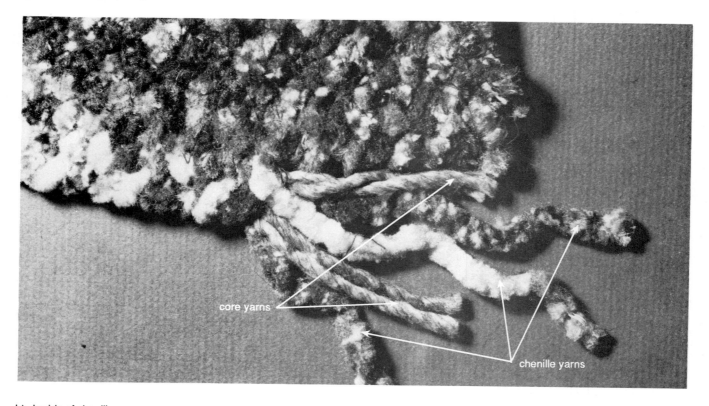

b) braids of chenille yarns

Figure 26.16 Braided rugs.

formance features that are especially important when the structures are to be used as walk-off mats and automotive floor coverings. The accelerated laboratory tests used to assess the abrasion resistance of floor coverings are detailed in Chapter 30.

Needlepunching

Needlepunched floor coverings are often referred to as indoor-outdoor carpet. These structures are manufactured in the following sequence. Various colors of 3- to 4-inch-long fibers are blended to achieve uniform distribution of the colors. Long webs, as wide as the needle loom and weighing approximately 0.5 to 1.0 ounce per square yard, are formed by laying the fibers flat. A thick batt of the desired weight, which typically ranges from 16 to 32 ounces per square yard, is formed by layering the webs at 45- or 90-degree angles to one another. For strength and dimensional stability, an adhesive-coated jute or nylon scrim may be centered in the batt or placed behind it. The batt is then tacked or prepunched to reduce its thickness and fed into a needle loom (Figure 26.17). Here, hundreds of barbed needles punch into the batt some 800 to 1,200 times per square inch, creating a mechanical chain-stitch

Figure 26.17 Needle board on a needle loom. (Courtesy of Fibers Division, Monsanto Chemical Co.)

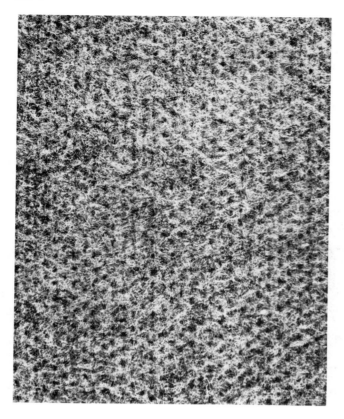

a) nonpile texture

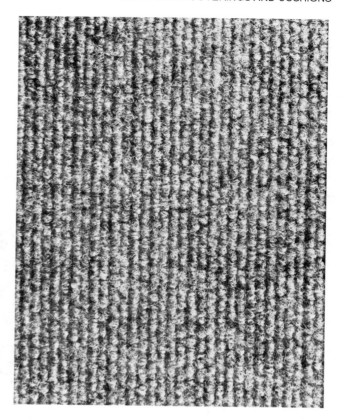

b) simulated loop pile textures

Figure 26.18 Needlepunched floor coverings.

among the fibers and locking them into the scrim and adhesive.

The barbed needles used in the punching operation produce flat carpet with a felt-like appearance (Figure 26.18a). Carpet having loop-like protrusions (Figure 26.18b) can be produced by using needles with crescent-shaped points for the final punches.

When needlepunched structures are to be installed outdoors, on patios and golf greens and around pools, their composition is chosen to withstand the ravages of sunlight, rain, and insects. They are permeable, so they can be hosed to flush away dirt. If these structures are installed wall-to-wall indoors, their permeability presents obvious problems when liquids are spilled on them.

SUMMARY

Machine techniques other than tufting used to produce soft floor coverings include weaving, fusion bonding, braiding, flocking, and needlepunching. Axminster, Wilton, and chenille weaving operations are relatively slow and expensive, but Axminster and Wilton weaving can produce patterns of intricate detail and many colors. Fusion bonding is increasingly used to produce rollgoods and carpet modules with fine, velour surface textures.

chapter *27*

Construction of Floor Coverings: Hand Techniques

- Hand-woven Pile Rugs
- Hand-constructed Nonpile Rugs

Hand operations produce rugs, not rollgoods. Some of these operations are carried out by highly organized, commercial organizations. In such cases, the quality of the products is carefully controlled and the marketing strategies that promote them are sophisticated. This is typical of the production and promotion of authentic Oriental rugs and rugs woven by Native Americans.

The distinctive styling of many hand-constructed rugs leads many people to use them as ornamental wall accents, perhaps as often as they use them as floor coverings. Whether placed on the floor or on the wall, most of these rugs are produced by weaving, but some are constructed in braiding, hooking, and felting operations. Hand weaving and hand knotting are generally combined to produce pile structures, and plain- or tapestry-interlacing patterns are used to produce many nonpile structures.

HAND-WOVEN PILE RUGS

Two types of hand-woven rugs, Oriental rugs and rya rugs, contain hand-knotted pile yarns. Another type, the Flokati rug, has a hand-pulled pile layer.

Oriental Rugs

Intricate motifs and many colors are found in the pile layers of Oriental rugs. Typical are geometric shapes, styl-ized dragons, rosettes, medallions, trees, flowers, vines, and many styles of borders. Historically, weavers executed only their own ancestral designs or those first produced in their geographic regions; the designs reflected the cultural heritage and life of the weavers. The origin of these rugs could be identified by their pattern, and they were known by such names as Persian, Turkoman, Chinese, Caucasian, and Indian. Today, most of the traditional patterns have been adapted by weavers throughout the world, and it is no longer possible accurately to identify the origin of a rug by its design.

Savonnerie rugs, which were first produced in France, present an example of pattern dispersion. The name derives from *savon*, French for "soap," because these rugs were first woven in a factory that had been earlier used for the production of soap. Today, the classic designs and soft pastel colors characteristic of these rugs, and of the fine, loop pile French Aubusson rugs, have been liberally copied by rug weavers in other countries. A Savonnerie rug woven in India is pictured in Figure 27.1. The design of Aubusson and Savonnerie rugs is often emphasized by hand carving.

The distinguishing feature of all authentic Oriental rugs is that each pile tuft is hand knotted. The Sehna (Senna) or Persian knot (Figure 27.2a) or the Ghiordes or Turkish knot (Figure 27.2b) is used. The Sehna knot can be tied to slant to the left or right, but must be tied the same way throughout a project. The Sehna knot com-pletely encircles one warp yarn and passes under the adjacent warp yarn; as a result, one pile tuft projects from every space between the warp yarns. When the Ghiordes knot is tied,

Figure 27.1 Savonnerie rug. (Courtesy of Peerless Imported Rugs.)

the pile yarns in horizontal rows. Normally, one or two filling or weft yarns are used in plain-weave interlacing between each crosswise row of pile knots. Increasing the number of filling yarns decreases the pile construction density.

The quality of Oriental rugs depends on the number of knots per square inch. Whereas the number of warp yarns per inch and the frequency of knot placement determine the crosswise density, the skill of the weavers, the size of the pile yarns, and the number of filling yarns per tuft row determine the lengthwise density. Antique Oriental rugs, those produced prior to the mid-1800s, often had as many as 500 knots per square inch. The famous Ardebil Mosque Carpet, produced in 1539–1540 and now housed in London, England, was woven with some 380 knots per square inch. Old or semiantique rugs, those woven during the latter part of the nineteenth century, and modern rugs, those produced during this century, generally have 100 to 225 knots per square inch, but some have as many as 324 knots per square inch.

Other important quality-related factors are pile height, fiber content, and level of luster. The use of natural dyestuffs for antique Oriental rugs resulted in a subdued, mellow luster. Synthetic dyestuffs developed in the mid-1850s simplified dyeing operations and were adopted by weavers. Because these colorants produce brighter colors than the natural dyestuffs, many of today's Oriental rugs are treated with chlorine or acetic acid and glycerine to simulate the prized sheen and soft luster of the older rugs: this processing is variously described as chemical washing, culturing, and luster washing. This treatment may weaken the fibers, but many producers and consumers consider the beauty of the rug more important than its wear-life.

both ends of the pile yarn extend from the same space; no pile tufts fill the alternate spaces. If other construction features are identical, a Sehna-knotted rug is finer than a Ghiordes-knotted rug, and the pattern is more sharply defined.

During the hand-weaving operation, several weavers may work simultaneously on the same project, knotting

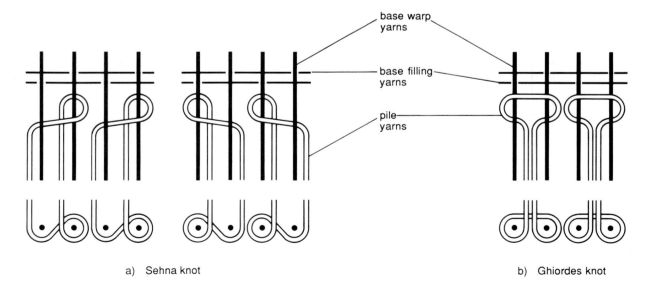

base warp yarns

base filling yarns

pile yarns

a) Sehna knot   b) Ghiordes knot

Figure 27.2 Knots used to form the pile layers in authentic Oriental rugs.

Economic considerations have largely been responsible for the diminished use of silk in Oriental rug pile yarns. Today, most of these rugs have pile yarns composed of wool and base yarns of cotton.

The labor-intensive, tedious, and slow production of hand-knotted Oriental rugs makes them relatively expensive, beyond the reach of many consumers. To lower the cost, manufacturers have increasingly produced rugs with traditional Oriental patterns on power looms, principally on Axminster looms. Machine-woven rugs, known as Oriental design rugs, generally have a sewn-on fringe, which may differ from the base warp yarns; in hand-knotted rugs, the base warp yarns extending from the ends of the rug form the fringe. Recently, computerized printing systems have been employed to increase the availability and affordability of these prized designs.

Rya Rugs

Rya rugs originated in Scandinavian countries where weavers hand knotted long pile yarns. Today, authentic rya rugs are still hand knotted, but machine-made rya rugs are also available; both are prized worldwide for their decorative value. Typically, yarns in related colors form the pile layer, and the designs are gently flowing and curved (Figure 27.3).

In rya rug construction, the pile yarns are knotted with the Ghiordes knot (Figure 27.2b) as in Oriental rugs. Rya rugs differ from Oriental rugs, however, in two principal ways. First, the pile height in rya rugs is considerably longer, ranging from 1 to 3 inches. As the pile height increases, the spacing between the pile rows can also increase, since the longer pile yarns will readily cover the base fabric. Second, more filling or weft yarns are used between each crosswise row of knotted pile yarns in rya constructions. These are interlaced with the base warp yarns in a plain- or tapestry-weave pattern. (The tapestry weave is a plain weave in which the filling yarns are crammed; see Chapter 35.)

So that the pile loops will be uniform in height, the yarn is continuously looped over a rya or flossa stick. The depth of the stick determines the pile height in the same way the wire height determines the pile height in Wilton and velvet carpet constructions. The stick is grooved to facilitate cutting the loops after a row has been knotted on it.

Pile yarns in authentic rya rugs are normally composed of wool. Along with the large amount of yarn used, the relatively high cost of the fiber makes the rugs comparatively expensive.

Flokati Rugs

Flokati (Flocati) rugs (Figure 27.4) are long pile wool structures woven in Greece. The pile yarn length is con-

Figure 27.3 Rya rug with long pile yarns in related colors. (Courtesy of Peerless Imported Rugs.)

trolled by the weaver who pulls a wooden rod inserted under the yarns. The loops are then cut by hand. After weaving, every authentic Flokati rug is immersed in a deep vat in a pool beyond a natural waterfall. Here, the swirling water causes the wool fibers to felt, converting the yarns into pointed strands. Like authentic rya rugs, these rugs use large amounts of wool and labor-intensive processing, making them comparatively expensive.

HAND-CONSTRUCTED NONPILE RUGS

Most hand-constructed nonpile rugs are woven in a plain or tapestry-based interlacing pattern. The motifs of these floor coverings, like those of Oriental rugs, often reflect the cultural heritage of the weavers.

Khilim Rugs

Khilim (Kelim, Kilim) rugs are woven in eastern European countries. These colorful floor coverings have graceful, stylized designs depicting flowers, animals, and other natural things (Figure 27.5).

The construction of Khilim rugs is similar to tapestry weaving: the filling yarns are woven in sections according to color. Unlike those in tapestry structures, however, the ends of all filling yarns in Khilim rugs are woven in, so the structure is reversible. In some cases, the weaving may produce slits or openings where the colors change in the design motif. These openings are finished and will not

Figure 27.4 Flokati rug, hand woven in Greece of long pile wool yarns. (Courtesy of The Wool Bureau, Inc.)

ravel (Figure 27.6). The slits may be retained as part of the design or they may be sewn together by hand.

Rugs Woven by Native Americans

Rugs produced by Native Americans, primarily the Navajo, Cheyenne, and Hopi peoples, are hand woven with a tapestry-related interlacing. Because the end of each filling yarn is woven in at the juncture of color changes, these rugs, like Khilims, are reversible. In contrast to the Khilim rug technique, however, the filling yarns are woven to avoid slits, with a dovetailing or interlocking technique (see Figure 35.3, page 386).

The designs used in these rugs are bold graphic symbols (Figure 27.7) or detailed patterns representing tribal life and culture. They are frequently adapted by weavers throughout the world. Today, these rugs are often chosen to act as wall accents.

According to the rules and regulations issued by the FTC pursuant to the Textile Fiber Products Identification Act, all hand-woven rugs made by Navajo Indians that car-

ry the "Certificate of Genuineness" supplied by the Indian Arts and Crafts Board of the United States Department of Interior are exempt from the provisions of the TFPIA. Here, the term "Navajo Indian" means any Indian listed on the register of the Navajo Indian tribe or eligible for listing thereon.

Dhurrie Rugs

Dhurrie (durrie, durry) rugs are nonpile, hand-woven rugs made in India. They have a plain, twill, or tapestry interlacing. These rugs may display crosswise striations, produced by interspersing various colors of heavy, hand-spun cotton filling yarns, or stylized designs executed with wool filling yarns (Figure 27.8).

Floor Mats

Floor mats composed of various grasses, coir, sisal, linen, hemp, or jute fibers are available in an extensive variety of sizes, shapes, and interlacings. Frequently, twill

Figure 27.5 Khilim rug. (Courtesy of Peerless Imported Rugs.)

Figure 27.7 Area rug with strong graphic designs characteristic of Cheyenne hand-woven rugs. (Courtesy of Peerless Imported Rugs.)

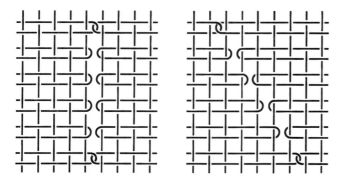

Figure 27.6 Slits found in Khilim rugs.

interlacing is used to create diamond, herringbone, and other geometric patterns over the surface. For larger floor coverings, several small mats can be sewn together.

Other Rugs and Mats

Rag rugs are hand woven in plain-weave interlacing. The filling component is formed by rolling and twisting new or previously used fabric into yarn-like structures. Other small rugs and mats are produced by braiding and felting operations. Some felted rugs are embellished with surface embroidery.

SUMMARY

Among the pile floor coverings produced by hand techniques are Oriental rugs, rya rugs, and Flokati rugs. Khilim, Navajo, and dhurrie rugs are examples of hand-woven, nonpile rugs. While Flokati and rya rugs are distinguished by the use of relatively long pile yarns, other hand-constructed rugs are generally distinguished by traditional motifs and colorations. Color styling is important to selection of these as well as machine-constructed floor coverings. The coloring of floor coverings is discussed in the following chapter.

Figure 27.8 Dhurrie rug. (Courtesy of Peerless Imported Rugs.)

chapter 28

Coloring Soft Floor Coverings

- Methods for Coloring Carpet and Rug Fibers
- Techniques Used to Color Carpet and Rug Yarns
- Dyeing and Printing Rollgoods and Rugs

When carpet and rugs are removed from the tufting machine, the loom, or the fusion-bonding apparatus, they are greige goods. Unless the fibers or yarns used were already colored, the goods may bear little resemblance to the colorful array of soft floor coverings displayed in showrooms and retail stores. The application of contemporary colors in fashionable styles helps assure that the finished goods will please residential and commercial consumers.

Carpet and rug fibers, yarns, and greige goods can be colored by the same basic techniques used with other textiles: dyeing, printing, or a combination of both. However, different equipment and procedures are often required for handling these heavier, wider, and bulkier structures, and larger amounts of dyestuff and water are needed to produce an acceptable level of color intensity. In recent years, increased energy costs and heightened concern for water conservation have led to the development of new and innovative techniques for dye application.

METHODS FOR COLORING CARPET AND RUG FIBERS

Two methods are used for coloring carpet and rug fibers before they are spun or thrown into yarns, or before they

are directly converted into greige goods. These methods include solution dyeing and fiber or stock dyeing.

Solution Dyeing

Solution dyeing, explained in detail in Chapter 8, is often used to color fibers that will be used in carpet produced for installation outdoors. Because such fibers must have little or no capacity to absorb moisture, they cannot absorb sufficient quantities of aqueous dye liquor. The relatively high cost of the pigments that they require may be weighed against the superior color retention achieved through solution dyeing. BASF Corporation has reported, for example, that its Zeftron® 500 solution-dyed nylon for commercial carpet retains it lightfastness after 500 hours of exposure in laboratory testing. Monsanto Chemical Company has reported that its solution-dyed acrylic fiber produced for use in outdoor surface coverings exhibited virtually no color change after 1,000 hours of exposure in the laboratory. Less stable colorants frequently exhibit color change after 60 or 80 hours of exposure.

Fiber or Stock Dyeing

Fiber dyeing, also explained in Chapter 8, is frequently used on man-made staple fibers to produce carpet yarns that simulate the soft, mellow patina of wool. The wool-like appearance is further enhanced when the colored fibers are spun on the woolen system.

TECHNIQUES USED TO COLOR CARPET AND RUG YARNS

Conventional techniques can be used to produce single-color carpet and rug yarns. A variety of space-dyeing operations and a warp-printing technique produce multicolored yarns.

Producing Single-colored Yarns

Package dyeing, skein dyeing, and beam dyeing produce a single, uniform color along the lengths of carpet and rug yarns. These yarns cannot be distinguished from those constructed of fibers of one color.

Package Dyeing. Except in one respect, the package-dyeing operation used for carpet and rug yarns is the same as that discussed in Chapter 8 and illustrated in Figure 8.3 (page 71). Because carpet and rug yarns have relatively large diameters, smaller amounts of the strands are wound on the packages.

Skein Dyeing. Skein dyeing of pile yarns is pictured in Figure 28.1. This method is efficient for dyeing smaller amounts of yarn, such as those required for custom-designed floor coverings; it is not efficient for coloring large quantities of yarns.

Beam Dyeing. Beam dyeing can be used to dye either yarns or greige goods. An apparatus used to beam dye yarns is shown in Figure 8.4 (page 72) and a machine used to beam dye rollgoods is shown in Figure 28.5.

Creating Variegated Pile Yarns

Variegated yarns have differently colored segments along their lengths. The segments may be equal or unequal in length; the junctures between colors may be sharp or muted. Several operations can create these unique color styles. One involves printing the yarns; others are dyeing techniques collectively known as space-dyeing operations.

Figure 28.1 Skein dyeing carpet pile yarns. (Courtesy of Fibers Division, Monsanto Chemical Co.)

Space-dyeing Operations. Yarn texturing and color application are combined in knit-de-knit space dyeing. Pile yarns, undyed or precolored, are rapidly knitted into a long, jersey-stitched tube (Figure 5.2c, page 35). One or more colors are then printed onto the tubing with dye jets before heat setting. Finally, the tube is de-knit or unraveled, producing variegated, crinkled pile yarns (Figure 28.2a). A carpet with a pile layer of these randomly colored yarns is pictured in Figure 28.2b.

to a sheet of yarns. The segments will have sharp color divisions, and the length of each color is easily controlled.

DYEING AND PRINTING ROLLGOODS AND RUGS

Dyeing operations used with rollgoods and rugs once could produce only solid-colored surfaces, and printing techniques only patterned surfaces. Advances in dye chem-

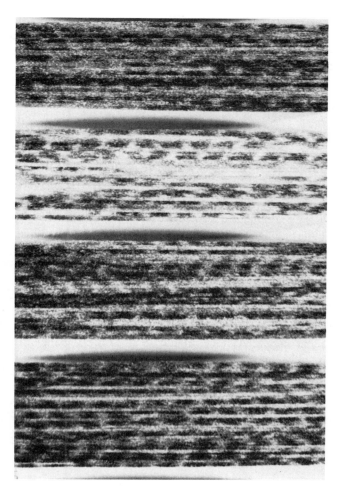

a) knit-de-knit space-dyed pile yarns

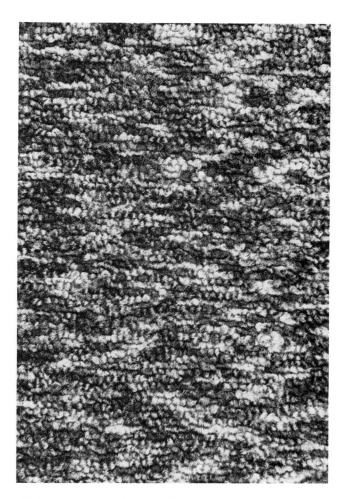

b) level loop space-dyed carpet

Figure 28.2 Knit-de-knit space-dyed yarns and carpet. (Courtesy of Fred Whitaker Company.)

Jet spraying also is used in skein space dyeing: in this operation, pressurized dye jets spray dye liquor onto skeins of pile yarns. A third space-dyeing method used dye-loaded needles, called astrojets, to give packages of yarn repeated, programmed "injections." This package-injection technique requires minimal handling of the yarns.

Warp Printing. In warp printing, engraved rollers, flat-bed screens, or rotary screens are used to apply color

istry and technology now enable colorists to use immersion processes for the production of multicolored designs and printing techniques for the production of solid-colored surfaces.

In dyeing operations involving the immersion or circulation of tufted greige goods in dye liquor, the primary backing may be thinly coated with an adhesive to stabilize the pile tufts. A secondary backing is not applied. Any secondary backing would add bulk and weight, making handling of the long lengths more difficult. A secondary backing of jute would absorb a large amount of dye liquor, increasing the cost of the dyestuffs, as well as the time and expense of drying the floor covering. However, prior to printing greige goods, a secondary backing is normally applied to add dimensional stability and ensure good registration of the colors in the motifs.

Producing Solid-colored Surfaces

Greige rollgoods and rugs may be dyed in a discontinuous or a continuous dyeing operation. Discontinuous operations are so named because the coloring process is interrupted when the wet carpet must be removed from the dyeing machine and dried elsewhere.

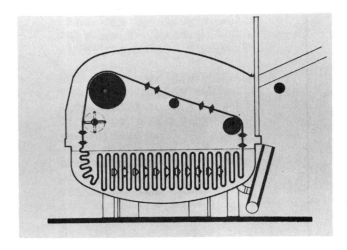

Figure 28.3 The interior of the Supraflor® carpet winch. (Courtesy of Bruckner Machinery Corporation.)

Discontinuous Dyeing. Because relatively small quantities or batches of carpet can be dyed in discontinuous-dyeing operations, they are often known as batch-dyeing operations. They are carried out in various vessels or becks, including a carpet winch, a jet beck, and a horizontal beam-dyeing machine.

In preparation for dyeing in a carpet winch (Figure 28.3), the ends of a batch of greige goods weighing approximately 2,000 pounds are sewn together and loaded into the beck. This weight roughly corresponds to 327 linear yards of goods. The full width of carpet is plaited or folded as it is fed into the dye liquor. If the plaiting operation is controlled so that it will produce folds from 8 to 16 inches deep and never creases the carpet in the same place twice, the development of crosswise surface markings will be minimized; avoiding these markings is especially important for velour and plush textures. The carpet is cycled through the dye liquor, which is continually filtered, for an average of 2 to 4 hours, and it is then rinsed, unloaded, and dried.

In preparation for dyeing in a jet beck, a batch of carpet in rope form is loaded into a long vessel (Figure 28.4). The unit is nearly 40 feet long, and can accommodate some 2,800 pounds of goods. Jets introduce the dye, and the carpet is cycled through the liquor. For effective dyeing of polyester, temperature and pressure can be elevated.

Beam-dyeing operations begin with the winding of an open width of greige goods on a perforated beam. The beam can accommodate approximately 218 linear feet of carpet that has a total thickness of 0.32 inch and a maximum width of 17.5 feet. The batch is loaded into a horizontal dyeing machine (Figure 28.5) and the dye liquor is forcibly circulated through the rolled goods.

Because the carpet is rolled in beam dyeing, soft, deep pile textures would be severely deformed. This technique is therefore generally restricted to the dyeing of low pile, loop textures. A distinct advantage of the operation is that

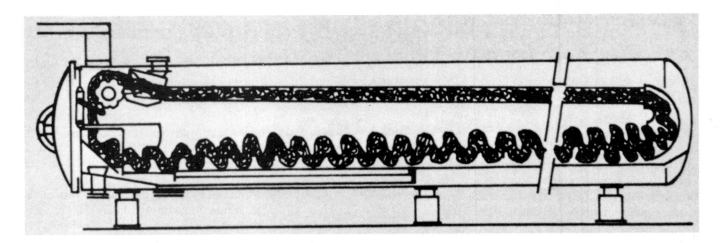

Figure 28.4 The interior of the MCS high temperature jet beck. (Courtesy of Keiltex Corporation.)

Figure 28.5 Supraflex® carpet beam-dyeing machine. (Courtesy of Bruckner Machinery Corporation.)

no crossmarks can develop because no folding is involved. When required, higher temperatures can also be used.

Two factors support the increased use of batch-dyeing operations. First, an increase in consumer demand for specialized colorations requires the use of equipment that can economically dye smaller amounts of greige goods. Second, the challenge of reducing the consumption of water and energy can be more effectively met with batch-dyeing operations than with continuous-dyeing methods. Specifically, the becks are designed to use comparatively low liquor ratios (pounds of liquor to pounds of carpet). Since water is the principal component in most dye liquors, this results in substantial savings in water cost and drying expenses.

Continuous Dyeing. Continuous-dyeing operations are used when large quantities of greige goods are to be dyed one color. Because several lengths of undyed carpet are generally sewn together, their construction and composition must be identical or quite similar if uniform color characteristics are to be reproduced. The dyeing systems,

known as ranges, comprise units for wetting the carpet pile, applying the dyestuff, steaming, washing, drying, and rolling up the dyed and dried rollgoods. These units are aligned so the carpet goes directly from one step to the next. Such operations do not require unloading of the dyed carpet and transporting it to other units for final processing, so they are said to be continuous.

As carpet is introduced into a continuous-dyeing range, it is wetted to increase dye absorption. In some systems, a squeegee-like blade transfers the dye liquor from a roller to the wet carpet surface. Steaming helps increase the movement or migration of the liquor through the pile layer, promoting uniform application of the dye and avoiding the problem of "tippiness," the concentration of color on the tips of the pile yarns. As the carpet continues through the system, it is washed, dried, and rolled.

Formerly, continuous-dyeing operations required comparatively high liquor ratios. In recent years, these ratios have been reduced by applying the dye in forms that are not highly aqueous solutions. In some cases, the dye is applied as a spray, that is, a mixture of air and dye; in other cases, the dye is carried on the surface of bubbles. One method involves depositing dye on the carpet as foamed dye liquor. The foam is an unstable froth, like the foam on beer, that collapses on the fiber and dyes it.

The spray, bubbles, or foam can be delivered through tubes, jets, or spray nozzles oriented toward the pile layer. They may also be delivered by blades and rollers, blowers, and rotary screens. In any case, the tremendous reduction in water usage in these new dye application methods has resulted in marked savings in processing costs.

Producing Multicolored Surfaces

Formerly, only mechanical techniques were used to produce multicolored floor covering surfaces, generally to print them with sharply defined motifs and pattern repeats. Today, mechanical operations have been refined also to produce randomized colorations, and some unusual color styles are being created through chemical techniques.

Cross Dyeing. The chemically dependent technique of cross dyeing was explained in Chapter 8. Carpet and rug producers generally use a blend of nylon variants, rather than generically dissimilar fibers, in this coloring operation.

Gum Printing. In gum printing, a gum compound known to resist dye absorption is applied to the tips of the pile yarns prior to dyeing. The gum will prevent dye absorption and migration, causing the upper portion of the pile layer to have a frosted appearance. "Frostiness" describes the absence of dye on the yarn tips. It is a planned color style, unlike "tippiness," the unplanned and unwanted concentration of dye on the yarn tips that occurs when dye migration is not sufficient to produce uniform intensity. Gum printing for frostiness has the drawback of consuming additional utilities in removing the gum.

TAK Printing. TAK (from Textile Austustings, a German carpet firm, and Kusters, the machinery supplier) printing units have been employed to add intense colors to precolored carpet surfaces. Because dye liquor, not dye paste, is used, some authorities refer to this operation as TAK dyeing. But because the application of the dye paste is mechanically controlled, most colorists prefer to label the operation as TAK printing.

In TAK printing, dye is doctored from a revolving roller as a sheet of liquor. As the sheet flows downward, it is cut or interrupted by laterally oscillating chains. The liquor is thus sprinkled or deposited as randomly placed droplets on the moving carpet.

Use of TAK printing units has diminished as consumer preferences for color styling changed and new equipment has been engineered. The Multi-TAK® unit developed by Kusters, for example, is somewhat more versatile than the conventional TAK apparatus. This unit can deposit liquor in simple geometric and wave-like patterns. The doctor blade has a notched or carved edge. During the printing operation, the blade oscillates laterally, and the liquor is removed from the roller only by the extended blade edges. Thus, the liquor flows in waves to the moving carpet. Attachments can be added to interrupt the descending streams and effect planned patterns.

Jet Printing. Jet-printing technologies are among the more recent and innovative developments for coloring soft floor coverings. In most cases, the same dye applicator units used to produce solid-colored surfaces in continuous-dyeing operations, including tubes, nozzles, blowers, and jets, are used in these operations. In jet printing, however, the delivery of the dye is precisely controlled to create detailed designs and pattern repeats. The engineering is so sophisticated in some systems that the intricate color placement and elaborate patterns of authentic Oriental rugs can be replicated.

The Foamcolor® unit developed by Kusters uses a computer to control jets that shoot air at streams of dye foam, deflecting them from their vertical path of descent. The Jet Foam Printer®, marketed by Otting, and the Colorburst® unit, manufactured by Greenwood, use photoelectric cells and solenoid systems to regulate the opening and closing of the valves controlling the flow of spray to print nozzles. The Millitron® system, owned by Milliken Carpets, has hundreds of dye jets directed toward the moving carpet surface. Printing is electronically controlled by a computer that triggers the jets to "shoot" the surface with dye liquor in a programmed sequence.

Some jet-printing systems have applicator components placed only 0.10 inch apart. This helps to ensure full coverage of the surface. To ensure the production of sharp, well-defined designs, greige goods are generally sheared and vacuumed prior to printing. Because no equipment is in contact with the floor covering during printing, the potential problem of pile distortion is avoided.

Along with a high rate of production, the utilization of relatively little water, dye, and energy makes jet printing a comparatively inexpensive operation. The cost advantages of the operation, however, may be offset by the high capital investment required initially to purchase and install the various units.

Screen Printing. Two challenges face colorists who use screen printing on pile floor coverings. First, care must be taken to avoid distortion of the pile yarns when the screens are in the printing mode. Second, the dye paste must be drawn into the pile layer or the colored design will be carried only by the yarn tips.

The Zimmer flat-bed screen printing operation is shown in Figure 28.6. The dye paste is drawn into the pile by an electromagnetic field. A needle belt advances

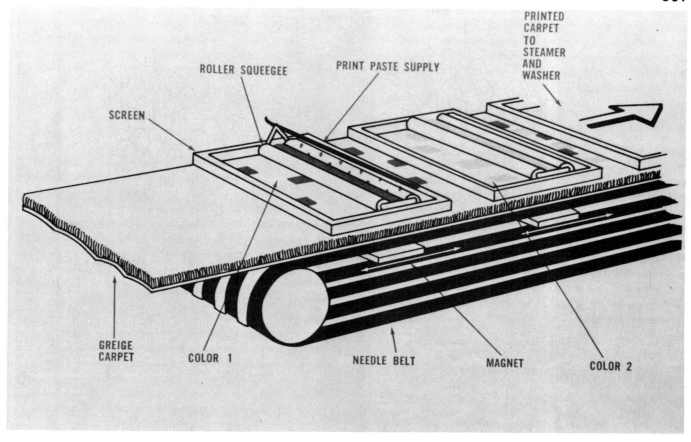

Figure 28.6 The Zimmer flat-bed screen printing machine. (Courtesy of Fibers Division, Monsanto Chemical Co.)

the carpet one pattern repeat at a time. Other flat-bed printing units use a vacuum system to pull the print paste into the pile yarns.

Rotary-screen printing is used infrequently to print soft floor coverings. In most cases, rotary screens have not been designed to supply the large amount of paste required for dyeing heavier pile layers. The recent introduction of a system that uses foam instead of paste, however, may increase the popularity of this high-speed printing technique.

Roller Printing. Because carpet and rugs are comparatively heavy textile structures and their printed pattern repeats are typically large, they cannot be printed with engraved metal-covered rollers. They can, however, be roller printed with large cylinders covered with three-dimensional sponge forms (Figure 28.7). The sponges are cut according to the shapes planned for the designs. All the shapes that are to be one color are positioned on the surface of one cylinder; the shapes to be a second color are placed on a second cylinder, and so on.

This method of roller printing is illustrated schematically in Figure 28.8. As the sponge-covered rollers rotate against the moving greige goods, the dye paste is transferred to the pile yarns. The printed designs have muted,

rather than sharply defined, edges. Use of this printing operation is decreasing as more efficient units, especially jet-printing systems, are put into service.

Color-box Printing. Color-box printing is also called deep dyeing. In preparation for this printing operation, a rectangular box with the dimensions of the planned pattern repeat is partitioned, so that three-dimensional wells that have the shapes of the planned designs are created. Each well is then filled with the appropriate color of dye. The greige goods are mounted face down, and the box is raised so the pile yarns are immersed into the various dye-filled wells. As is true of Stalwart roller printing, color-box printing is being replaced by more efficient printing techniques.

Following virtually every method of color application, the floor coverings are washed, rinsed, and dried. Dyed structures may be tentered, and some may be heat set. A secondary backing will be applied to tufted structures that were dyed. To restore distorted pile yarns to their upright position, the carpet will be passed against an angled blade that lifts the yarns. Cut pile textures may be sheared to create a uniform pile height and vacuumed to remove lint. A final inspection is made prior to shipment.

Figure 28.7 Preparation of the sponge-covered cylinders used in Stalwart printing. (Courtesy of Fibers Division, Monsanto Chemical Co.)

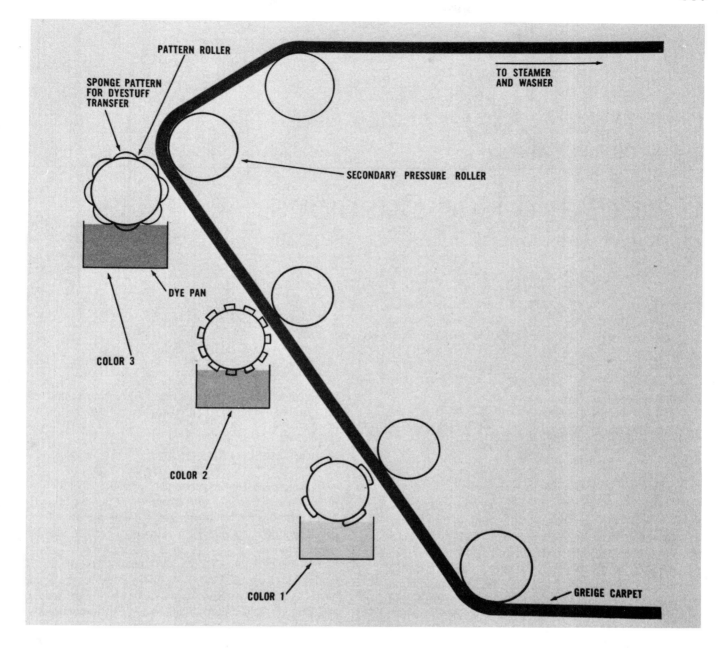

Figure 28.8 The Stalwart roller printing process. (Courtesy of Fibers Division, Monsanto Chemical Co.)

SUMMARY

Textile chemists, colorists, and engineers constantly strive to refine and improve methods of applying color to soft floor coverings. The urgent need to conserve energy and reduce production costs encourages this effort. Moreover, the rapid shifting of consumer style preferences re-quires that colorists be capable of an equally speedy response to remain competitive.

Whatever method of color application is used, the stability of the colorant is an important determinant of the ultimate serviceability of the floor covering. The laboratory tests for evaluating the fastness of colorants used in carpet and rugs are described in Chapter 30.

chapter *29*

Carpet and Rug Cushions

- Fibrous Cushion Structures
- Cellular Rubber Cushions
- Urethane Foam Cushions
- Listing Specification Data for Carpet Cushions
- Evaluating the Performance of Cushions

Many names—cushion, pad, padding, lining, foundation, underlayment—identify the structure placed between a carpet or rug and the floor. Today, members of the industry prefer to use the term cushion or carpet cushion. Carpet cushions vary in chemical composition, thickness, compressibility, resiliency, resistance to moisture and microbes, and cost. They also differ in acoustical value, insulative benefit, and the contributions they make toward extending the wear-life of the soft floor covering. Some cushions can only be used separately; others can be separate or permanently attached to the carpet back. Cushion-related variables should be considered in the light of the carpet or rug selected, the kind of "feel" preferred underfoot, the environmental and traffic conditions anticipated in end use, and the floor covering budget.

Professionals must understand the evaluation of carpet cushions, so that they can interpret the data provided by producers and understand requirements set forth by an authority with jurisdiction over certain installations. Professionals must be able to supply accurate data for custom projects. The information required depends on the type of cushion selected. The cushions available on today's mar-

ket fall into three major categories: fibrous cushions, cellular rubber cushions, and urethane foam cushions.

FIBROUS CUSHION STRUCTURES

Fibrous cushions are produced by needlepunching hair or jute fibers into felt-like structures. Four types of fibrous cushions are on the market: all hair, all jute, blends of hair and jute, and hair or jute fibers or both bonded between of latex.

All-hair structures are normally made of cleaned, stiff cattle hair (Figure 29.1a). Like all-jute cushions, all-hair cushions are relatively inexpensive, but both types tend to shift, bunch, and clump under heavy traffic conditions. For added stability, a loosely woven jute scrim may be centered in the batt prior to needlepunching. Antimicrobial agents are recommended to retard the growth of mildew and fungi and the odor and deterioration they cause. These cushions tend to exhibit aging; they can crumble and disintegrate after prolonged use. Because fibers are subject to moisture damage, the use of latex sheets as protective barriers is recommended when below-grade installation is planned. For skid resistance, as well as to compensate for the somewhat low compressibility and resiliency, the surfaces of the fibrous batts and latex sheets are generally embossed (Figure 29.1b).

Fibrous cushions are available in rolls up to 12 feet wide. Their weights range from 32 to 86 ounces per square yard.

continuous flat sheets or into three-dimensional forms. The three-dimensional cushions are variously referred to as waffle, ripple, or bubble sponge cushions; a typical profile is in Figure 29.2. The flat form is available in uniform thicknesses that range from 0.125 to 0.3125 inch.

a) all hair

b) jute fibers bonded between latex sheets

Figure 29.1 Fibrous cushions. (Photograph *b* is courtesy of Mohawk Carpet.)

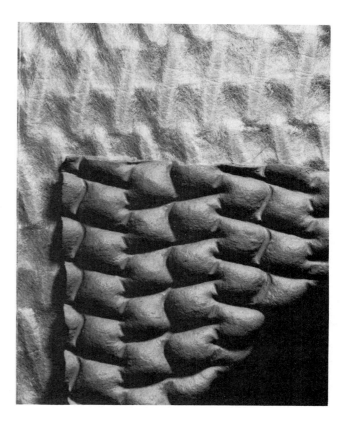

Figure 29.2 Bubble sponge rubber cushion.

CELLULAR RUBBER CUSHIONS

Cellular rubber cushions can be either foam rubber or sponge rubber. Both types can be made from natural or synthesized rubber compounds.

Sponge Rubber Structures

Sponge rubber cushions frequently contain chemicals, oils, and fillers that were added to the rubber compound for weight. The mixture is pulverized and then expanded into

Sponge rubber has larger cells and thicker cell walls than foam rubber; sponge structures are therefore more porous and less likely to retain odors. The cellular qualities also contribute buoyancy and softness, characteristics further enhanced when the cushion is three-dimensional. Sponge cushions are highly compressible and produce the plushness often sought in residential interiors and executive offices. Under heavy commercial traffic, however, the waffle forms do not provide uniform support: repeated deformation and flexing of the carpet backing can produce uneven surfaces. Moreover, the clay or ash fillers may grind against other components and crumbling may occur. Flat sponge rubber cushions can provide more uniform support for carpet used in areas of medium and heavy traffic, and better skid resistance for area rugs.

Sponge rubber cushions are available in rolls up to 12 feet wide. Their weights range from 41 to 120 ounces per square yard.

Foam Rubber Structures

Foam rubber cushions are manufactured by converting liquid latex and fillers into flat, continuous sheets. The sheets may be as thin as 0.125 inch or as thick as 0.625 inch. A spunbonded fabric is normally applied to the top of sponge and foam rubber cushions. The fabric facilitates handling during installation since it permits the carpet back to slide over the fabric without stretching and distorting the cushion. The spunbonded fabric that covers the cushion in Figure 29.3 has been reinforced with a woven scrim.

Figure 29.3 Foam rubber cushion covered with a scrim-reinforced spunbonded fabric.

Because foam rubber has smaller cells than sponge rubber, foam cushions provide firmer, more uniform support, but they may exhibit more odor retention. Foam rubber cushions are available in rolls up to 12 feet wide, and in weights ranging from 28 to 65 ounces per square yard.

In thinner forms, foam rubber cushions can be permanently bonded to the back of carpet structures (Figure 29.4). The assembly can then be laid on the floor without installing a separate cushion; for maximum stability, it can be glued to the floor.

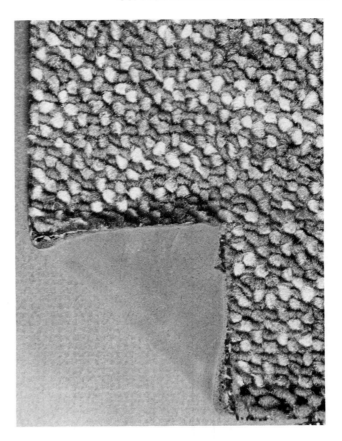

Figure 29.4 Permanently attached foam rubber cushion.

Minimum standards have been established for attached foam cushions in an effort to promote consistent quality. These standards are listed in Table 29.1. In this table, density refers to the amount of rubber per unit of volume; increasing the density would increase the weight of the cushion and the level of support provided. Compression loss, also known as compression set, is the extent to which the structure fails to recover its original thickness after being compressed 50 percent under a static load.

Compression deflection is the extent to which the structure resists compression force. Delamination strength is the force per inch of width required to separate the cushion from the carpet; it is measured as described in Chapter 25, using the test apparatus clamps shown in Figure 25.9 (page 276). Procedures for measuring other properties are discussed later in this chapter.

Several of the recommended specifications for attached foam cushions have been adopted as required standards by a number of federal agencies, including the office of Housing and Urban Development, the General Services Administration, and the Veterans' Administration. These authorities have also set forth additional requirements pertaining to fire performance. The test methods used to evaluate flammability are explained in the following chapter.

Table 29.1 RECOMMENDED MINIMUM SPECIFICATIONS FOR ATTACHED LATEX FOAM CUSHIONS

Weight	38 oz./sq. yd.
Thickness	1/8 in.
Density	17 lb./cu. ft.
Compression loss	maximum of 15% loss
Compression deflection	not less than 5 p.s.i.
Delamination strength	2 lb./in.
Accelerated aging	(a) heat aging: 24 hrs at 275 °F; after flexing, should remain flexible and serviceable. (b) Fade-Ometer aging: 20 hrs. exposure; sample should show only slight crazing.
Ash content	maximum of 50%

Courtesy of the Carpet and Rug Institute.

URETHANE FOAM CUSHIONS

Three types of urethane foam cushions are generally available for residential and commercial use: prime or conventional foam, densified prime foam, and bonded or rebond foam. The chemical composition of these cushions is basically the same, but they are manufactured by different processes, and their cellular structures differ.

Prime Urethane Foam Structures

Prime urethane foam cushions are manufactured by foaming the urethane polymer units into a continuous sheet, generally 6 feet wide. "Prime" distinguishes this kind of cushion from the bonded or rebond type.

Prime urethane foam has comparatively large cells shaped somewhat like ellipses, and the foam struts or columns among the cells are vertically oriented. This cellular form provides various degrees of compressibility, depending on density. Under load, these structures may "bottom out": the cushion suddenly flattens under force. Prime foams may contain powdered fillers for weight and polymer additives for increased stability.

Densified Prime Urethane Foam Structures

Densified foam cushions have a higher density then prime foam. The higher density is produced from a finer, elongated cellular structure and somewhat horizontal struts. No fillers are used. These cushions are said to be odorless, resilient, mildew-resistant, and resistant to bottoming out.

Bonded Urethane Foam Structures

Bonded urethane foam cushions are made by bonding and compressing together granulated pieces of prime urethane trim; the term rebond is sometimes used to identify these cushions. The strength of these structures largely depends on the strength of the prime urethane foam material used in the trim pieces.

All three types of urethane foam cushions are manufactured in several thicknesses, generally ranging from 0.375 to 0.750 inch, and all generally have a spunbonded facing to facilitate installation. In their thinner forms, these cushions can provide skid resistance to area rugs and runners. As do other types of cushions used for this purpose, the thin form minimizes the problem known as "rug walking" or "rug crawling," the tendency for rugs to shift or move off cushions under the stress of traffic.

The density of urethane cushions is usually within the range of 2.4 to 5.0 pounds per cubic foot. Cushions with higher densities have higher compression deflection values: they provide firmer support underfoot.

LISTING SPECIFICATION DATA FOR CARPET CUSHIONS

Specification listings detail the composition, construction, and performance features of a textile structure. Specification data may be prepared by the producer, or by the trained and experienced professional. The data reported by the producer include values obtained from the accelerated laboratory testing of their products. Professionals list the characteristics and properties they or their clients prefer, or those mandated for textile products used in a particular project. For certain installations, the professional must specify test methods and levels of performance to ensure that the structure conforms to standards established by the authority that has jurisdiction.

Specification listings for cushions are less extensive than those prepared for carpet and rugs (see Table 30.1, page 317). The data required will depend on the type of cushion selected, the anticipated traffic conditions, the carpet selected, and any mandated features. The recommended minimum specifications for attached foam cushions are listed in Table 29.1; Table 29.2 exemplifies the various features that may be specified for a densified prime urethane foam cushion.

The first item in Table 29.2 states the composition of the cushion; the second item states that a spunbonded fabric is to be applied to the top side of the structure; the next two items describe structural characteristics; and the remaining items detail performance features and levels. The values used are for illustrative purposes only. Laboratory testing confirms that a cushion exhibits specified characteristics.

Table 29.2 SAMPLE CUSHION SPECIFICATION/DATA LIST

Cushion compound: densified prime, unfilled polyurethane foam; clean and free of defects
Coating: spunbonded polypropylene olefin
Density: 5.0 lb./cu. ft.
Thickness: 0.265 in.
Compressive load deflection:

25% deflection	1.5 p.s.i.	minimum
65% deflection	6.5 p.s.i.	minimum
75% deflection	11.0 p.s.i.	minimum

Compression set: Maximum of 15% at 50% deflection
Tensile strength: 25 p.s.i. minimum
Elongation: 50% minimum
Flammability:　(a) FF 1-70/tablet test: passes
　　　　　　　(b) flooring radiant panel test: greater than 0.25 watt/sq. cm.

EVALUATING THE PERFORMANCE OF CUSHIONS

Some performance features, including compression loss and compression set, are important to all cushion materials. One performance variable, aging, is important only in cellular rubber cushions, and, as noted earlier in this chapter, delamination strength is a concern only with permanently attached cushions.

Accelerated Aging

In prolonged use, rubber cushion compounds may be affected by heat and exhibit aging in the form of cracking, crumbling, and sticking. To assure that the cushion will not show rapid aging, the structure can be evaluated in accelerated laboratory testing. In one procedure, latex cushion material may be exposed for 24 hours to a temperature of 275°F in a circulating air oven prior to evaluation. In a second accelerated procedure, a specimen may be placed in a Fade-Ometer® (Figure 21.4, page 226) for 20 hours in accordance with Federal Test Method Standard 191A, Method 5660. As stated in Table 29.1, foam latex samples should withstand these exposures with no more than slight discoloration or surface degradation. Upon flexing, a slight cracking or crazing is acceptable.

Compressibility

Compressibility evaluations measure the degree of resistance a cushion offers to being crushed or deflected under a static load. The measurements are made by following the procedures outlined in ASTM D 1564 and D 3574. In preparation for evaluating this performance quality, cushion specimens are cut into small squares (often 2 inches

square) and layered to a thickness of 1 inch. The plied structure is then placed on the platform of a testing unit (Figure 29.5). The support platform has perforations to allow for rapid escape of air during the test. A flat, circular foot is used to indent or deflect the layered specimens.

Figure 29.5 Compression deflection testing apparatus. (Courtesy of Custom Scientific Instruments, Inc.)

The force required to deflect or compress the specimen assembly a given percentage of its original thickness is measured for each of two replicate tests. Together with the percentage of deflection used, the average number of pounds per square inch (p.s.i.) required to compress the cushion material is reported to the nearest pound. Several federal agencies have mandated specific levels of compression load deflection (CLD); these vary with the type of cushion and the interior facility.

The compressibility of a cushion correlates with the degree of softness felt underfoot. Cushions having low CLD values are soft and easily compressed; cushions having high values are firmer, less compressible structures. Firmer cushions should be selected for interior floor space subjected to rolling equipment or wheelchairs.

Compression Set

Compression set is synonymous with compression loss. It describes the extent to which a structure fails to recover its original thickness after static compression. In most evaluation procedures, cushion specimens are layered to a thickness of 1 inch and deflected 50 percent. The compressed structure is then placed in an oven at 158°F for 22 hours. At the end of this period, the load is removed and the thickness is measured after a 30-minute recovery period. The compression set is calculated with the following formula: compression set = [(original thickness − thickness after compression)/original thickness] x 100. The average of two replicate tests is reported.

A high recovery of cushion thickness is desirable, and a minimum recovery level of 85 percent (maximum loss of 15 percent) is frequently recommended or mandated. As a cushion recovers from compression, it exerts an upward pressure that encourages the carpet also to recover. The actual level of recovery depends upon the particular combination of carpet and cushion.

Tensile Strength

The tensile strength of cushion structures is measured in the laboratory according to prescribed test methods, such as FTMS 191A, Method 5100. The value reported is the average of five replicate tests and is the force per unit of cross-sectional area necessary to cause rupture. Required minimum tensile strength values may range from 8 to 20 p.s.i.

Elongation

Elongation values describe how far a cushion structure extends before rupturing. The performance is evaluated as part of the procedure for evaluating tensile strength. The value reported is the average of five readings, each calculated by the following formula: % elongation at break = (length stretched/original length) x 100.

Because cushions are always used in combination with a carpet or rug, some performance evaluations are more meaningful when they are made on the floor covering assembly. This is especially true when such functional values as noise reduction and insulation benefits are being considered. In some cases the functional benefits of an assembly will be more strongly influenced by the cushion than by the carpet; in many cases, carpet and cushion both contribute to a functional value. Evaluations of floor covering assemblies are described in the following chapter.

SUMMARY

Most of the cushions available today can be classified in one of three major categories: fibrous felt cushions, cellular rubber cushions, and urethane cushions. Numerous variations exist within each category, in thickness; weight; density; compressibility; resiliency; resistance to moisture, heat, and microbes; and cost. The choice of a cushion involves an assessment of these features, as well as an analysis of the traffic levels and activities anticipated in the interior area to be carpeted. In light traffic areas, a thick, low density structure could be selected for greater buoyancy and softness underfoot. In areas where traffic is heavy, a thin, high density structure should be used. The cost of installing a separate cushion will normally be higher than using an attached cushion or no cushion, but certain performance benefits may partially offset the additional materials and installation charges. In all installations, the quality of the cushion should be consistent with that of the carpet: a high quality cushion cannot compensate for a low quality carpet, and a skimpy cushion cannot support a heavy, high quality carpet or rug.

chapter 30

Evaluations and Specifications for Soft Floor Coverings

• Listing Specification Data for Carpet
• Evaluating Functional Features
• Evaluating Performance Properties

For suppliers, producers, colorists, and converters of textile floor coverings and components, standard test methods and performance specifications are an important part of manufacturing and marketing efforts. Data gathered from this quality-control work help industry members identify the need for changes in the composition, manufacturing, or conversion of their products. The data also provide the basis for claims about performance made in promotional materials, whether targeted at the trade or at the consumer.

Contract designers, architects, commercial specifiers, and retailers must understand the test methods used to measure structural and performance qualities of carpet and cushions and the implications of the reported data. Such an understanding makes it possible for professionals to interpret data supplied by producers and determine the suitability of a carpet or an assembly for relevant traffic and other end use conditions. The informed professional also can prepare specification listings that cover specific features and levels of performance required by end use conditions or a regulatory agency.

LISTING SPECIFICATION DATA FOR CARPET

Because tufting is the dominant floor covering construction technique, the sample specification listing presented in Table 30.1 is written for a tufted structure. Sev-

eral of the items would, however, also be listed for woven and fusion-bonded carpet. Virtually all of the test methods listed in the table and discussed in this chapter apply to all textile floor coverings, regardless of their construction. The specific values listed in the table are for illustrative purposes only.

The first several items listed in Table 30.1 describe the appearance, composition, and construction features of the carpet. The following standard test methods and practices may be used to determine the data reported for these features:

ASTM D 629   Standard Methods for Quantitative Analysis of Textiles

ASTM D 861   Standard Recommended Practice for Use of the Tex System to Designate Linear Density of Fibers, Yarn Intermediates, Yarns, and Other Textile Materials

ASTM D 2260   Standard Tables of Conversion Factors and of Equivalent Yarn Numbers Measured in Various Numbering Systems

ASTM D 1244   Standard Practice for Designation of Yarn Construction

ASTM D 418   Standard Methods of Testing Woven and Tufted Pile Floor Coverings

ASTM D 2646   Standards of Testing Backing Fabrics

Table 30.1 SAMPLE CARPET SPECIFICATION/ DATA LIST

Style: Kamiakin
Surface texture: one level loop
Coloration: jet printed
Face fiber: 99% Super®XYZ nylon; 1% Stat-Redux®
    stainless steel for static control
Face fiber size: 20 dpf
Yarn size: 2.00/2cc (equivalent denier 5315)
Body construction: tufted
    gauge: 1/10
    stitches per inch: 8
    primary backing: 100% woven polypropylene olefin
    secondary backing: 100% woven jute
Pile height: 0.250 in.
Pile yarn weight: 40.0 oz./sq. yd.
Total weight: 65 oz./sq. yd.
Density Factor: 425,200
Average density: 4383
Weight density: 122,713
Structural stability:
    bundle penetration: 80%
    delamination strength: 2.5 lbs./in.
    tuft bind: 6.25 lbs.
Acoustical ratings:
    NRC .45 over 40 oz. hair pad; IIC 73 over 40 oz. hair
        pad (INR +22)
Insulative value: R-2 over concrete slab
Light reflectance factor: 15
Colorfastness
    crocking: 4.0 (AATCC 8)
    gas fade: 4.0 (AATCC 23)
    ozone fade: 3.0 (AATCC 129): 4.0 (AATCC 109)
    shampoo: 4.0 (AATCC 138)
Flammability
    FF 1-70: passes
    tunnel test (ASTM E 84): Class A
    flooring radiant panel test (NBSIR 75-950): CRF
        greater than 0.25 watts/sq. cm.
Static generation: 2,500 static volts at 70°F and 20%
    RH (AATCC 134)
Wear resistance
    floor tread test: 3.0 after 100,000 treads
    pilling: 3.0
    abrasion (Taber): not worn through to backing after
        10,000 cycles

As discussed in Chapter 10, trade names frequently distinguish fibers, especially those engineered to exhibit special properties. When a trade name is used to advertise a carpet, the fiber composition of the pile layer must be disclosed in accordance with the provisions of the Textile Fiber Products Identification Act.

Pile construction density, pile height, weight-related factors, and structural variables are specified to ensure that a floor covering will withstand the traffic conditions in the end use location, and will conform to mandated design standards if these apply. These construction features were reviewed in Chapter 25.

The remaining data in Table 30.1 detail the functional benefits and performance properties of a carpet. Test methods for determining the values reported for these characteristics are frequently identified in specification lists.

EVALUATING FUNCTIONAL FEATURES

Carpet and cushion assemblies may be designed and selected to provide such functional benefits as noise control and insulation. Carpet may also be selected to reduce energy consumption by contributing to the efficient management of interior light and by helping to lower the rate of heat exchange.

Acoustical Ratings

One of the more important functional benefits of floor covering assemblies is their acoustical value, the extent to which they prevent sound from becoming unwanted noise. The noise reduction benefits of carpet installed on walls and panels were discussed in Chapter 22; those of carpet and carpet and cushion assemblies are discussed here.

Sound Absorption. Homes are often filled with many electrical appliances and pieces of entertainment equipment, each one of which generates sound. Contemporary office designs frequently call for large open areas that will permit maximum flexibility in space utilization: such areas can contain numerous people, telephones, typewriters, and printers, all of which, again, generate sound. Commercial structures are often built to serve several firms and many employees and executives; places where people assemble, such as theaters, often house thousands; schools accommodate hundreds of students. In these interiors, sound is created by the constant movement of equipment and people, continual verbal exchange, and the like. Lowering the level of airborne and surface sounds in these environments is highly desirable; in some cases it is mandatory.

Table 30.2 presents the results of controlled testing for the sound absorption of various carpets with and without an all-hair cushion. The results are reported numerically as the noise reduction coefficient (NRC). Higher NRC values indicate greater sound absorption. The values reported in Table 30.2 reveal the effects of various structural features. Cut pile textures are somewhat more efficient in absorbing sound than loop pile textures. Increasing the weight of the pile layer or the height of the pile yarns in cut pile

Table 30.2 SOUND ABSORPTION OF CARPET

Carpet no.*	Backing	Pile wt.	Pile ht.	Surface	Pad	NRC
#1	67 oz. sponge rubber attached	44 oz	.25"	loop	none	.30
#2	coated	44 oz.	.25"	loop	40 oz. hair	.40
#3	uncoated	44 oz.	.25"	loop	40 oz. hair	.60

Backing		Pile wt.	Pile ht.	Surface	Pad	NRC
coated		44 oz.	.25"	loop	40 oz.hair	.40
uncoated		44 oz.	.25"	loop	40 oz.hair	.60
coated		40 oz.	.40"–.20"	loop	40 oz.hair	.65
coated		15 oz.	.25"	loop	40 oz.hair	.65
coated		43 oz.	.25"	loop	40 oz hair	.50
coated		40 oz.	.39"	loop	40 oz. hair	.60
coated		32 oz.	.56"	cut	40 oz. hair	.70
coated		43 oz.	.50"	cut	40 oz. hair	.70

*See carpet fabric key, Table 30.4.
Courtesy of The Carpet and Rug Institute.

structures will increase the sound absorption capabilities. In loop textures, pile height apparently has a greater positive influence than does pile weight. The Carpet and Rug Institute has reported that such structural variations produce similar effects when the carpet is glued directly to the floor. Regardless of the method of installation, the fiber content of the pile yarns has virtually no effect on sound absorption.

From the results listed in Table 30.2, a permeability principle can be established: the more permeable the structure, the more efficiently it will absorb sound. For example, the uncoated carpet having a pile weight of 44 ounces per square yard had an NRC of .60; when a latex coating was added and the permeability was reduced, an NRC value of .40 was recorded.

The same principle holds for cushion materials. As shown in Table 30.3, the more permeable hair and hair-jute cushions were more effective acoustically than the less permeable sponge rubber cushions of similar weight. The less dense, lower weight foam rubber cushion was also more effective than the higher density, higher weight sponge rubber cushion of the same thickness. Further, a comparison of the appropriate values in Tables 30.2 and 30.3 confirms the negative effect of permanently attaching cushions to the back of the carpet. Attaching the cushion reduces the permeability and thus the level of sound absorption.

Within an interior, surface noise is created by the routine activities of walking, running, and shuffling, and by the shifting of furniture and equipment. Experimental testing has indicated that carpet is significantly more effective in reducing surface noise radiation than is vinyl tile.[1]

Noise Transmission. Controlling impact and structurally borne sounds is especially important in multilevel structures, where impact sounds can be transmitted as noise to the interior spaces below. Evaluations of the acoustical role of carpet and cushions in such a situation are made in a chamber with 100 square feet of either concrete or wood joist flooring. The ISO R 140 Tapping Machine is used to impact the surface, and the noise transmitted to the room-like chamber below is picked up by a microphone (Figure 30.1).

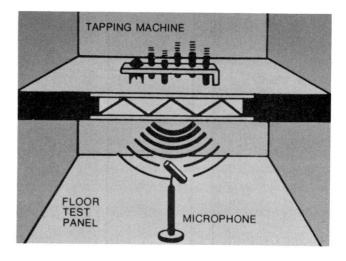

Figure 30.1 Impact noise testing facility. (Courtesy of The Carpet and Rug Institute.)

Table 30.3 SOUND ABSORPTION OF CUSHIONS
Cushions were tested under carpet having a pile weight of 40 oz./sq. yd.

Pad Wt.	Pad Material	NRC	
—	none	.35	▬▬▬▬▬
32 oz.	hair	.50	▬▬▬▬▬▬▬
40 oz.	hair	.55	▬▬▬▬▬▬▬▬
54 oz.	hair	.55	▬▬▬▬▬▬▬▬
86 oz.	hair	.60	▬▬▬▬▬▬▬▬▬
32 oz.	hair jute	.55	▬▬▬▬▬▬▬▬
40 oz.	hair jute	.60	▬▬▬▬▬▬▬▬▬
86 oz.	hair jute	.65	▬▬▬▬▬▬▬▬▬▬
31 oz.	3/8" foam rubber	.60	▬▬▬▬▬▬▬▬▬
40 oz.	hair jute[a] foam rubber	.50	▬▬▬▬▬▬▬
42 oz.	hair jute 1/8"[a] foam rubber latex	.60	▬▬▬▬▬▬▬▬▬
44 oz.	sponge rubber	.45	▬▬▬▬▬▬
86 oz.	sponge rubber 3/8"	.50	▬▬▬▬▬▬▬

[a]Tested foam side down.
Courtesy of The Carpet and Rug Institute

The ability of a floor, carpet, or cushion to minimize noise transmission is evaluated and reported numerically as an impact noise rating (INR) or as an impact insulation class (IIC). Higher values indicate greater noise control, that is, a reduced level of transmission. IIC values are roughly equal to the INR value plus 51.

The values reported in Table 30.4 show the effectiveness of various carpet and cushion features in reducing the level of noise transmission. In this series of tests, a concrete floor was used in the test facility. Concrete floors are generally used in commercial structures, and they are less effective in controlling impact sounds than the wood joist floors commonly used in residential construction. When tested without floor coverings, a 5-inch-thick concrete slab had an INR of –17 and a wood joist floor had an INR of –9.

The ratings in Table 30.4 show that increases in the weight of the pile layers of the test carpets improved their performance. All of the carpet and cushion assemblies tested were more effective than any of the test carpets alone. The rubber cushion specimens were more effective when used separately under the carpet than when permanently attached. Here, increased permeability had a negative influence, permitting more sound to be transmitted.

Insulative Value

Heat conductivity and heat resistivity are reciprocal terms referring to the rate at which a material conducts or transfers heat. The rate of heat transmittance is given numerically as the K-value or K-factor. Materials such as copper conduct heat rapidly and have relatively high K-values. Materials, including textile fibers, that have low K-values are poor heat conductors and can contribute insulative value.

R-values or R-factors numerically describe how effectively structures resist heat flow, that is, how effectively they insulate and prevent heat exchange. The following formula determines R-value: R-value = thickness/K-value. From the formula, it is apparent that resistance to heat flow is determined not only by the rate of conduction, the K-value, but also by the thickness of the structure. Increasing the thickness of a material does not increase its K-value, but does increase its R-factor, making it a more effective insulator.

Several trade associations jointly sponsored a research project to assess the effectiveness of carpet and cushions in reducing heat flow and subsequent heat loss by convection. Various carpet construction variables and types of cushions were tested over uninsulated wood floors over a vented crawl space and over a 6-inch-thick concrete slab. Heat was radiated downward from a hot plate to the surface of the carpet; the heat that flowed through the carpet or cushion or both was measured by a cold plate behind the assembly. Computer simulation was used to analyze the energy savings in residential and commercial structures of various sizes and shapes and located in different geographic areas.[2] As a result of this work, The Carpet and Rug Institute published the following findings:

1. The carpet samples tested, typical of those available during the time of the study, had R-values ranging from .55 to 2.46.

Table 30.4 IMPACT NOISE RATINGS OF VARIOUS CARPETS AND CUSHIONS ON A CONCRETE SLAB
Rating improves as pile weight increases.

Fabric No.	Pad description	Impact noise rating (INR)		Impact insulation Class (IIC)
no carpet or pad		−17		34
#1	none	+2		53
#2	none	+4		55
#3	none	+6		57
#5	none	+9		65
#6	none	+14		68
#8	3/16" sponge rubber attached	+17		69
#6	40 oz. hair & jute	+22		73
#6	urethane foam pad	+24		76
#6	44 oz. sponge rubber	+25		79
#6	31 oz. 3/8" foam rubber	+28		79
#6	80 oz. sponge	+29		80

0 2 4 6 8 10 12 14 16 18 20 22 24 26 28 30

Carpet Fabric Key

Carpet	Pile wt.	Pile ht.
#1	20 oz.	.35–.15"
#2	27 oz.	.20"
#3	32 oz.	.56"
#4	40 oz.	.25"
#5	44 oz.	.25"
#6	60 oz.	.25"
#7	44 oz. with attached 3/16" sponge rubber pad	.25"

Courtesy of The Carpet and Rug Institute.

2. The contribution of any component of the carpet or cushion test specimens to the total R-value depended more on the thickness of the component than on the fiber or yarn type.

3. R-values varied in direct proportion to thickness and pile density.

4. R-values were additive (R-value of carpet + R-value of cushion = R-value of assembly) for any combination of carpet and cushion.

5. Carpet installed on an uninsulated concrete slab provided greater savings than carpet installed on an insulated wood floor of the same area.

6. Energy savings varied substantially, depending on the R-value of the carpet and cushion assembly. For example, an assembly with an R-value of 4.0 provided an estimated energy savings greater than two times the savings estimated for carpet with an R-value of 1.0. Dollar savings varied according to local fuel charges and length of heating and cooling periods.

Light Reflectance Factor

Because light-colored textiles tend to reflect high quantities of incident light waves, light-colored carpet can reduce the energy consumed by artificial luminaires (light fixtures). The reflectance value of soft floor coverings can be measured and reported in terms of a light reflectance factor (LRF), the percentage of incident light that is reflected. The complement of the LRF indicates the amount of light absorbed. Thus, a LRF of 10 indicates that 10 percent of the incident light was reflected and 90 percent was absorbed.

Mohawk Carpet, a division of Mohasco Corporation, has suggested that carpet with a LRF greater than 10 will reduce both the number of luminaires and the wattage required to light an interior space. Table 30.5 details the relationship between various LRF values and interior illumination savings.

Table 30.5 EFFECT OF CARPET REFLECTANCE FACTORS ON INTERIOR ILLUMINATION

Theoretical number of luminaires required to light a:	Carpet light reflectance factor				
	30%	20%	15%	10%	0%
small office (140 sq. ft.)	2	2	2	3	3
large office (6,000 sq. ft.)	65	70	71	76	80
Total wattage required to light a:					
small office	272	272	272	408	408
large office	8,840	9,520	9,656	10,336	10,880
Watts per sq. ft. required to light a:					
small office	1.9	1.9	1.9	2.9	2.9
large office	1.5	1.6	1.6	1.7	1.8

Courtesy of Mohawk Carpet.

Because tracked-in dirt will reduce the light reflectance of carpet, anticipated soil accumulation must be considered when consumers wish to select more reflective carpet. Mohawk Carpet reommends a LRF of 15 as a practical upper limit for carpet to be installed in areas undergoing heavy traffic and soiling.

EVALUATING PERFORMANCE PROPERTIES

Besides the functional properties discussed in the preceding section, other properties, including colorfastness, flammability, static generation, and wear resistance, also help determine the in-use performance of textile floor coverings. Such properties should be evaluated prior to selection; again, professionals may be required to specify or select floor coverings exhibiting a mandated level of performance.

Colorfastness

Standard laboratory test methods are available to evaluate the stability of the colorants in most colored floor coverings. Generally, fastness to crocking, atmospheric gases, light, and cleaning agents are measured.

Fastness to Crocking, Gases, and Light. The standard test methods used to measure crocking, the transfer of dye from one surface to another, and gasfastness were discussed and illustrated in Chapter 14; standard test

methods used to measure lightfastness were discussed in Chapter 21. The designations of these test methods may be listed with the appropriate fastness ratings, as in Table 30.1.

Fastness to Shampoo and Water. Textile floor coverings are frequently tested for their fastness to water and to shampoo using the methods in AATCC 107 Colorfastness to Water and AATCC 138 Shampooing: Washing of Textile Floor Coverings. Either test method allows for analysis of the test results in terms of bleeding and staining, as well as in terms of color change. Test specimens are compared with the appropriate Geometric Gray Scale (Figures 14.9 and 14.10, page 145), and the numerical values recorded.

Flammability

As is true of other laboratory testing procedures, test methods that assess the potential flammability of soft floor coverings have been designed to simulate real-life conditions. Prior to marketing most carpet and large rugs, producers must subject them to the methenamine tablet test to confirm that they conform with the performance standards enforced by the Consumer Product Safety Commission. For use in some commercial interiors, carpet and rugs may be required to conform with additional flammability mandates. In such cases, the floor coverings are often tested in accordance with the procedures outlined in the flooring radiant panel test.

Methenamine Tablet (Pill) Test Method. This test method, designated ASTM D 2859, is designed to simulate a situation in which a textile floor covering is exposed to a small source of ignition, such as a burning match, an ignited cigarette, or a glowing ember. Structures that resist ignition and do not propagate the flame could reasonably be expected to contain a fire in Stage 1 (see Figure 11.1, page 103).

Test specimens and procedures. Eight specimens, each 9 inches square, are dried in an oven so that they will be free of moisture. Then, one at a time, the specimens are placed in a draft-protected burn chamber and covered by a steel flattening frame with an opening 8 inches in diameter. As pictured in Figure 30.2, a methenamine tablet, which is formulated to burn for 2 minutes, is placed in the center of the specimen and ignited. Testing is complete when burning of the tablet or the carpet specimen ceases, whichever occurs last.

Analysis of results. A char length measurement is taken on each of the eight specimens. Measurements are made of the shortest distance between the edge of the hole

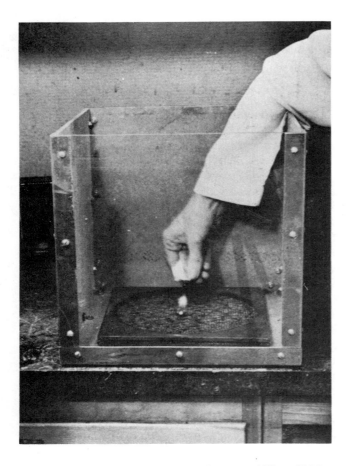

Figure 30.2 Methenamine tablet test. (Courtesy of Fibers Division, Monsanto Chemical Co.)

in the ring and the charred area. Smoke and toxic gases are not considered.

Adoption of the method. This test has been adopted as the method to be used in FF 1-70 and FF 2-70. The scope of FF 1-70 is limited to large carpets and rugs, those having an area greater than 24 square feet and one dimension greater than 6 feet. Carpet modules, because they are installed to cover large areas, are also subject to the provisions of FF 1-70. The scope of FF 2-70 includes floor coverings that are not large enough to fall within the scope of FF 1-70. Such structures include scatter rugs, bathroom rugs, and smaller area rugs. These standards became effective in 1971, and virtually all imported and domestic soft floor coverings offered for sale in the United States must conform to the provisions of the applicable standard.

A specimen meets either standard when the char area does not extend to within 1 inch of the hole in the ring. Seven out of the eight specimens must pass for the floor covering to pass. The provisions of FF 2-70 permit rugs that fail the test to be marketed as long as they carry a label warning: flammable (fails U.S. Consumer Product Safety Commission Standard 2-70: should not be used near source of fire).

Tunnel Test Method. This test method, also known as the Steiner Tunnel Test Method, measures the surface burning characteristics of building materials. It has been designated as ASTM E 84, NFPA 255, and UL 723. The testing apparatus (Figure 30.3) is structured to simulate a corridor, and the testing procedures and results are used to assess flame spread and smoke generation. The method is thus intended to evaluate the potential hazard of a textile floor covering in a Stage 3 fire (see Figure 11.3, page 104).

Test specimen and procedures. A floor covering specimen, 25 feet by 1 foot 8 inches, is mounted pile surface down on the ceiling of the tunnel chamber. The sample is then subjected to gas jet flames and heat for 10 minutes (Figure 30.4). Temperatures range from 1,600°F to 1,800°F. Testing is complete when 10 minutes have elapsed or the specimen has burned completely, whichever occurs first.

Analysis of results. Time and flame spread distance values are plotted graphically and compared with those recorded for asbestos-cement board (assigned a flame spread rating of 0) and select-grade red oak flooring (assigned a flame spread rating of 100) to arrive at a flame spread classification. Class A includes flame spread ratings from 0 to 25, Class B from 26 to 75, and Class C from 76 to 200. Smoke density values are determined separately.

Figure 30.3 Tunnel-like flammability test apparatus. (Courtesy of Fibers Division, Monsanto Chemical Co.)

Adoption of the method. In recent years, the use of the tunnel test as a method for evaluating the potential fire hazard of textile structures to be installed as floor coverings has been diminishing. Although the long, tunnel-shaped testing apparatus does indeed resemble a corridor, the method has two major shortcomings when correlated to end use. First, because the specimen is mounted on the ceiling, the test does not realistically portray real-life installations. Second, the method fails to incorporate the critical variable of the heat energy that will be radiating into a corridor in the event an interior fire progresses from Stage 2 to Stage 3. Nonetheless, testing by this method continues to be required for some installations, and is often recommended or required for carpet to be used as an interior finish on walls and ceilings (see Table 30.6).

Chamber Test. The chamber test, designated UL 992, evaluates the fire performance of flooring systems in corridors. The specimens and tunnel apparatus are smaller then those used in the tunnel test method, and the specimens are placed on the floor of the chamber. During testing, forced air sweeps the carpet surface. The flame spread and time factors are calculated and converted into a numerical index with a range from 0 to 25. In most cases, a UL Index of 4 or less would correspond to Class B in the tunnel test, and a UL Index of 8 would correspond to Class C. Because the chamber test, like the tunnel test, fails to account for the most important mechanism behind flame spread in corridors—ceiling radiation—it is no longer used extensively for evaluating floor coverings, either.

Flooring Radiant Panel Test Method. This test method has been designated as NBSIR 75-950, ASTM E 648, and NFPA 253. It accurately simulates real-life floor covering installation practices and the conditions characteristic of a Stage 3 interior fire. This test does assess the critical relationship between heat energy radiating from the ceiling and flame spread along a corridor floor covering. Because it has thus overcome the major shortcoming of the tunnel and chamber tests, the test method is increasingly used by authorities who have jurisdiction over the selection of interior floor finishes for commercial interiors.

The panel test apparatus is much smaller than the other tunnel-shaped furnace devices but, like them, it has a corridor-like design (Figure 30.5). An inclined panel radiates heat energy to the surface of the specimen. Because the level of heat radiating onto a corridor carpet would be highest at the point of spill-over, the panel is positioned at an angle of 30 degrees to the carpet specimen. The amount of heat energy radiating along the carpet during testing ranges from a maximum of 1.2 watts per square centimeter immediately below the panel to a minimum of 0.10 watt per square centimeter at the opposite end of the specimen.

Test specimens and procedures. A carpet specimen, with or without a separate or attached cushion, is cut 39 inches long and 7.87 inches wide and placed pile side up on the floor of the chamber. A gas flame is impinged on the surface of the specimen immediately below the preheated panel for 10 minutes. Air is allowed to flow through the chamber bottom and exit via a chimney-like opening. The test continues until the floor covering ceases to burn. Three replicate tests are normally required.

Analysis of results. A numerical value, the critical radiant flux (CRF), is determined by converting the distance of flame spread into watts per square centimeter. The CRF indicates the minimum heat energy that is necessary, or critical, to sustain burning of the floor covering and support flame propagation. The profile in Figure 30.5 shows that a carpet that stopped burning a distance of 19.68 inches (50 centimeters) down its length would have a CRF of 0.34 watt per square centimeter, whereas a carpet that burned the entire distance would have a CRF of 0.10 watt per square centimeter. Higher CRF values thus indicate safer systems. The CRF value reported is the average of the three replicate tests. No analysis is made of smoke generation.

Adoption of test method. The levels of fire performance of soft floor coverings mandated by municipal, state, and federal agencies are frequently based on recommendations set forth in the NFPA 101®Life Safety Code®. Table 30.6 summarizes recommendations

Table 30.6 NFPA 101® LIFE SAFETY CODE® INTERIOR FINISH AND INTERIOR FLOOR FINISH RECOMMENDATIONS

The following is a compilation of the interior finish requirements of the occupancy chapters of the *Code.*

Occupancy	Exits	Access to exits	Other spaces
Places of assembly—new*	A	A or B	A, B, or C
Places of assembly—existing*	A	A or B	A, B, or C
Educational—new	A	A or B	A, B, or C
Educational—existing	A	A or B	A, B, or C
Open plan and flexible plan*	A	A	A or B
			C on movable partitions not over 5 ft. (1.5 m) high
Child day-care centers—new	A	A or B	A or B
	I or II	I or II	
Child day-care centers—existing	A or B	A or B	A or B
	I or II	I or II	
Group day-care homes	A or B	A or B	A, B, or C
Family child day-care homes	A or B	A or B	A, B, or C
Health care—new	A	A	A
			B in individual room with capacity not more than four persons
	I	I	
Health care—existing	A or B	A or B	A or B
Detention & correctional—new	A	A	A, B, or C
	I	I	
Detention & correctional—existing	A or B	A or B	A, B, or C
	I or II	I or II	
Residential, hotels—new	A	A or B	A, B, or C
	I or II	I or II	
Residential, hotels—existing	A or B	A or B	A, B, or C
	I or II	I or II	
Residential, apartment buildings—new	A	A or B	A, B, or C
	I or II	I or II	
Residential, apartment buildings—existing	A or B	A or B	A, B, or C
	I or II	I or II	
Residential, dormitories—new	A	A or B	A, B, or C
	I or II	I or II	
Residential, dormitories—existing*	A or B	A or B	A, B, or C
	I or II	I or II	
Residential, 1- and 2-family, lodging or rooming houses		A, B, or C	
Mercantile—new*	A or B	A or B	A or B
Mercantile—existing Class A or B*	A or B	A or B	ceilings—A or B existing on walls—A, B, or C
Mercantile—existing class C*	A, B, or C	A, B, or C	A, B, or C
Office—new and existing	A or B	A or B	A, B, or C
Industrial	A or B	A, B, or C	A, B, or C
Storage	A, B, or C	A, B, or C	A, B, or C
Unusual structures*	A or B	A, B, or C	A, B, or C

*Exposed portions of structural members complying with the requirements for heavy timber construction may be permitted.
Notes:
Class A Interior Finish–flame spread 0–25, smoke developed 0–450.
Class B Interior Finish–flame spread 26–75, smoke developed 0–450.
Class C Interior Finish–flame spread 76–200, smoke developed 0–450.
Class I Interior Floor Finish—minimum 0.45 watt per sq. cm.
Class II Interior Floor Finish—minimum 0.22 watt per sq. cm.
Automatic Sprinklers—where a complete standard system of automatic sprinklers is installed, interior finish with spread rating not over Class C may be used in any location where Class B is normally specified and with rating of Class B in any location where Class A is normally specified; similarly, Class II interior floor finish may be used in any location where Class I is normally specified and no critical radiant flux rating is required where Class II is normally specified.
Reprinted with permission from NFPA 101-1985, Life Safety Code, Copyright 1985, National Fire Protection Association, Quincy, MA 02269. This reprinted material is not the complete and official position of the NFPA on the referenced subject, which is represented only by the standard in its entirety.

Figure 30.4 Gas jets in operation during tunnel testing. (Courtesy of Fibers Division, Monsanto Chemical Co.)

pertaining to interior finishes, such as carpet installed on walls, and to interior floor finishes. The materials used for interior finishes are classified in accordance with the tunnel test, and those used for interior floor finishes are classified in accordance with the radiant panel test. Because all large floor coverings must conform with FF 1-70, the NFPA does not recommend additional testing for floor coverings other than those installed in exit ways and corridors in certain occupancies.

Several local, state, and federal regulatory agencies, which have replaced the tunnel test with the panel test, also have established standards pertaining to smoke development. When these agencies have jurisdiction over an installation, smoke development must be measured in a separate test.

Smoke Chamber Test Method. This test method is assigned the designations ASTM E 662, NBS Technical

Note 708, and NFPA Research Test Method 258. It measures the smoke generation of solid materials under flaming and nonflaming (smoldering) conditions. The purpose of such testing is to identify materials that would generate large volumes of dense smoke, which would hinder quick and efficient egress by obscuring exit markers and would also hamper breathing.

Test specimens and procedures. A specimen, 3 inches square and up to 1 inch thick, is suspended vertically in an enclosed test chamber. Three replicate tests are conducted by exposing the specimen surface to an irradiance level of 2.5 watts per square centimeter; the individual tests are conducted by impinging six flamelets (small flames) across the lower edge of the specimen in combination with the radiant heat. A light beam is passed vertically through the smoke chamber. The test is completed when a minimum light transmittance value is reached or 20 minutes have elapsed, whichever occurs first.

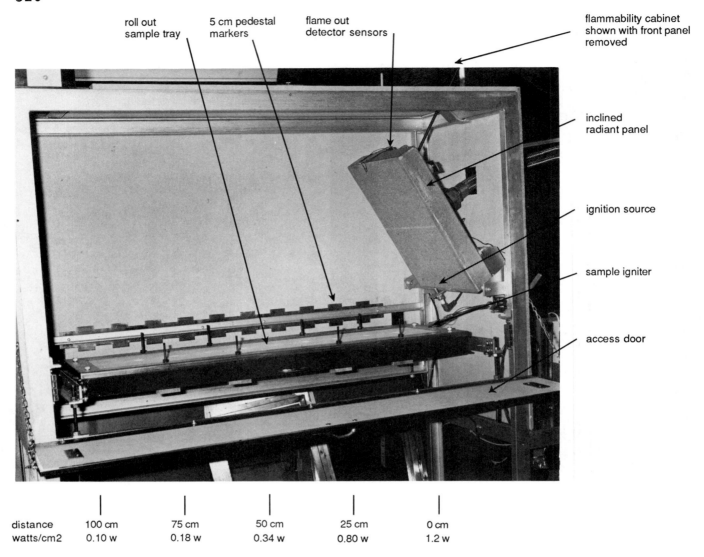

distance	100 cm	75 cm	50 cm	25 cm	0 cm
watts/cm2	0.10 w	0.18 w	0.34 w	0.80 w	1.2 w

Figure 30.5 Interior view of the radiant panel flammability test apparatus. (Courtesy of Custom Scientific Instruments, Inc.)

Analysis of results. A photometric system measures the continuous decrease in light transmission as smoke accumulates. These measurements are converted into specific optical density values.

Adoption of test method. Various city, state, and federal agencies have adopted this test method for materials installed in facilities they oversee. Required values vary from a low of 50 to a maximum of 450. In some cases, an agency may specify an average of the flaming and non-flaming tests; in other cases, only the results of the flaming tests may be involved.

The General Services Administration has combined CRF and smoke development limits to establish two classifications, and defined a third through FF 1-70. The three classes and the various GSA space to which they apply are listed below. These classes must not be confused with the

A, B, and C classes that categorize the results of tunnel testing.

Class A: a CRF of 0.50 watt per square centimeter or greater and a maximum specific optical density not over 450 flaming. Class A carpet is not needed in office buildings.

Class B: a CRF of 0.25 watt per square centimeter or greater and a maximum specific optical density not over 450 flaming. Class B carpet is required in unsprinklered corridors exposed to office space having a controlled equivalent fuel load of 6 pounds per square foot or less.

Class C: the face and back of the carpet and separate cushion pass FF 1-70. Class C carpet may be installed in all office areas and in corridors protected with automatic sprinklers.[3]

Other Test Methods. Floor coverings used in the occupant compartments of motor vehicles must comply with MVSS 302, while those used in the interiors of airplanes must comply with Paragraph 25.853 (b). The test methods and acceptance criteria included in these fire-safety standards were discussed in Chapter 16.

Static Generation

The test method generally accepted in the industry for evaluating the static propensity of floor covering assemblies is AATCC 134 Electrostatic Propensity of Carpets. The test procedure, designed to closely simulate actual end use conditions, is conducted in an atmosphere having 20 percent relative humidity and a temperature of 70°F. During the testing, a person wearing clean, neolite-soled shoes walks across a carpet while linked to an electrometer. This device measures the voltage building up on the body, and the recorded level is then reported in static volts. (The mechanisms of static voltage buildup were explained in Chapter 24.)

Frequently, federal mandates state that the control of static generation must be durable. In such cases, the agency having jurisdiction may require that floor coverings be cleaned in accordance with the procedures outlined in AATCC 138 Shampooing: Washing of Textile Floor Coverings prior to testing with AATCC 134.

Wear Resistance

The extent to which a carpet or rug exhibits satisfactory in-service performance with respect to appearance retention and durability is determined by several factors. The abrasion resistance of the floor covering will affect the extent to which fuzzing, pilling, and fiber loss occur. The resiliency of the structure will affect the degree to which the original thickness and luster are retained when the assembly is subjected to the static pressure of furniture legs, repeated loads of foot traffic, and the rolling stresses of moving equipment. If the original texture is lost, the consumer may regard the structure as "worn out," even though fiber loss may be negligible. Therefore, service performance analyses related to wear cannot be limited to abrasion-related performance; they must also include evaluations of texture retention.

Texture Retention. ASTM D 2401 Sevice Change of Appearance of Pile Floor Coverings is commonly referred to as the floor tread test. It evaluates the change in texture that results from exposure to service conditions in a corridor. The method is directed to appearance changes, such as matting, crushing, or change in pile configuration, that do not necessarily involve fiber loss by abrasion or the development of a threadbare appearance. For testing, the carpet specimens are cut approximately 13 inches long and 27 inches wide and secured to a corridor floor. If necessary, traffic may be guided to concentrate on the 27-inch-wide lane. A regular maintenance procedure, either vacuuming with suction only or with suction and a beater bar for pile restoration, is followed during the testing period.

At the end of the traffic exposure, photographs of the carpet test specimens or the test specimens themselves are visually compared with reference photographs. Five or more observers rate the textural change of each specimen according to the following scale:

0 = original or no noticeable change

1 = noticeable change

2 = definite change

3 = considerable, substantial change

4 = severe change

5 = near extreme change

Together with the average of the five ratings, the tread or traffic count (the number of persons walking over the specimens) and the type of vacuuming used during the test may be reported in specification listings, as shown in Table 30.1. Some producers elect to evaluate the appearance change after shampooing, as well.

Pilling Resistance. Carpet pilling is assessed with ASTM D 3512 Pilling Resistance and Other Related Surface Changes of Textile Fabrics: Random Tumble Pilling Tester Method. The apparatus used in the test (Figure 30.6) has cylindrical chambers lined with a mildy abrasive material.

In preparation for testing, the specimens are cut 4.1875 inches square, and the edges sealed to prevent fraying. The specimens are tumbled by a pair of impellers rotating at 1,200 revolutions per minute for 30 minutes. The specimens are then compared with standard reference photographs and rated according to the following arbitrary scale:

5 = no pilling

4 = slight pilling

3 = moderate pilling

2 = severe pilling

1 = very severe pilling

As noted in Chapter 25, manufacturers of tufted carpet seek to reduce the number of individual fibers that are

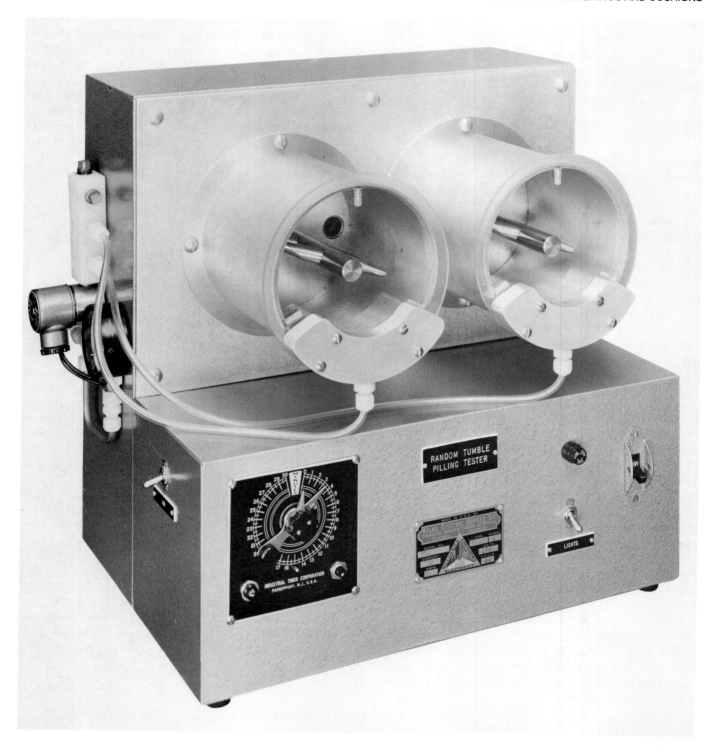

Figure 30.6 The Atlas random tumble pilling tester. (Courtesy of Atlas Electric Devices Company.)

teased to the surface and rolled into pills through the proper application of adhesive coatings. Part of their quality-control effort involves ascertaining how thoroughly the adhesive has penetrated the pile yarn bundle, to lock the fibers side by side.

Abrasion Resistance. ASTM D 3884 Abrasion Resistance of Textile Fabrics: Rotary Platform, Double Head Method is a standard test method used in the carpet and rug industry for the accelerated laboratory testing of the abrasion resistance of floor coverings. The apparatus used in the test has two flat platforms, or turntables, each supporting and rotating one specimen under two abradant wheels (Figure 30.7). The pressure of the wheels on the specimens can be controlled during the testing operation, and a vacuum unit may be employed to remove abraded particles continually.

During testing, the abradant wheels rotate in opposite directions (Figure 30.8). This results in abrasion marks that form a pattern of crossed, slightly curved, herringbone-like arcs over an area of approximately 4.5 inches.

Some producers evaluate the results in terms of the number of cycles (revolutions of the turntable carrying the specimen) required to cause exposure of the backing. Other producers measure the percent of pile weight loss or the percent loss of breaking load. The value reported is the average of five replicate tests.

Other Wear Resistance Tests. Some manufacturers have adapted the floor tread test for use in evaluating the service performance of carpet installed on stairs. Commonly referred to as the stair tread test, the method is directed to assessing the extent to which the carpet withstands abrasion, especially at the nosing of stairs. This is a long-term, service exposure test: carpet specimens are installed without a cushion on heavily trafficked stairs. Producers may evaluate the level of abrasion resistance visually; they may measure the pile weight loss; or they

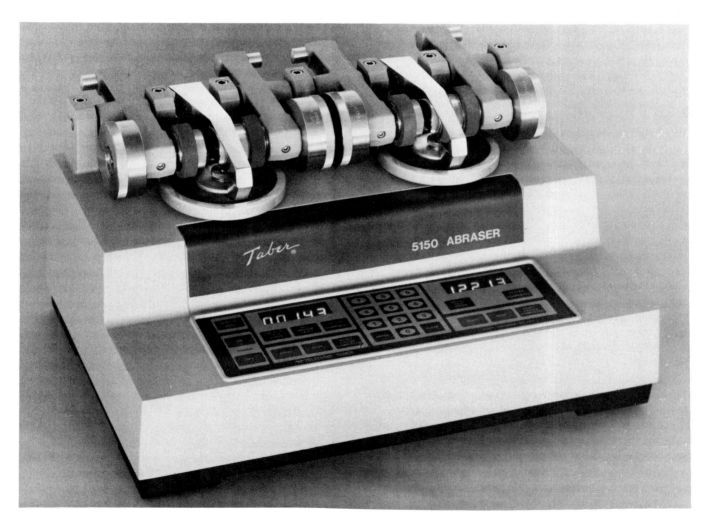

Figure 30.7 Taber Abraser with double heads. (Courtesy of Teledyne Taber.)

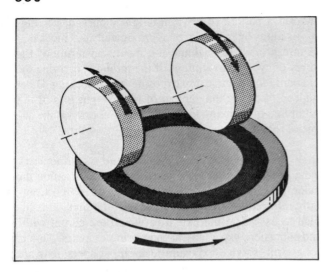

Figure 30.8 Directions of rotation of the abradant wheels and support platform during abrasion resistance testing. (Courtesy of Teledyne Taber.)

may record the traffic count required to expose the backing and create a threadbare appearance.

An accelerated laboratory test that predicts how well a carpet will perform on a stair edge is called the Tetrapod Wear Test. As pictured in Figure 30.9, the test carpet is installed in a cylindrical chamber that has a raised ridge to simulate a stair edge.

During testing, the rubber-tipped "feet" of the tetrapod tumble against the carpet surface as the cylinder revolves, simulating foot traffic. The change in texture is assessed visually and by measuring the change in pile thickness. The resistance to abrasion is assessed by measuring the loss in pile weight. Research has shown that the tetrapod test gives results that qualitatively resemble those obtained in long-term service exposure tests.[4]

SUMMARY

Soft floor covering manufacturers use prescribed test methods, as well as some adapted procedures, to evaluate the quality of their products and to predict their in-service performance. Members of the trade frequently use the results of these tests to promote the selection of their carpet and rugs.

For commercial interiors, selection prerequisites include not only an assessment of the traffic conditions and activities anticipated in the end use setting, but also an investigation of any legally mandated performance and structural requirements. Special requirements may exist regarding, for example, static generation, flammability, weight-related factors, and colorfastness. The interior designer and architect can use the test data provided by the producer to determine whether or not a stock product meets or exceeds requirements. When working on a custom project, the professional can specify the composition, construction features, and levels of performance desired or required.

NOTES

1. *Acoustical Benefits: Sound Conditioning with Carpet,* The Carpet and Rug Institute, Dalton, Ga., n.d.

2. *Advantages of Carpet and Rugs in Energy Conservation,* The Carpet and Rug Institute, Dalton, Ga., 1976.

3. *Building Firesafety Criteria,* PBS P 5290.9, General Services Administration, Washington, D.C., October 23, 1980.

4. Kenneth C. Laughlin and Gordon E. Cusick, "Carpet Performance Evaluation, Part I: The Tetrapod Walker Test," *Textile Research Journal,* Vol. 37, No. 7, July 1967.

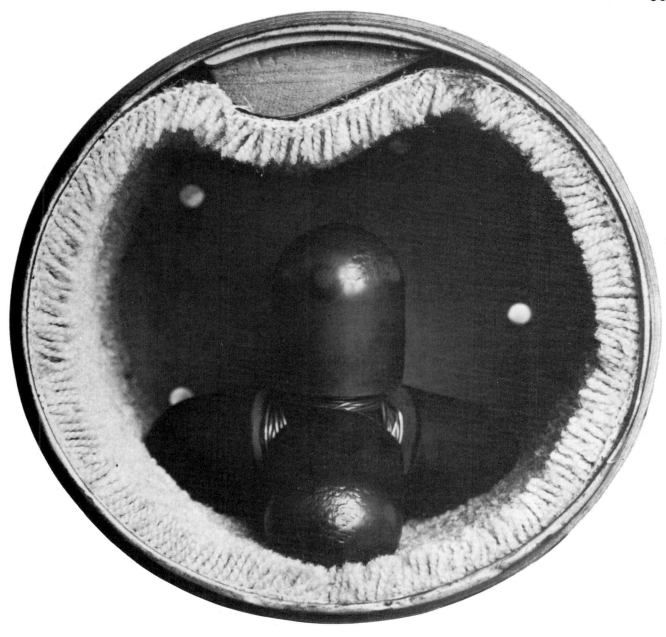

Figure 30.9 Tetrapod wear testing. (Courtesy of BASF Corporation Fibers Division.)

chapter 31

Installation and Maintenance of Floor Covering Assemblies

- Installing Soft Floor Coverings and Cushions
- Maintaining Textile Floor Coverings

To ensure long-term serviceability in their textile floor coverings and cushions, residential and commercial consumers should consider installation and maintenance factors as thoroughly as they do appearance and performance variables. Unless the floor covering assembly is carefully installed by qualified persons, ripples, bubbles, prominent seams, and mismatched patterns may appear. An insecure installation could be hazardous, as well as result in undue stress on the structure itself.

Cleaning and stain removal procedures, if part of a planned maintenance program, should not cause marked changes in texture, nor should they alter the original color of a product. The installation to be used and the maintenance program to be followed should be investigated prior to the final selection of the floor covering assembly.

INSTALLING SOFT FLOOR COVERINGS AND CUSHIONS

Residential consumers, contract designers, and architects should be familiar with the basic procedures used in wall-to-wall installations. This will prepare them for an accurate analysis of whatever factors will influence their choice of a method of installation. They should be familiar also with such features as pile lay and types of pattern repeats and with the principles governing seam placement and floor space measurements. Such familiarity is the foundation for correctly planning the carpet layout, deter-

mining the yardage required, and estimating the cost of the project.

Wall-to-wall Installation Methods

Three methods may be considered for the wall-to-wall installation of textile floor coverings. These include stretch-in, glue-down, and free-lay techniques. Before proceeding with any installation, the site must be properly prepared. Often, this preliminary work and installation should be done by skilled persons fully experienced in the procedures.

Site Preparation. An important part of site preparation is the removal of the previously installed floor covering assembly. Old carpets, if left in place, would prevent the new cushion from sliding smoothly into place during installation, causing it to become distorted and thus to prevent the proper stretching and smooth installation of the replacement carpet. Moreover, loading of a multilayered installation that included the old floor covering would result in severe and repeated flexing of the new assembly, promoting deterioration of the backing and the development of an uneven wear layer. For glue-down installations, sheet vinyl and linoleum must be removed for the new structure to adhere well.

Although the subfloor should be dry for all installations, dryness is especially critical for glue-down installations. New concrete floors, which may require up to four months to dry, should be checked carefully for dryness; so should subfloors that are close to or in contact with the ground, either on-grade (ground level) or below-grade. Ground moisture may be transported upward through the slab, facilitating the migration of alkaline compounds at the same time. The moisture can prevent good adhesion of the floor covering and foster microbe-related problems. The alkaline substance may react with the adhesive compounds that stabilize the carpet and with those that secure it to the floor, causing degradation and loosening of the carpet. In order to avoid such problems, the moisture condition must be resolved and the alkaline must be neutralized prior to installation.

The interior floor space to be covered should be smooth and free of cracks, crevices, and holes, for a more pleasing appearance and uniform support for the assembly. Rough areas should be sanded, and openings should be filled. Finally, the floor should be free of dust, lint, and grit.

Stretch-in Installations. Stretch-in installations involve stretching rollgoods and fastening them over pin-holding strips that have been secured to the perimeter of the floor space. These plywood strips, also known as tack-

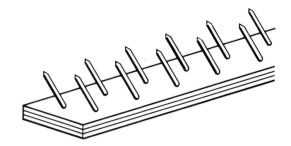

Figure 31.1 Pin-holding strip used in stretch-in installation projects.

less strips, are approximately 1.5 inches wide, and have rows of rust-resistant metal pins protruding upward at an angle of 60 degrees (Figure 31.1). The strips are up to 0.375 inch thick; the thickness of the strip is coordinated with the thickness of the cushion to be installed. When carpet lengths greater than 30 feet are being installed or when heavy traffic loads are anticipated, three rows of pins

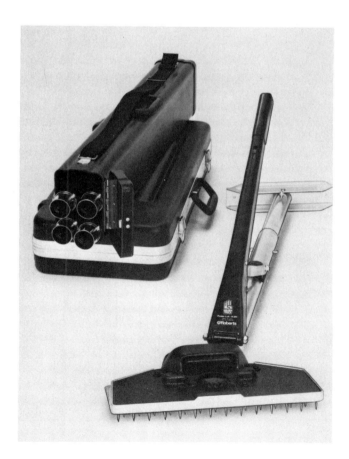

a) telescoping power stretcher

10-409—GOLDEN TOUCH KNEE KICKER

10-412—DELUXE KNEE-KICKER

b) knee kicker

Figure 31.2 Tools used to install rollgoods in stretch-in tackless projects. (Courtesy of Roberts Consolidated Industries.)

should be used; for residential installations and smaller commercial installations, two rows of pins should be sufficient.

The strips are nailed or glued to the floor, with the pins angled toward the wall. A gully or space slightly narrower than the thickness of the carpet is left between the wall and the strip. If a separate cushion is used, it is laid within the perimeter of the strips and stapled or glued to the floor.

When seams and pattern matching are required, the parallel edges of the floor covering must be carefully aligned and trimmed to fit tightly. Butting of factory edges is not recommended since they may be slightly irregular; there may be a slight excess of printed pattern repeats provided for trimming to an accurate match. After the rollgoods are cut, a thin bead of an adhesive should be applied to prevent edge raveling and fraying during subsequent handling, seaming, and use.

Seams may be formed by hand sewing or by applying various types of tape. Crosswise seams are often sewn. Hot melt tape is often used for lengthwise seams. This tape has a thermoplastic coating that becomes tacky when heated with a special iron. The carpet edges are sealed together by the adhesive when it cools. In lieu of hot melt tape, a strip of pressure-sensitive or adhesive tape may be placed behind the parallel carpet edges and a latex bead applied along the seam line to secure the join.

After the seaming is completed, the carpet is stretched, generally 1 to 1.5 percent in length and width, and anchored over the pins in the wooden strips. A power stretcher is used to place uniform stretch over the surface of the carpet, and a knee-kicker is used to grip and anchor the edges over the pins (Figure 31.2).

The procedures recommended for stretching tufted carpet are shown in Figure 31.3. The power stretcher is anchored at the base of the walls and telescoped as needed.

Stairway carpet may be installed with a stretch-in technique, using pin-holding strips and knee-kicker. It may also be glued down.

Glue-down Installations. Glue-down installations involve securing floor covering structures to the floor with an adhesive. When no cushion is used, the procedure may be referred to as direct-glue down; when an attached cushion is involved, the procedure is called glue-down. The same procedures are used in both operations, except that structures without a cushion are rolled onto the adhesive and structures with a cushion are pressed into the adhesive.

When installing rollgoods, the layout and seam placement must be carefully planned, and the floor measurements must be exact. If the carpet is too large, buckles and ripples may develop; if the carpet is too small, separation of the seams may occur. The cut edges of the carpet must be precisely marked, trimmed, and secured with a

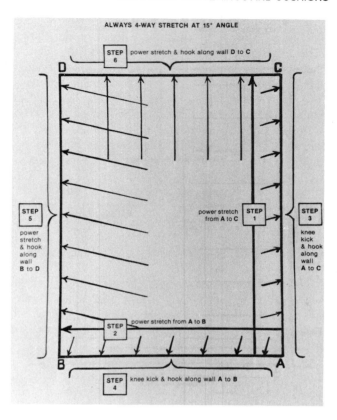

Figure 31.3 Stretching tufted structures. (Courtesy of The Carpet and Rug Institute.)

bead of latex. The selected adhesive is then spread over the floor with a notched trowel and the carpet is bonded to the adhesive.

When working with carpet modules, the installer should locate a starting point that will maximize the cut size of the perimeter modules. From this point, a grid is established and the selected adhesive is spread over the area. Each module is then slid into position, taking care to avoid catching any pile tufts in the joint. Successive tiles should be laid in a pyramid or stairstep manner (Figure 31.4). Perimeter modules can be precisely cut to fit the floor space.

The adhesive used to bond rollgoods and modules may be a nonreleasable (permanent) or a releasable type. Releasable adhesives may permit the floor covering structure to be repeatedly lifted and rebonded into position. This permits some degree of access to underfloor service trenches or to flatwire cable systems installed directly on the floor. It may also permit the rotation or removal of carpet modules.

Free-lay Installations. Free-lay installations may be considered for carpet modules when consumers wish to maximize the flexibility of the carpet tile, as long as heavy rolling traffic is not expected. Rolling casters on of-

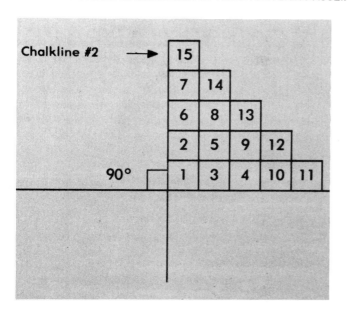

Figure 31.4 Pyramid technique recommended for positioning carpet modules. (Courtesy of Milliken and Company.)

fice chairs would have an insignificant effect, but such heavy items as hospital guerneys wheeled down corridors and automobiles driven into showrooms could have a "snowplow" effect, raising the edges of the modules.

Modules must have superior dimensional stability for free-lay use. This feature is often achieved with the application of a heavy secondary backing. Some free-lay tiles alternate layers of heavy-gauge vinyl and glass fiber scrims for the necessary stability (Figure 31.5).

In preparation for installation, a control grid is again planned to maximize the cut size of the perimeter nodules. Within this grid, specific crosswise and lengthwise rows of modules should be secured to the floor with adhesive or

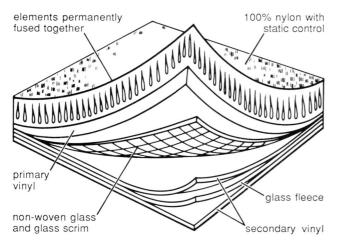

Figure 31.5 Fusion-bonded, free-lay tile with GlasBac™ secondary backing. (Courtesy of Interface Flooring Systems, Inc.)

double-face tape to minimize shifting. Selective glue-down leaves approximately 80 to 90 percent of the modules in the free-lay mode; tape, which is removed after installation, leaves all of the tiles held by gravity.

Like installations with releasable adhesives, free-lay installations permit easy access to floor and underfloor utility systems. Free-lay also offers maximum convenience in shifting modules.

Loose-laid Rug Installations

Cut edges of rugs and runners must be bound by sewing twill-woven tape over the raw edges or by serging (machine overcasting). Cushions used with loose-laid rugs and runners should be thin and about 1 or 2 inches narrower and shorter than the floor coverings. This allows the rug or runner to lie close to the floor and minimizes the tendency for the soft floor covering to advance off the cushion. On stairs, runners may be securely installed with brass rods (Figure 31.6).

Figure 31.6 Stair runner installed with brass rods. (Courtesy of Peerless Imported Rugs.)

Factors Affecting Choice of Installation Method

Besides the site-related considerations identified in the previous section, other factors may limit the type of installation chosen for soft floor coverings. These include traffic conditions, planned space utilization, and concern for noise reduction and energy conservation.

Traffic Conditions. The traffic conditions in the area to be carpeted include a number of variables. First, the anticipated number of persons who will walk over the floor covering should be estimated. At low and medium levels, 500 to 1,000 traffic counts per day, the carpet may be stretched-in over most types of cushions; at higher levels, the carpet may be stretched-in over a thin, high density cushion or over no cushion, or it may be glued down.

Second, it is important to consider what type of traffic will be usual. If people with canes, crutches, or limited vision will use the interior, area and room-size rugs and runners should be avoided, or their edges should be securely attached to the floor. When rolling traffic, such as wheelchairs and equipment, will impact the floor covering, strong consideration should be given to gluing the carpet structure directly to the subfloor. This installation technique will help to minimize shearing and seam separation.

A third traffic-related factor to consider is the amount of dirt and grit that will be tracked in. If a rapid rate of accumulation is expected, the specifier may elect to install carpet modules with a releasable adhesive or in a free-lay mode. The modules could then be rotated to minimize apparent and actual differences in appearance and texture throughout the interior. Soiled modules could be removed for off-site cleaning, and damaged modules lifted out and replaced.

Planned Space Utilization. Frequently, modern commercial offices have an open design; movable wall partitions define work stations. As personnel and activities change, the partitions can be moved to define new spaces consistent with current needs. For such interiors, the specifier may investigate the use of carpet modules instead of rollgoods. If rollgoods are installed to the base of each movable wall, shifting the wall would leave a bare strip of subfloor, which would have to be patched with carpet. If wall panels are placed over a carpet, eventual wall shifting may reveal unsightly lines, requiring a large amount of replacement carpet. These problems may be avoided through use of carpet modules.

As shown in Figure 31.7, a common grid can be planned for the placement of the modules. When a square falls on a wall, it can be cut to fit on either side of the wall (Figure 31.7b). Later, when the wall panels are shifted, the cut modules can be lifted and a row of full-size modules laid in place (Figure 31.7c).

Acoustical and Insulative Control. The need for noise control and insulation may call for the installation of a carpet and cushion assembly, rather than a carpet glued to the floor. As noted in Chapter 30, a separate cushion increases the level of sound absorption, and any combination of carpet and cushion provides greater reduction of impact noise transmission than does carpet alone. Chapter 30 also discussed the finding that the insulative values of a carpet and cushion are additive, and are higher when the two structures are used separately. If traffic conditions dictate the selection of a glue-down installation, less effective control over noise and energy consumption

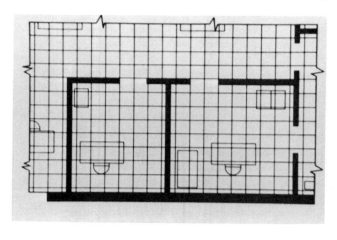

a) common grid for module placement

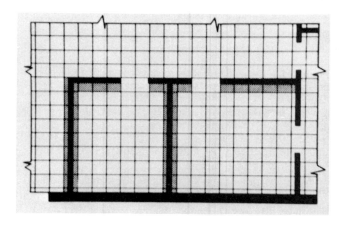

b) modules cut to fit base of wall panels

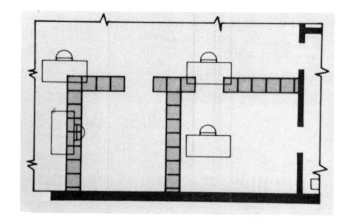

c) full size replacement modules

Figure 31.7 Use of carpet modules in interior space with movable walls. (Courtesy of Interface Flooring Systems, Inc.)

may be partially offset by increasing the pile yarn weight and pile height of the carpet.

Cost-related Factors. As discussed in Chapter 23, there may be per square yard charges assessed for site preparation, for installation of the new cushion, and for installation of the new carpet. Normally, the cost of installing a separate cushion and carpet will be higher than that of installing a carpet with no cushion or a cushion attached. When selecting a type of installation, however, the consumer may consider acoustical benefits and energy savings that separate structures help realize. If the value of these benefits outweighs the additional installation costs, a separate cushion should be chosen, provided budgetary limitations are not exceeded. Of course, it is advisable to investigate the comparative life-cycle costs of all floor covering options.

Determining Yardage Required

The number of square yards of carpet required for a project must be accurately calculated. If the initial order was insufficient, the additional yardage of a second order inevitably has slightly different color characteristics as a result of being dyed or printed in a separate operation. Of course, if the initial order is excessive, unnecessary materials costs will be incurred.

Careful planning and correct measuring can ensure that the yardage order is accurate. Attention must be given to the direction of pile lay, the placement of seams, and the size and nature of pattern repeats.

Measuring Floor Space. The following lists the important rules to observe when measuring floor space for carpet:

1. Between opposite walls, each of which is uninterrupted, measure the distance from baseboard to baseboard and record the information on a sketch of the floor plan.

2. Between opposite walls, one of which is interrupted by an opening, measure from the baseboard to the mid-

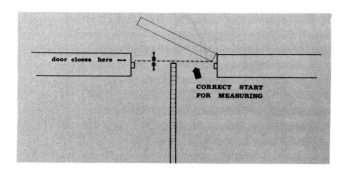

Figure 31.8 Measuring for carpet at a door jamb. (Courtesy of J.P. Stevens.)

point of an archway or to a point halfway under the bottom edge of the closed door (Figure 31.8). Record the measurement on the floor plan sketch.

3. Measure stairs as illustrated in Figure 31.9. Landings are treated as if they were large steps.

From 2 to 4 inches must be added to each of the recorded lengthwise and crosswise measurements. This will provide the yardage required for fitting and trimming.

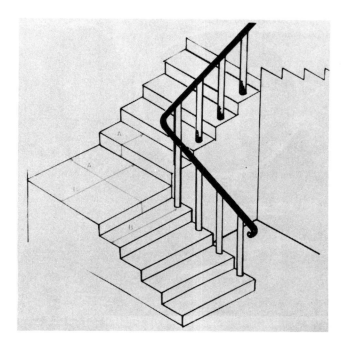

Figure 31.9 Measuring stairs and landings for carpet. (Courtesy of J.P. Stevens.)

Positioning the Pile Lay. The directional lay of pile yarns (Figure 9.3, page 83) must be uniform for all adjoining pieces of carpet. The layout should be planned so that the lay parallels the longest dimension of the largest room to be carpeted, as shown in Figure 31.10a. Unless pattern orientation or a similar feature must be considered, the pile lay direction should be away from the strongest source of light and toward entrance areas.

Figure 31.10b illustrates an incorrect layout. One length has been reversed and one length has been given a quarter turn. Because the quantity of light reflected by each section would be different, there would be marked differences in their apparent color. The carpet would appear darkest when the viewer is looking at the tips of the pile tufts and lightest when the viewer is looking at the sides of the yarns. Therefore, once the correct positioning of the pile lay direction has been established, all adjoining lengths of carpet of the same color and quality must be laid with their pile lay in the same direction.

Some interior designers and architects may purposely vary the pile direction of adjoining units in order to create

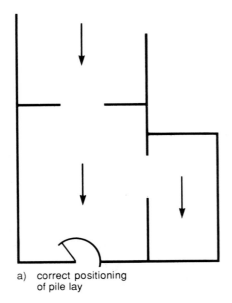

a) correct positioning
of pile lay

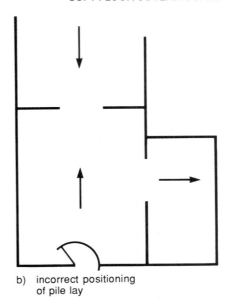

b) incorrect positioning
of pile lay

Figure 31.10 Planning pile lay direction.

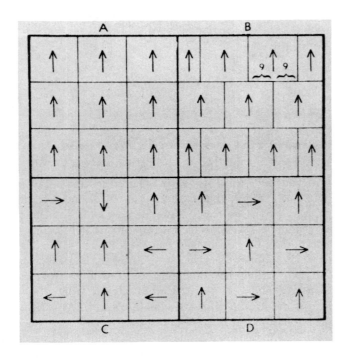

a) monolithic—corner to corner

b) monolithic—ashlar

c) random—corner to corner or ashlar

d) parquet

Figure 31.11 Four patterns for installing carpet modules with varied pile lay directions. (Courtesy of Milliken and Company.)

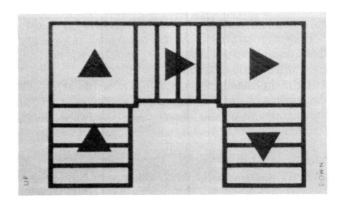

Figure 31.12 Direction of pile lay on angled stairs. (Courtesy of J.P. Stevens.)

marked differences in their apparent brightness. Examples of possible patterns for the placement of carpet modules are shown in Figure 31.11. In each of these four patterns, shading variations would alter the aesthetic characteristics of the installation.

When pile carpet is installed on stairs, the width of the carpet must parallel the width of the stairs so that carpet "grin," the exposure of the backing on the nose edges, will be minimized. With angled stairways, this will necessitate installation of the carpet with quarter turns of the pile lay (Figure 31.12). In such cases, the critical importance of avoiding exposure of the backing overrides concern for shade variations.

Planning Seam Placement. Several principles should govern the placement of seams. Whenever possi-

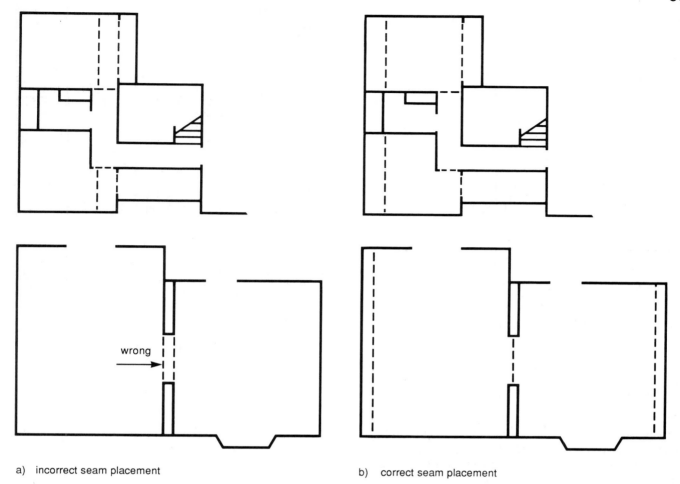

a) incorrect seam placement   b) correct seam placement

Figure 31.13 Planning carpet seam placement. (Courtesy of J.P. Stevens.)

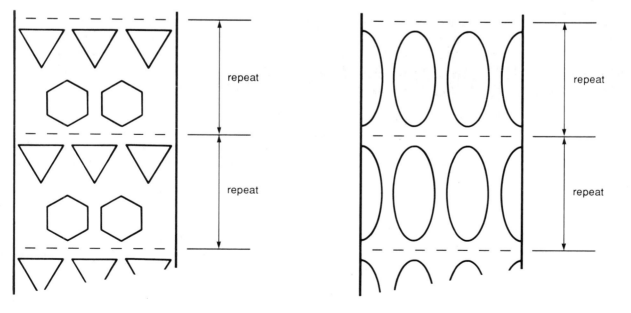

Figure 31.14 Set-match patterns.

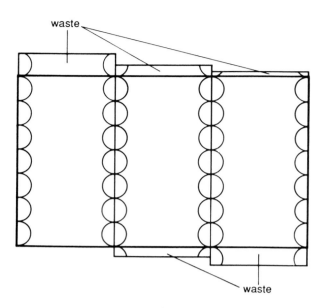

Figure 31.15 Matching set-match patterns.

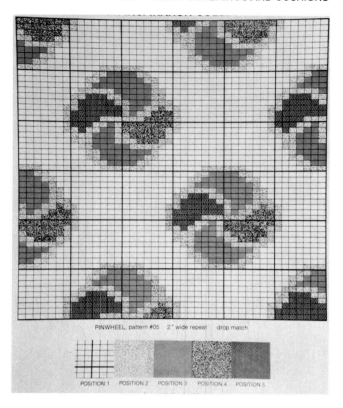

PINWHEEL, pattern #05   2" wide repeat   drop match

POSITION 1   POSITION 2   POSITION 3   POSITION 4   POSITION 5

Figure 31.16 Half-drop match pattern. (Courtesy of Mohawk Carpet.)

ble, seams should run lengthwise, parallel with the pile lay, not crosswise. Crosswise seams interrupt the pile sweep and are highlighted when the quantity of incident light is high. Seams should not run perpendicular to a doorway, although they may run across the opening (Figure 31.13b). A seam condition known as a "saddle" (Figure 31.13a) should be avoided by shifting the carpet and seaming it in a different location. For stability and safety, seams must not be located in traffic pivot areas and on stair treads.

Allowing Yardage for Matching Patterns. Patterned floor coverings have either a set-match or drop-match pattern repeat. The type of match and the lengthwise and crosswise dimensions of the repeat affect the yardage required.

Set-match patterns repeat themselves across the width of the carpet. Depending on the width of the repeat and the width of the carpet, the crosswise repeats may be fully completed or partially completed (Figure 31.14). In the latter case, the pattern is generally scaled so that the complement of the incomplete design is at the opposite edge.

Set-match patterned carpet should be cut at the next highest multiple of the pattern repeat length beyond the amount actually required. Thus, if the repeat is 12 inches long and 17 feet 6 inches are required, the carpet would be cut 18 feet long (18 is the next highest multiple of the 1-foot length); if the repeat is 36 inches long and 21 feet 6 inches are required, the carpet would be cut 24 feet long (24 is the next highest multiple of the 3-foot dimension). This cutting plan would provide the additional yardage needed for side matching. The installer would shift the

long edges of the parallel carpet lengths, matching the pattern. The waste would then be cut away, but not necessarily from one end of each length (Figure 31.15).

Drop-match patterns repeat themselves diagonally across the width of the carpet. In half-drop match patterns, the complementing portion of a design is located at a point up or down one half the length of the repeat, as shown in the draft in Figure 31.16.

Two methods may be used to cut carpet having half-drop match patterns. The first method is to cut on multiples of the repeat. If three 9-foot widths of carpet that has a 36-inch-long repeat are being installed in a room that measures 20 feet 6 inches in length, the first and third cuts would be cut on seven multiples or 21 feet. The second strip would then be cut 22 feet 6 inches, minimizing waste.

The second method is to cut on multiples of the repeat plus half a repeat. This method utilizes a half repeat to advantage. For example, a 12-inch pattern can be cut in lengths of 1 foot 6 inches, 2 feet 6 inches, 3 feet 6 inches, and so on. If three widths of carpet with a 36-inch repeat are being installed in a room that measures 22 feet 6 inches in length, all lengths can be cut seven and a half repeats, or 22 feet 6 inches long.

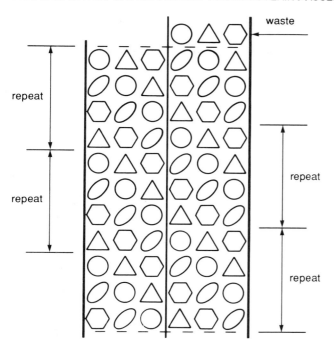

waste

repeat

repeat

repeat

repeat

Figure 31.17 Matching quarter-drop match pattern.

A second type of drop-match pattern is the quarter-drop pattern. This type of repeat is frequently seen in colonial patterns; it has four blocks to a repeat. The figures match one quarter of the repeat on the opposite edge (Figure 31.17). It is apparent that successive pieces of carpet must be shifted and aligned to preserve the diagonal pattern. According to the length required and the length of the repeat, quarter-drop patterns can be cut in multiples of the repeat plus one, two, or three blocks. Side matching can then be achieved by dropping one, two, or three blocks.

For all planned installations, it is advisable to sketch the layout of the carpet lengths on graph paper, noting the direction of pile lay, the placement of seams, and the orientation of patterns. The floor measurement and the calculations of the extra yardage needed for pattern matching should be rechecked. This plan will help ensure that the tally of the total number of linear feet and inches of carpet required is accurate; later it will serve as the cutting guide.

Linear measurements must be converted into square yards for ordering. Because most carpet is produced 12 feet wide, the conversions presented in Table 31.1 are based on this width. This conversion also facilitates an estimate of materials costs, since these charges are normally quoted on a per square yard basis.

When floor covering is received, it should be inspected to confirm that the quantity ordered was delivered and that the structure is free of unacceptable flaws and color variations. Most manufacturers will not assume responsibility for such defects after carpet has been cut.

After the carpet or carpet and cushion assembly has been installed, a planned maintenance program should be initiated. Without proper care, a carpet that has been carefully selected, correctly specified, and skillfully installed may "ugly out" long before it is worn out.

MAINTAINING TEXTILE FLOOR COVERINGS

To ensure that they retain a high level of appearance, textile floor coverings installed in residential and commercial interiors should be maintained through a planned program. Scheduled maintenance can keep the appearance from changing noticeably, in contrast to sporadic maintenance, in which cleaning is undertaken as a last resort after excessive soil has already accumulated and visibly altered the look of the surface.

The primary objective of planned maintenance programs is to prevent soil, ordinarily captured in approximately 20 to 30 percent of the carpet area, from being spread throughout the interior. A second equally important objective is to reduce the amount of grit that becomes embedded in the surface yarns. These objectives are met by strictly adhering to a schedule of regular, frequent vacuuming and cleaning, and, for localized areas that become highly soiled, stain removal. Commercial programs are available, but professionals and consumers may design appropriate plans themselves. However it is arrived at, a planned maintenance program delays or prevents the development of apparent changes in color caused by excessive soil accumulation; it also reduces changes in texture and luster caused when traffic grinds gritty soil against fiber surfaces.

Initially, some corrective measures may be required to mend an occasional flaw or to remove loose fibers. Thereafter, specific preventive, interim, and restorative procedures should be followed, with salvage procedures used as necessary. Each of these activities is scheduled after consideration of the level of appearance preferred by the carpet owner, the anticipated traffic load, and the rate and type of soiling expected.

Initial Care

Inspection of a newly installed carpet may reveal such problems as shedding, sprouting, missing tufts, and small dots of latex. Simple measures can correct these irregularities.

Shedding occurs when short lengths of fibers that have accumulated during manufacturing work to the surface. It is particularly characteristic of cut pile textures and will soon be corrected by regular vacuuming. The fiber loss

Table 31.1 CONVERSION OF FEET AND INCHES TO SQUARE YARDS OF 12-FOOT-WIDE CARPET

Example
74'5" of 12' width
74' = 98.67 sq. yds.
5"   =   .55 sq. yd.
_____
Total = 99.22 sq. yds.

Inches		Linear ft.	Sq. yds.	Linear ft.	Sq. yds.
Linear in.	Sq. yds.				
1	.11	25	33.33	64	85.33
2	.22	26	34.67	65	86.67
3	.33	27	36.00	66	88.00
4	.44	28	37.33	67	89.33
5	.55	29	38.67	68	90.67
6	.67	30	40.00	69	92.00
7	.78	31	41.33	70	93.33
8	.89	32	42.67	71	94.67
9	1.00	33	44.00	72	96.00
10	1.11	34	45.33	73	97.33
11	1.22	35	46.67	74	98.67
Feet		36	48.00	75	100.00
Linear ft.	Sq. yds.	37	49.33	76	101.33
		38	50.67	77	102.67
		39	52.00	78	104.00
1	1.33	40	53.33	79	105.33
2	2.67	41	54.67	80	106.67
3	4.00	42	56.00	81	108.00
4	5.33	43	57.33	82	109.33
5	6.67	44	58.67	83	110.67
6	8.00	45	60.00	84	112.00
7	9.33	46	61.33	85	113.33
8	10.67	47	62.67	86	114.67
9	12.00	48	64.00	87	116.00
10	13.33	49	65.33	88	117.33
11	14.67	50	66.67	89	118.67
12	16.00	51	68.00	90	120.00
13	17.33	52	69.33	91	121.33
14	18.67	53	70.67	92	122.67
15	20.00	54	72.00	93	124.00
16	21.33	55	73.33	94	125.33
17	22.67	56	74.67	95	126.67
18	24.00	57	76.00	96	128.00
19	25.33	58	77.33	97	129.33
20	26.67	59	78.67	98	130.67
21	28.00	60	80.00	99	132.00
22	29.33	61	81.33	100	133.33
23	30.67	62	82.67		
24	32.00	63	84.00		

Courtesy of Milliken and Company.

will not be significant. Sprouting refers to the protrusion of a tuft above the surface of the wear layer. This may result from the release of a small fold of pile yarn that was caught during manufacturing. The extended tuft should simply be clipped to the proper pile height; it must never be pulled. A missing tuft can be replaced by the floor covering dealer, in a procedure known as burling. During manufacturing, a small dot of latex is frequently used to join or splice ends of pile yarns. All visible bits of latex are removed by the factory inspector. If, however, some were hidden and appear in the new carpet, the installer or consumer can simply cut them out, removing any residue with a small amount of dry-cleaning fluid.

Another activity to be carried out after installation of a new carpet is the placement of chair pads under wheeled desk chairs and casters or rests under furniture. These will protect the pile layer from excessive abrasion, shearing, and crushing, prolonging the wear-life and helping to retain the original texture of the carpet.

Preventive Maintenance

Preventive maintenance procedures are protective procedures, employed to capture soil and grit in track-off, funnel, and concentrated traffic areas. If soil and grit particles are continually removed from the sites where they were initially deposited, the amount spread throughout a facility can be significantly reduced. Preventive measures can also help minimize spotting and staining.

Using Protective Mats. Because over 80 percent of carpet soil is tracked-in, preventive maintenance must begin with walk-off mats or runners placed outside and inside of entrance areas. Walk-off mats should also be placed where foot traffic may transfer wax and dust from hard-surfaced floors to carpet surfaces. In areas where commercial traffic is concentrated or channeled, such as lobbies, elevators, in front of vending machines and file cabinets, down corridors, and at doorways, protective mats should be strategically located to capture soil.

In all cases, walk-off mats and runners must be cleaned so they do not themselves become sources of soil and grit. In elevators, removable rugs or carpet modules can facilitate off-site cleaning and rotation.

Vacuuming. In most planned maintenance programs, a thorough vacuuming (five to seven passes of the sweeper over the surface) with an upright, rather than a canister, vacuum is recommended for track-off areas and primary traffic lanes every one or two days. For areas subjected to lower levels of traffic, vacuuming may be light (three passes of the sweeper) and as infrequent as every seven to ten days. Such light maintenance is reasonable for many areas: approximately 70 to 80 percent of all interior floor space is rarely walked on.

Figure 31.18 Planned carpet maintenance calendar. (Courtesy of Host/Racine Industries, Inc. Copyright 1980, 1981, 1982, 1983, 1984.)

An example of a planned maintenance schedule for a commercial interior is presented in Figure 31.18. Vacuuming, stain removal, and interim cleaning activities are listed. Track-off and funnel areas are scheduled for dry cleaning once every twenty days; stain removal and dry cleaning procedures are discussed later in this chapter.

Pretesting Cleaning Products. Pretesting stain removal and carpet cleaning products is an important preventive activity, because it minimizes the chance that products will damage the fibers, cause color transfer, produce color changes, or leave sticky residues. The Carpet and Rug Institute recommends the use of two types of pretests. In one test, approximately one teaspoon of the prepared product is worked into the fibers in an inconspicuous area of the floor covering. The fibers are then pressed between a clean, white tissue for about ten seconds. The tissue is examined for evidence of bleeding, and the fibers are examined for evidence of damage. The procedure should be repeated until a safe agent is identified.

In the second test, a half cup of the prepared product is poured into a clear glass dish. After the liquid portion of the product has evaporated, the residue is examined. If a dry, powdery residue is found, it would be reasonable to

Table 31.2 SPOT AND STAIN REMOVAL SUPPLIES

Absorbent dry powders—examples include Host® and Capture®

Abundant supply of absorbent white tissues and towels for blotting

Acetic acid or white vinegar solution (1/3 cup of vinegar to 1 cup of water)

Acetone or fingernail polish remover, non-oily type

Aerosol cleaners—commercial type available from floor covering dealers and in grocery stores

Alcohol, denatured or rubbing type

Ammonia solution (1 tablespoon to 3/4 cup of water)

Detergent (use 1 teaspoon of mild hand dishwashing type without oily conditioners to 1 cup of warm water or 1 tablespoon of dry powdered laundry type to 1 cup of water)

Dry-cleaning fluid—examples include Carbona®, Renuz-it®, and Energine®

POGR (paint, oil, and grease remover)—examples include Pyratex® and Buckeye®

Pre-soak laundry product (enzyme digester)

Squeeze bottles, medicine droppers, wooden scrapers

expect that vacuuming could remove such deposits from the carpet. If a sticky or waxy residue is found, it is evident that such deposits would remain in the carpet after cleaning, causing the fibers to adhere to one another and promoting rapid resoiling.

Minimizing and Removing Stains. Another important preventive activity is the prompt and efficient removal of solid and liquid substances deposited or spilled on the carpet. This will help to prevent spotting and staining. A few basic rules should be observed in this practice.

1. Act promptly. Foreign substances are more difficult to remove after they have aged.

2. Vacuum dry substances, scoop up excess thick substances, and absorb as much spilled liquid as possible before proceeding with further removal procedures. To avoid diluting and spreading spilled liquids, do not wet at this time. Immediately place absorbent towels over the spill and apply pressure with the hands or heels to promote transfer of the moisture from the carpet to the towels. Use a blotting action: rubbing could cause distortion of the pile. Continue blotting until no more of the spot shows on the towels. Next, cover the area with a half-inch-thick layer of absorbent tissues topped by a sheet of foil and place a heavy object (for example, a big-city telephone directory) on the foil-covered towels. Wait patiently over-

night while the liquid wicks into the towels. If some of the spill remains, proceed with the appropriate removal technique listed in Table 31.3 or Table 31.4.

3. Be prepared. Have a kit of cleaning agents and materials assembled for immediate use. A list of common stain removal supplies is listed in Table 31.2. It does not include carbon tetrachloride, gasoline, or lighter fluid, which are flammable and hazardous to human health. Label the containers and store them in a locked cabinet out of the reach of children.

Common stains and the procedures recommended for removing them from nylon fibers are listed in Table 31.3. Procedures recommended for removing stains from wool carpet fibers are listed in Table 31.4. Residential and commercial consumers may obtain additional stain removal guides and care instructions from retailers, fiber and carpet producers, and trade associations.

Pretests, described above, should precede the application of any stain removal agent.

When small bits of carpet fibers have been melted or singed, they can be carefully clipped and removed. If the damaged area is large, it must be cut out and replaced with a piece reserved at the time of installation.

Interim Maintenance

Interim maintenance activities are designed primarily to assure a high level of appearance retention for an extended period of time and to delay the need for restorative procedures. Interim maintenance is, specifically, the use of a restorative cleaning procedure in a localized area, such as a track-off area, every twenty or thirty-one days. A planned schedule will prevent soil accumulation in areas of heavy traffic from developing an appearance noticeably different from that of adjacent areas.

Interim cleaning may be done with a dry or a wet cleaning system. Frequently, dry cleaning is recommended so that no drying time is required and the area being cleaned can extend beyond the soiled area to prevent marked differences in appearance between the cleaned site and the adjacent areas. Some examples of dry-cleaning compounds are Capture®, produced by Milliken Chemical, DryCare™, produced by National Labs, Host®, produced by Racine Industries, Inc., and Blue Lustre® Dry, produced by Earl Gressmer Company. 3M Brand Carpet Protector Maintainer/Shampoo, produced for interim wet cleaning, deposits a fluorochemical stain repellent compound on the carpet during the cleaning process.

Other interim maintenance activities should be performed as needed. These may include the removal of pills, fuzz, and snags. Fuzziness may occur with loop pile textures when abrasion causes some fibers to rupture, leaving one end in the base of the yarn and one end protruding. The protruding length should be clipped away; it should not be pulled. Unsightly pills should be clipped away,

Table 31.3 REMOVAL OF SPOTS AND STAINS FROM NYLON FIBERS

Stain/Procedure		Stain/Procedure		Procedure A	Procedure E	Procedure I
Asphalt	A	Lard	A	Apply solvent	Detergent	Denatured
Beer	E	Linseed Oil	A	*POGR	Blot	alcohol
Berries	E	Machine Oil	A	Blot	Ammonia	Blot
Blood	B	Mascara	A	Apply solvent	Blot	Repeat, if
Butter	A	Mayonnaise	B	Detergent	Acetic acid	necessary
Candle Wax	G	Mercurochrome	E	Blot	Blot	Note: pretest
Candy (Sugar)	D	Merthiolate	E	Ammonia	Detergent	as for other
Carbon Black	A	Milk	B	Blot	Blot	solutions
Catsup	B	Mimeo Correction		Detergent	Water	
Charcoal	A	Fluid	C	Blot	Blot	**Procedure J**
Cheese	B	Mixed Drinks	E	Water		Detergent
Chewing Gum	G	Model Cement	L	Blot	**Procedure F**	Blot
Chocolate	B	Mustard	E		Detergent	Vinegar
Coffee	E	Nail Polish	L	**Procedure B**	Blot	Blot
Cooking Oil	A	Paint—Latex	A	Detergent	Acetic acid	Ammonia
Crayon	A	Paint—Oil	A	Blot	Blot	Blot
Creme de Menthe	F	Rubber Cement	A	Enzyme digestor	Ammonia	Detergent
Dye—Blue, Black,		Rust	D	Soak	Blot	Blot
Green	F	Shellac	I	Ammonia	Water	Water
Dye—Red	E	Shoe Polish	A	Blot	Blot	Blot
Earth	B	Shortening	A	Detergent		
Egg	B	Soft Drinks	E	Blot	**Procedure G**	**Procedure K**
Excrement	B	Soy Sauce	B	Water	Freeze with ice	Blot
Fish Slime	B	Starch	B	Blot	cube	Water
Foundation		Tar	A		Shatter w/blunt	Blot
Make-Up	A	Tea	E	**Procedure C**	object	Ammonia
Fruit Juice	E	Tooth Paste	B	Apply solvent	Vacuum out chips	Blot
Furniture Polish	A	Typewriter Ribbon	A	*POGR	Apply solvent	Detergent
Furniture Polish with		Urine—Dry	J	Blot	Wait several	Blot
Stain	H	Urine—Fresh	K	Apply solvent	minutes	Water
Gravy	A	Varnish	C	Blot	Blot	Blot
Hair Oil	A	Vaseline	A	Detergent	Repeat, if	
Hair Spray	A	Wax—Paste	A	Blot	necessary	**Procedure L**
Hand Lotion	A	White Glue	B	Water		Polish remover
Ice Cream	B	Wine	E	Blot	**Procedure H**	(non-oily)
Ink—Ball Point	A				Apply solvent	Blot
Ink—Fountain Pen	F			**Procedure D**	Wait several	Repeat
Ink—India	A			Detergent	minutes	
Ink—Marking Pen	A			Blot	Blot	
Ink—Mimeo	A			Acetic acid	Detergent	
Lacquer	C			Blot	Blot	
				Rust remover	Water	
				Blot	Blot	
				Detergent		
				Blot		
				Water		
				Blot		

Courtesy of Allied Fibers.

Table 31.4 REMOVAL OF SPOTS AND STAINS FROM WOOL CARPET FIBERS

This table includes advice on methods of treating stains and the order in which they should be tried. For instance, if clean water does not remove all traces of a beverage, try a solution of washing powder next. Most of the agents mentioned are easy to obtain; however, if you cannot get a dye stripper or hydrochloric acid, call a professional cleaner instead. A freezing agent is available in aerosol sprays, but you can use ice instead to harden chewing gum in order to remove it. CAUTION: Before proceeding to treat a stain, pretest your treatments on an inconspicuous part of the carpet to check for possible color change. Some recommended treatments may be toxic; therefore all precautions should be taken when handling these products.

Types of treatments

1. Carpet shampoo solution. It is important to use a neutral shampoo on wool carpets, not one that is alkaline. Never use carpet shampoos that smell of ammonia.
2. Evaporating spot remover or dry-cleaning fluid.
3. Warm water.
4. Cold water.
5. Laundry detergent (one teaspoon in one pint warm water).
6. Absorbent paper and hot iron.
7. White vinegar.
8. Rubbing alcohol.
9. Nail polish remover or acetone.
10. Turpentine or white spirits.
11. Vacuum.
12. Starch paste.
13. Scrape lightly with fingers or a coin.
14. Rug gently with coarse sandpaper.
15. Scape and vacuum.
16. Glycerine.
17. Call a professional cleaner.

Stains

Acids 1, 5, or 7
Alcoholic beverages 1, 2, 5, or 7
Beer 1, 5, or 7
Bleach 1, 5, or 7
Blood 1, 5, 7, or 12
Burn or scorch mark 13 or 14
Butter 1 or 2
Candy 1, 5, 7, or 15
Chewing gum 1, 2, 5, or 7
Chocolate 1, 2, 5, or 7
Coffee 16
Coffee with cream 16 followed by 5
Colas 1 or 4
Cosmetics 1, 2, 5, or 7
Crayon 1, 2, 5, 7, or 15
Cream 1 or 2
Egg 1, 5, or 7
Excrement (human) 1, 5, or 7
    (remove at once—chemicals in excrement
    attack dyestuffs)
Excrement (pet) 17
Fat and oil 6 then 2
    (do not use iron after solvent)
Floor wax 2
Fruit and juices 1, 2, 5, or 7
Furniture polish 1, 2, 5, or 7
Glue 8
Grass 1, 2, 5, or 7
Gravy 1, 2, 5, or 7
Grease 2 or 15
Household cement 1, 2, 5, or 7

Ice Cream 1, 2, 5, or 7
Ink (fountain pen) 4 or 5
Ink (ball point pen) 1 or 8
Iodine 8
Jam 3
Lipstick 1, 2, 5, or 7
Medicine 17
Metal polish 1
Mildew 17
Milk 1 or 3
Mud 5 or 7
Mustard 1, 5, or 7
Nail polish 2 or 9
Oils 2 or 1
Paint (emulsion) 4 or 1
Paint (oil) 10, 2, or 1
Perfume 1, 2, 5, or 7
Permanent ink 17
Rust 17
Salad dressing 1, 2, 5, or 7
Sauces 1, 2, 5, or 7
Shoe polish 1, 2, 5, 7, or 15
Soot 11, 1, 2, or 17
Tar 2
Tea 1, 5, or 7
Urine (human) 1, 5, or 7 (remove
    at once—chemicals in urine
    attack dyestuffs)
Urine (pet) 17
Urine (old stain) 17
Vomit 1, 2, 5, or 7
Wax 2 or 15
Wine 4, 5, 7, or 2

NOTE: While this advice is offered in good faith, no responsibility is accepted for claims arising from the treatments proposed. If stains fail to respond to treatments listed, call a professional carpet cleaner immediately.

Courtesy of The Wool Bureau, Inc.

although this is a tedious job. Snagged tufts are treated in the same manner as sprouting tufts. If rippling or seam separation is evident, the installer should be called to re-stretch or re-glue the structure and to secure the seams. Area and room-size rugs and runners should be reversed and modules rotated to even the level of wear and soiling. Furniture may be shifted a few inches to allow crushed areas to recover: recovery may be assisted by steaming the areas with an iron held approximately 4 inches above the surface. An occasional "raking" can help to keep the pile tufts in shag floor coverings erect.

Restorative Maintenance

Restorative maintenance involves an overall or wall-to-wall cleaning procedure. The frequency with which such cleaning operations should be undertaken depends on the rate of soil accumulation and the effectiveness of interim maintenance procedures. Of course, the owner's opinion about the acceptability of the surface appearance is usually decisive. Four major restorative maintenance procedures can be considered: dry extraction, dry foam, wet shampoo, and hot water extraction.

Dry Extraction. Dry extraction cleaning is also referred to as absorbent powder or absorbent compound cleaning. The soil-extracting particles are generally composed of water-based cleaning fluids or detergents and a small amount of solvent. Their minute size (they are magnified in Figure 31.19) results in an extremely high surface area to volume ratio that increases their capacity for absorption.

The particles are sprinkled over the carpet structure and vigorously brushed by hand or machine into the pile layer. There, the solvent releases the soil and the porous particles act like tiny sponges, absorbing the soil. Subsequent vacuuming removes the soil-holding particles. Examples of several dry extraction products were listed in the earlier discussion of interim cleaning.

The advantage of dry extraction cleaning is that the fibers are not wetted. This not only avoids the need for drying, but also the problem of overwetting the structure, which could lead to shrinkage and microbe-related problems. When a jute backing is present, overwetting could also cause a problem known as "browning," staining of the pile as the water wicks from the backing upward. Caution should be exercised when brushing the particles into the pile layer to avoid distortion of cut pile yarns.

Dry Foam. Dry foam cleaning is also called aerosol cleaning. The cleaning agent is generally a water-based shampoo that has been converted into foam. The foam is sprayed onto the carpet surface and worked into the pile layer with a hand-held sponge or with mechanically operated brushes. After the compound dries, the surface must be thoroughly vacuumed or rinsed with a damp sponge to remove the soil-foam residue. Some electrically powered units apply the foam and vacuum the carpet in a one-step operation (Figure 31.20).

Cleaning with dry foam may not be as thorough as other methods, especially if a large amount of soil is deeply embedded in the pile layer. The risk of overwetting the carpet is minimal.

Wet Shampooing. The wet shampoo method of carpet restoration is commonly referred to as the rotary brush method. The properly diluted detergent solution or foam is driven into the pile with one or two rotating brushes (Figure 31.21). A thorough vacuuming, preferably with a wet vacuum, must follow. Wet vacuums, unlike conventional vacuums, are engineered to suction fluids, as well as dry matter, from surfaces safely and efficiently.

While the mechanical action of the rotating brushes works the detergent solution into the carpet, it may also cause pile distortion, especially of cut surfaces. Care must be taken in applying the solution or foam to avoid overwetting the structure. Vacuuming of the soil-shampoo compound must be thorough, since any residue will accelerate resoiling.

Hot Water Extraction. Hot water or spray extraction cleaning is commonly called steam extraction, although extemely hot water is used, not steam. The properly diluted shampoo is driven into the pile as a spray by high-pressure jets; it is then immediately extracted by the vacuum component of the machine (Figure 31.22).

Because no mechanical brushing is used in this extraction method, pile yarns are minimally distorted. Spots and stains must be removed before the cleaning operation is begun so that the hot water will not set them. As in wet shampooing, the detergent must be thoroughly removed to retard rapid resoiling.

Salvage Maintenance

Salvage maintenance procedures may be required for extremely soiled carpet or for removing built-up residue. When such problems are evident, it may be advisable to use a combination of wet shampooing and hot water extraction. The mechanical action of the rotary brushes will help to loosen the soil, and the extraction will make for better removal.

SUMMARY

Carpet rollgoods may be installed with a stretch-in or glue-down technique. Modules may be glued to the floor, using a permanent or releasable adhesive; some may be free-laid. For all projects, yardage calculations must be

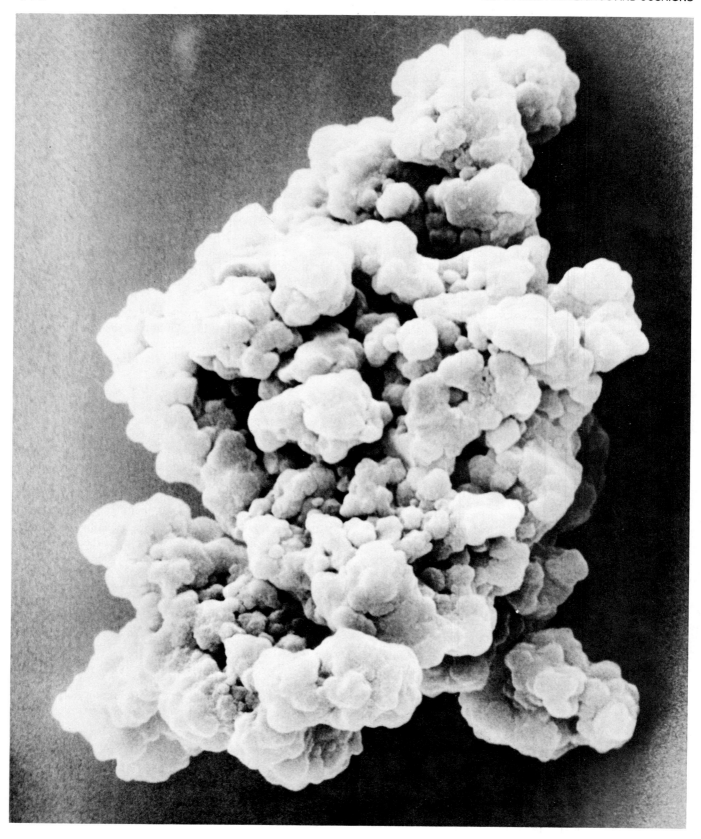

Figure 31.19 Capture® soil-extracting particles. (Courtesy of Milliken and Company.)

accurate. Installation procedures should generally be carried out by skilled personnel.

Effective procedures and adherence to a planned maintenance schedule can maintain the original appearance of textile floor coverings at a higher level for a longer period of time. Wear-life can also be extended this way, and the need for premature replacement avoided.

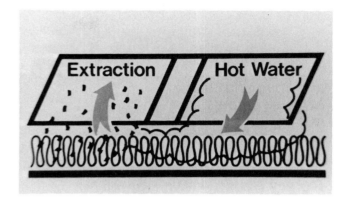

Figure 31.22 Hot water extraction cleaning. (Courtesy of Allied Fibers.)

Figure 31.20 Dry foam cleaning. (Courtesy of Allied Fibers.)

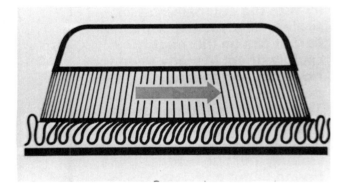

Figure 31.21 Wet shampoo cleaning. (Courtesy of Allied Fibers.)

five

TEXTILE ACCESSORIES
AND ACCENTS

Unit Five focuses on textile accessories and accents used in residential and commercial interiors. Several of these structures fulfill both decorative and functional needs. Chapter 32 examines the composition and construction of textile bath products. It also reviews the federal flammability standard that applies to bath rugs and mats. Chapter 33 covers the wide assortment of textile fabrics manufactured for use in bedding products, as well as the natural and synthesized fillings used in beddings and the flamma-

bility mandate with which mattresses and mattress pads must comply prior to marketing.

Chapter 34 presents various tabletop accessories, including tablecloths, napkins, table runners, and doilies. The final chapter describes and illustrates textile accents created by skilled artisans, and reviews techniques for producing hangings, needlework accents, lace, and distinctive handprinted fabrics.

chapter *32*

Textile Products for the Bath

- Towels and Toweling
- Bath Rugs and Mats
- Shower Curtains

Over the past two decades, fabric stylists and end product designers have created many decorative variations of such textile bath products as towels, rugs, mats, and shower curtains, so that these items are often as ornamental as they are functional. Manufacturers have also expanded the size range of towels, increased the types of materials used in shower curtains, and varied the shapes and constructions of small bath rugs and mats. Frequently, contemporary bath products are offered in coordinated ensembles, and sometimes they are part of elaborate ensembles that include bedding products as well.

Towels, toweling, bath mats, rugs, carpet, and textile shower curtains are subject to the provisions of the Textile Fiber Products Identification Act (see Chapter 10). Small rugs and bath mats are also subject to a federal flammability mandate, FF 2-70.

TOWELS AND TOWELING

Various fabrication techniques, including weaving, stitch-knitting, and bonding webs of fibers, are used to produce toweling. The major portion of today's toweling is composed of cotton.

Statistical Profile of Fiber Usage

In contrast to other interior textile products, which are primarily composed of man-made fibers, towels and toweling are primarily composed of cotton, as detailed in Table 32.1. The poundages listed include the fiber used in the production of woven dish towels, but they do not include the fiber used to produce bonded-web toweling.

Dominance of Cotton. The towel and towelings market has been and continues to be dominated by cotton. This natural fiber held more than 99 percent of the 1966 market, and although its use has decreased since the late 1960s, it nonetheless holds approximately 94 percent of the current market. Cotton is highly wickable, or able to move moisture along its surface by capillary action; it also is soft and has relatively high moisture absorption, features that make it an attractive and efficient fiber for toweling. Linen, which has slightly higher moisture absorption and produces less lint than cotton, is also used. The harsh hand and low abrasion resistance characteristic of linen, however, preclude its use in bath towels, and the comparatively high cost of the fiber limits its use in dish towels.

The increased consumption of the noncellulosic fibers reflects their growing use in strong spun yarns incorporated in the base of pile toweling. Although these fibers can be spun into yarns that simulate the appearance and hand of yarns composed of cotton, they do not provide the high absorbency needed for towels. Currently, textile re-

Table 32.1 FIBER USAGE IN TOWELS AND TOWELING
(million pounds)

		Man-made fibers[a]						Cotton	Wool
			Cellulosic		Noncellulosic				
Year	Total Fiber	Total	Yarn	Staple	Yarn	Staple		Cotton	Wool
1966	282.4	2.5	b	2.5	c			279.9	c
1985	351.1	22.3	c	0.9	0.2	21.2		328.8	c

[a]Man-made fiber end-use is divided between cellulosic (rayon plus acetate fibers) and noncellulosic (nylon, polyester, acrylic, olefin, saran, spandex, and textile glass fiber). Yarn includes monofilaments, and olefin "yarn" also includes film fiber and spunbonded polypropylene. Staple includes tow and fiberfill.

[b]Nominal amounts used (less than 50,000 pounds).

[c]Little or none of the fiber is used.

Sources: Textile Economics Bureau, Inc., *Textile Organon,* Vol. 43, No. 11, November 1972, 166, and Vol. 57, No. 9, September 1986, 210.

search chemists are investigating ways to make noncellulosic fibers more hydrophilic so that they will exhibit the requisite wickability. When an economically viable technique is perfected, the use of these fibers in flat and pile toweling will no doubt increase.

Manufacturing Toweling

Manufacturers use a variety of fabrication techniques to produce flat, nonpile toweling. They use a warp pile weaving operation to produce pile toweling.

Constructing Pile Toweling. Pile or terry toweling is also known as Turkish toweling. The components of this toweling are illustrated in Figure 32.1. One set of filling or weft yarns is interlaced with one set of base or ground warp yarns and two sets of pile warp yarns. If loops are planned for only one side of the fabric, only one set of pile warp yarns is used. Fabrics with loops on both sides have more fiber surface area for absorbing moisture, but they are also more expensive if the construction density is not reduced. For visual interest, the pile yarns appearing on each side can be of different colors.

The warp pile weaving operation used to produce terry toweling is known as the slack tension technique. During weaving, the base warp yarns are held under regular (high) tension, and the pile warp yarns are held under slackened tension. As the reed moves forward in the battening operation, it compacts the filling picks and pushes the slackened yarns into pile loops on the fabric surface. For greater durability, the number of picks per crosswise row of loops may be increased from three to four or five, but the number of picks must be limited to preseve the number of pile loops available for absorption. A Jacquard

mechanism may be used to produce elaborate, multicolored patterns in the pile layer (see Figure 32.2).

For economical production, terry looms are generally threaded for full-width weaving. When hemmed edges and ends are planned, the dimensions of individual towels are demarcated by the omission of pile yarns in narrow lengthwise and crosswise bands; when fringed ends are planned, the crosswise bands are also void of filling picks. A dobby mechanism may be used to produce woven-in border designs.

For increased efficiency and economy in both weaving and finishing, textile machinery engineers have developed extra-wide looms capable of simultaneously weaving multiple widths of toweling. Looms of the type pictured in Figure 32.2 can weave up to ten widths of toweling during one operation. The several widths of toweling have tucked-in selvages (see Figure 6.2b, page 45).

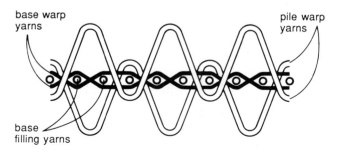

Figure 32.1 Cross-sectional sketch of terry toweling that has three filling picks per crosswise row of pile loops.

Figure 32.2 Loom engineered to weave multiple widths of terry toweling. (Courtesy of Sulzer-Ruti, Inc.)

Terry velour toweling has a conventional looped pile surface on one side, and a dense, cut pile surface on the other side. The sheared velour surface has a thick and luxurious appearance and hand, but the level of moisture absorption is relatively low since only the small tips of the yarns are exposed.

A small amount of terry is produced by a stitch-knitting operation known by the patent name Malipol. In this procedure, an expansion of the stitch-knitting technique described in Chapter 7, pile yarns are incorporated into webs of yarns that are layered and stitched.

Fabricating Flat Toweling. Flat toweling is generally produced by weaving yarns in a basic biaxial or dobby interlacing pattern or by bonding webs of fibers. Crash is a plain-woven fabric composed of coarse, irregular yarns spun from linen. The fabric is constructed into dish towels intended for the lint-free drying of glassware. Twill-woven toweling, often referred to as institutional toweling, is generally produced with brightly colored stripes on each long side and constructed into towels used in restaurants. Huck toweling (huckaback) is woven on a dobby loom and has small filling floats. These slightly raised floats, visible in the close-up photograph in Figure 32.3, improve the drying efficiency of the towel.

Disposable toweling is produced by bonding webs of fibers with heat or an adhesive. Some items are intended to be used once; others are for repeated use. For increased strength, a scrim of fine yarns may be anchored between the layered webs. The scrim-reinforced toweling pictured in Figure 32.4 is composed of cellulosic fibers.

Constructing Towels

Towels come in a variety of sizes and with a variety of edge and end finishes. Trims and embroidery embellish their surfaces.

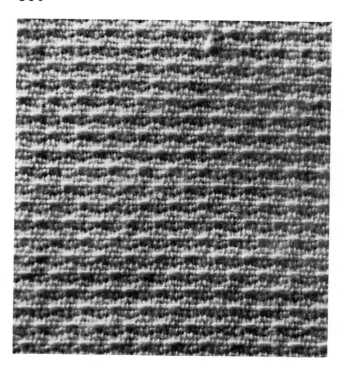

Figure 32.3 Huck toweling, a dobby-woven fabric with slightly raised filling floats.

Types and Sizes. The assortment available on today's market includes several types of towels. The approximate size ranges of the various types are listed in Table 32.2.

Table 32.2 TYPES AND SIZES OF TOWELS

Type	Inches, width x length
Dish towel	12 x 24 to 16 x 30
Fingertip/guest	9 x 14 to 11 x 20
Wash cloth	12 x 12 to 14 x 14
Face/hand towel	15 x 25 to 20 x 36
Bath towel	20 x 40 to 27 x 50
Bath sheet	35 x 66 to 45 x 75

Edge Finishes and Decorative Treatments. Terry toweling is cut along the flat lengthwise and crosswise bands spaced throughout the pile greige goods. Cutting produces unfinished towels of various sizes. The sides may be finished with a small, machine-stitched hem or with machine serging. The ends may be hemmed or left with a yarn fringe. Squares of pile fabric are cut for wash cloths, and the four raw edges are serged. For decorative interest, bands of embroidered fabric or trim may be sewn across towels and wash cloths, or the surface may be embellished with a Schiffli-embroidered monogram or motif.

Coordinated Items. Yarn-dyed, solid-colored, or printed toweling used to construct dish towels may also be used to produce such coordinated items as oven mitts, pot

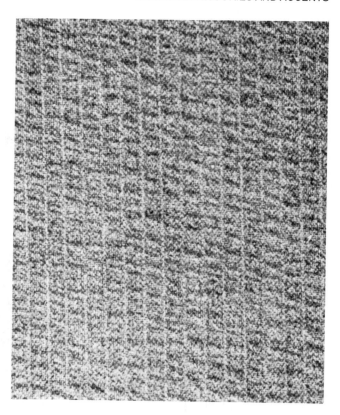

Figure 32.4 Kaycel® scrim-reinforced disposable toweling. (Courtesy of Kimberly-Clark Corporation.)

holders, small appliance covers, and aprons. The color styling and decorative treatment of bath towels may be replicated in bedding products; the several bath and bedding products are then offered and promoted as a coordinated ensemble.

Caring for Towels

Virtually all towels can be machine washed and dried, although some borders and trims may exhibit shrinkage. To avoid excessive fiber damage, white items should be bleached with chlorine compounds only when necessary, not routinely in each successive laundering. To avoid potential bleeding and staining problems, towels with intense, deep-toned colors should be laundered separately. To avoid excessive deposition of softening agents, which reduces moisture absorption, some liquid fabric softeners should be omitted every third or fourth time the items are laundered.

BATH RUGS AND MATS

Soft floor coverings are produced in various sizes and shapes for use in bathroom interiors. Bath rugs are larger and normally heavier than bath mats, and are used continuously for decoration, softness underfoot, or insulation. Bath mats are used temporarily to protect the floor from moisture and to prevent bathers from slipping. Both floor covering products are subject to a federal flammability mandate.

Constructing and Finishing Bath Rugs and Mats

Bath rugs are generally cut from tufted or knitted carpet that has a lower pile construction density and a greater pile height than carpet produced for other interior applications. For economy and ease of handling in use and care, no secondary backing is applied; for skid resistance, the adhesive compound is normally embossed. End-product producers cut various sizes of round, square, oval, and rectangular shapes from the wide carpet and finish the raw edges by hemming, serging, or binding with firmly woven tape. Frequently, rugs cut from the same solid-colored greige goods are tufted a second time to introduce a distinctive design to the surface; no additional backcoating is applied to these items to secure the added pile yarns. Other rugs may be embellished with various types of trim, including rhinestone tape, braid, and fringe.

Pile fabric produced for use as a bath rug may also be used to construct such other items as toilet lid and tank covers. Lid covers have an elasticized edge or a drawstring run through a casing to secure them in use and permit their easy removal for laundering.

Bath mats may be woven in narrow widths, with the selvages as the side edges and small hems finishing the ends, or they may be cut from wide fabric and hemmed on all edges. Two different colors of warp pile yarns may be used to produce mats with different colors of loops on each side, or several colors of pile yarns may be used to produce richly patterned, Jacquard-woven mats.

Flammability Standard

FF 2-70 Standard for the Surface Flammability of Small Carpets and Rugs became effective in December 1971. The scope of FF 2-70 includes soft floor covering items that have an area not greater than 24 square feet and no dimension greater than 6 feet.

Test Method and Acceptance Criteria. Items within the scope of FF 2-70 are tested in accordance with the procedures outlined in the methenamine tablet test. This test method is also specified in the flammability standard established for large carpets and rugs, FF 1-70 (see Chapter 30). The acceptance criteria, which are based on char length, are the same in both standards.

Labeling Requirement. Small rugs and mats that fail the tablet test may be marketed. They must, however, carry a permanently attached label bearing the following statement: flammable (fails U. S. Consumer Product Safety Commisson Standard 2-70; should not be used near sources of ignition).

SHOWER CURTAINS

Shower curtains may be constructed of textile fabric or polymer film sheeting. Both types are often produced as part of a coordinated bath ensemble.

Polymer Film Shower Curtains

Various types of polymer film sheeting are used to produce nontextile shower curtains. The sheetings differ in gauge or thickness, in the level of transparency, and in color styling. Some films are relatively thin, others relatively thick; some are opaque, others transparent; some are solid colored, while others have contemporary designs printed with opaque pigments.

Textile Shower Curtains

With the exception of heavy, stiff structures, virtually any textile fabric may be used for a shower curtain. To protect the fabric from water and soap residue, converters may coat the interior surface with a waterproofing compound, or the consumer may hang a thin film as a separate curtain lining.

SUMMARY

Unlike other interior furnishings, which are primarily composed of man-made fibers, towels are primarily composed of cotton because it provides softness, wickability, and good moisture absorption. Towels are available in a wide range of sizes and with a variety of decorative features and side and end finishes.

Bath rugs and mats are available in various sizes, shapes, colors, and textures. Like other soft floor coverings, bath rugs and bath mats are subject to a federal flammability mandate.

Shower curtains may be constructed of textile or nontextile fabrics. Along with towels and bath rugs and mats, shower curtains are frequently offered as part of a coordinated group of bath products.

chapter 33

Textile Bedding Products

- Fiber and Yarn Usage in Beddings
- Fillings Used in Bedding Products
- Mattresses, Mattress Foundations, and Mattress Protectors
- Pillows
- Sheets and Pillowcases
- Blankets
- Bedspreads, Quilts, and Comforters

The bedding products industry is an important segment of the interior textile industry; some 15 percent of the total fiber used for textile furnishings is channeled to the production of beddings.[1] The assortment of textile bedding products includes mattresses and box springs, mattress pads and mattress covers, sheets and pillowcases, quilts, comforters, sleeping bags, blankets, bedspreads, and pillows. All of these are produced in different sizes, and some have styling features as distinctive and varied as those typical of fashion apparel. Many of these items are multicomponent structures. Most beddings are composed entirely of textile fibers, but some products, including mattresses, box springs, and sleeping bags, contain some nontextile components.

FIBER AND YARN USAGE IN BEDDINGS

A statistical profile of the types of fibers used in residential and commercial bedding products is given in Table 33.1. The poundages listed in the first category, bedspreads and quilts, include the fiber used for producing the outer shells of comforters; the poundages listed in the second category, blankets and blanketing, include the fiber used for producing the bindings applied to the ends of the coverings; and the poundages listed in the last category, sheets and other bedding, include the fiber used to produce the outside cover of quilted pads, mattress pads, mattresses and innersprings, civilian cots, and sleeping bags. None of the poundages tabulated include any quantities of fiber used in fillings.

Since 1966, the total quantity of fiber used in bedding products has decreased from 810 million pounds to 660.9 million pounds. This decrease does not result from production of fewer square yards of fabric; rather, it reflects a shift in usage from the relatively heavy natural fibers to the lighter weight noncellulosic fibers.

Predominance of Noncellulosic Fibers

In 1966, approximately 80 percent of the bedding products market was held by cotton, 13 percent by rayon and acetate, 5 percent by noncellulosic fibers, and the remaining 2 percent by wool. In contrast, noncellulosic fibers dominated the 1985 market, collectively accounting for some 52 percent of the total fiber usage. However, the importance of cotton in contemporary products should not be overlooked; this natural fiber alone accounted for about 45 percent of the 1985 market.

Table 33.1 FIBER USAGE IN BEDDING PRODUCTS
(million pounds)

End-use	Year	Total fiber	Man-made fibers[a]	Cellulosic		Noncellulosic		Cotton	Wool
			Total	Yarn	Staple	Yarn	Staple		
Bedspreads/ quilts	1966	149.2	42.7	9.9	27.8	4.5	0.5	106.5	b
	1985	134.6	77.4	c	6.0	17.4	54.0	57.2	b
Blankets/ blanketing	1966	113.7	70.4	1.9	43.4	3.5	21.6	26.2	17.1
	1985	73.4	56.4	b	0.2	b	56.2	12.9	4.1
Sheets/ other bedding	1966	547.1	30.8	1.0	24.5	0.3	5.0	516.3	b
	1985	452.9	227.0	1.5	12.5	47.9	165.1	225.9	b

[a]Man-made fiber end-use is divided between cellulosic (rayon plus acetate fibers) and noncellulosic (nylon, polyester, acrylic, olefin, saran, spandex, and textile glass fiber). Yarn includes monofilaments, and olefin "yarn" also includes film fiber and spunbonded polypropylene. Staple includes tow and fiberfill.

[b]Little or none of the fiber is used.

[c]Nominal amounts used (less than 50,000 pounds).

Sources: Textile Economics Bureau, Inc., *Textile Organon,* Vol. 43, No. 11, November, 1972, 166, and Vol. 57, No. 9, September 1986, 210.

Disclosure of Fiber Composition

Most textile bedding products are subject to the labeling mandates set forth in the Textile Fiber Products Identification Act and its accompanying set of rules and regulations. Specifically, the scope of the TFPIA includes all beddings, which, by definition, include sheets, covers, blankets, comforters, pillows, pillowcases, quilts, bedspreads, pads, and all other textile fiber products used or intended to be used on or about a bed, not including furniture, mattresses, or box springs, or the outer coverings on these items. Fillings incorporated in bedding products primarily for warmth rather than for structural purposes are also included.

As explained in Chapter 10, products within the scope of the TFPIA must carry a label or hangtag that discloses the fiber composition, the name or registered number of the manufacturer, and the country of origin. Products having down or feather fillings should also be labeled in accordance with guidelines specifically established by the FTC for these materials; these guidelines are discussed in the next section.

Predominance of Spun Yarns

Staple fibers are used more extensively in bedding products than filament fibers, accounting for some 90 percent of today's market. All staple-length fibers, natural as well as man-made, must be spun to produce usable yarn structures; therefore, spun yarns predominate. In comparison with filament yarns, spun yarns are often judged to have a more attractive appearance and a softer, more comfortable hand, qualities many consumers prefer in their bedding products.

FILLINGS USED IN BEDDING PRODUCTS

Filling components in bedding products may be composed of natural or synthesized materials. Some materials are used in loose, lofty masses; others, in stabilized battings; and still others, in well-defined, three-dimensional forms.

Natural Filling Materials

Natural filling materials include down, feathers, wool, cotton, and kapok. Earlier, cotton and kapok were used alone, either loose or in the form of batting. Today, supply and delivery problems have reduced the use of kapok, and the low resiliency of cotton has prompted manufacturers to blend it with polyester. Although the use of wool as a filling material is limited, primarily because of its cost, some longer-staple wool fibers are occasionally used to produce lofty, three-dimensional battings for use in comforters.

Down and feathers are virtually always used loose in lofty masses. Bedding products filled with these materials should be labeled in accordance with the provisions of the Guides for the Feather and Down Products Industry.

Guides for the Feather and Down Products Industry. While labeling guides are advisory in nature, manufacturers should adhere to the recommendations included in them in order to avoid engaging in commercial practices that could be considered unfair or deceptive under the provisions of the Federal Trade Commission Act. Included in the Guides for the Feather and Down Products Industry, promulgated on October 29, 1971, are definitions of terms and recommended procedures for labeling products filled with these natural materials. Some of these terms and their definitions are listed below:

Down: the undercoating of waterfowl, consisting of clusters of light, fluffy filaments, i.e., barbs, growing from the quill point but without any quill shafts. (The quill is the tube or barrel of a feather.)

Plumules: down waterfowl plumage with underdeveloped soft and flaccid quill with barbs indistinguishable from those of down.

Down fiber: the detached barbs from down and plumules and the detached barbs from the basal end of waterfowl quill shaft, which are indistinguishable from the barbs of down.

Feathers: the plumage or out-growth forming the contour and external covering of fowl, which are whole in structure and which have not been processed in any manner other than by washing, dusting, chemical treatment, and sanitizing.

Waterfowl feathers: feathers derived from ducks and geese.

Nonwaterfowl feathers or land fowl feathers: feathers derived from chickens, turkeys, and other land fowl.

Quill feathers: feathers that are over 4 inches in length or that have a quill point exceeding six-sixteenths of an inch in length.

Feather fiber: the detached barbs of feathers that are not joined or attached to each other.

Crushed feathers: feathers that have been processed by a curling, crushing, or chopping machine, which has changed the original form of the feathers without removing the quill. The term also includes the fiber resulting from such processing.

Damaged feathers: feathers that have been damaged by insects, or otherwise materially injured.

Residue: means quill pith, quill fragments, trash, or foreign matter.

According to the provisions of the guides, industry products should be labeled as to the kind or type of filling material used. When the filling material consists of a mixture of more than one kind or type, then the proportion of each should be disclosed in the order of predominance, the largest proportion first. If the term "nonwaterfowl" or "land fowl" is used, it should be accompanied by the name of the fowl from which the products were obtained, for instance, chicken or turkey.

A certain leeway is permitted in the use of the terms down and waterfowl feathers. "Down" may be used to designate any industry product containing the following filling material:

1. Down, plumules,
   and down fiber . . . . minimum 80 percent
   Consisting of:
   Down and plumules. . . . . . . minimum 70 percent
   Down fiber . . . . .maximum 10 percent
2. Remainder .20 percent
   Consisting of:
   Down fiber, waterfowl feather fiber, and waterfowl feathers, and nonwaterfowl feathers and nonwaterfowl feather fiber.. . . . . maximum 2 percent
   Residue . . . . maximum 2 percent

A product should not be designated "100 percent down," "all down," "pure down," or by other terms of similar import unless it in fact contains only down, without regard to the tolerance detailed above.

"Waterfowl feathers" may be used to designate any plumage product containing the following filling material, free of quill and crushed feathers:

   Waterfowl feathers . . . . .minimum 80 percent
   Nonwaterfowl feathers . . . . . . maximum 8 percent
   Residue . . . . .maximum 2 percent

The name of a waterfowl species may be included if a minimum of 90 percent of the waterfowl plumage contained in the filling is that of the species.

Synthesized Filling Materials

Synthesized fillings include such materials as noncellulosic fibers, synthetic rubber, and polyurethane. Noncellulosic fibers are virtually always in staple or tow forms for use as filling material. They may be used in loose, lofty masses, known as fiberfill, or organized into battings of various thicknesses. Today, fiberfill is almost exclusively composed of polyester.[2] Batting structures composed of polyester, as well as those composed of polyester and cotton, may be stabilized by spraying resin throughout the layered fibers. Synthesized rubber and urethane compounds are generally foamed and formed into three-dimensional structures for use in pillows, into thick slabs for use in mattresses, and into thin slabs for use in quilts (see Figure 33.14).

Functions and Properties of Filling Materials

In mattresses, fillings provide support for the body; in bed pillows, they cushion the head; in decorative pillows, they impart and maintain a distinctive form. In most other bedding products, fillings are primarily intended for thermal insulation. Ideally, filling materials should be lofty or bulky without being heavy. They must be resilient to regain their original loftiness after being compressed, and they must be affordable.

To improve the loftiness and insulative value of fiberfill without increasing the weight, textile fiber chemists have engineered fibers with hollow interiors. Examples of fibers with tunnel-like cores include KodOfill® polyester, marketed by Eastman Chemical Products, Inc., and Dacron® Hollofil® polyester, produced by du Pont (Figure 33.1a). Dacron® 113 polyester has four microscopic openings in its interior, as shown in Figure 33.1b.

The fiberfill pictured in Figure 33.2 is composed of KodOfill® polyester. The open interiors of the fibers and the air pockets surrounding them provide a great deal of insulation. The quilted comforter pictured in Figure 33.8 is filled with this product.

In laboratory testing, the insulative values of goose down, wool, polyester, and olefin were found to be similar.[3] Down and feathers offer the advantage of being inherently lofty and lightweight, but their limited supply in comparison to demand and the labor involved in their retrieval make them comparatively expensive. Wool has excellent resiliency, but the fibers are comparatively heavy and expensive. Fiberfill is lofty, lightweight, and economical; unlike the natural filling materials, it is also nonallergenic.

Care of Fillings

Bedding products filled with wool batting must be drycleaned to avoid the agitation that can cause felting shrinkage. Some manufacturers recommend that down, feather, and polyester fillings be dry-cleaned to minimize shifting and clumping of the materials. Others recommend that the fillings be laundered and then tumble dried to encourage the materials to regain their original loftiness. In every case, the care procedures performed on the filling must be appropriate for the outercovering and vice versa. To prevent care practices that could cause unnecessary product

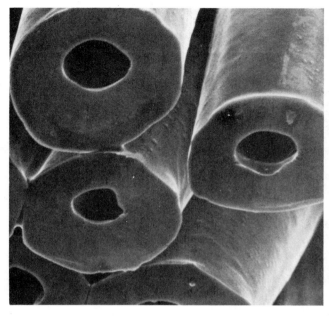

a) Dacron® Hollofil®

b) Dacron® 113

Figure 33.1 Photomicrographs of hollow Dacron® polyester fibers. (Courtesy of E.I. du Pont de Nemours & Co., Inc.)

Figure 33.2 Photomicrograph of KodOfill® polyester fiberfill. (Courtesy of Eastman Chemical Products, Inc.)

failure—a problem generally accompanied by the consumer losing confidence in the producer's name—many manufacturers voluntarily label their goods with care instructions.

MATTRESSES, MATTRESS FOUNDATIONS, AND MATTRESS PROTECTORS

Beds, and such dual purpose sleeping equipment as convertible sofas and studio couches, have two basic units, a mattress and a mattress foundation. Because mattresses, especially when used with a companion set of box springs, are comparatively expensive, covers and pads are often employed to protect them and prolong their use-life. Unlike other bedding products, mattresses and mattress pads are subject to a federal flammability mandate.

Mattress Foundations

With the exception of air-filled mattresses, intended to be placed on the floor or ground, and water-filled mattresses, which are placed within a plastic-lined, boxlike frame, all mattresses are used with a resilient foundation. These foundations may be flat or three-dimensional units.

Flat Bedspring Units. In some flat bedspring units, flexible metal bands are anchored to the ends of the bed frame by tightly coiled springs. Additional springs, placed crosswise, stabilize the parallel bands. In other flat bedspring units, metal bands are interlaced and held to the sides and ends of the frame with spring units. While these nontextile foundations are relatively inexpensive, they do not provide adequate support for everyday use and are normally used only with items intended for occasional use, such as cots and rollaway beds.

Box-spring Units. In box-spring units, hundreds of coiled springs are anchored to wooden slats and framing boards and to each other. Because box springs and mattresses are offered as a coordinated set, the fabric that decorates the mattress also covers the exposed surfaces of the foundation. For economy, a fine, lightweight fabric such as batiste or spunbonded olefin serves as a dustcover on the back of the springs unit. Various types and amounts of filling are used for top cushioning, and an insulator fabric is placed over the springs to prevent them from penetrating into the filling materials.

While the gauge of the wire used for the support springs in box-springs is generally higher than that used for the support springs in mattresses, the configuration of the coils in the units may be identical. In double deck springs, the tighter coiling of the lower portion is designed to provide firm support and the looser coiling of the upper portion is for resiliency (Figure 33.3a). The flat metal bands anchored over platform-top springs (Figure 33.3b) provide a more uniform surface than that created by open-top springs. The extra coils placed at the top of convoluted springs provide increased support when the foundation is depressed by the weight of the body (Figure 33.3c).

The quality of box-springs and innerspring mattresses depends on the gauge of the wires and the level of spring coiling. These features are the main determinants of the use-life of the units; they also help determine the length of any warranty offered by the manufacturer.

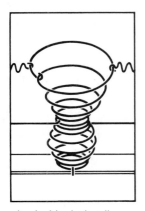

a) double deck coil

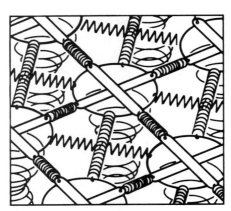

b) platform-top coil

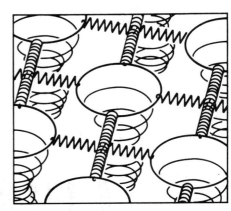

c) convoluted coil

Figure 33.3 Configurations of springs used in box springs and mattresses.

Mattresses

Mattresses are available with different interior components and construction features. They are produced in several sizes and covered with a variety of textile fabrics.

Interior Components. Mattresses are available in two constructions: innerspring and foam-core. Foam-core mattresses have a single interior component, a slab of rubber or urethane foam. In these units, the level of support varies readily with the density of the foam material. The several components in innerspring units are illustrated in Figure 33.4. The spring units may be anchored to one another by coiled wires, metal clips, or flexible metal bands, or each spring may be encased within a fabric pocket and all pockets sewn together to minimize side sway. An insulator fabric like that on box-springs prevents the springs from penetrating the upper filling layers. The degree of firmness can be increased by using a high gauge of wire for the spring units and by using resinated batting. Small holes should be built into the sides of mattresses to provide ventilation and preserve the freshness of the interior components.

Exterior Coverings. "Ticking" is a generic term for any fabric used to cover the exterior of mattresses, box springs, and pillows. Tickings may be plain or highly decorative. To capture the attention of the contemporary consumer, such elaborately patterned fabrics as damask are increasingly used today in place of the familiar twill-woven ticking with its blue or black stripes (Figure 33.5).

For long-term serviceability, tickings should be firmly woven of strong, smooth yarns. Less durable and less expensive coverings generally are made of coarse yarns and contain low thread counts and excess sizing.

Sizes. Mattresses are produced in a variety of sizes, with each size designated by name, not by dimensions. The names and characteristic dimensions of the more common mattresses are listed in Table 33.2.

Larger mattresses should have permanently attached side handles to facilitate the turning of the unit. As a precaution, consumers should measure their mattresses prior to purchasing bed coverings.

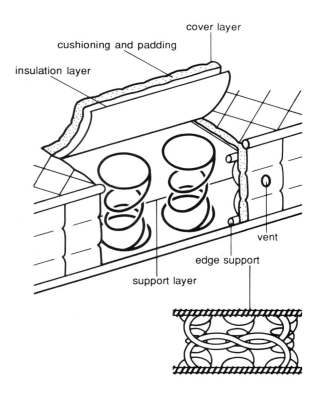

Figure 33.4 Cross-sectional sketch of an innerspring mattress.

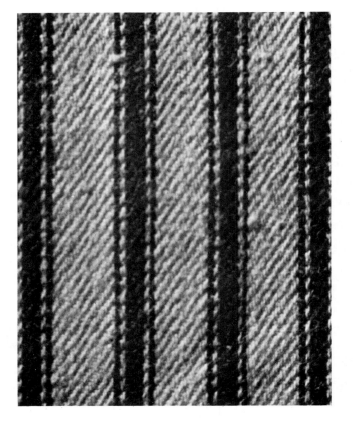

Figure 33.5 Twill-woven ticking characterized by lengthwise stripes.

Table 33.2 MATTRESS SIZES AND NAMES

Name	Inches, width x length
Rollaway bed or cot	30 x 75
Studio couch or daybed	28 x 74
Single bed	33 x 75
Twin bed	39 x 75
Twin bed, extra long	39 x 80
Three-quarter bed	48 x 75
Double bed	54 x 75
Double bed, extra long	54 x 80
Queen-size bed	60 x 80
King-size bed	78 x 80
California bed	72 x 80

Mattress Covers and Pads

Mattress covers protect mattresses from dust, moisture, and abrasion. Mattress pads provide these features and increased cushioning as well.

Covers. Mattress covers may be designed and constructed to completely encase the mattress or to cover only the exposed surfaces. Zippers or elasticized edges ensure a smooth fit. When maximum protection against moisture is needed, a vinyl film sheeting bonded to an acetate or nylon tricot may be used as the covering fabric. For protection against dust, a closely woven fabric composed of cotton or a blend of cotton or polyester may be appropriate.

Pads. Mattress pads are multicomponent structures that cushion and soften while they cover and protect the mattress. Most pads have a batting of polyester quilted between two woven or spunbonded fabrics. Some pads cover the sleeping surface only; others cover the sleeping surface and the vertical sides; and others completely encase the mattress. An example of an encasing style is the Bedsack®, produced by Perfect Fit Industries, Inc. The company also manufactures matching pads for box springs and bed pillows.

Mattress pads of wool have been used in hospitals and care-type facilities for some time, but have only recently been promoted for residential use. These structures are produced by locking slivers of lambs wool into a knitted base fabric composed of polyester. The fleece-like fabric is placed, pile up, under the bottom sheet, providing softness, warmth, and moisture absorption. The wool used in some of these "underblankets" has been treated with agents that minimize felting shrinkage, permitting the pad to be laundered. The name Superwash® may be used with pads that The Wool Bureau, Inc. has certified to be fully machine washable.

Reducing Microbial Action. Covers and pads, especially those produced for use in hospitals and nursing facilities, may be treated with agents that effectively reduce the action of such microbes as bacteria and fungi. Bacteria and fungi are extremely simple vegetative plant forms that lack chlorophyll. Bacteria can react with perspiration to cause odor and can cause infection and slow the healing process. Fungi, such as molds and mildew, feed on cellulosic fibers and sizings. These microbes are often described as "saprophytic" (from the Greek for "rotten growth"); they produce stains and odors, and weaken and rot fibers.

Antimicrobial chemicals can resist a microbe either by killing the pest or retarding its normal activities. Agents such as quaternary ammonium compounds (four organic groups bonded to nitrogen), metallic salts, and other organic compounds can help protect fibers. Converters are now able to apply these agents with others in a single operation, reducing production time and expense while affording fibers greater protection.

Flammability Standard

The Standard for the Flammability of Mattresses, FF 4-72, was established in an effort to protect the public against unreasonable risk of mattress fires leading to death, personal injury, or significant property damage. The most common mode of bedding ignition, a burning cigarette, is used as the ignition source in the test procedure.

Scope of FF 4-72. The provisions of FF 4-72 apply to domestic and imported mattresses. Included in the definition of mattresses are mattress pads; adult, youth, crib, and portable crib mattresses; bunk bed mattresses; corner group and daybed mattresses; rollaway and convertible sofa bed mattresses; high risers; trundle bed mattresses; and futons—flexible mattresses filled with cotton batting. Items specifically excluded from FF 4-72 are sleeping bags, pillows, mattress foundations such as box springs, water bed and air mattresses, and other items such as chaise lounges and sofa beds, which are distinct from convertible sofa beds. A convertible sofa bed is an upholstered sofa with a mattress concealed under the cushions; a sofa bed is an upholstered sofa with a hinged back that swings down flat with the seating cushions to form the sleeping surface.

Test Procedures. In testing, the bare sleeping surface of mattresses, including smooth, tape edge, and quilted or tufted locations, is exposed to at least nine ignited cigarettes that are 85 millimeters long and have no filter tips. These locations are also tested by placing nine additional burning cigarettes between two bed sheets that cover the mattress (Figure 33.6a). The muslin or percale sheets used must be 100 percent cotton, have no durable press resins or flame retardant agents, and be laundered one time prior to testing.

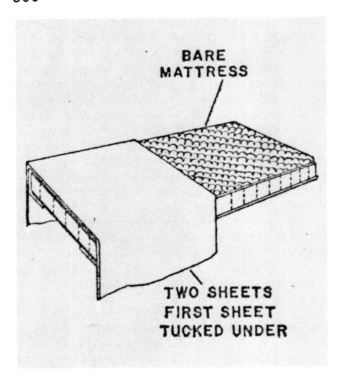

a) mattress preparation

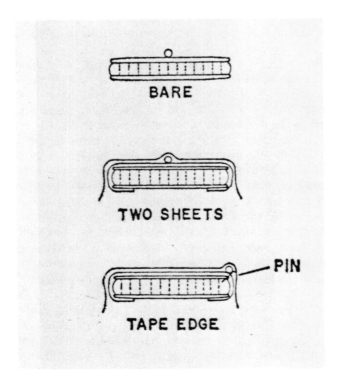

b) cigarette locations

Figure 33.6 Mattress preparation and cigarette locations used in FF 4-72. (*Source: Federal Register,* Vol. 38, No. 110, June 8, 1973, 15100.)

Mattress pads are tested in the same manner before they are laundered or dry-cleaned and again after they have been cleaned in accordance with prescribed procedures. Pads treated with a flame retardant agent must be labeled with precautionary care instructions to help prevent the use of agents or procedures that could impair the effectiveness of the finishing compound.

Acceptance Criterion. Individual cigarette test locations pass the test if the char length of the mattress or mattress pad surface is not more than 2 inches in any direction from the nearest point of the cigarette. All eighteen cigarette locations must pass the test in order for the mattress or pad to be marketed.

PILLOWS

Two categories of pillows, namely bed pillows and decorative pillows, are available on today's bedding products market. The same filling materials and ticking fabrics may be used in both types of pillows, but decorative pillows are produced in a wider variety of sizes and forms and their outer coverings have more elaborate styling features.

Sizes and Forms

Bed pillows are basically rectangular in shape, and most are 20 to 21 inches wide. Their length varies according to the width of the mattress with which they are intended to be paired. Standard pillows, intended to be used with a twin or double mattress, are 26 to 27 inches long; queen-size pillows are 30 to 31 inches long; and king-size pillows are 37 to 38 inches long.

Decorative pillows are available in various sizes and forms. Neckroll pillows are cylindrical forms 6 inches by 14 inches or a larger 7 inches by 17 inches; boudoir pillows, also called breakfast pillows, are 12 inches by 16 inches; bolster pillows are cylindrical or lozenge-shaped pillows that may be from 40 to 50 inches in length; Turkish pillows, which have gathered corners, are 16 inches square; European pillows are 26 inches square; round pillows are normally 12 inches in diameter; and a bedrest pillow has a back and arms.

Fillings and Tickings

Bed pillows and decorative pillows may be filled with fiberfill, down, feathers, or foam. In many items, the filling material is enclosed in a nonremovable casing that is then protected by a zippered casing. The interior casing fabric should have an extremely high thread count, around 220 when fine down filling materials are used, and the fabrics used for the pillow protectors must be machine washable. Commonly used fabrics include muslin, percale, twill-woven ticking, cotton damask, and more recently, spunbonded ticking composed of polypropylene olefin. The spunbonded ticking pictured in Figure 33.7 weighs 1.5 ounces per square yard; it has been printed for visual interest.

Figure 33.7 Evolution® spunbonded polypropylene olefin pillow ticking. (Courtesy of Kimberly-Clark Corporation.)

Decorative Coverings for Pillows

For nighttime use, bed pillows are inserted into the familiar pillowcases. These may be plain or have decorative hem treatments. For daytime display, bed pillows may be inserted into a pillow sham, a decorative casing, which often has contrasting piping and ruffles. Shams are generally styled to match decorative pillows placed on the bed.

Today, consumers are frequently offered an assortment of decorative pillows covered and trimmed to coordinate with a variety of products included in an ensemble (Figure 33.8). The pillows are covered with the fabric used in other items in the grouping, and they are finished with identical trimmings. The trimming may include such embellishments as monograms, contrasting piping or fabric banding, Schiffli-embroidered appliques, ribbons, and ruffles.

Besides decorative pillows, a coordinated ensemble may include a quilt, a bedspread or comforter, sheets, and pillowcases. It may also include round and square tablecloths, towels, curtain and drapery panels, and valences for windows and canopy beds.

SHEETS AND PILLOWCASES

The assortment of sheets and pillowcases offered to contemporary consumers includes items ranging from those of minimal aesthetic appeal to those with distinctive color styling and decorative border embellishments. Much of today's sheeting is stabilized and given a resin finish to improve end use serviceability.

Manufacturing Sheeting

Fabric manufacturers produce the major portion of sheeting fabric in a plain-weave interlacing. Generally, they use spun yarns composed of cotton and polyester.

Fiber and Yarn Usage. As detailed in Table 33.1, 516.3 million pounds of cotton were used in sheets and other beddings in 1966, thus accounting for nearly 95 percent of the market. By 1985, the consumption of cotton in these items fell to 225.9 million pounds, or only about 50 percent of the total. Over the same period, the market share captured by the noncellulosic fibers rose from less than 1 percent to slightly more than 47 percent. The significant increase in the use of noncellulosic fibers is largely the result of the overwhelming acceptance of durable press sheets by consumers. As explained in Chapter 9, durable press resins improve the resiliency of cotton fibers but also weaken them and reduce their abrasion resistance. In order to prolong the use-life of resin-treated sheeting, manufacturers altered the composition of the fabric, increasing the polyester content and decreasing the cotton content.

The predominance of spun yarns in all textile bedding products was mentioned earlier. In sheets and other bedding, more than 89 percent of all fibers used, natural and man-made, are in staple lengths. These fibers are converted into carded or combed yarns by spinning on the cotton system.

Fabricating Sheetings. Most sheeting fabrics have the same simple interlacing pattern, 1 x 1, but they may have different yarns and different thread counts. Muslin sheeting contains carded yarns and its thread count may be as low as 112 or as high as 140, although 130 is most common. A large amount of sizing is generally used on muslin that has a very low thread count. This increases fabric weight but not its durability, and few of these sized or "backfilled" fabrics are produced today. Percale sheeting's thread count may be as low as 168 or as high as 220; 180 is common. Most percale sheeting is woven from fine, combed yarns.

A relatively small amount of woven sheeting is produced with a satin-interlacing pattern. The floating warp yarns produce a smooth, luxurious sleeping surface, but they may be snagged and ruptured, interrupting the pattern of light reflection, producing a stain-like appearance, and shortening the use-life of the sheets. For better durability, manufacturers have decreased their use of warp yarns composed of acetate and increased their use of nylon and poly-

Figure 33.8 Coordinated bedroom ensemble. (Courtesy of Eastman Chemical Products, Inc.)

ester. The shift in fiber usage is accompanied by a decrease in moisture absorption and comfort.

Knitted sheets are produced with a jersey or a tricot stitch. The inherent stretchability offered by the inter-looped yarns helps to keep the sheets fitting smoothly, but those composed of cotton exhibit relatively low elastic recovery. A broken loop in a jersey-stitched product initiates the development of the unsightly, ladder-like effect know as a run, and the loops in tricot-stitched sheets may snag and pill.

Coloring and Finishing Sheetings. Today, 85 percent of sheeting fabric is printed.[4] Rotary screen printing, explained in detail in Chapter 8, is the predominant technique: patterns range from those whose tiny motifs

cover virtually all of the surface to those whose large motifs combine with sizeable areas of white or solid-colored ground. Frequently, producers seek to enhance their position in the market by enlisting the assistance of well-known fashion fabric and apparel designers to create patterns and select the coloration. Currently, solid-colored sheets are in higher demand than formerly. They are cutting into the market not for printed styles, however, but for white sheets.[5]

A limited quantity of sheeting fabric is made with duplex print. Duplex prints are produced by printing identical or different design motifs on both sides of the fabric. Because more dye paste and two sets of screens are used, duplex prints are relatively expensive; this restricts their widespread production and selection.

Sheeting greige goods may be preshrunk to encourage relaxation shrinkage. Woven goods processed through the compressive shrinkage operation developed by The Sanforized Company, a division of Cluett, Peabody & Company, Inc., may be marketed with the licensed trade name, Sanforized®. Goods carrying this name have been certified to exhibit no more than 1 or 2 percent residual shrinkage, unless dried in a dryer. A significant portion of sheeting greige goods is treated with durable press resins to avoid the need for ironing after laundering (durable press processing was explained in Chapter 9).

Converters have responded to the demands of energy-conscious consumers by increased use of napping treatments on sheeting. In napping operations, the ends of many fibers are raised to the surface; fabrics napped on both sides are called flannel. In use, the raised fibers entrap air and provide thermal insulation. Flannel sheets are generally composed of 100 percent cotton, making them relatively expensive but providing the comfort sought by consumers.

Constructing Sheets and Pillowcases

Sheets and pillowcases have few construction details, but are produced in a variety of sizes and types. Decorative trimmings may embellish their hems.

Types and Sizes. Three styles of sheets are produced: flat, semi-fitted, and fitted. Flat sheets are hemmed at both ends and may be used as top or bottom sheets. Semi-fitted sheets are hemmed at one end and have contour corners at the other. This infrequently seen style is intended for use only as a top sheet. Fitted or contour sheets have four contour corners and can be used only as bottom sheets. The sheeting selvages provide a finished edge on the sides of all sheets; tape blinding or elastic banding finishes the lower edges of contour corners.

For the construction of cases for bed pillows, sheeting fabric is cut into rectangular shapes of specific dimensions. The fabric is folded lengthwise, right sides together, stitched across one end and the side having raw edges, and then turned. The hem treatment used for the top hem of the coordinating flat sheet is also used to finish the open end of the cases.

Sheets and pillowcases are constructed in various sizes for use with various sizes of mattresses and pillows. Typical dimensions are listed in Table 33.3; actual dimensions vary among producers. It should be noted that the size of flat sheets that producers report is measured prior to hemming.

Hems and Border Embellishments. The hems that finish flat sheets and pillowcases may be simple or highly decorative. A simple hem (Figure 33.9a) is normally 1

Table 33.3 TYPES AND SIZES OF SHEETS AND PILLOWCASES

Type and name	Inches, width x length
Flat sheets	
crib	45 x 68
twin	66 x 104
double or full	81 x 104
queen	90 x 110
king	108 x 110
Fitted sheets	
crib	29 x 54
twin	39 x 75
double or full	54 x 75
queen	60 x 80
king	78 x 80
Pillowcases	
standard	21 x 35
queen	21 x 39
king	21 x 44

inch deep at the bottom of sheets and 3 to 4 inches deep at the top of sheets and the end of cases. Decorative hems (Figures 33.9b, 33.9c, and 33.9d) have such border embellishments as delicate lace, scalloped eyelet trim, and contrasting piping.

Coordinated Items. The sheeting fabric produced and used for a set of sheets and pillowcases frequently also appears in other items offered with the sheets and pillowcases in a coordinated ensemble, such as curtains, draperies, valences, tablecloths, sheet casings, and dust ruffles. Dust ruffles, also known as bedskirts, bed petticoats, and platform skirts, are fabric panels that drape from the top of the foundation to the floor; the panels are normally pleated or, as in Figure 33.8, gathered. Sheet casings are covers that protect comforters from soil accumulation and abrasion; their releasable closures permit their easy removal for laundering.

BLANKETS

Blankets are primarily used for warmth. Conventional structures provide warmth by reducing the transfer of body heat to the interior; electric blankets provide warmth by

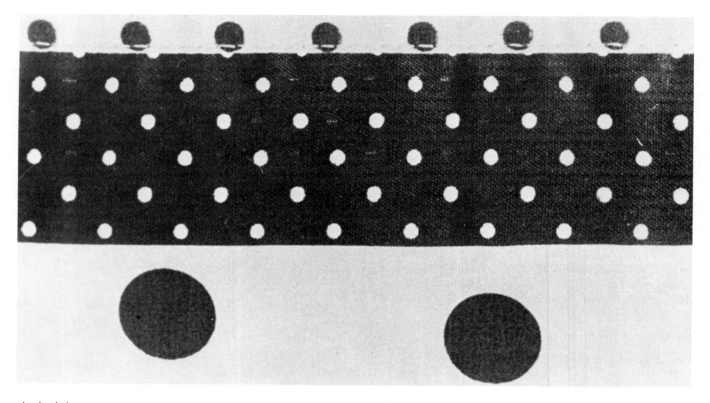

a) simple hem

b) lace trim

Figure 33.9 Simple and decorative hem treatments for flat sheets and pillowcases. (Springs Industries, Inc.)

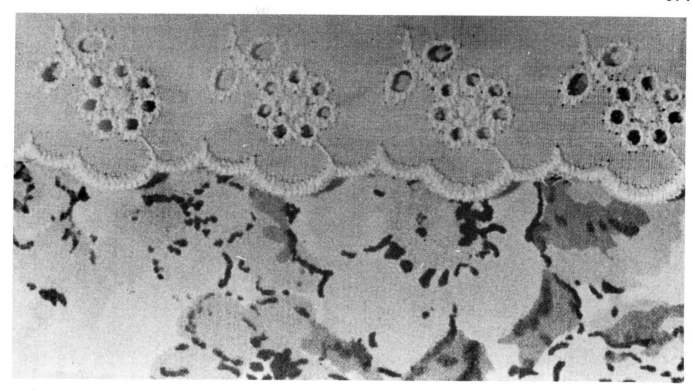

c) scalloped eyelet

d) piping

Figure 33.9 Simple and decorative hem treatments for flat sheets and pillowcases. (Springs Industries, Inc.)

generating heat. The blanketing fabrics used to produce these coverings may be produced from yarns or, bypassing the yarn stage, directly from fibers.

Manufacturing Blanketing

Blanketing may be manufactured from yarn structures, using simple and decorative biaxial weaves, knitting, and tufting. It may also be manufactured directly from fibers, through a flocking or needlepunching operation. Like other bedding products, blankets are primarily composed of noncellulosic fibers. Unlike other bedding products, however, some blankets are composed of wool fiber, and a limited number of contemporary blankets are composed of camel hair.

Fibers and Yarns Used. Over the past twenty-year period, the use of the noncellulosic fibers in blanketing has steadily increased; collectively, these fibers now hold about 77 percent of the market. The growth of the noncellulosic fibers in other bedding products has largely been at the expense of cotton; their growth in the blanket market has largely been at the expense of rayon, acetate, and wool. The man-made cellulosic fibers are relatively weak, wool is relatively expensive, and products composed of any of these three fibers generally must be dry-cleaned. At the same time, a significant decrease in the consumption of cotton in this market has also occurred.

As detailed in Table 33.1, most fibers used in blankets and blanketing are staple length. These fibers are usually processed into yarns on the woolen or cotton spinning systems.

Weaving Blanketing. Plain weaving and leno weaving are used to produce a large amount of blanketing. The leno-woven blanket pictured in Figure 33.10 is lightweight and lofty for thermal insulation. The filling yarns were spun on the woolen system and the warp yarns on the cotton system.

Double-faced or reversible blanketing, with different colors on each side, is produced by weaving one set of warp yarns and two sets of filling yarns together. One set of filling yarns is carried to the face and one set to the back. The sets of filling yarns may have different colors or different fiber compositions. If the fiber compositions differ, a cross-dyeing operation could be used to produce the two colors in one immersion procedure (see Chapter 8).

The blanketing in electric blankets is often produced by interlacing four sets of yarns into a doublecloth fabric. The interlacing is planned so that pocket-like channels are created, which will prevent the wires from shifting through the structure.

Knitting Blanketing. Knitted blanketing, which is generally constructed on a raschel knitting machine, may

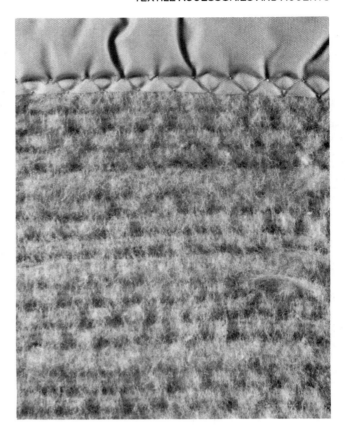

Figure 33.10 Leno-woven thermal blanket.

have a simple or a complex interlooping pattern. The thermal efficiency of this fabric can be engineered by varying the size of the yarns and the knitting gauge used.

Tufting Blanketing. Tufting, used extensively for the production of soft floor coverings and increasingly for upholstery coverings, can be adapted for the production of blanketing. The pile yarns are punched into the base fabric, using a gauge of 5/64 or 6/32 inch and six to fourteen stitches per lengthwise inch. By napping the pile surface, the raised fibers have the effect of increasing the diameter of the pile yarns, helping to secure them in the fabric. The back is napped to soften the surface and further stabilize the pile yarns.

Needlepunching Blanketing. The use of a needlepunching operation for the commercial production of blanketing began in the mid-1960s. In the Fiberwoven Process®, developed by Chatham Manufacturing Company, a 5-inch-thick batt is prepared by cross-layering twelve to eighteen webs of staple-length fibers on each side of a web of yarns. The batt is fed into a machine where more than 13,000 pairs of closely spaced, barbed needles punch into the batt, entangling the fibers into a mechanical chain-stitch. The extensive needling, approximately 2,000 punches per square inch, reduces the depth of the batt to about 1/4 inch. Subsequent napping raises some surface fibers, softening the appearance and improving the thermal efficiency.

Flocking Blanketing. Lightweight, warm blankets can be produced by flocking nylon over the surfaces of a thin slab of polyurethane foam. Together, the flocked fiber and the cellular foam serve to minimize heat transfer.

Coloring and Finishing Blanketing. Blanketing may be constructed with colored fibers or yarns or the greige fabric may be piece dyed or printed. Whatever fabrication technique is used, virtually all blanketing fabrics are napped.

Constructing Blankets

Most blankets are approximately 84 inches long and they are finished 20 inches wider than the mattress with which they are intended to be used. The side edges are generally machine overcast, and the ends are enclosed within tightly woven binding (see Figure 33.10). For electric blankets, insulated wires are inserted into the channels before the edges are finished.

Caring for Blankets

Naphthalene compounds, available in such familiar forms as moth balls, crystals, blocks, and sprays, can be used in storage areas to protect wool blankets from attack by moth larvae. Naphthalene fumes do not kill moth adults or larvae; rather they repel them by giving the wool fibers and the immediate area a noxious odor, so unattractive to moths that they will seek other places for laying their eggs. A note should be added about safety: if internalized, naphthalene compounds are potentially hazardous to humans. To prevent their being ingested by young children, moth balls and crystals may be knotted inside sheer hosiery; the porous construction of the hosiery will not hinder the effectiveness of the fumes.

To avoid felting shrinkage, blankets composed of wool fiber should be dry-cleaned, unless information on the label directs otherwise. Blankets composed of most other fibers can generally be laundered, unless care instructions voluntarily provided by the producer state otherwise. Electric blankets must always be laundered; dry-cleaning solvents may damage the insulating material covering the heating wires.

Flammability of Blankets

Currently, no federal flammability standard exists for blankets, although a finding of need for such a standard was issued on June 5, 1970. Today, the Consumer Product Safety Commission is involved with blanket producers in the development of a voluntary standard focusing primarily on improving the safety of electric blankets.

BEDSPREADS, QUILTS, AND COMFORTERS

Comforters and quilts are multilayer bed coverings stabilized through some kind of quilting. Many bedspreads are also produced in this manner.

Commercial Quilting

Commercial quilting may be done by sewing or by melding. The quilting operation serves to join the separate layers and sometimes to impart a surface pattern as well.

Techniques. Machine stitching and pinsonic melding are used in commercial quilting operations. The equipment used in machine stitching operates in the same manner as a conventional sewing maching, except that many needles stitch at the same time. In pinsonic melding, a wide cylinder with raised designs is rolled over the multilayer structure while heat and sound waves meld the layers at the contact points. The meld points simulate the appearance of sewn quilting stitches (Figure 33.11).

Patterns. Three patterns are typical of commercial quilting. In channel quilting, the stitches or meld points are aligned in parallel rows (Figure 33.12a). In pattern quilting (Figures 33.12b and 33.12c), the quilting lines develop a surface pattern with slightly three-dimensional motifs. Such quilting is frequently used on solid-covered fabrics. In outline quilting (Figure 33.12d), the stitches follow the outline of pattern motifs, making them stand in slight relief.

Bedspreads

Most bedspreads are chosen primarily for their styling and decorative fabric. Others, especially quilted ones, are selected for their insulative value.

Styles. Various styles of bedspreads, ranging from tailored to ruffled styles, are illustrated in Figure 33.13. The appearance of any of these styles changes dramatically when executed in different fabrics. The qualities of the fabric must always be appropriate for the styling features of the spread. For example, although a heavy fabric would be suitable for use in a throw style, it would not drape properly in a style with gathered or shirred sides.

Fabrics. Virtually any fabric may be used for a bedspread. Several fabrics, such as gingham and printed per-

Figure 33.11 Fabric quilted by pinsonic melding.

Pile bedspread fabrics are produced by weaving, knitting, or tufting. Corduroy, a woven filling-pile fabric, is often used for tailored spreads, and velvet, a woven warp-pile fabric, is often used for throw spreads. Pile knitting produces the simulated fur fabrics often used for throw-style coverings. These three-dimensional coverings are fabricated by incorporating combed fibers into a knitted base fabric.

Tufting is used to produce chenille spreads and candle-wick spreads. In chenille spreads, the pile tufts are closely spaced and cut, producing the caterpillar-like appearance of chenille yarns; true chenille yarns are not used. In candle-wick spreads, the pile tufts are individually spaced, but, viewed collectively, form a design. The designs resemble those created by a hand-stitching technique in which heavy yarns produced for use as candlewicks are used for the em-broidered motifs (see Chapter 35). After tufting, the level of twist of the pile yarns is reduced, causing them to "bloom" or increase in diameter, and the base fabric is shrunk to effectively lock the pile yarns in position.

Quilts and Comforters

Quilts and comforters are multicomponent bed coverings. Either structure may be used in lieu of a bedspread.

Quilts. Commercially produced quilts usually have a printed face fabric, a fibrous or polyurethane batting, and a coordinating solid-colored or printed back fabric (Figure 33.14). Patterned machine stitching is normally used to stabilize the layers. Today, lofty comforters are increasingly replacing such quilts on the beddings market.

Comforters. Comforters are usually filled with down, feathers, or fiberfill. They may also be filled with a loose batting of polyester. The close-up photograph in Figure 33.15 shows the use of a spunbonded interior lining fabric to prevent migration of the filling fibers through the outercovering. The same fabric may be used on the face and

cale, are flat, essentially two-dimensional, smooth fabrics; others, including taffeta and ribcord, show a slightly raised rib effect; others, such as clipped dot or spot fabrics, Schiffli-embroidered organdy, and eyelet, have slightly raised designs created by extra yarns; and still others, including corduroy, velvet, simulated fur fabrics, and tufted fabrics, exhibit the conspicuous depth of a pile layer.

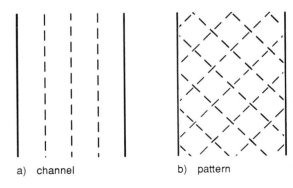
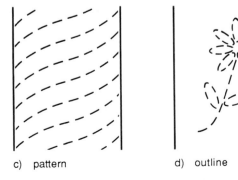

a) channel   b) pattern   c) pattern   d) outline

Figure 33.12 Quilting patterns.

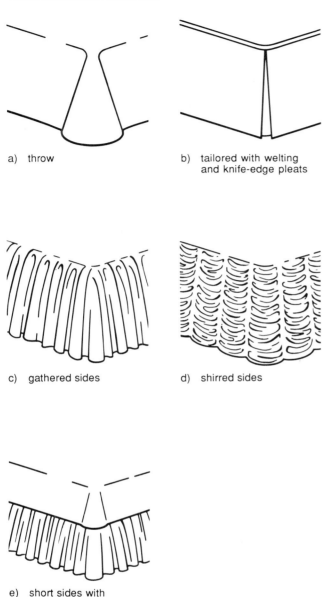

a) throw

b) tailored with welting and knife-edge pleats

c) gathered sides

d) shirred sides

e) short sides with dust ruffle

Figure 33.13 Typical bedspread styles.

Figure 33.14 Machine-made quilt with a polyurethane batting and pattern quilting.

back, or for greater in-use flexibility, different fabrics, for instance, a solid-colored fabric and a printed fabric, may be used. To minimize the need for cleaning, manufacturers often recommend that comforters be enclosed in a sheet casing. Sheet casings have releasable closures that permit them to be easily removed for laundering.

Most comforters are channel quilted to minimize shifting and clumping of the filling. Some products also use a system of crosswise baffles. Sleeping bags are often constructed in this manner, making them, in effect, folded comforters with zipper closures.

SUMMARY

Several bedding products, including mattresses, mattress pads, quilts, and comforters, are multicomponent structures. They are generally filled with polyester fiberfill, but other filling materials, including loose masses of down or feathers, foamed compounds, and battings composed of wool, cotton, or cotton and polyester, are also used.

Bedding products may be purchased singly or in coordinated ensembles. Some products, such as mattresses and bed pillows, serve functional purposes; other products, such as sheets, pillowcases, and comforters, are selected for their functional and decorative attributes; and still other products, such as decorative pillows and dust ruffles, are completely ornamental.

NOTES

1. Textile Economics Bureau, Inc. *Textile Organon*, Vol. 56, No. 9, September 1984, 185.
2. *Ibid.*, 192.
3. W. C. Kaufman, D. Bothe, and S. D. Meyer, "Thermal Insulating Capabilities of Outdoor Clothing Materials," *Science*, Vol. 215, February 5, 1982, 690–691.
4. James A. Cooney, "Printed Sheets: One Answer to the Challenge of the 80s," *American Dyestuff Reporter,* Vol. 70, No. 2, February 1981, 16.
5. Marita Thomas, "For Bed and Bath: Solids, Detailing, Flannels Dominate," *Modern Textile Business,* April 1982, 11.

Figure 33.15 Comforter with a spunbonded interior lining to prevent fiber migration and to increase insulation.

chapter 34

Textile Accessories for Tabletops

- Producing Tabletop Coverings
- Labeling Textile Table Accessories

Because many of today's tabletops have a heat, chip, and stain resistant finish, the use of such coverings as tablecloths and placemats is often optional. Nonetheless, these items frequently enrich the dining experience. They may be selected to add warmth and beauty to the table, to carry out a decorative theme, to set a casual or formal mood, or to complement the table service. Even when table coverings are needed to protect fine wood or to camouflage a damaged surface, the assortment of contemporary products is so varied that consumers may choose the items mostly on the basis of their aesthetic features.

At the outset, two terms, napery and linens, should be distinguished. Napery is a general term for tablecloths and napkins. Although the term is no longer widely used in commercial activities, it is used in certain labeling mandates. Earlier, "linens" described sheets, towels, tablecloths, napkins, and related products composed entirely or primarily of linen fiber. The use of linen fiber in these goods has declined significantly, but many merchandisers and consumers continue to refer to them as linens.

Some tabletop accessories are specifically produced for use on dining room tables. Several other items are produced for use on tables and other furniture situated throughout interiors.

PRODUCING TABLETOP COVERINGS

The assortment of products produced for use on tabletops includes such items as tablecloths, napkins, doilies, placemats, and silencers. With the exception of silencers, all of these items are visible in use; therefore, they are designed to be attractive additions to the table surface, and often to complement the interior setting as well. Silencers, which are placed under tablecloths and concealed from view, serve purely functional purposes.

Components

Most tabletop coverings are composed of textile fibers. Some distinctive nonfibrous structures are also available.

Fibers and Yarns. Together with rayon and various noncellulosic fibers, several natural cellulosic fibers, including cotton, linen, ramie, sisal, and raffia, are used in dining table products, doilies, and dresser scarves. Raffia, a fiber obtained from the leaves of various species of palm trees, is used in long, narrow, yarn-like bands to make woven placemats. Sisal, a relatively stiff fiber obtained from the leaves of the sisal plant, is effectively used to produce woven placements and hot pads, examples of which are pictured in Figure 34.1.

Figure 34.1 Hand-woven placemat and hot pad composed of sisal.

When stiff fibers, such as linen and ramie, are used in large items that are normally folded for storage or use, they may be unable to withstand the repeated flexing, and eventually may split on the crease lines. To avoid this problem, fabrics composed of these fibers should be stored flat or rolled, and crease positions should be shifted when possible.

Most yarns used for table products are spun. For economy and ease of care, spinsters frequently use staple-length rayon and polyester to produce yarns that resemble those spun of linen. For improved dimensional stability and resiliency, polyester is increasingly used alone or blended with cotton in various sizes of yarns.

Nonfibrous Materials. Some contemporary placemats are multicomponent structures, made of a layer of aluminum foil or metallized polymer film faced with a clear fabric, such as Mylar® polyester film produced by du Pont, and backed with a conventional textile fabric; such mats have a mirror-like quality. For the placemat pictured in Figure 34.2, clear and colored film sheetings have been

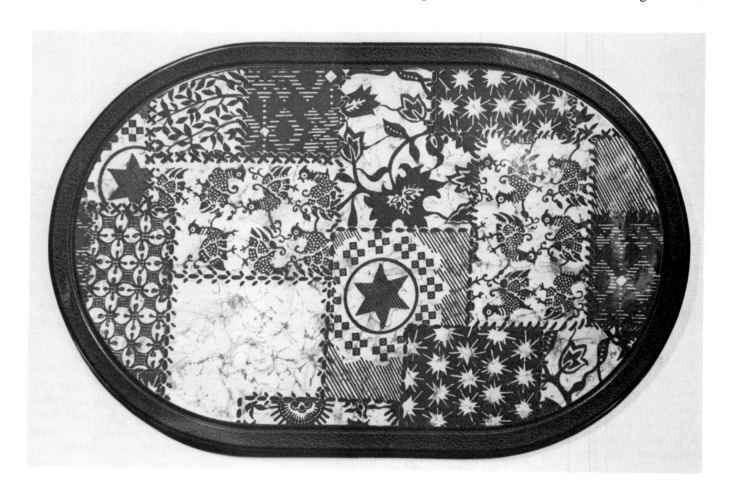

Figure 34.2 Placemat with fabric printed to simulate batik and patchwork quilting encased between film sheetings.

used to encase a simulated batik textile fabric. Batik printing is explained in Chapter 35.

Several nonfibrous placemats are composed of polymer foam that has been expanded into a thin, fabric-like structure. For increased visual interest, these mats are generally printed with colorful design motifs.

Manufacturing Table Covering Fabrics

Table coverings are produced by weaving, stitch-knitting, knotting and twisting, spunbonding, and extrusion. Color may be added before or after fabrication, and finishing agents and processes may be used to alter the appearance and improve serviceability.

Fabricating. Woven table coverings may have a casual, contemporary appearance or a formal, traditional appearance; most styles carry no specific fabric name. Elaborate Jacquard interlacing patterns are used to create the distinctive surfaces of single and double damask. The motifs in single damask have a five-shaft satin weave, with each warp yarn floating over four filling yarns; the motifs in double damask have an eight-shaft satin weave, with each warp yarn floating over seven filling yarns. The ground in these fabrics is generally woven in a twill- or sateen-interlacing pattern. Although damask tablecloths and napkins are normally white or a solid pastel color, the yarns in the varied interlacings reflect incident light in different directions and in different quantities, enabling the viewer to see the distinctive patterns (Figure 34.3).

Figure 34.3 Close-up of motifs in damask tablecloth.

Stitch-knitted tablecloths and napkins are produced by chain-stitching across webs of yarns, a technique described in Chapter 7. The technique is fast and economical, but rupturing of the chain-stitches can initiate runs. This is the problem with the napkin pictured in Figure 34.4.

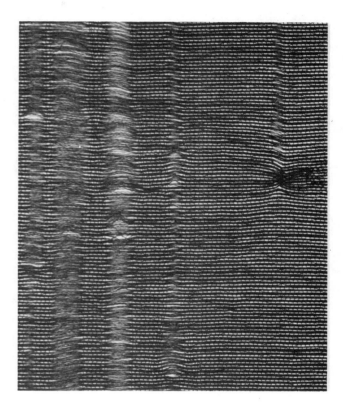

Figure 34.4 Stitch-knitted napkin with a run caused by rupturing of the chain-stitches.

A wide variety of lace fabrics is produced for use as tablecloths, dresser scarves, and doilies. Machine-made Nottingham lace, originally used only for curtains, is used in the doily pictured in Figure 34.7. Frequently, lace fabrics are placed over a solid-covered fabric for a color accent that emphasizes the intricate motifs in the lace.

Extrusion of such polymer compounds as polyvinylchloride produces film fabrics that are then supported by conventional woven or knitted fabrics and cut for use as tablecloths. Extrusion is also used to produce film structures that are then laminated to produce items like the placemat pictured in Figure 34.2.

Spunbonding is increasingly used for the rapid and economical production of fabrics for table coverings. The spunbonded fabric pictured in Figure 34.5 has been printed with a pattern traditionally woven from dyed yarns.

Coloring and Finishing. Table covering fabrics may be manufactured from colored components or color may be

Figure 34.5 Spunbonded table covering. (Courtesy of Kimberly-Clark Corporation.)

Figure 34.7 Nottingham lace doily.

Figure 34.6 Table napkin enriched with embroidery.

applied by dyeing or printing the greige goods. Visual interest may also be added with embroidery (Figure 34.6).

Converters may use a process known as beetling to increase the surface luster of fabrics composed of linen. In the operation, heavy wooden planks hammer the fabric and flatten the cross section of the yarns. This process is often used on damask to increase the amount of light reflected from the floating yarns, increasing the visual distinction between the motifs and the ground.

Greige fabrics intended for use as silencers will be napped to raise the ends of the fibers to the surface, converting the flat goods into thick, flannel-like fabrics. The added thickness will help the silencer to absorb the impact force of dishes and silverware, reducing noise and protecting the table surface.

Fabrics composed of natural and man-made cellulosic fibers may have small amounts of chemical cross-linking resin added to them to improve wrinkle recovery and reduce mussiness. The use of these agents is critical for fabrics composed of linen since the untreated fabrics have extremely low resiliency and require a great deal of moisture and pressure in ironing. Fabrics composed of cotton and polyester are often treated with a larger amount of resin for durable press or no-iron performance. Fabrics composed of thermoplastic fibers can be heat set to improve their resiliency and dimensional stability.

Soil release compounds may be used with tablecloths and napkins to help the fibers release food stains. These compounds are designed to function in unison with detergent molecules in the laundry solution. The detergent molecules will reduce the surface tension of the water; in effect, this makes the water "wetter" by causing it to spread rather than bead. At the same time, the fluorocarbon-based finishing agent will increase the surface energy of the fibers, making them more hydrophilic, so the water can more readily carry the detergent molelcules into the fiber crevices and emulsify and remove the soil and stain material. Because soil release compounds increase the hydrophilic nature of fibers, they are particularly helpful when used with such hydrophobic fibers as polyester and nylon, and with fabrics having a durable press finish. Durable press resins reduce absorbency and thus lessen the efficiency of the detergent in removing soil. Visa® is a trade name that indicates the use of a soil release treatment developed by Deering Milliken.

Constructing Tabletop Accessories

Tabletop accessories are constructed in assorted sizes and shapes for different uses. Producers employ various techniques to finish the raw edges.

Types and Sizes. Accessories constructed for use on dining tables include tablecloths, runners, placemats, and napkins. These items are available in square, round, oval, and rectangular shapes in various sizes. Tablecloths should be selected to cover the tabletop and drop from 5 to 10 inches on all sides. Runners are approximately 12 inches wide, and they, too, should drop from 5 to 10 inches, as they do in Figure 34.9. Placemats are generally rectangular, but many are round or oval. Rectangular placemats are typically 12 inches by 18 inches. Small cocktail napkins are 5 inches square; larger napkins are 12 to 22 inches square.

Accessories constructed for use on cocktail tables, side tables, end tables, dressers, and the like include such items as mats, scarves, coasters, and doilies (Figure 34.7). These products, like dining table accessories, are available in a wide variety of sizes and shapes.

Edge Finishes. The raw edges of fabric used for tabletop items may be finished with a small hem, binding, or fringe, or with machine serging, which may be plain or decorative. When plain overcasting stitches are used on fabrics having relatively large yarns, the stitches often cover only one or two yarns. With continual use and cleaning, the covered yarns and stitching may slide off the edge of the item (Figure 34.8a). The decorative overcasting stitches shown on the napkin pictured in Figure 34.8b extend over several yarns, providing a more secure edge finish.

The edges of textile placemats are fringed and reinforced with machine zig-zag stitching (see Figure 34.1), serged with plain or decorative stitching, or finished with a small hem. They are also frequently bound with bias-cut fabric (Figure 34.9).

LABELING TEXTILE TABLE ACCESSORIES

Two federal labeling mandates apply to the labeling of textile tabletop accessories. One regulation, the Textile Fiber Products Identification Act, pertains to fiber composition; the other, a trade regulation rule, pertains to representation of product size.

a) plain serging slipping from fabric edge

b) decorative serging secured over fabric edge

Figure 34.8 Machine serging on edges of tablecloth accessories.

Figure 34.9 Bias binding used to finish the edges of placemats and a runner. (Courtesy of Eastman Chemical Products, Inc.)

Textile Fiber Products Identification Act

The provisions of the TFPIA apply to tablecloths, napkins, doilies, and dresser and other furniture scarves. Specifically exempted are table placemats made principally of plastic. Most textile tabletop accessories therefore must be labeled with the fiber composition and other information required by this act, which was discussed in detail in Chapter 10.

Trade Regulation Rule

The Trade Regulation Rule Relating to the Deceptive Advertising and Labeling as to Size of Tablecloths and Related Products became effective on February 1, 1965. In this rule, the Federal Trade Commission requires that any representation of the "cut size" of tablecloths and related products, such as doilies, table mats, dresser scarves, placemats, table runners, napkins, and tea sets, in advertising or labeling must be accompanied by the words "cut size" and the clear and conspicuous disclosure of the dimensions of the finished size.

SUMMARY

Accessories produced for use on tabletops may be composed of textile fibers or nonfibrous materials. Many table covering fabrics are fabricated by weaving, stitch-knitting, knotting and twisting, and, more recently, by spunbonding. Items intended for use on dining tables may have a soil-release finish to help preserve a stain-free appearance. Items produced for use on occasional tables, dressers, and the like are available in a range of sizes and shapes as varied as that of the dining table accessories.

Virtually all textile tabletop products must be labeled in accordance with the provisions of the Textile Fiber Products Identification Act. When producers make a reference to the "cut size" of most textile tabletop accessories in advertising or labeling, they must also provide the dimensions of the finished size.

chapter 35

Textile Accents Created by Artisans

- Decorative Textile Hangings
- Needlework Accents
- Bobbin-work Accents
- Hand-printed Accents

The assortment of interior textile products available today is not limited to items produced in industrial operations. It also includes a wide variety of products created by skilled artisans, who may work independently or cooperatively. These artists produce such items as quilts, tapestries, macramé panels, needlepoint pictures, and hand-printed fabrics. Some of these products are produced as "one-of-a-kind" items and some in large quantities; many are promoted and marketed as aggressively as are machine-made goods. Because many consumers equate "hand-made" with quality and uniqueness, many of the items carry a label not only stating that they were made by hand, but also that they were made exclusively for the store or mail-order firm selling them.

Some hand-made textile products are selected entirely on the basis of their beauty and are used only as decorative accents. Other products are also chosen for their aesthetic qualities, but they serve both decorative and functional purposes.

DECORATIVE TEXTILE HANGINGS

Decorative textile hangings may be essentially flat or markedly three-dimensional. Among the more frequently used structures are macramé hangings and tapestries.

Macramé Hangings

Macramé hangings are produced by knotting and twisting textile yarn, cord, or rope. Several of the various knots used in macramé work are illustrated in Figure 35.1 Macramé panels may be dense, with many knots, or open, with relatively few knots. Artists may elect to incorporate such nontextile materials as tree branches, wooden beads, and seashells as they knot the strands.

Tapestries

Tapestry is a nonpile fabric that may be woven on a high warp (vertical) loom or on a low warp (horizontal) loom. A cartoon, which is a color-keyed mirror image of the planned pattern, is placed behind or under the warp yarns threaded and tensioned on the loom. Working on the back of the fabric, the weaver uses the cartoon as a guide for interlacing the various colors of yarns to create the motifs.

Tapestry weaving is plain weaving in which the filling or weft yarns are beaten or crammed to completely cover the warp yarns. The filling yarns are not carried from selvage to selvage; rather, they are interlaced to create a particular shape or to introduce specific details within a motif and then clipped to hang fringe-like on the fabric back (Figure 35.2a). The filling yarns may or may not be perpendicular to the warp yarns or parallel to one another (Figure 35.2b).

Because the filling yarns are woven in within the perimeter of a motif, adjacent motifs with vertical or dia-

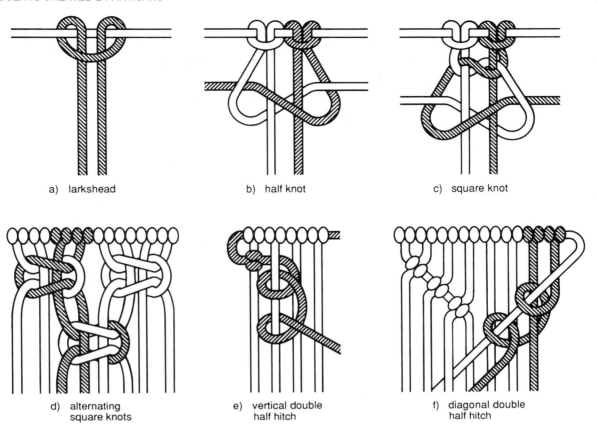

a) larkshead   b) half knot   c) square knot

d) alternating square knots   e) vertical double half hitch   f) diagonal double half hitch

Figure 35.1 Various knots used in macramé work.

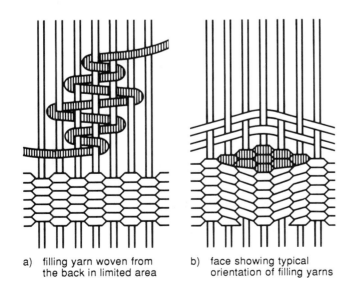

a) filling yarn woven from the back in limited area

b) face showing typical orientation of filling yarns

Figure 35.2 Tapestry weaving.

gonal design lines will be separated by a nonraveling slit unless the weaver employs a technique that prevents their formation. As noted in Chapter 27, such slits are typically seen in Khilim rugs (see Figure 27.6, page 299); they are purposely avoided in rugs woven by Native Americans. To avoid the formation of slits, weavers may elect to use dovetailing or interlocking (Figure 35.3), or they may turn and weave the pattern so that the warp yarns parallel the floor when the finished tapestry is hung.

During the Middle Ages, well-known artists were often commissioned to design a set of related tapestries, with each piece to depict a part of a story. The completed masterpieces, each woven by several weavers, were generally hung in the interiors of castles and churches, fulfilling both an aesthetic need and a functional purpose. The richly colored and intricately detailed works transformed the dark, bleak, and cold stone walls into dramatic and beautiful backdrops, while they also reduced drafts and heat transfer. Among the best known surviving medieval works are the "Lady with the Unicorn" series, a set of six tapestries now belonging to the Cluny Museum in Paris, France, and the "Unicorn Tapestries," six large works now owned by the Metropolitan Museum of Art and hanging in The Cloisters in New York City.

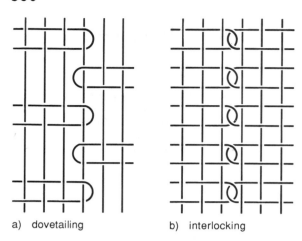

a) dovetailing   b) interlocking

Figure 35.3 Techniques used to avoid the formation of slits in tapestry.

Figure 35.4 Contemporary tapestry having stylized motif woven in related colors.

Many of today's hand-woven tapestries are also fine works of art. Frequently, their motifs are stylized or geometric designs woven in related colors (Figure 35.4), rather than the realistic figures in numerous colors that typify the fifteenth century masterpieces. Contemporary tapestries are usually one of a kind, and they are hung primarily for their aesthetic impact, not for any insulative value they might add.

Other Contemporary Hangings

Hand weavers often create distinctive wall hangings on a standard harness loom by combining several interlacing patterns, strategically positioning pile yarns, and substituting a wide variety of materials for some of the yarns. Today's fiber artists also create unique wall hangings through off-loom techniques. Such things as hula-hoops are used to support the yarns and provide added visual interest. (See the hanging pictured in Figure 27.7, page 301.)

NEEDLEWORK ACCENTS

Skilled artisans use textile yarns or fabrics to create such items as needlepoint pictures, crewel pillow coverings, quilts, doilies, throws, laces, and soft sculptures. They may hold on to completed projects for personal use or sell them in a wholesale or retail market. In some cases, an artist is commissioned to design and produce a needlework item for use as an accent in a specific interior, such as a corporate office, an airport lounge, or a bank.

Embellishing Fabric Surfaces

Fiber artists use various techniques to embellish fabric surfaces for use as accents in interiors. Among these are needlepoint stitching, embroidering, and quilting.

Needlepoint Stitching. In needlepoint stitching, also referred to as canvas embroidering, yarns are used to cover all or part of the surface of a canvas fabric. Typically, the surface has a solid-colored ground surrounding a multicolored, detailed pattern, or the design repeats identical or mirror-image geometric motifs (Figure 35.5).

Needlepoint projects may be done with either single-mesh canvas, which is plain woven, or double-mesh (penelope) canvas, which has closely spaced pairs of warp and filling yarns. The term mesh refers to one intersection of the yarns used in the canvas; the compactness of construction of the fabric is designated by the number of meshes per inch. Fine canvas, with eighteen or more meshes per inch, is used for petit point work. These projects usually have small motifs and are framed and hung as wall accents or placed on tabletops. Medium canvas, with ten or twelve meshes per inch, is used in such needlepoint items as dining chair seat coverings, a rendition of a company logo, and backgammon and other game boards (see Figure 35.5). Coarse canvas, with three to seven meshes per inch, is used to construct rugs.

Needlepoint work uses Persian yarns and tapestry yarns. Persian yarns are loosely twisted three-ply strands

Crewel, floss, pearl, and candlewick yarns are used for embroidery work. Crewel yarns are fine, two-ply strands composed of wool; floss yarns are loosely twisted, six-ply strands composed of mercerized cotton; pearl yarns are fine cords formed by plying three two-ply yarns composed of

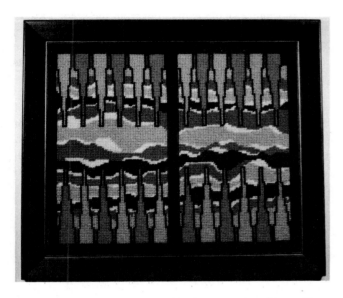

Figure 35.5 Needlepoint-stitched backgammon board framed for use as a wall accent.

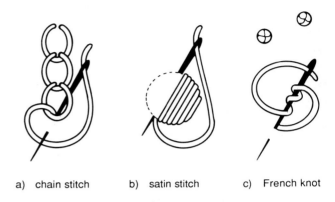

a) chain stitch b) satin stitch c) French knot

Figure 35.7 Common embroidery stitches.

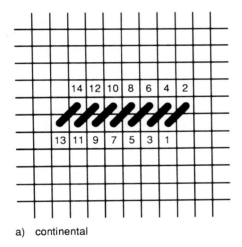

a) continental

Figure 35.6 Frequently used needlepoint stitches.

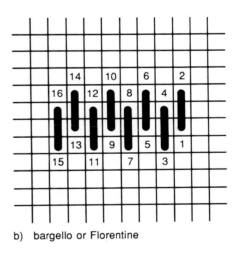

b) bargello or Florentine

composed of wool. Frequently, the plied yarns are untwisted and a single strand is used in stitching. Tapestry yarns are highly twisted, four-ply yarns, which are used without being separated. Example of frequently used needlepoint stitches are shown in Figure 35.6.

Embroidering. Embroidering is the stitching of colored yarns in decorative patterns on a portion of a base fabric, leaving the other portion unadorned to serve as the ground and accentuate the slightly raised motifs. Embroidered fabrics are used as the outer coverings of decorative pillows and as cases for bed pillows. They are also framed and hung as wall accents, and cut and finished for use as tabletop accessories.

mercerized cotton; and candlewick yarns are four-ply yarns composed of unmercerized cotton. Since these yarns vary in texture, size, and luster, they produce distinct appearances when used in any of the many embroidery stitches, examples of which are illustrated in Figure 35.7.

Embroidery techniques are primarily distinguished by the type of yarn used, not by differences in the stitches used. One exception is candlewicking in which the design motifs are created by the extensive use of French knots. The knots are used singly, but collectively they create a recognizable pattern (Figure 35.8).

Appliquéing. In most appliqué work, shaped pieces of coordinating or contrasting fabric are placed over the face

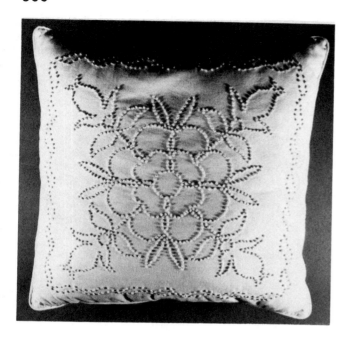

Figure 35.8 Candlewicking embroidery used to embellish the outer covering of a decorative pillow. (Courtesy of Norma Mayfield.)

of a second fabric. The raw edges are turned under and blind stitches or embroidery stitches are used to secure the appliqué. Appliquéd fabrics are constructed into decorative pillow coverings, bedspreads, and tablecloths, and are used as the face fabric in quilts.

An intricate appliqué technique is employed by needlework artisans in South America to produce molas. Molas have multiple layers of fabric and are typically characterized by highly stylized animal motifs (Figure 35.9). Various colors of fabrics are layered and a large, shaped area is cut from the top fabric. The raw edges are turned under, and the folded edge is stitched to the second fabric. A slightly smaller shape is then cut from the second fabric and the raw edges are turned and stitched to the third fabric; this reverse appliqué sequence is repeated until the base fabric is reached. Molas are prized as framed wall accents and decorative pillow coverings.

Quilting. With quilting stitches, artisans join three layers: a face fabric, a fibrous batting, and a backing or lining fabric. The face fabric may be an appliquéd fabric, a solid-colored or printed fabric, or constructed of small pieces of coordinated fabrics. In patterned quilts, the several pieces are shaped to create a specific pattern repeat; today, skilled quilters often cut and sew selected fabrics to replicate traditional patterns (Figure 35.10). In crazy quilts, the pieces are irregularly shaped and they vary in size and color styling. The "patches" in patchwork quilts are often square or rectangular. Finishing touches differ from quilt to quilt. The patchwork face fabric pictured in Figure 35.11 has been embellished with embroidery stitches.

Quilting stitches should be uniformly placed to stabilize the layered structure. As shown in Figure 33.12 (page 374), the stitches may be sewn in parallel rows, in crisscrossing lines, or in undulating waves, or they may follow the outlines of printed motifs or appliqués. Since the stitches create a three-dimensional effect, they may be used to introduce a surface pattern to a solid-colored surface or to augment the visual interest of a printed fabric.

Two quilting variations used on interior textile products include trapunto quilting and shadow quilting. Trapunto quilting is done by placing quilting stitching around a single motif in a pattern repeat. The interior of the quilted shape is then filled by inserting batting material

Figure 35.9 Mola, a textile accent produced by a reverse appliqué technique. (Courtesy of Ruth E. Weibel.)

Figure 35.10 Hand-stitched quilts with motifs adapted from traditional patterns. (Courtesy of Susan T. Farmer.)

through tiny slits cut in the backing fabric. For long, narrow shapes, a yarn or cord may be drawn between the face and back fabrics. Trapunto quilting is particularly effective when used for decorative pillow coverings with large motifs.

Shadow quilting is done by covering an appliquéd face fabric with a sheer fabric such as organdy or voile. Quilting stitches are then placed around the outlines of the appliqués, joining the layers together. The colored appliqués have a softened or shadowed appearance. This technique is often used for crib quilts.

Interlooping Yarns

Fiber artisans use one needle in crocheting and two needles in knitting to interloop yarns into interior accent pieces, some of which are both decorative and functional. They create such products as afghans, doilies, arm covers, and head rests.

Creating Soft Sculptures

In recent years, talented artisans have used textile fabrics and fillings to create life-sized soft sculpture forms. These are designed to be used as decorative pillows, suspended hangings, or as free-standing items. Often, soft sculptures enhance the decorative theme of an interior, as do cactus forms in a room with an American Southwest

decor or hanging fish forms in a seafood restaurant. The forms are also effective as eye-catching conversation pieces.

BOBBIN-WORK ACCENTS

Small, hand-held bobbins are used to produce open fabrics known as bobbin lace and tatted lace. Although several bobbins are used to produce bobbin lace and a single bobbin produces tatted lace, both techniques involve the crossing and twisting of yarns.

Bobbin Lace

Multiple pairs of bobbins are used to twist and cross yarns in the production of bobbin lace. The small wooden bobbins are wound with a length of yarn and hung below the work area to keep the yarns under slight tension. With practice, skill, and patience, artisans manipulate the several bobbins in twisting and crossing motions (Figures 35.12a and 35.12b). These motions are combined to execute various stitches, two of which are illustrated in Figures 35.12c and 35.12d.

Bobbin lace may be designed and constructed for such interior uses as open casements in window treatments. It may also be produced for use as coverings for decorative pillows.

Figure 35.11 Close-up of a patchwork quilt face fabric embellished with various embroidery stitches. (Courtesy of Norma Mayfield.)

Tatted Lace

In tatting, the artisan deftly moves one small bobbin to twist fine yarns into open fabric structures. Tatting often produces such small items as doilies and other tabletop accessories.

HAND-PRINTED ACCENTS

Using hand-carved blocks or resist printing operations, artisans create distinctive block prints, batik prints, tie-dye prints, and ikat prints. Because hand-printing procedures are time- and labor-intensive, these prints are comparatively expensive.

Block Prints

In preparation for block printing, all shapes of the planned design that will be the same color are carved to stand in relief on the face of a block of wood. A separate block is prepared for each color to be printed. The block pictured in Figure 35.13 is unusual in that it is curved instead of square; it can be used to print medallion-like motifs.

During printing, the artisan dips the face of the carved design into the dyestuff and then presses it onto the fabric surface. Since the printer may pick up different amounts of dye paste each time and exert different amounts of pressure with each printing action, various levels of intensity may be seen for the same hue, as in Figure 35.14.

Batik Prints

Beeswax is the resist agent in traditional batik printing. It is melted and applied with a tjanting tool to all areas of the fabric that are to resist penetration of the dye liquor. The tjanting has a small copper cup and a tiny spout. In use, the tool functions somewhat like a fountain pen, and skilled artisans can apply fine lines of wax to create intricate details within the motifs.

After the wax hardens, the fabric is immersed into a dye bath; only the nonwaxed areas absorb the dye. The wax is then removed from the fabric by boiling. The artisan again applies melted wax, this time to all areas—including those that are to remain the first color—that are to resist the second dye liquor. If a "crackle effect" characterized by linear striations is planned, the artist randomly cracks the hardened wax at this time. Piece dyeing then results in absorption of the second color in all unwaxed areas, as well as in those areas below any cracks (Figure 35.15). This sequence of wax removal, wax application, and immersion is repeated until all planned colors have been applied.

Tie-dye Prints

In tie-dying, folds, gathers, and knots, which are introduced in the fabric and secured with waxed thread, function as the resist medium. These are selected and positioned according to the motifs and pattern scale planned. When the fabric is immersed into the dye bath, the tied-off areas resist penetration of the dye liquor. The fabric is then opened flat and again tied off and immersed in a second dye bath. The processes will be repeated in sequence until all planned colors and designs have been introduced. The tie-dye fabric pictured in Figure 35.16 was produced through two folding and immersing operations.

Ikat Prints

In ikat printing, specific portions of bundles of warp and filling yarns, not fabric, are wrapped to resist dye

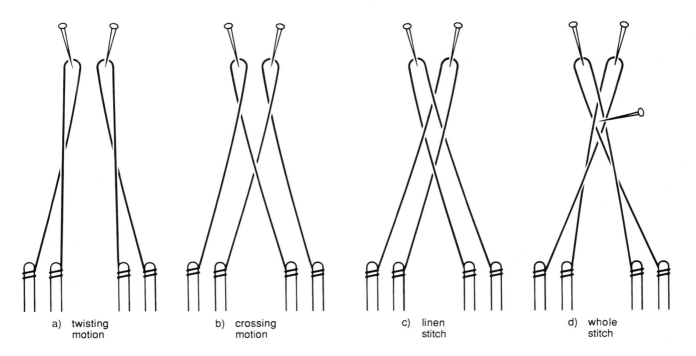

a) twisting
motion

b) crossing
motion

c) linen
stitch

d) whole
stitch

Figure 35.12 Basic motions and stitches used in the production of bobbin lace.

Figure 35.13 Carved block used in block printing.

Figure 35.14 Authentic block print.

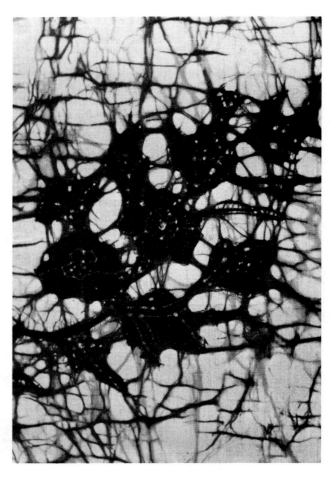

Figure 35.15 Authentic batik print with crackle effects.

penetration. The wrapping is carefully positioned to create the planned motifs. Subsequent dyeing results in absorption of the dye liquor by the unwrapped yarn portions only. Portions of the wrapping may be removed and additional colors applied. Because the aqueous dye liquor migrates through the yarns and varied levels of relaxation shrinkage may occur after weaving, ikat motifs have a striated appearance (Figure 35.17).

Although consumers may prefer an authentic block, batik, tie-dye, or ikat printed fabric, many find the yardage costs exceed their interior furnishings budget. Recognizing this dilemma, manufacturers often simulate the hand-printed patterns with high-speed, commercial printing techniques. Professionals and consumers can readily distinguish authentic prints from most simulated ones by examining the back of the fabric. Except for block prints, all authentic hand prints have the same depth of color on both sides of the fabric.

SUMMARY

An extensive variety of interior textile accents are created by talented, skilled artisans, including macramé hangings, tapestries, embroidered fabrics, quilts, laces, soft sculpture forms, and fabrics with distinctive hand prints. Frequently, consumers may purchase these hand-made items directly from the artist. Although many hand-created products carry a relatively high price, they are nonetheless often prized textiles in residential and commercial interiors.

Figure 35.16 Authentic tie-dye print.

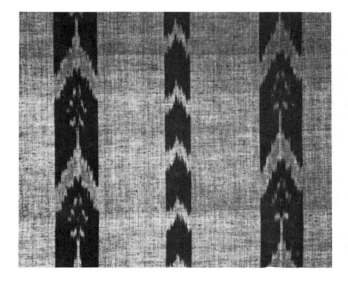

Figure 35.17 Authentic ikat print.

appendix A

Man-made Fiber Generic Classes and Trade Names

Pursuant to Section 7(c) of the Textile Fiber Products Identification Act, the Federal Trade Commission (FTC) established generic class names and definitions for manufactured fibers marketed in the United States.* Several trade names used by producers to distinguish their fibers and fiber variants are listed separately in alphabetical order.

FTC GENERIC CLASS DESIGNATIONS

(a) *acetate*. A manufactured fiber in which the fiber-forming substance is cellulose acetate. Where not less than 92 percent of the hydroxl groups are acetylated, the term triacetate may be used as a generic description of the fiber.

(b) *acrylic*. A manufactured fiber in which the fiber-forming substance is any long-chain synthetic polymer composed of at least 85 percent by weight of acrylonitrile units ($-CH_2-CH-$)
$$|$$
$$CH$$

(c) *anidex*. A manufactured fiber in which the fiber-forming substance is any long-chain synthetic polymer composed of at least 50 percent by weight of one or more esters of a monohydric alcohol and acrylic acid ($CH_2=CH-COOH$)
Not currently manufactured in the United States.

(d) *aramid*. A manufactured fiber in which the fiber-forming substance is a long-chain synthetic polyamide in which at 85 percent of the amide ($-C-NH-$)
$$||$$
$$O$$
linkages are attached directly to two aromatic rings.

(e) *azlon*. A manufactured fiber in which the fiber-forming substance is composed of any regenerated naturally occurring proteins. Not manufactured in the United States.

(f) *glass*. A manufactured fiber in which the fiber-forming substance is glass.

(g) *metallic*. A manufactured fiber composed of metal, plastic-coated metal, metal-coated plastic, or a core completely covered by metal.

(h) *modacrylic*. A manufactured fiber in which the fiber-forming substance is any long-chain synthetic polymer composed of less than 85 percent but at least 35 percent by weight of acrylonitrile units, ($-CH_2-CH-$)
$$|$$
$$CN$$

---

*The International Organization for Standardization has established some twenty-three generic names and promotes their use in textile commerce outside the boundaries of the United States. The Textile Economics Bureau, Inc., states that the ISO names cupro, viscose, acetate, triacetate, acrylic, modacrylic, nylon or polyamide, polyester, and glass are similar to the FTC designations. Other ISO names include modal (regenerated cellulose obtained by processes that result in a high tenacity and a high wet modulus), alginate (metallic salts of alginic acid), chlorofibre (similar to the FTC's saran and vinyon), elastane (similar to the FTC's spandex), elastodiene, fluorofibre, polycarbamide, polyethylene and polypropylene (similar to the FTC's olefin), polyurethane, trivinyl and vinylal (similar to the FTC's vinal). Full descriptions of these names may be reviewed in International Standard #2076, "Generic Names of Man-made Fibers."

except fibers qualifying under subparagraph (2) of rubber generic class definition and fibers qualifying under anidex generic class definition (as amended, effective March 13, 1966 and November 3, 1969).

(i) *novoloid*. A manufactured fiber containing at least 85 percent by weight of a cross-linked novolac.

(j) *nylon*. A manufactured fiber in which the fiber-forming substance is a long-chain synthetic polyamide in which less than 85 percent of the amide $(-C-NH-)$

$$\overset{\|}{O}$$

linkages are attached directly to two aromatic rings (as amended, effective January 11, 1974).

(k) *nytril*. A manufactured fiber containing at least 85 percent of a long-chain polymer of vinylidene dinitrile $(-CH_2-C(CN)_2-)$ where the vinylidene dinitrile content is no less than every other unit in the polymer chain. Not currently manufactured in the United States.

(l) *olefin*. A manufactured fiber in which the fiber-forming substance is any long-chain synthetic polymer composed of at least 85 percent by weight of ethylene, propylene, or other olefin units except amorphous (noncrystalline) polyolefins qualifying under category (1) of rubber generic class definition (as amended, effective March 13, 1966).

(m) *polyester*. A manufactured fiber in which the fiber-forming substance is any long-chain synthetic polymer composed of at least 85 percent by weight of an ester of a substituted aromatic carboxylic acid, including but not restricted to substituted terephthalate units

$$p(-R-O-\overset{\|}{\underset{O}{C}}-C_6H_4-\overset{\|}{\underset{O}{C}}-O-)$$

and parasubstituted hydroxybenzoate units

$$p(-R-O-C_6H_4-\overset{\|}{\underset{O}{C}}-O-)$$

(as amended, effective September 12, 1973).

(n) *rayon*. A manufactured fiber composed of regenerated cellulose, as well as manufactured fibers composed of regenerated cellulose in which substitutents have replaced not more than 15 percent of the hydrogens of the hydroxyl groups.

(o) *rubber*. A manufactured fiber in which the fiber-forming substance is composed of natural or synthetic rubber, including the following categories: (1) a manufactured fiber in which the fiber-forming substance is a hydrocarbon such as natural rubber, polyisoprene, polybutadiene, copolymers of dienes and hydrocarbons, or amorphous (noncrystalline) polyolefins; (2) a manufactured fiber in which the fiber-forming substance is a copolymer

of acrylonitrile and a diene (such as butadiene) composed of not more than 50 percent but at least 10 percent by weight of acrylonitrile units.

$$(-CH_2-\underset{\underset{CN}{|}}{CH}-)$$

The term lastrile may be used as a generic description for fibers falling within this category; (3) a manufactured fiber in which the fiber-forming substance is a polychloroprene or a copolymer of chloroprene in which at least 35 percent by weight of the fiber-forming substance is composed of chloroprene units.

$$(-CH_2-\underset{\underset{Cl}{|}}{C}=CH-CH_2-)$$

(As amended, effective March 13, 1966).

(p) *saran*. A manufactured fiber in which the fiber-forming substance is any long-chain synthetic polymer composed of at least 80 percent by weight of vinylidene chloride units $(-CH_2-CCl_2-)$.

(q) *spandex*. A manufactured fiber in which the fiber-forming substance is a long-chain synthetic polymer composed of at least 85 percent of a segmented polyurethane.

(r) *vinal*. A manufactured fiber in which the fiber-forming substance is any long-chain synthetic polymer composed of at least 50 percent by weight of vinyl alcohol units $(-CH_2-CHOH-)$ and in which the total of the vinyl alcohol units and any one or more of the various acetal units is at least 85 percent by weight of the fiber. Not currently manufactured in the United States.

(s) *vinyon*. A manufactured fiber in which the fiber-forming substance is any long-chain synthetic polymer composed of at least 85 percent by weight of vinyl chloride units $(-CH_2-CHCl-)$.

SELECTED FIBER TRADE NAMES

Trade name	Generic class	Distinguishing feature	Producer
Acrilan	acrylic		Monsanto Chemical Company
Anso	nylon		Allied Fibers
Anso IV	nylon	soil repellent	Allied Fibers
Anso IV HP	nylon	soil repellent, high dpf	Allied Fibers
Antron	nylon		E.I. du Pont de Nemours & Co., Inc.
Antron III	nylon	antistatic	E.I. du Pont de Nemours & Co., Inc.
Antron XL	nylon	high dpf, soil hiding	E. I. du Pont de Nemours & Co., Inc.
Arnel	triacetate		Celanese Corporation
Avlin	polyester		Avtex Fibers, Inc.
Avril	rayon	high wet modulus	Avtex Fibers, Inc.
Bekinox	metallic	stainless steel, antistatic	Bekaert Steel-wire Corporation
Beta	glass	low dpf	Owens-Corning Fiberglas Co.
Bi-Loft	acrylic		Monsanto Chemical Company
Brunsmet	metallic	stainless steel, antistatic	Brunswick Corporation
Camalon	nylon		Camac Corporation
Caprolan	nylon		Allied Fibers
Chromspun	acetate	solution dyed	Eastman Kodak Company
Coloray	rayon	solution dyed	Courtaulds North America, Inc.
Cordura	nylon		E.I. du Pont de Nemours & Co., Inc.
Creslan	acrylic		American Cyanamid Company
Dacron	polyester		E.I. du Pont de Nemours & Co., Inc.
Dacron Hollofil	polyester	hollow interior	E.I. du Pont de Nemours & Co., Inc.
Estron	acetate		Eastman Kodak Company
Fiberglas	glass		Owens-Corning Fiberglas Corp.

Tradename	Generic Class	Distinguishing features	Producer
Fibro	rayon		Courtalds North America, Inc.
Fi-Lana	acrylic		Monsanto Chemical Company
Fortrel	polyester		Celanese Corporation
Herculon	olelfin	polypropylene	Hercules Incorporated
Kevlar	aramid		E.I. du Pont de Nemours & Co., Inc.
Kodel	polyester		Eastman Kodak Company
KodOfill	polyester	hollow interior	Eastman Kodak Company
Kynol	novoloid		American Kynol Inc.
Lycra	spandex		E.I. du Pont de Nemours & Co., Inc.
Marquesa	olefin	bulked filaments	Amoco Fabrics and Fibers Co.
Marquesa Lana	olefin	bulked, wool-like	Amoco Fabrics and Fibers Co.
Marvess	olefin		Phillips Fibers Corporation
Nomex	aramid		E.I. du Pont de Nemours & Co., Inc.
Nypel	nylon		Allied Fibers
Orlon	acrylic		E.I. du Pont de Nemours & Co., Inc.
Pa-Qel	acrylic		Monsanto Chemical Company
Patlon	olefin	fibrillated ribbon	Amoco Fabrics and Fibers Co.
Remember	acrylic		Monsanto Chemical Company
SEF	modacrylic	self-extinguishing	Monsanto Chemical Company
Shareen	nylon		Courtaulds North America, Inc.
So-Lara	acrylic		Monsanto Chemical Company
Trevira	polyester		American Hoechst Corp.
Trevira Pentron	polyester	pentalobal, soil repellant	American Hoechst Corp.
Ultron	nylon		Monsanto Chemical Company
Ultron Z	nylon	soil shedding	Monsanto Chemical Company
Ultron 3D	nylon	high dpf	Monsanto Chemical Company
X-Static	nylon	silver coated, antistatic	Sauquoit Industries
Zeftron ATX	nylon	pentalobal, hollow voids, soil hiding	BASF Corp.
Zeftron 500 ZX	nylon	soil hiding, solution dyed	BASF Corp.

appendix **B**

The International System of Units—SI/Metric

The information in this appendix is courtesy of PPG Industries, Inc., 1984.

SI BASE UNITS

Quantity measured	Unit of measure	Symbol
Length	meter	m
Mass[a]	kilogram	kg
Time	second	s
Electric current	ampere	A
Thermodynamic temperature[b]	kelvin	K
Amount of substance	mole	mol
Luminous intensity	candela	cd

[a]The kilogram is the unit of mass but not of force. The Newton (N) is the unit of force. (For more detailed explanation of mass and force, refer to ASTM E 380.)

[b]While the kelvin is the correct SI unit of thermodynamic temperature, in practice, degree Celcius (°C) is most commonly used (1K = 1°C).

PREFIXES USED WITH THE SI METRIC SYSTEM

Prefix	Symbol	Multiplying factor		
tera	T	1 000 000 000 000	=	10^{12}
giga	G	1 000 000 000	=	10^{9}
mega	M	1 000 000	=	10^{6}
kilo	k	1 000	=	10^{3}
hecto	h	100	=	10^{2}
deka	da	10	=	10^{1}
deci	d	0.1	=	10^{-1}
centi	c	0.01	=	10^{-2}
milli	m	0.001	=	10^{-3}
micro	μ	0.000 001	=	10^{-6}

For additional prefixes, refer to ASTM E 380.

CUSTOMARY INCH-POUND MEASURES AND EQUIVALENT SI UNITS

Inch-Pound Measure and symbol		Equivalent metric measure and symbol	
inches	in.	centimeters	cm
inches	in.	millimeters	mm
feet	ft.	meters	m
yards	yd.	meters	m
miles	mi.	kilometers	km
square yards	yd^2	square meters	m^2
ounces (avdp.)	oz.	grams	g
pounds (avdp.)	lb.	kilograms	kg

CUSTOMARY UNITS OF MEASURE IN SI UNITS

Length

1 meter (m) = 100 cm	=	1000 mm
1 millimeter (mm)	=	0.001 m
1 centimeter (cm)	=	0.01 m
1 decimeter (dm)	=	0.1 m
1 dekameter (dam)	=	10 m
1 hectometer(hm)	=	100 m
1 kilometer(km)	=	1000 m

Capacity

l liter (L) = 100 cL	=	1000 mL
1 milliliter (mL)	=	0.001 L
1 centiliter (cL)	=	0.01 L
1 deciliter (dL)	=	0.1 L
1 dekaliter (daL)	=	10 L
1 hectoliter (hL)	=	100 L
1 kiloliter (kL)	=	1000 L

Weight

1 gram (g) = 100 cg	=	1 000 mg
1 milligram (mg)	=	0.001 g
1 centigram (cg)	=	0.01 g
1 decigram (dg)	=	0.1 g
1 dekagram (dag)	=	10 g
1 hectogram (hg)	=	100 g
1 kilogram (kg)	=	1 000 g

SELECTED INCH-POUND/SI METRIC CONVERSION FACTORS AND REFERENCES

Quantity	Inch-pound units	SI units	To Convert	
			Inch-pound units to SI	SI units to Inch-pound
			Multiply by:	Multiply by:
Length	inch	mm	25.400	0.03937
	inch	cm	2.5400	0.3937
	foot	m	0.3048	3.2808
	yard	m	0.9144	1.0936
	mile	km	1.6093	0.6214
Mass	ounce (avdp.)	g	28.3495	0.0353
	pound (avdp.)	kg	0.4536	2.2046
	ton (2,000 lbs.)	t	0.9072	1.1023
	ton (2,240 lbs.)	t	1.0161	0.9842
Force	pound	N	4.4482	0.2248
Volume	ounce (fluid)	mL	29.5735	0.0338
	quart (liquid)	L	0.9464	1.0567
	gallon	L	3.7854	0.2642
	quart (dry)	L	1.1012	0.9081
	bushel	L	35.2391	0.0284
	$inch^3$	cm^3	16.3871	0.0610
	$feet^3$	dm^3	28.3168	0.0353
	$yard^3$	m^3	0.7646	1.3079
Area	$inch^2$	cm^2	6.4516	0.1550
	$feet^2$	m^2	0.0929	10.7639
	$yard^2$	m^2	0.8361	1.1960
	acre	hectare	0.4047	2.4710
Temperature	°F	°C	$5/9(°F - 32°)$	$9/5°C + 32°$
Density	lb/in^3	g/cm^3	27.6799	0.0361
	lb/ft^3	kg/m^3	16.0185	0.0624
Velocity	ft/sec	m/s	0.3048	3.2808
	yd/min	m/min	0.9144	1.0936
	mi/hr	km/h	1.6093	0.6214
Energy	ft lb	J	1.3558	0.7376
	BTU	kJ	1.0551	0.9478
	kWh	MJ	3.6000	0.2778
Pressure	lb/in^2	kPa	6.8947	0.1450
Textile	oz/yd	g/m	31.0034	0.0323
	oz/yd^2	g/m^2	33.9057	0.0295
	turns/in(tpi)	turns/m(tpm)	39.3700	0.0254
	yds/lb	m/kg	2.0159	0.4961

*Definitions and symbols for the complete international system are given in ASTM E 380.

appendix *C*

Scientific Organizations, Government Agencies, and Trade Associations

Scientific Organizations

American Association of Textile Chemists and Colorists
(AATCC)
P.O. Box 12215
Research Triangle Park, NC 27709

American National Standards Institute, Inc. (ANSI)
1403 Broadway
New York, NY 10018

American Society for Testing and Materials (ASTM)
1916 Race Street
Philadelphia, PA 19103

National Fire Protection Association, Inc. (NFPA)
Batterymarch Park
Quincy, MA 02269

Government Agencies

Architectural and Transportation Barriers Compliance Board
U.S. Department of Health and Human Services
330 C Street, SW
Washington, DC 20201

Committee on Barrier Free Design
U.S. President's Committee on Employment of the Handicapped
1111 20th Street, NW
Washington, DC 20210

Consumer Product Safety Commission (CPSC)
Washington, DC 20207

Federal Aviation Administration (FAA)
U.S. Department of Transportation
800 Independence Ave., SW
Washington, DC 20591

Federal Housing Administration
U.S. Department of Housing and Urban Development
Washington, DC 20410

Federal Trade Commission
6th and Pennsylvania Ave., NW
Washington, DC 20580

General Services Administration
7th and D Streets, SW
Washington, DC 20407

National Bureau of Standards
Washington, DC 20234

National Highway Traffic Safety Administration
U.S. Department of Transportation
400 7th St, SW
Washington, DC 20590

National Technical Information Service
U.S. Department of Commerce
5285 Port Royal Road
Springfield, VA 22161

Office of Civil Rights for the Handicapped
U.S. Department of Health and Human Services
330 Independence Ave., SW
Washington, DC 20201

U.S. Government Printing Office
Washington, DC 20402

Trade Associations

American Furniture Manufacturers Association
P.O. Box 2436
High Point NC 27261

American Textile Manufacturers Institute, Inc. (ATMI)
1101 Connecticut Ave., NW, Suite 300
Washington, DC 20036

Association of Interior Decor Specialists, Inc. (AIDS INTERNATIONAL)
2009 N. 14th Street #203
Arlington, VA 22201

Belgian Linen Association
280 Madison Ave.
New York, NY 10016

California Furniture Manufacturers Association (CFMA)
1933 South Broadway
Los Angeles, CA 90007

Canadian Carpet Institute (CCI)
280 Albert St., Suite 502
Ottawa, Ont. KIP5G8

Carpet Cleaners Institute
1411 W. Olympic Blvd.
Los Angeles, CA 90015

Carpet Cushion Council (CCC)
21780 Partridge Lane
Farmington Hills, MI 48018

Carpet Manufacturers Association of the West (CMAW)
100 N. Citrus St. #235
W. Covina, CA 91791

Carpet Manufacturers Marketing Association, Inc. (CMMA)
1514 West Walnut Avenue
Dalton, GA 20720

Carpet and Rug Institute (CRI)
P.O. Box 2048
Dalton, GA 20720

Cotton Incorporated
1370 Avenue of the Americas
New York, NY 10019

Decorative Fabrics Association (DFA)
950 3rd Avenue
New York, NY 10022

Furniture Manufacturers Association of Grand Rapids (FMA)
220 Lyon Street NW
Grand Rapids, MI 49502

International Home Furnishings Representatives Association (IHFRA)
666 Lake Shore Drive
Chicago, IL 60611

International Linen Promotion Commission
280 Madison Avenue
New York, NY 10016

Jute Carpet Backing Council
30 Rockefeller Plaza
New York, NY 10020

Jute Manufacturers Development Council
19 W. 44th St., Suite 503
New York, NY 10036

Man-Made Fiber Producers Association (MMFPA)
1157 17th St., NW, Suite 310
Washington, DC 20036

National Association of Decorative Fabrics Distributors (NADFD)
6022 West Touhy Ave.
Chicago, IL 60648

National Association of Floor Covering Distributors (NAFCE)
13-186 Merchandise Mart
Chicago, IL 60654

National Cotton Batting Institute (NCBI)
1918 North Parkway
Memphis, TN 38112

National Cotton Council of America (NCCA)
1030 15th St., NW, Suite 700
Washington, DC 20036

National Home Fashions League, Inc. (NHFL)
107 World Trade Center
Dallas, TX 75258

National Home Furnishings Association (NHFA)
900 17th St., NW, Suite 514
Washington, DC 20006

Northwest Furniture Manufacturers Association
(NWFMA)
Box 2233
Tacoma, WA 98401

Retail Floor Covering Institute (RFI)
1889 Merchandise Mart
Chicago, IL 60654

The Society of the Plastics Industry (SPI)
355 Lexington Avenue
New York, NY 10017

Southwestern Furniture Manufacturers Association
(SWFMA)
9061 World Trade Center
P.O. Box 58258
Dallas, TX 75258

Synthetic Turf Council
P.O. Box 326
Dalton, GA   30720

Upholstered Furniture Action Council (UFAC)
Box 2436
High Point, NC 27261

The Wool Bureau, Inc.
1360 Lexington Ave.
New York, NY 10017

appendix *D*

Bibliography

Advantages of Carpet and Rugs in Energy Conservation, Dalton, Ga.: The Carpet and Rug Institute, 1976.

AATCC Technical Manual, Research Triangle Park, N.C.: American Association of Textile Chemists and Colorists, published annually.

Alexander, Patsy R., *Textile Products: Selection, Use, and Care,* Boston: Houghton Mifflin, 1977.

Annual Book of ASTM Standards, Philadelphia: American Society for Testing and Materials, published annually.

Benjamin, I. S. and S. Davis, *Flammability Testing for Carpet,* NBSIR 78-1436, Washington, D.C.: U.S. Department of Commerce, National Bureau of Standards, April 1978.

Beutluck, Tradek, *The Technique of Woven Tapestry,* New York: Watson-Guptill Publications, 1967.

Birrell, Verla, *The Textile Arts,* New York: Harper & Row, 1959.

Cammann, Nora, *Needlepoint Designs from American Indian Art,* New York: Charles Scribner's Sons, 1973.

Carpet and Rugs, 12th ed., North Canton, Ohio: The Hoover Company, 1983.

Carpet Specifier's Handbook, 2nd ed., Dalton, Ga: The Carpet and Rug Institute, 1976.

Cook, J. Gordon, *Handbook of Polyolefin Fibres,* London: Merrow Publishing Company, 1967.

Cook, J. Gordon, *Handbook of Textile Fibres,* Vols. 1 and 2, London: Merrow Publishing Company, 1968.

Corbman, Bernard P., *Textiles: Fiber to Fabric,* 6th ed., New York: McGraw-Hill, 1983.

Diamond, Sidney A., *Trademark Problems and How to Avoid Them,* revised edition, Chicago: Crain Books, 1981.

Frings, Gini Stephens, *Fashion: From Concept to Consumer,* Englewood Cliffs, N.J.: Prentice-Hall, 1982.

The Govmark Book on Flammability Standards and Flammability Test Methods of Textiles, Plastics and Other Materials Used in Home and Contract Furnishings, Bellmore, N.Y.: The Govmark Organization, Inc., 1982.

The Govmark Book of Reprints of Flammability Standards and Flammability Test Methods of Textiles, Plastics and Other Materials Used in Home and Contract Furnishings, Bellmore, N.Y.: The Govmark Organization, Inc., 1982.

Harries, Nancy G., and T. E. Harries, *Textiles: Decision Making for the Consumer,* New York: McGraw-Hill, 1974.

Held, Shirley E., *Weaving: A Handbook for Fiber Craftsman,* New York: Holt, Rinehart and Winston, 1973.

Hilado, Carlos J., ed., *Flammability of Fabrics,* Westport,

408

Conn.: Technomic Publishing Co., Inc., 1970–74.

Hollen, Norma, Jane Saddler, and Anna L. Langford, *Textiles,* 5th ed., New York: Macmillan, 1979.

Joseph, Marjory L., *Essentials of Textiles,* 2nd ed., New York: Holt, Rinehart and Winston, 1980.

Joseph, Marjory L., *Introductory Textile Science,* 5th ed., New York: Holt, Rinehart and Winston, 1986.

Larsen, Jack Lenor, and Jeanne Weeks, *Fabrics for Interiors,* New York: Van Nostrand Reinhold Company, 1975.

Lewin, Menachem, and Jack Preston, eds., *Handbook of Fiber Science and Technology: Volume III, High Technology Fibers: Part A,* New York: Marcel Dekker, 1984.

Lewin, Menachem and Stephen B. Sello, eds., *Handbook of Fiber Science and Technology: Volume I, Fundamentals and Preparation, Part A and Part B,* and *Volume II, Functional Finishes, Part A and Part B,* New York: Marcel Dekker, 1983–84.

Lewis, Alfred Allan, *The Mountain Artisans Quilting Book,* New York: Macmillan, 1973.

Linton, George E., *The Modern Textile and Apparel Dictionary,* 4th ed., Plainfield, N.J.: Textile Book Service, 1973.

Lyle, Dorothy S., *Modern Textiles,* 2nd ed., New York: John Wiley & Sons, 1982.

Lyle, Dorothy S., *Performance of Textiles,* New York: John Wiley & Sons, 1977.

Moncrieff, R. W., *Man-made Fibers,* 6th ed., New York: John Wiley & Sons, 1975.

NFPA 101® Life Safety Code®, Quincy, Mass.: National Fire Protection Association, Inc., 1981.

Perrone, Lisbeth, *The New World of Needlepoint,* New York: Random House, 1972.

Pizzuto, J. J., *Fabric Science,* revised by Arthur Price and Allen C. Cohen, New York: Fairchild Publications, 1974.

Reznikoff, S. C., *Specifications for Commercial Interiors, Professional Liabilities, Regulations, and Performance Criteria,* New York: Whitney Library of Design/Watson-Guptill Publications, 1979.

Robertson, Seonaid, *Dyes from Plants,* New York: Van Nostrand Reinhold Company, 1973.

Shoshkes, Lila, *Contract Carpeting,* New York: Whitney Library of Design/Watson-Guptill Publications, 1974.

Smith, Betty F., and Ira Block, *Textiles in Perspective,* Englewood Cliffs, N.J.: Prentice-Hall, Inc., 1982.

Souchal, Genevieve, *Masterpieces of Tapestry from the Fourteenth to the Sixteenth Century,* New York: The Metropolitan Museum of Art, 1973.

Specifier's Guide for Contract Carpet Installation, 1st ed., Dalton, Ga: The Carpet and Rug Institute, 1980.

Springer, Jo, *Pleasures of Crewel,* New York: Universal Publishing Company, Inc., 1973.

Standard Practice for Installation of Textile Floorcovering Materials, CRI Standard 104, Dalton, Ga.: The Carpet and Rug Institute, March 1982.

Tortora, Phyllis G. *Understanding Textiles,* 2nd ed., New York: Macmillan, 1982.

Wingate, Isabel, *Dictionary of Textiles,* 6th ed., New York: Fairchild Publications, 1979.

Wingate, Isabel, and June F. Mohler, *Textile Fabrics and Their Selection,* 8th ed., Englewood Cliffs, N.J.: Prentice-Hall, 1984.

Woodhouse, J. Michael, *Science for Textile Designers,* London: Paul Elek (Scientific Books) Ltd., 1976.

Periodicals

American Dyestuff Reporter
630 Third Avenue
New York, NY 10017

American Fabrics and Fashions Magazine
Doric Publishing Company
343 Lexington Avenue
New York, NY 10016

Daily News Record
Fairchild Publications, Inc.
7 East 12th Street
New York, NY 10003

High Performance Textiles
Elsevier International Bulletins
Journal Information Center
52 Vanderbilt Avenue
New York, NY 10017

Home Furnishings Daily
Fairchild Publications, Inc.
7 East 12th Street
New York, NY 10003

Interiors
Billboard Publications, Inc.
1 Astor Plaza
New York, NY 10036

Modern Textile Business (formerly *Modern Textiles)*
Vista Publications Inc.
9600 West Sample Road
Coral Springs, FL 33065

Textile Chemist and Colorist
P.O. Box 12215
Research Triangle Park, NC 27709

Textile Organon
Textile Economics Bureau, Inc.
101 Eisenhower Parkway
Roseland, NJ 07068

appendix E

Glossary

The parenthetical numbers following descriptions identify figures in the text that illustrate the term.

Abaca Bast fiber used for cordage; also called Manila hemp.

Abrasion resistance Ability of a textile structure to resist damage and fiber loss by friction.

Absorption Penetration of gases or fluids into fibers or within yarn and fabric interstices.

Adsorption Holding of gases, fluids, or solid materials on fiber surfaces.

Afterglow Smoldering combustion occurring after flames are extinguished.

Alpaca Hair fiber retrieved from Peruvian sheep of the llama species.

Angora Hair fiber retrieved from Angora rabbits.

Aniline finish Denotes use of aniline dyestuffs with leather; not a finish.

Antimacassars Fabric covers used to protect upholstery from hair oil.

Antique satin Sateen-woven drapery fabric with simple warp yarns and slub filling yarns (20.8).

Bast Classifies cellulose fibers retrieved from stem portion of plants, e.g., jute, linen, ramie, and hemp.

Batik print Hand print produced by artisans who apply melted wax to fabric areas that are to resist dye penetration (35.15).

Batiste Sheer, plain-woven fabric composed of fine, combed cotton yarns or spun polyester yarns; used for curtain treatments and Tambour-embroidered panels (20.19).

Bearding Development of long fiber fuzz on loop pile floor coverings; caused by snagging and poor penetration of pile yarn bundle by adhesive.

Below-grade Below ground level.

Bengaline Filling-rib woven upholstery fabric having equally sized and spaced ribs that number approximately twenty-four per inch (12.4c).

Berber yarn Speck yarn, hand-spun by peoples of northern Africa, composed of naturally colored wool; simulated by spinning fiber-dyed acrylic (23.7).

Bicomponent fiber Fiber composed of two or more generically similar polymer compounds.

Biconstituent fiber Fiber composed of two or more generically dissimilar polymer compounds; components may be in a side by side, sheath-core, or matrix-fibril arrangement.

Birdseye piqué Dobby woven curtain fabric with small, diamond-shaped designs (20.9b).

Bleeding Loss or migration of color when dye mixes with fluids.

Block print Hand print produced by artisans who press a hand-carved, dye-covered block (35.13) onto fabric surface (35.14).

Blotch print Color style in which fabric background is printed, leaving undyed design motifs (20.21).

Bobbinet Transparent net with six-sided openings that appear round; produced by raschel stitching; used as a base for Tambour-embroidered appliqués (20.29).

Bouclé yarn Complex yarn with pronounced, closed loops that vary in size and spacing (5.11c, 19.3b).

Bow Distorted yarn alignment in woven fabric; filling yarns curve below straight crosswise grain (9.5a, 14.1a, 14.2).

Boxing Wrapping strips of fabric around front and sides of upholstered cushions and throw pillows (15.3, 15.4c).

Broadloom Carpet produced 54 or more inches wide; does not identify a method of construction and carries no implication of quality.

Brocade Jacquard patterned upholstery and drapery fabric; motifs are created with extra filling yarns interlaced in a filling-faced twill or sateen weave; ground is plain, twill, satin, or filling-rib weave (12.14).

Brocatelle Jacquard patterned upholstery and drapery fabric; motifs are created with heavy warp yarns interlaced in a satin weave; ground is twill; extra yarns pad the motifs (12.15).

Browning Staining of pile yarns as water wicks upward from overwetted jute carpet and rug backing yarns.

Bulked continuous filament *(BCF)* Filament-length fiber given a multidimensional configuration to increase the apparent volume (5.1).

Bullion Fringe composed of metallic-colored strands; used as decorative trimming.

Burling Repair of imperfections in textile floor coverings.

Burnt-out print Print produced with acid instead of dyestuff; weak acid is used to etch out or destroy an acid-degradable fiber in selected fabric areas, leaving a transparent ground composed of an acid-resistant fiber; also known as etched-out print (20.25).

Cable yarn Simple yarn formed by plying two or more cords.

Calico Lightweight, plain-woven fabric characterized by small, colorful, printed motifs and solid-colored ground (20.1).

Cantonnière Rigid overhead window treatment mounted flush to the wall, framing the window; has a curved cornice and side panels that extend to the floor (17.5c).

Carded yarns Yarns spun of both long and short cotton fibers and having a relatively low degree of fiber alignment.

Carpet Singular as well as plural form of term used to identify textile floor covering securely attached to the floor (carpets and carpeting are incorrect forms).

Cascades Nonrigid side window treatments composed of gathered fabric falling in folds of graduated length; normally hung behind ends of swagged valence.

Casement General term for curtain and drapery fabrics that have medium weight and some degree of transparency (20.15, 20.26, 20.27, 20.28).

Cashmere Fine, soft fiber retrieved from Cashmere goat.

Chain warp yarns Warp yarns used in machine-woven floor coverings (26.1).

Challis *(challie)* Plain-woven drapery lining fabric composed of spun yarns of rayon or acetate; highly drapable.

Char length The distance of fabric damage produced by flame in standard flammability test methods.

Chenille yarn Yarn-like strand cut from leno-woven fabric that has fine warp yarns and coarse filling yarns; fluffy strand is said to resemble a caterpillar (5.12).

Chintz *(glazed chintz)* Plain-woven fabric characterized by brightly colored floral or geometric motifs and high surface luster (20.2).

Cloque Jacquard-woven, doublecloth upholstery fabric in which the back yarns are strategically interlaced to create the appearance of quilting stitches on the fabric face (12.21).

Cohesiveness The ability of textile fibers to adhere to one another mechanically.

Coir Fiber retrieved from husk of coconut; used in pile layer of track-off mats (26.15).

Collagen Protein compound in leather fibers.

COM See *customer's own material.*

Combed yarns Yarns spun of long cotton fibers having a relatively high degree of fiber alignment.

Combustible Material capable of undergoing combustion.

Combustion Chemical process in which combustible materials combine with oxygen to produce heat and light (flame).

Compressibility The ease with which a textile structure can be crushed or reduced in thickness.

Compressional loft Ability of a textile structure to recover from compression and regain its original loft; also known as compressional resiliency.

Compression deflection The extent to which a structure resists compression force (29.5).

Compression loss The extent to which a structure fails to recover its original thickness after being compressed under a static load; also known as compression set.

Conditioning, textile Placing test specimens in a controlled atmosphere of $70 \pm 2°F$ and $65 \pm 2\%$ relative humidity for a minimum of 24 hours prior to measuring a given property.

Conduction Mechanism by which heat energy, electrical charges, and sound waves are transmitted through solids, liquids, and gases.

Continuous filament See *filament.*

Convection Transmission of heat energy by air movement.

Cord yarn Simple yarn formed by plying two or more plied yarns (5.6).

Corduroy Woven or tufted fabric whose cut pile surface has a pronounced nap; used for covering furniture, windows, and walls (6.15, 6.16, 12.22).

Corkscrew yarn Complex yarn formed by twisting a fine yarn around a heavy yarn; also known as spiral yarn (5.9d).

Cornice Rigid overhead treatment mounted over drapery heading and hardware (17.5a).

Covering power The ability of a textile structure to cover or conceal a surface without undue weight.

Crease resistance Misnomer; creases are planned, wrinkles are not.

Cretonne Plain-woven drapery fabric characterized by large, printed motifs and a dull surface.

Critical radiant flux *(CRF)* Numerical value determined by converting the distance of flame spread to watts per square centimeter after completion of the flooring radiant panel test; indicates the minimum heat energy necessary to sustain burning of a floor covering that leads to flame propagation (30.5).

Crocking Transfer of color from one material to another as a result of surface rubbing (14.8).

Crushed velvet Velvet characterized by varied levels of surface luster (12.24).

Curtains General term for textile window covering fabrics hung without linings (17.1).

Customer's own material *(COM)* Textile or nontextile fabric supplied to end-product manufacturers by consumers.

Damask Jacquard-patterned upholstery and drapery fabric; motifs have plain, filling-rib, or sateen interlacings; ground is satin or twill weave (12.11, 12.12).

Deck Portion of furniture frame that supports the seat cushions.

Delamination Separation of attached layers in a textile structure (25.9).

Denier Weight per unit of length measurement of a fiber or yarn; numerically equal to the weight in grams of 9,000 meters of the strand.

Density Mass or amount of matter per unit of volume of a fiber or other textile structure; reported as pounds per cubic inch or grams per cubic centimeter.

Density factor Product resulting from the multiplication of yarn size, needle count, and stitches per inch used in a pile floor covering (25.12).

Dimensional stability The ability of a textile structure to maintain its original size and shape after use and care.

Dimity Sheer, warp-rib woven curtain fabric (6.9, 20.6).

Directional pile lay See *nap.*

Doctor blade Squeegee-like metal blade used to clean nonengraved portion of metal-covered printing rollers or to transfer dye liquor from a roller to the surface of greige goods (8.5).

Dotted swiss Voile curtain fabric having small flocked or woven-in dots (20.18).

Drapability The ability of a fabric to form graceful configurations, such as folds in curtain and drapery panels.

Draperies Lined textile fabric panels hung to drape gracefully at windows (17.2)

Drapes A verb meaning "hangs gracefully"; incorrectly used as a synonym for draperies.

Drawing Stretching a manufactured filament to improve its interior order, especially to increase the orientation of the polymer chains.

Duck Plain- or 2 x 1 basket-woven fabric composed of two-ply yarns. Used for exterior awnings.

Effective face weight Weight of the pile yarns in the wear layer of a textile floor covering, not in the backing.

Egress The act of leaving an interior in the event of fire; the exit way or means of egress should be free of obstrucions.

Elastic modulus Initial resistance to deformation stress exhibited by a fiber or other textile structure.

Elastic recovery The extent to which a fiber, yarn, or fabric recovers from extension.

Elasticity The ability of a textile structure to be extended and to recover from the extension; also known as stretchability.

Elevator effect Euphemism for the sagging and shrinking of curtain and drapery panels composed of conventional rayon fibers when the level of relative humidity fluctuates; also known as hiking and yo-yo effect.

Elongation The ability of a fiber, yarn, or other textile structure to extend or elongate; normally measured and reported as percent elongation at the rupture point.

End One warp yarn.

Etched-out See *burnt-out print.*

Extruding Mechanical spinning of manufactured filaments; polymer solution is extruded or forced through openings in a spinneret (3.3).

Eyelet Curtain fabric with holes surrounded by Schiffli embroidery (20.20).

Fabric openness The ratio of the open areas of a fabric to its total area (18.1).

Faille Filling-rib upholstery and drapery fabric with somewhat flat ribs that number approximately thirty-six per inch (12.4b).

Felting Intermeshing of the scales covering wool fiber that results in matting and shrinking of the yarns and fabric; caused by heat, agitation, and moisture.

Fenestration Design, arrangement, and proportions of the windows and doors in an interior.

Festoon Ornamental trimming draped over a valence or other overhead window treatment.

Fiber variant Manufactured fiber that is chemically related to other fibers in its generic class but distinguished by a structural feature, such as diameter or cross-sectional shape, or by the inclusion of a polymer additive.

Fibrillation Breaking off of minute slivers of glass from high denier glass filaments as a result of flexing and abrasion.

Filament An extremely long textile fiber, measured in yards, meters, miles, or kilometers; also known as a continuous filament.

Finials Decorative pieces attached to the ends of curtain and drapery rods.

Fireproof fiber A fiber that is unaffected by heat, e.g., asbestos.

Flame propagation Flame spreading.

Flame resistant fiber Fiber exhibiting relatively high decomposition and ignition temperatures.

Flame yarn Complex yarn produced by twisting a simple yarn around a single slub yarn that has large and elongated areas of low twist (5.9b).

Flammable fiber Fiber that is relatively easy to ignite and sustains combustion until it is consumed.

Flashover Situation in which all combustible materials burst into flame (11.4).

Floss yarns Loosely twisted, six-ply strands composed of mercerized cotton; used in hand embroidery.

Friezé *(frisé)* 1. Upholstery fabric produced by an over-the-wire construction technique; characterized by small loops that may be cut or uncut (12.25). 2. Name assigned to pile floor covering surfaces composed of yarns of maximum twist (23.6d).

Frostiness Absence of dye on yarn tips; planned and executed by gum printing operations.

Frosting Loss of color as a result of abrasion-induced fiber loss.

Fugitive dye Textile colorant exhibiting poor colorfastness.

Full-grain leather Leather having unaltered grain markings.

Fusion bonding Fabrication technique in which pile yarns are embedded into a vinyl compound coating a base fabric (26.11).

Galloon Narrow, tape-like length of trimming; often contains metallic strands.

Gauge 1. Fractional distance between needles on tufting machines; reported in whole number fractions. 2. Number of loops per inch of width in knitted constructions. 3. Thickness of polymer film sheeting.

Gauze See *theatrical gauze.*

Ghiordes knot Hand-tied knot used in the production of rya rugs and some Oriental rugs; also known as Turkish knot (27.2b).

Gimp yarn Yarn formed by spirally wrapping one yarn around another, or by braiding three or more strands around one central yarn; interior yarn is completely covered and outer yarns are often metallic strands.

Glass curtains Sheer curtains hung next to the window glass; may or may not be composed of glass fiber.

Goose-eye twill Dobby-woven upholstery fabric with small, diamond-shaped motifs said to resemble the eyes of a goose (12.9c).

Greige goods Unfinished fabrics.

Grin Exposure of the backing in floor covering with low pile construction density (23.4).

Grospoint Upholstery fabric produced by an over-the-wire construction technique; has larger loops then friezé; often used to cover office desk chairs (12.26).

Guides Collection of labeling provisions issued by the FTC; serve to inform members of one segment of the interior textile industry how to avoid engaging in unfair and deceptive labeling practices; advisory in nature.

Hand The tactile qualities of a fabric, perceived by touch; also known as handle.

Hawser yarn Simple yarn formed by twisting two or more ropes together.

Heat conductivity Rate at which a material conducts heat; reported as K-value; reciprocal of heat resistivity.

Heat sensitivity See *thermoplasticity.*

Heat setting Use of heat to stabilize thermoplastic fibers, improving their dimensional stability and that of yarns and fabrics composed of them; also improves resiliency.

Heather Descriptive of the color styling produced by spinning or throwing variously colored fibers.

Herringbone 1. Variation of the basic twill weave in which the direction of the visual diagonal is continually reversed (6.10c). 2. Upholstery fabric produced with a herringbone weave (12.7).

Homespun 1. Another name for the plain weave. 2. Plain-woven upholstery and drapery fabric composed of heavy, coarse yarns that resemble hand-spun yarns (12.1a).

Hopsacking *(hopsack)* Plain- or- basket-woven upholstery fabric composed of irregular yarns and resembling sacks used to gather and store hops (12.1b).

Houndstooth check Broken-check motif said to resemble the tooth of a dog; produced by interlacing different colors of strategically placed yarns in a twill weave (12.5).

Hydrophilic fiber Fiber having strong attraction for water; also known as water-loving fiber.

Hydrophobic fiber Fiber having low attraction for water; also known as water-hating fiber.

Ignition temperature Temperature at which a combustible material combines with oxygen, igniting to produce heat and such other combustion by-products as light and smoke; also known as kindling temperature.

Ikat print Hand print produced by artisans who tie off selected areas of bundled warp yarns and dye them prior to weaving (35.17).

Impact insulation class *(IIC)* Numerical value used to indicate the effectiveness of a carpet and/or cushion in reducing noise transmission; IIC values are roughly equal to INR values plus 51.

Impact noise rating *(INR)* Numerical value used to indicate the effectiveness of carpet, cushion, or both in reducing noise transmission; INR values are roughly equal to IIC values minus 51.

Insulation See *R-value.*

Jabots Non-rigid side window treatments composed of pleated fabric; lower end may be level or angled; normally hung in front of ends of swagged valance (17.4).

Jaspé Descriptive of color style in which space-dyed yarns are woven in arrow, lengthwise bands to produce the effect of irregularly placed stripes; similar to strié.

Kindling temperature See *ignition temperature.*

K-value Numerical value that reports the rate at which a material conducts heat.

Lambrequin Rigid overhead window treatment with a straight cornice and side panels that protrude some distance from the wall and extend some distance down the sides of the window (17.5b).

Lampas Jacquard-woven drapery fabric with detailed motifs created by combining satin and sateen interlacing patterns; often composed of two sets of identically colored warp yarns and one or more sets of variously colored filling or weft yarns; patterns are typical of those seen in the seventeenth and eighteenth centuries (20.17).

Leaf Classifies cellulose fibers retrieved from the leaf portion of plants, e.g. abaca, banana, sisal.

Life-cycle cost *(LCC)* The total cost of a product durings its expected use-life; includes initial purchase costs, installation charges, and long-term maintenance expenses; the total LCC values of several products may be amortized according to their respective life expectancies to show the annual use-cost of each.

Light reflectance factor *(LRF)* Numerical value indicating the percentage of incident light being reflected by a carpet surface; complement of the LRF indicates the percentage of incident light being absorbed.

Limiting oxygen index *(LOI)* Numerical value identifying the amount of oxygen required to support the combustion of a textile fiber.

Liquor ratio Ratio of pounds of dye liquor to pounds of greige goods.

Liseré Jacquard-patterned upholstery and drapery fabric; an extra set of warp yarns is used to produce detailed motifs in lengthwise bands, which are interspersed with satin-woven stripes (12.13).

Llama Hair fiber retrieved from the South American llama.

Lofty Quality of bulk without weight.

Loop or curl yarn Complex yarns with open, airy loops (5.11d).

Marled Descriptive of the color styling produced by spinning together two differently colored rovings (8.2).

Marquisette Transparent, lightweight leno-woven curtain fabric composed of fine, monofilament yarns (20.14).

Matelassé Jacquard-woven upholstery fabric in which mutual interlacings between back and face yarns produce the appearance of quilting stitches; a third set of filling or weft yarns pads the motifs and emphasizes the quilt-like form (12.20).

Migration Movement of dye through fabric; results in varied levels of intensity.

Mildew Growth caused by spore-forming fungi; may result in discoloration, odor, and tendering.

Mohair Hair fiber retrieved from Angora goat; often used in loop or curl yarns.

Moiré Finish characterized by a wood-grain or water-marked effect (9.2, 17.8).

Monk's cloth Basket-woven fabric composed of coarse, irregular yarns; used for curtain and drapery treatments (20.5).

Monofilament yarn Simple yarn composed of a single filament; used in sheer curtain fabrics and as transparent sewing thread.

Monomer Basic building block of textile fibers; several monomers are linked end to end to form polymers.

Mordant Compound, usually metallic salt, used to increase the attraction between fibers and dyestuffs.

Moresque Descriptive term used to identify color effect of ply yarn formed by twisting different colors of single yarns.

Multifilament yarn Simple yarn composed of several filaments.

Nap Directional orientation of yarns in pile layers; also known as pile sweep, pile lay, and directional pile lay (9.3).

Napery General term for tablecloths and napkins.

Needle count Number of needles per crosswise inch on tufting machines.

Needlepoint weave Misnomer; used for Jacquard-woven tapestry having the appearance of hand-stitched needlepoint (12.17).

Ninon Sheer, plain-woven curtain fabric with every third warp yarn omitted (19.2, 20.3).

Noise Unwanted sound.

Noise reduction coefficient *(NRC)* Numerical value that indicates the effectiveness of textile floor and wall coverings at absorbing sound.

Noncellulosic fibers Man-made fibers manufactured from compounds other than cellulose, e.g., polyester, nylon, acrylic, olefin.

Noncombustible fiber Fiber that does not burn or contribute significant amounts of smoke; may undergo pyrolysis.

Nottingham lace Flat lace or net with warp and filling yarns; machine-made (34.7).

Nub yarn Complex yarn with tightly compacted projections created at irregular intervals along its length (5.10a).

Nylon cap Web of nylon fibers needlepunched into face of primary backing; color-coordinated with pile yarns (25.3).

Ombré Descriptive of the color styling produced by a gradual change in the level of intensity of a single hue.

Organdy Sheer, plain-woven fabric having a parchment-like hand; produced by degrading cotton fibers with weak sulfuric acid; used in curtain treatments.

Osnaburg Plain-woven drapery fabric made of coarse, irregular yarns; originally produced in Osnaburg, Germany, for use in grain and cement sacks (20.4).

Ottoman Filling-rib woven upholstery fabric; has large, flat ribs of equal size and spacing or of unequal size and spacing (12.4d, 12.4e).

Over-the-counter fabric Refers to lengths of piece goods or fabric sold by retail distributors; also called OTC fabric.

Panné velvet Velvet with a pronounced nap, high surface luster, and a smooth hand; used for dining chair seats and upholsterd furniture.

Passementerié French term for trimmings, edgings, and the like.

Pick One filling or weft yarn.

Pigment print Color styling in which opaque pigments are applied (20.24).

Pile construction density Value indicating number of pile tufts per square inch; with tufted constructions, calculate by multiplying the needle count by the stitches per inch; with woven constructions, calculate by multiplying the pitch divided by 27 by the number of rows or wires per inch.

Pile height The length of the pile tufts above the backing.

Pile lay See *nap*.

Pile sweep see *nap*.

Pile thickness Average thickness of the pile material above the backing.

Pile yarn integrity Ability of pile yarns to retain their original level of twist.

Pile yarn weight The weight of the yarns used in the wear layer and those portions of the pile yarns that extend into the backing layer; expressed in ounces per square yard.

Pills Unsightly bunches or balls of fiber formed on fabric surfaces.

Pinwale piqué Dobby-woven curtain fabric with fine, lengthwise wales or ridges; also known as plain piqué (20.9a).

Pitch Number of pile tufts per 27 inches of width in a woven floor covering.

Ply yarn Yarn formed by twisting two or more single yarns.

Pockets Areas in Jacquard-woven, doublecloth fabrics in which the face yarns and back yarns are not interlaced (12.19).

Polymer Compound composed of extremely long, chain-like molecules.

Pyrolysis Process in which high temperature causes the decomposition of textile fibers and other organic materials.

Radiation Mechanism by which heat is transferred in the form of waves or rays.

Ramie Cellulosic fiber retrieved from stem portion of plants.

Ratiné yarn Complex yarn with small, uniformly spaced loops of equal size; projections may resemble rick-rack trim (5.11b).

Relaxation shrinkage Shrinkage of yarns; occurs when yarns recover or relax from strains imposed by manufacturing stresses.

Rep (repp) Filling-rib woven upholstery fabric with fine ribs, slightly larger than those seen in taffeta (12.4a).

Residual shrinkage Shrinkage of fibers; fibers become progressively shorter during use and care.

Resiliency Ability of a textile structure to recover from deformations other than elongation; recovery from folding and bending is commonly referred to as wrinkle recovery and recovery from compression as crush recovery; see also *compressional loft*.

Rollgoods Soft floor coverings available in widths of 9, 12, and 15 feet and long lengths.

Rope yarn Simple yarn formed by plying two or more cable yarns.

Rows per inch The number of crosswise rows of pile tufts per lengthwise inch in Axminster and chenille floor coverings.

Rug Soft floor covering which is loose-laid on floor or over wall-to-wall carpet.

R-value (R-factor) Numerical value indicating how effectively a structure resists heat flow, that is, how effectively it insulates and prevents heat exchange; R-value equals the thickness of the structure divided by its K-value.

Sateen 1. Lining fabric produced with a sateen interlacing. 2. Variation of basic satin weave in which filling yarns float, that is interlace infrequently, on the face (6.11b).

Scrim Flat woven fabric with low thread count; used as backing in tufted floor coverings and as reinforcing layer in needlepunched carpet, hair cushions, and spunbonded fabrics (25.2a, 29.1a, 29.3).

Seed yarn Complex yarn with tiny nubs (5.10b).

Sehna knot Hand-tied knot used in the production of some authentic Oriental rugs; also known as Persian knot (27.2a).

Self-extinguishing fiber Fiber that stops burning when the source of ignition heat is removed.

Serging Machine overcasting (34.8).

Shading coefficient (S/C) Numerical rating that indicates light transmission in relation to temperature flow; calculated by dividing the total amount of heat transmitted by a window and window covering combination by the total amount of heat transmitted by a single pane of clear glass 1/8 inch in thickness.

Shots Filling yarns used in machine-woven floor coverings (26.1).

Skew Distorted yarn alignment in woven fabric; filling yarns slant below straight crosswise grain (9.5b, 14.1b, 14.3).

Slub yarn Complex single yarn with fine and coarse segments along its length, which are produced by varying the level of twist used in spinning (5.7a).

Smoldering Flameless combustion.

Specific gravity The density of a fiber relative to that of water at 4°C, which is 1.

Speck yarn Complex single yarn having small tufts of differently colored fibers incorporated along its length; used in tweed fabrics (5.7c).

Spinneret Shower head–like device used for mechanically spinning man-made fiber filaments (3.3).

Spiral yarn Complex yarn formed by twisting a heavy yarn around a fine yarn (5.9c).

Splash yarn Complex yarn having elongated nubs along its length (5.10c).

Split leather Leather fabric produced from an inner layer of hide; lacks natural grain markings.

Spontaneous combustion Combustion process initiated by heat rather than flame.

Spunbonding Fabrication technique in which a web of filaments is stabilized with heat or adhesive binders (25.2c).

Spunlacing Fabrication technique in which webs of fibers are mechanically entangled (7.10).

Staple A relatively short textile fiber; measured in inches or centimeters.

Stitch-bonding Fabrication technique in which knitting stitches are used to stabilize webs of fibers (20.30).

Stitch-knitting Fabrication technique in which knitting stitches are used to anchor webs of yarns; also known as knit-sewing (20.28).

Strié (straié) Descriptive of color style in which yarns of various shades of the same hue are woven in narrow, lengthwise bands to produce the effect of irregularly placed stripes; similar to jaspé (12.7, 12.11b).

Stuffer yarns 1. Extra warp yarns running in a plane and supporting wales or other woven-in dobby designs (20.10). 2. Extra warp yarns running in a plane in the back of woven floor coverings, adding weight, strength, dimensional stability, and thickness (26.1).

Tambour embroidering Machine stitching that resembles hand chain-stitching (20.19, 20.29).

Tapestry 1. Jacquard-woven upholstery and drapery fabric in which bands of colored yarns appear selectively on the face and produce stripes on the back (12.16, 12.17, 12.18). 2. Hand-woven fabric in which the filling or weft yarns are interlaced within the perimeter of a motif, clipped, and left hanging fringe-like on the back (35.2a, 35.4).

Tapestry weave   Plain weave in which the filling or weft yarns are crammed to completely cover the warp yarns (35.2b).

Tenacity   The force per unit of linear density necessary to rupture a fiber, yarn, or thread; reported as grams per denier (g.p.d. or g/den) or grams per tex (g.p.t. or g/tex).

Tendering   Weakening of fibers.

Tensile strength   The force per unit of cross-sectional area necessary to rupture a fabric; reported as pounds per square inch (p.s.i.) or grams per square centimeter.

Tex   Weight per unit of length measurement of a fiber or yarn; numerically equal to the weight in grams of 1,000 meters of the strand.

Textile   Formerly used only in reference to woven fabrics; now applied to fibers, yarns, and fibrous fabrics manufactured in various ways; not applicable to leather and film fabrics.

Theatrical gauze   Plain-woven, stiffened curtain fabric having slightly higher thread count than cheesecloth; also known as gauze.

Thermoplasticity   Property that allows a fiber to be softened and stabilized with controlled heat and that results in melting at higher temperatures; also known as heat sensitivity.

Thick-and-thin yarn   Complex single yarn characterized by variations in diameter that are created by varying extrusion pressure (5.7b).

Thread   Fine, yarn-like strand used for sewing.

Thread count   The number of warp yarns and filling yarns in one square inch of greige goods; indicates compactness of construction.

Threshold of human sensitivity   The level of static voltage that produces a noticeable shock for most people when it discharges from their bodies; the level is normally 2,500 static volts.

Tidies   Decorative covers placed on the backs and arms of furniture.

Tie-dye print   Hand print produced by artisans who tie off selected areas of fabric so that they resist penetration of dye liquor (35.16).

Tippiness   Unwanted concentration of dye on yarn tips; result of poor dye migration.

Toile de Jouy   Plain-woven fabric printed with landscapes, floral motifs, or other pictorial designs in various shades of a single hue on a cream-colored background; first produced in Jouy, France; used for draperies (20.23).

Top-grain leather   Leather having minor corrections of the natural grain markings.

Tow   1.   A rope-like bundle of manufactured filaments having crimp but no twist.   2.   Linen fibers approximately 12 inches long.

Trade practice rule   Collection of labeling provisions issued by the FTC in response to requests by members of a limited segment of the industry; advisory in nature; several trade practice rules have been superseded by guides.

Trade regulation rule   Collection of mandatory labeling provisions issued by the FTC.

Triaxial weaving   Fabrication technique in which two sets of warp yarns and one set of filling yarns are interlaced at 60-degree angles (6.20).

Tufting   Fabrication technique in which pile yarns are inserted into a preformed base fabric (7.8).

Valence   Overhead window treatment composed of fabric; may be pleated, scalloped, shirred, or draped as a swag (17.4).

Velvet   Upholstery fabric produced by a doublecloth construction technique; has a cut pile surface created with an extra set of warp yarns (6.17, 12.23, 12.24).

Velveteen   Upholstery fabric produced with an extra set of filling yarns; has dense cut pile surface.

Voided velvet   Velvet characterized by the absence of pile yarns in selected areas (12.23).

Voile   Sheer, crisp, plain-woven curtain fabric; often flocked with dots to produce dotted swiss (20.18).

Waffle piqué   Dobby-woven curtain fabric resembling the grid of a waffle iron (20.9c).

Warp print   Color style produced by printing the warp yarns prior to weaving; distinguished by striated or blurred appearance; used for draperies (20.22).

Wear layer   The face or pile yarns above the backing in pile floor coverings.

Weft   Another name for filling yarns; also known as woof.

Weft insertion   Fabrication technique in which weft or filling yarns are inserted through loops of a tricot-stitched fabric (7.4, 20.27).

Welt   Fabric-covered cord inserted in seam lines of upholstered furniture coverings (15.3, 15.4b, 15.5).

Wickability   The ability of a fiber to transport moisture along its surface by capillary action.

Wires per inch   The number of wires used per lengthwise inch in the construction of Wilton and velvet carpet; also the number of crosswise rows of tufts per lengthwise inch in Wilton and velvet carpet, since one wire is used per row of tufts.

Woolen yarn   Yarn spun of both long and short wool fibers and exhibiting a relatively low degree of fiber alignment.

Worsted yarn   Yarn spun of long wool fibers and exhibiting a relatively high degree of fiber alignment.

Wrinkle recovery   Recovery from folding and bending deformations, minimizing fabric mussiness; see *resiliency*.

Yarn count   See *yarn number*.

Yarn number   Numerical designation of the fineness or size of a yarn; based on length per unit of mass (weight) or mass (weight) per unit of length; also known as yarn count.

Index